CISTERCIAN STUDIES SERIES: NUMBER TWO HUNDRED-SIX

# PRAYER

## The Spirituality of the Christian East

*Volume 2*

**Cistercian Publications**
Editorial Offices
The Institute of Cistercian Studies
Western Michigan University
Kalamazoo, Michigan 49008-5415
www.spencerabbey.org/cistpub

*The work of Cistercian Publications is made possible in part by support from Western Michigan University to The Institute of Cistercian Studies.*

CISTERCIAN PUBLICATIONS BOOKS ARE AVAILABLE AT THE FOLLOWING ADDRESSES:

The United States: Liturgical Press
Saint John's Abbey Collegeville, MN 56321-7500
sales@litpress.org

The United Kingdom and Europe: The Columba Press
55A Spruce Avenue
Stillorgan Industrial Park
Blackrock, Co. Dublin
Ireland
info@columba.ie

Canada: Bayard-Novalis
49 Front Street East, Second Floor
Toronto Ontario M5E 1B3
cservice@novalis-inc.com

CISTERCIAN STUDIES SERIES: NUMBER TWO HUNDRED SIX

# PRAYER

## The Spirituality of the Christian East

*Volume 2*

by

Tomaš Špidlík SJ

Translated by

Anthony P. Gythiel

CISTERCIAN PUBLICATIONS

Kalamazoo, Michigan

A translation of Tomaš Špidlík, *La spiritualité de l'Orient chrétien*. II. *La prière*.
Orientalia Christiana Analecta 230. Rome: Pontificium institutum studiorum orientalium, 1988.



*The work of Cistercian Publications is made possible in part by support from Western Michigan University to The Institute of Cistercian Studies.*

The translator and editor express their appreciation to
The Office of Research and Sponsored Programs at Wichita State University, Wichita, Kansas, for a translator's grant which made this work possible.

ISBN-13: 978-0-87907-879-9 (v. 1, hardcover)
ISBN-10: 0-87907-879-0 (v. 1, hardcover)

ISBN-13: 978-0-87907-979-6 (v. 1, paperback)
ISBN-10: 0-87907-979-7 (v. 1, paperback)

ISBN-13: 978-9-87907-706-8 (v. 2, paperback)
ISBN-10: 0-87907-706-9 (v. 2, paperback)

Library of Congress Cataloging-in-Publication Data may be found on page 542.

*Printed in the United States of America*

# CONTENTS

## CHAPTER 10. HESYCHASM



## CONCLUSION

# FOREWORD

'PRAYER IS A STATE OF THE INTELLECT, actualized only through the light of the Holy Trinity by means of ecstasy.'[1] This is one of the many 'definitions' of prayer found in the spiritual writings of the christian East. Extremely varied, they agree in one assertion alone: the true nature of prayer is unutterable; the true master who teaches us to pray is the Holy Spirit. Should we be surprised then, if most of the writings of this spiritual tradition are treatises on prayer? One even gets the impression that prayer is almost the exclusive theme, and that other subjects are touched upon only as they relate to prayer. What is the content of these treatises? To what end were they composed? The variety of forms reflects their intent and the circumstances that prompted writers to take up the pen to address so difficult a subject.

Poets admit that for them writing is a compulsion, a command they cannot disregard. Anyone who has had a remarkable experience feels obliged to share it with others. When the heart is seized by great joy, eagerness 'unwinds the tongue', exclaims Saint Gregory of Nazianzus, the poet among the Fathers.[2] Strong emotion is expressed in words which, like a violent wind, 'enters the cracks to produce a sound'.[3] How can anyone keep secret the divine inspirations received during prayer, the mystical visions experienced at privileged moments, especially when the recipient possesses literary talent and the gift of words? Keeping silent under such circumstances would surely mean being ungrateful to God.

When Symeon the New Theologian, the great byzantine mystic, speaks of his experiences of enlightenment, he does so in the form of a 'Thanksgiving to God' for the favors he was deemed worthy of receiving.[4] Gregory of Nareg was not called 'the armenian Pindar' without good reason. His *Sacred Elegies*[5] are unsurpassed in the perfection of their form, and his personal experience—an experience received exclusively in prayer—is communicated with an amazing freshness.

Yet not everyone has the gift of eloquence, or chooses not to use it out of humility. In every civilization there have been great masters who wrote nothing at all. Yet their teaching survived because disciples carefully noted down their instructions and recorded them for posterity. Some saints' *Lives* were written for the express purpose of revealing the marvelous divine gifts received by men and women of God during prayer. Who would be able to imagine the inner struggles of Saint Antony during his nights in the desert, had Saint Athanasius not described them for the profit of those who pray?[6] While Saint Symeon the New Theologian kept secret certain details of his mystic journey, his disciple, Nicetas Stethatos, gave an account of them in the biography of his master.[7]

A pattern of spiritual instruction came more and more to dominate treatises on prayer. It was the task of the spiritual fathers to introduce their 'sons' into the life of the Spirit, where prayer plays a fundamental role. Prayer must be taught, explained, and supervised—as is true for the practice of the virtues. 'To beginners, the law of prayer is burdensome, like a despotic master', Ilias the Ekdidos wrote.[8] In egyptian monastic circles, exhortations to the spiritual life were usually very brief, given in the form of 'apophthegms', 'sayings'—yet this simplicity of form frequently concealed a life-long experience.

Evagrius was so fascinated by this simplicity that he tried to imitate it in his little work *On Prayer*,[9] really a treatise that reveals a clearly developed pattern of thought presented in the form of short insights presented in no apparently fixed order. Cassian is close to Evagrius; in his views on lofty mystical exaltation he certainly belongs to the same tradition. The aim of his *Conferences,* however, was more comprehensive. He did not want to advocate a particular pattern, but set out faithfully to collect all the teachings of the elders. As a result, his chapter dealing exclusively with prayer[10] takes on the appearance of a general, though succinct, handbook.

This style was later to be continued and perfected, especially when anthologies and collections of the maxims of the ancients dominated the literature of spirituality. Later compilers assured their readers of their fidelity in transmitting the teaching of the Fathers without adding to or removing from it. Indeed, this was often their only merit, and not one to be belittled. Let us bear in mind that this type of spiritual reading continued until the publication of the *Philokalia,* that pre-eminent collection of instructions on prayer.[11]

Despite its abundance of classical texts, the *Philokalia* nonetheless represents a particular stream of thought, for it is an anthology of texts typical of the hesychast movement. The aim of Ignatii Brianchaninov a century later was similar. Because he no longer limited himself mechanically to reproducing the texts themselves, but in addition explained the teaching of the Fathers in his own words, his treatises on prayer[12]—while remaining traditional—take on the character of a logical synthesis, structured in terms of a personal, conscious reflection.

Being rational, human persons spontaneously reflect on what they learn and discover. Upon reflection, they synthesize the data to produce an overview. Questions are asked and answers are formulated—a method the greek Fathers learned during their studies. Thus, Origen's little work *On Prayer*[13] has all the good qualities of a treatise on speculative theology and remains relevant even today.

On the other hand, in the East, thanks to the monks, the 'positive' method largely prevailed over 'scholastic' theology. Spiritual authors never tired of pointing out the great danger that rational concepts, the products of aristotelian logic, might replace spiritual vision given only to those who are pure of heart.

The present book—conceived as Volume Two of our *Systematic Handbook,*[14] because it studies the last two chapters in depth—remains in the tradition of eastern 'positive' theology while adapting itself to standards of modern-day research. No attempt will be made to follow any system other than that suggested by the chapter divisions, by subject matter, or by the documents presented. We are aware of certain disadvantages: the overlap among the various traditions is easily obliterated and may create the impression of detracting from the progressive rhythm of the individual life.

This is, inevitably, the weak aspect of any handbook that attempts to offer a broad overview in a limited number of pages. Real life, by contrast, leans towards a saying clearly stated by Mark the Ascetic: 'There are many differing methods of prayer. No method is harmful. If it were, it would be not prayer but the activity of Satan.'[15] Also, 'Progress should be visible in our life. We should offer prayers to God in accordance with our state in life.'[16]

To anyone who is seeking in this handbook less general and more nuanced instruction, we can give no better advice than this: find a suitable apophthegm, one chosen from the heart. The tradition of the Christian East offers an enormous wealth of them, each more beautiful than the next.[17]

## Notes

In the footnotes, references to English translations of primary and secondary sources have been provided for the convenience to readers. This reference does not infer that the translations have been taken from these sources, and in many cases page references within the translations have not been given.

1. Evagrius, *Cent. Suppl.* 30. See Irénée Hausherr, 'Par delà l'oraison pure', *Hésychasme et prière,* OCA 176 (Rome, 1966) 11.

2. *Oratio* 6.1; PG 37:721A.

3. *Carmina* 1.1.13, vv. 19–20; PG 37:1229A.

4. *Catéchèses* 34–36; SCh 113 (Paris, 1965) 304ff; de Catanzaro, CWS, 347ff.

5. SCh 78 (Paris, 1961).

6. *Life of Antony;* PG 26:838–976. For English translations, see 'Source Citations for Frequently Cited Works', below, page 373.

7. Greek text and french translation by Irénée Hausherr in OC 12 (Rome 1928).

8. 'A Gnomic Anthology', Part Two, no. 107, in *The Philokalia. The Complete Text,* 3:46.

9. *Chapters on Prayer (De oratione);* PG 79:1165–1200; translated by I. Hausherr, *Les leçons d'un contemplatif* (Paris, 1960); English translation by John Eudes Bamberger, *The Praktikos: Chapters on Prayer,* CS 4 (1970).

10. The *Conferences,* Chapter 9; SCh 54:38–73; Ramsey, ACW, 57:329–363; Luibheid, CWS, 101–140.

11. See p. 462.

12. See p. 113.

13. *De oratione;* PG 11:415–561; GCS 2:295–403; translated by John O'Meara, *Origen: Prayer,* ACW 19 (1954).

14. *The Spirituality of the Christian East: A Systematic Handbook,* translated by Anthony P. Gythiel, CS 79 (Kalamazoo: Cistercian Publications, 1968); originally published as *La Spiritualité de l'Orient chrétien,* OCA 206 (Rome 1978).

15. 'On the Spiritual Law: Two Hundred Texts', 22; *The Philokalia. The Complete Text* , 1:111.

16. See *La loi spirituelle,* 153, translated C. A. Zirnheld, *Spiritualité orientale* 41 (Bellefontaine, 1985) 58.

17. The translator expresses his thanks to the Office of Research Administration at Wichita State University for a grant which made this translation possible, and to Dr Rozanne Elder for editing the text.

# 1

## AN OVERVIEW OF THE SOURCES

THE CONTENT of this opening chapter can only be very modest. Who could possibly present, in a few pages, a complete picture of the works on prayer so numerous in the East? What is more, classifying authors according to their differing leanings is difficult, and there is no doubt that these exist. Among the various ways of praying, each writer selected the one which suited him: liturgical, solitary, vocal, mental, and on it goes. But no one felt compelled invariably to remain within the confines of that choice. The various ways of praying also express continual progress in the dialogue with God. From reciting vocal prayers to mystical vision, there are stages. But progress is linked, not so much to the various 'schools' or to circumstances of place and time, as to each writer's spiritual development, and this often varies greatly, even in the same author.

This being so, we will limit ourselves by way of introduction simply to presenting the authors studied in this book. To this will be added a brief description of the books and of the forms and terms of liturgical prayer typical of the various rites, but not yet belonging to the vocabulary of general culture.

### THE FATHERS AND THE SPIRITUAL WRITERS

#### *The Ancient Fathers*

The earliest documents of the post-apostolic age contain important instructions on liturgical prayer and the confession of sins. Through them, the characteristics of christian prayer begin to be clearly delineated.[1] The conclusion of *The First Letter* of Clement of Rome is preceded by a beautiful prayer.[2] A sacramental, ecclesiastical, and christological mysticism appears in the *Letters* of Ignatius of Antioch († *c.* 110–117).[3] *The Shepherd of Hermas* is a short treatise, the oldest known, on the discernment of spirits. In it, the soul, in her relationship to God, is viewed as the scene of a struggle within the human person between the spirit of wickedness and the Spirit that comes from God.[4]

The prayers inserted into the texts of the Apocrypha are of interest to modern researchers because they are the earliest manifestations of christian poetic activity.[5] The *Acts of the Martyrs* present many brief examples of private prayer.[6] Specific instructions on worship and popular devotions are found in the Apologists. Justin Martyr († probably 165) describes the Sunday liturgy, the veneration of angels, and the 'reasonable' character of the christian 'sacrifice' (λογικὴ θυσία).[7] For Saint Theophilus of Antioch, the human person is essentially in dialogue with God, since the Word *(Logos)* of God conversed with him right from the creation.[8] Confronting his opponents, the false gnostics, Irenaeus of Lyons († after 193) taught the 'true gnosis' *(gnôsis alethes),* which is a gift of the Holy Spirit and is practised in prayer.[9] The pre-eminent witness to eucharistic prayer in the 'Apostolic Tradition' is Hippolytus of Rome († *c.* 235). Devotion to Christ animated his entire theology; the essential duty of the all–renewed creation consists in adoration.[10]

### *The Alexandrian Fathers*

In the writings of the alexandrian Fathers, prayer occupies the central place in the spiritual life. In egyptian monastic circles people described how to achieve perfection in practical terms. Clement of Alexandria († before 215) introduced the term 'contemplation' *(theoria)* into the christian vocabulary, and identified contemplation with christian perfection.[11] This trait was to be developed more profoundly by Origen († *c.* 254), who may be viewed as one of the first mystical writers.[12] His treatise, *On Prayer,*[13] is the first of this genre and deals directly with the theoretical and practical problems of how a Christian should address and converse with God.[14] Later, Methodius of Olympus († 311), influenced by Origen, taught in *The Banquet* a method of prayer to help virgins discipline their imagination.[15]

It was primarily Origen who cleared the way for a mystical interpretation of Scripture, a tradition which continued uninterruptedly in Alexandria. Didymus the Blind († *c.* 398) felt it was his personal vocation to guide Christians to a spiritual reading of Scripture so they could be schooled by the Spirit of Truth.[16] The same tendency is found in Cyril of Alexandria († 444), whose seventeen books on *The Adoration and Worship of God in Spirit and in Truth*[17] exemplify an allegorical-typological reading of Scripture.[18]

### *Monastic Writings*

Everything we read in *The Life of Antony* by Athanasius († 373) about the discernment of spirits and the struggle against demons was written with a view to the life of prayer the egyptian monks attempted to lead.[19] The *Letters* of Ammonas, Antony's faithful disciple, are important in the history of christian mysticism; in them, the ascent of the soul is compared to the ascent of Elijah.[20] The pachomian documents by Pachomius († 346) and his successors seek ways of harmonizing fervent personal prayer with the tightly structured community life.[21]

The origenist theses of Evagrius of Pontus († 399) did not prevent him from being a key witness to the spirituality of the egyptian desert. He was to remain one of the important masters of contemplation. His teaching, contained in his *Chapters on Prayer,* condensed in an aphoristic style and masked under the name of Nilus, would be meditated upon and copied by eastern monks at all periods.[22] The *Lausiac History* by his disciple Palladius († between 420 and 430) helped to make the monastic ideal of the life of prayer known far and wide.[23] The testimony of Cassian († *c.* 435) on the same subject is still more detailed. His originality consists in pointing out, more systematically than his predecessors, the lower forms of prayer before giving a description of how the prayer life progresses to the highest degrees of contemplation of the evagrian type ('the fiery prayer'). Editions usually include an *Index* of passages as they relate to the various themes.[24]

The spiritual teaching of the *Apophthegmata* is profound, though fragmentary. Chapter Nine of the Systematic Collection gathers the sayings of interest to us under the heading, 'That One Should Pray Without Ceasing and With Soberness'.[25] The very title indicates the ideal of what is called 'ancient hesychasm'.[26] To this egyptian tradition may be added that of the monks of Palestine and Sinai. In the ascetic world described in the *Spiritual Meadow* of John Moschus († 619), visions, ecstasies, and miracles are routinely described because prayer establishes an intimate communion between the inhabitants of heaven and the saints on earth.[27] John Climacus in *The Ladder of Paradise* († *c.* 644) describes the transition from *praxis* to contemplation *(theoria);* the last four Steps delineate the final phase of the process of union with God. Step Twenty-eight, one of the most beautiful in the entire work, is devoted specifically to prayer. In it, the common teaching is presented in great detail in the form of aphorisms. At the same time, John Climacus lets himself be carried away by an enthusiasm which gives this chapter a lyrical intensity.[28]

### *The Golden Age of Greek Patristics*

As the legislator of the cenobitic life, Saint Basil († 379) in his *Rules* dealt especially with psalmody in common.Yet as he was also a great contemplative, his *Homilies on the Hexaemeron*[29] are an excellent guide to 'the contemplation of nature' *(theoria physikē).* His *Homily on the Martyr Julitta* contains important observations about prayer in general.[30] The connection between *theoria* and *praxis* was the crucial problem in the life of Gregory of Nazianzus († 390). His personal conclusions were accepted by tradition on account of his great influence.[31] The treatise by Saint Gregory of Nyssa († probably in 394) entitled *The Life of Moses* was decisive in creating the terminology of the mysticism of darkness and influenced the great mystics of the East and the West, frequently through Pseudo-Denys.[32]

It would be hard to find anyone among the Fathers who more diligently prepared the faithful to partake of the mysteries of the christian liturgy and to receive the Body and Blood of Christ worthily than did Cyril of Jerusalem (*c.* 386/387) in his mystagogic *Catechetical Lectures.*[33] As for John Chrysostom († 407), we need only look at the *Index* in the Migne edition[34] to discover the wealth of information about prayer to be found in his homilies. His main preoccupation was in teaching christian people how to pray, and in explaining the meaning of worship in the Church. But in him one also finds numerous passages on sobriety of mind and guarding the heart—virtues typical of the hesychasts.[35] Chapter Four of his *Homily on Anne* constitutes a short treatise on prayer.[36]

The biblical commentaries of Diodore of Tarsus († before 394) and of Theodore of Mopsuestia († 428) provide examples of a reading of Scripture quite different from that of the Alexandrian School.[37]

The *Spiritual Homilies* of Pseudo-Macarius († 390) had an influence upon Eastern contemplation which parallels that of Evagrius, whose intellectualism was tempered by a more heart-felt, emotive mysticism.[38] As part of the macarian corpus in Migne are found the short books *On Prayer,*[39] *On the Ascent of the Soul,*[40] and *On Guarding the Heart.*[41] For Hesychius of Jerusalem (5th century) contemplation consisted of a spiritual understanding of Scripture: this presupposes a requisite spiritual discernment in every Christian.[42]

Maximus the Confessor († 662) set prayer within the process of the deification *(theosis)* of the human person and of the world. Within this same content, one should read the *Four Centuries on Charity:*[43] *agapē,* the queen of virtues, is the gate that leads to deifying *gnosis.*[44] The writings of John of Damascus († *c.* 750) encompass the entire range of theology. His key concept, however, is as follows: the Christian, beginning right now, has no other goal than to find God, who is reached in prayer because it is an ascent to God. During the iconoclast controversy, John became one of the main defenders of orthodoxy in his three treatises *On the Divine Images.*[45] He did not view this question as peripheral, but as a consequence of the Christ-centered cosmological vision elaborated by Maximus the Confessor.

That such a vision must be lived during the liturgy was realized more and more. The *Explanation of the Divine Liturgy*[46] by Germanus I, patriarch of Constantinople († 733), lacks the theological scope of Maximus the Confessor's *Mystagogy*[47] or of later works (those by Theodore of Andida in the eleventh century and

Nicolas Cabasilas in the fourteenth), but it brought to the attention of the faithful what is essential in liturgical symbolism.[48]

*The Byzantines*

During the byzantine period, the Greeks developed prayer formulas while the monks directed their zeal to perfecting the methods of prayer learned from patristic writings. From the beginning two different trends became apparent. On the one hand, those who were somehow associated with the 'Studite Reform' focused primarily on common, liturgical prayer. On the other hand was solitary prayer, the ideal of the hesychasts.

Theodore the Studite († 826) became a mystic by suffering for Christ. While he did not write explicitly on prayer, the *Typikon* of his monastery was to become the classical norm for liturgical prayer.[49] Theodore opted for a 'return to the Fathers'. To encourage such reading, traditional teachings needed to be gathered into a single book. Thus anthologies were created: the *Questions and Answers* of Anastasius the Sinaite (9th century),[50] the *Synagogē* of Paul Evergetinos[51] and the *Pandects* of Nikon of the Black Mountain (both 11th century).[52] The teaching on prayer found there is clearly traditional. The *Mēterikon* of Isaiah the Monk (12th–13th century) deliberately leaned towards athonite hesychasm.[53]

Prayer was not a theme avoided by learned byzantine writers in university circles. Photius († 898?) developed the doctrine of the veneration of images more than his predecessors; his great devotion to the *Theotokos* derived from his personal experience.[54] Michael Psellos († *c.* 1079), a deeply speculative mind, wrote a *Commentary on the Song of Songs* in the form of a patristic *catena*.[55]

The byzantine fondness for the splendor of liturgical celebration re-awakened the ancient mystagogic tradition, the contemplative participation in the rites of the Church. *A Commentary on the Divine Liturgy* by Nicholas Cabasilas († *c.* 1380) is viewed as one of the masterpieces of universal piety.[56]

For a history of byzantine hesychasm, one event must be singled out first: in the tenth century, two monks of Saint Sabas, Abramios and Patricios, translated the works of Isaac the Syrian (Isaac of Nineveh) into Greek. Through this channel, the contemplative mysticism of Evagrius entered Byzantium.[57] In the person of Symeon the New Theologian († 1022), the 'luminous experience of God' would begin to be lived behind the walls of the studite monasteries in Constantinople. In athonite monastic circles, this great mystic, together with his inseparable companion Nicetas Stethatos, would later receive due honor.[58]

*Athonite Hesychasm*

Three famous 'Sinaites' constitute the link between the ancient tradition of Egypt and the hesychasts of Mount Athos: Hesychius (eighth-tenth century?), author of *Centuries on Sobriety and Virtue;*[59] Philotheus of Batos (ninth-twelfth century), for whom the aim of prayer was 'to inscribe Jesus in the heart luminously';[60] and Gregory of Sinai († 1346), who came to Mount Athos as a missionary of the new mysticism.[61]

On Mount Athos, Nicephorus the Hesychast, in the second half of the thirteenth century, became famous in the history of spirituality as the person who initiated the psychosomatic method. His work *On Sobriety and On Guarding the Heart* explains the technique of deep breathing while reciting the Jesus prayer.[62] The most important extant witness to the spirituality of the athonite monks is that preserved in the *Triads for the Defense of the Holy Hesychasts* by Gregory Palamas († 1359). These rich texts, centered around the concept of *theosis* (deification), are viewed as a compendium of the faith and also of the experience of apophatic mysticism.[63] Gregory's views were strongly supported by his friend Philotheus Kokkinos († 1377).[64]

Most of the hesychast authors are to be found in the *Philokalia.* Since their names are generally not well known, we will list them here, while indicating where information about them can be found[65]: John of Karpathos (fifth-seventh century);[66] Abba Philemon (sixth–eighth century);[67] Thalassius the Lybian (fifth–seventh century);[68] Theodore of Edessa (ninth, or fourteenth–fifteenth century?);[69] Ilias the Ekdidos (eleventh–twelfth century?);[70] Theophanes the Monk (identity and dates uncertain); Peter of Damascus (twelfth century);[71] Theognostos (thirteenth century);[72] Theoleptus of Philadelphia († 1326);[73] Callistus, patriarch of Constantinople († 1397); and Ignatius Xanthopulos (end of the fourteenth century);[74]

Callistus Telikudes (second half of the fourteenth century);[75] Callistus Kataphygiotes (Kataphrygiotes) (end of the fourteenth–beginning of the fifteenth century);[76] and Symeon of Thessalonika († 1429).[77]

The 1782 edition of the *Philokalia*—a collection of ascetic and mystical texts assembled by Macarius of Corinth († 1805) and Nicodemus the Hagiorite († 1809)—gave rise to a renewal of hesychast prayer after centuries of spiritual aridity. The *Philokalia* may rightly be viewed as a 'breviary' of hesychasm.[78]

### *The Copts*

By 'coptic' is generally understood the literature initially written in pachomian monastic circles in the language of the Egyptians. Numerous translations from the Greek are included; among these, of course, are passages on prayer: to it the monks did, after all, assign the first place in their lives. Aside from such translations, coptic literature possesses few works, and even then, what was translated was often apocryphal.[79] It remains true, however, that for the liturgy the *Euchologion* attributed to Serapion of Thmuis, a fourth-century disciple of Antony the Great, emerges as an important work. In the anaphora that bears his name is found the *Sanctus,* the *epiclesis* to the Son, not to the Holy Spirit. It is a mixture of egyptian liturgy and his own creativity.[80]

The byzantine period (451–641) and the epoch in which the Coptic Church was formed hardly favored the development of a spiritual literature, given the great debates of the time. Under the Arabs (641–1517), and even more under the Turks (1517–1798), persecutions alternated with periods of relative peace.

More important is the literature written in Arabic after the ninth century. Abu'l Bakr Ibn al-Muqaffa (tenth century), a prolific writer, speaks of the Eucharist and of confession, but from a somewhat polemic or canonical point of view. The *Treatise on Preparation for Holy Communion,* written by Michael the Syrian, the patriarch of Antioch, and sent to Egypt toward the end of the twelfth century, is in the same vein: it instills the need for confession against those who denied this. Among thirteenth-century polemical works is an *Abridged Contemplation* of a homiletic type by Abu Ishaq Ibn al'Assal. During the decadence of the fifteenth century, Patriarch Gabriel V (1409–1428) codified the administration of the sacraments and the celebration of the Mass in his *Ritual.*[81]

To understand the characteristics of prayer among the Copts, one needs to consult primarily liturgical texts, and also to take into account popular devotions, above all pilgrimages.[82]

### *The Syrians*[83]

'Syrians' refers not only to the inhabitants of Syria, but also to those whose rites use or used the syriac language—the language of most of the syriac church Fathers and of many writers of that period. After the arab conquest, which is to say, during the second period, authors were moved to write more and more in Arabic. Although the christological controversies divided the Syrian Church very early, Monophysitism and Nestorianism had little influence on spiritual doctrine. By way of orientation, we may divide syriac literature into four periods: 1) From the beginning to the fifth century; 2) From the fifth century to the arab conquest; 3) From the arab conquest to the tenth century; 4) After the tenth century.

1. The *Didascalia Apostolorum (Teaching of the Apostles),* preserved in a syriac version which dates perhaps back to the third century, contains precious information on liturgical prayer, baptism, and repentance.[84] With a curious gnostic hymn inserted into the apocryphal *Acts* of the Apostle Thomas, Bardesanes appears to have been the creator of syriac religious poetry.[85] Among the twenty-three *Demonstrations* by Aphrahat (Aphraates), which date back to the years 337 and following, is found *Demonstration IV, On Prayer,* which deals with the whole of christian life.[86] According to the *Liber Graduum (Book of Steps),* a work written in the fourth century, the conduct of the Christian rests on three foundations: fasting, prayer, and almsgiving.[87]

Ephrem [of Edessa], 'the harp of the Spirit' and great classic of the Syrian Church, is unsurpassed as an exegete, polemicist, preacher, and poet. Authentic or not, his numerous hymn-prayers have taken on a liturgical function in almost all eastern churches.[88] Into the same books were inserted short poems by Balai (first half of the fifth century) which lack neither vivacity nor elegance.[89] Isaac, to whom are ascribed more than two hundred of the best loved poetic works in syriac literature, is a name which undoubtedly covers two homonyms: one, the orthodox Amid who lived in the first half of the fifth century; the other, a Monophysite of Antioch in the second half of the same century.[90]

John the Solitary (of Apamea) was a monk of the same era. His thought is dominated by the hope of life in the world to come. One is already in communion with it when—having reached the pneumatic stage—one receives in prayer a revelation of the mysteries of God.[91] The syriac text of the *Asketikon* of Isaiah of Scetis, or of Gaza (fifth century), is extremely rich, though its origins remain obscure. In it, as in a watermark, one perceives a preoccupation with safeguarding intimacy with God.[92]

2. Among monophysite authors of the fifth and sixth centuries, the two most eminent are Jacob of Sarug († 521) and Philoxenus of Mabbug († 523). Jacob's poetic work has always prompted the admiration of the Syrians, who call this author 'the flute of the Holy Spirit, the harp of the Orthodox Church'. Even in the other churches of the East, he is venerated as the master of liturgical hymnography.[93] To Philoxenus, also a major writer, are ascribed three Liturgies, a Baptismal Rite, and Prayers.[94] To these two authors may be added a heterodox mystic, Stephen Bar Sudayle († 543), to whom is attributed the *Book of Hierotheus,* the extreme point in the evolution of origenist mysticism.[95]

Following Rabbula († 435/6), bishop of Edessa, the last 'orthodox' writer and also an hymnographer,[96] come the Nestorians, beginning with Barsauma († 491–496) to whom a liturgy is attributed. The School of Edessa was directed by Narsai 'the leper' († early sixth century), who is said to have written three hundred-sixty metrical homilies and a number of liturgical texts.[97] Among the works of Henana, one of the giants of the School of Nisibis in the second half of the sixth century is found a commentary on the sacramental liturgy.[98] The large monastery of Izla, where Babai of Nisibis († 628/9) and Babai the Great († 628)[99] wrote, was a center of religious poetry. Gregory of Cyprus (sixth-seventh century) instructed monks on the nature of contemplation, the vision of invisible nature, and 'the joy and openness of speech *(parrhesia)* before God'.[100] The *Explanation of the Offices* by Abraham Bar Lipheh (probably in the early seventh century) is a mystical and symbolic text noted for its simplicity.[101]

3. The most remarkable jacobite author of the seventh century, Jacob of Edessa († 708), wrote various liturgical texts as well as making a translation of the Homilies of Severus of Antioch.[102] The liturgical treatises of Moses Bar Kepha, a monk and jacobite bishop († 903), are cited frequently and numerous copies of them are found in the Near East.[103]

In his *Book of Perfection,*[104] Martyrius Sahdona, a seventh-century monk and nestorian bishop, frequently deals with prayer. He insists on the dispositions one should bring to participation in the holy mysteries, on meditation on the word of God, and on the prayer of the heart.[105] The evagrian 'mysticism of light', of the 'formless' vision,[106] of the Trinity and Christ, is described by Joseph Hazzâyâ, an eighth-century nestorian monk.[107] The great master of 'spiritual prayer', Isaac of Nineveh [Isaac the Syrian] (seventh century) enjoyed great success not only among Syrians but also in byzantine and slavic monasticism.[108] The influence of Evagrius [of Pontus] can also be seen in the *Discourse on Solitude* by Dadišo Quatraya in the seventh century.[109] The writings of the nestorian hermit John of Dalyatha in the eighth century are highly esteemed because of his sensitive treatment of such things as spiritual consolations, the struggle against distraction, and the knowledge of the mysteries.[110]

4. The tenth century marks a decline in the syrian language. The Nestorians apparently resisted Arabic better. We should take note of *An Explanation of the Church Services,* a liturgical treatise of great interest attributed to George of Mossul (tenth century).[111] *The Treatise on the Usefulness of Prayer* is the work of a brilliant writer of the Assyro-Chaldean church, Elias bar-Senaya, metropolitan of Nisibis († 1046).[112] George Warda, in the thirteenth century, was the author of a collection of liturgical hymns entitled *Warda* ('The Rose') after his surname.[113]

Of the Jacobites, we need mention only two names: James (Dionysius) Bar Salibi († 1171), famous for his *Explanation of the Liturgy;*[114] and Gregory Abu'l Faradj, surnamed Barhebraeus († 1286), the last glory of his Church; among his learned writings are religious poems marked by a certain charm.[115]

*The Armenians*

Armenian literature, like syriac, is essentially religious.[116] Even in writing a work on history, the armenian author seems to have been preoccupied not so much with the events themselves as with the action of Providence within them. Thus the author easily moves to spontaneous prayer, and following upon this is a great number of hymns, prayers, and ascents to God, some of which are among the most beautiful of universal, mystical literature. Prayer Collections *(Aghothagirq)* abounded.

Hymnographic tradition attributes to Mesrob († 439), the creator of the armenian alphabet, the composition of the lenten troparia. These troparia introduce into this church a spiritual atmosphere of prayer: a personal awareness of human guilt and, at the same time, the hope of forgiveness.[117] Isaac Sahak (the Great) († 438) is presumed to be the author of *k'aroz* (a type of litany within the divine Office), and of certain hymns for Great Week.[118] To the patriarch John Mandakouni († 490) we owe two great liturgical collections still in use.[119] Of the literary production of Stephen of Siounie († *c.* 735), a few fragments of an *Explanation of the Breviary* have survived.[120]

'The armenian Pindar', Gregory of Nareg († *c.* 1010), a mystic monk who greatly influenced the poetic and spiritual life of his nation, won immortal fame through his *Book of Prayer* or *Sacred Elegies.*[121] The volume's general title *olberguthion* ('wailing, lamentation') indicates the author's vivid awareness of sin, and the mysticism of the love of the Redeemer.[122]

*Jesus, Only-begotten Son of the Father*[123] is the english translation of one of the most important poems of Patriarch Nerses IV Šnorhali, 'the Gracious' († 1173). Nerses is fond of emphasizing that prayer is a colloquy; the two speakers in it are 'Jesus Christ, Only-begotten Son of the Father, and himself, Nerses, who became a son by grace'.[124]

For Mekhitar of Sebasteia, the founder of the Mekhitarists († 1749), the choir office lies at the heart of monastic life; it sanctifies the intellectual, manual, and especially apostolic work of the monks.[125]

*The Georgians*

Georgian spiritual literature is rich in translations and reflects the byzantine tradition. Many monasteries owned texts by all the classical authors of patristic times: Evagrius, Cassian, Pseudo-Macarius, John Climacus, Isaac the Syrian, Martyrius Sahdona, Thalassius, and still others. Georgian tradition has preserved for us some texts by eastern, especially egyptian, authors which byzantine literature did not know or did not keep: certain *Letters* by Ammonas, the *Letter* of Arsenius, and yet more.[126]

*The Russians*

In Russia there existed from the beginning a liturgical, mystagogic tradition[127] alongside that of the hesychasts.[128] Yet explicit treatises on prayer appeared only with the spiritual renewal of the eighteenth century. Among the writings of Tikhon of Zadonsk († 1783), we take special note of *The Spiritual Treasure Gathered from the World,*[129] even though this work was directly inspired by the text of an anglican bishop, Joseph Hall († 1656). The very title of Tikhon's book is typical of the method of prayer known in the East as 'natural contemplation'.[130]

Paisius Velichkovsky († 1794)[131] should be viewed as the moving force behind the renewal of hesychast prayer in russian monasteries through his edition of the slavonic *Philokalia.*[132] From him we also have a text entitled *To the Opponents and Detractors of Spiritual Prayer,* that is, the Jesus Prayer.[133]

A new edition of the *Philokalia,*[134] no longer in Church Slavonic, but in the living language, was later published by Ignatii Bryanchaninov († 1867), an advocate of the patristic renewal in spirituality. He also wrote a work *On the Prayer of Jesus.*[135] The most recent edition of the *Philokalia* by Theophan the Recluse (Govorov) († 1894) is the most complete.[136] In his numerous works and letters, this author frequently speaks of prayer, insisting that true prayer is that prayer which addresses God 'unceasingly through the voice of the Spirit in the heart'.[137] *My Life in Jesus Christ,*[138] the spiritual diary of the twentieth-century thaumaturge John of Kronstadt (†1909), contains beautiful reflections on prayer, especially liturgical prayer.

Western readers have come to know the Jesus Prayer through *The Way of a Pilgrim,* translated into several languages.[139] More detailed information may be found in an anthology of russian authors on the prayer of the heart entitled *The Art of Prayer,* put together by Chariton, a monk of Valamo.[140]

Among religious thinkers, we should also mention Vladimir Solovyof († 1900); everything he says about the problem of knowledge is closely linked to christian contemplation.[141]

## LITURGICAL DOCUMENTS

### *Major Byzantine and Armenian Service Books*

In 1645, L. Allatius wrote a large volume of essays on the ordering of the service books used in the greek church.[142] They are twelve in number, though, if needed, an addition is possible.

Three are biblical: the *Evangeliarion* (Book of the Gospels); the *Praxapostolos* (Epistles and Acts); and the Psalter *(Psalterion).* The *Euchologion,* a book for the celebrant, we may translate as 'Rituale', but without any distinction between the Pontifical, the Missal, and the Ritual. It contains the entire sacramentary (an excerpt containing the most important functions of the priest is called 'Service Book', *Hieratikon*). The *Leiturgikon* (Slavonic, *Sluzhebnik*) also forms part of the *Euchologion,* and contains the three ordinaries of the liturgy, as well as the offices of Matins and Vespers. The *Horologion* contains the ordinary of the canonical office, and in an appendix, (though not in their entirety) the temporal cycle, the sanctoral, and the troporia for each day.

The *Octoechos,* 'The Book of Eight Tones', contains the temporal cycle: the *Little Octoechos* includes eight offices for Sundays; the *Great Octoechos* or *Parakletike,* one for each day of the week as well. The *Triodion* contains the propers for the ten weeks before Easter; the *Pentekostarion* the services for paschaltide. The *Heirmologion* is a manual for the use of cantors. The *Menaion* contains the services for fixed feastdays. Historical notes on the lives of the saints are gathered in a collection called the *Synaxarion* or *Menologion.* The same motives that led to the creation of the breviary and the missal in the West led to an attempt to unify the liturgical books in the East under the name of *Anthologion* (Slavonic, *Sbornik* or *Tsvietoslov,* meaning *florilegium*).

The armenian[143] directory or *Tonatc'oyc'* corresponds to the greek *Typikon*. The *Pataragamatoyc'* or *Xohrdatehr,* 'The Book of Mystery', is the book for the liturgical celebrant. The Gospels and Epistles for the liturgy are found in the lectionary, *Čašoc'* (literally, 'the noonday meal'). The *Haysmawurk,* 'this day', contains homilies for Sundays, together with short saints' lives. The Book of Hours, *Zamagirk',* is analogous to the greek *Horologion.*[144] The *Maštoc',* the equivalent of the latin *Rituale,* is a handbook for the priest in the exercise of his ministry. The psalter is called *Salmosaran;* the hymnal *Talaran,* and the antiphonary *Sarakan*. The *Ganjaran* is a book of litanies.

### *Coptic and Ethiopic Books*

The *Euchologion (Hulaki)* is the most important liturgical book of the Copts.[145] It contains the ordinary of the Mass, of the offering of incense, and some other services. In the *Diaconal* are found the variable parts used by the deacon and the faithful. The *Difnar* is the *Menologion*. The *Book of Holy Pascha,* or the lectionary of *Holy Week,* contains the 'order' and the prayers for the services for that week. In the *Pontifical* are found the rituals reserved to the bishop; in the *Ritual,* those of the sacraments. The *Synaxarion,* the *Martyrologium,* is attributed to Peter el-Gamil (in the twelfth-thirteenth century). The annual *Psalmodia* contains the odes, the *Theotokia* (hymns in honor of the *Theotokos*), and the doxologies (hymns for the feasts or in honor of the saints). The *Psalmodia of Kiahk* includes the services of the *Theotokos* proper to the month of Kiahk, before Christmas. The *Horologion* or *Agpeya (al-Agbiyah)* contains the eight hours of the monastic office, together with several other chants and special offices.[146]

Ethiopic liturgical books,[147] whether translated directly from the Greek during the most ancient period or composed *ex novo* in Ethiopia, are of a fairly ancient date. The Ethiopic Church uses seventeen anaphoras found in the *Quedassie,* the Missal. Furthermore, there are several books of plainchant: the *Mewaše'et* (Book of Responses), the *Zig* (Festal Antiphonary), the *Deggua* (Antiphonary for the Year), the *Soma Deggua* (Antiphonary for Lent), the *Me'eraf* (Common Service), and the *Zemmarie* (songs to accompany the distribution of Holy Communion to the faithful). We should add the *Synaxarion* for the feasts of the Saints, and the *Masehafa Gessawye,* the lectionary.

*The Syrian Liturgy*

The *Hudrâ,* or 'Cycle', the oldest liturgical book of the Chaldaean Church,[148] contains the services for all feast days, except for some quite recent compositions. In the *Gazzâ* ('Thesaurus') are found the poetic parts of *Lelya* (Nocturns) for feasts and the commemorations of saints. The *Kaškull* ('containing everything'—that is, the entire text) is a collection of the services of the *Hudrâ* for feast days. The *Warda* ('Rose') is an anthology of antiphons by the poet George Warda († before 1300) and other authors. The *Abu Halim* contains some prayers for *Sapra* (Matins) composed for the most part by the nestorian patriarch Elias III Abu Halim († 1190).[149] The *Ktaba da-qdam wa-d-batar* ('The Book of Before and After') contains a two-week cycle of services: used alternately on even and odd Sundays. The cycle begins on the Sunday after Easter. Three *Lectionaries* are used for the liturgy: the Old Testament and Acts; the Epistles; and the Book of the Gospels.[150] The chaldaean service has no readings except during the Holy Triduum. The *Naqpayatha d'raze* ('Supplement to the Mysteries') contains liturgical chants.[151]

The number of manuscripts of liturgical books to be found among the west Syrians (Jacobites) is surprising. The abundance and variety may be explained by the fact that each priest copied out a certain number of anaphoras. Printed texts were very rare. For this reason the Synod of 1930, held at the monastery of Mar Mattai, decided to unify all these texts with the intention of publishing them.[152]

It is understandable that, as soon as the Syrian Catholic Church was founded in 1662,[153] the Congregation for the Propagation of the Faith was interested in editing the books to be used in worship. Nevertheless, the Syrian Catholic bishops, gathered at the Synod of Charfe in 1888, determined that the liturgical books of their rite were still too varied, and 'without codification'. They decided to edit, in Syriac and Arabic, the following seven books: 1. The *Shehim,* the festal office with the calendar. 2. The *Finkith,* services for non feast days, along with the book entitled *Houssay (Absolutions).* 3. The book containing everything that pertains to the eucharistic liturgy. 4. The *Diaconarium,* with everything that concerns the deacon and the choir. 5. The book called *Sinoûs* (Ritual). 6. The *Festarium, Meadenana,* containing benedictions, processions, and other special ceremonies. 7. The *Pontifical,* with the functions reserved for the bishop. In addition, Syrian Catholics also have a *Breviary* in seven volumes.[154]

Today, the Maronite Church has several editions of its liturgical books[155]: the *Missal;*[156] the *Diaconal,*[157] which contains the 'diaconika', variable acclamations by the deacon; the *Lectionaries,* that is, the *Book of the Gospels,* the *Epistle Book,* the *Lectionary of the Old Testament* for the divine office[158] (in recent editions, readings have also been incorporated into the *Missal,* the *Diaconal,* and the *Fanqītō*). The *Šhîmtō* ('Simple') is the ordinary office for the week, including Sunday. The *Fanqītō* ('Tome') is a book of festal services in two volumes. There is a supplement to it, the *Temeštō* ('Office'), containing fifty more recent offices.[159] The *Book of Holy Fasting,* containing the propers of Lent and Holy Week, exists only in manuscript.[160] The Holy Week office is found in the *Hašō,* 'the Book of the Redeeming Passion'.[161] The *Ritual* contains the celebrations and benedictions of the great annual feasts.[162]

Until the arrival of the Portuguese, Malabar 'Syrians' followed the same liturgy as the east Syrians of Mesopotamia. Unfortunately, no manuscript earlier than the sixteenth century has been preserved. After the separation, the Jacobites and the Syro-Malabar Catholics adopted the antiochian rite. In 1766, a Roman Commission proposed to give the Syro-Malabar clergy the same Missal as the Chaldaeans of Mesopotamia, until someone noticed that the calendar and the system of pericopes differed.[163] The *Ritual* had been translated from Latin into Syriac well before the end of the sixteenth century. What prompts the editions of present-day liturgical books is a desire to rediscover the spirit of their own liturgical tradition.

## LITURGICAL POETRY

### *Greek Hymnography*

Prayer appeals to the deepest, most intimate forces of our being and provides poetry with a rich, profound inspiration. In the early christian communities, piety flowed out 'in psalms and hymns and spiritual songs' (Col 3:16; Eph 5:19). By the term 'hymnography', we traditionally understand all the songs in the liturgy which are neither canonical psalms nor biblical canticles, but form part of the liturgical celebration, especially that of the Hours.[164] Various stylized forms of prayer circulated in jewish and gnostic circles, and under their influence christian hymnography developed.[165] To the extent that relationships between christian and greek culture narrowed, the forms of greek poetry also strongly influenced christian poetry.

In the fourth century, more than one Christian had the ambition of competing with greek classical poetry. The poetic works of Gregory Nazianzus counts more than eighteen thousand lines.[166] The works of Ephrem the Syrian († 373) were very early translated into Greek, and what is called the *Greek Ephrem* (containing pieces that are not by Ephrem) has become a source of inspiration for the various eastern liturgies.[167]

In the sixth century, Romanus Melodius († 556) was recognized as a classic author of liturgical poetry. He must have composed more than a thousand hymns—most of them having twenty-four stanzas—based on free rhythm and a tonic accent.[168] George of Pisidia (first half of the seventh century) wrote in iambic trimeter.[169] Andrew of Crete († 740) is the author of *The Great Canon,* a penitential text of two hundred fifty stanzas used in the liturgy of Great Lent.[170] Following his example, Cosmas the Melodist and his adopted brother John Damascene composed *idiomela* and Canons.[171]

The hymnographic compositions of the Byzantines—monks, priests, and laity—are very numerous. They celebrate Christ and the saints and edify the christian people by 'homilies in verse'. To name only a few, there were Cosmas of Maiuma († 760); Joseph the Studite († 832), brother of Theodore the Studite, several of whose compositions are found in the *Triodion,* the office of 'Great Lent';[172] Joseph of Thessalonika († 832), Theophanes († 847);[173] Joseph the Hymnographer († 886);[174] Metrophanes of Smyrna († *c.* 900);[175] the Emperor Leo VI († 912);[176] John Kyriotes, called 'the Geometer' (tenth century);[177] and John Mauropous (eleventh century).[178] We note, too, that religious poetry was also cultivated in the greek-byzantine monastic circles in Italy. [179]

*Forms of Hymnology in the Byzantine Rite*[180]

The liturgical genre typical of the byzantine rite is the *Canon* (Greek, κανών), a collection of scriptural canticles or 'Odes' (Ωδαί, Slavonic, *pěsni*), accepted as canons for liturgical use. As early as the seventh century, under syrian influence, poetic texts came to be inserted between lines taken from Scripture. Soon they pervaded everything, until today the scriptural odes are sung only rarely, with the exception of the Canticle of the Virgin, the *Magnificat.*

The *Kontakion* (Κοντάκιον, Slavonic, *kondak*), inspired by syrian metrical homilies, is the oldest non-psalmodic contribution. The ancient *Kontakia* contained a model stanza and *iki* (Οἶκος Slavonic, *ikos,* strophe)—often twenty-four of them. The best known among the authors of kontakia is Romanus Melodius († 556). The *Akathist Hymn* is an entire *Kontakion.* Today, the *Kontakion* is placed after the sixth canticle of the canon of *Orthros* (the Morning Service).

Troparion (Τροπάριον, Slavonic, *troparj*), from the Greek *tropos* (mode, manner, tone), is a generic term used to designate a poetic liturgical stanza with a simple structure and rhythmic cadence. It is often a development of the psalmodic antiphon. *Troparia* bear various names depending on their content, the place they occupy in the liturgical Office, or their melody: A *Triadikon* (Τριαδικόν, Slavonic, *troïčnyj, troïčen*), honors the Trinity. A *Doxastikon* (Δοξαστικόν, Slavonic, *slavnik*) is sung after the first part of doxology, the 'Glory be to the Father and to the Son and to the Holy Spirit.' A *Theotokion* (Θεοτοκίον, Slavonic, *Bogorodičen*) honors the Mother of God, the *Theotokos.* A *Dogmatikon* (Δογματικόν, Slavonic, *Dogmatik*) is a qualitative name given to the *Theotokion* of the evening service (*Lucernarium,* in Latin) because of its specific theological formulations. A *Sticheron* (Στιχηρόν, Slavonic, *stichira*) is a troparion inserted between psalm verses (στίχοι); a series of *Stichera* constitutes an *Anatolikon* (Ἀνατολικον, Slavonic, *vostočen*) or *Aposticha* (Ἀπόστιχα, Slavonic, *Stichovna*). *Evlogitaria* (Εὐλογητάρια, Slavonic, *tropari voskresny*) accompany the verse, 'Blessed art Thou, O Lord' (Ps 118/119:2). *Anavathmi* (Ἀναβάθμοί, Slavonic, *stepenny*) are three very short troparia inspired by the songs of ascent (Psalms 119-133 / 120-134). *Kathisma* (Κάθισμα, Slavonic, *kafisma*) is the part of the service when people may be seated (by contrast, they stand during the *Akathist Hymn*), but it is also the name of the troparion which follows the Little Collect *(Ektenia)* during *Orthros*. The twenty kathismata of the psalter are divided into three *Stases* (Στάσις, *statija*), also called *Antiphons*. The *Apolytikion* (Ἀπολυτίκιον, *otpustitelnyi*) is a troparion sung at the end of Vespers and *Orthros*. *Hypakoê* ('Υπακοη, *ipakoi,* 'response') is a troparion that originated in Jerusalem for Sundays and feastdays. *Prosomion* (Προσόμιον, *podoben*) is strictly speaking not a melody, but is sung according to a melody common to other troparia; by contrast an *Idiomelon* ('Ιδιόμελον, *samoglasěn*) sung according to a proper melody. *Irmos* (Εἱρμός, *irmos,* 'series') originally served as the melodic, rhythmic model for the other odes of the canon; when it is repeated by the two choirs at the end of the ode, as on feast days, it is called *katavasia* (Καταβασία, 'descent'). The *Prokimenon* (Προκείμενον, *prokimen*) is not a troparion but the verse placed before a psalm, to which it serves as a response.

The litany of prayers usually reserved to the deacon are, by their number, one of the characteristics of the byzantine rite. We may distinguish among the Great and Little *Collect* (Συναπτη', Slavonic, *ekteniya*), the *Ektenia* ('Εκτενή, *sugubaja*), with a prolonged response; a triple *Kyrie eleison* ('Lord, have mercy') at each invocation, and the *Petition* (Αἴτησις; Slavonic, *prositelnaja ekteniya*). Each verse ends with the words, 'We pray' or 'We beseech thee', to which the response is 'Grant this, O Lord'. *Lity* (Λιτή, Slavonic, *litya*), 'entreaty, supplication', with a procession to the narthex of the church is a rite characteristic of the ancient liturgy of Constantinople. Among the chants, the evening hymn 'O joyful light' (Greek, *phôs hilaron,* (φῶς ἱλαρον, Slavonic, *světe tichij*) is one of the rare remaining examples of early christian hymns.[181] The *Exapostilarion* ('Εξαποστελάριον, *exapostilarij*) is the chant that precedes Lauds after the canon of Orthros. During Lent, it is called *Photagogikon* (φωταγογικόν, *světilen*), an appeal to the morning light. The *Trisagion* (Τρισάγιον, *tisvjotoe*)—'Holy God, Holy Almighty, Holy Immortal'—is an acclamation taken from Isaiah 6:3. Mentioned in the acts of the Council of Chalcedon and originally christological, it has been given a trinitarian interpretation. A very popular refrain, it is sung at almost all services. The *Doxology* (Δοξολογία, *slavoslovie*) glorifies the Trinity at the end of a prayer, like the *Ekphonesis* (Slavonic, *vozglas*): 'Glory be to the Father'. But it is also the hymn 'Glory to God in the highest', which occurs at the end of Orthros. *Eothinon* ('Εωθινόν, *utrennaja stichira*) is the *Doxastikon* of Lauds, corresponding to one of the eleven gospels of the Resurrection on Sunday.

Far and away the most famous hymn is unquestionably the *Acathist,* a hymn of jubilation and of praise to Mary.[182]

### *Syriac Poetry*[183]

The success of Ephrem's compositions inspired many imitators. Numerous works were written in verse to imprint religious teachings firmly on the minds of the people. Between syriac and hebrew poetry there is a certain similarity: the grouping of lines by two, the use of acrostic stanzas, and the 'response'—that is, the repetition at the beginning of a stanza of a concept contained in the preceding strophe. The basic principle of syriac metrics, which is not found in Hebrew, however, is the fixed number of syllables in a line.

Religious poetic compositions may be divided in two groups: metric homilies *(memre)* and hymns *(madrashe).* The metric homilies—poetic discourses of a narrative or epic genre—are written in lines of the same meter of five, seven, or twelve syllables. The 'hymn' is not known to the Syrians; the poems we designate by this term were called 'instructions'. Unlike the homilies, they represent the lyric genre and are capable of all its variations, running from a verse of four syllables to one of ten. The Syrians are very fond of the genre they call *sughitha* or canticle, which takes dialogue form (somewhat analogously to the latin *Victimae paschali laudes,* 'Christians, to the Paschal victim').

Beginning in the ninth century, when the use of Arabic began to supplant Syriac, the Syrians, in imitation of arabic poetry, introduced rhyme into their metrical compositions along with often affected, artificial turns of phrase.

### *Armenian and Georgian Hymnology*

The liturgical hymnology of the Armenians took on its enduring appearance from the thirteenth century on, thanks to Vardan Vardapet († 1271), the Catholicos James Klajetzi († 1287), and John Vardapet Ernzkatzi († 1325). The printed edition of the armenian hymnal in 1664 fixed its form and its content was estimated at 1166 hymns.[184]

The Georgians' liturgical poetry grew out of the translation of greek texts, a work probably begun in Jerusalem. Although such texts are usually called *jambiḳoni*, they are not iambic poetry, but prose, having generally twelve syllables; rhyme is rare, and acrostics are favored. The best known poets are Gregory of Khandzta († 861), John Minčchi, and John Mtbevari, bishop of Tbethis (tenth century). About the year 980, Mikhael Modrekeli gathered a great collection of hymns.[185] The translation of the most important byzantine collections by George the Hagiorite († 1065) decisively enriched the georgian literary patrimony.[186]

### *Ethiopian Liturgical Chant*

The Ethiopians have several collections of chant. They were fond of some genres not pertaining to the liturgy: the *salâm,* which consists of one or more five-line stanzas, the first of which opens with the word *salâm,* 'greetings to'. The *malkee* (image, portrait) praises the main members and organs of a saint's body. The *quenê* are short compositions sung by their authors during liturgical functions, especially on Sunday, at the moment of 'the throwing of incense'.

Marian hymnody is especially rich. The collection *Matshafa Kidâna Mehrat (The Book of the Covenant of Mercy)* was written in rhymed prose toward the end of the fifteenth century in the monastery of Lake Tsana. The *Weddâsê Mâryâm (In Praise of Mary),* of egyptian or syrian origin, served as a model to other collections. The *Argânona Dengel* (*Organ of the Virgin*) must have been composed about 1440, in imitation of the *Weddâsê Mâryâm*. Finally there is the *Lâhâ Mâryâm (Mary's Lamentations),* sung on Good Friday and reminiscent of the *Stabat Mater dolorosa.*[187]

## *Notes*

1. See Adalbert Hamman, *La prière,* 2: *Les trois premiers siècles.* (Tournai 1963).

2. English translation by Robert M. Grant and Holt H. Graham, *First and Second Clement,* The Apostolic Fathers, 2 (New York: Thomas Nelson, 1965) 92ff; also translated by Edgar J. Goodspeed, *The Apostolic Fathers. An American Translation* (New York: Harper, 1950); and by James A. Kleist, Clement of Rome: 'The Epistle to the Corinthians', in *The Epistles of St. Clement of Rome and St. Ignatius of Antioch,* ACW 1 (1961). See Ferdinand Cavallera, 'Clément de Rome (saint)'. DSp 2/1 (Paris, 1953) 962–963.

3. English translation by Robert M. Grant, *Ignatius of Antioch,* The Apostolic Fathers, 4 (London-Camden-Toronto: Thomas Nelson); also by Goodspeed (above, n. 2) and by Kleist (note 2). See Pierre-Thomas Camelot, 'Ignace d'Antioche'. DSp 7/2 (1971) 1250–1266.

4. Translated by Graydon F. Snyder, *Hermas,* The Apostolic Fathers, 6 (Nelson, 1968); also by Goodspeed (above, n. 2). See Joseph Paramelle and Pierre Adnès, 'Hermas (Le Pasteur d')'. DSp 7/1 (1968) 316–334.

5. Gustave Bardy, 'Apocryphes à tendance encratique (Actes des Apôtres)'. DSp 1 (1936) 752–765.

6. See Johannes Quasten, *Patrology,* 4 volumes (Utrecht-Brussels 1950; rpt 1986) 1:176–185.

7. Justin Martyr, *Apologia I pro christianis,* 67; PG 6:429BC; translated by Leslie W. Barnard, *St. Justin Martyr: The First and Second Apologies,* ACW 56 (New York, 1997).

8. *Ad Autolycum* 2. 22; SCh 20 (Paris, 1948) 154; translated ANF 2:89–121: *Theophilus to Autolycus* (1885, rpt. 1994).

9. See Louis Doutreleau and Lucien Regnault, DSp 7/2 (1971) 1939–1969; A[ntonio] Orbe, 'Ireneo'. DP I (1983) 1791 8 (bibliography), 'Irenaeus'. EEC I, (New York: Oxford University Press,1992) 413–416, translated by Adrian Walford. All subsequent references are to the EEC edition.

10. See Marcel Richard, 'Hippolyte de Rome'. DSp 7/1 (1968) 531–571.

11. Walther Völker, *Der wahre Gnostiker nach Clemens Alexandrinus.* (Berlin, 1952).

12. Henri Crouzel, 'Origène'. DSp 11 (1982) 933–961.

13. *De oratione;* PG 11:415–561; GCS 2:295–403; translated by John J. O'Meara, *Origen: Prayer, Exhortation to Martyrdom,* ACW 19 (1954).

14. See Wilhelm Gessel, *Die Theologie des Gebetes nach 'De oratione' von Origenes.* (Paderborn, 1975).

15. *Methodius of Olympus: The Symposium, A Treatise on Charity,* translated H. Musurillo, ACW 27 (1958). See Herbert A. Musurillo, 'Méthode d'Olympe'. DSp 10 (1977) 1109–1117.

16. See Gustave Bardy, 'Didyme d'Alexandrie'. DSp 3 (1957) 868–867; P(ierre) Nautin, 'Didymus the Blind of Alexandria', EEC 1 (1992) 235–236.

17. *De adoratione et cultu in Spiritu et veritate;* PG 68:133–1125.

18. Hubert du Manoir, 'Cyrille d'Alexandrie (saint)', DSp 2/2 (1953) 1672–1683; (M[anlio] Simonetti, 'Cyril of Alexandria', EEC 1 (1992) 214–251.

19. Basilius Steidle, *Antonius Magnus Eremita* (Rome, 1956) 356.

20. Greek text in PO 11 (Paris 1916) 432–454; Syriac in PO 10 (1915) 539–555; Latin in PG 40:1019–1066; English translation. by Derwas J. Chitty, *The Letters of Ammonas: Successor of St Anthony* (Oxford: Fairacres Press 1979; available in the United States from Cistercian Publications).

21. English translation by Armand Veilleux, *Pachomian Koinonia*, 3 volumes (Kalamazoo: Cistercian Publications, 1980–1982). See Heinrich Bacht, 'Pachôme (saint)'. DSp 12/1 (1984) 7–16. See also Philip Rousseau, *Pachomius: The Making of a Community in Fourth-century Egypt* (Berkeley, 1985).

22. *De oratione tractatus;* PG 79:1165–1200; french text and commentary by Irénée Hausherr in RAM (1934; rpt. 1959, 1960); offprint, *Leçons d'un contemplatif* (Paris 1960); translation by John Eudes Bamberger, *Evagrius Ponticus. The Praktikos: Chapters on Prayer.* CS 4 (Spencer-Kalamazoo: Cistercian Publications, 1970).

23. English translation by Robert T. Meyer, *Palladius: The Lausiac History,* ACW 34 (1991). See Bernard Flusin, 'Pallade d'Hélénopolis'. DSp 12/1 (1984) 113–126.

24. See, e.g. the Index in SCh 64:241 *(oraison),* 243 *(prière);* SCh 109:524 *(oratio).* See Michel Olphe-Galliard, 'Cassien (Jean)', DSp 2/1 (1953) 214–276. See also the Index in the english translation by Colm Luibheid, *John Cassian: Conferences* CWS (New York 1985) 207 (Prayer).

25. PL 73:941–943.

26. F. Cavallera, in DSp 1 (1936) 765–770.

27. Erpidio Mioni, in DSp 8 (1974) 632–640.

28. Guerric Couilleau, DSp 8 (1974) 369–389.

29. SCh 26bis (1968); english translation by Agnes C. Way, *Saint Basil: Exegetic Homilies*. FCh (New York 1973) 3–135.

30. *Homilia in martyrem Julittam;* PG 31:237–262.

31. Jacques Rousse, in DSp 6 (1967) 932–971; J[ean] Gribomont, 'Grégoire de Nazianze', DP 2: 1707–1712; 'Gregory Nazianzen', EEC 1:361–362.

32. Mariette Canévet, in DSp 6:971–1011. *Gregory of Nyssa: The Life of Moses,* translated by Abraham J. Malherbe and Everett Ferguson, CWS (New York 1978), CS 9 (Kalamazoo 1978).

33. SCh 126 (1966); see Gustave Bardy, in DSp 2/2 (1953) 2683–2687. English translation by Leo P. McCauley and Anthony A. Stephenson, *The Works of Saint Cyril of Jerusalem,* 2. FCh (1970) 143–206.

34. PG 64:329–330 *(oratio),* 364–366 *(preces).*

35. Antoine Wegner, in DSp 8 (1974) 331–335.

36. *De Anna sermo IV;* PG 54:660–668.

37. M[anlio] Simonetti, 'Diodoro di Tarso', DP I, 976–978; 'Diodore of Tarsus', EEC 1:236–237]; *idem,* 'Teodoro di Mopsuestia', DP 2:3382–3386; 'Theodore of Mopsuestia', EEC 2:824–825.

38. Vincent Desprez and Mariette Canévet, in DSp 10 (1977) 20–43. *Fifty Spiritual Homilies: St Macarius the Great,* translated by A. J. Mason (Willits, CA: Eastern Orthodox Books, 1974); *Pseudo-Macarius: The Fifty Spiritual Homilies and the Great Letter,* CWS, translated by George A. Maloney (1992).

39. *De oratione;* PG 34:853–866.
40. *De elevatione mentis;* PG 34:889–908.
41. *De custodia cordis;* PG 34:821–852.
42. See Jean Kirchmeyer, in DSp 7/1 (1968) 399–408.
43. Critical edition by Aldo Ceresa-Gastaldo, *Capitoli sulla carità* (Rome, 1963). English translation by Polycarp Sherwood, *St Maximus the Confessor. The Ascetic Life; The Four Centuries on Charity,* ACW 21 (Westminster: Newman Press, 1955). See also Irénée-Henri Dalmais, 'Maxime le Confesseur'. DSp 10 (1977) 836–847; Andrew Louth, *Maximus the Confessor* (London: Routledge, 1996).
44. Basile Studer, in DSp 8 (1974) 452–466.
45. *De imaginibus oratio* I, II, III;, PG 94:1231–1420. English translation by D. Anderson, *On the Divine Images* (Crestwood, New York: St Vladimir's Seminary Press, 1980).
46. *Mystica contemplatio;* PG 98:383–454.
47. *Mystagogia;* PG 91:657–718. English translation by George C. Berthold, *The Church's Mystagogy.* CWS (New York 1985) 181–226; and by D. J. Stead, *Church, The Liturgy and the Soul of Man: The Mystagogia of St. Maximus the Confessor* (Petersham, MA: St Bede's Publications, 1982).
48. Jean Darrouzès, 'Germain I de Constantinople (saint)', DSp 6 (1967) 309–311.
49. *Descriptio constitutionis monasterii Studii;* PG 99:1704–1720.
50. *Interrogationes et responsiones;* PG 89:311–824.
51. Eds. Venice (1783), Constantinople (1861), Athens (1900, 1901, 1957); see Aimé Solignac, 'Paul Evergetinos'. DSp 12/2 (1984) 562–564.
52. See Charles de Clercq, *Les textes juridiques dans les Pandectes de Nicon de la Montagne Noire.* Sacred Congregation for the Eastern Church, Codif, canon. orient., Fonti II, 30 (Venice, 1942); see also Marcel Richard, 'Florilèges grecs'. DSp 5 (1962) 475–512.
53. Daniel Stiernon, 'Isaïe, moine byzantin', DSp 7/2 (1971) 2080–2082.
54. Pélopidas Stéphanou, 'Photius', DSp 12/1 (1984) 1397–1408.
55. Hans-Georg Beck, *Kirche und theologische Literatur im byzantinischen Reich* (Munich, 1959) 538–541.
56. Sévérien Salaville, 'Cabasilas (Nicolas)', DSp 2/1 (1953) 1–9. Cabasilas, *A Commentary on the Divine Liturgy,* translated by J. M. Hussey and P. A. McNulty (London: SPCK-Crestwood, New York: St Vladimir's Seminary Press, 1960).
57. J. Lemaitre (Hausherr), in DSp 2/2 (1953) 1792ff; see Aimé Solignac, 'Nicétas Stéthatos'. DSp 11 (1982) 224–230.
58. Basil (Vasilii) Krivochéine, *Syméon le Nouveau Théologien, 949–1022. Vie-Spiritualité-Doctrine* (Chevetogne, 1980); English translation by Anthony P. Gythiel, *In the Light of Christ: Saint Symeon the New Theologian (949–1022). Life-Spirituality-Doctrine* (Crestwood, New York: St Vladimir's Seminary Press, 1986). See also Aimé Solignac, 'Nicétas Stéthatos'. DSp11 (1982) 224–230.
59. Jean Kirchmeyer, 'Hésychius le Sinaïte', DSp 7/1 (1968) 408–410.
60. Aimé Solignac, 'Philotée de Batos', DSp 12 (1984) 1386–1389.
61. Jean Darrouzès, 'Grégoire le Sinaïte', DSp 6 (1967) 1011–1114.
62. Daniel Stiernon, 'Nicéphore l'Hésychaste', DSp 11 (1982) 198–203.
63. Jean Meyendorff, 'Palamas (Grégoire)', DSp 12 (1984) 82–107; *Triades,* Spicilegium sacrum Lovaniense. Etudes et documents; fasc. 30–31; critical edition and french translation by John Meyendorff, 2 vols. (Louvain 1959); 2d revised ed. (1974); english selections translated by Nicholas Gendle, *Gregory Palamas: The Triads,* CWS (New York: Paulist Press, 1983).
64. Aimé Solignac, 'Philothée Kokkinos', DSp 12/1 (1984) 1389–1392.

65. Kallistos Ware, 'Philocalie', DSp 12/1:1336–1352.
66. Daniel Stiernon, 'Jean de Karpathos', DSp 8 (1974) 589–592.
67. 'Abbé Philémon', DSp 8:1113.
68. Kallistos Ware, 'Thalassius le lybien', DSp 12/1 (1984) 1340.
69. 'Théodore le Grand', DSp 12/1:1340.
70. Jean Darrouzès, 'Elie l'ecdidos', DSp 4/1 (1960) 576–578.
71. Kallistos Ware, 'Théophane le moine. Pierre Damascène', DSp 12/1 (1984) 1341.
72. 'Théognoste', DSp 12/1:1341.
73. 'Théolepte de Philadelphie', DSp 12/1:1341.
74. 'Calliste et Ignace Xanthopoulos', DSp 12/1:1342.
75. 'Calliste Tèlikoudès', DSp 12/1:1342.
76. 'Calliste Kataphygiotès (alias Kataphrygiotès)', DSp 12/1:1342; Hans-Georg Beck, *Kirche,* 784–785.
77. Martin Jugie, 'Syméon de Thessalonique', DThC 14/2 (1941) 2976–2984.
78. Kallistos Ware, 'Philocalie', DSp 12/1 (1984) 1336.
79. Tito Orlandi, 'Copto', DP 1:774–780. 'Coptic', EEC 1 (1992) 199–201.
80. Adalbert Hamman, 'Serapione di Thmuis', DP 2: 3150. 'Serapion of Thmuis'. EEC 2 (1992) 768.
81. Martin Jugie, 'Monophysite (Eglise copte)', DThC 10/2 (1929) 2251–2306.
82. *Ibid.,* 2267ff.
83. Jean-Baptiste Chabot. *Littérature syriaque* (Paris 1935).
84. R. H. Connolly, trans., *Didascalia Apostolorum. The Syriac Version translated and accompanied by the Verona Latin fragments.* (Oxford 1929).
85. René Lavenant, 'Bardesane'. DP I:746–752. 'Bardesanes', EEC 1 (1992) 110.
86. Lavenant, 'Afraate', DP 1:58–61. 'Aphraates'. EEC (1992) 54; Irénée Hausherr, 'Aphraate (Afrahat)', DSp 1 (1936) 746–752.
87. Antoine Gauillaumont, *Liber Graduum,* DSp 9 (1975) 749–754; Maria Grazia Bianco, *Liber,* DP 2:1944–5. *Liber,* EEC 1:485. English translation by Robert Kitchen and Martien Parmentier, *Liber Graduum. The Syriac Book of Steps* (Kalamazoo: Cistercian Publications, 2004); excerpts translated by Sebastian Brock in *The Syriac Fathers on Prayer and the Spiritual Life* (Kalamazoo: Cistercian Publications, 1987) 41–61.
88. Edmond Beck, Demetrios Hemmerdinger-Iliadou, and Jean Kirchmeyer, 'Ephrem', DSp 4 (1960) 788–822; Frédérick Rilliet, 'Efrem Siro', DP 1:1103–1107. 'Ephrem the Syrian', EEC 1 (1992) 276–277. Sebastian Brock, *The Luminous Eye: The Spiritual World Vision of Saint Ephrem.* CS 124 (Kalamazoo: Cistercian Publications, 1992).
89. Joseph-Marie Sauget, 'Babai', DP 1:468. 'Babai the Great', EEC 1 (1992) 106.
90. François Graffin, 'Isaac d'Amid, Isaac d'Antioche', DSp 7/2 (1971) 2010–2011; Michel Van Esbroeck, 'Isacco di Amida, Isacco di Antiochia', DP 2:1828 ;'Isaac of Amida, Isaac of Antioch', EEC 1 (1992) 416.
91. Bruce Bradley, 'Jean le Solitaire (d'Apamée)', DSp 8 (1974) 764–772; J[oseph]-M[arie] Sauget, 'Giovanni di Licopoli', DP 2:1568–70 ['John of Lycopolis', EEC 1 (1992) 445]. Excerpts translated by Sebastian Brock, *The Syriac Fathers on Prayer and the Spiritual Life* (Kalamazoo: Cistercian Publications, 1987) 77–100.
92. Lucien Regnault, 'Isaïe de Scété ou de Gaza', DSp 7/2 (1971) 2083–2095; Jean Gribomont, 'Isaia di Sceti (e di Gaza)', DP 2:1831–1832; 'Isaiah of Scete (and Gaza)', EEC 1 (1992) 417. *Isaiah of Scetis: Ascetic Discourses,* translated by John Chryssavgis and Robert Penkett (Kalamazoo: Cistercian Publications, 2002).
93. François Graffin, 'Jacques de Saroug', DSp 8 (1974) 56–60; Jean Gribomont, 'Giacomo di Sarug', DP 2:1512–1513; 'Jacob of Sarug', EEC 1 (1992) 429.

94. François Graffin, 'Philoxène de Mabboug', DSp 12 (1984) 1392–1397; Frédéric Rilliet, 'Filosseno di Mabbug', DP 1:1372–1374; 'Philoxenus of Mabbug', EEC 2 (1992) 684. Excerpts translated by Sebastian Brock, *The Syriac Fathers on Prayer and the Spiritual Life* (Kalamazoo: Cistercian Publications, 1987) 101–133.

95. Antoine Guillaumont, 'Étienne Bar Soudaïli (ou Soudailê)', DSp 4/2 (1961) 1481–1488; J[oseph]-M[arie] Sauget, 'Stefano Bar Sûdaylê', DP 2:3306–3307; Stephen Bar Sûdaylê', EEC 2 (1992) 794.

96. J.-M. Sauget, 'Rabbula di Edessa'. DP II, 2967–8; 'Rabbula of Edessa'. EEC II. (1992) 729. Robert Doran, *Writings from Fifth Century Edessa: The Man of God, Rabbula, and Hiba* (Kalamazoo: Cistercian Publications, forthcoming 2006).

97. René Lavenant, 'Narsai (Narsete) (399–502)', DP 2:2342–2343; 'Narsai or Narses (399–502)', EEC 2 (1992) 583.

98. J.-M. Sauget, 'Henanâ di Adiabene', DP 2:1727–1728; 'Henana of Adiabene', EEC 1 (1992) 374.

99. Michel Van Esbroeck, 'Babai bar Nesibnaye il Piccolo'. DP I, 463–464; 'Babai bar Nesibnaye (the Less)'. EEC I (1992) 106; J.-M. Sauget, 'Babai il Grande'. DP I, 463; 'Babai the Great'. EEC I (1992) 106. Excerpts translated by Sebastian Brock, *The Syriac Fathers on Prayer and the Spiritual Life* (Kalamazoo 1987)135–165.

100. Jean Kirchmeyer, 'Grégoire de Chypre', DSp 6 (1967) 920–922.

101. Jean-Baptiste Chabot, *Littérature syriaque*, 59ff.

102. J.-M. Sauget, 'Giacomo di Edessa', DP 2:1508–1509; 'Jacob of Edessa', EEC 2 (1992) 428–429. François Graffin, 'Jacques d'Edessa', DSp 8 (1974) 33–35.

103. François Graffin, 'Moïse Bar Képha', DSp 10 (1977) 1471–1473.

104. CSCO, 201–2.

105. Louis Leloir, 'Martyrius (Sahdona)', DSp 10 (1977) 737–742. Angelo Di Berardino, 'Martirio (Sahdona)', DP 2:2154–2155; 'Martyrius (Sahdona)', EEC 1 (1992) 536. Excerpts translated by Sebastian Brock, *The Syriac Fathers on Prayer and the Spiritual Life*, 197–239.

106. See below, Chapter 8, p. 243.

107. Robert Beulay, 'Joseph Hazzâyâ', DSp 8 (1974) 1341–1349.

108. Élie Khalifé-Hachem, 'Isaac de Ninive', DSp 7 (1971) 2041–2054. René Lavenant, 'Isacco di Ninive', DP 2:1892–1830; 'Isaac of Nineveh', EEC 1 (1992) 416. Hilarion Alfeyev, *The Spiritual World of Isaac the Syrian* (Kalamazoo: Cistercian Publications, 2001).

109. Antoine Guillaumont, 'Dadišo Qatraya'. DSp 3 (1957) 2–3.

110. Robert Beulay, 'Jean de Dalyatha', DSp 8 (1974) 449–45. S[ever] J. Voicu, 'Giovanni di Dalyatha (Saba)', DP 2:1159; 'John of Dalyatha', EEC 1 (1992) 445.

111. Chabot, *Littérature syriaque* (1935) 115ff.

112. Emmanuel-Karim Delly, in DSp 4/1 (1960) 572–574.

113. Chabot, *Littérature*, 137ff.

114. François Graffin, 'Jacques (Denys) Bar Salibi', DSp 8 (1974) 29–30.

115. F[rançois] Nau, 'Barhébraeus', DThC 2/1 (1910) 401–406.

116. Irénée Hausherr, 'Arménienne (spiritualité)', DSp 1 (1936) 862–876.

117. Boghos Levon Zekiyan, 'Mesrop (dit Maštoc')', DSp 10 (1977) 1070–1074. S[ever] J. Voicu, 'Mesrob', DP 2:2231–2232; 'Mesrob (Mesrovp or Mastoc')', EEC 1 (1992) 556.

118. Athanase Renoux, 'Isaac le Grand', DSp 7/2 (1971) 2007–2010. S[ever] J. Voicu, 'Sahak il Grande', DP 2:3062–3063; 'Sahak the Great', EEC 2 (1992) 752.

119. André Rayez, 'Jean Mandakouni', DSp 8 (1974) 621–622. S[ever] J. Voicu, 'Giovanni Mandakuni', DP 2:1571; 'John Mandakuni', EEC 1 (1992) 443.

120. Joseph Karst, 'Étienne de Siounie', DSp 4/2 (1961) 1524–1525.
121. *Le livre de prières.* Introduction, traduction de l'arménien et notes par Isaac Kéchichian, SJ avec une préface de Jean Mécérian SJ, SCh 78 (Paris: Cerf, 1961).
122. Isaac Kéchinian, 'Grégoire de Narek', DSp 6 (1967) 927–932.
123. English translation by J. S. Wingate, *Jesus, Son Only-begotten of the Father* (New York 1947); french translation by Isaac Kéchichian, *Jésus, Fils unique du Père,* SCh 203 (Paris: Cerf, 1973).
124. *Jesu. Fils unique;* SCh 203:229.
125. Boghos Levon Zekiyan, 'Mékhitar et Mékhitaristes', DSp 10 (1977) 940–950.
126. Gérard Garitte, 'Géorgienne (littérature spirituelle)', DSp 6 (1967) 244–256. *A Systematic Handbook,* 16–17, 363–364. Tomaš Špidlík, 'Georgiano monachesimo', DIP 4 (1977) 1054–1055.
127. K.Ch. Felmy, *Die Deutung der göttlichen Liturgie in der russischen Theologie* (Berlin-New York, 1984).
128. Tomaš Špidlík, *Les grands mystiques russes* (Paris 1979) 129ff.
129. *Works* (in Russian), volume 3 (Moscow 1899).
130. Špidlík, *Les grands mystiques,* 65–72.
131. Kallistos Ware, 'Philocalie', DSp 12/1 (1984)1343ff.
132. See Špidlík, *Les grands mystiques,* 173ff.
133. Translated into French by Igor Smolitsch, *Moines de la sainte Russie* (Paris 1967) 98–104.
134. Saint Petersburg, 1857.
135. Saint Petersburg, 1967; English selections translated by Lazarus [Moore], *On the Prayer of Jesus: From the Ascetic Essays of Bishop Ignatius Brianchaninov,* 2d ed. (London 1965).
136. Published by the monastery of Saint Panteleimon on Mount Athos, 1877–1905; rpt. Jordanville, New York (1963–1966).
137. Tomaš Špidlík, *La doctrine spirituelle de Théophane le Reclus, Le Coeur et l'Esprit,* OCA 172 (Rome, 1965): chapter IV: L'oraison ou la 'respiration de l'Esprit', 239–291.
138. French translation published by Bellefontaine in 1979, in the collecton *Spiritualité orientale* 27. *My Life in Christ,* translated by E. E. Goulaeff (Jordanville, New York, 1994).
139. See below, Chapter 10, p. 331.
140. Chariton de Valaam, *L'art de la prière, Anthologie sur la prière du coeur,* Spiritualité orientale, 18 (Bellefontaine 1976). *The Art of Prayer,* translated by E. Kadloubovsky and E[lizabeth] M. Palmer (London: Faber and Faber, 1966).
141. Tomaš Špidlík, 'Solov'ev', in *La mistica, fenomenologia e riflessione teologica* (Rome 1984) 645–668.
142. *De libris ecclesiasticis Graecorum dissertationes duae . . .* (Paris 1645); cf. Sévérien Salaville, *Liturgies orientales, notions générales, éléments principaux* (Paris: Librairie Bloud & Gay, 1932)178ff; translated by John M. T. Barton, *An Introduction to the Study of Eastern Liturgies* (London: Sands & Co., 1938) 185ff.
143. *Acta et decreta concilii nationalis Armenorum Romae habiti, anno Domini 1911* (Rome 1914) 305–314; Louis Petit, 'Arménie', DThC 1/2 (1923)1963ff. Malachia Ormanian, *A Dictionary of the Armenian Church,* translated by B. Norehad (New York 1984). Z. Baronian,'Cărtile de slujbă ale Bisericii armene', in *Biserica Orthodoxă Română,* 88 (1980) 1082–1091. Anton Baumstark, *Liturgie comparée, Principes et Méthodes pour l'étude historique des liturgies chrétiennes* (Paris-Chevetogne: Éditions de Chevetogne, 1953) 256ff; translated F. L. Cross, *Comparative Liturgy* (Westminster, Md: Newman, 1958).

144. There is a complete latin translation of the *Žamagirk' Hajastaneajc ekelecvoj* under the title *Breviarium Armenium sive Dispositio communium Armeniacae Ecclesiae precum a sanctis Isaaco patriarcha, Mesrobio doctore, Kindio atque Joanne Mantagunensi habita, nunc primum in Latinam linguam translatum* (Venice 1908); *The Book of the Order of Common Prayers of the Armenian Apostolic Orthodox Church* (Evanston, IL, 1964).
145. G. Graf, *Geschichte der christlichen arabischen Literatur,* volume 5, Studi e Testi 118 (Città del Vaticano 1944–1953) volume 1: 644–652; H. Malak, 'Les livres liturgiques de l'Église copte', in *Mélanges E. Tisserant,* Studi e Testi, 233, (Città del Vaticano 1964) volume 3:1–35.
146. Translation of the *Horologion. The Agpeya, being the Coptic Orthodox Book of Hours* . . . (Los Angeles, 1982); *Agpeya, Das Koptische Stundengebet* (Würzburg, 1984).
147. Bernard Velat, 'Éthiope'. DSp 4/2 (1961) 1456ff. Velat, 'Études sur le me'eraf'. *Proche Orient Chrétien* 33 (1983) 9ff.
148. Eugène Tisserant, 'Nestorienne (Église)'. DThC 11/1 (1931) 317–23. C. Mousses, *Les livres liturgiques de l'Église chaldéenne* (Beirut, 1955) vol. 1. J. Mateos, *Lelya-Sapra,* OCA 156 (Rome, 1959) 3–37. S. Pudichery, *Ramsa: an Analysis and Interpretation of the Chaldean Vespers* (Bangalore, 1972). P.G. Badger, *The Nestorians and their Rituals* (London, 1892) vol. 2:19–25.
149. Mateos, *Lelya-Sapra,* 66ff.
150. Mousses, *Livres liturgiques,* 3ff., 29–51. A. J. MacLean, *East Syrian Daily Offices.* (London, 1984) 264–290. *L'Orient syrien* 3 (1958) 358–386; 12 (1967) 211–240, 371–388, 525–548.
151. Mousses, *Livres liturgiques,* chap. 5.
152. Ignace Ziadé, 'Syrienne (Église)'. DThC 14/2 (1941) 3024ff.
153. *Ibid.,* 3025.
154. *Synodus Sciarfensis Syrorum in Monte Libano celebrata anno 1888.* (Rome, 1897) 37–39. A[nton] Baumstark, *Liturgie comparée* (Paris-Chevetogne: Editions Chevetogne, 1953) 242–245; *Comparative Liturgy,* translated by F. L. Cross (Westminster, Md.: Newman, 1958)]. Baumstark, *Festbrevier und Kirchenjahr der syrischen Jakobiten* (Paderborn, 1910) 29–97.
155. Michel Breydy, *L'Office divin dans l'Église Syro-Maronite.* (Beirut, 1960) 56–78. P. Dib, *Études sur la liturgie maronite.* (Paris, 1964) chapters 2–3. B. Gemayel, *Prière du Croyant, selon l'année liturgique maronite,* 3 vols. (Beirut, 1967–1968). Louis Hage, *Le chant de l'Église maronite,* vol. 1. (Beirut, 1972). Michel Hayek, *Liturgie maronite, Histoire et textes eucharistiques* (Paris, 1964). Jean Tabet, *L'Office commun maronite* (Kaslik, 1972). Michel Hayek, 'Maronite (Église)'. DSp 10 (1980) 631–644.
156. Hayek, *Liturgie maronite,* 61ff. Dib, *Études,* 34–77.
157. Hayek, 84–94. Dib, 77–87.
158. Hayek, 94–102. Dib, 159–64.
159. Dib, 151–152.
160. Breydy, *L'Office divin,* 63. Dib, 152ff.
161. Breydy, 62ff.
162. Dib, 100–104.
163. Eugène Tisserant, 'Syro-Malabare (Église)'. DTH 14/2 (1941) 3157. We are grateful to Robert F. Taft for reviewing these notes on the liturgical books.
164. Aimé Georges Martimort, *L'Église en prière* IV, *La liturgie et le temps* (Paris, 1983) 228; translated by Matthew J. O'Connell, *The Church at Prayer,* vol. IV: *The Liturgy and Time* (Collegeville, Minnesota: The Liturgical Press, 1986), 'The Liturgy of the Hours', 151–175. G. Del Ton, G. Schirò, and A. Raes, 'Innografia'. *Enc. Cattolica* 7 (1951)

28–39. J. P. Foucher, *Poésie liturgique, Orient, Occident* (Mame, 1963). Jacques Fontaine, 'Innologia'. DP II, 1781–1783 (bibliographie.); 'Hymn-Hymnology'. EEC I (1992) 400–1 (bibliography).
165. Robert T. Taft, 'Select Bibliography on the Byzantine Liturgy of the Hours'. OCP 48 (1982) 358–370; particularly, 365ff.
166. Jean Gribomont, 'Gregorio di Nazianzo'. DP II, 1710; 'Gregory Nazianzen'. EEC I (1992) 361–2.
167. Demetrios Hemmerdinger-Iliadou, 'Ephrem grec'. DSp 4/1 (1960) 800–815.
168. S[ergio] Zincone, 'Romano il Melode'. DP II, 1528 ['Romanus Melodus'. EEC II (1992) 740].
169. Daniel Stiernon, 'Gregorio di Pisidia'. DP I, 1528. [George of Pisidia'. EEC II (1992) 343].
170. Johannes Irmscher, 'Andrea di Creta'. DP I, 192–193. ['Andrew of Crete'. EEC II (1992) 38].
171. Irmscher, 'Cosma di Maiouma'. DP I, 749; 'Cosmas of Maiuma'. EEC I (1992) 204.
172. Daniel Stiernon, 'Joseph Stoudite (saint)'. DSp 8 (1974) 1405–1408.
173. Stiernon, 'Méthode (saint)'. DSp 10 (1977) 1107–1109.
174. Stiernon, 'Joseph l'Hymnographe'. DSp 8 (1974) 1349–1354.
175. Stiernon, 'Métrophane de Smyrne'. DSp 10 (1977) 1126–1129.
176. Stiernon, 'Leon VI (le Sage)'. DSp 9 (1975) 615–639.
177. Jean Darrouzès, 'Géomètre'. DSp 6 (1967) 235–236.
178. Daniel Stiernon, 'Jean Mauropous'. DSp 8 (1974) 624–626.
179. Agostino Petrusi, 'La spiritualité gréco-byzantine en Italie Méridionale'. DSp 7/2 (1971) 2193–2206.
180. *La prière des Églises de rite byzantin,* vol. IV (Chevetogne, 1968): *Dimanche, Office selon les huits tons,* Ὀκτώηχος, 595ff.
181. E. R. Smothers, 'Phôs hilaron'. *Recherches des Sciences Religieuses* 19 (1929) 266–283.
182. Elio Peretto, 'Acatisto'. DP 1:27–28; 'Acathistus'. EEC 1 (1992) 5.
183. Jean Baptiste Chabot, *Littérature syriaque* (Paris, 1935) 30ff.
184. Nerses Ter-Mikaëlian, *Das armenische Hymnarium, Studien zu seiner geschichtlichen Entwicklung* (Leipzig, 1905).
185. G. Deeters, 'Georgische Literatur', in *Handbuch der Orientalistik* 7: *Armenisch und Kaukasische Sprachen* (Leiden-Cologne, 1963) 137.
186. Jean Kirchmeyer, 'George l'Hagiorite (saint)'. DSp 6 (1967) 240–242.
187. G. Nollet, *'Le culte de Marie en Éthiopie',* in Hubert du Manoir, *Maria, Études sur la Sainte Vierge,* vol. I (Paris, 1949) 363–413.

## 2

# THE DIVINE-HUMAN DIALOGUE

### *The Necessity of Prayer*

THE LANGUAGE OF THE EAST is rich in symbols. To emphasize the importance of prayer, what could be more appropriate than the piling-up of metaphors? Prayer, John Chrysostom writes, is 'a harbor for the storm-tossed, an anchor for the shipwrecked, a staff for those who totter, the treasure of the poor. Prayer is a refuge in sadness, an argument for joyousness, a cause of uninterrupted pleasure, the mother of philosophy.'[1] In another text, it is 'the light of the soul',[2] 'a chance for salvation, the Church's strong wall and unshaken rampart, the terror of demons'[3]; it is as indispensable to monks as water is to fish,[4] and a sword to the hunter.[5]

Paul Evergetinos defines prayer as 'the monk's mirror'[6]; according to the ethiopian *Paterikon,* it is 'his bride'[7]; for John of Kronstadt, 'Prayer is the breathing of the soul . . . our spiritual food and drink'.[8]

Western medieval scholastics searched for 'convenient reasons' to demonstrate the necessity of prayer. They strongly emphasized the human person's radical incapability of achieving salvation by himself or herself alone. We hear an echo of discussions against Pelagianism when prayer is presented as a necessary 'aid', and the obligation to pray as being imposed 'by a divine law, some sort of contract'. Strangely enough, the Gospel 'Ask' (Mt 7:7: 'Ask and you shall receive') emerges as an 'urgent exhortation', while prayer itself would not be an absolute obligation.[9]

The perspective of Easterners is much broader. To show that a Christian must pray, they emphasize not so much the corruption of human nature by sin as the original deification of the human person, our renewal in Christ, and our participation in the trinitarian life—hence, our disposition 'to dialogue' with heaven. For the sinner, prayer is the search for a lost paradise, for the original *parrhesia* ('frankness of speech'), free access to heaven. The situation of the Christian, John Chrysostom writes, is this: 'God on earth, man in heaven: all became intermingled. Angels joined the choirs of man, man dwelt with the angels and the other heavenly powers.'[10]

Theophan the Recluse confirms this 'natural' need to pray by an analysis of the anthropological trichotomy traditional in the East.[11] The human person is made up of three elements: 'the part of the body, that of the soul, and that of the spirit. Each has its needs and powers, as well as its own ways of displaying them.'[12] We should not deny the claims and needs of the body, for these are natural appetites. The soul is active in the spheres of knowledge, the will, and the feelings. And the spirit? It prays. Prayer may therefore be called 'the breathing of the spirit'.

> As the lungs expand to draw in the life-giving elements of air by breathing, so do the depths of our soul open and expand during prayer, and our spirit mounts up to God to receive the gift that allows us to be united with him. And as the oxygen received by the blood is then conveyed to the entire body to vivify it, so the gift received from God permeates everything that is in us and vitalizes our entire inner being.[13]

We may therefore say that 'prayer is the spiritual barometer that allows us to "become aware of ourselves"'.[14]

In the process of the human person's 'spiritualization', prayer is more than an effective aid: it is the pre-eminent means of salvation. 'Just as sight is the most worthy of the senses, so also is prayer the most divine of virtues,' Evagrius writes.[15] 'When prayer takes possession of us', Ignatii Brianchaninov writes, 'it gradually transforms us, and spiritualizes us as a result of our union with the Holy Spirit.'[16]

In the East, we know, the perfection of the spiritual life is viewed as the resplendence of the image of God in man.[17] Now, according to the Greek Fathers, 'the image of God in man' is the image of Christ, the Logos,[18] born eternally in the contemplation of the Father. In conformity with this sublime example, the human person is born spiritually in prayer.

Progressive growth manifests itself as the acquisition of wisdom, *gnosis.*[19] Christian *gnosis,* however, is not 'sterile' knowledge: it is a conscious understanding of the creative, saving word of God, the word which calls for the human person's response.[20] Prayer, a dialogue with God, is therefore typically christian wisdom, true philosophy.[21]

This priority given to prayer in progressing along the path of perfection is not explicable only by the fact that the East is more contemplative. Is prayer not also viewed as 'the soul of the apostolate'? On this point, too, the East has its own perspective. In the West, this requirement is often presented as follows: we must pray, otherwise our works of charity will remain sterile, without divine blessing. The eastern monks performed their works of charity principally by praying. But for this prayer to be effective, the practice of charity was a precondition.[22]

The perspective may be different, but the practical conclusion remains the same: we must learn how to pray, do our best to pray, and pray to be able to pray. Someone once came to ask a solitary to accept him as a disciple. The solitary asked him: 'What do you need, brother?' The other replied: 'I have come to pray, father'.[23] Abba Agathon said: 'Nothing is more laborious than prayer. There are moments of relaxation for every virtue, but prayer does not permit any, until our last breath.'[24]

## *Definitions of Prayer*

While christian prayer is like the breathing of our deified nature, only rough definitions, drawn from human experience can be given of it. The profound nature of prayer, even the very possibility of its existence, is revealed only to those who enter into this sanctuary. The 'definitions' which come from such experience only describe one or another particular aspect of it.[25]

As the unquestioned master of 'definitions' of spiritual realities, John Climacus opens his 'argument' *(logos)* on prayer as follows:

> Prayer by reason of its nature is the converse and union of man with God, and by reason of its action upholds the world and brings about reconciliation with God; it is the mother and also the daughter of tears, the propitiation for sins, a bridge over temptations, a wall against afflictions, a crushing of conflicts, work of angels, food of all the spiritual beings, future gladness, boundless activity, the spring of virtues, the source of graces, invisible progress, food of the soul, the enlightening of the mind, an axe for despair, a demonstration of hope, the annulling of sorrow, the wealth of monks, the treasure of solitaries, the reduction of anger, the mirror of progress, the realization of the future, a sign of glory. For him who truly prays, prayer is the court, the judgment hall and the tribunal of the Lord before the judgment to come.[26]

Meanwhile, three definitions have become famous in the christian tradition: a petitioning of God; an ascent of the mind; and conversation with God. As a communication of the human person with God, prayer is viewed primarily as 'asking God for what is appropriate'.[27]

The ancients had already spoken of the 'ascent of the spirit to God'—a definition taken over by Evagrius.[28] This ascent is viewed as a going up, because 'the mind cannot see, until it reaches the top of the mountain; the spiritual mountain is knowledge of the Holy Trinity, and its summit is difficult of access'.[29] It is an ascent of the mind—that is, of the higher part of our being—in keeping with the advice: 'Keep your eyes lowered while you are praying. Deny your flesh and your desires and live according to the spirit.'[30]

Because the human person raises himself or herself to God who is Father, the ascent is not limited simply to 'seeing' (*horasis,* in the platonic sense)—but it becomes a conversation, 'a continual intercourse of the spirit with God'.[31] *Homilia* (communication) and its equivalent *conversatio* (dialogue) denote something which is both deeper and more encompassing than even inner words: an encounter, habitual intercourse, persistent frequent meetings. The translation 'with God' takes away the essential aspect of movement from πρὸς θεόν (towards God).

John of Damascus unified all these aspects in the following formulation, taken over by many others: 'Prayer is an ascent of the mind to God, or a request to God for what is appropriate'.[32]

To avoid the danger of platonic intellectualizing, it was necessary to explain and adapt νοῦς, mind, the organ of this ascent, or to replace it by 'heart', to designate the totality of the spiritualized human person. What is more, ways had to be found to express clearly what one would dare ask of God, the source of all goodness, and in what manner the human person, an earthbound being, could make his or her voice heard in heaven.

### *Various Types of Prayer*

Bound up with life, prayer follows innumerable forms and manifestations. Prayer has therefore been given many different names which authors have used with great spontaneity. So, for example, Martyrius Sahdona viewed prayer indiscriminately as 'taking our stand in the Office for the utterance of praise that sends our minds towards God, supplications made in his presence, metanies (genuflections), prayers of petition accompanied by spiritual groaning of the heart, fervour of spirit when we are set on fire by love, eagerness of mind as we gaze undistractedly on God'.[33]

In *The Ladder* of John Climacus, we read that 'The attitude of prayer is one and the same for all, but there are many kinds of prayer and many different prayers'. He too enumerates randomly the various postures that can be observed among the monks in church.[34]

Yet the very fact that so many different names are used is indicative of an attempt at classification; and so it was that certain terms gradually acquired a specific meaning: oral, mental, affective prayer, meditation, contemplation, and on it goes.[35] The authors who used such terms spontaneously sought to classify them into some order. The problem lay in finding an adequate criterion.

All masters adjust their teaching to the progress of their disciples. They try to determine which type of prayer will be appropriate for beginners, for those who had made some progress, and for the perfect. Thus, John the Solitary describes prayers that are suitable for 'the somatic, psychic, and pneumatic'.[36] They all address their petitions to God. According to Evagrius, however, the requests formulated by those who concentrate on *praxis* differ from those formulated by persons aspiring to *theoria* (contemplation).[37]

Attempts have sometimes been made to define the four basic forms of prayer on the basis of an analysis of the four terms found in 1 Tm 2:1, 'petitions, prayers, intercessions, thanksgiving'.[38]

A basic, but significant, classification can be created by the two main definitions of prayer: a petition addressed to God; and an ascent of the mind towards God. With some reservations, we may say that such a distinction reflects the evolution from biblical prayer towards the contemplative ideal of the Greek Fathers.

The anthropological character of eastern spirituality justifies taking the distinction suggested by Theophan the Recluse as the one which most adequately classifies the various degrees corresponding to the structure of the composite human being. The proposed formulation points out the predominant element:

1. Bodily or vocal prayer *(telesnaja, molitvoslovnaja);*
2. Mental prayer *(umnaja);*
3. Prayer of the intellect and of the heart; or only of the heart, of feeling *(umnoserdečnaja, serdečnaja, čuvstva);*
4. Spiritual or contemplative prayer *(duchovnaja, sozercatel'naja).*[39]

What appears to be missing in this structure is the dimension of the will. Yet Theophan was well aware of the role of the will in prayer when he spoke of 'laborious' prayer.[40] Moreover, he realized that the term 'mental prayer' can be applied also to the three degrees that follow vocal prayer. The distinction between private and community prayer could certainly be added, although that distinction does not fall within the outline of spiritual progress according to the dynamics of the human 'trichotomy'.

These categories will help us to arrange the subject matter in chapters. We will deal first with prayer as a petition, and will then follow the framework sketched out by Theophan. But we must first answer the preliminary question: to whom is prayer addressed?

### *Prayer to the Father*

Prayer is an ascent of the spirit to God, a request addressed to God, a dialogue with God. Only with a person can we converse. Unlike systems of philosophy, a living religion has a personal view of the deity, a certain concept of the divine 'fatherhood', known from experience. This dimension is very explicit in Scripture, which is the revelation of a God who lives and reigns. Scripture contains no treatise *De Deo:* it does not stand back, as if to describe its object from a distance. It asks us, not to speak about God, but to listen to him and respond to him. What prompted Israel to call God its father was a living experience, not reason. The *Leitmotiv* in psalmic prayer is *batah,* 'to put one's trust in'.[41] Jesus Christ fulfills judaic reflection on the fatherhood of God. He invites us to live like a child who entreats its father (Mt 7:7-11) and trusts him (6:24-34). The life of believers is therefore marked by prayer to the Father.

The Church Fathers instinctively viewed the Lord's Prayer as the pre-eminent christian prayer (sometimes with an anti-jewish touch). Their explanations are usually based on johannine or pauline texts about the divine filiation.[42] 'The one who loves God constantly lives and speaks with him as a Father', Evagrius writes.[43]

A beautiful meditation entitled 'The Father and his Children', by Tikhon of Zadonsk sought to develop this concept in greater detail: 'Children are born of a father; renewed and made children of God by grace. Christians too, are born of God. Character traits resembling those of the father are found in the children. Father and children speak to one another with tenderness.'[44] And it continues in this vein.

### *Sons through the Son, in the Holy Spirit*

Conscious of the sublime dignity of being able to pray in this manner, the spiritual writers insist above all on the moral purity of the person who wishes to address God as Father. 'Before we approach God', Gregory of Nyssa advises, 'we should first examine our life, whether we have something of the divine kinship in ourselves, and so make bold to use this word [Father]. For the one who commanded us to say Father does not permit us to speak a lie.'[45] To the modern reader, a surprising aspect of the ancient commentaries on the Lord's Prayer is the insistence with which they viewed this prayer as a rule of life because prayer is in vain if life is not in harmony with it.[46] The Father-child relationship presupposes a resemblance.

This fact does not deal with the question of whether reflection is able to clarify such a personal relationship with God. The concept of 'God-the-Father' conveys a mystery that is inaccessible precisely because this mystery represents a person who is sovereignly free.[47] Yet the Gospel is 'the proclamation of Jesus Christ in accordance with that mystery which for ages was kept secret but now is revealed' (Rom 16:25ff.). The Inaccessible makes himself known by his grace, through Jesus Christ, in the Holy Spirit. This is why patristic commentaries on the Lord's Prayer always have an underlying trinitarian character, even when it is now explicitly stated.[48]

When Christ revealed the identity of the Father and of God, he set this revelation within another mystery, which the traditional formulations epitomize by two movements: one descending—every good comes to us from the Father, through the Son, in the Holy Spirit; the other, ascending—we ascend to the Father, through the Son, in the Holy Spirit.[49]

## *The One Mediator*

To express its spiritual momentum, early Christianity borrowed its formulations and usages from Judaism. Yet Christians knew that the 'servant' prophesized by Isaiah had arrived, and that Christ is the Saviour and Mediator. The Church was conscious of this newness. All prayer, Justin Martyr writes, has its source in 'the crucified High Priest' who founded his Church as 'a house of prayer and worship'.[50]

For a prayer to be heard, it must be uttered in the name of Christ.[51] He is the true Mediator between God and human beings (1 Tim 3:5ff.). The pseudo-mystical trends that proliferated in late antiquity, as well as those of all religions, attempted to 'bridge the gulf between the visible and invisible world'.[52] For the great philosophers, the unity of the visible and invisible world could not be conceptualized without some intermediary. In Plato, this function is exercised by *Eros*,[53] who is between (μεταξύ) the two worlds. The plotinian 'world soul' played an analogous role.[54] A well-developed doctrine of the Logos-Mediator is found in Philo.[55]

The Church Fathers grasped and understood what Philo was only able to guess at: that the Word of God was made flesh to be the Mediator of the New Covenant.[56] Christ is Mediator as a man endowed with the fullness of grace, because 'God was in Christ, reconciling the world to himself'.[57] Christ does not stand *between* God and the people, nor does he represent God as an angel could, since he himself is 'the source of eternal salvation' (Heb 5:9).[58] It is through him then that God speaks to the people; it is through him that the human voice ascends to God, and shares in the eternal dialogue between the Father and His Word.

## *In the Spirit*

The nearness between our spirit and God is established above all in prayer, which is uttered 'in the Spirit'.[59] According to the beautiful expression of Theophan the Recluse, prayer is 'the breathing of the Spirit'.[60] Speaking to God presupposes some form of inspiration, since the human person in prayer is 'under the guidance of the Spirit of God' (ὁδηγουμένος ὑπὸ τοῦ θείου πνεύματος).[61]

The activity of the Spirit during prayer has never been questioned in the East, but it has rather been exaggerated by charismatic trends as, for example, among the Messalians.[62] This activity is manifested especially in the following manner: it unites our prayer to that of the Son, gives it the power to obtain what it asks for, reveals an understanding of the mysteries, and joins individual prayers in the one single voice of the Church.

Without the Spirit, prayer would not be christological. For Saint Paul, being 'in Christ Jesus' (Rom 8:1) means living by 'the Spirit' (Rom 8:2). The Paraclete is 'the Spirit of adoption', in whom we cry, *'Abba,* Father' (Rom 8:15, Gal 4:6).[63] The Spirit lets us repeat the gestures of Christ, because he is the Spirit of Jesus. He prolongs the thanksgiving of Jesus in the breaking of the bread, and enables us to repeat the prayer of Jesus.[64]

Saint Paul guides Christians to the knowledge that comes from the Spirit of God, thanks to which we can truly 'understand the gifts bestowed on us by God', and express them in words 'taught by the Holy Spirit' (1 Cor 2:6-16), who 'helps us in our weakness; for we do not know how to pray as we ought' (Rom 8:26).[65]

The Spirit always reveals himself in the Church as the source of prophecy and knowledge *(gnosis).* 'No one is capable of revealing and interpreting the heavenly mysteries if he does not partake of the Spirit,' writes Hippolytus.[66] Basil often commented on the subject, borrowing freely from the pages in which Plotinus links the inward richness of the mind to the World Soul.[67] 'We believe in . . . the Holy Spirit, . . . who teaches all things and brings all things to remembrance, as many as he hears from the Son . . . , who is good and leads into all truth and establishes all that believe in sure knowledge.'[68]

Knowledge is enlightenment. But since the term 'light' is applied either to the Spirit or to the Son, the verse 'In thy light we shall see light' (Ps 35:10) is often interpreted as follows: through the illumination of the Holy Spirit, we shall see 'the true light that enlightens every man that comes into the world' (Jn 1:9).[69]

During the preparation for the Liturgy, the armenian rite invokes the Spirit as 'the interpreter of the profound mysteries of the almighty will of the Father of Emmanuel'.[70]

Finally, the Spirit gathers the scattered prayers of the faithful into the one voice of the Church of Christ. According to Basil, 'the Spirit is a whole divided into parts, according to the distribution of charisms'[71]; or, as Cyril of Jerusalem writes, as 'the light (that) with one casting of its radiance, brightens everything'.[72]

## Epiclesis

Every prayer uttered in the Spirit contains an implied *epiclesis*. In Greek, ἐπίκλησις carries the meaning 'invocation' and it is used by liturgists and theologians to designate a prayer of the *anaphora*—or canon of the Mass—asking for divine intervention (almost always that of the Holy Spirit) upon the gifts and upon the communicants. The formulation usually follows the *anamnesis* (recollection, commemoration) and therefore comes after the words of Christ, 'This is my Body; this is my Blood'.

A theological principle is emphasized by this structure of the eucharistic canon. The eucharistic prayer is trinitarian. The consecration therefore is attributed to the three divine Persons: to the Father, in so far as it represents an act of divine power; but it is the priesthood of the Son that renews the mystery of the Last Supper on the altar; finally, this mystery is the special work of the Holy

Spirit, to whom every activity of sanctification is attributed. The invocation of the Holy Spirit is highly developed in the eastern liturgies because the church writers readily emphasized the parallelism between the Incarnation and the consecration, both brought about by and performed through the power of the Holy Spirit.[73]

In some patristic texts, the entire *anaphora*, not just this particular prayer, is viewed as the great 'invocation', and is called *epiclesis.* Outside the Eucharist, the term is sometimes used to designate invocations of the Holy Spirit during liturgy. 'All the sacraments and ecclesiastical rituals of the eastern Church are indeed a solemn, explicit profession of orthodox pneumatology,' Cyprian Kern writes.[74] In collects and prayers, the Paraclete is invoked that he may descend and perform the blessing of the baptismal waters or of the oil of the sick, or may crown the newly married couple, and so forth.

The short prayer that introduces the services of the byzantine rite—'Heavenly King, Spirit of Truth, Who art in all places and fillest all things: come, and abide in us, and save our souls'—may be compared to the *Veni Sancte Spiritus* ('Come, Holy Spirit') of the Latins.

### *Devotion to the Humanity of Christ*

*Omnis oratio dirigitur ad Patrem:* all prayer is addressed to the Father. In conformity with this ancient rule, Origen maintains that we do not pray to Christ, but to the Father through Christ.[75] Nevertheless, this rule was not strictly followed, even by the man who formulated it. Popular devotion was often addressed to Christ. While being stoned, Stephen the Deacon repeated the last words of Christ on the cross. But he addressed them to Christ instead of calling upon the Father as the Saviour had done: 'Lord, Jesus, receive my spirit!' (Acts 7:59). Invocations to Christ were frequently heard on the lips of the martyrs. While being brutally beaten, Senator Dativus addressed this prayer to the Lord: 'Lord Jesus Christ, let me not be confounded!'[76] The God to whom the Desert Fathers addressed themselves was very frequently Christ.[77] The place of Christ in the apocrypha is so central that it almost obscures the role of the Father within the liturgical celebrations.[78] The *Kyrios* ushered in the new times.

*Kyrios* (Lord) is the divine title. It is often said that eastern spirituality is characterized by a strong awareness of the divine transcendence, and that in the Incarnation, Christ's divinity is emphasized more strongly than his humanity.[79] It is indeed difficult to speak of a devotion of Christians of the early centuries to the humanity of Christ. In his glory, they no longer had any reason to view him as a mere man. Their prayer was addressed 'to Christos as to a God', according to the testimony of Pliny the Younger in his famous *Letter to Trajan.*[80]

But did this vivid awareness of the Lord's glory bring with it a diminished esteem for his appearance 'in the flesh'? The heresy of docetism prompted the orthodox Fathers to pay more attention to the humanity which the Word of God had not spurned. Christ, God and man, has actualized in his person the encounter between divine transcendence and human finiteness, without sacrificing the one or ignoring the other.[81]

One could insist further that the Fathers were not preoccupied with devotion, and that in their reflections they adopted a view that was primarily polemical and intellectualizing. The liturgical witness is persuasive in this respect. The function of liturgy, too, was to highlight the divinity of Christ proclaimed at Nicaea. The great feasts gave christian poets a chance to write hymns in honor of the God-man. Themes that had been familiar to preachers were taken up again, but with a more exuberant lyricism.[82] Pilgrimages led to the places where the Saviour had lived. In Bethlehem, the grotto of the Nativity had been venerated long before the Peace of the Church under Constantine; a magnificent basilica equal to the Holy Sepulchre drew the attention of pious believers to this place. By representing scenes from the gospels, art and the apocrypha satisfied the attachment the people felt for the events and deeds of the life of Christ.

Later on, icons 'not made by hands' *(acheiropoietes,* μανδύλιον, *mandulion,* from the Arabic *mandîl* or *mindîl)* represented the glorious face of Christ: the face of God reflected in the human face of the only Son, the image of the Father.[83]

It should be noted that in the liturgical texts of the byzantine feast of the Holy Face there is a display of themes concerning the veneration of icons, which are to be venerated specifically because they represent the divine-human face of Christ.[84]

*Contemplating the Mysteries of the Life of Christ*

In principle, the Fathers are in agreement when they state that all knowledge about God remains fundamentally linked to Christ, and that mystic union with God is proportional to our actual participation in the mystery of the God-man.[85] By nature, the Saviour is the perfect image of the Father, his 'face'.[86] This image is then stamped in the heart of the believers.

In Philotheus of Sinai, a nice detail refers to a mystic 'photograph':

> And so, every hour and every moment let us zealously guard our heart from thoughts obscuring the mirror of our soul, which should contain, drawn and imprinted on it (φωτεινογραφεῖσθαι), the radiant image of Christ who is the wisdom and the power of God the Father.[87]

A distinction is often made between two levels of mystical experience. On the first is the experience of the incarnate Christ; on the higher level, the humanity of Christ directs contemplation toward Christ God.[88]

For Origen, contemplation of the humanity of Christ remains linked above all to Scripture, which is totally inspired with a view to the incarnation of the *Logos* (Word). Starting from the texts, contemplation of the mysteries of Christ is practiced in a special manner on the basis of spiritual meanings, and is far from being an abstract theory; all the thought processes are modeled on the most humble gestures of the Savior: 'The soul, attracted by the fragrance of the perfumes of the Word, is carried along in its wake'.[89] A good definition of the imitation of the Word, in Origen, was given not long ago: it is 'the application to oneself of the episodes of the life of Christ (through allegory, and universalizing)'.[90]

Ultimately, the adoption of the sentiments of Christ makes of the Christian another Christ. The divine image in us, Gregory Nazianzus writes, is purified through contact with the luminous model from on high.[91] It is actualized in the union with Christ, whose actions become the norm for ours,[92] and whose feelings become the model for our own: the peacefulness of Christ teaches us gentleness.[93]

## *Imitating the Saints*

Just as Christ is for us the image of the substance of the Father (Heb 1:2), so the saints are models in whom we find some reflection of the human-divine Exemplar to whom they attempted to conform their life.[94] This theme is sounded as early as the first Letter of Paul, our oldest document on the Church: 'You became imitators of us and of the Lord' (1 Thess 1:6).

*Exempla* played an important role in the moralizing literature of the ancients. We need only recall the famous line of Seneca, often repeated by Christians: *Longum iter est per praecepta, breve et efficax per exempla:* 'The way is long if one follows precepts, but short and productive if one follows examples.' A collection was made of examples from the Old and New Testaments: Abraham, Moses, Elijah, John the Baptist, and many others comparable to the heroes of pagan literature—and this quickly became traditional.[95]

We should therefore not be surprised if the christian tradition has always viewed meditation on or the reading of saints' lives as a tonic for the spiritual life, a comfort, an encouragement. Collections, often voluminous collections, were made: the byzantine *Menaia* contains twelve volumes, one for each month *(men).* The syrian *Fanqito* has been published in seven volumes; hardly less would be needed for a complete edition of the chaldean *Gazza.* The coptic *Difnar* and the armenian *Šarakan* are more restrained.[96]

## *Ecclesiastical* Anamnesis

A purely external model would reduce the christian mystery to a profane mimicry. Our union with the saints is within the Body of Christ. That remembrance of the saints was evoked during the eucharistic prayer as an *anamnesis* of the life of the Church from the very beginning is not without importance. By means of these eminent figures this commemoration makes present the history of salvation which is being accomplished alongside the history of the world since Pentecost.

The eastern churches established their sanctoral very early. While that of the non-byzantine churches contains almost no names later than the sixth century, the byzantine sanctoral , by contrast, tended to be ecumenical, especially after the tenth century, by incorporating the most famous saints from various regions of the empire.[97] The Russians have proved to be even more receptive of recent saints. Following the example of Rome, they have elaborated a procedure for canonization, while maintaining that the legitimacy of the veneration must be the result of a *de facto* situation: the consensus of the christian people being viewed as expressive of the faith of the Church.[98] The central core of this faith, then, is that 'the saints live after death', as John of Kronstadt writes, and that they are very close to us during the liturgy:

> I often hear . . . the Mother of God singing her wonderful, heart-penetrating song . . . . At times, I hear the song of Moses; the song of Zacharias . . . . Here is a proof for you of the immortality of men's souls. How is it that all these people have died, and yet are governing our lives after their death—they are dead and they still speak, instruct and touch us?[99]

The various eastern churches have all, to a greater or lesser degree, assigned an important place to the veneration of the saints of the Old Testament. Such veneration apparently originated in the annual commemoration of the dedication of a church built in their honor in the Holy Land.[100] To the feasts of the saints should be added the commemoration of the councils to be found in the calendar of most churches.[101]

The psychological and national importance of the veneration of the saints should not be minimized. For believers, the saints represent a spiritual family, whose presence, especially at church, creates an atmosphere of spiritual warmth and tenderness. The saints' feast days on the liturgical calendar were embellished by proverbs and popular aphorisms alluding to all aspects of daily life. For peasants, one was 'a sowing saint', another 'makes hay', and so on. It is not difficult to understand why people were opposed to the introduction of the gregorian instead of the julian calendar: indeed, according to the new dating, many of these customs totally lost their meaning.[102]

*The Saints' Intercession*

The eastern liturgies invoke Christ, at the conclusion of prayers, 'together *with* the pure and blessed Virgin Mary, the Mother of God, *with* the angels and *with* all the saints'.[103] Unity in Christ cements the solidarity among all the members of the Church, in heaven and on earth. Heavenly beatitude is of a communal, ecclesiastical nature. The problem is knowing how to phrase the invocation of a certain patron, a specific saint, in order to obtain his or her personal intercession.

In the West, Catholic theologians strongly insist on the fact that the universal mediation of Christ is in no way lessened by the subsidiary mediation of the saints, and that their invocation is optional.[104] Eastern Christians, as we said, cannot imagine God or Christ except in the midst of saints: the mediation of Christ is a mystery of the *total* Christ, in all his members. The prayer of an individual is always incorporated into the intercession of the saints, who are the real mortar between the 'living stones' of the Church.[105]

While living here below in the ecclesiastical community, human persons maintain their own personalities and unique relationships with others; the latter are not destroyed in celestial society, but are in fact strengthened because they have been purified. The Orthodox faith professes that 'Our Lady, the Mother of God, the angels and all the saints are as near to me when I call upon them with a pure, whole heart as my own soul, and hear me, as I hear myself'. John of Kronstadt, who wrote these words,[106] wondered, 'How is it that the saints see us . . . ?' He replied,

> The saintly soul, having become united to God as to its spiritual sun, sees, through the medium of its spiritual sun which lights the whole universe, all persons and the needs of those who pray.[107]
>
> Therefore, how easy it is to communicate with the saints! It is only necessary to purify the eye of the heart, to fix it firmly upon a saint known to you, to pray to him for what you want, and you will obtain it.'[108]

Macarius Bulgakov asked the same question in his *Orthodox Dogmatic Theology*.[109] He makes a comparison with the gift of spiritual insight *(diorasis)* of the saints who are still on earth, and adds: 'Why not admit that all the souls of the just in heaven receive from God the gift of being so enlightened that, when standing before his throne, they see in the person of God everything that happens on earth?'

## *Veneration of the Mother of God*

All of eastern piety, according to Vladimir Lossky, consists of the celebration of what is the goal of our salvation: overcoming the abyss between God and man. This is why there is added to the Christians' devotion to an incarnate divine hypostasis, Jesus Christ, a deified human hypostasis, Mary, whom Gregory Palamas calls: 'the boundary between the created and the uncreated'.[110]

We hear about 'the eschatologism of the eastern Church'.[111] Is the mystery of Mary not one of the most effective expressions of this hope? 'The last glory of the Mother of God', Lossky continues, is 'the *eschaton* realized in a created person before the end of the world'.[112]

> Tradition shows us the Mother of God in the midst of the disciples on the day of Pentecost . . . . The Mother of God received with the Church the last and only thing she lacked, so that she might grow to mature manhood, to the measure of the stature of the fullness of Christ.[113]

In pre-revolutionary Russia, close to a thousand icons of Mary were venerated in the liturgical calendar under various names—for example, 'Our Consolation', 'Provident', 'Softening of our evil hearts', and so on. The icon called *Pokrov* (Protection) represents the Virgin covering the entire earth with her mantle. The icon *Znamenye* (Sign, Miracle) shows Mary in the *orans* posture, with the Word of God on her breast. This is symbolic of the deifying contemplation which makes God present in the soul. On the icon of the Ascension, the Virgin represents the Church imploring the descent of the Spirit and the second coming of the Saviour.[114] The veneration of the Mother of God represents one of the typical traits of eastern Christians because devotion to the

*Theotokos* (God-bearer) agrees well with the characteristics of eastern spirituality.[115]

### *Angels*

In Scripture, God is surrounded by innumerable angels (Dn 7:10), who are like his army, his court. The greek term *angelos* originally referred to a human messenger whose person was sacred because he was charged specifically with negotiating treaties in times of war. The term was then reserved for messengers of the gods, as, for example, Hermes.[116] For the Hebrews, an angel was a messenger who transmitted divine commands and announced heavenly blessings.[117]

As mediators between human beings and God, the angels never cease ascending above the heavens to offer God our good thoughts, our repentance,[118] and prayers, and to descend from there laden with gifts, especially inspirations and enlightenings.[119] In this statement by Origen, we hear an echo either of Scripture or of Plato in writing about the role of intermediary spirits *(daemones).*[120]

In the East, numerous texts speak about the function of the angel in prayer, during the Liturgy, and in the discernment of thoughts: 'When the angel of the Lord visits us, he dispels by his word alone every conflicting force acting in us, and brings it about that the light of our spirit operates without deception'.[121]

Viewed by the Greeks as pure intelligences *(logikoi),* were angelic powers not kin to those who sought to free themselves from the fetters of the flesh, to ascend to 'the intelligible' and lead 'the angelic life' of monks?[122] Angels are rational beings in whom there is an overabundance of knowledge *(gnosis);* contemplation *(theoria)* is their special food.[123] Thus, 'the angel communicates knowledge of true prayer'.[124] From remote antiquity, devotion to angels has made churches and sanctuaries rise from the earth; on the calendars of all churches, feasts of the angels frequently occur under various names.[125]

## *Notes*

1. John Chrysostom, *Contra Anomoeos* 7; PG 48:768AB.
2. Chrysostom, *Peccata fratrum non divulganda* 5; PG 51:358.
3. Chrysostom, *De precatione 2;* PG 50:784.
4. *Ibid.,* 781.
5. Chrysostom, *Comparatio regis et monachi* 4; PG 47:394.
6. *Synagogé,* vol. IV, 10B, 17 (Athens, 1966) 251.
7. CSCO 278 (*Aethiop.* 54) (Louvain, 1967) 156.
8. *Moja žizň vo Christe,* 311; *My Life in Christ* translated from the Saint Petersburg edition by E. E. Goulaeff (Jordanville, New York: Holy Trinity Monastery, 1994). Used by permission.
9. See Anton Fonck, 'Prière'. DThC 13/1 (1936) 204ff.
10. John Chrysostom, *In Matthaeum, homilia* 1, 2; PG 57:15D.
11. Tomaš Špidlík, *La doctrine spirituelle de Théophane le Reclus. Le coeur et l'Esprit.* OCA 172 (Rome, 1965) 239ff.
12. *Načertanie christianskogo nravoučenija* [Christian Moral Teaching] (Moscow, 1895) 189.
13. *Ibid.,* 406.
14. *Ěčto jest' duchovnaja žizň* [What the Spiritual Life Is] (Moscow, 1897) 165.
15. *Chapters on Prayer,*150; Hausherr, *Les leçons d'un contemplatif. Le traité de l'oraison d'Évagre le Pontique* (Paris, 1960) 181; *Evagrius Ponticus. The Praktikos: Chapters on Prayer,* CS 4:79.
16. Russian text in *Soěčineija,* vol. II (St Petersburg, 1865) 209–375. French translation by Hieromonk Symeon, *Approches de la prière de Jésus,* Spiritualité orientale 35 (Bellefontaine 1983). In English, excerpts can be found in *On the Prayer of Jesus,* translated by Lazarus (Moore) (London: John Watkins, 1965).
17. *A Systematic Handbook,* 55ff.
18. *Ibid.,* 57.
19. *Ibid.,* 328.
20. Tomaš Špidlík, *La sophiologie de S. Basile,* OCA 162 (Rome, 1961) 27ff.
21. Tomaš Špidlík, *Grégoire de Nazianze,* OCA 189 (Rome, 1971) 132ff.
22. See below, p. 178.
23. Louis Leloir, *Paterica armeniaca* 5, 46, R; CSCO 361:118.
24. *Ibid.,* 149. Cf. *Apophthegmata patrum* (Alphabetical Collection), Agathon 9, translated by Benedicta Ward, *The Sayings of the Desert Fathers* (Kalamazoo: Cistercian Publications, 1975) 22: Whatever good work a man undertakes, if he perseveres in it, he will attain rest. But prayer is warfare to the last breath.
25. Before giving their definitions of prayer, medieval theologians gathered those they had inherited from the Fathers; see, e.g., Thomas Aquinas, *Summa theologiae* 2-II, 83, 1; Suarez, *Opera omnia, tract.* IV, *lib.* 1 (Paris, 1859) 4ff.; Arthur Vermeersch, *Quaestiones de virtutibus religionis et pietatis* (Bruges, 1912) 57. See A[nton] Fonck, 'Prière'. DThC 13/1 (1936) 169ff.
26. *Scala paradisi* 28; PG 88:1129AB; translated Lazarus Moore, *St John Climacus: The Ladder of Divine Ascent* (Willits, California: Eastern Orthodox Books, 1973) 250.
27. Basil, *Homilia in martyrem Julittam* 3; PG 31:244A.
28. *Chapters on Prayer,* 35; PG 79:1173D; Hausherr, *Leçons,* 53ff; CS 4:60.
29. *Cent.* 19.17.
30. Nilus (=Evagrius), *Chapters on Prayer,* 110; *Leçons,* 142; CS 4:73.

31. *Chapters on Prayer,* 3; *Leçons,* 16f; CS 4:56.

32. *De fide orthodoxa* 3.24; PG 94:1089D. Thomas Aquinas, *Summa theologiae* 2-II, 83, 1c. *Expositio in epistola D. Pauli ad Colossenses* I, 3. See Émile Bertaud, 'Élévations spirituelles'. DSp 4/1 (1960) 553–558; Pierre Pourat, 'Colloque'. DSp 2/1 (1953) 1123–1130.

33. The *Book of Perfection* II, 8 (71); CSCO 253, *Syri* 111, 20; translated by Sebastian Brock, *The Syriac Fathers on Prayer and the Spiritual Life,* CS 101 (Kalamazoo: Cistercian Publications, 1987) 231.

34. *Scala Paradisi* 28; PG 88:1129D; Moore, *Ladder,* 251.

35. Michel Dupuy, 'Oraison'. DSp 11 (1982) 836ff.

36. Irénée Hausherr, *Jean Solitaire (Pseudo-Jean de Lycopolis). Dialogue sur l'âme et les passions des hommes,* OCA 120 (Rome, 1939) 7ff., 37ff.

37. See p. 178.

38. See p. 53.

39. *Piœma o duchovnoj žizni [Letters on the Spiritual Life]* (Moscow, 1903) 112, 170; Špidlík, *Théophane le Reclus,* 244ff.

40. Špidlík, *Théophane, ibid.*

41. Ps 25:2, 55:24. Paul Ternant, 'Pères et Père'. VTB (1970) 962–971; 'Fathers & Father'. DBT 169–174.

42. Aimé Solignac, 'Pater noster'. DSp 12/1 (1984) 388–413.

43. *Chapters on Prayer,* 54; Hausherr, *Leçons,* 79; CS 4:63.

44. *Sokrovišče duchovnoe . . .* [The Spiritual Treasure Gathered from the World] in *Works.* vol. III (Moscow, 1899) 14–17; French translation in T. Špidlík, *Les grands mystiques russes* (Paris, 1979) 66–72.

45. *De oratione dominica, homilia* 2; PG 44:1148AB; translated by Hilda C. Graef, *Gregory of Nyssa, The Lord's Prayer,* ACW 18 (1954) 43–44.

46. Aimé Solignac, 'Pater noster'. DSp 12/1 (1984) 402.

47. Karl Rahner, 'Geheimnis', in Heinrich Fries, *Handbuch Theologischer Grundbegriffe,* vol. I (Munich, 1962) 447–452.

48. Solignac, 'Pater', 396.

49. *A Systematic Handbook,* 44ff.

50. *Dialogus cum Tryphone Judaeo* 86; PG 6:681C; *Dialogue with Trypho,* ANF, 1 (1885, rpt. 1994). Origen, *De oratione* 10. 2; GCS 2:320, 2022. See Adalbert Hamman, *La prière* (Tournai, 1963) 2:112.

51. See p. 332.

52. Vladimir Soloviev, *La justification du bien,* III, X, 2 (Paris, 1939) 414; translated. by Natalie A. Duddington, *The Justification of the Good: An Essay in Moral Theology* (New York: Macmillan, 1918) 414.

53. *Symposium* 202E–203A.

54. *Enneads* IV, 3, 11.

55. H. Kleinknecht, 'The *Logoi* of Philo of Alexandria', in Kittel IV (1956) 88–89.

56. Heb 8:6, 9:15, 12:24, 7:22.

57. 2 Cor 5:19.

58. Tomaš Špidlík, *Grégoire de Nazianze,* OCA 1889 (Rome, 1971) 87ff.

59. Origen, *De oratione* 2; PG 11:421; translated by John J. O'Meara, *Origen: Prayer,* ACW 19 (Westminster, Md: Newman, 1954)]. See M. De Goedt, 'Die Interzession des Geistes im christlichen Gebet (Rom 8:26-7)', in *Concilium* 8 (1972) 654–660.

60. Špidlík, *Théophane le Reclus,* 239ff.

61. *Contra Celsum* VII, 44; GCS 2, 196.3; ANF 4:628.

62. Antoine Guillaumont, 'Messaliens'. DSp 10 (1980) 1074–1083.
63. Basil, *De fide,* Prol. 4; PG 31:685BC; W. K. L. Clarke, *The Ascetic Works of Saint Basil* (London, 1925) 96. See Irenaeus, *Adversus haereses* 5.8.1; PG 7:1141BC.
64. Acts 7:59ff.= Lk 23:34, 46. Acts 21:14= Lk 22:42.
65. See Origen's explanation, *De oratione* 2.3; GCS 2:301, 10–15; translated Rowan A. Greer, *Origen,* CWS(1979) 84.
66. *Commentaire sur Daniel* 2.1-2; ed. M. Lefèvre (Paris, 1947) 130.
67. P. Henry, *Études Plotiniennes,* vol. I, *Les états du texte de Plotin* (Paris, 1938) 159–196.
68. *De fide,* Prol.; PG 31:685BC.
69. Basil, *Liber de Spiritu Sancto* 47; PG 32:153B; SCh 17bis (1968) 468; Translated by David Anderson, *On the Holy Spirit* (Crestwood, New York: St Vladimir's Seminary Press, 1980) 74. Athanasius, *Epistola I ad Serapionem;* PG 26:573C–576A. Gregory Nazianzen, *Oratio* 31, *Theologica* 5; PG 36:136BC; LNPF, ser. 2, vol. 7 (1894, rpt 1994).
70. From the french translation: Venice (1851) 9.
71. *De Spiritu Sancto* 26; PG 32:181AB; SCh 17bis, 376; Anderson (above, n. 69), 93ff.
72. *Catechesis* XVI, *de Spiritu Sancto* I.22; PG 33:949B; FCh 2:89.
73. Sévérien Salaville, 'Epiclèse eucharistique', *Catholicisme* 4 (1956) 302–307.
74. *Irénikon* 24 (1951) 183.
75. *De oratione* 33.1; PG 11:557ff; GCS 2:401, 14–6; ACW 19:137–139.
76. *Actes de SS. Saturninus,* Dativus 7–8; ed. Th. Ruinart (Ratisbon, 1895).
77. Lucien Regnault, 'La prière continuelle 'monologistos' dans la littérature apophthegmatique'. *Irénikon* 47 (1974) 467–493.
78. Adalbert Hamman, *La prière* 2 (Tournai, 1963) 225.
79. Vladimir Lossky, *Essai sur la théologie mystique de l'Église d'Orient* (Paris, 1944) 242; *The Mystical Theology of the Eastern Church* (Crestwood, New York, 1976) 215. See *A Systematic Handbook,* 39ff.
80. Letter 10.96, *Lettres,* Budé, vol. 4; ed. M. Durry (Paris, 1947) 96.
81. See Cyril of Jerusalem, *Thesaurus* 32; PG 75:504AC.
82. Anton Baumstark, *Liturgie comparée* (Chevetogne, 1953) 173; translated F. L. Cross, *Comparative Liturgy* (Westminster, Md.: Newman, 1958).
83. Jean-Augustin Robilliard, 'Face (Dévotion à la Sainte Face)', DSp 5 (1964) 26–33.
84. Christoph von Schoenborn, *L'icône du Christ. Fondements théologiques élaborés entre le I<sup>er</sup> et II<sup>e</sup> Concile de Nicée* (325–787), Paradosis 24 (Fribourg, 1976).
85. Charles Kannengieser, 'La contemplation de l'humanité du Christ'. DSp 7/2 (1969) 1043–1049.
86. Clement of Alexandria, *Paedagogi Liber* I.7; PG 8:320A; GCS 1:114; ANF 2:223–224. *Idem., Stromata* 5.6.34,1; PG 9:57B; GCS 2:348; ANF 2:452–454.
87. Philotheus of Sinai, 25, in the *Philokalia* 2 (Athens, 1958) 282; translated by G. E. H. Palmer, Philip Sherrard, Kallistos Ware, *The Philokalia: The Complete Text,* vol. 3 (London: Faber and Faber, 1984) 25; and by E. Kadloubovsky and G. E. H. Palmer, *Writings from the Philokalia on Prayer of the Heart* (London 1951) 333.
88. Kannengieser, 'Contemplation', 1048.
89. Origen, *Commentary on Matthew* 14.17; translated by Hans Urs von Balthasar, *Parole et Mystère chez Origène* (Paris, 1957) 52. *In canticum canticorum;* PG 13:95A; GCS 58, 103, 27; ACW 26:58ff.
90. Henri Charles Puech, 'Un livre récent sur la mystique d'Origène', *Revue d'histoire et de philosophie religieuses* 6 (1933) 287.

91. *Oratio* XXXII, 15; PG 36:189D–192A.

92. *Oratio* XL, *In sanctum baptisma,* 30; PG 36:401B; LNPF, ser. 2, vol. 7:371.

93. *Oratio* XIX, 13; PG 35:1065AB. *Oratio* XLII, *Supremum vale,* 1;, PG 36:473A; LNPF, ser. 2, vol. 7:389.

94. See 1 Cor 4:10, Phil 3:17, 1 Cor 11:1, 1 Thess 1:6-7.

95. Hélène Pétré, 'Exemplum-époque patristique'. DSp 4/2 (1961) 1886–92. *A Systematic Handbook,* 41.

96. Irénée-Henri Dalmais, *'Rites et Symboles', Les liturgies d'Orient* (Paris, 1980) 179; translated by Donald Attwater, *Eastern Liturgies* (New York: Hawthorn, 1960).

97. *Ibid.,* 176ff.

98. *Ibid.,* 177.

99. *Moja žizň vo Christe* (St Petersburg, 1905) 5; *My Life in Christ* (Jordanville, New York: Holy Trinity Monastery, 1994) 4.

100. Dalmais, *Liturgies,* 177.

101. *Ibid.,* 170.

102. Špidlík, *Les grands mystiques russes.* (Paris, 1979) 309ff.

103. The idea was developed by Origen in *Libellus de oratione,* 11; PG 11:448ff; translated by J. O'Meara, *Prayer,* ACW 19 (1954).

104. See B. Köttig, 'Heiligungverehrung'. HTG I, 1, 633ff; 'Saints (culte des)'. EF IV, 186ff.

105. Sergius Boulgakov, *L'Orthodoxie* (Paris, 1932) 169; translated and revised by Lydia Kesich, *The Orthodox Church* (Crestwood, New York: St Vladimir's Seminary Press, 1988) 116ff. See *Handbook,* 158.

106. *Ma vie en Christ* (Bellefontaine, 1979) 196; *My Life in Christ* (New York, 1994) 409.

107. *Ibid.,* 32 [English 2].

108. *Ibid.,* 67 [English 42–43].

109. Volume II (Paris, 1860) 663ff.

110. Vladimir Lossky, *Á l'image et à la ressemblance de Dieu* (Paris: Aubier-Montaigne, 1967); translated by John E. Erickson and Thomas E. Bird, *In the Image and Likeness of God* (New York: St Vladimir's Seminary Press, 1985) 208.

111. *Handbook,* 65.

112. Lossky, *A l'image,* 206; *In the Image,* 208.

113. *Ibid.* 205–206.

114. Tomaš Špidlík, 'L'ecclesiologia di una icona russa', *Asprenas* 27 (1980) 239–245.

115. *Handbook,* 158–199.

116. Plato, *Cratylus* 407e. W. Grundmann, 'ἄγγελος in the Greek and Hellenistic World'. Kittel I (1964) 74–76.

117. Joseph Duhr, 'Anges'. DSp 1 (1936) 580–625.

118. Origen, *In Leviticum, homilia* 9.9.8; PG 12:520BC; translated Gary W. Barkley, *Origen. Homilies on Leviticus,* FCh 83 (1990).

119. *Contra Celsum,* V.4; PG 11:1186B; *Origen Against Celsus,* ANF 4 (1907).

120. *Symposium* 202E.

121. *Libellus de oratione,* 74; Hausherr, *Leçons,* 108; Bamberger, 67.

122. García M. Colombás, *Paraíso y Vida Angélica* (Montserrat, 1958), and *Paradis et vie angélique* (Paris, 1961).

123. Evagrius, *Cent.* 3.4.

124. *Ibid.,* 46.

125. Joseph Duhr, 'Anges', 598.

## 3

# PRAYER AS SUPPLICATION

*Addressing Petitions to God*

IN PRIMITIVE RELIGIONS, need seems to be the main reason prompting man to pray. Overwhelmed by evils, the human person tries to get the attention of the deity by invocations and offerings of gifts. Hence the familiar expressions such as: 'Listen! Hear our prayer! Have pity on us! Accept!' Or, 'We offer unto thee, receive favorably!'[1] These are known from Scripture and the entire christian tradition. The main incentive for prayer is still the same as ever, therefore, and retains its validity.

The Fathers—and christian authors in general—acknowledged this situation; an awareness of our misery prompts us to seek protection with God. 'And you say, What need have I of prayer?' John Chrysostom exclaims. 'On this account you need it, because you think that you can do without'.[2] Evagrius gives this definition of supplication (δέησις): 'A conversation of the mind with God, joined to supplications asking for help in times of struggle, and for graces in hope'.[3]

*Giving Thanks*

When the human person becomes aware of his or her misery, the face of divine mercy is revealed. This unshakable scriptural conviction apparently originated during the experience of Israel in Exodus: 'I have indeed seen the misery of my people. I have heard them crying' (Ex 3:7). Giving thanks goes hand in hand with a revelation of mercy. According to Paul, the pagans' cardinal sin was that 'they did not honor him as God or give thanks to him' (Rom 12:21). Indeed, the giving of thanks is rarely found in the large collection of hymns created by mesopotamian devotion,[4] while its frequent occurrence in Scripture prompts exuberant outbursts: 'O give thanks unto the Lord, for he is good, for his mercy *(hesed)* endures forever' (Ps 106:1).

This leads us to the distinction between two kinds of prayer: supplication and thanksgiving. However, since the time of Origen, attempts have been made to establish four types of prayer, or at the least four elements to be found in all prayer: petitions (supplications), prayers, intercessions, and thanksgivings (ποεῖσθαι δεήσεις προσευχᾴς, ἐντεύξεις, ευχαριστίας)—1 Tm 2:1; see Phil 4:6).[5] It was clearly Paul's authority that led to the creation of careful, and sometimes artificial, distinctions. But a close reading of Origen's explanation reveals that, practically, these four kinds of prayer are reduced to two. *Deēsis* (supplication) consists of asking for things needed. *Proseuche* (prayer), having a higher objective, is made by a more noble soul and contains a doxology. *Enteuxis* (intercession) is a request made by someone who has great confidence, with *parrhesia* (freedom of speech, familiarity), as by someone who has free access to God. Lastly, *eucharistia* (thanksgiving) expresses gratitude for blessings received.[6] Thus, the first three are petitions described in terms of a lower or a higher aim. The fourth is an expression of gratitude. Cassian, who follows this distinction among four kinds of prayer, justifies it by saying: 'One must not believe that the Holy Spirit uttered anything casually or without reason through the Apostle [Paul]'.[7]

In more recent times, scholars no longer feel obligated to follow the pauline terminology mechanically. Nonetheless, they habitually distinguish among three types of biblical prayer: supplication, thanksgiving, and praise—praise being the most prominent because it is the most disinterested.[8]

In Scripture, praise and thanksgiving are actually intertwined in the same movement of the soul and, on the literary level, in the same texts.[9] Exegetes note that praise is a form of thanksgiving, and that there is indeed no hebrew word for 'thanks'. In semitic fashion, one gives thanks by praising and glorifying the giver.[10] This is in fact confirmed by the innumerable 'eulogies' (*eulogia,* good words, praise) in the eastern liturgy. The litanies *(ekteneiae)*, petitions of all sorts, open with 'Blessed be God' and end as follows: 'For unto thee do we ascribe glory, honor, and praise'.

### *The Prayer of Supplication in Divine Pedagogy*

Schematically, the structure of prayer may be presented as follows: a certain need prompts a request; the granting of it compels one to give thanks. A question then arises: this outline is well adapted to 'natural religion', but does it correspond to the spirit of Scripture, where it is God who takes the initiative, addresses himself to the human person, is the first one to speak, and expects an answer?

Actually, the fact that the human person feels a need to pray already presupposes a divine pedagogy, as the Fathers noted in their reflections on the meaning of 'physical evil'.[11] At creation, in Paradise, Adam listened to the word of God in everything, and responded to the Creator with his entire heart and mind.[12] As a result of sin, the human intellect broke off the dialogue with God and no longer listened to the words of God. We should therefore do everything possible, Basil writes, 'to convince man that God, the just judge, exists. Man will then believe that there is a God . . . and he will be terrified.'[13] Even when terrifying or threatening, it is once more the voice of God that speaks through calamities. The severity of the afflictions sent by the Lord is compared to an education, a *paideia*.[14] A prayer for mercy, even when it is based on our need, is in fact already a human response to the pedagogy of Providence.

Patristic observations about the meaning of physical evil are correct, but they have an apologetic dimension: they seek to convince someone who does not see the finger of God in events, and who complains instead of thanking Providence. In Scripture, the divine pedagogy is more complete. God threatens the sinner but at the same time he nourishes the faith of his people through signs, miracles, and wondrous deeds which are the outward signs of his protection. The remembrance of such signs is nourished by the liturgy in the celebration of feasts, 'a memorial of the great deeds of Yahweh' (Ps 111:4).[15]

By all his blessings, God is proven worthy of praise and thanksgiving. At all times in Israel praise was linked to the liturgy, but especially after the building of the Temple, when worship became more rigidly structured. In the New Testament, it is the Lord who receives our praise.[16] Growing out of Scripture, praise was always to remain paramount in Christianity, sprinkling liturgical prayer with Alleluias, 'Glory to the Father' or 'Glory to thee, O Lord'—animating prayer to the point of permeating and transforming it into a pure 'praise of his glory' (cf. Eph 1:12).

This climate allows us to understand why petitioning does not occupy first place. On the contrary, it accompanies the remembrance of blessings received. Jewish piety bases its certainty of being heard on this remembrance, which is seen in the very formulation of prayers. The invocations, 'Hear, Lord, answer our prayer', are preceded by a 'Remember'. Μνήστητι ('Remember') is a *Leitmotiv* in jewish prayer and was to be again in Christianity.[17]

Thus, for example, the prayer of Hermas consists primarily in glorifying God, in extolling his works. Thanksgiving to God rises from the action of God in the life of the believer: 'I gave thanks to the Lord for all his benefits to me'.[18] John Climacus recommends therefore that we begin with a sincere thanksgiving, follow it with a confession of sins, and only then should we present our petitions. He learned this, he says, from a brother who had heard it from an angel. This ties in with a long tradition, and is also in perfect agreement with the liturgy.[19]

We encounter the same thing again at the very heart of christian prayer, the eucharistic prayer. In the anaphora of *The Apostolic Tradition,* we read: 'At the end of the meal, the bishop introduced the *eucharistia* in the following manner, "Let us give thanks" or "We give thanks to the Lord our God"'. The reasons for this thanksgiving are scriptural, but above all personal. They derive from a living experience of the goodness of God. A petition follows at once: 'Have mercy, O Lord our God, upon your people Israel, on your city of Jerusalem, on Sion', and so forth. Another act of thanksgiving is developed parallel to this: 'Blessed art thou, Lord our God, eternal king, who nourishes the entire world with your goodness, your grace, your mercy, and tender compassion. You give food to all living things, and your mercy endures forever. Because of thy great goodness, we never lack nourishment.'[20]

*Prayer Granted*

A difficult problem arises, not merely on the theoretical but on the existential level: Why is it that our prayers are not always granted? Indeed, the gospel states very clearly: 'Whatever you pray for in faith, you will receive' (Mt 21:21; 17:19).

Within the context in which these words were written, we certainly understand that what was emphasized was not so much the 'whatever you pray for' as 'faith'. The hebrew mentality has been described as 'subjective',[21] as being more interested in the disposition of the person who prays than in the object of the petition. The blind man in the Gospel explicitly states that God does not listen to sinners (Jn 9:31). This attitude is noticeable in the documents of judaeo-christian times: their apparent concern is not so much with the tenor of prayer as it is with the inner conditions for it.[22]

The greek environment, by contrast, displayed an 'objective' tendency. Thus, it was easier to ask the question: which prayer could be granted and which not. We can pray for everything that is good: concretely, Cassian says, for all that is contained in the Lord's Prayer. Asking for something evil or something sinful is forbidden and would insult God.[23]

But in both mindsets, the problem is resolved only in its main lines. In a sense, no one can address God because every human person is 'a sinner'. As for the 'sinful thing', doubts arise as to what is on the borderline between good and evil, especially because our judgment is clouded by ignorance. From this we would have to conclude, with Clement of Alexandria, that only the prayer of a 'gnostic' is always heard.[24]

While following the same line of reasoning, Origen approached the problem in a way that is theologically more correct. He emphasizes that we are here in the presence of a mystery accessible only to the Holy Spirit, since only the voice of the Holy Spirit ascends to the Father.[25] The good will of human beings which expresses desires cannot always harmonize them with the Spirit; we do not know the true intentions of the economy of salvation, 'we do not know how to pray properly' (Rom 8:26), and this is why 'the Spirit comes to help us in our weakness' *(ibid.)*. According to Origen, this happens as follows: we pray, but the Holy Spirit 'arrives'. His voice is stronger than ours, which is stirred by ignorance *(agnosia)*.[26] Thus, our prayer is always heard, but according to the voice of the Spirit (which is also ours because the Spirit is part of 'me').[27]

The general principle guiding the formulation of petitions is therefore the same that controls every christian word and deed: they must 'agree with' the Spirit,[28] or, to express the same principle from the point of view of christology, with the *Logos;* for the *Logos,* Origen says, is present in our prayer as High Priest, Intercessor, and Mediator of our oblations to the Father.[29] When persons 'agree', the subjective and the objective dimension coincide easily.

We discern the same principle in the language of Scripture, which exhorts us to prayer that is 'full of faith' (Mt 21:21). This means much more than a psychological 'confidence'. Those who 'believe' follow Christ earnestly in word and deed: they have received the same Spirit as the disciples of Jesus (Acts 11:27).[30]

If we are aware of the essentially ecclesiastical dimension of such 'faith', should we be greatly surprised if doubts have arisen as to the validity of the prayers (especially sacramental prayers) uttered by heretics and schismatics?[31] Nonetheless, such doubts originated from theoretical reflections or from a polemical context. The fact that someone uses certain erroneous formulations or lives in an all-too-narrow ecclesiastical circle does not imply that the foundations of his faith in God the Father have disappeared. Moreover, such faith in God the Father is not absolutely assured among even the best Christians.

When Cassian deals with this problem, he carefully notes: 'We will bring forward the marks of prayer which we have heard from the Lord, as far as we have tried them'.[32] Prayer must be 'full of faith'. He interprets such 'faith' first in the sense of 'confidence', 'when no hesitation intervenes and breaks down the confidence of our petition'.[33] In order not to remain on the purely psychological level, he indicates, on the authority of Abba Germanus, 'that this confidence flows from purity of conscience'. 'But for us', he adds, 'whose heart is still smitten by the pricks of sin, how can we have it, as we have no merits to plead for us, whereby we might confidently presume that our prayers would be heard?'[34]

The insistence on faith in prayer is found on every page of the spiritual journal of John of Kronstadt, a nineteenth-century russian thaumaturge:

> Remember that God, during your prayer, is waiting for your affirmative answer to the question which he is inwardly asking you: 'Believe ye that I am able to do this (Mt 9:28)?' To which question you must from the depth of your heart reply, 'Yea, Lord'.[35]
>
> The heart that doubts that God can grant what it asks for is punished for this doubt: it is painfully oppressed and contracted by doubt. Do not anger Almighty God even by a shade of doubt—especially you, who have already experienced many and many times, the omnipotence of God.[36]
>
> Men have fallen into disbelief because they have either completely lost the spirit of prayer, or never had it at all, nor have it now—in short, because they do not pray.[37]

To the texts that exhort us to pray with faith should be added those in which Jesus teaches his disciples to pray in his name: 'Whatever you ask in my name, I will do' (Jn 14:30; cf. 15:16; 16:23). These texts should be studied within the context of the farewell discourses after the Last Supper. In his conclusion to the allegory of the vine (Jn 15:1ff), Christ gives his disciples a central command, to love one another, as an expression of the love the Son has for the Father (15:10) and the Father for the Son (17:23). Abiding in the words of Christ (15:7) is *the* condition for prayer to be granted. It is therefore not a matter of a power that is linked to a name, as in magic. The Christian who prays in the name of the Lord Jesus becomes aware of his benevolent presence near us and in us; and so we say our prayer with the most perfect confidence.[38]

### *The Will of God—The Norm for Petitions*

Faith is understood as the free acceptance of the Word of God. The Word of God, as Basil then says, 'impels the will'.[39] Praying with faith therefore means concretely to accept the will of God as normative for one's own desires. 'Do not set your heart on what seems good to you but rather what is pleasing to God when you pray', Evagrius writes. And he adds, 'This will free you from disturbance and leave you occupied with thanksgiving in your prayer'.[40]

Cassian confirms this doctrine on the authority of the apostle John:

> We should constantly meditate on the saying of the blessed evangelist John, that saying by which all doubt regarding this matter is dissolved, 'We have the assurance of being heard by God if we ask for something that accords with his will'(1 Jn 5:14). . . . This is what we are taught to say in the Lord's prayer with the words 'Thy will be done', your will, not ours.[41]

All this may seem very discouraging after the beautiful exhortations that came earlier. Could it therefore be that the Lord does not really agree with our desires? Is being subservient the one thing that is left to us?

To reply to the objection, let us recall what the eastern ascetics understood by 'one's own will' (in Latin, *voluntas propria*) and its total eradication.[42] This is a matter not of human activity and initiatives, then, but only of their deviations toward evil. In this sense, a request inspired by 'one's own will' can obviously not be granted by God. By contrast, spiritual persons—the thaumaturges among them—were aware that God did indeed perform *their* will. They forced him, so to speak, to change his eternal designs. We may read, for example, the episode in the Life of Seraphim of Sarov in which he caused to live someone who according to the plans of Providence, 'had to die'.[43]

How is this possible? Origen's argumentation about the foreknowledge of God[44] actually coincides with the very subtle explanation given by L. S. Frank,[45] who holds that human cooperation in creative activity over the course of history intersects with God's creation of the concrete world 'in the beginning'.

In spite of all such explanations and restrictions, the free dialogue between God and man remains a mystery. It happens, as

Clement of Alexandria notes, that God listens to sinners. Why? We can think of two possible answers: either because what he gives them is not profitable or because in his immense goodness he listens to them.[46] The second reason is typical of Scripture: God is merciful 'for the sake of his name',[47] because his mercy endures forever. This is the reason for the marvelous events in the history of salvation.[48] Spiritual persons, who knew how to simplify, did not dare venture to do an analysis of these 'high deeds'; they preferred to contemplate them in order to pray more fervently.

## *The Order of the Petitions*

'Send new portents, do fresh wonders!' Ben Sirach begged (Si 36:5), expressing the hope of all of Israel after the Exile, disappointed as he was by a return that was less brilliant than the announced new Exodus. Christ came to fulfill this expectation, but by discouraging any taste for the spectacular. God will always work miracles, but they are only the beginnings of what they signify. They bring a 'pledge (*arrhae,* earnest money) of eternal salvation', and are responsible for creating the great miracle, that of a conversion in faith.[49]

An analogous progression is at work in the life of each human person who prays. In our misery, we always ask for God's help but that help is shown in various ways, depending on the degree of our understanding of the mystery of salvation. The needs a human person experiences at the beginning are principally material. We therefore ask God for protection against death, war, illness, hunger, and so on. The more spiritual we become, the more we realize that our true misery is spiritual. Christians are so convinced of this that they view sin as the only real evil. Calling for mercy therefore coincides first of all with prayer for the remission of sin and the restoration of grace. Such a renewal of divine blessings brings with it a gradual healing from the consequences of sin. According to several Greek Fathers, what is most harmful and perturbs our prayer petitions is ignorance (ἀγνωσία).[50] The contemplatives therefore prefer to ask for a better, more searching understanding of divine mystery.

Within this context we may mention the scale of values suggested by Evagrius; it corresponds to the degrees of the spiritual life. At the beginning comes *praxis,* then 'natural contemplation' *(theoria physike),* and finally *gnosis,* which blossoms only where *apatheia,* a peaceful state of soul, reigns. 'First of all pray to be purified from your passions. Secondly, pray to be delivered from ignorance. Thirdly, pray to be freed from all temptation and abandonment.'[51] This structure seems abstract, but it unquestionably summarizes the experience of the spiritual masters. They taught their disciples to pray according to a specific progression, because they wanted to raise them to the highest degrees of prayer.

### *Asking for 'Great Things'*

The formulation of Evagrius is based on the experience of solitary monks, that is, of those who already were spiritually advanced. Most christian people start from a less elevated level by asking for the little things of daily life. To a 'gnostic', such requests may seem small, but the Church has always encouraged them. 'What is desirable can also be asked through prayer.'[52] Indeed, the liturgy offers litanies 'for all the needs of the faithful'. It is significant, however, that—in the Eastern Church—such prayers 'for all needs' are generally said by the deacon together with the people, while the priest recites 'more elevated' prayers behind the iconostasis.

This approach corresponds to the principle set down by Clement of Alexandria and Origen: 'When you pray, ask for "great things"'. The sublimity of the blessings one asks for is an indication of the view one has of the greatness of God.[53] But how can we measure what is 'great' or 'little' in prayer, if we do not know what to ask for (Rom 8:6)? Origen follows a schematic classification of values. He exhorts us to ask for 'spiritual things', and not to 'harass' the divine goodness with 'earthly' concerns—they are like shadows that follow things, and we should not be directly concerned with them.[54] He even interprets in this sense the passage in the Lord's Prayer about 'daily bread': by this appeal, spiritual men ask God for *gnosis.*[55]

It is obvious that such an appraisal of values can be justified only if we are careful not to forget that the terms 'spiritual', 'material', or 'carnal' are not understood in a philosophic sense by christian authors. Origen's advice is valid only if we give spiritual realities their typically christian meaning, by viewing them as they relate to the Holy Spirit.[56] The Holy Spirit who joins the human person at prayer makes the value of 'spiritual' needs felt. But these are different, depending on our particular vocation. Those who do not listen to the voice of the Spirit will never be able to know what is truly great and what can be asked of God with persistence. This is why preference has often been given to being guided in prayer by a 'spiritual' father. What was asked of him was a *politeia,* 'a word', which was accepted not only as a rule of life, but especially as a rule for prayer.[57]

### *Prayer for the Forgiveness of Sins*

Clement of Alexandria contends,[58] while disagreeing on this point with the eastern tradition of 'compunction' *(katanyxis),*[59] that this request is reduced to a minimum in the prayer of the 'gnostic', since he approaches God only after having been purified by observing the commandments. From the beginning the petition for remission of sins has occupied a special place in christian prayer, as the apostle James testifies: 'The prayer of faith will save the sick person and the Lord will raise him up again; and if he has committed any sins, he will be forgiven. So confess your sins to one another, and pray for one another to be cured.'[60] Prayer as it relates to the forgiveness of sins is also the central theme in *The Shepherd* of Hermas.[61]

The expression 'confessing one's sins' (ὁμολογεῖν—acknowledge, ἐξομολογεῖσθαι—confess) is often found in these texts; according to biblical usage, it is polyvalent. For John Chrysostom, every prayer for forgiveness embodies a 'confession'. 'The one who says, "have mercy on me", utters a confession *(exomologesin)* and recognizes his sin; those who have fallen ask for mercy.'[62] This prayer has a special force:

> the one who says 'have mercy' will receive forgiveness of sins, and the one who has obtained mercy will not be punished. The one who says 'have mercy' acquires the kingdom of heaven; for God, in his mercy, not only frees man from punishment, but also makes him worthy to possess the blessings to come.[63]

Asking for forgiveness already is, then, a type of 'confession'; and in the christian community, this was to become a sacrament. Though there has been some hesitation,[64] the christian East never doubted the specific value of prayer said for the remission of sins in the sacrament of confession. On the other hand, it opposed the tendency to minimize the power of any prayer for the forgiveness of sins, whether it was said for oneself or for others.

Spiritual direction normally concluded with a prayer asking for forgiveness. Because the spiritual father was not necessarily a priest, a certain confusion in the documents may easily have created the impression that laypersons heard confessions.[65] The uncertainty is increased because of the fact that in the East (except among the Armenians), the sacramental absolution was in the deprecatory form.[66] All this, however, merely indicates one thing: that it was clearly recognized that the sacrament of penance and repentance in the general sense go hand in hand, and that each prayer for the remission of sins must be viewed as one of those that are most certainly answered. Indeed, it is obvious that we then pray according to the will of God. Sincerity in prayer is therefore sufficient.

In the West, absolution from sin assumed the form of a judgment. It is interesting to point out that John Climacus applied this metaphor to prayer: 'For him who truly prays, prayer is the court, the judgment hall and the tribunal of the Lord'.[67] Numerous apophthegms confirm that 'prayer forgives sins and decrees healing'.[68] The endless *Kyrie eleisons* of the liturgy and the long 'catanyctic' prayers of the monks express this in their own way.

### *Praying for Others*

Certain abuses have thrown doubt upon the value of such prayers. Saint Antony refused to pray for someone who had done nothing to improve his relationship with God.[69] John Chrysostom too complained about those who let others pray for them; it is much better to pray for oneself.[70] In the Middle Ages, several objections were raised against 'prelates and monks' praying for others, but these were directed against scandalous abuses, especially simony.[71]

On the other hand, Scripture, together with general experience, witnesses to the essentially communal character of petitions addressed to God; prayer is then made 'on behalf of all and for all' (the offertory of the byzantine liturgy immediately following the Lord's words of institution).

Christian prayer is always uttered 'in the Spirit of God'.[72] And the surest sign of the Spirit is charity. Prayer motivated by love will therefore be especially valuable. 'Why has our sincere prayer for each other such great power over others?' John of Kronstadt wonders. 'Because of the fact that by cleaving to God during prayer I become one spirit with him, and unite with myself, by faith and love, those for whom I pray, for the Holy Spirit acting in me also acts at the same time in them, for he accomplishes all things.'[73]

There are certain questions which are pointless. For example, is it better to pray specifically for one person or for everyone in general? The answer is obvious: if prayer is an expression of love, it is practised according to 'the order of charity'.[74] We also understand that those who have reached the summit of this spiritual ascent prefer to pray for all without distinction. Thus we read in the story of the martyrdom of Polycarp: 'When he had at last ended his prayer—in which he remembered everyone who had met him at any time—both small and great, both known and unknown to fame, and the whole world-wide Catholic Church—the moment of departure arrived'.[75]

Praying for everyone has always been viewed as the chief obligation of monks.[76] Therein lies their angelic, spiritual, and priestly function, Evagrius says. 'It is a part of justice that you should pray not only for your own purification but also for that of every human being. In doing this, you will imitate the practice of angels',[77] for 'the task of angels is to care for sick souls, to lead them to the perfection of health'.[78] 'Intercession is a petition addressed to God by spiritual persons for the salvation of others.'[79] Why by 'spiritual' persons? As long as one is not pure, preoccupation with others becomes a hindrance to prayer.[80] Interceding for others is a priestly function: 'Therein lies the priesthood of the spirit'.[81] 'The one who pleads with God for all rational beings',[82] assumes a priestly function.

While praying for others, we should request what we ask for ourselves: preferably 'great and heavenly things', the forgiveness of sins, and, in general, everything that is a true good. Consequently, the Fathers severely condemned prayers 'against enemies' used by pagans and in the Old Testament. Evagrius writes: 'Strive to avoid entreating against anyone in your prayer so that what you have been building up you do not destroy by making your prayer a defilement'.[83] 'You are begging the Legislator', John Chrysostem insists, 'to violate his own laws.'[84]

What is to be said, then, about the 'imprecatory' psalms? Gregory of Nyssa notes that when 'saints pray for the destruction of all that is hostile and contrary to nature, this may put into the heads of the ill-instructed the idea that they are greatly incensed against people'. When Christians sing with the psalmist, 'May sinners vanish from the earth, and the wicked exist no more' (Ps 103:35), the object of their prayer is the destruction of sin, not of sinners.[85] For monks, the greatest enemies are evil thoughts *(logismoi);* it is against these that the imprecations of the psalms are directed.[86]

### *Praying for the Dead*

The entire christian tradition justifies praying for the dead. Theological speculations have sometimes tried to circumscribe or limit the time for such supplications,[87] but the faith of the early Church, always alive among christian people, moved in the opposite direction. There has been a tendency not to distinguish the moment when prayer is said *for* someone from the moment when it becomes a prayer addressed *to* someone. An example is found in the ethiopic liturgy: 'We pray thee *for* the saints, prophets, martyrs and confessors; *for* the Blessed Virgin Mary . . .';[88] such a lack of precision indicates that the value of praying for one another was accepted without taking time or space into account. It is a prayer characteristic of the eschatological state.

Burial customs are extremely diverse because there are no rules imposed in the name of an ancient tradition. Let us note, however, that, unlike what happened in the roman rite, the East has preserved a great richness by incorporating elements that were borrowed from pre-christian sources that varied by region. Two customs are noteworthy in the byzantine tradition: the kiss given to the deceased before burial, and the formula of absolution placed in the hand. In one form or the other, furthermore, this absolution is found everywhere. The Copts recite 'the absolution of the Son', a very beautiful formula that follows the ritual of purification at the beginning of the eucharistic liturgy.[89]

*Praying for Temporal Benefits*

We have seen that Origen did not approve of petitions for material goods being addressed to God. However that may be, christian people made a practice of praying 'for all needs', and the Church has approved this custom by incorporating numerous forms of litany into the liturgy. Augustine defended them *ex professo* on the basis of the following principle: 'What we can desire, we can ask of God'.[90] He is not alone. It takes only a little experience to teach us that the result of giving too much advice on how to pray may lead 'ordinary' Christians to lose their sense of relationship with God as a Father.

To bolster the confidence of Christians, people told of the miracle of rain obtained by the prayer of christian soldiers in the army of Marcus Aurelius.[91] At all times, litanies have been recited for the sick, for those who travel, for the fruits of the earth, and on it goes.

*Persevering in Prayer*

Following the example of the young Church in Jerusalem 'constant in prayer' (Acts 1:14), the Christian should persevere in prayer. This theme is often dealt with in the context of the prayer of petition, when it seems that God does not hear our voice. In such circumstances, the same exhortations always recur. In the *Monastic Constitutions* attributed to Basil we read: 'Do not become fainthearted if you do not immediately receive what you have asked for'.[92] We could cite innumerable other texts on the subject: 'Do not be anxious and strain yourself so as to gain an immediate hearing for your request',[93]—and so on.

To explain the slowness of divine grace, authors appealed to divine pedagogy. Prayers prolonged by long expectation serve to prepare us to receive the eternal gifts worthily.[94] Evagrius, however, gives us a more profound answer: persevering prayer is in itself already a gift which is superior to what we ask: 'For what greater thing is there than to converse intimately with God and to be preoccupied with his company?'[95]

The frequency of the requests can become a means of arriving at unceasing prayer and contemplation. It creates a salutary attitude. John Chrysostom writes:

> When I tell someone 'Ask God, beseech him, implore him', he replies, I have asked once, twice, three, ten, twenty times, and have received nothing at all!' Brother, do not cease until you receive. The aim of prayer is the gift received. Cease when you have received or rather, do not cease even then, but persevere.[96]

Such perseverance in prayer brings with it a frequent repetition of the same words. By 'speaking much' would there not be a danger of falling into the 'wordiness' (πολυλογία) the gospel warns us against (Mt 6:7)? Origen's answer to this objection goes back to a typically greek, thoroughly metaphysical reflection on the One and the many. Between what is one and things that are manifold there is no contradiction, provided the latter are not disharmonious. What is 'too much' is what is incompatible with the first principle of being. In this case, it would be a request that is contrary to the will of God, a prayer for things that cannot be reconciled with the spiritual life.[97] Despite its philosophic formulation, Origen's thought is simple: it is the aim of prayer which determines how many or how few words to use and which unites them.

*Miracles*

Prayer is sometimes granted in what is called a 'miraculous' way. The term 'miracle' has no equivalent either in Hebrew or in Greek. It is expressed by a constellation of terms which may be divided in two groups: 1) 'great deeds' (μεγαλεῖα, *magnalia*), 'marvels' (θαυμάσια)—which emphasize the amazement caused by an act of almighty God; 2) The couplet 'wonders' and 'signs' (τέρατα and σημεῖα) describes the miracle's twofold aspect as an extraordinary and significant phenomenon. Recognized by faith, the miracle allows access to the very mystery of God. The dialogue God wants to initiate with the human person consists specifically in this.[98]

Divine intervention causes no problem for Christians, since the world does not exist without God, who allows it to exist. During the first three centuries of the christian era, the 'miracle' was never questioned. Nor can it be reduced to being merely an exceptional phenomenon. It is attributed to a power that surpasses human ability, yet it cannot be a mere portent: the element of meaning is an integral part of the phenomenon. Meaning is inherent in the very act and somehow coincides with it.[99]

Eastern and western hagiography abound with tales of the miraculous. Yet we can say in a very general way that miracles are affirmed only after the death of their real or supposed authors. While they were alive, they were horrified at being perceived as wonder workers. The farther we are removed from their life, the greater becomes the reputation of their miracles. 'Think of the illustrious Fathers', Evergetinos writes, 'how—ignorant as they were, Abba Paul the Simple, Abba Pambo, and the other God-bearing Fathers—they even raised the dead, performed great miracles, and received power against demons . . . .'[100]

The aim of such *laudationes temporis acti* (praises of olden times) is not to make anyone long for wonders or feed a taste for the supernatural and the exceptional, but to cause regret for lost realities and to rediscover the faith, the simplicity, the intimacy the ancients had with God. Miraculous deeds are mentioned only as signs of God's approval of the prayer life of the great Saints. The 'simplicity' with which the christian thaumaturges work miracles proves that 'frankness with God' (*parrhesia,* free speech),[101] a relationship of dialogue with their Creator, and a filial spirit towards the Father represent the 'natural' condition of the spiritual person.[102]

An 'old man' says in the *Apophthegmata:*

> It is not appropriate for me to chase away someone's demon or heal the sick. The only thing I ask of God is not to let a demon enter me, and to purify me from impure, indecent thoughts; through this, I will become great. For if someone purifies himself of such thoughts and says his prayers promptly, he will be placed with the wonder-working Fathers in the kingdom of heaven.[103]

In another apophthegm we read: 'If someone has acquired purity, all things are obedient to him as [was the case] with Adam before he transgressed God's commandment'.[104]

## Notes

1. See Friedrich Heer, *Das Gebet,* 5th ed. (Munich, 1923); translated by Samuel McComb, *Prayer: A Study in the History and Psychology of Religion.* (New York: Oxford University Press, 1958).

2. *In epist. I ad Thessal.* 1, 3; PG 62:397. (For a recent anthology of patristic prayers, see Tomaš Špidlík, *Breviario Patristico* (Turin, 1971); translated. by Paul Drake as *Drinking From the Hidden Fountain. A Patristic Breviary: Ancient Wisdom for Today's World* (London: New City Press-Kalamazoo: Cistercian Publications, 1994)–ed.)

3. *Cent. Suppl.* 31.

4. André Ridouard and Jacques Guillet, 'Action de grâces'. VTB, 12; 'Thanksgiving'. DBT, 598–600.

5. Thomas Aquinas, *In IV Sent., dist.* XV, *p.* IV. a. 3. Aquinas, *Summa theologiae* II–II, *q.* 83, a. 17.

6. *Libellus de oratione* 14; PG 11:460–461A; translated by John O'Meara, *Origen: Prayer*, ACW 19 (1954).

7. *Conferences* 9. 99. 14; SCh 54 (1958) 50ff.; LNPF 11:391.

8. Anton Fonck, 'Prière', DThC 13/1 (1936) 183.

9. André Ridouard, 'Louange'. VTB, 680; 'Praise'. DBT, 442–445.

10. Augustin Bea, 'Gebet im Alten Testament', LThK2, 4 (1960) 539.

11. *A Systematic Handbook,* 135ff.

12. Tomaš Špidlík, *La sophiologie de S. Basile,* OCA 162 (Rome, 1961).

13. *Regulae brevius tractatae* 81; PG 31:1140BC; see W. K. L. Clarke, translator, *The Ascetic Works of Saint Basil: the Shorter Rules* (London, 1925).

14. *In epist. ad Hebraeos, homilia* 30.12; PG 63:209C.

15. Paul Ternant, 'Signe'. VTB, 1230–1236; DBT, 360–364.

16. André Ridouard, 'Louange'. VTB, 680–684; 'Praise'. DBT 442–445.

17. For example, Jgs 16:28, 2 Kgs 20:3, Jb 4:7, Acts 10:31, Lk 23:42. Adalbert Hamman, *La prière*, 2: *Les trois premiers siècles* (Tournai, 1963) 25ff.

18. *The Shepherd of Hermas,* Fifth Parable, 1, 1, Ninth Par., 14, 3; translated by Joseph M. F. Marique, *The Shepherd,* in *The Apostolic Fathers,* FCh (1947).

19. *Scala paradisi* 28; PG 88:1132A; Luibheid and Russell, CWS, 275f.

20. French trans. by Louis Bouyer, *La vie de la liturgie* (Paris, 1956) 149ff; Hamman II, 231ff.

21. Th. Boman, *Das hebräische Denken im Vergleich mit dem griechischen* (5th ed., Göttingen, 1968) 172ff.

22. See Hamman, *La prière* 2:67.

23. *Conferences* 9. 24–25; SCh 54 (1958) 61ff.; translated by Colm Luibheid, *John Cassian, Conferences,* CWS (1985).

24. *Stromata,* 6.14; PG 9:366BC; *The Stromateis or Miscellanies,* ANF 2 (1908).

25. *Libellus de oratione* 14; PG 11:464A.

26. See p. 214.

27. *A Systematic Handbook,* 20ff.

28. Gregory Nazianzen, *Oratio* XXXII, 1; PG 36:176A.
29. *De oratione* 10, PG 11:445D.
30. Jean Duplacy, 'Foi'. VTB, 475–86;'Faith'. DBT, 158–63.
31. Panaghiotis N. Trembelas, *Dogmatique de l'Église orthodoxe catholique, 3* (Chevetogne, 1968) 52ff.
32. *Conferences,* 9.31; ACW 57: 349; CWS, 119; LNPF 21:398.
33. *Ibid.,* 32; ACW 349; CWS, 120; LNPF 398.
34. *Ibid.,* 33; ACW 349; CWS, 120; LNPF 398ff.
35. *My Life in Christ* (London, 1897, New York, 1994) 8.
36. *Ibid.,* 8.
37. *Ibid.,* 24.
38. Jacques Dupont, 'Nom'. VTG, 827–832; 'Faith'. DBT, 377–380.
39. Špidlík, *La sophiologie de S. Basile,* 10.
40. *Chapters on Prayer,* 89; Hausherr, *Leçons,* 123; CS 4:70.
41. *Conferences* 9.34; ACW 58:349–353; CWS, 122; LNPF 398–400.
42. *A Systematic Handbook,* 256.
43. I. Goraïnoff, *Séraphim de Sarov,* 101, Spiritualité orientale 11 (Bellefontaine, 1973) See also C. Cavarnos and M. B. Zeldin, *St. Seraphim of Sarov* (Belmont, Mass., 1980).
44. Cf. *De oratione,* 6; PG 11:436D.
45. L. S. Frank, 'La realtà e l'uomo, Metafisica dell'essere umano', in *Il pensiero religioso russo, Da Tolstoy a Lossky,* translated by P. Modesto (Milan, 1977).
46. *Stromata,* 7.2; PG 9:501B.
47. See Ps 24:11; 43:6; 43:26 (Vulgate enumeration)
48. Ps 135 (Hebrew 136).
49. Paul Ternant, 'Miracle'. VTB, 757–67. ['Miracle'. DBT, 360–6].
50. *A Systematic Handbook,* 185ff.
51. *Chapters on Prayer,* 37; *Leçons,* 55; CS 4:61.
52. See Anton Fonck, 'Prière', DThC 13/2 (1936) 230ff.
53. *Stromata,* 1.24; PG 8:905B. Origen. *De oratione* 14.1; GCS 2:330, 7–9; ACW 19: 53. Ambrose, *Expositio in psalmum* 118.11; PL 15:1549A: 'Et tu cum oras, magna ora, id est, ora quae aeterna sunt, non quae caduca': 'And when you pray, ask for great things; ask for things that are eternal, not transitory'. Augustine, *Enarratio in psalmum* 62.14; PL 36:755; LNPF 8.
54. *De oratione* 14.1 (see n. 53).
55. *Ibid.,* 27, 1; GCS 2, 363ff; ACW 19:92ff.
56. *A Systematic Handbook,* 29ff.
57. Irénée Hausherr, *Noms du Christ et voies d'oraison,* OCA 157 (Rome, 1960) 162ff; translated by Charles Cummings OCSO, *The Name of Jesus,* CS 44 (Kalamazoo, 1978) 165ff.
58. *Origen's Treatise on Prayer* (London, 1954); translated by E. G. Jay, Intro., 30ff.
59. Irénée Hausherr, *Penthos, La doctrine de la componction dans l'Orient chrétien,* OCA 157 (Rome, 1944); translation by Anselm Hufstader, *Penthos: the Doctrine of Compunction in the Christian East.* CS 53 (Kalamazoo, 1982).
60. For the text analysis, see Hamman, *La prière* I1:226ff.
61. See Hamman, *La prière* 2:68ff.
62. *De Anna sermo* 4. 6; PG 54:667.
63. *Ibid.*
64. *A Systematic Handbook,* 191ff.
65. *Ibid.,* 192
66. Alfred Vacant, 'Absolution', DTh 1 (1903) 244ff.

67. *Scala paradisi* 28; PG 88:1129B; Luibheid and Russell, CWS, 274; Moore, 250.

68. Martyrius Sahdona, *Livre de la perfection* 2.8 (40); CSCO 253 (Syri 111) 11ff; translated by Sebastian Brock, *The Book of Perfection* 40, in *The Syriac Fathers on Prayer and the Spiritual Life,* CS 101 (Kalamazoo: Cistercian Publications, 1987) 219. See Irénée Hausherr, *Penthos* (1944) 26ff (above, note 43).

69. *Apophthegmata Patrum,* Anthony 16; PG 65:80C; translated Benedicta Ward, *The Sayings of the Desert Fathers,* CS 59 (1975) 4.

70. *In psalmum* 145.6; PG 55:527.

71. DThC 13/1 (1936) 232ff.

72. See, e.g., Mt 5:44, Jas 5:16.

73. *My Life in Christ* (New York, 1994) 414.

74. *A Systematic Handbook,* 153.

75. *The Martyrdom of St. Polycarp,* trans. by James A. Kleist, ACW 6 (1948) 93.

76. John Chrysostom, *De beato Philogonio* 6.3; PG 48:752. *Idem., Comparatio regis et monachi* 4; PG 47:390.

77. Evagrius, *Chapters on Prayer*, 39; *Leçons*, 58; CS 4:61.

78. *Cent.* 5.7; cf. Hausherr, 59.

79. *Cent, Suppl.* 33; Hausherr, 58.

80. Evagrius, *Chapters on Prayer,* 25; *Leçons,* 39; CS 4:59.

81. *Lettre* 49; Hausherr, 60.

82. *Cent.* 5.46; Hausherr, 59ff.

83. *Chapters on Prayer,* 103; *Leçons*, 139; CS 4:72.

84. *Non esse desperandum* 11; PG 51:363.

85. *De Oratione Dominica, oratio* I; PG 44:1129ff. See Hilda C. Graef, translator, *St. Gregory of Nyssa: The Lord's Prayer,* ACW 18 (1954). See also Maximus the Confessor, *De caritate* 1. 56, SCh 9 (1943) 80; translated by Polycarp Sherwood, *St. Maximus the Confessor, The Ascetic Life. The Four Centuries on Charity,* ACW 21.

86. *A Systematic Handbook,* 248ff.

87. See Martin Jugie, *Theologia dogmatica christianorum orientalium* IV (Paris, 1931) 134ff.

88. J. M. Harden, *The Anaphoras of the Ethiopic Liturgy* (London, 1928) 78ff.

89. Irénée-Henri Dalmais, *Les liturgies d'Orient* (Paris, 1959); translated by Donald Attwater, *Eastern Liturgies* (New York: Hawthorn Books, 1960).

90. DThC 13 (1936) 230ff.

91. Tertullian, *Apologeticus adversus gentes* 5; PL 1:346. Eusebius, *Historiae ecclesiasticae,* 5.5; PG 20:441–445.

92. *Constitutiones monasticae*; PG 31:1337B. Iosif of Volokolamsk, *Prosvetitel* [Illuminator] (Kazān, 1857) 360ff.

93. Evagrius, *Chapters on Prayer,* 34; *Leçons,* 51; CS 4:60. Martyrius Sahdona, *Livre de la perfection* 2. 8 (74); CSCO 253 (Syri 111) 21; Brock, *The Syriac Fathers on Prayer and the Spiritual Life,* 232.

94. *Constitutiones monasticae;* PG 31:1337B.

95. *Chapters on Prayer,* 34; *Leçons,* 51;CS 4:60.

96. *In dimissionem Chananaeae* 10; PG 52:457.

97. *Libellus de oratione* 21; PG 11:481AB; translated by John J. O'Meara, *Origen: Prayer,* ACW 19 (1954).

98. Xavier Léon-Defour, 'Miracle', *Catholicisme* 9 (1982) 259.

99. *Ibid.,* 266.

100. *Synagogē,* 2, chapter 32 (Constantinople, 1961) 41.

101. Irénée Hausherr, *Direction spirituelle en Orient autrefois,* OCA 144 (Rome, 1955) 51; translated by Anthony P. Gythiel, *Spiritual Direction in the Early Christian East,* CS 116 (Kalamazoo: Cistercian Publications, 1990) 58ff.
102. *A Systematic Handbook,* 100.
103. Louis Leloir, *Paterica armeniaca* 10, 81R; CSCO 371, 111.
104. *Ibid.*, 18, 11A; CSCO 377:47.

# 4

## BODILY PRAYER

*The Body During Prayer*

THE BODY IS AN IMPORTANT ELEMENT in dialogue between corporeal beings. Even if we communicate with others especially through words, we should not forget that human persons express themselves with their entire body. From ancient times the question has been raised as to what extent bodily members can be a help or a hindrance in the conversation with God, who is spirit.

The God of Scripture, unlike the god of the intellectualizing philosophers, revealed himself to humankind by taking on flesh, by 'stammering with children', as Origen says.[1] The human person replies in the same manner, through gestures and the voice, by lifting up hands (Ps 62:4) and eyes (122:1), by bending the knee (Eph 3:14), and crying to the Lord (Ps 3:3).

The Jews did not question the value of such outward expressions, except when they failed to correspond to the disposition of the heart or when people wanted to imprison the dialogue with God within such a sensory framework. Indeed, God knows the human heart and speaks to the human person without using words. He also hears the most intimate voices of our being (Ps 7:10). We should not be surprised therefore to find exhortations in Scripture that move in two different directions. On the one hand, ceremonies are prescribed, prayers are composed and recited; on the other, God proclaims through the mouth of the prophets: 'When you stretch out your hands I turn my eyes away. You may multiply your prayers, I shall not be listening' (Is 1:15).

These same attitudes are found again in christian writers. Over the years, the language of ritual in the various religions was codified to the extent that prayer seemed impossible without external elements. Such an outlook gave rise to the exaggerated ritualism so typical of the official religions of late antiquity. The Fathers were compelled to fight such a mentality. John Chrysostom writes: 'What is necessary is not the bodily posture you adopt [in prayer] but your inner disposition (οὐδὲ σχήματος ἀλλὰ φρονήματος)'.[2] 'Paul prayed while lying in prison . . . , the thief stretched out on the cross.'[3] 'What good is it', Origen warns, 'to go down on one's knees before God, if in his heart man kneels before the devil.'[4]

These warnings were inspired not simply by the ritualism of the pagan world; the ascetics were always conscious of the inherent temptations in everything that deals with the body when it is given free rein. To understand fully the import of such warnings, we should put them in their polemical context. Understood too literally, they could lead to a maiming of the expressive power of prayer.

### *The Meaning of the Body*

A passage by Basil in favor of 'bodily' prayer recurs like a *Leitmotiv:* 'Consider the power that is given by the soul to the body [*te sarki,* to the flesh], and what sympathy the body renders the soul in return'.[5] Iosif of Volokolamsk makes the following comment: 'Let us be concerned first over physical elegance and good order and then over internal observance'.[6] Since inner attention leads in turn to outer attention, one should pray 'with elevated thought, and with a contrite heart, and then visibly display the character of your heart by means of posture, good order of the hands, and a meek and quiet voice'.[7] Long before Iosif, Origen had written that the devout person 'bears in prayer the image of the characteristics befitting the soul'.[8]

The first aspect, the influence of the body on the disposition of the soul, has been studied exhaustively in connection with the 'somatic' method of hesychast prayer.[9] The second aspect, suggested by Origen, is represented to perfection in the liturgical rites.[10] Multiplying quotations about such a commonly accepted teaching would be unprofitable. Nonetheless, we would like to prevent a possible ambiguity over some texts that differentiate between the 'spiritual' element and the 'bodily' element in prayer. The external attitudes of which Evagrius speaks in contrasting them to the 'feelings of spiritual prayer' are not only physical postures but also the still too human attitudes of the intellect, compared to 'the spiritual intelligence contemplating the Blessed Trinity'.[11]

In addition, through prayer, the body itself is on its way to 'spiritualization', and to recovering its proper nature. Ignatii Brianchaninov writes:

> During prayer, thanks to the ineffable mercy of God . . . our corruptible body itself will turn toward prayer—the body that was created with the desire for God, but which, as a result of the Fall, has been contaminated by desires proper to animals. Then the human person is utterly seized by prayer: even the hands, feet, and fingers participate in prayer in an ineffable but entirely real and perceptible manner; they are filled with a power human language would be powerless to explain.[12]

### *Traditional Gestures*

Certain physical attitudes, inherited from the past and accepted in christian circles with a new symbolism, have become a traditional language to express and awaken feelings of prayer. In general, there are three postures which may be viewed as being fundamental: standing upright with hands raised—an image of the lifting up of the mind; kneeling—to express repentance; seated, for the quiet listening to the divine words that are either external or a discourse of the heart.

The language of the hands makes such postures more expressive. They are lifted or folded in supplication or at rest when the mind should remain recollected. But the most expressive and typically christian hand sign is the sign of the cross.

*Praying with the face turned toward the East* was also a practice among pagans and Jews.[13] The Christians quickly adopted it,[14] and it became a kind of profession of faith[15] because of the symbolism that came to be added to it. It is in the East that light originates, Clement of Alexandria notes.[16] Christ is this light.[17] In

Cappadocia and among the eastern Fathers, it was readily recalled that paradise, where man conversed with God, was in the East.[18]

*With hands lifted.* Standing, with hands spread wide and eyes lifted up to heaven, seems the most appropriate position for prayer, according to Origen.[19] Moreover, this posture was well known to the pagans[20] and to the Bible,[21] as it was to John Chrysostom.

### *The Sign of the Cross*

Making the sign of the cross is one of the early christian practices attested to abundantly in both texts and monuments.[22] In these texts we see how Christians signed themselves on the forehead; but a line from Tertullian bears witness that the custom involved much more. Writing to a woman, he tells her, *cum lectulum tuum signas*,[23] make the sign on going to bed. Prudence recommends that at this moment the sign be made not only on the forehead but also on the heart.[24]

From the beginning, the faithful ascribed a spiritual efficacy to the sign of the cross. Holy things were consecrated with the sign of the cross, for 'everything that is to be sanctified is consecrated by the sign of the Lord's cross with the invocation of the name of Christ', Augustine writes.[25]

It seems that these signs of the cross were made then with one finger rather than with the entire hand.[26] It is not unlikely that they were multiplied on each part of the body, first on the forehead, then on the breast and upon the lips, instead of making a single sign covering, so to speak, the entire body. The introduction of the present form is attributed to eighth-century monks.[27] Then the sign of the cross was made by joining together the first three fingers of the right hand while keeping the others folded, and by bringing the three joined fingers to the forehead, the breast, the right shoulder and the left. This manner of signing oneself is still that of the eastern Church (with a variant among the 'Old Believers' in Russia).[28] In the Latin Church, a change was introduced in the thirteenth century when the modern practice was adopted, with the open hand touching the left shoulder before the right.

Was the sign of the cross accompanied by a formula? If we recall that baptism consisted of an outpouring of water, accompanied by the sign of the cross and the words, 'In the name of the Father, of the Son, and of the Holy Spirit', it is hard—given this solemn circumstance—not to accept that a constant, universal practice was not established. But the sign of the cross may have been made not only with a fixed formula. It may and must commonly have been made with improvised formulas or invocations. Even in our own day, the practice of signing oneself in eastern liturgies is frequent and spontaneous.

### *Genuflections and* Metanies[29]

Human beings have used bows, genuflections, prostrations, and similar gestures in their relationship with God from time immemorial. In the East, there exists a particular form of respect, the *metania* (profound bow). A distinction is made between the 'little prostration' *(mikra metanoia)* which consists of a deep bow with the right hand touching the ground, and the 'great prostration' *(megale metanoia),* which is made by bending the knees until both hands touch the ground or by kneeling down and kissing the earth.[30]

Bending the knee in prayer (γονυκλισία), Origen notes,[31]

> is a symbol of that prostration and submission that Paul speaks of when he says: 'I fall on my knees to the Father of our Lord Jesus Christ, that Father from whom all fatherhood in heaven and on earth takes its title' (Eph 3:14). This spiritual bending of the knee, so called because all creatures worship God and humble themselves before him when they hear the name of Jesus, is, to my mind, what the Apostle is thinking of when he says: 'Everything in heaven and on earth and under the earth must bend the knee before the name of Jesus' (Phil 2:10).[32]

The meaning of this posture has not been lost with time. Theoleptus of Bulgaria († 1326) insists: 'Let each genuflection be accompanied by the spiritual [noetic] invocation of Christ; prostrating oneself soul and body before the Lord will make the God of souls and of bodies bend easily'.[33]

Genuflections and *metanias* are used widely as a monastic penance. Theodore the Studite, for example, imposed ten *meta-*

*nias* upon someone who had left church more than once without notice; and one hundred upon someone who had listened to a detractor.[34] Multiple *metanias* were used most frequently among the ascetics; Alexander the Sleepless *(akoimetos)* enjoined four hundred and ninety each day, to attain the 'seventy times seven' of the gospel (Mt 18:22).[35]

## *Oral Prayer*

What has been said about the expressive value of the body in general may be applied analogously to oral prayer. In the tradition there existed two conflicting positions: for and against vocal prayer. There was no need to tell pagans newly converted to Christianity that prayer was done by recitation. But it had to be made clear that, without the inward disposition, the recitation of formulas was merely an external element of little value. Christian prayer is not a magic formula. The petition addressed to God, Basil says, is not 'circumscribed by words', and is not 'made up of syllables'.[36]

The biblical story of Hannah, mother of the prophet Samuel, gave John Chrysostom a chance to explain this doctrine: Hannah prayed in the presence of Yahweh, but no one heard her voice (1 Sm 1:13). But 'she was heard not because of the clamor of her voice, but because of an inward cry of the heart'.[37] If christian prayer required oral recitation, Chrysostom concludes, how would we be able to do it everywhere, in the marketplace or during work?[38]

We should not be misled by the invective of polemics. Ignatii Brianchaninov warns: 'If the saintly Fathers speak of the sterility of oral and vocal prayer when it is not combined with attentiveness, one should not conclude from this that they rejected or scorned this prayer in itself'.[39]

> Numerous illustrious Fathers practiced oral and vocal prayer their entire life, and that did not prevent them from being filled with the gifts of the Spirit. The reason for their progress lies in the fact that with them the mind, heart, soul, and the entire body were joined with their voice and lips; they uttered prayer with their entire soul, their entire strength. In one word: their prayer expressed their whole being.[40]

To conclude: 'the mouth and tongue that apply themselves often to prayer and to a reading of the word of God become sanctified'.[41]

*The Educational Significance of Oral Prayer*

A great variety of grounds can be argued in favor of the recitation of formulas. Some have a rather psychological or pedagogic nature, while others are linked instead to the doctrine of the Incarnation. Here, for example, are the reasons enumerated by Theophan the Recluse.[42]

All the spiritual masters and the Church herself highly esteem oral prayer, especially because it is the necessary preparation for more advanced prayer. The language of prayer is a special language and should be studied like any other. We begin with prayer books and then we may venture to speak freely with God.[43] 'The flower precedes the fruit. Spiritual prayer is the fruit, and we must work hard to bring it to fruition.'[44] 'Even with those who have already reached the higher stage of inner prayer, the lips do not always remain closed, but here the external element of prayer, oral prayer, does not precede inner prayer, but follows it.'[45] In practice, however, it is not always the same element that precedes the other so that one moves spontaneously from one prayer to the other. 'All the great masters of prayer made a rule of prayer for themselves, and followed it. They began their devotions with specific prayers, which they abandoned as soon as they were able to pray spontaneously.'[46]

*The Power of Words*

'The function of words'—that would be the title we could give Theophan's psychological reflections. They carry weight, certainly, although they do not deal directly with the main issue: in the economy of salvation, the word has been promoted as an instrument of dialogue not merely between people, but also on the level of communication between God and the human person. Used in prayer, the human word becomes a reflection of the Word and participates in the mystery of the incarnation of the *Logos*. The Word, a divine Power, gives its servant a tongue that is 'as sharp as a sword', Gregory Nazianzus writes.[47] The tongue of a priest, by being joined to the Word, 'has great power';[48] it 'puts the sick back on their feet,[49] it purifies the assembly of the faithful and makes of it one heart, so that, joined together in the Spirit, they sing one triumphal hymn to the deity.[50]

The value of words is not the same for the Greeks and for the Bible. Concerning the power and the efficacy of the word, the Fathers held views which, compared to the theories of the ancients, differed from them in many original features. Socrates and Plato overcame skepticism, but for them communication between rational beings remained questionable. Despite its elegance and its flights, the platonic theory of language remains deeply pessimistic. In themselves, words do not have great value. If our mind did not preserve a remembrance of the heavenly world of the Ideas, we would learn but little from words, even less than from the sensory vision of objects.[51]

For the Old Testament prophets, discoursing on the link between inward thought and its outward manifestation was out of the question. What they wanted to establish was a link between the human word and that of God. Jeremiah was conscious of the impact of the words he uttered: they were like a 'hammer shattering a rock' (Jer 23:29). Their divine power seemed to form one body with his voice and the syllables he uttered.[52] The Christians would not pose the problem any differently. While speaking of the incarnate *Logos,* the Fathers allude to theories of language.[53] Basil enlarged the question when he gave weight to the service words render to the mutual communication between God and man, or among persons with a view to the unity of the Church.[54] Origen never tired of admiring the divine *Logos* who, moved by his benevolence toward humankind, wanted to 'stammer with children'.[55] The gift of words in the human person was viewed as a reflection of the divine action whereby the Father engenders his Word.[56]

The ancient philosophers thought that they were saving the value of language by relating it to the 'Idea' or to 'being'.[57] With the New Testament, the issue became christological. For Origen, the fullness of 'being' or of the 'Idea' is found in the *Logos* of God. It is in him that the human word finds communion *(koinonia)* with being.[58] Thus, only 'to the one who worships the Word are [given] discourse and word', Gregory of Nazianzus wrote.[59] The human word, a weak instrument in itself, partakes of the divine power through its union with the Word who created the universe.[60]

### *The Sacred Character of Oral Prayers*

Within this context, we are led to attribute an almost sacramental power to the words of prayer or even—much to be feared—an almost magical one. To accuse Origen of magic would be absurd.[61] Yet he maintains that the power of the psalms is not limited to our understanding of the words. Through their relationship with the body of Christ, the divine words are strong.[62] Even when we recite them without understanding them, their recitation already is a 'material' contact that resembles the conduct of the woman with an issue of blood who touched Jesus' garment and was healed.[63] The material recitation is like the practice used in charming snakes.[64] Abba Poemen also made an observation about this. The snake charmer does not always understand the words he uses, but the serpent understands and obeys them. Similarly, if we do not grasp the meaning of the psalms perfectly, the demons understand and they flee, terrified.[65]

On this topic, Nicholas Cabasilas mentions the case of Ardalion the clown who at the theater enacted the role of the martyrs in mockery but as a result of playing this role was converted.[66] There is a similar story in *The Way of a Pilgrim* about a restless boy who was instructed to repeat the Jesus Prayer.[67] There is also the story of a captain who was cured of his drinking by reading the Bible without understanding the meaning of the words.[68] In the book entitled *On the Mountains of Caucasus* we find the case of the hermit who for fifteen years repeated the Jesus Prayer vocally without being concerned about his inner dispositions, until the external prayer finally moved into his heart.[69]

The power of words in prayer is a frequent theme in John of Kronstadt. Here is a typical passage:

> Reverence every word, every thought of the Word of God, of the writings of the holy Fathers, and, amongst them, the various prayers and hymns which we hear in church or which we read at home,

> because they are all the breath and words of the Holy Spirit. It is, so to say, the 'Holy Spirit himself', who 'makes intercession' for us, and through us, 'with groanings which cannot be uttered' (Rom 8:26).[70]

One participates in the Holy Spirit, not in any magical way, but through one's own holiness. This is how Ignatii Brianchaninov explains it: 'The prayer of the saints is quickened by attention and the divine grace which reestablish the unity of man's faculties scattered by sin; this explains why it manifested such supernatural power and produced such a prodigious impression on the hearers'.[71] An example confirms this: 'It is said that when Saint Hilarion of Souzdal read the Akathist in church, the words flew from his lips as if they were fire, reaching the audience with an inexplicable power and efficacy'.[72]

*Reciting Fixed Formulas or Free Prayer?*

Even if we admit that it is possible to speak freely to God, we still notice a certain contempt in the history of spirituality for the recitation of fixed texts; what was feared was the danger of a magical mind set.[73] But we know that the great majority of Christians willingly let themselves be guided by good prayer books.[74] The tradition—that is, the spiritual experience of centuries—is recorded in such texts, and the voices of individuals are harmonized into the one voice of the Spirit that speaks in the Church.[75]

This does not prevent free prayer, praying in one's own words, from being viewed as being normally superior to the recitation of someone else's texts, except, as Theophan the Recluse notes, in one case: when free prayer is the result of sloth.[76] In normal situations, the principle is this: prayer is better to the extent that one is less bound to reading.[77] Even if such free prayer is monotonous, it resembles—in a comparison made by John Climacus—the unembellished lisping of children which wins a Father's heart more easily than does over-sophisticated discourse.[78] Nonetheless, in everyday life one cannot seek exclusively what is in itself best. From ancient times the advice has been to alternate psalmody with free prayer, not only in common but also in private prayer.

Their alternation is needed for a good spiritual balance. In a letter by John, the spiritual master of Gaza, we read: 'As for psalmody and recitation from memory, do not force yourself, but act according to the strength the Lord gives you. As to reading and prayer, do not deprive yourself of it: do a little of the one and a little of the other, and [thus] you spend the entire day by pleasing God. Indeed, our Fathers, who were perfect, had no specific rule.'[79] John Climacus believed that daytime was better for psalmody and night better for free prayer[80]: this is easy to understand if we think how difficult it was in those days to find a candle!

From the pedagogical point of view, it is clear that we should begin with specific prayers[81] and then move to free prayer: 'When you have finished reciting the prescribed prayers', Theophan the Recluse writes, 'continue praying, following your inspiration.'[82] Someone who is in the habit of praying by following his own thought, neglects the texts and often even leaves them aside altogether: 'The perception or vision of spiritual realities occurs during prayer, but recited prayer does not offer this advantage, which is a gift of personal prayer, however brief, joined to pious thought'.[83] A particular form of free prayer is glossolalia.

### *Glossolalia*[84]

Saint Paul counts speaking in tongues among the charisms (1 Cor 12:4, 10), which are 'manifestations of the Spirit'. In the assembly (15:9, 28), interpretation is needed for the edification of the hearers, while in private the person who speaks in tongues 'speaks to God'. He is 'speaking in the Spirit and the meaning is hidden' and he 'builds up himself' (14:2, 4).

The Fathers in their day had no experience of the gift of tongues which could have instructed them in their exegesis of 1 Cor 12–14 and Acts 2. John Chrysostom states explicitly: 'This entire passage is very obscure. The obscurity is caused by our ignorance of what had occurred then but now no longer take place.'[85] The only allusions to a real exercise in the gift of tongues are found in Irenaeus[86] and in Tertullian, in a work that belongs to his montanist period.[87] It is possible that the montanist practice of speaking in tongues contributed to the disappearance of this charism in orthodox circles. Augustine asked forcefully: 'Who nowadays would expect the imposition of hands to prompt speaking in tongues?'[88]

On the other hand, the classic spiritual authors have drawn attention to phenomena which might be the equivalent of the gift of tongues in the New Testament. They catalogued them under the rubric 'spiritual drunkenness',[89] a state in which the divine consolation seizes the mystic with such force that he finds himself unable to express his experience in a conceptual language and pours out strange, inarticulate words. The Greek Fathers follow Origen who speaks of 'jubilation' (ἀλαλαγμος).[90] The russian and syrian 'Fools for Christ' rejected words as a means of communication and created the impression that 'they were unable to utter coherent words'.[91]

## *Long Prayers or Short?*

Since the value of oral prayer is relative,[92] advice will vary depending on mind-sets and circumstances. Let us summarize some ideas that come from a parish priest, John of Kronstadt, a popular preacher. In principle, he is in favor of prolonged prayer: 'Why is long-continued prayer necessary? In order that by prolonged, fervent prayer we may warm our cold hearts, hardened in prolonged vanity.'[93] This long service of the lips is then like a preparation: 'Sometimes during a long-continued prayer only a few minutes are really pleasing to God and constitute true prayer and true service to God'.[94] Yet since 'not all men can receive this precept, but only those to whom it is given' (Mt 19:11), 'it is better for those who are not capable of long prayers to say short prayers, but with a fervent spirit'.[95]

There are also those who tire quickly of praying. The reason, John of Kronstadt says, is the lack of a sense of the presence of God, 'because we do not vividly represent to ourselves the Lord, who is at our right hand'. 'Look upon him unceasingly with the eyes of your heart, and then, even if you stand praying all night, you will not grow weary.'[96] The intense awareness of God's presence is not necessarily absent from rapid recitation. 'Is it possible to pray rapidly without damaging the quality of the prayer? It is possible to those who have learned to pray inwardly with a pure heart. . . . as rapidity in this case does not injure the sincerity of the prayer.'[97]

## Polylogia

The gospel condemns the *polylogia* (wordiness) of the pagans who 'imagine that the more they say the more likely they are to be heard' (Mt 6:7). Cassian has this to say about the egyptian Fathers: 'They care not about the quantity of verses but about spiritual understanding. . . .' The superior should 'take every possible care that the length of the psalms not weary [the younger monks] and that the cantor not lose the fruits of understanding the text'.[98] Evagrius likewise declares: 'Do not take pleasure in the great number of psalms, for it throws a veil on your heart. One word of intimacy is better than a thousand from a distance.'[99] Lastly, John Climacus says: 'Wordiness in prayer often distracts the mind and leads to phantasy, whereas brevity makes for concentration'.[100]

It would seem that monks, with their long prayers, hardly followed such wise advice. In any case for them, applying it mechanically would be out of the question. Origen was already aware[101] that *polylogia* could not be defined quantitatively. The ascetics spoke the same language when they recommended that the 'quantity' of words should match their 'quality', that is, their sincerity and power to penetrate into the mind and heart.[102] 'When praying', John of Kronstadt writes, 'keep to the rule that it is better to say five words from the depth of your heart than ten thousand words with your tongue only. . . . If you have no time to say all the prayers, it does not matter. . . .'[103] Setting a time for prayer every day is better than the amount of prayers to say.[104] Could this rule be applied to official, liturgical prayers? Not easily, because of the structure of the cenobitic life and of the divine office. Therefore another solution to the multiplicity of words had to be found.[105]

### *Recitation in Common*

At this point free prayer gives way to fixed formulas. While prayer in common was highly esteemed,[106] it remains true that those who lived the cenobitic life knew from experience the disadvantages of common recitations, especially if, like John Climacus, they had been nourished by the spirituality of the desert: 'In singing with many it is impossible to pray with the wordless prayer of the spirit'.[107] From this easily derives 'the confusion of voices which distracts attention from the psalms'.[108] Prayer in common is subject to the temptation of vainglory,[109] especially for those who have beautiful voices and sing well.[110] But the trouble can also arise from neighbors, each of whom has his own rhythm: 'For brisk chanting suits some, and more leisurely singing suits others. For the former are struggling with captivity of the mind, and the latter with ignorance.'[111] Thus, 'the dispositions of the religious are not all the same'.[112]

Here is the advice of John Climacus on how to keep the mind free even within the mold of recitation in common: 'Your mind should be engaged in contemplation of the words being chanted or read, or you should say some definite prayer while you are waiting for the alternate verse to be chanted'.[113]

### *Chant*[114]

The philosophers of antiquity attached great importance to music because of its influence on human emotions. They outlawed certain melodies and certain musical instruments as arousing feelings of sensuality and recommended others,[115] for music can become a powerful aid in purifying the passions of the soul.[116]

The desert Fathers were often strict about psalmody that was too ornate. On this subject, Paul Evergetinos, a good witness to the tradition, writes: 'A fisherman catches fish with a hook and a worm; similarly, it is with troparia and the chants themselves that the devil carries the monk away into vainglory, the desire to please, pleasure seeking, and soon impurity, for chanting has nothing to do with the monk who truly wants to be saved'.[117] Theodore the Studite declared, 'One does not come to the monastery to do calligraphy, to sing . . . or to wear beautiful garments'.[118]

But these same monks were often torn between this demand for austerity and their love of music. Cassian, also a witness of the desert, recognized the blessing of a melody that moves the heart: 'Once while I was chanting a verse of the psalms I was moved to the prayer of fire. Sometimes the musical expression of a brother's voice has moved sluggish minds to the most intense prayer. I have known it happen that the superiority and the seriousness of someone giving voice to the psalms has stirred a great onset of zeal in those who were attending.'[119]

Theodoret of Cyrrhus believed that a beautiful melody can provide a useful and easily remembered lesson: 'by adding the pleasure of music to what is useful'.[120] According to Hyperechius, thanks to chant the road is less long and the burden less heavy: 'Let spiritual song be on your lips, O monk, so that it may lift the burden of temptations that will assail us'.[121]

*Psalms*

'Psalmody is the work of incorporeal powers.'[122] The view that monks, by singing psalms, imitate the heavenly spirits is found explicitly or implicitly in many passages of ancient monastic literature.[123] 'A psalm chases away demons, attracts the protection of angels, and gives us weapons against the terrors of the night.'[124] 'The singing of psalms quiets the passions and calms the intemperance of the body.'[125] Hence this advice from Cyril of Phileotes: 'Even when you put your hand to work, let your lips sing hymns and your mind be occupied with prayer'.[126] He himself 'sometimes repaired his neighbors' nets, not for pay, but to combat *acedia* (boredom, listlessness) and for love of his brothers, while ceaselessly having psalms on his lips'.[127] 'He hastened to learn the psalter by heart', and 'was able to explain with understanding numerous psalms to others'.[128] Normally the monks were obliged to recite the entire psalter daily.[129] On the other hand, Evagrius notes: 'Psalm-singing is a many-sided image of wisdom; prayer is the prelude to immaterial and uniform knowledge'.[130] The expression 'many-sided wisdom', 'manifold wisdom' *(polypoikilas sophia)* comes from Saint Paul (Eph 3:10). In the language of Evagrius, it indicates the inferior contemplation which is preoccupied with the 'reasons' of creation[131]—hence the almost unavoidable distractions. 'It is a great thing to pray without distraction, but to chant the psalms without distraction is still greater.'[132]

Let us read how vividly Cassian describes this fact of experience:

> The mind skips along from psalm to psalm, leaps from the gospel to Saint Paul, from Paul to the prophets, from there to spiritual story. Ever on the move, forever wandering, it is tossed along through the whole body of Scripture, unable to settle on anything, unable to reject anything or to hold on to anything, powerless to arrive at any concentrated and judicious study, a dilettante and speedy taster of spiritual ideas rather than their creator and possessor.[133]

According to the testimony of the same author,[134] in Egypt there was no prescribed number of psalms to be recited; each monk, on the advice and under the guidance of a spiritual master, had to find 'the reasonable portion that suited him personally'.[135]

## Notes

1. *Contra Celsum* 5, 2; GCS 2:46, 13; ANF 4:543; also translated by Henry Chadwick, *Origen: Contra Celsum* (Cambridge University Press, 1976).
2. *De Anna sermo* 4.5; PG 54:668.
3. *Ibid.*, 4, 6.
4. *Homilia in Judices* II, 3; GCS 30: 475, 17–19.
5. *Homilia in illud, Attende tibi ipsi* 7; PG 31:216B.
6. Rule in Makarij, *Velikija Minei Četii,* September (St Petersburg, 1868) 506; translated by David M. Goldfrank, *The Monastic Rule of Iosif Volotsky*, CS 36 (Kalamazoo: Cistercian Publications, 1983, revised edition 2000) 70. T. Špidlík, *Joseph de Volokolamsk*, 107.
7. *Rule*; Goldfrank , 71.
8. *Libellus de oratione* 31. 2; PG 11:552A; GCS 2, 396, 11–5; ACW (1979) 165.
9. See p. 340.
10. See p. 99.
11. *Cent.* 3.30; *Chapters on Prayer,* 28; *Leçons,* 44; CS 4:59.
12. In Russian (St Petersburg, 1965) 265; *Approches de la prière de Jésus* (Bellefontaine, 1983) 99; selections are found in *On the Prayer of Jesus*, trans. by Lazarus (Moore) (London, 1952).
13. Wilhelm Gessel, *Die Theologie des Gebets nach 'De oratione' von Origenes* (Paderborn, 1975) 132ff.
14. Origen, *De oratione*, 32; GCS 2:400, 22–26; *Homilia in Jos.* 25.3; GCS 30:455, 2–4.
15. For an unusual account of this habit, see the *Pratum spirituale / Pré spirituel*, SCh 72 (1964) 144 ; translated by John Wortley, *The Spiritual Meadow (Pratum Spirituale) of John Moschos*, CS 139 (Kalamazoo: Cistercian Publications, 1992).
16. *Stromata* 7.7.43; CGS 3:32, 33ff; 33,1.
17. Origen, *De oratione* 32; PG 11:552A.
18. Basil, *Liber de Spiritu Sancto* 27; PG 32:189C ff;. translated by David Anderson, *St Basil the Great: On the Holy Spirit* (Crestwood, New York: St Vladimir's Seminary Press, 1980). See E. Weigand, 'Die Ostung in der Frühchristlichen Architektur', in *Festschrift*

*Sebastian Merkle,* re-edited by W. Schellberg (Düsseldorf, 1922) 370–381. See also Augustine, *De sermone Domini in Monte* 21.18; PL 34:1277.

19. *De oratione,* 31.2; GCS 2:396, 11–15.

20. Homer, *The Iliad,* 1, 450. Homer, *The Odyssey* 13, 355. Virgil, *The Aeneid* 3, 176ff. Friedrich Heiler, *Das Gebet,* 5th ed. (Munich, 1923) 101ff; English translation by Samuel McComb, *Prayer: A Study in the History and Psychology of Religion* (London, 1932, rpt New York, 1958). See E. von Severus, 'Gebet I', *Reallexikon für Antike und Christentum,* vol. 8 (Stuttgart, 1941) 1231ff.

21. Ex 9:29. Ps 28:2. Jb 11:13ff. 1 Tm 2:8.

22. See, e.g., Clement of Alexandria, *Stromata,* 6.11; PG 9:305, Origen, *Selecta in Ezechielem, cap.* 9; PG 13:800D, Tertullian, *De corona militis* 3; PL 2:98. See also Henri Leclercq, 'Croix (Signe de la)', DACL III/2 (1914) 3139–3144.

23. *Liber II Ad uxorem* 5; PL 1:1408.

24. *Cathemerinon* 6, v. 129; PL 59:839.

25. *Contra Faustum Manichaeum* 12.30; PL 42:207; LNPF 4:155–345.

26. Epiphanius, *Adversus haereses* 30.12; PG 41:428.

27. P. Bernardakis, 'Le culte de la croix chez les Grecs', *Echos d'Orient,* 5 (1901) 194.

28. See N. Subbotin, *Sources for the history of the raskol (schism) in the first period of its existence* (Moscow, 1975–1890)—in Russian.

29. Émile Bertaud, 'Génuflexions et métanies'. DSp 6 (1967) 213–226.

30. L. Clugnet, *Dictionnaire grec-français des noms liturgiques en usage dans l'Église grecque* (Paris, 1895) 99.

31. *Libellus de oratione* 31; PG 11:552; GCS 2:396, 21, 26; ACW 19 (1954) 130ff.

32. Jean Daniélou, *Origen,* translated by Walter Mitchell (New York: Sheed and Ward, 1955) 31.

33. The greek *Philokalia* (Athens, 1966) 11; *The Philokalia. The Complete Text* 4:185.

34. *Epitimia* 13 and 27; PG 99:1736.

35. See DACL 1 (1907) 313, and PO 6:680.

36. *Homilia in martyrem Julittam* 3; PG 31:244A.

37. *De Anna sermo* 4. 5; PG 54:667.

38. *Ibid.* See Ambrose, *Expositio in Psalmum* 117.18; PL 15:1471B.

39. *Approches de la prière de Jesus,* 45 (in Russian, 201). See note 12.

40. *Ibid.,* 49 (205).

41. *Ibid.,* 48 (204).

42. Tomaš Špidlík, *Théophane le Reclus,* 245ff.

43. *Piœma k raznym licam . . .* [Letters to Various Persons]) (Moscow, 1892) 326.

44. *Načertanie christianskago nravoučenija* [Christian Moral Teaching]) (Moscow, 1895) 409.

45. Ibid., 410.

46. *Čto jest duchovnaja žizň* [What the Spiritual Life Is]. 47 (Moscow, 1897) 170ff.

47. *Epistola* 171; PG 37:280C–281A.

48. *Ibid.*

49. *Oratio* 24, *In laudem S. Cypriani* 7; PG 35:1177A; LNPF ser. 2, 7:203–434.

50. *Oratio* 4, *Contra Julianum* 4.12; PG 35:541B.

51. *Cratylus* 383ff. R. Goegler, *Zur Theologie des biblischen Wortes bei Origenes* (Düsseldorf, 1963) 50ff. Špidlík, *Grégoire de Nazianze,* 138ff.

52. O. Prokosch, 'Wort Gottes im AT', in Kittel 4 (1942) 96ff.;'Word of God in the Old Testament', Kittel 4 (1967) 91–100.

53. See, for example, Irenaeus, *Adversus haereses* 2. 42; Harvey, 345. Tertullian, *Adversus Praxeam* 5; CSEL 47: 233, 12–13; 234, 3–14; ANF 3: 597–627.

54. Špidlík, *La sophiologie de S. Basile*, 8, 12, 246ff.
55. *Contra Celsum* 5.42; GCS 2: 46, 13; ANF 4:395–669.
56. Špidlík, *Grégoire*, 144ff.
57. F. Mayr, 'Prolegomena zur Philosophie und Theologie der Sprache', in Herbert Vorgrimmler, *Gott in Welt, Festgabe für Karl Rahner*, vol. I (Freiburg-im-Breisgau, 1964) 39–84.
58. Goegler, *Zur Theologie*, 222.
59. *Oratio* 41.1; PG 36:429A.
60. *Oratio* 20.9; PG 35:1076BC.
61. See Gessel, *Die Theologie*, 233f.
62. Henri Crouzel, *Origène et la connaissance mystique* (Paris-Bruges, 1961) 253ff; translated by A. S. Worrall, *Origen*, (San Francisco; Harper & Row, 1989).
63. *Commentarium in Matthaeum* 11.6–8; PG 13:924; ANF. 4: 409–512.
64. *Homilies on Joshua* 20.1; GCS 7:416ff. See Henri de Lubac, *Histoire et Esprit, L'intelligence de l'Écriture d'après Origène*, Théologie 16 (Paris, 1950) 323ff.
65. Louis Leloir, *Paterica armeniaca* 5, 52;CSCO 361:52–53.
66. *De vita in Christo*, liber 2; PG 150:556ff; translated by Carmino J. deCatanzaro, *The Life in Christ*, (New York: St. Vladimir's Seminary Press, 1974) 92ff.
67. *Irénikon* 4 (1928) 75ff; translated Helen Bacovcin, *The Way of a Pilgrim* and *The Pilgrim Continues His Way* (New York: Doubleday, Image Books, 1992) 92ff.
68. *Irénikon* 4 (1928) 30ff.
69. Schemamonk Ilarion, *Na gorach Kavkaza* (Batalpašink, 1910).
70. *My Life in Christ* (New York, 1994) 308. Translation used by permission.
71. *Approches de la prière de Jésus*, 49 (in Russian, 206). See also, note 12.
72. *Ibid.*
73. Beda Thum in LThK 4 (1960) 537ff. Friedrich Wulf, *ibid.*, 547.
74. Anton Fonck in DThC 13/1 (1936) 190ff.
75. Boris Bobrinskij (Bobrinskoi), *La prière et la liturgie dans la vie de l'Église orthodoxe* (New York, 1953) 244ff—in Russian. Agapij, monk of Valaam, in *Umnoe delanie o molitve Iisusovoj* (Valamo, 1936) 469.
76. *Čto jest duchovnaja žizň* [*What the Spiritual Life Is*] (Moscow, 1897) 279.
77. *Letters* (Moscow, 1898) 73.
78. *Scala paradisi* 28; PG 88:1132A; translated by Lazarus Moore, *St. John Climacus: The Ladder of Divine Ascent* (Willits, California: Eastern Orthodox Books, 1973).
79. Translated by Lucien Regnault, *Maîtres spirituels au désert de Gaza* (Solesmes, 1967) 69.
80. *Scala paradisi* 27; PG 88:1117C.
81. Theophane the Recluse, *Čto jest (Spiritual Life)* 170ff.
82. *Ibid.*, 172.
83. *Pisma* [*Letters*] (Moscow, 1892) 446.
84. Francis A. Sullivan, 'Langues (don des)', DSp 9 (1976) 223–227.
85. *In epist. I ad Corinthios, homilia* 29.1; PG 61:239B.
86. *Adversus haereses* 5.6.1; SCh 152 (1969) 74; *Irenaeus Against Heresies*, ANF 1 (1908).
87. *Adversus Marcionem* 5.8; PL 2:490; *Tertullian Against Marcion*, ANF 3 (1925) 271–474.
88. *De baptismo contra Donatistas* 3.16.21; PL 43:148ff.
89. Ignacio Ipparaguire, 'Ivresse spirituelle'. DSp 7/2 (1971) 2312–2338; see below, Chapter 8.
90. *Selecta in psalmos* 46; PG 12:1436D. See Aimé Solignac, 'Jubilation'. DSp 8 (1974) 1471–1478.

91. Leontius of Neapolis, *Vita S. Symeonis* 6; PG 93:1725B. See Tomaš Špidlík, '"Fous pour le Christ" en Orient'. DSp 5 (1964) 755ff.

92. See Thomas Aquinas (2-II-83, 14): 'The quantity of a thing should be commensurate with its purpose, for example, the quantity of medicine should be measured by the needs of health. Fittingly, therefore, prayer should last only as long as it arouses the fervour of interior desire, but when it exceeds this measure and cannot be continued without weariness it should be discontinued'. [Translation from *St Thomas Aquinas: Summa Theologiae* (New York: McGraw-Hill, 1964) 89].

93. *My Life in Christ* (New York, 1994) 345.

94. *Ibid.*, 26.

95. *Ibid.*, 114.

96. *Ibid.*, 122.

97. *Ibid.*, 19.

98. *The Institutes* 2.11.1–2; SCh l09 (1965) 77; ACW 58:44; LNPF ser. 2, 11:209.

99. *Paraenetikos*, ed. Frankenberg, 561.

100. *Scala Paradisi* 28; PG 88:1132; Moore (above, n. 78) 251; Luibheid, CWS, 275.

101. *Libellus de oratione* 21. 2; GCS 2: 345, 19–24. See *ibid.* 16.1; GCS 336, 6ff. See the translation by Rowan A. Greer, *Origen: an Exhortation to Martyrdom, Prayer*, CWS (1979).

102. *Umnoe delanie o molitve Jisusovoj* [*Dialogues on the Jesus Prayer*]) (Valamo, 1936) 408.

103. *My Life in Christ* (New York, 1994) 113.

104. Špidlík, *Théophane le Reclus*, 247.

105. See p. 89.

106. See p. 94.

107. *Scala* 19. 6; PG 88:937D; Moore, 169.

108. *Ibid.*, 4.91;713D; cf. Moore, 89.

109. *Ibid.*, 28.24; PG 113A.

110. See p. 87.

111. *Scala* 28. 62; PG 88:1140B; Moore, 258; CWS 281.

112. *Ibid.*

113. *Scala* 18.7; PG 88:937D; Moore, 169. See P. Miquel, *La liturgie une oeuvre d'art, L'oeuvre de Dieu célébrée par son peuple*, Vie monastique 13 (Bellefontaine, 1981) 139.

114. Miquel, *ibid.*, 53–66.

115. Plato, *The Republic* 398E–99D. Aristotle, *Politics* V, 4, 3–4.

116. Aristotle, *Politics* V, 7, 5. Basil, *Sermo de legendis libris gentilium* 7; PG 31:581D–584A; translated by F. M. Padelford, *Address to Young Men on the Right Use of Greek Literature: Essay on the Study and Use of Poetry by Plutarch and Basil the Great* (New York, 1902) 97–120.

117. *Synagoge* II.19. 5. See also *Sentences des Pères du désert, nouveau recueil* (Solesmes, 1970) 177. Irénée Hausherr, *Penthos. La doctrine de la componction dans l'Orient chrétien*, OCA 132 (Rome, 1944) 120–123; translated Anselm Hufstader, *Penthos: The Doctrine of Compunction in the Christian East*. CS 53 (Kalamazoo: Cistercian Publications, 1982).

118. *Grandes Catéchèses* I. 82, quoted by P. Miquel, *Liturgie*, 58.

119. *Conferences* 9.26; SCh 54 (1958) 62; CWS (1985) 117; LNPF second series, 11:396.

120. Quoted by P. Miquel, *Liturgie*, 60.

121. *Ad monachos adhortatio* 137; PG 79:1488A.

122. *La vie de saint Cyrille le Philéote*, ed. by E. Sargologos (Brussels, 1964) 289.

123. Garcia M. Colombás, *Paradis et vie angélique* (Paris, 1961) 203–227.

124. Basil, *Homilia in psalmum* I. 2; PG 29:212D.

125. Evagrius, *On Prayer,* 83; *Leçons,* 115; Bamberger, 69.
126. *La vie de saint Cyrille,* 289.
127. *Ibid.*
128. *Ibid.,* 345ff.
129. J. Bois, 'Les Hésychastes avant le XIVe siècle', *Échos d'Orient* 5 (1901) 6ff.
130. *Chapters on Prayer* 85; *Leçons,* 119; CS 4:63.
131. *Ibid.*
132. Evagrius, *Capita practica ad Anatolium* 41; PG 40:1232C; translated by E. Kadloubovsky and G. E. H. Palmer, 'To Anatolius: Texts on the Active Life', *Early Fathers from the Philkalia* (London: Faber and Faber, 1953) 102.
133. *Conferences* 10.13; SCh 54 (1958) 94; LNPF, series 2, 11:409; cf. CWS (1985) 139.
134. *Institutes* 3.2–3; SCh 109 (1965) 92ff; ACW 58:59–62; LNPF ser. 2, 11:212ff.
135. Pierre Miquel, *La liturgie une oeuvre d'art . . .* (Bellefontaine, 1981) 144.

# 5

# LITURGICAL PRAYER

## THE COMMUNAL NATURE OF LITURGICAL PRAYER

### *The Christian Assembly*

The *ekklesia* is a 'sacred convocation' of the people drawn together in a liturgical assembly. The term *ekklesia* refers first to the concrete assembly of the faithful gathered in the same place (Acts1:13-14; 2:42-47), then to a group of believers living in a certain city, and finally to the totality of believers scattered all over the world. We are incorporated into this assembly by a liturgical rite, baptism (Acts 2:38-41, 47). The high point of the assembly in church is the 'breaking of the bread' (Acts 2:42, 46; 20:7, 11), a sharing at the table of the risen Christ who presides over this meal invisibly (Lk 24:30-35; 1 Cor 11:20)[1], inviting us to participate in the life in the heavenly liturgy of the Holy Trinity.

In the East, John Chrysostom's praise of the communal prayer in church has often been quoted:

> Yes, you can pray at home, but not as well over there as you can in church. . . . Here, there is something more, namely harmony and unanimity, the bond of love, and the prayers of the priests. Indeed, the priests preside for this reason: that the prayers of the community, which are weaker, may rise to heaven, joined to theirs, which are stronger.[2]

Dare we object that the eastern liturgies betrayed their ecclesiastical function when they became typically monastic? In fact, the monasteries have always and everywhere been concerned with the dignity of liturgical celebrations, to the extent that the liturgy was in danger of becoming a worship reserved for monks and removed from the people. The coptic liturgy, long and slow, is perhaps the most 'monastic' of all: the gestures are significant, but there is little external ceremony. Yet, more than in any other liturgy, the people are associated with the celebration, up to the heart of the eucharistic anaphora.[3] This corresponds well to the general trend in the East: monastic spirituality is pre-eminently an ecclesiastical spirituality. All Christians are invited to participate in it according to their condition, 'to lead the monastic life, even when they are married'.[4] The monastery is an image of the Church universal.

Mutual intercession concretely expresses this ecclesiastical union in the broadest context. Joined more intimately to Christ and the Spirit, and thereby the object of the Father's greater love, Christians pray more intensely for one another. The link between the *epiclesis* and the intercessions which prepare for or prolong it, is attested to by the oldest eucharistic documents. If we take as an example the syriac anaphora of Saint James, the order of the intercessions ('mementos'), also called 'canons', is as follows:

—the first is for the intention of the Church orders, the patriarchs and bishops;
—the second is for the faithful brothers and sisters;
—the third for the kings;
—the fourth for the Blessed Virgin, the apostles, confessors, and martyrs;
—the fifth is for the doctors;
—the last one for the deceased.[5]

It is worth noting that, aside from this, the sense of church unity is very pronounced in syriac liturgical texts.[6]

*The Unifying Power of the Rites*

The unifying sanctification of the rite is vital to anyone who is conscious of the fact that the human person—bound to a tradition and the recipient of an entire geographic and historic viewpoint expressed within a culture—finds his or her normal development only within the bosom of a community.[7] The liturgy is a language: it makes use of words, places, and times.[8]

The Church, the union of believers in the Spirit, finds her concrete 'impression' in the rites and then becomes an 'expression', a summary of the piety of the group. The Christian East has always been very conscious of this, and it has viewed, as a 'particular church', those who pray together according to a specific ritual tradition. Thus, liturgy regulates spiritual life: it provides words and gestures, forms of devotion to more individualistic temperaments. 'There are many of us', Theophan the Recluse writes, 'and all of us have great needs, but for every need we find help in the church. On the other hand, each one is free to find for himself what is necessary.'[9] John of Kronstadt writes: 'The voice of the readings in church, the hymns, prayers, and supplications, is the voice of our own souls . . . ; it is the voice of all humankind . . . . Wonderfully beautiful are these prayers and hymns; they are the breathing of the Holy Spirit.'[10]

Within this context, the unity of the Church is visible above all in this community of prayers. Those who pray together are *one*. The Church, in essence, is universal because all pray for all. Yet the various ethnic and social groups pray in their own way, according to their mind-set and their traditions. From this it follows that the universal Church is made up of local churches, the liturgical language of which may vary one from the other. The eastern churches, distinguished by the variety of their rites and languages, are aware of the importance of such diversity, an expression of the manifold wisdom of God (Eph 3:10).

## THE DOXOLOGICAL CHARACTER OF LITURGICAL PRAYER

### *The Splendor of God's Glory*

The Church enters history like a mystic appearance of Christ. In the thought of modern Orthodox authors, she is a living icon of the Saviour, as he himself is the image of the Father.[11] Gregory of Nyssa long ago stated that the one who contemplates the Bride sees the face of the Bridegroom.[12] In biblical terms, this epiphany is expressed as the manifestation of the glory of God.[13]

The expression 'the glory of Yahweh' denotes God himself in so far as he manifests himself in his majesty and power, in the splendor of his holiness. The Old Testament knows two types of manifestations or epiphanies of the divine glory: the great deeds of God; and his appearances. The essential revelation in the New Testament is the link between glory and the person of Christ, who is 'the reflection of God's glory and bears the impress of his own being' (Heb 1:30), 'the Lord of glory' (1 Cor 2:8).

The liturgy which is essentially a 'remembrance' *(anamnesis)* evokes all the great deeds God performed in Christ. The heavenly glory of the Saviour, made visible on earth, shines through its words and symbolic rituals. The Orthodox authors of our day[14] like to emphasize the 'doxological' dimension of the liturgy, which corresponds to the human person's obligation to recognize and celebrate the glory of God. While the concept of *glory* is a key concept in hebrew thinking, that of *honor* (τιμή) represents an element imported into the sacred books through contact with alexandrian culture.[15] But in the New Testament and the greek liturgy, *timé* is almost always associated with *doxa* (δόξα, glory), especially in the 'doxologies'.[16] In the Latin Fathers there exists a current of thought which, under the influence of Cicero, seeks to establish the right God has to receive special honor from humankind.[17]

As a group, however, the Fathers do not distinguish between the 'honor' and the 'glory' of God. They place the glory of God in the profession of his creative glory, in the holiness of the christian life, and, of course, in worship,[18] which commemorates the blessings of God with thanksgiving. The 'doxological' dimension of the liturgy truly coincides with 'remembrance' *(anamnesis)* and 'thanksgiving' *(eucharistia).*

## *The Liturgy as Instruction in Truth*

As the 'icon of Christ', the Church in her liturgy emphasizes the two major aspects of any sacred image: teaching the mysteries of God and imparting grace. This God who manifests his glory is the One who teaches human beings the mysteries of his own life. An entire tradition assigns a favored place to the liturgy as 'essential theology': either it expresses an accepted belief or it precedes the proclamation of a dogma. 'There is a close connection between dogma and devotion which are inseparable in the consciousness of the Church,'[19] writes Paul Evdokimov. 'In their very formulation, the dogmas defined by the Ecumenical Councils belong to the doxological genre; this is why such formulas are so easily incorporated into the very body of the liturgy and structure it dogmatically'.[20] The saying *Lex orandi est lex credendi* (the rule of prayer is the rule of faith) is an abbreviated formula taken from the *Indiculus de gratia Dei* by Prosper of Aquitaine.[21]

### *The Contemplative Dimension of the Liturgy*

In discussing the contemplative life, Philo noted that in the present life, action and contemplation are intertwined. But among therapeutes (healers) such activity consisted of prayers and liturgical chant. The liturgy is therefore 'action' with a view to contemplation.[22] The contemplative mind of the East has always understood this. The eastern liturgies are the splendid flower of the civilization of peoples transfigured by Christianity. The art of the icon is incorporated into the celebration whose sacred character it structures. God reveals his glory visibly.

The *Sursum corda* ('Lift up your hearts') which precedes the anaphora therefore assumes a special importance because of its antiquity and universality. Theodore of Mopsuestia writes: 'The high priest alerts the people by saying "Let us lift up our hearts" to signify that we who are supposed to perform this awesome liturgy on earth should look to heaven, on high . . . .'[23]

As compared with his contemporaries, Theodore seems to go one step further when he emphasizes the realism of the *presence* of the mystery. With a description that anticipates the mystical explanations of the following centuries, we find in him one of the elements that will be developed in later byzantine and syrian mystagogies.[24]

### *The Mystical Nature of the Liturgy*

Saint Paul teaches that preference should be given to thanksgivings that are intelligible, so that the uninitiated may be edified by them (1 Cor 14:16-17); but such transparency in prayer is very relative. The object of christian contemplation is a mystery,[25] and the revelation of it is necessarily symbolic. So the liturgy is performed at the conjunction of mystery (the supra-rational) and symbol (the infra-rational).[26] By its very nature, a symbol 'points to something else'[27]: it is a starting point from which to arrive at the heights of union with God.

Latin theology developed this particular aspect of the liturgy gradually with the term *sacramentum,* which Tertullian and Augustine interpreted by emphasizing the aspect of 'sign' *(signum).* Classical theology described the *sacramentum* as 'an efficacious sign', thereby restricting its use to the sacraments viewed as channels of grace *ex opere operato.* More recently, giving liturgical theology a more solid foundation by composing a 'doctrine of the mysteries' *(Mysterienlehre)* has been recommended.[28]

The exploration of mystery has been helped by the contemplative and monastic nature of the eastern liturgies, by this transition from the visible to the invisible, from the human to the divine.

## *The Allegorical Interpretation of the Liturgy*

Liturgists are periodically tempted to 'allegorize' the rites, that is, to submit them to an analysis that conceptualizes the disparate elements. The candle is a figure of Christ; the wax is humanity; the wick, divinity; the flame, the Spirit, and so on. Medieval commentators transformed the Mass into a mime of the Passion.[29] Such intellectualizing, which is often misplaced, takes away the basic meaning of the symbol and uproots the primitive perception of the image from its native soil.[30]

Used to allegorical interpretations of Scripture and of nature (in 'natural contemplation'),[31] eastern authors easily assigned a place to it in their mystagogical commentaries,[32] while not always avoiding rather contrived interpretations. The symbolic meaning of the rites is clarified *ex professo* in a treatise which may be called a classic, *A Commentary on the Divine Liturgy* by Nicholas Cabasilas:

> This practice of demonstrating, exhorting or prophesying by means of action is very ancient. . . . And we are told of one of the

> divinely inspired Fathers that when he was asked what a monk was, he made no reply, but removed his cloak and trampled it underfoot. . . . In the same way, the priest expresses in words or represents by his gestures all that he knows of the solemn sacrifice. . . .[33] The whole scheme of Christ's work, as we have seen, is depicted in the Host during the liturgy; there we see the symbol of the infant Christ, of Christ led to death, crucified, and pierced with a lance. Then we see the bread transformed into the most holy Body which actually endured these sufferings, and rose from the dead, and ascended into Heaven, where it sits at the right hand of the Father . . . .[34]

### *The Beauty of the Liturgy*

It has often been said that beauty is the characteristic trait of the eastern liturgies. It was not always like this: the liturgy of the ancient monks was simple and stark. Poemen reports that Abba Paphnutius 'was great and avoided small liturgies'.[35] It irritated Pambo to see his disciple impressed by the beauty of the rhythmic chants he had heard at Saint Mark's in Alexandria: 'In his opinion, the monks had not sought solitude to bellow like oxen . . . or amuse themselves by dancing before God, by composing and warbling beautiful phrases'.[36]

The sumptuosness of churches was also criticized. A *Life* of Pachomius relates how he had an oratory destroyed which he accused himself of having erected to his own glory rather than that of God: 'When he came to himself, he said that it was through the machination of the demon that he had admired the beauty of the house'.[37]

Soon, however, another view prevailed. In response to criticism, the Fathers defended the richness of the worship. The beauty of the house of God should give the faithful a foretaste of the beauty of heaven. The 'sweetness of the church' should be transparent in the liturgical functions to create an impression of 'heaven on earth'.[38] According to the legendary story in the *Chronicle* ascribed to Nestor, it was the liturgical pomp of Byzantium that led to the conversion of Russia.[39]

And yet beauty is not always the daughter of opulence and false luxury. Basil had already adopted the stoic view of the beautiful as a harmony that appeases the soul.[40] Along the same lines, Pavel Florensky identified beauty with the unity of the Holy Trinity and its repercussions in the christian life.[41] Beauty, then, is the natural ambience of someone who, while praying, understands the full spiritual wealth of the Church. Various elements should contribute to the splendor of the liturgy: the building,[42] icons,[43] vestments, candles, incense, bells, and chanting.[44]

It is especially in the armenian rite where the absence of an iconostasis has contributed to letting the movements of the numerous officiants in their rich vestments be exposed to view. While preparing himself for the liturgy, in the presence of such splendor, the priest says; 'Lord, make me, your unprofitable servant, worthy of the spiritual ministry of your glory . . . since you alone are shrouded in splendor'.[45]

According to the russian *Pastoral Handbook*,[46] candles signify not only the purity of life of those who pray, but also the light of grace of the mystery. As for incense, so great a value was attributed to it that no one was allowed to do without it, even in simple functions.[47]

Unlike Mount Athos, where a piece of wood called *symbolon* is used [to call monks to prayer], the Slavs are very fond of bells, which may have different names depending on their function. Thus, for example, an invitation to a simple liturgy is made with the sound of one bell *(blagovest),* to a solemn liturgy with two bells ringing one after the other *(perezvon).* The beginning of the liturgy and the chanting of the Gospel are announced by three bells ringing together.[48]

## *The Traditional Teaching*

If the liturgy is to remain the authentic expression of dogma, any improvisation of liturgical prayers and often even any change of text or gestures would meet with opposition in the East and the West. Iamblichus, in the late third century, contrasted the fidelity of the barbarians in their ceremonies to the incessant innovations of the Greeks: 'If all the names and powers of prayers are now lost, it is because they [the Greeks] in their desire to innovate never cease changing and because of the thoughtlessness of the Hellenes. Indeed, by nature, the Greeks love novelties.'[49] He then dismissed reforms in worship for reasons we would call sociological, psychological, and ethnological.

In christian circles, Minucius Felix reminds us that the antiquity of a rite confers on it a special holiness: 'The older . . . the holier' *(tantum sanctitatis . . . quantum vetustatis).*[50]

While temperamentally given to change, the Greeks were nonetheless sensitive to another aspect of the liturgy: in the immutability of ritual, the human person senses a certain participation in eternity, in the cosmic order. The byzantine emperor Constantine VII Porphyrogenetus expressed this concept in the preface to his work on court ceremonies: 'May the imperial power, exerting itself with rhythm and moderation, reproduce the harmonious movement the Creator gives to this entire Cosmos, and the Empire will seem more majestic to our subjects, and thereby more pleasing and admirable'.[51]

But should this 'cosmic' dimension, which suggests immutability, not agree with the economy of salvation which is essentially historical, and subject to change? Theophan the Recluse held that the 'Old Believers' were wrong in refusing to admit the mutability of various non-essential forms. Some evolution in the rites of the Church would not be evil. He warned, nevertheless, that everything introduced into the Church comes by the grace of God, by Providence. Why not view this external order as a school in which to educate Christians, form their taste, discipline, and guide them? 'As the breathing of the body refreshes and vivifies the entire organism, so the observance of church rules refreshed and vivifies the entire spiritual life.'[52]

Others, however, while recognizing the warning of Saint Paul against the untimely speaking in tongues (1 Cor 12:1ff), regret that this type of charismatic prayer no longer has a place in the liturgical framework. The *Didache* permitted it: 'Allow the prophets to render thanks as they desire'.[53] In the *Apostolic Tradition,* Hippolytus of Rome uses two striking expressions: 'with moderation', and 'in conformity with orthodoxy'. 'It is not at all necessary for the bishop to pronounce the same words . . . . If someone is able correctly to make a great, exalted prayer, this is good. But if he prays with moderation, let no one prevent him, provided the prayer be correct and in conformity with orthodoxy.'[54]

But in the East, the pre-eminent mark of orthodoxy is above all the tradition *(paradosis),* which did not, of course, favor improvisations, but would not stifle creativity. Are the eastern liturgies, with their troparia and hymns, not an eloquent testimony to a living, religious poetry? The coptic liturgy has remained the most 'traditional'. Abba Pambo early showed his hostility to poetic innovations. One of his disciples who had been sent to Alexandria had learned troparia at the sanctuary of Saint Mark the Apostle. The old man held this against him: 'Woe to us, my child! The times are near when the monks will abandon solid food, the word of the Holy Spirit, to devote themselves to hymns and tunes. . . . Let me tell you, my child: the times will come when Christians will corrupt the books of the holy apostles and divine prophets, when they will scratch out sacred Scripture to write troparia and hellenic discourses. . . .'[55] Pambo's prophecies have been fulfilled impressively in the eastern liturgies, but has this been such a disaster?

## THE CHARACTER OF *ANAMNESIS* AND *EUCHARISTIA*

### *The Memorial of God's Great Deeds*

The essential element of jewish celebrations was praise addressed to God for the history of salvation. Therein lies the essence of *anamnesis* (remembrance). Christians know that the work of salvation is accomplished by the Son in the Holy Spirit. The specific mark of the christian *anamnesis* appeared when Hippolytus viewed the celebration of the eucharistic economy as being first and foremost a celebration of the trinitarian economy.[56]

From the two anaphoras attributed to Basil[57] and that contained in *The Apostolic Constitutions*[58] originated an ancient development devoted to the *anamnesis* of the great deeds of the Old Testament. But at the same time, one of the traits most typical of all three texts is a complete remembrance of the mysteries of Christ, including his death, his resurrection, ascension, and even the judgment to come.[59] This 'remembrance' or 'memorial' of the Saviour is sacramental. The East has always viewed the sacraments within the framework of the liturgy. The authors like to extend the sacred efficacy of *anamnesis* to the entire liturgy, at least in some way. Sergius Bulgakov speaks of 'the religious realism' of the eastern rites[60]; Boris Bobrinskoy of their 'eucharistic character' so that on Christmas Christ is really born in churches and really dies at Easter, and then rises.[61]

### *Feastdays: A Solemn* Anamnesis

In the history of humankind, a feastday is an experience verging on contemplation; a chance to escape from daily toil, a readiness to savor a higher experience.[62] According to Plato, 'the gods . . . have ordained feasts of thanksgiving as periods of respite from human troubles'.[63] In the flow of time, feasts are an image of eternity. In Scripture, the Sabbath is linked to the sacred rhythm of the week, which it closes with a very strict day of rest.[64]

The position of the Sabbath at the end of the week is important. Scripture, the revelation of eternal God, opens and closes with references to time. God is perceived in his interventions here below, and this makes the history of the world a sacred history. Eternity does not appear to be a flight from time, as it is in Plato. A feast puts us in contact, so to speak, with eternity through a transfiguration of time or 'simply by repeating an archetypal, mythical gesture'.[65] It is an *anamnesis,* an understanding of the primordial reality in the midst of ordinary time.[66]

A feast day is a cyclical and historic *anamnesis*. Two dimensions of time are superimposed within human experience: one that regulates the cycles of nature (cosmic time) and the one that unfolds in terms of events (historic time). God rules both equally and guides them towards the same end.[67] Pagan feasts were linked most frequently to the cycles of nature (the winter solstice, the rite of spring). The new reality brought to the notion of feast by the judaeo-christian revelation is that, from then on, feasts were linked, no longer to the seasonal cycle, but to historical events: to what God had done for his people. But in the New Testament, the supreme event is the death and resurrection of Christ and then the coming of the Spirit.[68] For the Christian, all feasts are of a paschal nature.

No feast is celebrated once and for all. It is in the nature of a feast to be repeated in time, at regular intervals, but the tenor of the feast differs every time depending on historic or local circumstances.[69] A feast commemorates a past, indestructible event, but its perfection is still in germ. A feast expresses the desire for an eschatological celebration: this explains the efforts of Christians to celebrate their feasts better and better.

### *The Spiritual Celebration of Festivals*

The attitude of the early ascetics toward the celebration of feasts sometimes surprises us. Following the pagan sages,[70] certain Greek Fathers insisted on the festive character of the life of the just person. Origen writes: 'To the perfect Christian, who is ever in his thoughts, words, and deeds serving his natural Lord, God the Word, all his days are the Lord's, and he is always keeping the Lord's day'.[71] 'A life in accordance with the divine Word consists in one entire and never-ceasing festival.'[72]

Festivities were severely criticized by the ancient monks who reacted against the worldly, and sometimes immoral, atmosphere of pagan and even christian feast days. A feast should not provide the monk with an opportunity to relax his vigilance. So we read in the *Apophthegmata:* 'If your mind tells you to prepare various dishes for a feast, do not listen to it. This would be to feast in the jewish manner; the Jews make such preparations. For a monk, good nourishment consists of compunction and tears.'[73] His heart should be pre-occupied only with the expectation of the heavenly feast. Theodore the Studite declares: 'For the monk, there is no celebration on earth'.[74] In his turn, Evagrius says, 'God's feast is true knowledge'.[75]

These admonitions, well intended but polemical, run the risk of making us forget that the meaning of feasts lies in an historic contemplation 'of Providence' learned in the rhythm of life. 'This is why popular feasts recapitulate various elements: solidarity, the praise of power, the expression of happiness, a taste for the mysterious . . . . For the Christian, feasts are lived spiritually, but the body can take part in them, since feasts are viewed as an anticipation of the eternal feast.'[76]

All the same, an insistence on the spiritual character of celebrations always remains timely. John of Kronstadt says:

> The festivals ought to influence our life, to vivify and kindle our faith in future blessings, and maintain in us a pious and gentle disposition. Yet they are mostly spent in sin and folly and met with unbelieving, cold hearts, often wholly unprepared to feel the great mercies which God has vouchsafed to us through the . . . event or person whose feast day is celebrated.[77]

## *Thanksgiving*—Eucharistia

The giving of thanks corresponds to the gifts being remembered. Christian liturgical texts have inherited the verbs for giving God thanks from the semitic language by way of the Septuagint 'ομολογέω (to acknowledge, to give thanks), αίνάω (to praise), δοξάζω (to give honor to), and εύλογέω (to praise). But the new terms εύχαριστέω (to express gratitude) and εὐχαριστια (thanksgiving) came into the New Testament, showing the originality and importance of christian thanksgiving in response to the grace given by God in Jesus Christ. As *anamnesis,* a remembrance of everything God has done and will do for us, the Eucharist is first of all a 'Thanksgiving'. Here, Cabasilas writes, God has given us 'reasons for thanksgiving'.[78]

The interpretation of the Eucharist as a glorification of the Name is linked to the jewish cultic substratum of the early Church. This is certainly true, but a typically christian aim immediately emerged from it in the lines of Phil 2:6-11—'at the name of Jesus every knee should bow'—in which some exegetes detect a pre-pauline christian hymn of thanksgiving. This glorification of the Name recurs in the concluding doxology of several eastern anaphoras: among the Copts and the Ethiopians (the anaphoras of Mark, Cyril, and the Apostles); among the Syrians of the West (the anaphoras of James, and the twelve Apostles) and the East (the anaphora of Addai and Mari in the *textus receptus*); and especially among the Byzantines (the anaphoras of Basil and Chrysostom), and also in others. In these doxologies, however, the glorification of the Name takes on an explicitly trinitarian coloring.[79]

For a long time this thanksgiving was above all collective and liturgical. However, John Chrysostom insisted on the communicant's personal feelings of gratitude for the gift of the Eucharist:

'He himself gives you his own flesh, and you do not even find words to thank him; you would not even give thanks for what you receive?'[80] Martyrius Sahdona addressed harsh words to those who leave church hurriedly:

> And once they have received the Living Sacrament they push their way out in haste, before the communal thanksgiving is made. They never quit the table which belongs to the belly that perishes before everyone else has had his fill and departed, yet they quit and leave the Table of the Bread of Spiritual Life in a matter of fact way, without rendering thanks to God, not even with words merely on their lips. Do you realize what you are doing, O man? I hesitate to say who it is that you resemble, for it would be something hard to listen to. Nevertheless it must be said, by way of a warning. That person who leaves the spiritual Table of the Mysteries and goes out before the priest's final thanksgiving is showing a resemblance to Judas.[81]

## LITURGICAL ESCHATOLOGISM

### *The Expectation of the* Parousia

Through the eucharistic communion and partaking in the banquet of the Kingdom, by the praise and vigils associated with the Watch-Angels, by consulting and imitating the Fathers and the saints and martyrs—in short, through an entire life anchored in eschatology, the soul is already sheltered in the blessed reality of the age to come.

Moreover, a 'purgatorial' present reverberates with the memory of the announced Parousia; it is a twilight condition dominated simultaneously by the hope of an ascent to the light and a fear of falling. This corresponds to the human person's spiritual makeup, according to which the soul is a link between the body she animates and the Spirit which vivifies her. The soul is torn between two opposite forces: one pulls her back toward original nothingness and one invites her to ascend to the final fullness.[82]

In this situation, the idea of expectation is central. Though common to all liturgies, it is emphasized especially in the Maronite

Church. The words of the Virgins (Mt 25:1-13) are a frequent theme for meditation. Someone 'must come', 'is about to arrive', 'will show up', 'will stand in the middle' of the assembly. 'To be ready', 'to await', 'to look at the East', 'to fix one's gaze', 'to look longingly', 'to hold', 'not to doze off', 'to remain vigilant', 'not let oneself be distracted', 'to keep the lamp burning'—an entire vocabulary of hope has been marshalled to keep the soul in a state of alert. All this is summarized in two hymns in the breviary: 'The light has appeared to the just, a joy for the upright hearts' (Office of Lauds); 'Light your lamps, brothers, for the Bridegroom is about to arrive' (Sunday Vespers).[83]

## *The Nature of the* Epiclesis

The prophets characterized the new, definitive covenant they promised as an outpouring of the Spirit. The One who rested on the Messiah (Is 11) will be poured out on all humanity (Jl 3:1-5). On the day of Pentecost, Peter recognized that these promises had been fulfilled (Acts 2:16ff.), and from that very first day, the Church has been conscious of living this eschatological gift.

The entire spiritual tradition of the East witnesses to the presence of the Spirit in the ecclesiastical body of Christ, today as once on Pentecost. 'Pentecost is a permanent feast . . .', John Chrysostom writes; 'if the Spirit were not present, there would be no Church.'[84] But the Church lives and expresses this eschatological situation in a paradoxical situation—within the dynamics of time. She sings the canticle of the marriage feast of the Lamb (Rv 19:1-7), while being on an earthly pilgrimage. She is viewed as the Bride, saying with the Spirit, 'Come!' (Rv 22:17). Although conscious of possessing the Spirit, the Church invokes him in the *epiclesis,* so that he may descend not only on the eucharistic 'gifts', but also 'upon us'.[85]

## *Penitential Eschatology*

The expected Bridegroom is also Judge. Thus, to the exalted remembrance of the Lord is added a reminder of ourselves, of our past, which is merged with that of the world. A highly vivid awareness of sin is deeply embedded in liturgical piety. This untiringly reminds each one of us of our unworthiness and insists on the need for repentance. This is an inheritance from monasticism,[86] reinforced by the frequent use of the ejaculatory prayer *Kyrie eleison* ('Lord, have mercy').

An *Anonymous Commentary on the Kyrie eleison,* probably from the end of the byzantine period, states:

> The mercy of God is nothing but the grace of the Holy Spirit, the grace which we sinners must request from God by saying *Kyrie eleison* continuously. Those who know that they are in need of all these things [the spirit of strength, wisdom, fear, love, peace, purity, and humility] and who ask them of God in his great love, while saying the *Kyrie eleison,* will certainly receive what they ask for: they will obtain God's mercy and his divine grace.[87]

### *The Eschatological Meaning of the Divine Office*

Prayer unfolds in time, but essentially it transcends time. That saintly people 'lose a sense of time' while praying is not merely the psychological result of an intense concentration: what really happens is a transfer into eternity. Prayer is made 'through Christ'. Yet the time of Jesus is not simply one of earthly duration; he guides time to its fulfillment and entirely governs it. The time of prayer is in itself sacred by the mere fact that it belongs to 'the age to come'. It tends no less towards the fullness to come and is directed toward the Day of the Lord. The early Church lived with this constant impression of its nearness: 'the time will not last long' (1 Cor 7:29). The custom of sanctifying the main hours of the day and night goes back to the beginning of Christianity, even to the judaic tradition.[88] What was essentially new in christian prayer resulted from the discovery the disciples made concerning the role Christ played in the economy of salvation. The *Apostolic Tradition* by Hippolytus played a prominent part in fixing the hours of prayer. Indeed, he suggests a timetable that covers the entire day and night. By inviting the Christian to unceasing prayer based on regular hours and privileged moments, Hippolytus places the passion of the Lord at the center of his concerns, as a way of anchoring his prayer.[89]

The transition from private to official prayer occurred in the fourth century and can be laid at the door of the ascetics. The monks living in community began to solemnize the hours of prayer.[90] But the monastic office was not always that of the non-monastic churches. Shortly before the fall of Thessalonika in 1430, its archbishop, Saint Symeon, was still referring to two byzantine offices which were parallel yet entirely different: the chanted office *(asmatikos)* proper to cathedrals and public churches (an office on its way to extinction), and the monastic office. By 'monastic' office, Symeon naturally understood the palestinian or sabaite office introduced to Constantinople by Theodore the Studite at the end of the eighth century and subsequently adopted by all the monasteries of the empire—becoming in the fifteenth century the only office in use in the entire Byzantine Church.[91]

We can mention recent studies on the origin and structure of the Divine Office in other eastern churches,[92] while simply pointing out the two main spiritual dimensions of the Prayer of the Hours: the sanctification of time, and the time of inspiration.

### *The Sanctification of Time*

Cosmic time is not a profane concept; all ancient religions considered it sacred. Such mythic hallowing led to the establishment of a calendar of feasts.[93] In the Church, the Divine Office seeks to sanctify the cycles of nature in terms of three moments: the day; the week; and the year.

The first aim of the arrangement of the Divine Office is to provide for the sanctification of the principal times of day and night. At an early date each of these was associated with the memory of a moment in our Redeemer's passion; and in some churches the chief stages of man's creation and fall were added as a sort of background.[94] 'In the Old Testament the passing of a week marks the rhythm of Creation (Gn 1); for Christians it is the period of the recurring celebration of the Lord's Passover, of the triumph of the risen Christ over sin and death. Sunday as a feast of the resurrection is very marked in eastern liturgies.'[95]

The organization of the liturgical year seems to have begun in Jerusalem, but it developed differently in different churches—

nowhere more rigorously than among the eastern Syrians, where the entire year was divided into periods of seven weeks each.[96]

### *The Divine Office—A Time of Inspiration*

Divine inspirations during prayer anticipate eschatological time, as it were. In Scripture, the history of salvation is not subject to the law of eternal return. It is guided at a deeper level by God's design, which unfolds in it and is manifested through it. God calls people into his service without warning; if we do not use this time right, we lose our vocation. 'Today if only you would listen to him! Harden not your hearts' (Ps 94 [95]:7-8).

These divine inspirations arrive unexpectedly, even in monastic life, precisely because they are free. Nonetheless, according to the testimony of numerous authors, the time when the psalter was recited by the community was considered privileged. According to Isaac the Syrian, certain monks 'leave their Psalms from time to time, and they fall on their faces on account of the gladness which moves in their soul'.[97]

## THE SACRAMENTS

### *The Christian Life Is Sacramental*

In discussing the number seven in connection with the sacraments, Panagiotis N. Trembelas states that, 'Despite their separations and successive schisms, the local churches are in agreement on this point'; 'the uncertainty that prevailed in the East as in the West regarding the exact number of the sacraments was due above all to the fact that the essential meaning of the term 'sacrament' had not been clearly defined'.[98] The link between the sacraments and the Incarnation is very clear.[99] According to Theophan the Recluse, pseudo-spirituals who reject such natural means are like someone who wants to cross a river by means of some spiritual power, while boats and bridges are at his disposal. Such a person will wait in vain for the power of the Spirit. And while others cross to the other side, he will be left on the riverbank, alone.[100]

The spiritual life then is sacramental. Let us have a look at the aspects that are especially emphasized in eastern spirituality.

### *The Contemplative Nature of the Sacraments*

'The sacraments', Trembelas continues, 'are simultaneously signs and carriers, symbols and channels of grace . . .'. To use the expression of Irenaeus,[101] they are the mysterious operations of God *(Dei operationes).*[102] In them, the supernatural and supra-sensory character is so dominant that John Chrysostom could exclaim: 'Christ has given us nothing sensory, only spiritual realities under sensory signs'.[103] In this perspective, emphasis is placed above all on the efficacy of the rites: they bring to pass what they signify *(efficiunt quod significant).* The visibility of the symbols came to be de-emphasized—we might add that here a slight tendency towards a kind of sacramental iconoclasm may be detected.

In the East, the evolution of the liturgical rites has brought forward the other term more and more: what the sacraments bring about, they also signify and make visible. If they anticipate the heavenly Jerusalem, they should appear as a manifestation of the visibility of the Church. The evocative rituals that were developed aid the reading of the invisible in the visible. This is the reason behind the celebration of sacraments with such outward pomp that it became an obstacle to their easy administration in everyday life (for example, the rite of the Anointing of the Sick).

### *Eschatological Prayers*

Emphasis on the unfailing efficacy of the sacraments easily led to an exaggerated stress on how they differed from other prayers in the Church. In reality, the words of each prayer uttered in the name of Christ possess spiritual power; and it can be said of each ecclesiastical rite that it brings about what it signifies.[104] How valid is such a comparison? The West sometimes ran the risk of attributing all power to the sacraments, thereby minimizing other prayers. Easterners have sometimes been upbraided for doing the opposite, forgetting what differentiates the sacraments from rites or prayers called 'sacramentals' *(sacramentalia),* just as they really do not make a sufficiently sharp distinction between Scripture and other spiritual books.[105] If a certain 'pan-sacramentalism' is noticeable among the faithful, this tendency may be explained by the eschatological character of the Eastern Church.[106] In its whole liturgy can be seen what, properly speaking, belongs only to the seven sacraments—a foretaste of the age to come. The prayers of the Church—sacramentals have power through the prayer of the Church, *per orationem Ecclesiae*—are viewed, so to speak, in their (future) christologically perfect state, while they are still 'in the process of becoming', and belong to the life of the Church in progress.

### *The Ecclesiological Character*

The sacraments are administered and received in the Church, and only in her. 'Thus', Trembelas concludes, 'we arrive at a question which has been raised over and over again and even now, in discussing intercommunion in the sacraments . . . . On this complex question, it is hardly necessary to recall that with respect to the sacraments celebrated by schismatics and heretics, the eastern Orthodox-Catholic Church has always held a position, the basis of which differs from that of the western Church.'[107] The discussions continue.

But the ecclesiastical significance of the sacraments is apparent in the inner life of the various churches. In the East, 'private masses', communion outside the liturgy, and administering the sacraments in abbreviated form have not been looked on with favor, and the main reason for this has been as follows: in the East, the essential elements (called the 'matter' and 'form' of the sacraments) are not easily isolated from the liturgy, separated from the rites which Westerners call accessory. The disadvantagc of this tradition is that it becomes increasingly difficult to administer the sacraments in a secularized society or in exceptional cases. In an authentically christian setting, the richness and the unity of the rites are, by contrast, manifestations that recall the divine-human life of the Church.

### *Preparation for the Sacraments*

A sacrament, wrote Theophan the Recluse, is like a framework that supports one's inner attitude and ensures its stability. Human thoughts are fluid, but as soon as they are written down they endure. Thus the sacrament of penance fixes our feelings of contrition. The repentant sinner has softened his inward attitudes, and reception of the sacrament gives them a new form, marks them with its imprint, like a seal on wax.[108] It is self-evident, he adds, that sacraments are not magic rites. They are like fire: if the wood is damp—that is, if the soul is passion ridden—the inner warmth does not make itself felt immediately after receptions of the sacrament.[109] At various times, manuals of spiritual preparation for any given sacrament have appeared given detailed instructions in terms of their viewpoint. In patristic times, everything was centered on the great event of solemn baptism, the entry into the Church.

### *Baptism*

The spirituality of baptism is a modern concept, but those who spread it have rediscovered the book of Nicholas Cabasilas, *The Life in Christ,* where the entire christian life is described as the development of the divine root implanted in the human person at baptism.[110] The *Baptismal Instructions* of John Chrysostom,[111] among others, focus our attention on what a christian initiation into the Church consisted of at one time. Let us briefly summarize the spiritual themes that recur most frequently.

> *The Christian Identity.* The glory of the stars, and that of emperors, is nothing compared to that of Christians.
>
> *A Sense of Church,* especially of the local church, so typical of the christian East. Although Chrysostom does not systematize this concept, it is found frequently in his *Instructions.*
>
> *The Good Fight.* Evil lies at the gate. His series of warnings should be understood within this context.
>
> *Witness.* Christians live in the world and are to be its salt and its light.
>
> *Eschatological Tension.* We live on earth as in an inn, which we will one day have to leave to return to our homeland. The martyrs wonderfully symbolize this *pascha* (Easter Passover,

*pesah*), which is at one and the same time painful and glorious, and toward which we are all moving.

*Confirmation (Chrismation)*

Regarding confirmation, we need only note that it was viewed as the fulfillment of baptism, which is why it was administered to little children. Beginning with Origen[112] and Cyprian,[113] the Fathers describe this rite as the perfection of christian initiation. Confirmation was even called 'completion' *(šumloyo)* by the Syrians of Antioch. Of what does this perfection consist? The gift it confers is expressed in terms of 'effusion', 'sending', 'pledge', 'charisms', and 'seal', depending on whether it is linked to the laying on of hands, to a lengthy prayer, or to chrismation with its short formula; but it is always defined in relationship to the Holy Spirit. Cyril of Jerusalem viewed chrismation as 'the antitype of the Holy Spirit by whom Christ himself was anointed'.[114] The ritual of the Nestorians begins by reminding Christ 'that he has promised to make all of us heirs to his kingdom'. In the midst of nature, which always and inexorably consigns the flesh to corruption, human beings need the Spirit to confirm our hope of resurrection, to find within ourselves the sign, the pledge *(rahbuna),* that we have become children of the Kingdom.[115]

*Frequent Communion*

There was no uncertainty in the thought of the ancient Fathers concerning frequent communion.[116] 'Every day', Clement of Alexandria states, 'Christ gives himself as bread and drink of immortality.'[117] Origen categorized as Jews those who attended the sacrifice infrequently because 'Christians eat the flesh of the Lamb every day'.[118]

We may question whether the desert hermits attended Mass regularly. In fact, those solitaries who did not go to the Sunday *synaxis* (assembly) and in whose cell a priest sometimes celebrated the Eucharist[119] or those to whom an angel brought Holy Communion[120] were the exception. Absence from the *synaxis* was commonly viewed as a scandal.[121] The solitaries prepared themselves for it carefully. Poemen spent a whole hour in preparation,[122] other solitaries the entire night.[123] Among the Desert Fathers, even visions and eucharistic miracles were not unknown. Some saw angels at the right side of the altar and the Holy Spirit in the form of an eagle descending on the gifts, on the blood of Christ in the chalice. An image of the priest on fire during the divine liturgy corresponds to a common conception among the Desert Fathers.[124] John of the Thebaid's only food was Communion.[125]

And yet, repeated laments by the Fathers indicate that the affection of christian people, and even the monks, for this eucharistic food began to cool. On the other hand, in the testimony of John Cassian,[126] we meet timid souls who received communion only once a year. Respect, tied to an exaggerated fear—the opposite of ancient casualness— was a new motif that began to surface in monastic circles. In some eastern circles, according to the testimony of John Chrysostom,[127] some persons claimed to enhance the celebration of the feast of Pascha by restricting the reception of communion to this one day.

A more serious and more persistent obstacle was bound to arise from the more and more perfect dispositions required of the faithful before receiving communion. It appears that the monasticism of Basil had something to do with this more rigorous discipline.[128] In the early Church the third and fourth centuries were the golden age of frequent communion. In the periods that followed, a forgoing of eucharistic communion came to be more and more noticeable, and all attempts by church writers to reverse it were unsuccessful.

In the East as in the West, there has been a eucharistic renewal in recent years, as, for example, in Russia at the end of the last century. In this sense, Theophan the Recluse wrote in a letter: 'Partaking of the sacraments of Christ is often a good thing. If you can, do it even more than once a month.'[129] In another letter, he insisted: 'If those around you are surprised by frequent communion, you should not stop doing it. On the contrary, you should accustom the others to consider such a practice as normal.'[130] This was not always easy. As a student, Ignatii Bryanchaninov practiced weekly confession and communion (the year was 1822), and he was reported to the authorities by the chaplain of his school in

Saint Petersburg for having joined a secret political society.[131] Gradually this attitude changed.

*The Effects of the Eucharist*

The effects of the Eucharist are best seen in the titles given this sacrament in the liturgies. They indicate the double movement of the encounter between God and humankind. On the human side, this is 'an assembly' under the sign of a 'memorial' to offer 'a sacrifice' to God. On God's side, the 'consecration' of this oblation offered by human beings leads him to be present with, to be by his very 'proximity' within reach of, his servants who have become his friends. Through the 'breaking-dividing' of the body and blood of Christ, the human person enters 'into communion' with God.

In the maronite rite, the Liturgy is called assembly *(knouchoyo)*, communion, participation *(chaoutofouto)*, reconciliation *(qourobo)*, oblation *(qourbono)*, sacrifice *(debahto)*, memorial *(ouhodono, dokhrono)*, consecration *(qoudocho)*, new covenant *(diyatiqihdato)*, fullness of perfection *(gmirout gmiraoto)*, and so on.[132] The people offer God an 'oblation' so that it may be consecrated. God then becomes 'a living blaze', 'a devouring fire' that burns away sins, 'efficient grace', 'the leaven of life', 'pledge of the resurrection of the dead'.[133]

To systematize all this: in the East, three effects received special emphasis: union, transformation, and purification.

The first effect of communion is the creation of a mysterious, sacramental union between Christ and us, and in Christ among ourselves. 'Through the Sacrament', John of Kronstadt wrote, 'Thou art wholly with us, and Thy Flesh is united to our flesh, whilst Thy Spirit is united to our soul; and we feel this life-giving, most peaceful, most sweet union, we feel that by joining ourselves to Thee in the Holy Eucharist we become one spirit with Thee . . . .'[134] The union of the Church in the Eucharist is a frequent, albeit traditional, theme in modern Orthodox theology.[135] According to Nicholas Cabasilas, in the Eucharist we see 'on the one hand, the harmony of the Old and New Testaments, and on the other, that angels and human persons form one Church, a single choir'.[136]

The Eucharist unites souls and events across time and space. It is a memorial not merely of the past but also of the time to come, when Christ will appear in his glory. The prayers given the name '*anamnesis*' (remembrance) thus summarize what is, according to the syriac term used to designate them, *mdabronoûto* (economy), the entire economy of Christ: beginning most frequently with his death and resurrection but sometimes—as in the anaphora of Saint Mark and more particularly in the anaphora *Charar*—with the Annunciation and including conception, birth, baptism, preaching, passion, death, burial, resurrection, and ascension, right up to the memorial of the *parousia* (the Second Coming).[137]

The goal of this union is the kingdom of heaven, transformation, and sanctification. Cabasilas writes:

> The faithful are called saints because of the holy thing of which they partake, because of him whose Body and Blood they receive. Members of his Body, flesh of his flesh and bone of his bone, as long as we remain united to him and preserve our connection with him, we live by holiness, drawing to ourselves, through the holy mysteries, the sanctity which comes from that Head and that Heart.[138]

John of Kronstadt provided numerous examples taken from his own experience with parishioners to show how this transformation produces miraculous effects, even in the body: 'I glorify the wonders accomplished by thy Holy Mysteries upon thy believers, to whom I have administered them; I glorify the innumerable cures which I have witnessed; I glorify Their all-saving action in myself'.[139] Theophan the Recluse had earlier provided a similar testimony.[140]

While distributing communion in the byzantine rite, the priest says 'unto the remission of sin, and unto life everlasting'. The maronite Mass ends with a thanksgiving for 'forgiveness' obtained and for 'life everlasting' bestowed: 'May my desires vanish through the eating of your body, and my passions be extinguished by drinking from your chalice. . . . And may I, through you, deserve the remission of sins in this world and in the next.'[141]

The egyptian solitaries viewed the Eucharist as a purification. Poemen said:

> In the same manner as deer, nourished by insects and serpents, but burned by the poisons they secrete, hasten to the running streams . . . so do the solitaries—wounded by the devil's bite, poisoned by the evil desires and the imaginings which he suggests to them—ardently desire to find freshness and joy on Saturday and Sunday at the fountain which is Christ, by touching his body and blood.[142]

If this 'penitential' aspect of the Eucharist surprises us, we should remember that in the East the renewal of life in God is viewed as a 'purification'.[143]

### *The Eucharist and Mystical Experience*[144]

The Eucharist is the sacrament of mystical experience because it fulfills the promises of Christ made in the farewell discourses and in the priestly prayer of Jn 14:12-26; 15:1-12; 17:20-26, as they were interpreted by the great mystics in the wake of Cyril of Alexandria.[145]

In addition, Psalm 22 [Heb 23], viewed as the prophetic announcement of baptism or christian initiation, was sung during the paschal eve, and the catechumens learned it by heart on the occasion of the rite of *traditio*. From this exegetical perspective, the various verses of the psalm were given a distinctly typological interpretation. The 'table prepared' by the Shepherd was seen as a figure of the eucharistic banquet; in the 'overflowing cup' (or, as the LXX translate it, ' the inebriating chalice'), the Fathers, beginning with Origen and Cyprian, saw a symbol of the special grace imparted by the Eucharist: mystical ecstasy.[146] The drunkenness the eucharistic wine causes is a 'sober inebriation'.[147] If this inebriation or ecstatic enjoyment is sometimes produced by contemplation of the Word or spiritual 'chewing', as Origen and the school of Alexandria taught,[148] it usually is the effect of sacramental communion.[149] On this subject, the testimony of Gregory of Nyssa is very explicit.[150] Here we find an aspect that would be greatly developed by subsequent eastern mysticism.[151]

### *Confession*

'Roman Catholics', P. N. Trembelas writes, 'differentiate, and with reason, between penitence as a virtue, in the general sense of the term, and penance as a sacrament instituted by Christ.'[152] In the spiritual writings of the East, a certain confusion, a lack of precision, between penitence and penance led to an understanding of the mystery of the forgiveness of sin within the totality of revelation. Moreover, penitence fostered the development of spiritual direction, which also implied a confession of faults and a prayer by the spiritual father, even when he was not a priest, for the forgiveness of sins.[153]

Works entitled 'Εξεμολογητάρια, corresponding to the latin *Penitentiales,* contain an enumeration of the various categories of sins as well as of penances or *epitimias* which the priest imposes for each of them in sacramental confession.[154] The formulas and the sequence of the penitential rites vary from one Church to the other. Almost everywhere, however, we notice an adaptation and an extension of the rites which were first established for the reconciliation of apostates or public sinners.[155] When these rites became too complex and unworkable—for example, for the Coptic Church under arab domination—the doctrine and the use of the sacrament passed through a long eclipse.[156]

We can say in general that frequent access to sacramental confession always depended more on the prudence of those who administered the sacrament than on the canonical instructions governing its reception, or, to follow Trembelas,[157] on the art of understanding its pedagogic character.

## *Anointing the Sick*

The administration of this sacrament contained rites that were often very complex. Among the Copts, as among the Byzantines, seven priests participated, each reciting the epistle, the gospel, a psalm, and a prayer. The Copts call the anointing of the sick *kandil,* the lamp, because the oil that serves as the matter of the sacrament was poured in a lamp with seven branches. The *kandil* is given not only to the sick but also to those in good health, as a sort of supplement to the sacrament of penance and an immediate preparation for communion.[158] Because of the solemnity of the ritual, this sacrament was not administered very frequently in the East.

*Marriage*

Although established late, the rite of marriage is in its essence common to the various eastern Churches. With the exception of the chaldaean rite, a sharp distinction is made between the Service of Betrothal (or of the Rings) and the Service of Crowning (the marriage service), even though the two rituals are part of a single celebration. The prayer of the byzantine rite that precedes the crowning says: 'Unite thy servant and thy handmaiden; for by thee is the husband joined unto the wife. Unite them in one mind; wed them into one flesh, granting to them the fruit of the body and the procreation of fair children, and let their conduct be blameless.' After the crowning, the priest says: 'O Lord our God, . . . cause their marriage to be honorable. Preserve their bed blameless. Mercifully grant that they may live together in purity; and enable them to reach a ripe old age, walking in thy commandments with a pure heart.'[159]

These liturgies have a more didactic nature than did patristic writings, for, with the exception of John Chrysostom[160] and Augustine, the Fathers generally neither developed nor wrote an exhaustive theology of marriage. In recent times, a 'mystique of marriage' has been developed by Vladimir Soloviev (†1900). In his treatise *The Meaning of Love*[161] he articulates in an expressive manner how virginity and celibacy appear as the natural perfection of marriage, but only for those who contemplate their mutual relations in the married life spiritually. Thus, life together becomes a *theoria physikē* (natural contemplation) which uplifts souls and leads them toward life eternal.[162]

*The Priesthood Is for the Benefit of the Church*

The christian faith, as it has been expressed since the apostolic period, holds that the priesthood is a sacrament which produces a spiritual effect, and in a definitive manner. The grace that is imparted is, however, of no direct benefit to the person who receives it, as is true of baptism, but is for the benefit of the Church and of the people whom God saves through her.[163]

Ordination does not remit sins, despite the contrary hypothesis of a few authors.[164] The Fathers understood the difference between the hierarchy of holiness and that of ministries. Narsai multiplied metaphors to describe the priestly ministry:

> The mysteries of the Church cannot be celebrated without a priest because the Holy Spirit does not allow anyone else to celebrate them. The Holy Spirit accomplishes this through the hands of the priest, even when the latter would be altogether in a state of sin.[165]

This conviction is set forth strikingly by Gregory Nazianzus: a ring engraved with the royal image impresses the same image on wax whether the ring is golden or iron.[166] But such texts are in a certain sense polemic: their intent was to safeguard the essential dogmatic position. In practice, the monks had such a high esteem for the priestly function that they deemed themselves unworthy of it and avoided ordination.

The *Apophthegmata* and other monastic sources mention several monks who refused the priesthood out of humility and on whom it was imposed by force. Among others was Abba Isaac, who became a priest of the Cells.[167] He hid by running away, and when captured, he stopped resisting only at the moment they were about to bind him. Such behavior became widespread in the ancient Church.[168] In the Coptic Church, a ritual consisting of putting the newly designated patriarch in chains until his ordination—to vanquish his humility, real or feigned—has been carried on for centuries.[169] The spirit of vainglory, Evagrius notes vividly, foretells that certain monks 'will attain to the priesthood. It has men knocking at the door, seeking audience with them. If the monk does not willingly yield to their request, he is bound and led away.'[170]

### *Priestly Spirituality*

Set aside to serve the community, the ministers of Christ are also consecrated to God in a new manner, and their consecration includes a demand for holiness. During the liturgy, the celebrant is adorned with ornaments, each of which is accompanied by a verse from Scripture which points out its spiritual meaning.

To develop the principles of priestly spirituality does not enter into the scope of our study. Leaving aside numerous other passages scattered throughout the writings of the Fathers, we will limit ourselves to mentioning the real treatises on priestly holiness. They are: *Oration II (Apologeticus de Fuga)* by Gregory Nazianzus,[171] the six books *On the Priesthood* by John Chrysostom,[172] and the *Regula Pastoralis (Pastoral Rule)* of Gregory the Great.[173]

The most significant traits are clearly indicated in the rites of ordination: faith, availability to the Spirit, intimate union with Christ in the mysteries.

With the *Apostolic Constitutions* there appeared the custom of putting the Gospel-book on the head or shoulders of the elect during the consecration. Also, from early on, he had to make an explicit profession of faith.[174] The Syrians and Maronites place ordination at the end of the eucharistic anaphora. 'This is to enable the consecrator, before laying on his hands, to touch the sacred elements three times, as if to signify that it is from immediate contact with Christ that he draws the graces he is about to communicate to the elect.'[175]

John of Kronstadt, the only canonized diocesan priest in the Russian Church, refers frequently to priestly holiness: 'A priest is an angel and not a man; everything worldly ought to be left far away behind him. O Lord, "let thy priests be clothed with righteousness" (Ps 132:9); let them always remember the greatness of their calling and do not let them be entangled in the nets of the world and the Devil.'[176]

## *Notes*

1. Pierre Grélot, 'La liturgie dans l'Écriture', DSp 9 (1976) 873ff.

2. *De incomprehensibili Dei natura,* 3.6; PG 48:726; translated by Paul W. Harkins, *St. John Chrysostom. On the Incomprehensible Nature of God,* FCh 72 (1984). See Tomaš Špidlík, *Joseph de Volokolamsk,* OCA 146 (Rome, 1956) 104ff.

3. Irénée-Henri Dalmais, *Les liturgies d'Orient,* '*Rites et Symboles*'. (Paris, 1980) 64; translated from the 1959 edition by Donald Attwater, *Eastern Liturgies* (New York: Hawthorn Books, 1960).

4. John Chrysostom, *Adversus oppugnatores vitae monasticae,* 3.15; PG 47:373A. See *A Systematic Handbook,* 288ff.

5. Michel Hayek, '*Liturgie maronite. Histoire et textes eucharistiques* (Paris, 1964) 193ff.

6. Guillaume De Vries, 'Le sens ecclésial chez les Syriens (jacobites et nestoriens)'. DSp 4 (1960) 436–442.

7. Dalmais, *Les Liturgies*, 35.

8. Pierre Miquel, *La liturgie une oeuvre d'art, L'Oeuvre de Dieu célébrée par son Peuple,* Vie monastique 13 (Bellefontaine, 1981) 14.

9. *Pisma* [Letters] (Moscow, 1892) 263ff.

10. *My Life in Christ* (New York, 1994) 316.

11. See, for example, Sergius Bulgakov, *L'Orthodoxie* (Paris, 1932) 10; translated by Lydia Kesich, *The Orthodox Church* (Crestwood, New York: St Vladimir's Seminary Press, 1988) 6.

12. Gregory of Nyssa, *In Cantica canticorum commentarius, passim;* PG 44:755ff.; translated Casimir McCambley OCSO, *Saint Gregory of Nyssa: Commentary on the Song of Songs* (Brookline, Massachusetts: Hellenic College Press, 1987). See; G. I. Gargano, *La teoria di Gregorio di Nissa sul Cantico dei Cantici,* OCA 216 (Rome, 1981).

13. Donatien Mollat, 'Gloire', VTB, 504–11; 'Glory'. DBT, 202–205.

14. Paul Evdokimov, *L'Orthodoxie* (Paris, 1959) 239ff.

15. J. Schneider, 'timē, timaô', Kittel 8 (1972) 169ff.

16. Rom 16:27, 1 Tm 1:17, Rv 4:9, 4:11, 5:12-13, 7:12.

17. Lactantius, *The Divine Institutes*, 4.28; PL 6:535ff; ANF 7:9–223.

18. Aimé Solignac, 'Honneur de Dieu', DSp 7/1 (1969) 704–717.

19. *À l'image et à la ressemblance de Dieu.* (Paris, 1967) 193; translated by John H. Erickson and Thomas E. Bird, *In the Image and Likeness of God* (Crestwood, New York: St Vladimir's Seminary Press, 1986) 196.

20. 'L'Esprit Saint et l'Église d'après la tradition liturgique', in *L'Esprit Saint et l'Église, Actes du symposium . . .* (Paris: Fayard, 1969) 85.

21. *De gratia Dei et libero voluntatis arbitrio,* 8; PL 51:209. For a discussion on the meaning of this maxim, see Miquel, *La liturgie*, 15–20.

22. *Peri biou theôretikou* [De vita contemplativa]; translated by F. H. Colson, *Philo,* The Loeb Classical Library, vol. 9. See René Arnou, 'Contemplation chez les anciens', DSp 2/2 (1953) 1726.

23. *Homélies catéchétiques,* 6.3; edited R. Tonneau and R. Devreesse, Studi et Testi 145 (Rome: Vatican City, 1949) 538ff; translated in A. Mingana, *Commentary of Theodore of Mopsuestia on the Lord's Prayer and on the Sacraments of Baptism and the Eucharist,* Woodbrooke Studies 6 (Cambridge, 1933).

24. Emmanuel Lanne, 'Liturgie eucharistique en Orient et en Occident (1er-4[e] siècles)', DSp 9 (1976) 890.

25. See p. 203.

26. Marie-Dominique Chenu, 'Anthropologie et Liturgie', *La Maison-Dieu* 12 (1977) 54.

27. See p. 240.

28. Irénée-Henri Dalmais, 'Liturgie: problèmes théologiques', DSp 9 (1976) 937ff.

29. See Miquel, *La liturgie,* 49ff.

30. See Thomas Aquinas, *Summa theologiae* III.83. 5.

31. See p. 183.

32. K. Ch. Felmy, *Die Deutung der göttlichen Liturgie in der russischen Theologie.* (Berlin-New York, 1984).

33. Chapter VI, 3–6; SCh 4bis (1967) 83; translated by J. M. Hussey and P. A. McNulty. *A Commentary on the Divine Liturgy* (London: SPCK, 1960) 34–35.

34. Chapter XXXVII, 2; SCh 227ff; *A Commentary,* 90.

35. *Apophthegmata,* Poimen, Suppl. 3; Jean-Claude Guy, *Recherches sur la Tradition grecque des 'Apophthegmata Patrum',* Subsidia Hagiographica 36 (Brussels, 1862) 30.

36. Louis Leloir, *Paterica armeniaca* 1.27; CSCO 353:12ff.

37. *Vie du bienheureux Pachôme* 50; PO 4: 476; cf. First Bohairic Life of Pachomius, 25, translated by Armand Veilleux, *Pachomian Koinonia,* 1: *The Life of Saint Pachomius and his Disciples,* CS 45 (Kalamazoo: Cistercian Publications, 1980) 47–48.

38. Sergius Bulgakov, *Le ciel sur la terre.* (Munich, 1928). Pierre Miquel, *La liturgie une oeuvre d'art. L'Oeuvre de Dieu célébrée par son Peuple,* Vie monastique 13 (Bellefontaine, 1981) 195–208.

39. *Povest vremennych let,* ed. by A. S. Lichačev (Moscow-Leningrad, 1930) vol. I:74ff. See Špidlík, *La spiritualità russa.* (Rome, 1981) 33–36.

40. Špidlík, *La sophiologie de S. Basile,* OCA 162 (Rome, 1961) 227ff.

41. *Stolp i utverždenie istiny* [*The Pillar and Foundation of Truth*] (Moscow, 1914); french translation, *La colonne et le soutien de la vérité* (Lausanne, 1974) 69ff.

42. Sergius Bulgakov, *The Orthodox Church.* (London, 1935) 150.

43. See below, 307.

44. Tomaš Špidlík, 'La preghiera presso i popoli slavi', in R. Boccassino, ed., *La preghiera,* vol. 2 (Rome, 1967) 797ff.

45. *Rite arménien,* french trans. (Venice, 1851) 4.

46. (Moscow, 1899) 207.

47. *Ibid.*, 106.

48. Špidlík, 'La preghiera', 801ff.

49. *Les Mystères d'Égypte* 7.5, Belles Lettres (1966) 194. A Neoplatonist, Iamblichus was not commenting on christian worship.

50. *The Octavius,* 6.3; ANF 4:176.

51. Edited in *Belles Lettres,* vol. 1 (1935) 1. See Miquel, *La liturgie,* 167ff.

52. *Pisma k raznym licam . . .* [*Letters to Various Persons*] (Moscow, 1892) 278. See Špidlík, *Théophane le Reclus,* 180ff.

53. Chap. 10, trans. by Francis X. Glimm, *The Didache or Teaching of the Twelve Apostles,* FCh (1947) 180.

54. *Apostolic Tradition,10;* SCh 11:41; translated by B. S. Easton, *The Apostolic Tradition of Hippolytus* (Cambridge, 1924).

55. Pambo, in Paul Evergetinos, *Synagogē* II, 11 (Constantinople, 1961). Miquel, *La liturgie,* 57.

56. Emmanuel Lanne, 'Liturgie eucharistique en Orient et en Occident (1er-4e siècles)', DSp 9 (1976) 891ff.

57. B. Cappelle, 'Les liturgies "basiliennes" et saint Basile', in Jean Doresse and Emmanuel Lanne, *Un témoin archaïque de la liturgie copte de saint Basile* (Louvain, 1960) 45ff.

58. *Apostolic Constitutions,* 8; ed. F. X. Funk, vol. 1:496–514.

59. Lanne, *'Liturgie eucharistique',* 893.

60. *The Orthodox Church* (London, 1935) 150.

61. In Sergei Verchovskoj, *Pravoslavie v žizni* [*Orthodoxy in Life*] (New York, 1953) 244ff.

62. H. Cox, *La fête des fous. Essai sur les notions de fête et de fantaisie* (Paris, Editions du Seuil, 1971) 124.

63. *The Laws* II, 653D.

64. Ceslas Spicq and Pierre Grélot, 'Sabbat'; VTB, 1151–1183; 'Sabbath', DBT 551–552.

65. Mircea Eliade, *Patterns in Comparative Religions,* translated by Rosemary Sheed. (New York: Meridian Books, 1958) 398.

66. Pierre Miquel, *La liturgie une oeuvre d'art, L'oeuvre de Dieu célébrée par son Peuple,* Vie monastique 13 (Bellefontaine, 1981) 181.

67. Michel Join-Lambert and Pierre Grélot, 'Temps', VTB, 1273–1284; 'Time', DBT, 600–606.
68. Miquel, *La liturgie,* 185.
69. *Ibid.,* 179.
70. Plato, *The Laws* II, 803C.
71. *Contra Celsum, liber* 8.22; PG 11:1549C; ANF 4:647.
72. *Ibid.;* 1552B; 648.
73. *Apophthegmes,* nos. 593–5; ed. Lucien Regnault, *Les sentences des pères du désert:* Nouveau recueil. (Sable-sur-Sarthe: Solesmes, 1970) 116.
74. *Responsiones ad interrogata quaedam;* PG 99:1731C.
75. *Sententiae ad fratres;* PG 40:1279B (latin text, 'Festivitas Dei scientia vera').
76. Miquel, *La liturgie,* 191.
77. *My Life in Christ* (New York, 1994) 48.
78. *Explication de la divine liturgie* 52.4; SCh 4*bis* :297ff; *A Commentary on the Divine Liturgy* (London: SPCK, 1960) 116ff.
79. Emmanuel Lanne, 'Liturgie et vie spirituelle dans les Églises chrétiennes'. DSp 9 (1976) 886.
80. *De baptismo Christi;* PG 49:371ff.
81. *Livre de la perfection,* 2.8 (34–35); CSCO 263 (Syri 111): 10; translated Sebastian Brock, *The Book of Perfection,* in *The Syriac Fathers on Prayer and the Spiritual Life,* CS 101 (Kalamazoo: Cistercian Publications, 1987) 216.
82. Irenaeus, *Adversus haereses* 5.9.1–2; Harvey, vol. 1:242–243; ANF 1:534–535.
83. Michel Hayek, 'Maronite' (Église)'; DSp 10: 641ff.
84. *De Sancto Pentecoste, homilia* I.1 and 4; PG 50:454D, 459A.
85. See J. Klinger, *Geneza sporu o epikleze . . .* (Warsaw, 1969).
86. Irénée Hausherr, *Penthos. La doctrine de la componction dans l'Orient chrétien,* OCA 132 (Rome, 1944); translated by Anselm Hufstader, *Penthos. The Doctrine of Compunction in the Christian East.* CS 53 (Kalamazoo: Cistercian Publications, 1982).
87. *Philokalia,* vol. 5 (Athens, 1963) 67–72.
88. Irénée-Henri Dalmais, *Les liturgies d'Orient. 'Rites et Symboles'* (Paris, 1980); translation of the 1959 ed. by Donald Attwater, *Eastern Liturgies.* (New York: Hawthorn Books, 1960).
89. Guy-Marie Oury, 'Office divin en Occident', DSp 11 (1982) 685–707.
90. *Ibid.,* 691. See D. de Reynal, *Théologies de la Liturgie des Heures.* (Paris, 1978).
91. Miguel Arranz, 'Office divin en Orient', DSp 11 (1982) 707–720.
92. See DSp 11:720.
93. Michel Join-Lambert and Pierre Grélot, 'Temps', VTB, 1273–1284; 'Time', DBT, 600–606.
94. Dalmais, *Les liturgies d'Orient* (above, n. 88) 170; *Eastern Liturgies,* 131.
95. *Ibid.,* 171; 132.
96. *Ibid.,* 173, 133.
97. *Mystic Treatises by Isaac of Nineveh* 550, chap. 80; translated by A. J. Wensinck (Amsterdam, 1923) 369.
98. *Dogmatique de l'Église orthodoxe catholique,* vol. 3 (Chevetogne: Desclée de Brouwer, 1968) 75.
99. Theophan the Recluse, *Letters* (Moscow, 1892) 107ff.
100. *Ibid.,* 254ff.
101. *Contra haereses,* 2.30.7; PG 67:820.
102. *Dogmatique,* 22.

103. *In Matthaeum homilia* 72,4; PG 58:743.
104. See pp. 38, 98.
105. See p. 133.
106. *A Systematic Handbook,* 66.
107. *Dogmatique,* 48.
108. *Put ko spaseniju* [*The Way to Salvation*] (Moscow, 1908) 159ff.
109. *Pisma* [*Letters*] (Moscow, 1892) 459.
110. *De vita in Christo;* PG 150:491–726; translated by Carmino deCatanzaro, *The Life in Christ* (Crestwood, New York: St Vladimir's Seminary Press, 1974).
111. *Huit catéchèses baptismales inédites;* SC 50bis (1970); translated by Paul W. Harkins, *St. John Chrysostom: Baptismal Instructions,* ACW 31 (1963).
112. *Peri archôn (De principiis),* I.3.2; PG 11:147BC; GCS 5:50; translation in ANF 4.
113. *Epistola ad Jubajanum* 9; PL 3:1115A; translated by Rose B. Donna, *Saint Cyprian: Letters,* FCh 51.
114. *Catechesis* 21.1; PG 33:1089A; SCh 126: 122; translated by Leo P. McCauley and Anthony A. Stephenson, *The Works of Saint Cyril of Jerusalem,* vol. 2, FCh 64 (1970).
115. Louis Ligier, *La Confirmation. Sens et conjoncture oecuménique hier et aujourd'hui,* Théologie historique 23 (Paris, 1973).
116. Joseph Duhr, 'Communion fréquente', DSp 2 (1953) 1234–1292.
117. *Liber quis dives salvetur* 23; PG 9:628; *Who Is the Rich Man That Shall be Saved?,* ANF 2:598.
118. *In Genesim, homilia* 10.3; PG 12:218.
119. Louis Leloir, *Paterica armeniaca* 9, 12; CSCO 361:230–231.
120. *Ibid.,* 18, 67; CSCO 377:99.
121. *Ibid.,* 18, 36; CSCO 68. 18, 20B; CSCO 55.
122. *Ibid.,* 11, 8A; CSCO 371:120.
123. *Ibid.,* 7, 49R; CSCO 361:193.
124. Louis Leloir, *Désert et communion. Témoignages des Pères recueillis à partir des Paterica arméniens,* Spiritualité orientale 26 (Bellefontaine, 1978) 176ff.
125. Rufinus, *Historia monachorum* 15; PL 21:434; translated by Norman Russell, *The Lives of the Desert Fathers: The* Historia Monachorum in Aegypto, CS 34 (Kalamazoo: Cistercian Publications-London: Mowbray, 1980) 93.
126. *Conference* 23.21; SCh 64 (1959); LNPF 11 (1904) 526.
127. *In Epistola I ad Timoth., homilia* 5.3; PG 62:529–530.
128. *De baptismo, liber* I; PG 31:1577. *Regulae brevius tractatae* 172; PG 31:1196; translated by W. K. L. Clarke, *The Ascetic Works of Saint Basil* (London, 1925). P. Humbertclaude, *La doctrine ascétique de saint Basile de Césarée* (Paris, 1932) 243–247.
129. *Pisma* [Letters] (Moscow, 1892) 333.
130. *Ibid.,* 391ff.
131. Serge Bolskakoff, *I mistici russi* (Turin, 1962) 148; *Russian Mystics,* CS 26 (Kalamazoo: Cistercian Publications, 1977) 145.
132. Michel Hayek, *Liturgie maronite* (Mame, 1964) 143ff.
133. Hayek, 145.
134. *My Life in Christ* (New York, 1994) 21. Used by permission.
135. K. Ch. Felder, *Die Deutung der göttlichen Liturgie in der russischen Theologie* (Berlin, New York, 1984).
136. *A Commentary on the Divine Liturgy* 20.3; SCh 4bis:149; translated by J. M. Hussey and P. A. McNulty (London: SPCK, 1960) 59.
137. Hayek, *Liturgie,* 188.

138. *A Commentary,* 36.1; Hussey-McNulty 89; see John of Kronstadt, *My Life*, 114, 294.
139. *My Life,* 319.
140. *Put ko spaseniju* [*The Way to Salvation*] (Moscow, 1908) 25ff.
141. Hayek, *Liturgie,* 221. See L. Khawand, *Le pardon dans la liturgie eucharistique maronite* (typescript thesis, Accademia Alfonsiana, Rome, 1971).
142. Louis Leloir, *Paterica armeniaca* 18, 3b; CSCO 377:58. *Ibid.,* 7, 37; CSCO 361:63. Cf. Ps 42:2 [1].
143. *A Systematic Handbook,* 182ff.
144. Ephrem Longpré, 'Eucharistie et expérience mystique, DSp 4/2 (1961)1586–1621.
145. *In Joannis Evangelium,* 10.4.21; PG 74:285B, and 10.14.23;290C.
146. Jean Daniélou, *Bible et liturgie*, Lex orandi 11 (Paris, 1951) 247–248 ; *The Bible and the Liturgy* (Notre Dame Press, 1956) 183–4].
147. See p. 263.
148. Hans Lewy, *Sobria ebrietas. Untersuchungen zur Geschichte der antiken Mystik,* Beihefte zur Zeitschrift für die neutestamentische Wissenschaft und die Kunde der alterer Kirche (Giessen, 1929) 113–114. Tomaš Špidlík, 'La mistica del sangue inebriante', *Il Sangue che rivela l'amore* (Rome 1987) 201–208.
149. *Ibid.,* 115–118.
150. *In Cantica Canticorum, homilia*e 5–6; PG 44:873AB; 989C; McCambley, 109–138.
151. Jean Daniélou, *Platonisme et la théologie mystique. Essai sur la doctrine spirituelle de saint Grégoire de Nysse,* Théologie 2 (Paris, 1944) 271ff.
152 *Dogmatique de l'Église orthodoxe catholique* (Chevetogne: Desclée de Brouwer, 1969) vol. 3:218.
153. *A Systematic Handbook*, 284ff.
154. See the *Exomologetarion* of Nicodemus the Hagiorite (Venice, 1794). See also S. Smirnov, *Drene-russkij duchovnik* [*The Spiritual Father in Old Russia*] (Moscow, 1914) 32ff.
155. Iréné-Henri Dalmais, *Les liturgies d'Orient* (Paris, 1980) 116ff; translated from the 1959 edition by Donald Attwater, *Eastern Liturgies* (New York: Hawthorn Books, 1960).
156. Martin Jugie, 'Monophysite (l'Église copte)', DThC 10 (1929) 2285ff.
157. *Dogmatique*, 295f.
158. Jugie, 'Monophysite', 2288.
159. Dalmais, *Les liturgies,* 155ff; Attwater, 116ff.
160. Tomaš Špidlík, 'Il matrimonio-sacramento di unità nel pensiero di Crisostomo', *Augustinianum* 17 (1977) 221–226. *Idem,* 'La concezione cristologica del matrimonio nell'antica liturgia orientale', *Bessarione* 1 (1979) 139–152.
161. *Smysl ljubvi* [Works] (Brussels, 1966) vol. 3:3–60; translated by Jane Marshall, *The Meaning of Love* (London: Geoffrey Bles, 1946).
162. Tomaš Špidlík, *La spiritualità russa* (Rome, 1981) 72–112.
163. Joseph Lécuyer, *Le sacrement de l'Ordination. Recherche historique et théologique, Théologie historique* 65 (Paris, 1983) 271.
164. *Ibid.,* 266.
165. See P. Gignoux, in 'L'initiation chrétienne', Lettres Chrétiennes 7 (Paris, 1963) 237.
166. *Oratio* 40, *In sanctum baptisma* 26; PG 36:396BC; *Oration on Holy Baptism,* LNPF 7:369.
167. *Apophthegmata Patrum,* PG 65:224BC; *Sayings,* 99.

168. Yves Congar, 'Ordinations "invictus coactus", de l'Église antique au canon 214', *Revue des sciences philosophiques et théologiques* 50 (1966) 169–197.
169. Martin Jugie, 'Monophysite (l'Église copte)', DThC 10 (1929) 2262.
170. Praktikos 13; Sch 171:529; Bamberger, 19.
171. *Oratio* II, *Apologetica;* PG 35:408–513; *In Defense of his Flight to Pontus,* LNPF 7:204–227.
172. *De sacerdotio;* PG 48:623–692; *Treatise on the Priesthood,* LNPF, 9 (1903).
173. *Regulae pastoralis liber,* PL 77:9–128; translated by Henry Davis, *St. Gregory the Great: Pastoral Care,* ACW 11 (1950).
174. Irénée-Henri Dalmais, *Les liturgies d'Orient,* 129; Attwater translation, 109.
175. *Ibid.*
176. *My Life in Christ* (New York, 1994) 23.

# 6

# MEDITATIVE READING

## THE SPIRITUAL BOOK

### *Spiritual Communion*

CHRISTIAN AND MONASTIC *lectio divina* (divine reading) has unquestionably been influenced by Judaism.[1] Yet Origen would be the first openly to advocate the practice of divine reading (θεία ἀνάγνωσις).[2] We know that he had been trained by jewish masters. He undoubtedly learned from them that way of scrutinizing the word of God and applying oneself to it (προσέχειν). This verb will recur almost always to characterize spiritual reading.

We realize how inadequate it is to use the term 'reading' to describe our contact with spiritual books, when for ancient monks it was more a matter of 'communion', of a dialogue with God. Cyprian of Carthage formulated one of the fundamental laws of spiritual reading when he said: 'Be constant in prayer as in reading; now speak to God, now let God speak to you'.[3]

Above all, it is a matter of understanding the personal, concrete message God gives us through books. It is while listening to a reading in church that Antony decided to leave everything and follow Christ.[4] It is because they are spiritual that books possess the power of the Spirit operating in the world. 'Truly great and mighty is the power of God's word', Martyrius Sahdona exclaims. 'For the word of God has changed the offspring of vipers into children of God (see Mt 3:7, 9). So let us constantly sow it within the hard soil of our heart, waiting for it to soften it so that the wheat-ear of life may sprout up in it.'[5]

Reading then should be like a seed or like spiritual food. Chewing on Scripture is a symbol that is entirely biblical, but it is Origen who incorporated it into the tradition. To him, Scripture and the Eucharist appeared to be intimately linked, since Scripture is one of the 'embodiments' of the Word of God.[6]

The dimensions of the Word of God are manifold. Ephrem writes: 'The Lord has colored his word with kaleidoscopic beauty, so that all those who scrutinize it may contemplate what they love. In his Word, he has concealed all treasures, so that each of us may find richness in our meditation.'[7]

### *A 'Second Navigation'?*

All spiritual writers agree that we should appropriate the truth to be found in sacred books and make it our own. Nonetheless, the fundamental attitude towards written revelation may vary enormously. Two metaphors illustrate this difference well: the 'second navigation' and 'purification of Jacob's wells'.

The first expression is very old,[8] but it was deliberately used by a confirmed traditionalist, Iosif of Volokolamsk,[9] whose position can be summarized in a few words. The apostles saw Christ with their own eyes and they heard his voice. The Church Fathers were filled with the Spirit and were able to let themselves be guided by their own inspiration. Contemporary people, however, have become unworthy of being enlightened by the Spirit. This is the reason why God has given us Sacred Scripture. 'The first navigation is made with sails—that is, through the Holy Spirit; the others with oars—that is, the Sacred Scriptures.'[10] The sinner no longer hears the inner voice of conscience, which has had to be replaced by obedience to what is written.

Origen was of a different opinion, as was Dorotheus of Gaza, who followed him. In the beginning, the human person had no other rule of conduct than the inner conscience. But 'the Philistines filled with dirt all the wells dug by Jacob (Gn 26:15)'. It is not a matter of replacing such 'wells' by something else: they need to be purified by reading spiritual books.[11] The main result of meditating on Scripture is the awakening of conscience. It is therefore not surprising that reading tends to lessen as the spiritual life progresses. The author of the *Life* of Saint Symeon Salos states this very clearly: 'Only those who are still at the lower rung, and the imperfect, need laws and biblical explanations; but for those who love God, the conscience is perfectly sufficient to choose the good'.[12]

While the first point of view is dangerously 'bookish', the second advocates charismatic freedom for the perfect. But who has the right to consider himself or herself perfect? This is why the correct view will follow a middle course between these two attitudes.[13]

### *The Bible*

From the beginning, reading Scripture occupied a large place in monastic asceticism. *The Bohairic Life of Pachomius* mentions that the disciples of Pachomius 'read from the Scriptures every day and . . . recite them'.[14] The study of Scripture remained the fountainhead of Basil's ascetic and monastic doctrine, 'the most important path to the discovery of duty'.[15] In Syria, the monks praised by John Chrysostom, 'having performed their morning prayers and hymns, proceed to the reading of the Scriptures. There are some too who have learned to transcribe them.'[16] Martyrius Sahdona admonished that: 'the Word of God is at the same time the seed and the water; and even though we have a heart like stone (cf Mt 13:5), it will be softened and split by the water of the Spirit, that it can bring forth holy fruit that is pleasing to God'.[17]

The Fathers, then, strove to have access to the Scriptures. Epiphanius said: 'Everyone who is able to do so should acquire (a copy of) the Scriptures, for the mere fact of seeing them makes a man reluctant to sin. Reading them, on the other hand, is an invitation to righteousness and invigorates the soul.'[18] John Chrysostom[19] tells of christian women and children who carried the gospel book hung around their neck wherever they went. If the women and children of believers easily acquired versions that were probably radically abbreviated, the monks would not have found themselves in less favorable circumstances. Serapion gave his gospel to a poor man so that he could repay his debt, and he explained: 'I have sold him who continually told me: "Sell your possessions, and give to those in need"'.[20]

Given the difficulty most ascetics had in acquiring the least incomplete possible copy of the Scriptures, however, the preferred means of contact with Scripture was the liturgical proclamation of the Word of God in the Sunday assemblies or in the shorter liturgies in cells and groups.[21]

*The Extended Meaning of 'Divine Scriptures'*

Ancient monks read the 'Divine Scriptures', that is, the books of the Bible. Over the centuries, however, we must point out, the term 'Divine Scriptures' acquired a much broader meaning in the spiritual literature of the East. It referred not only to Scripture, but still more to the writings of the Fathers and also to everything that could be read, once pagan books had been eliminated.

In Byzantium, patristic writings that had perceptibly defeated heresies shared the authority of inspired books. Theodore the Studite, for example, singles out Saint Basil for special praise because 'Christ spoke through his mouth', and because someone who follows him, 'follows the guidance of the Holy Spirit'.[22] Nikon of the Black Mountain (eleventh century) spoke simply of 'Divine Scripture' when he referred to his *florilegium,* even though the essentials of his reference texts consisted of conciliar Canons and extracts from the Fathers.[23]

In Russia, even after the publication of the Bible of Gennadius in 1499, writers continued to express themselves as Nikon had done. Thus, it was entirely normal for Nilus of Sora (Nil Sorsky) to speak of 'the blessed Fathers of the Divine Scriptures'.[24] From a theoretical point of view, this designation was justified in the first russian dogmatic-apologetic handbook, *Prosvetitel' (The Enlight ener),* by Joseph of Volokolamsk (Josif Volotsky): 'We have received doctrine from the prophets, the gospel, and the apostles, and also from the saintly Fathers filled with the Holy Spirit'.[25] Anyone who rejects the writings of the Fathers, therefore, is 'neither a believer nor a Christian'.[26] 'Everything we have said about the writings of the apostles equally applies to the writings of the saintly Fathers and of Saint Ephrem—at the time, there was an ongoing discussion about his writings on the end of the world—everything he has written is true and useful to the soul.'[27]

*Patristic Anthologies*

The East has always appealed to the authority of the Fathers.[28] Even so, acquiring their writings or owning them was not always easy. More than one monk changed residence and selected another monastery with the sole aim of finding an abundant supply of books.[29] What can we say about those who in the eleventh century had tragically to flee from arab raids? It was for their benefit that Nikon of Raithou or of the Black Mountain—in Syria—composed his *Pandects,* a semi-spiritual, semi-canonical compilation of texts on various subjects.[30] He was not the first to compile such an anthology. It is generally accepted that the *Hiera*, a damascene anthology in three books, formed the base of the *Sacra Parallela.*[31] *Questions and Answers,* a compilation attributed to Athanasius the Sinaite is a fairly important collection and was widely disseminated.[32] In 1048, an inhabitant of Constantinople, a certain Paul, withdrew from the world and founded the monastery of the Evergetis. For the edification of his monks, he composed a massive spiritual anthology in four books of fifty chapters each, entitled *Synagogē,* and also referred to under the title the *'Evergetinos'.*[33]

The point of view that guided the composition of these anthologies often varied greatly. Some of them centered around questions of dogma, others had a moral aim, especially dealing with monastic asceticism. The *Philokalia* is the most impressive collection on prayer, especially hesychast prayer. In ancient times, liturgical life required a variety of texts which had to be adapted to the cycle of annual celebrations: the homiliaries.

*Patristic Homilies*

The greek term ὁμιλία means 'gathering' or 'assembly', and came to be applied to a religious discourse before the christian assembly. Whether taken down by *tachygraphoi* (speed writers) or written out, sermons and homilies by a single author were easily grouped in more or less homogeneous 'collections'. The collection came to be called a 'homiliary' (a later term) when it was organized according to the cycle of the liturgical year and corresponded to the sacramentary.[34] The function of a homiliary was spiritual edification. The

*Hypotyposes (Constitutions)* of the monastery of Studios prescribed that after Matins on Wednesdays, Fridays, and Sundays during Lent 'the catechesis of our God-bearing Father Theodore' be read.[35] The reading was followed by an exhortation from the *hegumen* (abbot).

In general, the structure of byzantine homiliaries[36] is straightforward and deals with the following four groups: 1) *Panegyrics,* collections for the feasts of Christ and the saints; 2) *Homiliaries* in the narrow sense: patristic collections organized according to the liturgical year—as Lent, Pascha, the Sundays of the year; 3) *Menologia,* compilations of a hagiographic rather than homiletic nature, intended for spiritual reading according to the months of the liturgical year—hence their name, *men* (month), *logos* (word), and not to be confused with the *Synaxaria,* condensed hagiographic collections corresponding approximately to the roman martyrologies; and 4) *Mixed Collections.*

The syriac homiliaries are in continuity with the ancient jewish-palestinian tradition and synagogue preaching, though a strong influence of byzantine homeletics is noticeable in them.[37] Most georgian homiliaries are translations from the Greek.[38] We know that the ancient armenian homiliary reflects the liturgical usages of the church of Jerusalem in the fifth century.[39] The arabic homiliaries cover various segments of the christian Church: the melkite, the coptic, and so on.

### *Biographies of Saints*

Christianity was not the first to conceive the idea of preserving the memory of its heroes and saints. The influence of edifying classical *Lives* on comportment is well known.[40] At the time when Diogenes Laertius wrote his *Vitae Philosophorum (Lives of Eminent Philosophers),* the Christians began carefully preserving the acts of their martyrs and often accounts of their passion. The *Vita et passio Cypriani* of Pontius is a true spiritual biography.[41]

In the East, the *Life of Saint Antony* by Athanasius[42] was read far and wide from the outset and served as a model for many other saints' lives. Gregory of Nyssa composed the *Life of Macrina,* his own sister, as an example of holiness of life.[43] The *Religious History* of Theodoret of Cyrrhus[44] is a collection of notes devoted to saintly personalities of the East.

It is not easy to choose among the numerous *Lives* that appeared over the course of the following centuries. From the perspective of the history of spirituality, even the most imaginative of them deserve attention because they summarize better than any other treatises the then-current views of holiness. To a large extent the pious stories of hagiographers determine the concept of perfection.

## THE SEARCH FOR THE SPIRITUAL SENSE

### *Beyond the 'Letter'*

Reading is part of human instruction. Normally people learn how to read at school. One understands the meaning of what is written relative to one's level of intelligence. But the meaning of the Scriptures is spiritual. The human intellect cannot, on its own, understand the Scriptures. It behooves us therefore to recall the fundamental principle of patristic exegesis: the advocates of the 'mere letter' cannot grasp the inspired doctrine without being illogical.[45] 'The one who evaluates the writings', Basil maintains, 'must be equipped with almost the same preparation as the one who composed them. Someone who is not engaged in agriculture is not able to judge agricultural work. . . . I maintain that not everyone is allowed to examine the words of the Spirit by himself; it can be done only by someone who possesses the Spirit of discernment. . . .'[46]

According to Origen, the historical and the spiritual meanings are like the flesh and the divinity of the Word. In his Scripture, as in his earthly life, the *Logos* needs a body. Just as, in Christ, we should not stop at the man who can be seen but, beyond the flesh that hides him from physical eyes, perceive God who is in him, so we should pierce the outward history offered to us in the sacred books, especially those of the Old Testament, to penetrate into the spiritual mystery that lies concealed therein.[47]

The Desert Fathers sometimes experienced a combination of reticence and fear in the face of Scripture, as is expressed, for example, in the answer Poemen gave to Abba Ammonas: 'If you cannot keep silent, it is better for you to speak according to the words of the elders, and not according to Books. It is dangerous for a man to speak about the (sacred) Books.'[48]

The meaning of a text is understood not merely by studying it but much more by praying to discern it. The One who inspired the sacred writers can also inspire their interpreter.[49] When questioned about the meaning of a passage from Leviticus, Antony fell to prayer: 'My God, send Moses to me, so that he may teach me (the meaning of) these words'.[50] Isaac the Syrian gives this advice: 'Do not approach the mysterious words in the Scriptures without prayer and without asking help from God, saying, "Lord, grant me to perceive the power that is in them". Deem prayer to be the key to discerning the truth in Scripture.'[51]

### *'Search the Scriptures'*

An understanding of the spiritual sense is a gift of God, an illumination, but does not preclude the need for human effort. Severianus of Gabala, a syrian author (at the end of the fourth—beginning of the fifth century) made the following comments on the words of Christ, 'Search the Scriptures' (Jn 5:39):

> Search them, but not by frivolous reading; pore over them, examine them, study the depths of their sentences. Indeed, God who has put the Scriptures at our disposal has veiled the meaning of their oracles. He has given us the Scriptures, but without disclosing their hidden interpretation. He has left this to the disciplined zeal of your efforts in order to sharpen your mind and to verify whether you serve the Scriptures or do violence to them.[52]

Thus, the interpretation of sacred texts is an art not unlike others:

> God has given us nature, but has concealed art. All the materials and framework have been put at our disposal, but art was born from the mind of man. So it is with Scripture.[53]

Within this context, various 'methods' of searching the Scriptures were enunciated and often designated by a specific name. When disciples asked their masters how to pray, they obviously also wanted to learn how to search the Scriptures to discover the hidden spiritual treasures. The 'methods' that were taught were of a twofold nature: on the one hand, certain types of exegesis had become traditional;

on the other, certain methods of 'meditating on' the texts proved to be effective as a preparation for illumination by the Spirit.

### *Typology and Allegory*

In the spiritual exegesis of Scripture there are evident differences between schools, especially between that at Alexandria and that at Antioch,[54] between 'allegorical' and 'literal' exegesis. No one can deny that typology is found at the point where New Testament exegesis and patristics meet in the life of the ancient christian community.[55] Typology could assume several aspects. The most ancient, and the foundation of all the others, is the eschatological typology which the Old Testament presents to us. The prophets announced that at the end of time God would accomplish works that are analogous but superior to those he had performed in the past. The essential affirmation of the New Testament lies in showing that this typology has been fulfilled in Jesus Christ. But the life of Christ does not exhaust the realities of the New Covenant. That life continues in the Church, which is the Body of Christ, and in the members of the Church who, in their entire life and in most diverse circumstances, are the stones of the true temple.

Consequently, there are several types of typology.[56] Matthean exegesis, which appeared in Hippolytus of Rome, in the *Catechetical Lectures* of Cyril of Jerusalem, and in many others, was fond of drawing analogies between the Old Testament and the concrete life of Christ. Sacramental typology was to find its place in mystagogical catecheses.[57] But ascetic writers preferred the so-called moral typology.

### *Moral Exegesis*

The unfailing sign of a fruitful reading lies in its application: of what use would a knowledge of the texts of Scripture be if such knowledge were not to change our life completely? Such a moral exegesis predominated in Alexandria. This trend was already evident in Clement, where the influence of Philo contributed to making it more explicit. It would become predominant in Origen but not exclusively so.[58]

This was not merely a matter of gathering all the explicit commandments of the New Testament to sketch out a code of life, as Basil did in his *Moralia (Ta ethika),* but of finding a christian meaning even in the 'material' prescriptions of the Old Testament regarding circumcision, exhortations to make war upon enemies, the bloody sacrifices, and so on. A moral significance was given even to such simple statements as, for example, that Christ ascended or descended. As the spiritual life progresses, this moral (or tropological) typology evolved more and more towards the 'mystical' (or anagogical).[59]

We need give only a few references. Origen, in his spiritual interpretation of the opening verse of the *Song of Songs,* 'Let him kiss me with the kisses of his mouth', writes:

> As the third point in our exposition, let us bring in the soul whose only desire is to be united to the Word of God and to be in fellowship with him, and to enter into the mysteries of his wisdom and knowledge as into the chambers of her heavenly Bridegroom. . . . And let us understand that by the 'mouth' of the Bridegroom is meant the power by which he enlightens the mind. . . . And this is the truer, closer, holier kiss, which is said to be granted by the Bridegroom—Word of God to the Bride—that is to say, to the pure and perfect soul . . . .[60]

### *The Mystical Exegesis of the Syrians and the Armenians*

What characterizes the exegesis of these churches is not a particular form of figurative interpretation, but a tendency to restrain this form, especially when it leads to an allegorism that seems to forget the original meaning. Theodore Bar Koni asked himself this question: 'What difference [is there] between the historical and the allegorical interpretation, and who invented it?' His answer:

> Great, and not small, is the difference between the historic and the allegorical interpretation: as much as the latter consists of impiety, blasphemy, and falsehood, so much (is) the former, truth and confession. Indeed, it is the misguided Origen who invented this device of allegorism.[61]

But if we concentrate too much on the historical meaning, how can we find the link between the past which is being narrated and present-day actual life? Without this vital union, reading would lose its most important dimension. On this point, the spiritual writers are in agreement. But they go their separate ways when they look for some connection with what is past or far removed. Here the difference in world views notably intervenes.

The Greeks, in their 'formal' way of thinking, did not easily succeed in imagining that we could pass from one reality to the other except *per pontem analogiae* (over the bridge of analogy): things are identical if they have the same form; and the more similar they are, the closer they are to each other. To indicate that a biblical event applies to us, it is therefore necessary to show that something similar proves to be true in our own life.

Fundamentally different in the semitic world view and elsewhere was the way of seeing relationships. For a Semite, the link between the two realities exists and is intensely lived if one discovers their common root. The Hebrews felt they were one people because they had one father: Abraham. Calling oneself a son of Abraham meant to be in him, to be included in his history and his promises.

A similar world view existed in the climate of most syriac homilies and was also at work in the poetry of the Armenians. What was lacking in their meditations on Scripture was the moral application. We get the impression that they relate mere facts. Yet at the same time we sense that such facts affect us intimately—that what is at stake is our common roots, and that we re-live these mystically. Judging by the evidence, the readings always have a sacred, liturgical, almost sacramental dimension. Thus, the reading of Scripture was part of the liturgical *anamnesis,* in which the past becomes eternally present.

## MEDITATION

### *Haga—Meletan—Meditari*

In the Old Testament, the idea 'meditation' is expressed by terms deriving from the root *haga,* terms often translated in Greek by μελετᾶν (to study, to meditate upon), in Latin, *meditari, medita-*

*tio*. The original root meaning was 'to make a soft murmuring sound'. The seat of 'meditation', its organ, was primarily the throat, the larynx. Meditation can have a religious as well as a neutral value; there even is a hostile 'meditating' against God (Ps 2:1, *populi meditati sunt inania,* 'the peoples meditated empty things'). Even so, the physical, aural component is usually accompanied by a spiritual or mental component: 'Blessed is anyone who delights in the law of Yahweh and murmurs his law day and night' (Ps 1:2). Meditation then comes from 'the heart' (Is 33:18).

The translation of the hebrew term by the greek *meletan* or latin *meditari* already expands its meaning: the term now means 'to take care of', 'to attend to', or more specifically, 'to take to heart'. The latin term conveys the idea of 'practising', 'accustoming oneself'.

In the New Testament, the only significant text on this topic is 1 Tm 4:15, where Paul recommends that his disciple 'take to heart' the reading of Scripture, the exhortations, the teaching, the gift which he had received. 'To ponder' words or events 'in one's heart', as Mary did (Lk 2:19, 51), already is a form of *meditari.*[62]

Following the lines of the Old Testament, christian meditation was directed from the beginning at the word of God. The first characteristic of meditation then is recall and repetition of texts from Scripture, making of them food for the soul. This idea was expressed by the metaphor of *ruminatio,* ruminating, musing upon. The concept of *ruminari-ruminatio* was inspired by Lv 11:3 and Dt 14:6, where the ruminants were classified among the clean animals. Applied to Scripture and set parallel with 'meditation', this concept, which is already found in chapters 10 and 11 of the *Epistle of Barnabas,*[63] would be taken over by the greek and latin Fathers and by the coptic tradition.[64]

The method used by pachomian monks for meditation is remarkably close to the biblical *meditari:* what they did was recite verses from the Psalms or short biblical texts in a low voice. The *Rule* of Pachomius never tires of repeating the recommendation *de Scripturis aliquid meditari* (meditate on something from Scripture). Number 36: 'The one who strikes the signal to assemble the brothers for meals shall recite while striking [the simandra].' Number 37: 'Let him who gives desserts to the brethren at the refectory door meditate on something from Scripture as he gives it.'[65]

Cassian notes that for the eastern monks this exercise, practised all day long during manual labor, replaced the canonical hours celebrated by western monks.[66] We may therefore conclude ironically: 'It is not that the ancients were unaware of meditation; it is just that the moderns have shortened it'.[67] Meditating is synonymous with 'praying unceasingly'.

### *Learning by Heart*

The greek verb μελετάω, Theophan the Recluse taught, refers to the activity of learning the word of God by heart.[68] Whatever the etymology of the greek term, it is certain that this was the practice of the monks in the early centuries of the Church.[69] Theophan himself was attached to this practice, and he recommended it frequently:

> Trying to define all the profit there is in learning certain passages from Scripture by heart is impossible. In the soul, the same phenomenon is produced as the one that occurs when corruptible fruit is put in sugar. The sugar penetrates into all its pores, the sweetness permeates it and preserves it from corruption. Likewise, when the soul is well impregnated by the words of God she has learned by heart, she rejects the corruption of evil or vain thoughts, and is filled with the sweetness of the remembrance of things divine.[70]

The following advice given by the same author is also invaluable. The goal of reading is to let the word of God penetrate the heart, where it becomes prayer. One should therefore make a selection among the texts and choose only those that move the heart or translate into words the feelings one already has. Once they are associated with a sacred text, our feelings are, so to speak, 'adorned' with Scripture.[71]

### *The 'Testimonies' of Scripture*

Making *excerpta* (extracts) from a weighty tome is both an ancient and a modern custom.[72] According to the testimony of Suetonius, Augustus loved to gather from the classical authors moral texts which he addressed to those in need of exhortation.[73] The *Testimonium libri ad Quirinium* indicates that the Christians did the same while reading Scripture.[74] The *Moralia* of Basil[75] or the *Pandects* of Antiochus the Monk[76] are veritable handbooks of ethics and scriptural asceticism.

Normally, the goal of reading was not to compose learned anthologies. Cyprian presents an easy method of reading and meditating on texts. Deeply convinced of the unity between the two Testaments and of the symbolic values of expressions, readers committed to memory, by means of associations, the various scriptural *topoi* (topics), terms, and metaphors. All this had to be channeled in one direction: Christ and the spiritual life.

While reading the story of the stone which Jacob had put under his head (Gn 28:11), Cyprian was reminded that Christ is the true stone (1 Cor 10:1), that David killed Goliath with a stone (1 Sm 17:40ff.), and so on.[77] By such spontaneous associations, scriptural terms were charged with a rich symbolism of which patristic homilies offer abundant evidence.

## *Discursive Reason in Meditation*

In one of his letters, Theophan the Recluse tells of how he came across the method of meditation regarded as being typical of catholic piety. He stated his intention to translate Saint Frances de Sales from the French, 'because he is so practical'; and he also informed his reader that he had already begun working on the russian text of 'a french book of meditations'. But he never finished it, and he gave as his reason: 'It is a catholic book. Unfortunately, Catholics never understand what true prayer is!' They concentrate, he reckoned, on rational reflections, and they think this is already prayer.[78]

A long tradition led this author to be suspicious of διάνοια, discursive, dialectic, 'aristotelian' reason ('kantian', modern russian authors would say). The organ of contemplation is the *nous,* the intuitive intellect.[79] If people were afraid of speculative theology,[80] how much more should they avoid rationalism in prayer. Indeed, the eastern authors frequently insist on this point in their writings.[81]

Who was more speculative than Origen? And yet he warns: 'It is not right that prayers should take the form of teaching; they should only be supplications for good things from God'.[82] It is easy to fall into pride while speculating, Maximus the Confessor informs us: 'As parents feel an affection for the offspring of their bodies, so also the mind is naturally attached to its own reasonings'.[83]

But we should not allow ourselves to be misled by such texts to the extent of believing that the contemplatives forbade any use of the discursive reason during prayer. With authors who are well-informed, the elements of the rational order dominate more and more. Theophan, who was quoted as a witness against rationalism, did not believe he was contradicting himself when he stated: 'The life according to the will of God is truly reasonable to the highest degree'.[84] And he suggested a method for using reason during meditation.[85]

Certain Byzantines took up the explicit defense of discursive reasoning, Theoleptus of Philadelphia,[86] for example, at the beginning of the fourteenth century. In order to 'penetrate into the sanctuary of the *nous* (mind)', he writes, 'one must pass through some type of meditation, by following the path of *dianoia*'. By praying according to *dianoia,* 'the soul will cross over to the remembrance of God *(mneme theou)*'.[87] The entire soul with its various faculties must apply herself in prayer.[88]

The problem, as Theophan the Recluse notes correctly, does not lie in the use of reflection in prayer, but in the rationalism which is inherent in human thought.[89]

### *'The Use of the Faculties'*

What has been said about reason is equally valid for the other human faculties. Ignatii Brianchaninov states that 'in their writings, the holy Fathers frequently mention under the same rubric mental prayer, the prayer of the heart, and that of the soul'.[90] He calls prayer of the soul a prayer 'performed with the whole soul, with the participation of the body itself, when one prays with one's whole being—that is, when one's whole being becomes like a single mouth uttering the prayer'.[91]

The meditation methods taught in the West since the time of the ignatian *Exercises*[92] have no other goal. The whole person should participate in meditation: body, memory, mind, will, and affections, so that the 'colloquium' which ends such an effort may be an encounter that is fully responsible and personal.

In spite of his doubts about the correctness of a certain 'french book of meditations', Theophan fairly faithfully adopted the same method of teaching mental prayer. We should first select a theme for personal meditation. In the main, this will be the gospel text: 'Read the Gospel . . . , while meditating on it, to derive from this the personal applications you need'.[93] One could also follow the liturgical prayers according to the church calendar.[94] But since 'all our prayers proceed from dogmas',[95] any divine truth is worthy of meditation[96]; a very easy method consists of taking a truth from the catechism daily.[97]

The best times for meditation are morning and evening.[98] First of all, let the truth be well understood and clear.[99] A practical goal emerges at once: one should visualize situations in which the truth will find a practical application: Read the Gospel, compare your life to it, and see whether it corresponds to it.[100] In outline, Theophan makes four practical recommendations for making a truth of the faith one's own: 1) Do not argue too much: understand this truth well and present it to the heart at once, in the manner most apt to affect it; 2) Do not move quickly from one point to the other before the first point has reached the heart; 3) Attach an appropriate image to the thought, because images make a deeper impression and are more easily remembered. Or also, and preferably, relate several thoughts to a single image: for example, visualize a sword above your head to evoke judgment, sin, and death. 4) Enshrine the truth in a short sentence that expresses it, and repeat this often.[101] Any desire to come to the end of the proposed matter should always be rejected as a temptation. On the contrary, full attention should be centered on kindling the feelings.[102] If one truth moves the heart more than another, this is normal. It is good then to return to it and be 'nurtured' by it for a long time.[103]

In this connection, one may remember the famous *annotacio* two of *The Spiritual Exercises of Saint Ignatius:* 'it is not an abundance of knowledge that fills and satisfies the soul but rather an inner understanding and savoring of things'. A direct influence of this book on Theophan is not excluded. He undoubtedly knew the *Pneumatika gymnasmata (Spiritual Exercises)* of Nicodemus the Hagiorite[104] which are essentially a commentary on the *Exercises* by Father Pinamonti.

In itself, this fact is quite eloquent. It would be difficult to find a better expert on the eastern tradition of prayer than Nicodemus. If he adopted the western method of meditation without difficulty, this is because he saw that it was in the tradition of the 'neptic' (watchful) Fathers, his acknowledged masters.

## *The Use of the Imagination in Prayer*

Theophan's third recommendation, 'to attach some image to the thought', is surprising coming from him. The intellectualist mystics were unanimous in condemning any use of the imagination.[105] Their ideal hovered 'above forms and figures' [106] and imposed an inner iconoclasm. Their theoretical approach predominated in the East for centuries.[107] But in practical reality, the imagination always regains its legitimate rights. An inner iconoclasm cannot coexist with the veneration of images.

Opposition to purely noetic mysticism manifested itself even in theory. Contrary to alexandrian spiritualism, the antiochian Theodoret did not mind being lavish with turns of phrases such as, τήν θείαν θεωρίαν φανταζομένος or τῆ τῆς θεωρίας φαντασία, the 'imaginings of contemplation'. 'He [Zeno] devoted himself to divine contemplation, that is, he perceived the vision of God',[108] and even 'contemplation made visible'.[109]

The *phantasia* (imagination) played an important role in gnoseology and in the ethics of the stoa.[110] We recall how, in Philo of Alexandria, 'they [the therapeutes] . . . imagine *(phantasiousthai)* nothing other than the divine excellences and powers'.[111] Theodoret had read Philo, and for him 'the remembrance of God' consisted of 'imagining the divine beauty'.[112] Theodoret was not the only one to sin against the strict laws of the Alexandrians. Gregory Nazianzus, not satisfied by the use of the term 'imagining, representing' in speaking of our contemplation here below applied it to the vision of Moses,[113] even to that of Saint Paul.[114]

The spirituality of the 'remembrance of God'[115] is not afraid of sensory images, because 'memory' uses them, and the popular devotion evident in the veneration of icons had defeated the hypernoetic ideology, the enemy of the concrete and of art.[116]

With all due respect for the teaching of the *Philokalia,* Theophan sought to insert within the context of modern psychology what the Fathers had said about the imagination.[117] He explains how the judgment, to be informed, needs the 'material' provided by the senses. But between the direct perception of the senses and reasoning intervene the memory and imagination. These last two are even more important for judgment than the outer senses. They present images according to the laws of association, but also depend on the will and the heart. Finally, a mysterious cause may also intervene: the inspirations of one's Guardian Angel.[118]

Abstract concepts of images accompany the imagination. Those who have the mind of Christ possess this art of correct representation which a finely-tuned sense allows them. By contrast, sinners have little chance of arriving at this because their images are corrupt and distorted from the beginning.[119] One alienates oneself from the real to fall into the realm of the lie, where the imagination twirls around the selfish 'me', the merry-go-round of daydreaming.[120]

We have, therefore, an obligation to cultivate our imagination. The spirituality of the Fathers emphasized the negative dimension of this inner education: renouncing all vain, useless images. Theophan did not limit himself to this. He recommended at the same time filling the memory with profitable representations, appropriate to the cultivation of the remembrance of God.[121] Training the imagination must be done especially with the young, because first impressions endure and influence the character all life long. Christian parents, then, should guide their child's imagination towards objects of faith and fill its memory with religious representations.[122] This is also one of the goals of 'meditating on' the Scriptures.

## *Notes*

1. Louis Leloir, *Désert et communion, Témoignages des Pères du Désert recueillis à partir des Paterica armeniens,* Spiritualité orientale 26 (Bellefontaine, 1978) 283ff. Jacques Rousse, 'Lectio divina', DSp 9 (1976) 470ff.

2. *Letter to Gregory the Miracleworker,* 4; *Lettre à Gregoire le Thaumaturge;* SCh 148 (1969) 192.

3. *Epistola* I.15; PG 4:226B; ANF 5:280.

4. *Life of Antony,* 2; PG 26:841C; Vivian and Athanassakis, CS 202:58–59; Meyer, ACW 10.

5. *The Book of Perfection,* 5.8 (53); CSCO 254 (Syri 111):15; translated Sebastian Brock 'The Book of Perfection', *The Syriac Fathers on Prayer and the Spiritual Life,* CS 101 (Kalamazoo: Cistercian Publications, 1987) 224.

6. Henri de Lubac, *Histoire et Esprit.* (Paris, 1950) 355f.

7. *Commentaire de l'Evangile concordant ou Diatesseron* I,18–19; SCh 121:52–53.

8. The term *deuteros plous* is already found in the classics, even in Aristotle, as a proverbial expression. See Henricus Stephanus, *Thesaurus linguae Graecae* (Paris, 1842–1847) vol. 6:1240. See Gregory of Nazianzus, *De vita sua,* 5.497; PG 37:1063.

9. Tomaš Špidlík, *Joseph de Volokolamsk. Un chapitre de la spiritualité russe,* OCA 146 (Rome, 1956) 9.

10. *Prosvetitel'* [*Illuminator*]) (Kazan, 1857) 582ff.

11. Origen, *Homilies on Genesis,* 12; GCS 6:112; SCh 7:212; FCh 71:183. Pseudo-Basil (Evagrius), *Letter* 8.2; ed. Courtonne (Paris, 1957) 23. Dorotheos, *Instructions,* 1.6; SCh 92:155; translated Eric P. Wheeler, *Dorotheos of Gaza: Discourses and Sayings,* CS 33 (Kalamazoo: Cistercian Publications, 1977).

12. *Vita S. Symeonis Sale Confessoris;* PG 93:1169C.

13. Tomaš Špidlík, 'Le concept de l'obéissance et de la conscience selon Dorothée de Gaza', *Studia Patristica* XI (1972) 72–78. See *A Systematic Handbook,* 285ff.

14. *Bohairic Life,* 183; ed. L.Th. Lefort, CSCO 107 (1952) 105; translated by Armand Veilleux, *The Life of Saint Pachomius and His Disciples,* Pachomian Koinonia, 1, CS 45 (Kalamazoo, Cistercian Publications, 1980) 218.

15. *Epistola* 2; PG 32:228BC. Tomaš Špidlík, *La sophiologie de S. Basile,* 155ff.

16. *In 1 ad Timotheum* 14.4; PG 58:646BC; LNPF 13:457.

17. *The Book of Perfection,* 2.8 (53); CSCO 253 (Syri 111):15; Brock, *The Syriac Fathers on Prayer and the Spiritual Life,* CS 101:224.

18. Louis Leloir, *Paterica armeniaca* 1, 10Rb; CSCO 353:27.

19. *Ad populum Antiochenum, homilia* 14.4; PG 49:196.

20. Louis Leloir, *Apophthegmata armeniaca* 13, 8R; CSCO 371, 189. Reference to Lk 12:33.

21. Leloir, *Désert et communion,* 245.

22. *Epistolarum liber* 2.164; PG 99:152OC.

23. *The Pandects.* See below, n. 30. Charles de Clercq, *Les textes juridiques dans les Pandectes de Nicon de la Montagne Noire,* Sacred Congregation for the Eastern Church, Codif. canon. orient., *Fonti* II, 30 (Venice, 1942).

24. *Tradition and Rule* [in Russian]; ed. M. S. Borovkova Maïkova (St Petersburg, 1912) 5.

25. *Prosvetitel'* (Kazan, 1857) 471.

26. *Ibid.,* 468.

27. *Ibid.,* 428. See Špidlík, *Joseph de Volokolamsk,* OCA 146 (Rome, 1956) 10ff. *Idem, Les grands mystiques russes* (Paris, 1979) 213ff.

28. *A Systematic Handbook,* 6ff.

29. Špidlík, *Les grands mystiques,* 210.

30. Aimé Solignac, 'Nicon de la Montagne-Noire', DSp 11 (1982) 319–320.

31. Marcel Richard, 'Florilèges grecs', DSp 5 (1964) 475–512.

32. *Interrogationes et responsiones;* PG 89:312–824. Richard, 'Florilèges'. 500.

33. The full greek title of the *Synogogē* is *Synagogē ton theophthogon rhematon, kai didaskalion ton theophoron, kai hagion Pateron (A Collection of the Inspired Words, and of the*

*Teachings of the God-bearing and Saintly Fathers),* ed. Nicodemus the Hagiorite and Macarius of Corinth (Venice, 1782). *Mikros Evergetinos (The Shorter Evergetinos),* ed. Kallikinos monachos (Athens, 1977). For the various editions, see Richard, 'Florilèges'. 503.

34. Henri Barré, 'Homéliaires', DSp 7/1 (1969) 597–606.

35. *Constitutiones Studitanae* 16; PG 99:1709C. See 3; PG 1717C.

36. Réginald Grégoire, 'Homéliaires orientaux', DSp 7/1 (1969) 606–617.

37. *Ibid.,* 613ff.

38. Michele Tarchnišvili, *Geschichte der kirchlichen georgischen Literatur,* Studi e Testi 185 (Rome: Città del Vaticano, 1955) 424–429.

39. A. Renoux, 'Un manuscrit du lectionnaire arménien de Jerusalem (*cod. Jerus. arm.* 121)', *Le Muséon* 74 (1961) 361. Grégoire, 'Homéliaires', 607.

40. Gustave Bardy, 'Biographies spirituelles. Antiquité chrétienne', DSp 1 (1936) 1624–1634. Irénée Hausherr, 'Époque byzantine', DSp 1:1634–1646. *A Systematic Handbook,* 41.

41. A. Harnack, *Das Leben Cyprians von Pontius,* TU 39/3 (Leipzig, 1913).

42. *Bios kai politeia (Vita et conversatio S.P.N. Antonii),* PG 26; 835–976 (translations, above, n. 4).

43. *The Life of S. Macrina;* PG 46:960–1000; translated Virginia W. Calahan, *Saint Gregory of Nyssa: Ascetical Works,* FCh 58, 163–191; translated Joan M. Petersen in Joan M. Petersen, ed., *Handmaids of the Lord,* CS 143 (1996) 51–86.

44. *Historia religiosa;* PG 82:1283–1496; translated by R. M. Price, *A History of the Monks of Syria: The Religious History of Theodoret of Cyrrhus,* CS 88 (Kalamazoo, Cistercian Publications, 1985).

45. Origen, *Commentary on Saint John,* 10.43; GCS 4:221; ANF 9:297–408.

46. *Homilies on the Hexateuch, Leviticus,* 1.1; GCS 6:289ff.

47. Henri de Lubac, *Histoire et Esprit. L'intelligence de l'Écriture d'aprène* (Paris: Aubier, 1950) 93–94. See Basil, *Liber de Spiritu Sancto* 21; PG 32:165AB; translated David Anderson, *St. Basil the Great: On the Holy Spirit* (Crestwood, New York, St Vladimir's Seminary Press, 1980) 82–83. Gregory Nazianzen, *Oratio* 20.2; PG 35:1068AB.

48. *Apophthegmata syriaques* 17; PO 11:420.

49. Jean Daniélou, *Origène* (Paris, 1948) 38; translated Walter Mitchell, *Origen* (New York: Sheed and Ward, 1955) 24.

50. Louis Leloir, *Paterica armeniaca* 11, 3R; CSCO 371:132. Leloir, *Désert et communion,* 251ff.

51. A. J. Wensinck, *Mystic Treatises* (Amsterdam, 1923) par. 329, chapter 45, page 220.

52. *Homily* 7: *Seberiani Gabalorum episcopi Emesensis Homiliae* [Armenian and Latin] (Venice, 1927) 268 and 270. Leloir, *Désert,* 247ff.

53. *Ibid.*

54. Manlio Simonetti, 'Esegesi patristica', DP I1211–1213;'Exegesis, Patristic', EEC 1:309–311. *Idem, Lettera E/O Allegorica, Un contributo alla storia dell'esegesi patristica,* Studia Ephemeridis 'Augustinianum' 23 (Rome, 1985).

55. Jean Daniélou, 'Exégèse et typologie patristique', DSp 4/1 (1960) 132–138.

56. *Ibid.,* 136ff. Daniélou enumerates five main forms of typology: matthean, johannine, ecclesial, mystical, and eschatological.

57. See p. 99.

58. Daniélou, *Origène* (Paris, 1948) 145ff; [99 *Origen* (New York, 1955) 139ff.

59. Daniélou, 'Exégèse et typologie', 137.

60. *In Canticum canticorum, homilia* 1; PG 13:85C; SCh 37bis:7; ACW 26:60–62.

61. *Livre des Scolies,* Memra 5.19; CSCO 431 (*Syri* 197):296.

62. Emmanuel von Severus, 'Das Wort "meditari" im Sprachgebrauch der Heiligen Schrift', *Geist und Leben* 26 (1953) 365–375. E. von Severus and Aimé Solignac, 'Méditation: de l'Ecriture aux auteurs médievaux', DSp 10 (1980) 907–914.

63. SCh 172 (1971) 156–158; ANF 1:143–144.

64. É. Amelinau, *Histoire des monastères de la Basse Egypte* (Paris, 1894) 39, 152–156.

65. See also nos. 3 and 28; Amand Boon, *Pachomiana latina.* (Louvain, 1932)14, 20ff; translated by Armand Veilleux, 'Precepts', *Pachomian Chronicles and Rules,* Pachomian Koinonia, vol. 2 (Kalamazoo: Cistercian Publications, 1981) 131 [in the Veilleux translation, Number 37 does not mention meditation–ed.]

66. *The Institutes,* 3.2; CSEL 17:34; ACW 58:59; LNPF 11:212–213.

67. Irénée Hausherr, *Penthos,* OCS 132 (Rome, 1944) 76; translated Anselm Hufstader, *Penthos: The Doctrine of Compunction in the Christian East,* CS 53 (Kalamazoo: Cistercian Publications, 1982) 64. Heinrich Bacht, *Das Vermächtnis des Ursprungs,* excursus IV. *Meditatio in den ältesten Mönchsquellen* (Würzburg, 1972).

68. *On Psalm 118* (Moscow, 1891) 64. Špidlík, *Théophane le Reclus,* 267.

69. Heinrich Bacht, '"Meditari" in den ältesten Mönchsquellen', *Geist und Leben* 28 (1955) 360–373. René Draguet, *Les Pères du désert* (Paris, 1949) 155.

70. *On Psalm 118,* 68ff.

71. *Put ko spaseniju* [*The Way to Salvation*] (Moscow, 1908) 219. *Čto jest duchovnaja žizň* [*What the Spiritual Life Is*], 47 (Moscow, 1897) 172.

72. A. Quacquarelli, *Retorica e iconologia* (Paris, 1982) 1ff.

73. Suetonius, *De vita Caesarum,* Aug. 89.2.

74. PL 4:673–780.

75. PG 31:691–870.

76. *Pandectes Scripturae divinites inspiratae;* PG 31:1431–1850.

77. *Testimonium libri ad Quirinium* 2.16; ed. W. Hartel, CSEL 3/1:83 ff.

78. *Pisma* [Letters] (Moscow, 1899) vol. 6:205.

79. See p. 170ff.

80. See p. 161ff.

81. See p. 249ff.

82. *Commentary on Matthew,* 12.6; GCS 6:77,30; ANF 14:454.

83. *Centuries on Charity,* 3.58; SCh 9:141; translated by Polycarp Sherwood, *Maximus the Confessor: The Ascetic Life. The Four Centuries on Charity,* ACW 2 (1955)184; *Maximus the Confessor. Selected Works,* CWS (1985) 69.

84. *Načertanie christianskago nravoučenija* [*Christian Moral Teaching*] (Moscow, 1895) 209.

85. See p. 144.

86. Sévérien Salaville, 'Formes de prière d'après un byzantin du XIVe siècle', *Echos d'Orient* 39 (1940–1942) 1–25.

87. *De abscondita operatione in Christo;* PG 143:393C.

88. *Ibid.,* 389.

89. Tomaš Špidlík, *Théophane le Reclus,* 20ff.

90. *Approches de la Prière de Jésus,* 96 (in Russian, 250ff.); selections translated by Lazarus [Moore], *On the Prayer of Jesus* (London, 1952).

91. *Ibid.*

92. Cardinal Lercaro, *Metodo di Orazione Mentale* (Milan, 1969); translated by T. F. Lindsay, *Methods of Mental Prayer* (Westminster, Maryland, 1957).

93. *Pisma* [Letters] (Moscow, 1898) vol I:72.

94. Špidlík, *Théophane le Reclus,* 269ff.

95. *Letters,* 151.
96. *Letters,* 205ff.
97. *Puť ko spaseniju* [The Way to Salvation] (Moscow, 1908) 234.
98. *On Psalm 118* (Moscow, 1891) 64ff.
99. *Pisma* [Letters] 205ff.
100. *Ibid.,* 72.
101. *Put ko spaseniju* [The Way to Salvation], 121ff.
102. *Pisma* [Letters], 227.
103. *Ibid.*
104. (Venice, 1800; Athens, 1869).
105. See p. 212.
106. See p. 243.
107. Sergius Bulgakov, *The Orthodox Church* (London, 1935) 170: 'Orthodox mysticism is without imagery; without imagery, also, is the way which leads to it, that is, prayer and meditation'.
108. *Historia religiosa* 12 (PG 82:1396C; CS 88:96f), 18 (1425D; 126f), 24 (1460A, 154f).
109 *Oratio de divina charitate;* PG 82:1501B. J. Lemaitre, DSp 2/2:1859.
110. Michel Spanneut, *Le Stoïcisme des Pères de l'Église de Clément de Rome à Clément d'Alexandrie* (Paris, 1957) 225. Clement of Alexandria, *Stromata* 2.54, 5–55,1; GCS 2:145; SCh 38:78.
111. *De vita contemplativa;* ed. F. C. Conybeare (Oxford, 1895) 61ff.
112. *Historia religiosa* 21; PG 82:1445D; CS 88:108. See also *In epistola ad Hebraeos* 11.1; PG 82:757B.
113. *Oratio* 10.2, *In seipsum;* PG 35:828C and *Oratio* 20.1,1ff; 1065; LNPF ser. 2, vol. 7:203–434.
114. *Oratio* 32.16, *De moderatione in disputando;* PG 36:192.
115. See p. 364.
116. See p. 307.
117. Špidlík, *Théophane le Reclus,* 17ff.
118. *Načertanie christianskago nravoučenija* [*Christian Moral Teaching*] (Moscow, 1895) 250ff.
119. *Ibid.*
120. *Ibid.*
121. *Ibid.*
122. *Puť ko spaseniju* [*The Way to Salvation*] (Moscow, 1908) 34ff.

# 7

# CONTEMPLATION

## THE CONTEMPLATIVE EAST

### *Mary Eastern—Martha Western?*

THE EASTERN CHURCH has insisted on the need for contemplation proportionate to the abilities of each believer. In this, she saw the demands of a faith that, if it ceased to grow deeper, would discredit itself .[1] More than one spiritual writer therefore has praised the joys of contemplation. Messalianism in particular maintained the absolute need for contemplation as the only way to attain holiness.[2] Then hesychasm, that great orthodox movement, was but a manifestation of that same desire to contemplate God already in this life.[3] The Eastern Church has therefore been compared to Mary, in contrast to the Western Church—Martha.[4]

The problem of christian perfection is that of assimilation to divine perfection. Contemplation, having as its goal 'divine things' or God himself, tends to simplify the human spirit to the extent that its eye 'considers God alone', *Dei solius intuitus,* in Cassian's words.[5] Consequently, the kingdom of God is established in us by spiritual knowledge[6]; any other activity, even perfectly praiseworthy, scatters the mind because it is centered on an earthly object. Here, Cassian follows Evagrius, for whom the entire spiritual life is directed toward contemplation.[7]

We should point out that these authors include charity itself in their definition of contemplation. If all things have been created because of the knowledge of God,[8] charity will be defined as 'the higher state of the reasonable soul, whereby it is impossible to love something on earth more than the knowledge of God'.[9]

Contemplation is a foretaste of heaven;[10] it is, which is the same thing, a return to paradise[11] where man cultivated immortal plants, that is, divine thoughts.[12]

Within this context, the ethics of the Greek Fathers present virtue as knowledge and sin as ignorance ('αγνωσία). In attacking the monk, the demons have as their main object depriving him of knowledge *(gnosis).*[13] 'The mind is impure, first, in having false knowledge . . . ,'[14] in lacking the true contemplation of the world.[15] Vladimir Soloviev taxes the East with 'being numbed by a lazy passivity under the guise of contemplation'.[16] If there is any truth to this reproach, that tendency is not linked only to temperament: the spiritual authors, almost all monks, were primarily responsible for it. But according to the legislation of Justinian, the only goal of the monastic was contemplation.[17] 'The monk', Abba Bessarion said at the moment of his death, 'must be all eye, like the cherubim and the seraphim'[18] who see the face of God unceasingly (see Mt 18:10).

### *Two Mentalities: An Objection Against Contemplation*

'All of us who have the use of sight', wrote Clement of Alexandria, 'contemplate (ϑεωροῦμεν) what is offered to it.'[19] The term *theoria* (contemplation) expresses an ideal, it reflects a mentality. The Hellenes, at the beginning of their history, were in some way like a wide open eye, gifted with a rare perspicuity of sight and contemplation. Their classical culture would adopt the definition of aesthetics given by Plotinus, 'the beautiful is that which pleases the eye *(pulchrum quod visum placet)'*.[20] It is true that the greek sage *(sophos)* would soon turn away from the senses, which provide only an opinion (δόξα), and seek the truth (ἀλήϑεια, λόγος) in purely intellectual knowledge.[21] But even then, this knowledge would be conceived by analogy with visual perception: the object of knowledge or the essence of things received the same name as the visible image: ἰδέα or εἶδος, an image perceived by the eye of the mind.[22]

An entirely different tonality resounds through the religion of the Old Testament and in the Judaism derived from it, which may be called 'the religion of verbal revelation'.[23] The vision of Moses is characterized as a face to face 'conversation' (Ex 33:11). The prophets whom God sent to his people began their message with the typical exhortation: 'Hear the word of Yahweh' (Am 7:16, Jer 2:4). The most serious reproach made to the messianic people is that they 'have not listened' (Hos 9:17, Jer 7:13).

Visual from the beginning of their civilization, the Greeks were fond of knowing the essence of things. Their philosophy aimed at pure knowledge, which was abstract—or at least not very imperative. By contrast, the entire judaic system was centered around the *Law,* the moral code with its list of obligations and prescriptions for every circumstance of life. Nothing in it called for intellectual speculation, while every word and the sum total of it encouraged obedience to the commandments.[24]

Thus, the question is sometimes asked whether the enthusiasm of the Fathers for contemplation *(theoria)* was derived from Scripture or whether it might not have been inherited from philosophy, an adaptation to the hellenistic world view.[25]

The objection is a modern one. Yet Symeon the New Theologian had already foreseen it. His reply makes sense: 'For those who are spiritual, hearing and contemplation are one and the same . . . .'[26] 'Holy Scripture thus habitually uses the vision of God to mean hearing and hearing to mean vision. Thus, too, the divine Paul called his unutterable visions and illuminations "speech", and said that he had "heard" these things and put them into writing.'[27] Moreover, long before Symeon, Basil envisioned the ideal of contemplation in auditory terms to remain closer to the vocabulary of Scripture.[28] What is more, a marvelous synthesis of the two mentalities, auditory and visual, is found in the New Testament. The *Logos*, the Word of God, became incarnate, to appear visibly. The Son of God is the image of the invisible Father, from all eternity (Col 1:15). To Philip, who had asked him, 'show us the Father', he was able to reply: 'Anyone who has seen me has seen the Father' (Jn 14:9). By fixing on the historical person of Jesus, the human eye contemplates God.[29]

These brief notes show us already that christian contemplation has deeper foundations than those that could be deduced from the visual mentality of the Greeks, which does not mean that the terminology may not have been inspired by the hellenistic tradition.

## *A Study of the Vocabulary*

A study of the vocabulary of the Greek Fathers brings out a great many terms used within the context of *theoria* (seeing, contemplation).[30] From the same root as *theoria* are derived 'spectacle' (θέαμα), that which is seen (for example, the many sights of the truth enjoyed by the apostles)[31]; 'theorem' (θεώρημα), a principle of science or of doctrine; *theates* (θεατής), one who contemplates the *Logos*: likewise, *theoretes* and *theoros* (θεωρητής): one who contemplates, a spectator; *theoretikos* (θεωρητικός): contemplative, speculative; *to theoretikon* (τό θεωρητικόν): the contemplative; and ή θεωρητική δύναμις, the soul's contemplative power or faculty.

From the verb ὁρᾶν (to look) is derived *horasis* (ὅρασις), either the faculty of spiritual sight or that which is seen, a vision. *Τὸ διορατικόν* designates the contemplative faculty, clear-sightedness (Latin: *perspicuitas*); βλέπειν (to look, see) is infrequent; τρανοῦν means 'to see very distinctly'.

'Perception' or 'comprehension' is expressed by νοεῖν (seeing) and words of the same root: *noësis* (νόησις, a perceiving, reflection), *noëma* (νόημα, that which is perceived, a thought); *to noumenon* (τὸ νοούνμενον, the intelligible); *noëtos* (νοητός, perceived, intelligible); *noëtikos* (νοητικός, noetic); but especially the *nous* (νοῦς: mind).[32] Used very frequently are *ennoia-ennoein* (ἔννοια, έννοεῖν) both referring to the concept one has of something. *Epinoia* (ἐπίνοια, a thinking of) and ἐπίνοεῖν are applied to someone who is capable of representing incorporeal reality to himself;[33] *chorein* (χωρεῖν) is translated as 'hold, contain', and 'take in, comprehend'.

Even *dianoia* (διάνοια: a thought) and its derivatives can designate the power or faculty of spiritual understanding: when it is illumined by the Word, it is equivalent to *nous* and to *hegemonikon* (ἡγεμονικόν, the guiding principle).

Found less frequently are *episteme* (ἐπιστήμη, understanding, knowledge) and *epopteia* (ἐποπτεία: inspection—ἐποψία in Pseudo-Denys): witnessing the mysteries.

But the greek religious vocabulary uses above all two terms to refer to contemplation: *theoria* and *gnosis* (θεωρία, γνῶσις). In general, one may say that *theoria* is of philosophic, and *gnosis* of religious origin.

Let us also note that the Latin *contemplatio* is derived from *templum,* the space which the diviner delimited as the field of his observations.[34]

## Theoria

The word *theoria* is derived from *thea* (θέα, vision), and consequently expresses the idea of seeing in a more emphatic way[35]: to watch, to go to a spectacle, and by extension (when applied to the mind), to reflect, meditate, philosophize. Mere seeing can thus be accompanied more and more by reasoning. When such reasoning becomes scientific, we have what is called 'a theory', in contrast to practice. Thus, the word *theoria* can be defined fairly well, but its meaning in specific texts is harder to define.

The distinction between the three lives (βίος ἀπολαυστικος, πολιτικός, θεωρητικός, the life of enjoyment, the political, and the contemplative lives)[36] was implicitly accepted, if not always formulated by the pre-socratics—but what type of *theoria* are we dealing with? In a general sense, any existence devoted to study is a contemplative ('theoretical') life; any sage may be called a contemplative. But with the classical authors of greek philosophy, *theoria* had, we might say, a more technical meaning, and referred to the contemplation of which the object was the prime being, God. Such *theoria* required a preparation; it implied a mental method, a concentration of the intelligence from which care for the city and the public life could divert attention.[37] To restrict *theoria* to the intelligible was certainly in the platonic tradition,[38] which was confirmed by Aristotle.[39] But it is the very thing that makes the human person happy, and is therefore the goal of life.[40]

Of the Gospel writers, only Luke uses the word *theoria,* and then only once, as if by chance, in connection with Christ on the cross: 'the crowds had gathered to see the sight' (Lk 22:48). But in this sense, the word loses nothing of its greatness. Through the visible aspect of this scene of horror, the mystery of faith hidden for ages was unveiled to the eyes of faith and became manifest to the saints precisely and especially through this spectacle.[41]

But this is only a remote reference. Early spirituality did not have the problems that subsequently agitated the perceptions of countries being evangelized. Strictly speaking, the term *theoria* is absent from the vocabulary of the Apostolic Fathers. It made its appearance only with Clement of Alexandria and Origen, but after that it was used frequently.[42]

The term expresses an ideal, it reflects a frame of mind. Its greek origin was so apparent that the Syrians rarely tried to translate it; Jerome himself merely transcribed it in his latin translation of Origen.[43]

## Gnosis

We know that *gnosis* preeminently characterized certain eastern religions.[44] From the etymological point of view, the verb γνῶμαι (to know) does not appeal to any particular organ of sensory knowledge, unlike *είδέναι* (to know, the infinitive of *oida*, 'I know') which refers explicitly to 'seeing', 'vision'. *Gnosis* is not even a matter of the mind exclusively: the will can be part of it, as is evident from γνώμη, which means judgment, a tendency of the will, a resolution, a disposition. For Clement of Alexandria, *gnosis* is 'that light which penetrates the soul as a result of obeying the commandments'.[45]

The greek use of the term was easily contaminated by the influence of Scripture. The expression 'knowing God'—that first appeal addressed to the heart of the human person—is used in the Bible, not in the context of an abstract knowledge, but within the context of life. Indeed, for a Semite, 'to know' (in Hebrew, *yd'*), expresses an existential relationship. 'To know' something means to have a concrete experience of it. Thus, one knows grief (Is 53:3), sin (Ws 3:13), good and evil (Gen 2:9-17). One knows God by entering into his Covenant (Jer 31:34), and one is led gradually into intimacy with him.[46]

In practice, however, while reading texts, we should distinguish carefully between the various meanings of *gnosis,* which ranges from secular knowledge to religious and mystical contemplation;

and even this last, as a true *gnosis,* differs essentially from the *gnosis* of the so-called gnostics.[47]

### *The Definition of Contemplation*

According to Plato, *theoria* is the vision of what is most excellent in beings, 'the Beautiful itself', *(to kalon),* divine beauty, God himself.[48] Although the God of the Christians is not the god of the philosophers, the terms can remain identical. With the spiritual masters of the christian East, the meaning of *theoria* was soon crystallized in a definition which follows, however, a false etymology: *theoria* meant *theon horan,* to see God in everything.[49]

If prayer is defined as 'an ascent of the mind to God', do we have to say that contemplation is identical with prayer? It is surely difficult to measure the boundaries of the various meanings of words in particular cases. What remains true is that only in prayer does one acquire true *gnosis.* For Evagrius, the highest degree of prayer is *theologia,* superior contemplation[50]; hence this remarkable maxim: 'If you are a theologian you truly pray. If you truly pray you are a theologian.'[51]

If *theoria* is defined as 'seeing God', two questions will be of paramount interest to us: how can God be seen in this world, while our gaze is occupied by created things? and which human 'faculty' is capable of such vision?

## THE OBJECT OF CONTEMPLATION

### *The Knowledge of Beings*

If contemplation is 'vision', its object is that the human person be able to 'see', in the most general sense of the term. And because it is a 'knowing', contemplation deals with everything that is knowable, intelligible. For the Greeks, this included all being. What was then transferred to contemplation were the names given to philosophy, the knowledge of beings (ϑεωρία τῶν ὄντων[52]), including the Supreme Being.

Reality is one, but human knowledge varies depending on whether its interest centers on some object or other, but also depending on a special attitude towards them, the particular vantage point from which they are viewed. The contemplatives, too, select their viewpoint. If contemplation is spiritual knowledge, their attitude toward all being will have to follow this demand. The *'gnoseology'* of the contemplatives will have its own rules and principles, and the greek tradition formulated them quite clearly.

### *Contemplation Is Not a Vision of the 'Surface' of Things*

At the beginning of their history, the Hellenes were in some ways like a wide-open eye, gifted with a rare perspicacity of sight and speculation.[53] The greek *sophos* (sage) went out to conquer the world: 'to know everything that happens all over the earth'.[54] But on his march he was soon to have a strange experience: disappointment. This visible cosmos, this world filled with wonders and adventures—what is it really and truly? He received from it no more than superficial, deceptive impressions. So he turned away from the senses which provide only an opinion (δόξα), to seek the truth (ἀλήθεια, λόγος) in intellectual knowledge alone.[55]

In the wake of Plato,[56] Proclus,[57] and many others, the Fathers taught , in turn, that in order to contemplate the truth, the soul must be freed from sensory seeing, because 'whatever is perceived by the senses is alien to God'.[58] The traditional 'purification of the senses' was not to have the same meaning with the christian contemplatives; it was differently understood by them and the Platonists.[59] But the fundamental principle would remain beyond dispute: the object of true contemplation is not what is accessible to bodily sight.

### *Philosophic Contemplation and Its Object*

Once the distinction which underlies philosophy was accepted—the distinction between appearances and reality, between the way of opinion and that of the truth—another distinction was then made between what is understood on the basis of sense perception (αἰσθήσει θεωρητόν) and what was attained through rational contemplation (λόγῳ θεωρητόν).

For Democritus, the object of contemplation were the principles of which the soul is composed—the spheric 'ideas' which were not yet completely separated from matter and the power of which was that of fire.[60] This is also true for the pythagorean 'number'. The decisive step was taken by Plato. True knowledge has as its object neither the visible things nor their constituent elements nor even the order that makes a totality of them, but the invisible world of essences, of 'Ideas': 'Beauty itself (αὐτὸ τὸ καλόν), pure, undefiled not adulterated, divine Beauty (τὸ ϑεῖον καλόν').[61]

For Aristotle, the *logos* expresses and defines essence. Following Aristotle, Maximus the Confessor would say that 'the *logos* of human nature is to have body and soul'.[62] The stoic *logos* was essentially cosmic: it was a rational breath pervading all matter, like the soul in the body.[63]

In picking our way through the labyrinth created by the evolution of the term *logos* in philosophy, we should never lose sight of the fundamental principle that the *logos* expresses reality, as opposed to appearances. But what *is* reality? The answer differed from one school to the other.[64] With Plotinus, the meaning of the term escalated to a mysticism which brings it close, at least outwardly, to the depth of johannine thought (Jn 1:1): 'The beginning is *logos* and everything is *logos* (ἀρχή οὖν λόγος καί πάντα λόγος)'.[65]

## *The Object of Spiritual Contemplation Is Not the Philosophic* Logos, *the Idea, the Definition*

Cicero summarized the tradition of the ancient philosophers as considering things with the reason for the purpose of seeking their essence. . . that is to philosophize.[66] But Christians were deeply convinced that such knowledge was not yet the true *gnosis,* contemplation.

The danger of proclaiming as God what is but a product of our mental activity is great. The error of the Arians was to apply ready-made, clear concepts from dialectics, and for this they earned the reproach made of the Cappadocian Fathers for having turned theology into mere disputation (τεχνύδριον).[67] They had fallen victim to the 'idolatry of concepts', stated Gregory of Nyssa,[68] and Gregory Nazianzen echoed this verdict. What is this idolatry? 'One looks at visible things, and one gives to one of them the name of God. . . .'[69] More insidious, more dangerous, than the idolatry of sensory things is that of rational concepts.

## *'Simple' Knowledge and 'Spiritual' Knowledge*

Deeply convinced that rational theoria was not yet true gnosis, the spiritual writers made a distinction and a contrast between knowledge that is 'simple' (ψιλή) and knowledge that is 'spiritual' (πνευματική).[70] 'There is a twofold knowledge of the world: the pragmatic, at which even the impious arrive, and the spiritual, which is reserved for the saints.'[71] 'Simple knowledge' is 'sterile', incapable of subordinating itself to the kingdom of God.[72]

This terminology originated with the Stoics, who distinguished theoretical knowledge—the goal of which was the truth—from the practical, from action. But they maintained that both needed to go together.[73] Philo of Alexandria was to write, fully in the stoic spirit, that 'simple knowledge (θεωρία ψιλή), without practice is not profitable to the wise'.[74]

The Christians did not understand 'simple knowledge' in the same sense as did the Stoics, because the *praxis* they required went further than that of the philosophers.[75] *Theoria* and *praxis* are like two poles which are either opposite or complementary. To move one was to move the other. Christian *praxis* is 'the life in Christ' according to his example. Spiritual knowledge will therefore be a participation in the knowledge of Christ, a revelation in the broad sense of the term.

## *The Monks' Hostility to Rational Knowledge*

Such scorn of 'simple knowledge' explains the low esteem the eastern monks had for certain cultural forms and for rational knowledge in general. According to Pseudo-Macarius, such knowledge is like 'a great city, but deserted, and whose walls are broken down; if it is taken by the enemy, its greatness is of no use . . . By contrast, the unlearned *(idiotai)* who are partakers of grace are like little towns, fortified by the power of the cross.'[76]

This became a commonplace in byzantine theology. No one emphasized this contrast more strongly than Symeon the New

Theologian: The Holy Spirit 'was sent by the Son to people: not to the perfidious and the ambitious, not to rhetoricians and philosophers, not to those who are curious about pagan writing, not to readers of profane books, not to the comedians of life, not to wits, artists of the word, not to those who carry famous names, not to the favorites of the powerful . . . but to those who are poor in spirit'.[77]

Because of this conviction, the ascetics willingly bragged about their want of instruction (ἀπαιδευσία, ἰδιωτεία). The text of Acts (4:13) was often commented upon: those of the Sanhedrin were amazed at the fearlessness shown by Peter and John as they witnessed, 'considering that they were unlettered common men *(agrammatoi idiotai)'*.[78] Evagrius, the intellectual, summarized the eastern tradition well when he stated that 'The knowledge of Christ needs, not an intellectual soul, but a seeing soul'.[79] Or again, 'Rational knowledge—despise it, because it is not profitable to us on our way'.[80]

In syrian literature, *The Book of Steps* promises the wisdom of heaven to those who reject earthly knowledge.[81] The words of the Apostle, 'we are fools for Christ's sake' (1 Cor 4:10), served as a basis and a justification for the way of life of the *saloi, yourodivye,* 'fools for Christ',[82] whose spiritual clear-sightedness was acquired by a radical renunciation of human wisdom.

## *The* Theoteles Logos

If christian contemplation is not 'mere knowledge', if it is not an understanding of the philosophic *logos,* how should its object be defined? The 'causal reasons' *(rationes seminales)* of the Stoics, the definition of Aristotle, and the platonic Idea still explain only the 'surface' of true reality, for the latter at its core tends to God, and is not understandable aside from its relationship with Providence. The true *logos* of things is therefore the *theoteles logos* (θεοτελής λόγος, the divinely perfect), the logos that 'tends toward God',[83] 'the one towards which the inward thoughts *(rationes)'* of beings tend.[84]

To contemplate then means to understand beings in their ultimate truth, in their providential function, in their relationship to God, and, more precisely, to the creative redeeming Word.[85] On this point, Christians are in agreement that not one of the philosophers knew this true depth of reality. Such knowledge is essentially religious. Animals look at the world without understanding its *rationes*, its reasons; human beings, for the most part, perceive them only with difficulty. 'Only the just and the saints understand them according to the Wisdom of God and truly contemplate them.'[86] Maximus the Confessor expressly stated that the spiritual *logoi* are not to be identified with matter and form,[87] in other words, with 'the physical *logoi (rationes)* of things'.[88] The latter are still the 'surface', 'a second surface', we might say, after the surface perceived by the bodily senses. But can one identify this spiritual *logos* within God himself, hidden in his work?

The best thing to do would be to transcribe the following passage from Chapter 32 of Maximus' *Questiones ad Thalassium.*

> What is the meaning of 'so that they might seek God, and by feeling their way toward him, succeed in finding him?' (Acts 17:27). [Answer:] The one who views the entire corporeal cult of the Law not according to the senses, but finds each of the visible symbols with the mind, understands the divinely perfect reason *(theoteles logos)* hidden in each; such a person finds God in the logos.[89]

This brief note is enough to help us understand that the spiritual *logos* is not yet God; at the same time, one finds God in it. It is therefore a mysterious reality of this world, yet nevertheless divine. How can it be described?

### *The Various 'Incorporations' of the Logos*[90]

The *logos theoteles* reveals God. But God manifests himself in his Word. Origen classified the various manifestations of the *logos*. The first is in creation. As Creator (*demiourgos,* δημιουργὸς),[91] the Word *(logos)* pervades all beings. Through him, matter becomes the cosmos[92] in which God himself takes pleasure; if God saw that it was good (Gn 1:9), this is because he contemplated the *logos* of things.[93]

The Son is therefore the One who contains the *logoi* (reasons) of creation. The Word embodies the principles of beings; he is the unity of these *logoi* which are one body in him: he is the knowledge of their relationships.[94] The *logos* is one, 'although composed of numerous θεωρήματα (principles), of which each θεώρημα is a part'.[95]

> Numerous *logoi* intervene in the administration of the heavenly realities and in the government of earthly realities, and all, as parts of the entire cosmos, concur and converge towards the one fulfillment which is their recapitulation *(anakephalaiosis)* in Christ . . . and if one may say so, of all things, the bringing together under one head *(synkephalaiosis)*.[96]

Thus contemplation is an understanding of the various 'incarnations' of the *logos,* the 'christological' meaning of each event. (Not for nothing, therefore, is it that the famous Jesus Prayer seeks to link the remembrance of the Saviour to all things that can be seen). The object of *theoria* therefore bears upon the various 'sacred books'. We should read them as is appropriate: one after the other, and all of them together.[97]

Scripture appears as the first incorporation of the *logos*. The One who is by nature invisible can be seen and touched in the letter that makes him visible. There is a connaturality between Scripture and the human soul. Both, Origen says, are a temple in which the Lord dwells, a paradise in which he walks. 'What is called in Scripture "the spiritual meaning", is called "the image of God" in the soul. The faithful soul, sensitive to this relationship, contemplates God in herself.'[98]

Yet not only the soul, but also the universe should be the subject matter of spiritual reading. Everywhere in the Book of Nature shine the *logoi*, the rays of light emanating from the Logos and to varying degrees luminous. In the fullness of time, the *Logos* became flesh and shone forth in Christ. A method of contemplation therefore imposes itself on Christians: to seek to imitate Christ, to follow the *Logos* by following Christ. The voice of Christ is addressed to the Church: it speaks in her. She is its efficient sign. This voice insures the luminous presence of Christ in the Church. The contemplative understands this voice, which resounds in the entire life of the Church, in her mysteries, and above all in the eucharistic liturgy.

The *Logos* of God who dwelt among us is therefore the key to all that is offered for contemplation: Scripture, visible nature, the Church, the Eucharist, and the human soul. In all these multiple theophanies, contemplatives discover *one* meaning. Origen writes:

> The *Logos* of God, who was in the beginning with God, is not wordiness *(polylogia),* not *logoi* (words). The *Logos* of God is one Word made up of numerous sentences, of which each is part of the same totality, the same *Logos* . . . Apart from him, even if one speaks of truth, there simply is no unity, no harmony, no aspiration toward the same All.[99]

*The Voice of the Universe*

In the revealed Word it is God who speaks. 'They have mouths, but do not speak' (Ps 115:5; Bar 6:7). This satire on 'voiceless idols' (1 Cor 12:2) emphasizes one of the most typical traits of the living God in biblical revelation. He speaks to man 'at many moments and in various ways' (Heb 1:1).

Origen never wearied of admiring the divine Word who, impelled by his benevolence toward humankind, wanted to 'stammer with children'[100] by becoming incarnate in the symbols of the visible cosmos.

For Basil, the universe is no more than the actualization of the powerful Word of God.[101] Consequently, it is not hard to understand why the visible natural things deserve the name 'voice of God'. They are true words, addressed to human beings, who should hear and understand them. In his homilies, Basil returns to this subject several times, and not merely because he likes to enumerate the various species of animals, plants, and fish: 'Listen to the fish. . . . Do not despise fish because they are unable to speak.'[102] 'Inanimate things have received a voice from God, inasmuch as Scripture indicates that every creature proclaims the Creator with but a single shout.'[103]

The *logos theoteles* we discover in contemplation is therefore this 'Word of God moving through all creation, having begun at that time, active up to the present, and efficacious until the end, even to the consummation of the world'.[104]

## *The Will of God*

'When we speak of a "voice" with reference to God', Basil points out, we understand the divine word not 'as a sound sent out through the vocal organs, not as air molded by the tongue'; 'his Word is, we believe, in the command of his will'.[105] The will of God sustains all being, gives all its meaning and goal, a life filled with activity and joy. 'For the voice which was then heard and that first command became, as it were, a law of nature and remained in the earth.'[106] 'Thus everywhere the water hastened to obey the Creator's command. Who could count the species which the great and ineffable power of God caused to be suddenly seen and moving?'[107]

Yet there is a great difference between unreasoning creatures and human beings. The first obey through instinct, while we should be obedient by virtue of reason, our 'house-companion' (ὁ σύνοικος λόγος).[108] The word of God gives us a conscious life. We should lend our ear to any manifestation of the divine will. For humans, grasping the *theoteles logos* means understanding the divine intention (τὰ θεῖα θελήματα)[109] for beings, 'the divine arrangement (τὴν θείαν διάταξιν) which extends even to the tiniest beings'.[110] In this way, the human person cooperates with the Providence of the Father.

## *The 'Wisdom of the World'*[111]

To understand the divine will is to see in the created world 'a wise, well-ordered arrangement (σοφὴ καὶ εὔτακτος θιακόσμησις)',[112] for 'his wisdom and providence frequently shine out in the smallest things. . . . It is appropriate for us to say with the Prophet, 'How magnificent are Thy works, O Lord! In wisdom hast Thou made them all' (Ps 103:24).[113] This Wisdom *(Sophia),* Basil explains, is the one who was 'beside the master craftsman, delighting him' (Pr 8:30). Wisdom is not to be identified simply with created things. Her specific function is 'to lead us to the knowledge of God'.[114]

Here Basil attempts to draw a sublime distinction. On the one hand, the creatures speak to us of God, but 'no utterance at all, no speech, not a sound is to be heard' (Ps 19:3). At the same time, there is within creation 'a wisdom that shines forth in the world of visible things—a wisdom which lacks only a voice to proclaim that she was created by God. Such wisdom is by itself *(automatos)* not suitable to created things.'[115] Creatures carry some traces of God, but in the strict sense of the term they are of themselves not what one could call 'a discourse of God'. There are, hidden within beings, 'words of a primordial Wisdom', the foundations of which were built into the making of the world before all other created things'.[116] Through this sublime distinction, a comparison may be made with the famous eastern icons of the Divine Wisdom and with modern 'sophiologies'.[117] Yet this function of Wisdom is also similar to the concept of *logos* in Origen. On the one hand, *logos* is the 'rational principle' of beings; but is subsequently identified with the *Logos,* the Son of God.[118] In like manner, this 'wisdom of the world', 'created wisdom', cannot, if it is to lead us to God, remain enclosed in the limited circle of the cosmos: she transcends toward the Holy Spirit and the Son, uncreated Wisdom.[119]

For those who contemplate God by means of the 'wisdom of the world', the meaning of the *logos theoteles* is to see the intentions of Providence in a world that is deified.

### *The Eschatological Vision*

To seeing the world 'whither it tends' is to transfer the vision of what the world now is to what it is to be on the day of the Lord. One often hears of the eschatologism of the Eastern Church,[120] as if the contemplatives sought to turn away their eyes from the present world to direct all their attention to the future. It is in this sense that, for example, Joseph of Volokolamsk wrote: 'Know that you have done nothing great when you left all that is visible: heaven, earth, people. Remember that you are nothing in so far as body and soul are concerned.'[121]

Such an attitude was rightly criticized by Vladimir Soloviev as a remnant of Platonism. At the same time, this very author taught the contemplative dimension of christian eschatology masterfully.

We may summarize his thought as follows: everything that is visible to the eye can ultimately not be judged according to abstract, 'static' criteria. The meaning of each event, each thing, each thought and feeling should be discovered from a 'dynamic' perspective. That is, the present reality should be viewed as a preparation for the ultimate goal of the human person's life, the final meeting with Jesus Christ. From this vantage point, in *Three Conversations (The Story of Anti-Christ),*[122] Soloviev judges the life of various christian churches; in *The Meaning of Love*[123] he views family life eschatologically; in the treatise *The Spiritual Foundations of Life,*[124] he traces the general dynamics of the evolution of the cosmos and human history. In short, to view the present world realistically is to discover the One who is coming (ἐρχόμενος), who comes, and is to come, in whom is all truth.[125]

## THE ORGAN OF CONTEMPLATION

### *The* Nous—*The Divine Faculty*

God, being simple, embraces all that exists in one, eternal intuition. The composite structure of the human person, by contrast, contains a variety of organs correlated to their function. To enable us to see the material world, God has given us the physical eye. What is intelligible is seen by the eye of the mind.[126] And what 'organ' does man have to discover the divine reality which constitutes the object of contemplation? This was a question the mystics asked themselves frequently.[127] The question was scarcely debated in the days of the Greek Fathers, since in their circles the answer had already been given.

One need hardly point out how much greek antiquity emphasized the excellence of the mind that ascends to a knowledge of the heavenly realities : 'the true lover of knowledge is always striving after being; the keen edge [of the mind] will not be blunted until they have attained the knowledge of the true nature of every essence by a kindred power in the soul'.[128] It is thanks to such an affinity, κατὰ τὸ ξυγγενές,[129] that the soul is able to aspire to the higher world, be united with it, and find eternal blessedness in it.

God is an eternal thought which eternally thinks itself, Aristotle said.[130] In like manner, what properly belongs to the human mind, according to the neo-platonists, is that it rests in itself, and is turned inward toward itself. This is the 'pure spirit' of the Enneads, the organ or faculty capable of grasping The One.[131] The divine origin of the mind is one of the dogmas of the hermetic writings.[132] Philo made of the intellect a copy of God, either direct or indirect, which explains why we are able to contemplate things divine.[133]

In the alexandrian tradition, especially after Origen, and in the latin tradition from Hilary, Ambrose, and Augustine onwards, the *nous* and the *mens* are the locus of the image of God in man by reason of their specifically spiritual nature.[134] Consequently, the *nous* is the *locus Dei:* it is 'clear sighted' by nature *(to kata physin dioratikon);*[135] it is the organ of contemplation. 'What God is in nature and essence' wrote Gregory Nazianzus, 'will be discovered when that within us which is godlike and divine—I mean our mind and reason—shall have mingled with its Like, and the image shall have ascended to the Archetype, of which it now has the desire. . . .'[136]

## *The* Nous *Alone?*

The turn taken here by the greek intellectual tradition was a dangerous one. It is not only by the *nous* (the mind, reason) that man enters into contact with God, but it was by the *nous* alone that one is able to attain such a sublime union. Everything else is but an impurity added to man's true nature, an impurity from which one should gradually be purified. This was Plato's opinion.[137]

Evagrius, in his turn, identified 'the state of pure intelligence' (κατάστασις νοός) with 'the state of prayer' (κατάστασις προσευχής). Its highest degree—theology—he defined as: 'the state of the intellect is the intellectual peak on which shines the light of the Holy Trinity at the time of prayer'.[138] Thus, 'undistracted prayer is the highest understanding of the intellect'.[139] The Lord descends directly into the intellect to infuse into it the knowledge he pleases; human beings and demons derive their knowledge 'from the changing states of the body'.[140]

The Fathers took great pains to correct, properly understand, and christianize this platonic thesis. We can follow the gradual evolution. First, a demarcation line had to be drawn between *diatribe* (secular dialectic or argument) and spiritual vision. Next they emphasized that the contemplative *nous* is intuitive, and that it has to be purified in order to see clearly, which the philosophers also taught. Christian purification, however, is different: it goes deeper and includes the entire christian life, the *praxis* which is therefore a necessary condition of *theoria*.[141] At the same time, the mystics located the highest experience of the divine no longer on the level of the intellect, but on that of love. Finally, taking all such 'corrections' into account, the spiritual authors preferred to abandon the term *nous* / mind to return to the biblical 'heart' which better expresses all these dimensions in their unity.[142]

### *The Intuitive* Nous

Philosophy implies research, study, and reasoning; it is the object of teaching, of *diatribe* (dialectic). This is not contemplation, not according to Plato and not according to the christian mystics. During contemplation *(theoria),* Plato says, insight strikes like lightning, suddenly (ἐξαίφνης)[143]; it consists in being together, it is a kind of marriage.[144] The Stoics too distinguished between two ways of knowing God: sometimes it occurs at the end of a rational process; sometimes it is a gift, spontaneous, intuitive (πρόληψις). The latter occurs especially during sleep and ecstasy and there is a discontinuity between it and what prepares it.[145]

The Fathers knew this twofold path to God: one is 'according to knowledge', through reasoning; the other is 'not through knowledge' (ἀνεπιστημόνως), 'according to the common prolepsis'.[146] True contemplation is the revelation made to the purified intellect: it is sudden (ἐξαιφνης), effortless, without toil or technique (καμάτου χωρίς): 'In the same manner as a countryman, looking for a good place in which to plant some wild trees, unexpectedly comes upon a treasure, so will the humble, simple ascetic, his soul devoid of earthly shagginess, be like the blessed Jacob who, when asked by his father, "Son, how did you succeed so quickly?" replied, "Because Yahweh your God made things go well for me"(Gn 27:20)'. When, during contemplation, God of his own wisdom communicates to us the most learned theorems and the most intelligent reasons, without toil on our part (καμάτου χωρίς) and when we do not expect it, let us think that we have suddenly (ἐξαίφνης) found a spiritual treasure. [147]

In modern times, Theophan the Recluse explained the same experience by means of terms borrowed more or less from german idealistic philosophy. Understanding (*razsudok,* speculative reason) is capable of grasping the idea which the Divine Artist has put in the picture of creation. An appeal must be made to *razum,* a kind of 'aesthetic sense'.[148]

### *The Spiritual Senses*

Intuition pertains to the senses. Why not give this name also to the intuition of the intellect? Evagrius protested against those who wanted to exclude from the operations of the mind (*nous*) what everybody accords to the senses: the immediate apprehension of its object.[149] An analogy with the physical senses helps to explain certain subtleties which spiritual intuition experiences but is unable to express. Following Origen,[150] Evagrius states: 'The *nous* has five spiritual senses through which it sees and senses the *logoi* (reasons) of things. Sight shows the beings as objects; by hearing, it receives the words that concern them; thanks to smell, it delights in the holy scent that allows no admixture (what delights is the palate); thanks to touch, it acquires a real certainty about them.'[151]

The advocates of the 'school of feeling'[152] made subtle reflections about the particular functions of the various senses. Spiritual sight perceives the light of the Holy Trinity[153]; hearing allows one to hear the voice of divine inspiration[154]; the olfactory sense perceives the perfume of the virtues and the stench of evil and the Evil One[155]; taste discerns the goodness and sweetness of God[156]; the sense of touch gives 'certainty', as to 'doubting' Thomas (Jn 20:24ff).

There is no problem with the terminology as such. However, those who belonged to the 'intellectual' trend were quick to point out that what matters here are the senses of the mind *(nous).* Others preferred to speak of 'spiritual senses'. The Holy Spirit who sees everything (see 1 Cor 2:10) communicates his vision not only to the intellect but to the human person as such, and 'spiritualizes' all the person's faculties and entire being. To what degree? The credibility of the various 'spiritual feelings' is one of the fundamental problems of the religious experience.[157]

## *The Illuminated* Nous

The illumination of the mind is a concept which, even in philosophy, is akin to revealed religion. Despite the statements about the *nous* being a divine faculty, its best ideas come to it from outside, by an inspiration, a light, from on high.

Christians often probed Ps 35:10, 'In Thy light shall we see light'. Basil explained this by writing: 'In the illumination of the Spirit *(en tǫ photismǫ tou Pneumatos)* we shall see true light that enlightens everyone coming into the world' (Jn 1:9).[158]

The grace needed for contemplation is the light of knowledge (φώς γνώσεως), according to an expression which runs through spiritual literature.[159] John Cassian, profiting from the experience of the Desert Fathers, used the expression 'prayer of fire' for the highest degree of illumination by which God manifests himself as the consuming fire of love and the light that illumines the intellect.[160] Clement of Alexandria brings together the sacramental and the mystical characters of illumination: 'Being baptized, we are illumined; being illumined, we are children of the Father'.[161] Therefore, wrote Irenaeus, 'those who see the light are within the light', and 'those who see God are in God'.[162]

As a consequence, this light does not remain outside the eye: our human faculties are illumined inwardly. 'As the power to see is found in the healthy eye', Basil writes, 'so is the activity *(energeia)* of the Spirit in the purified soul. . . . As art resides in the one who possesses it, so the grace of the Holy Spirit [remains present] in the one who has received it.'[163] The Orthodox believe that the Holy Spirit 'operates as the inner reality of human nature',[164] though as the divine Giver, he comes from outside.[165] Thus, one understands the discussion about the nature of this light of knowledge and the hesitation expressed by Evagrius:

> Concerning this light, the servant of God Ammonios and I asked Saint John of the Thebaid whether it is the nature of the mind which is luminous and the light comes from this, or whether the mind is illumined by something from outside'. He replied to us: 'No man can settle that question; but in any case, without the grace of God the mind could not be illumined during prayer, and delivered from the numerous enemies, bent on destroying it'.[166]

## *To Understand the* Logoi, *the Human Person Must be* Logikos

The christological dimension of the divine grace needed for contemplation is expressed well by the term *logikos.*[167] Justin had already seized upon this word.[168] Having established a certain equivalence between Christ and the *logos* of the stoics, he indicates how the *Logos* (Word of God) is dispersed in humankind as 'seed of the Word' and 'seed of the Truth'.

Origen admitted openly that without an intimate union with Christ, there can be no true *gnosis*. For him, the true model of the gnostic was the apostle John, resting on the breast of Christ.[169] The term *logikos* (λογικός) therefore acquired a supernatural meaning: it expresses how 'creatures endowed with reason' *(logikoi)* partake of 'Reason' in the divine Logos. This is why it is not easy to distinguish between the *gnosis* due to human activity and that which is a gift of God, so intimately are the two elements intertwined and difficult to separate.[170]

Aside from this 'subjective' meaning expressing the participation by rational creatures in the Logos, the term *logikos* also has an 'objective' meaning: this 'reasonable food', which refers to the mysterious realities in beings who are poised on the brink of the spiritual knowledge of the world.[171] Christ, then, both is the One through whom one sees and the One who is seen in contemplation.

## *From Faith to* Gnosis

The life of light is the divine life in the human person.[172] As sanctification progresses, it increases, beginning at baptism and simple faith. According to Origen, *gnosis* is the perfection of faith.

Then 'one no longer simply believes, but one understands the religious realities with much greater insight'.[173]

Clement of Alexandria and Origen have frequently been accused of professing the same gnostic 'elitism' they combatted in heresy. This reproach is unjust because it freezes into fairly constricted 'categories' or 'classes' the continuing ascent to which every Christian is called.[174]

What is more, the progression from faith to *gnosis* does not occur in the purely intellectual realm of instruction. Only later did people attempt to reduce the christian life to the now traditional diptych, in the East as in the West: faith and works.[175] The partition has not been without its dangers. From this defective view of faith at the time of the Reformation arose pointless discussions over justification 'by faith alone'. In Saint Paul, the word 'faith' can designate the entire christian life.[176]

When Clement of Alexandria speaks of faith, he is thinking far more of life according to faith, that is, *praxis*. Those who do have faith, the faithful, are those who observe the commandments, especially charity, and so they are able to understand God-Charity.[177] For Gregory Nazianzus, a return to the faith of the Gospel after vain speculations is the *praxis* which sums up all the virtues.[178] 'Faith', Symeon the New Theologian writes, 'is to die for Christ and his commandments.'[179] From this perspective, the progression from faith to knowledge *(gnosis)* is the equivalent of the transition from *praxis* to *theoria* (contemplation).

Even so, from the outset, the element of 'knowledge' is implicit in the concept of faith, and is associated with 'wisdom'.[180] Such wisdom is the result of an illumination, a revelation. Ignatius of Antioch writes: 'There is one God, who has manifested himself through Jesus Christ his Son, who is his Word born out of silence'.[181] It is through this mystery that we have received the faith.

There exists a development in faith, for the apostles asked the Lord to increase theirs (Lk 17:5). We truly believe only if we understand. Knowledge marks a development in our understanding of the realities of faith. As perfect knowledge, *gnosis* is therefore the fulfillment of faith.[182]

But faith is the necessary beginning of knowledge. Those who do not believe, do not see.[183] *Gnosis* is 'contemplation begotten of faith'.[184] Before arriving at contemplation, the Christian is called to live by faith. The person who teaches about God *(theologos),* warns Diadochus of Photice, does not abandon the plane of faith, even if he may on occasion have the psychological sense of going beyond it.[185] *Theoria,* according to Pseudo-Denys, has as its necessary prerequisite the imitation *(mimesis)* which baptism constitutes.[186] According to Paul Evdokimov, only the 'violence' of faith is able to break the seals of the Book of Life.[187]

'Faith is the complement of reason', Gregory Nazianzus writes,[188] or rather, it frees our spirit from the blindness caused by sin.[189] For John of Damascus, the great teacher of the Orthodox faith, faith is itself a purification of the mind. By being nurtured on Scripture, the mind becomes more spiritual and reaches a purity that allows it to contemplate God.[190]

If such a statement seems 'unecumenical', let us recall an explanation given by Evagrius: 'Faith is an internal good (ἐνδιάθετον ἀγαθόν), one which is found even in those who do not yet believe in God'.[191] It exists implicitly, fundamentally, even among non-christians.

Before arriving at the vision of God, we humans are called to live by faith, with the assurance of realities which we cannot yet contemplate, but which are innate in us and unfold as we mature (1 Cor 13:11-12). Having believed in the Son, we should 'do what is beyond the faith: contemplate the Logos, and in this contemplation of the Logos contemplate the Father'.[192]

Maximus the Confessor established this scale: 'Christian philosophy has three objects: the commandments, doctrine, the faith. The commandments separate the mind from the passions; doctrine introduces it to the knowledge of creatures; faith brings it to the contemplation of the Holy Trinity.'[193]

## *The Purified* Nous

Purity, a concept common to ancient religions, was a condition required for approaching sacred realities. According to the original concept, which usually tends to be deepened, it was acquired through rites of purification and lost through contact with matter. In Scripture, the concept of purity tends to become moral.[194]

Greek philosophy insisted on purification for the sake of *theoria:* only the pure can behold the Pure.[195] The theme was taken up by the Fathers, but in a different context.[196] At first it concerned moral purification, with sin as its main target. Later, purification was to be extended to everything constituting a seduction to sin and everything following it as a consequence. Such purification is the equivalent of *praxis,* 'the spiritual method for cleansing the affective part of the soul'.[197] It therefore leads to *theoria.*

With the Fathers, *katharsis* (purification) coincided with perfection as the restoration of our original, primitive condition.[198] It therefore included the fullness of life eternal: the Mother of God who is 'most pure' is fully deified.[199] The first condition of contemplation then is purification from sin, repentance, because 'the Bridegroom does not like to mingle with an alien soul'.[200]

*Logismoi,* evil thoughts, are the fountainhead and the root of all sin.[201] So the demons who try to prevent the monks from praying strive against them 'by means of thoughts'.[202] Peaceful prayer therefore presupposes the art of fighting the enemies competently: 'If Moses, when he attempted to draw near the burning bush, was prohibited until he should remove the shoes from his feet, how should you not free yourself of every thought that is colored by passion seeing that you wish to see One who is beyond every thought and perception?'[203]

Among the *logismoi*, anger (*orge*) most disturbs the normal activity of the mind.[204] The remembrance of injuries (μνησικακία) is an obstacle to prayer.[205] On this point, the evagrian *Chapters on Prayer* merely convert into short aphorisms the doctrine which the author treats tirelessly in his other works: 'Whatever you might do by way of avenging yourself on a brother who has done you some injustice will turn into a stumbling block for you at the time of prayer'.[206] Among the other vices, melancholy, acedia, 'the noonday demon',[207] weighs on the soul of the person who prays. Such sadness 'according to the flesh'[208] is chased away by 'sadness according to God', compunction *(penthos).*[209] Hence the advice of Evagrius: 'Pray first for the gift of tears so that by means of sorrow you may soften your native rudeness. . . .'[210]

The perfect moral purification, 'the kingdom of heaven', is *apatheia,* 'passionlessness of the soul'.[211] It consists of the soul's complete immunity to the passions and the external thoughts which never cease to assail her, yet without shaking her. Prayer then becomes 'a state of the intellect which destroys all earthly thoughts'[212] or, as Gregory Nazianzus has it, the perfectly purified soul 'becomes each day more like a spotless mirror of God and of heavenly things. Light is added to light; our darkness gives way to the Light.'[213]

The ascent of the soul toward contemplation requires successive purifications, then. In the East, the moral effort at purification has traditionally been called *praxis*. And it is that which leads to *theoria*.

## *PRAXIS* LEADS TO *THEORIA*

### *Formulations*

The formulations that had become classical from Origen's time on are of two kinds[214]:

1. οὔτε γὰρ πρᾶξις οὔτε θεωρία ἄνευ θατέρου: no *praxis* without *theoria,* and no *theoria* without *praxis.*[215]
2. Πρᾶξις γὰρ θεωρίας ἀνάβασις: it is through *praxis* that one ascends to *theoria.*[216] This second axiom came somehow to be proposed as a motto by the spiritual masters.[217]

A great many equivalent expressions are found: virtues lead to knowledge;[218] the road to knowledge passes through the observance of the commandments;[219] 'spiritual knowledge is born when we begin to act from fear of God';[220] 'mystical contemplation is revealed to the mind after the soul has recovered her health';[221] and others that are similar.

The consequences of this maxim for the concept of contemplation and the entire christian life are far-reaching. For Gregory Nazianzus, it is a question no longer of reasoning about God in the manner of Aristotle (ἀριστοτελικῶς), but of being schooled by the fishermen of Galilee.[222]

Being generic, this formulation can be adapted to various levels depending on the meaning one wishes to give it. Several meanings are possible. Let us examine them one by one, without prejudging whether the authors consciously considered all the various meanings.

### *Purification Must Precede Illumination*

*Praxis*, according to the definition given by Evagrius, is 'the spiritual method for cleansing the affective part of the soul'.[223] If *praxis* is identified with purification *(katharsis)*, its priority to *theoria* is acceptable to all: Platonists, Stoics, and Christians.[224] Differences arose only when it came to determining concretely of what such a purification consisted: of the flesh, of the senses, from evil thoughts, from sin.[225] A common principle was accepted without difficulty: 'Where there is purification, there also is illumination'.[226] The vision of 'the pure light' requires a radical purification by the contemplatives.[227]

### *The Virtues Lead to Knowledge*

Practising the virtues is the positive aspect of *praxis*.[228] The Easterners insist on the importance of the virtues in coming to know God. Since only like knows like, the house of the soul should be decorated before the light of the knowledge of the divine mysteries is kindled in it.[229] It would be dangerous to venture into *theoria*, unless the virtues precede it.[230]

### *Charity Is 'the Door to* Gnosis*'*[231]

*Praxis* summarizes all the virtues. Of them, charity is the first and encompasses all. 'God is love' (1 Jn 4:8-16). And, 'without love, God cannot be apprehended',[232] 'affection being the ambassador of knowledge (τὸ φίλτρον πρόξενον . . . γνώσεως)'.[233] Evagrius claimed that, 'we do everything for the sole aim of attaining knowledge [of God]',[234] and Philoxenus of Mabbug explained that: 'Although the spiritual life of the mind is divine contemplation, Blessed Paul exclaims: I do not aspire to it outside of charity. . . .'[235]

Everyone, including Evagrius, assigned love of neighbor and of God enough of a role to safeguard orthodoxy. 'The first and greatest of the commandments is charity, thanks to which the mind sees the first love, that is, God.'[236]

In our day, some might detect in this axiom a trait typical of the East, in contrast to the 'rationalistic' West.[237] Boris Vyšeslavcev stated that 'Leonardo da Vinci's expression, "a great love is the child of a great knowledge", is prophetic of all recent intellectualizing. We Christians of the East can say the opposite, "a great knowledge is the daughter of a great love".'[238] The exhortation which precedes the recitation of the creed in the Byzantine Rite states, 'Let us love one another that with one accord we may confess, "I believe in God the Father. . . . "'

### *The Life in Christ Leads to Illumination*

The Fathers were deeply conscious of the intimate connection between one's moral behavior and one's participation in the life divine. The virtues are a measure of our deification.[239] And since we are created 'in the image', according to Christ,[240] the virtues, for Origen, became merged with Christ: He is the virtues, while we hold them in possession.[241] He is at the same time Justice, Wisdom, and Truth. This is why the practice of such virtues is a true participation in the essence of Christ.[242]

Jesus is 'the true light', and those who are attached to him through the virtues are 'illumined'. Gregory Nazianzus illustrates this: just as Moses, in order to receive but a glimpse of God, withdrew into the hollow of the rock when God passed by, to see him without being blinded, so should we seek shelter in the Rock, the Word Incarnate.[243] There is no other possibility.[244] As a consequence, the life in Christ is the indispensable *praxis* before we devote ourselves to *theoria* at any level. 'Always advancing toward the light', Gregory Nazianzus writes, 'I made for myself a rule of life, impelled by divine motions, having Christ as helper, life companion, and guide.'[245]

### *Descent* (katabasis) *Is Turned into Ascent* (anabasis)

*Praxis* is the ascent to contemplation: Πρᾶξις ἀναβασις θεωρίας. Do we realize that such an expression is a kind of oxymoron?

Indeed, *theoria* is the pre-eminent ascent *(anabasis). Praxis* expresses the reverse movement: the word of God descending from on high, emanating from the will of God and expecting fulfillment in mission. The soul's *eros* motivates the human person's upward movement. Yet we would never reach the summit if, in our effort, we did not encounter the *agape,* the love of God, which precedes us. Freely accepted in the human soul, *agape* compels us to turn back, as it were, to step down from the lofty spiritual heights to the humble realities of the flesh. But because such an abasement imitates that of Christ in his incarnation and death, it also shares, in Christ, in the mystery of his glorious resurrection and ascension. The descent *(katabasis)* then turns into an ascent *(anabasis),* one which this time leads to the desired goal, union with God. 'You want to become a theologian and worthy of the Deity? Observe the commandments, move forward in the [divine] precepts', Gregory Nazianzus advises. 'For *praxis* is the step toward contemplation.'[246]

### *From the Visible to a Knowledge of the Invisible*

How is it possible to arrive at the invisible God by means of visible creation? The problem was as crucial to ancient philosophy as the search for a formula to change base metal into gold was to medieval alchemists. Christians know this secret: the *Logos* of God becomes understandable 'through the body'.[247] *Praxis,* in Plotinus' terminology, is defined as a corporeal, 'impure', activity, that is to say, enslaved to the influences of the sensory world, tainted by the matter towards which it tends.[248] For this reason, Plotinus emphatically contrasted *theoria* to *praxis.*[249]

We know that in christian circles, the Euchites refused to perform manual, 'material', labor under the pretext of devoting themselves to prayer *(euche).*[250] Orthodox monasticism, by contrast, did not on principle eliminate manual labor; the activity of the body by means of the senses, if it is done in Christ, does not distract from, but leads to, *theoria,* the contemplation of divine realities.

### *The Whole Person Enters into Relationship with God*

In greek philosophy, *sophia* (wisdom) more and more assumed a noetic, intellectual character. In order to live well, Socrates taught, one need only think well, since virtue *(arete)* is nothing but a knowledge of the good. *Gnosis* will always have a tendency to locate human perfection in the speculative faculties which impede any spontaneity.[251] But biblical 'knowing' is a vital experience which is not tied to any particular faculty. It is an activity of the whole person.[252]

If such emphasis is put on the value of the *praxis* that leads to *theoria,* might this also stem from a reaction against the exaggerated intellectualism of greek philosophy? The spiritual life is above all a 'life', and therefore *praxis*. In 'vital', living, contemplation, all the human person's energies and faculties come into play. Prayer is a vital activity; and for prayer to be complete, the whole person must partake of it.

### *The Theology of Time and Eternity*

Greek philosophy differentiated time from eternity, as one contrasts illusion from reality. Consequently, philosophic *theoria* will attempt to escape the temporal conditions of life. Christian *praxis,* on the contrary, is preeminently historical, linked to the coming of Christ in the flesh, engaged in the present. But it leads to *theoria,* it reasserts the value of time by linking it to eternity.[253]

### *The Ascetical-Mystic Union*

To imitate Christ means to follow him on the way of the cross, of renunciation, and asceticism. In the 'mystical' state, there is a more direct union with God. The Eastern authors speak of such union when they deal with progress in *theoria*. The modern terms 'asceticism' and 'mysticism' may therefore be substituted for the older terms *praxis* and *theoria*. The ancient principle '*praxis* leads to *theoria*' is then converted into that of the ascetic-mystic union. In such a union, we correctly see 'the doctrinal foundation of all the forms of monasticism'.[254]

## THE DEGREES OF CONTEMPLATION

### *The Evagrian Scheme*

How we determine the degrees of contemplation is a relative matter, set according to what criterion we chose. Evagrius' enumeration corresponds to what may be called the 'objective' point of view; Gregory of Nyssa's follows instead a 'subjective' criterion.

Evagrius classified the vices according to their object.[255] The various contemplations he catalogued similarly, according to the reality contemplated. The ancients divided all that existed into the visible and the invisible. Consequently, Evagrius speaks of two *theoriae:* 1) that of the visible or corporeal (τῶν σωμάτων) or that of the realities perceived by the senses (τῶν αἰσθητων); 2) that of the invisible, incorporeal, intelligible realities (τῶν νοητῶν), the spiritual (τῶν πνευματικῶν).[256]

But this cosmic 'dichotomy' is not satisfactory because the God of Scripture does not belong to any of the created categories: he transcends them. A third contemplation had therefore to be added: the contemplation of the Holy Trinity *(theologia).* 'Theology' differs greatly from the inferior *theoriae.* Evagrius calls theology 'the first', while 'the second' is subdivided into that of the realities visible and invisible.[257] With this 'trichotomy', Evagrius codified a well-established tradition.[258]

What is more, he advocated a still longer list: 'There are five basic types of knowledge which contain all the others: the first, according to the Fathers, is knowledge of the blessed Trinity; the second and the third are knowledge of incorporeal and corporeal beings; the fourth and the fifth are knowledge of the judgement and of divine Providence'.[259]

Why the last two were added to the trichotomy was never clearly understood. This division is of no great historical importance, therefore, except in Maximus the Confessor.[260] Nonetheless, we can appreciate an important addition in the contemplation of judgement and of providence. While the first three are viewed from a static perspective, the fourth and fifth contemplate events in their dynamic, historical evolution. This is the point of view that best corresponds to Scripture, whose authors contemplate events and the connection between them.

In the other traditional scheme, that of Gregory of Nyssa, the degrees are differentiated not according to what is contemplated—for that is always God—but rather according to the manner by which one seeks to arrive at contemplation. Gregory explains this classification in Homily 11 on the Song of Songs: 'The manifestation of God to Moses began in the light (διὰ φωτός) later God spoke to him in a cloud (διὰ νεφέλης); and finally, after he had become more perfect, Moses saw God in the darkness (ἐν γνόφῳ)'.[261]

*Natural Contemplation*[262]

The contemplation of nature includes the ancient study of *physis* (the natural world), hence its names: θεωρία φυσική (natural contemplation), θεωρία τῶν ὄντων (contemplation of beings), τῶν γεγονότων (of the created), γνῶσις τῶν ὄντων (knowledge of beings). But such knowledge goes beyond 'physical' knowledge: the 'beings' are an object of contemplation because they lead us to God. While surveying the work of creation, Basil exclaims: 'I have seen these wonders [of nature] myself and I have admired the wisdom of God in all things'.[263]

A kind of religious knowledge of the cosmos appeared among the Stoics, who are considered the founders of an authentic deistic rationalism: the one Logos-God, immanent in the world, does not manifest himself to man by means of a revelation from the heights of an extracosmic heaven; he can be discerned from the world and his activities, especially from the harmony of the cosmos.[264] Sometimes the *Logos*-God was a rational conclusion; sometimes a spontaneous, natural given *(datum)* obtained by a knowledge that anticipates the intellectual work, some type of instinct (πρόληψις).[265]

The theological foundation of christian contemplation is different. It is not a 'cosmic religion'.[266] The Fathers never dreamed of diminishing the distance that separates the Creator from his creation. But, in its origin, the world is sustained by the creative word of the first Being; and this command, Basil says, 'remains in the earth and the earth does not cease serving the creator'.[267] Such 'service' must be coherent with the entire program of creation: the world 'provides guidance to the mind for the contemplation of the invisible, as the Apostle says (Rom 1:20)'; it is 'a training place for rational souls and a school for attaining the knowledge of God'.[268] But instead of 'God', let us say 'divine revelation', since this presents itself in different dimensions which give various colorings to natural contemplation.

### *'The Moral Exegesis' of the Cosmos*

The basilian *Homilies on the Hexaemeron* call for a continuous effort 'to have a mind trained for the consideration' of what is proposed.[269] Precisely because this is an 'outpouring of God's infinite mercy, . . . we must cling, not to the world, but to God', says John of Kronstadt.[270] One transcends the visible through an activity of the mind, which interprets, exegetes, the book of nature, and acts more or less in the same way it does in interpreting Scripture.[271]

The original trend in spirituality was 'practical'.[272] So a moral lesson was sought in everything God had revealed. With the spiritual authors, examples borrowed from nature arose out of a twofold tradition; that of debate *(diatribe)* which by preference took the creatures deprived of reason as the point of comparison, and the evangelical tradition into which the preaching of Jesus had introduced this means of exhortation. Thus, for Basil, the weeded vineyard is an image of the purified soul[273]; the cunning of the octopus, 'which assumes on every occasion the color of the rock to which it fastens itself', clarifies the baseness of those who 'adapt themselves to the needs of every occasion', and so on.[274]

We often find in the spiritual writers a curious mixture of secular erudition and scriptural overtones. As in the scriptural realm, we find, on the one hand, a tendency toward scientific rigor and, on the other, an inclination toward amiable or contrived fantasies. Hence we see a learned asceticism among the Syrians and among the heirs of Alexandria the exercises of the imagination .[275]

Let us simply add a recent passage from John of Kronstadt: 'If you wish to get pure air into your room, for example, or . . . go for a walk in the fresh air, think of the pure and of the unclean heart. . . . If you are fond of dressing elegantly, or when you put on your clothes, think of the . . . garment of righteousness'.[276]

## The Inspiration for Praising God

All the Fathers proclaimed that God can be known through his works. Let us read the opening passage of the *Apology* of Aristides: 'And when I saw that the universe and all that is therein is moved by necessity, I perceived that the mover and controller is God'.[277] 'The world makes manifest the One who ordered it', wrote Irenaeus.[278] Here the religious climate of the era is present to us. The *Corpus Hermeticum* never tires of repeating that for every educated person, the world has become the multifaceted face of God.[279]

However, the goal of the contemplatives was neither to find an apologetic proof for the existence of the Creator nor to construct abstract considerations about the divine qualities by starting from creation. What they tried above all to discover were signs of the goodness of the Father, of Providence, in order to be able to praise God.[280]

This discerning, 'dioratic', vision becomes doxological. The dioratic recognizes the divine Wisdom at work in the world and 'glorifies God'. This is a contemplation analogous to that of the apostles on Mount Tabor; it is a participation in the knowledge which God himself has of his own work: 'God saw that it was good' (Gn 1:19). Origen explains: 'All these sensible realities, including heaven and everything in it, are perhaps, if one lifts up the eyes, the fields "already white for harvest" (Jn 4:35), for the reason *(logos)* of each one clearly appears to those who, by their transformation into this image, "from glory to glory" (1 Cor 3:18), have received eyes like the ones that saw how good creation was'.[281]

## The Beauty of the World

Natural contemplation *(theoria physike)*, though essentially religious, does not promote a romantic feeling for nature. If monasteries are often found in magnificent places, we should not too hastily attribute the choice of location to artistic preoccupations.[282] Generations of monks have read, for example, the anecdote about Abba Silvanus, who covered his face after being rapt in ecstasy, and said: 'Why should I seek to see this earthly light, which is of no use?'[283]

Such austerity seems, however, to contradict what we frequently find in other texts. God himself saw that his work was beautiful (Gn 1:9—the greek word allows this double translation: good-beautiful). Basil asked, 'Why does God take pleasure in his creation?' He answered: 'Beauty is that which is brought to perfection according to the principle of art and which contributes to the usefulness of its end. Someone, therefore, who proposed to himself a clear aim for his work, having recourse to his own artistic principles, approved them individually as fulfilling his aim.'[284]

We might say that such a concept of the beautiful is too functional, too practical. But Basil's view of sensory beauty is not unique. For simple beings, beauty—like light, according to Platonists—is associated with 'joy and pleasure'.[285] As for composite beings, beauty depends on 'the symmetry of the parts',[286] which is a stoic concept.[287] But all this is not that important.

The pseudo-basilian *Commentary on Isaiah* creates a distinction, the terminology of which could be attributed to Basil only with great difficulty, even though the concept would certainly fit him. 'The one who is physical' contemplates the beauty of visible things, while 'the one who is metaphysical' recognizes the intimate reasons why such things are very beautiful.[288] The prophet weeps over those who wear themselves out from morning till night without reserving time to raise their eyes to the heavens so as, from their beauty, to arrive at a conception of their Creator.[289]

There appears to be a profound, hidden reason for such frequent considerations about the beauty of the world. Those who tend to contemplate the truth by reciting psalms reach a point when the number of formulations makes them stop. Their prayer then becomes 'monologistic', with everything contained in one simple invocation.[290] The same also holds true for those who read the book of nature. At the beginning, they struggle hard to discover ingenious analogies. Then all of creation strikes them as having one single quality—the beauty which, by directly fostering remembrance of the Creator, fills the soul with gratitude and love. Contemplation is simplified. It has become, so to speak, 'one single thought', monologistic: from the perception of sensory beauty emerges the ineffable, spiritual beauty of God.[291] 'The truly beautiful is that which surpasses human understanding and power and can be contemplated by the mind alone.'[292]

Theophan the Recluse does not deviate from this patristic thought when he says that 'aesthetic feelings' dwell in the heart which is the seat of the Spirit, and that it is through such a spiritual 'aesthetic sense' that we understand the concept which the Author of nature has willed to express in his work.[293]

## *The Contemplation of Invisible Realities*

The existence of spiritual beings—angels and demons—is one of the essential assertions in the polemic of Origen. A knowledge of these intelligible beings constitutes the summit of 'divine philosophy'. 'The study called inspective is that by which we go beyond things seen and contemplate somewhat of things divine and heavenly, beholding them with the mind alone, for they are beyond the range of bodily sight.'[294]

Knowledge of the intelligibles belongs to 'the mystery of the Resurrection to come'. But 'even now the Son is preparing our knowledge of that day and that hour'. This becomes a matter of seeing how, behind the surface of world events, the angelic forces, good and bad, struggle above us and in us. We are at stake in their wars. The battles of the people of God against idolaters symbolize 'the combats of the heavenly armies'.[295]

Closest to these invisible realities is our soul, which seems to be some type of closed battlefield where flesh and spirit are engaged in spiritual warfare.[296] 'But in the case of monks', Evagrius writes, the demons strive against them 'for the most part by means of thoughts.'[297] As a result of a long watchfulness, one acquires a special 'sense', an intuition for discerning 'spirits' and the 'reasons' for their warfare.[298] According to Diadochus of Photike, the Holy Spirit is 'the lamp' of such knowledge.[299]

It is through a knowledge of spirits, subordinated to Providence, that the spiritual person begins to understand the true meaning of events in the visible world.

Could we say that 'the contemplation of invisible realities' can be reduced in practice to being clear sighted in the discernment of thoughts? It would be better to say in the discernment of 'spirits'. In this context, 'spirit' is identical to 'thought', but by using this term we are able to place thoughts in a more profound context. Origen's remark is well founded: spiritual people discover more and more that the struggle between good and evil, fought on the battlefield of the human heart, reflects the struggle of Jesus against the Enemy.

An eloquent example is provided by the personal development of Vladimir Soloviev. We may distinguish three periods in his life. At the beginning, he believed that it was enough to explain Christianity well so everyone would accept it. Then he realized that in order to say 'yes' to a message, people need a long, careful education. In the third period of his life, marked by visions of the devil, Soloviev professed that in order to choose God, man must fight the Evil One who resists Christ everywhere. Those who see this are few.[300]

### *The Contemplation of Providence*[301]

Our lives, marked by human weakness and inconstancy, are littered with aborted projects and decisions poorly kept. All of Scripture testifies to the fulfillment of God's plan in history.[302] The face of God is that of a Father who watches over his creation. It is this aspect which the word Providence evokes,[303] a word which has no equivalent in Hebrew and for designating which the Greek uses πρόνοια (forethought, care) only twice.[304] Yet the prophets continually proclaim the sovereignty of God, who knows eternally everything that will happen (Is 44:7), whose 'outstretched arm made the earth' (Jer 27:5ff), in whose hands is the government of the earth, and whose creation 'exults in discharging his orders' (Si 10:4; 39:31).

The Fathers had to defend God's fatherly providence against the fatalistic 'physical concatenation' of which the Stoics spoke.[305] Some, the more philosophical, understood the difficulty of explaining this mystery of God's personal activity despite the necessary laws of nature.[306] But the spiritual authors knew that one does not succeed in proving Providence through argumentation: it has to be experienced, 'touched', 'felt' in one's personal life and recognized in the entire march of history.

The contemplation of providence often inspired the meditations of coptic authors. Already in ancient Egypt, wisdom was viewed as a discovery of the benevolent attitude of God, beyond the cosmic order celebrated in religion by formal rites. 'He governs the people, the flock of God, for he made heaven and earth for their benefit; for them he chased away the water monster; he made the air so that their nostrils live.'[307]

Furthermore, treatises 'On Providence' proliferated also in greek literature at the time of Clement of Alexandria. Their apologetic tone was mixed with a living spiritual experience.

Knowing the ways of Providence was particularly necessary to spiritual fathers in guiding others. The name 'prophet' was added to the name of certain great directors of souls.[308] They often possessed the charisma of διόρασις, vision through space or matter, and of προόρασις, vision through time.[309] Their clear-sightedness was due to a special intervention of God but it was also associated, by natural linkage, with purity of soul, as Gregory of Nyssa specifically explained.[310]

Can this art be learned? Certainly, no one would deny the need for illumination from on high. In addition, the reading of Scripture presents on every page reflections which show the hand of God in everything that happens. In the story of Joseph, for example, we see the mysterious activity of God who makes even what is evil serve his plan of salvation: 'The evil you planned to do me has by God's design been turned to good, to bring about the present result: the survival of numerous people (Gn 50:20).'

Reading the history of Israel is an exercise which can teach us how to read the history of our own life. The examination of conscience[311] should therefore not be limited to a mechanical scrutiny of our actions against the principles of a static morality. Rather, it is the art of reading the events and encounters of each day spiritually; of not ending the day until we have understood its meaning by contemplating the divine intentions (θεῖα θελήματα) whether in our virtues or our faults.

## *Contemplation of Judgment*

Providence and judgment are one and the same reality seen from two different points of view or at two distinct stages.[312] The Providence of God becomes judgment, punishment for sin, without ceasing to be providence for the sinner. Belief in the judgment of

God is a fundamental given of religion. Having control over the events, God could not fail to guide them so that the wicked will be punished (cf. Gn 18:23ff).'

The essential element of christian repentance is the acknowledgment of one's sins and self-condemnation,[313] an envisioning of the fear of God and his judgments. The realization that such judgments are carried out already here on earth is a special grace that leads to a conversion of heart. By way of example we may cite the reflection of Joseph's brothers: 'Clearly, we are being punished for what we did to our brother' (Gn 42:21).

To someone who views life's sufferings from this angle, divine punishments are like a new theophany which suits the sinner because they awaken in him the fear of God and at the same time implement the forgiveness of sins, 'deliver us from faults, and are a cause of justification'.[314] The meaning of this judgment differs considerably from Origen to Evagrius. One of the weakest aspects of Origenism is that it views our earthly existence as a judgment already passed on sins committed in the astral world.[315]

## Theologia

The word *theologia* seems to have appeared for the first time in Plato,[316] in the sense of a discourse on the gods, as distinct from *metereologia,* a discourse dealing with heavenly matters which are not divine.[317] The first is essentially the domain of poets, the second of sages.[318] In the writings of Aristotle, mythical discourse on the gods became more and more a science or a philosophy, the object of which is the divine Being. It finds its crowning achievement in the rational science of God, the unmoved mover of the first heaven.[319] For Plutarch,[320] ϑεολογικὴ φιλοσοφία constitutes one of the three essential divisions of philosophy, alongside dialectic-rhetoric and ethics-politics. Thus, the word has a rational, one would say, secular meaning.

The term *theologia* recurs frequently in the writings of Gregory Nazianzus.[321] For him, the true 'theologians' are those greatly favored by God: Moses, Elijah, and Paul.[322] To the person who, following their example, wants to become 'a theologian worthy of the divinity', Gregory gives this advice: 'Observe the commandments; move forward in the precepts of God'.[323] Access to the mountain of theology is off limits to the impure,[324] to the constructs of purely human reasoning, to mere disputation *(technydrion)*.[325] As a consequence, theology is acquired by *praxis*, 'the contemplation of heavenly things'.[326] To Christians, 'heavenly things' are revealed by the Son. In *Oration Twenty-eight,* Gregory contrasts *theologia* to the *blasphemia* of those who refuse the divine prerogative of the Word of God.[327] To be a theologian is to be the 'herald of God',[328] in the specifically christian sense of proclaiming the divinity of Christ.[329] Gregory felt that he was bringing the same testimony and claimed for himself the title *theologos,* theologian.[330]

In the eastern tradition, John the Evangelist is called *Theologos* because at the beginning of his gospel he testifies to the divinity of the *Logos*.[331] He thereby introduces us into the mystery of the Holy Trinity, into the contemplation of the pre-eminent 'heavenly things'. It follows that for Evagrius, theology is the highest degree of *theoria,* 'the contemplation of the Holy Trinity'.[332] Even so, it is not easy to explain what such contemplation consists of. The mystics will be able to tell us something about this.

## *The Heavenly Vision*

*Theoria* will reach its perfection only in the beatitude of heaven. On earth it will always remain imperfect. Here below we do not see God in his true essence, but only 'according to our economy'.[333] With rare exceptions, the Fathers did not conceive of the possibility of a real anticipation of seeing God face to face.[334]

Here below, the nature of this 'face to face' vision remains a mystery. Eastern theological reflection, even with the developments brought to it by the palamite controversy, does not seek to lift the veil. Is the heavenly *theoria* different from the earthly? We would like to know this, but the texts are not explicit about it. Besides that, it is difficult to interpret a doctrinal orientation which is neither fully homogeneous nor coherent, though its constant preoccupation has been to safeguard the transcendence of God. What is more, certain biblical passages that are particularly significant—such as 1 Jn 3:2 ('we shall be like him, for we shall see him as he is')—are missing from the antiochian canon.[335]

Whatever these differences, some essential themes should be remembered. First, the transcendence of the beatific vision when compared to our terrestrial experience of the spirit on earth.[336] The boundary line is less pronounced among the Antiochians, to the extent that their theology—even when it brings in the contemplation of the glorified humanity of Christ[337]—seems to dwell by preference on the quantitative aspect of the beatific vision rather than on its qualitative: on 'knowing more' rather than 'knowing differently'. And it seems inclined to understand such a vision in terms of our knowledge here below. The alexandrian tradition, by contrast, presents a praiseworthy effort to think of beatitude in terms of the ultimate vocation of the spiritual being. Vision is then a term of reference which is able to enlighten the faith and bring out its provisional structures.[338] Actually, the two trends correspond to the two different aspects of christian eschatology: the world to come will be 'the same' world and also 'an other'.

## *Notes*

1. Basil, *Homilia de fide,* 1; PG 31:464BC.
2. Antoine Guillaumont, 'Messaliens', DSp 10 (1980) 1074–1083.
3. See p. 319.
4. Ernst Benz, *Die Ostkirche im Lichte der protestantische Geschichtsschreibung von der Reformation bis zur Gegenwart* (Munich, 1952) 181. *A Systematic Handbook,* 328ff.
5. *Conferences,* 1.8; SCh 42:81; ACW 58:47; CWS, 43; LNPF 11:298.
6. *Ibid.*
7. Irénée Hausherr, *Les leçons d'un contemplatif. Le traité de l'Oraison d'Évagre le Pontique.* (Paris, 1960); *Evagrius Ponticus: The Praktikos and Chapters on Prayer,* CS 54 (Kalamazoo: Cistercian Publications, 1970).
8. Evagrius, *Centuries* 1.50; Frankenberg, 91. *Centuries* 1.87;123.
9. *Centuries* 1.86;123. See Maximus the Confessor, *Capitum de charitate centuria* 1.1;PG 90:961A; translated Polycarp Sherwood, *St. Maximus the Confessor: The Ascetic Life. The Four Centuries on Charity,* ACW 21 (1955).
10. John of Damascus, *Homilia in transfigurationem Domini* 20; PG 96:576Aff, see 585D.
11. *Ibid.,* 10:561B. Gregory Nazianzus, *Oratio* 16.9, *In patrem tacentem;* PG 35:945C; LNPF, ser. 2, 7:247ff. Evagrius, *Capita practica ad Anatolium* 1.3; PG 40:1121D; translated E. Kadloubovsky and G. E. H. Palmer, 'To Anatolius: Texts on Active Life', *Early Fathers from the Philokalia* (London, 1963) 98ff. Maximus the Confessor, *Ambiguorum liber;* PG 91:1088A.
12. Gregory Nazianzen, *Oratio* 21.2; PG 35:1084C; LNPF, ser. 2, 7:269ff.
13. *A Systematic Handbook,* 185ff.

14. Maximus the Confessor, *Centuries* 3.34; SCh 9; ACW 21:179.
15. Tomaš Špidlík, *Grégoire de Nazianze,* 75.
16. See Michel d'Herbigny, *Un Newman russe, Vladimir Soloviev* (1853–1900). (Paris, 1911) 170 ; translated by A. M. Buchanan, *Vladimir Soloviev: A Russian Newman* (London, Washbourne, 1918). Soloviev, *Works* (St Petersburg, n.d.) vol. IV:1–5.
17 *Novella* 133.
18. Louis Leloir, *Paterica armeniaca* 10,.44; CSCO 37:20.
19. *Stromata* 1.16; Staehlin 2,12,13; ANF 2:299ff.
20. G. Rudberg, 'Hellenistisches Schauen', *Classica et Mediaevalia* 5 (1942) 1599–1586. Gerhard Kittel, *'akouô,* Kittel 1 (1964) 216–220. G. Michaelis, 'ὁράω', Kittel 5 (1967) 315–382.
21. See p. 159.
22. André-Jean Festugière, *Contemplation et vie contemplative selon Platon* (Paris, 1953) 28.
23. O. Procksch, in Kittel 4 (1967) 4.
24. Rolf Goegler, *Zur Theologie des biblischen Wortes bei Origenes* (Dusseldorf, 1963) 28.
25. P. van der Aalst, 'Contemplation et Hellénisme', *Proche-Orient Chrétien* 14 (1964) 151–168.
26. *Ethical Discourses,* 3.253; SCh 122:409; translated Alexander Golitzin, *St Symeon the New Theologian: On the Mystical Life. The Ethical Discourses,* (New York, 1995) Vol. 1:127.
27. *Ibid.,* 231ff; SCh 407; Golitzin,125.
28. Tomaš Špidlík, 'L'idéal du monachisme basilien', in P.J. Fedwick, *Basil of Caesarea: Christian, Humanist, Ascetic.* (Toronto, 1981) 361–374.
29. See Špidlík, *Grégoire de Nazianze,* OCA 189 (Rome, 1971) 1–13.
30. Henri Crouzel, *Origène et la 'connaissance mystique,'* (Desclée de Brouwer, 1961) 375ff.
31. *Ibid.,* 378.
32. *Ibid.,* 41.
33. *Ibid.,* 389ff.
34. See Varro, *De lingua latina, lib.* 6. Pauly-Wissowa, *Real-Encyclopädie der classischen Altertumswissenschaft,* (Zweite Reihe, 9. Halbband [1934]) s.v., *templum,* 480–485.
35. René Arnou, DSp 2/2:1717.
36. *Nicomachean Ethics,* I.5,1095a.
37. André-Jean Festugière, *Contemplation et vie contemplative selon Platon* (Paris, 1936) 42ff.
38. *Ibid.,* 95ff.
39. J. Lemaitre, in DSp 2/2:1811.
40. Aristotle, *Nicomachean Ethics,* I.5, 1095.
41. Irénée Hausherr, 'Τήν θεωρίαν ταύτην', *Bolletino di Regina Mundi,* no. 11:10–17. *Idem, Hésychasme et prière,* OCA 176 (Rome, 1966) 247–253.
42. Lemaitre, in DSp 2/2:1762.
43. *Ibid.,* 1763.
44. J. Dupont, *Gnosis. La connaissance religieuse dans les Epîtres de saint Paul,* 2nd ed. (Louvain-Paris, 1960). Pierre-Thomas Camelot, 'Gnose chrétienne', DSp 6:509–523. Henri Crouzel, *Origène et la 'connaissance mystique'.* (Desclée de Brouwer, 1961).
45. Stromata 3.44; Stählin 2: 216, 20. André Mehat, *Étude sur les 'Stromates' de Clément d'Alexandrie* (Paris, 1966) 421–488.
46. Jean Corbon and Albert van Hoye, 'Know', DBT, 296–299.

47. Walther Voelker, *Der wahre Gnostiker nach Clemens Alexandrinus,* TU 57 (Berlin, 1952).

48. *The Republic* VII.532C.

49. Pseudo-Plutarch (*De musica* 27) makes *theos* the root of both *theorein* and *theatron,* the theater having been intended originally to honor the gods. This false etymology was still used in the fourteenth century by Callistus Cataphygiotes (*De vita contemplativa* 2 and 19; PG 147:836B, 859B). The strongest justification Denys brings to his theory of *thea* or *theoria* apparently lies in the eytmology he proposes of *theos, theotes*: *theotes de he panta theomene pronoia kai . . . panta peritheousa* (*De divinis nominibus,* PG 3:696C).

50. See p. 190.

51. *Chapters on Prayer* 60; PG 79:1180B; Hausherr, *Leçons,* 85; CS 4:65.

52. *A Systematic Handbook,* 336.

53. Špidlík, *Grégoire de Nazianze,* 2ff.

54. *The Odyssey* XII, v. 192.

55. Festugière, *Contemplation* (Paris, 1936) 28.

56. *Politics,* 273d.

57. *Alcibiades* II, 990.

58. Gregory Nazianzen, *Oratio* 38-*In theophania,* 10; PG 36:321B; LNPF, ser. 2, 7:348.

59. See p. 283.

60. H. Diels, *Die Fragmente der Vorsokratiker,* 4th ed. (Berlin, 1912) 2:36, 4ff.

61. *Symposium,* 210e–212a.

62. *Ambigua;* PG 91:1341D.

63. Špidlík, *La sophiologie,* 8ff.

64. Špidlík, *Grégoire de Nazianze,* 3ff.

65. *Enneads* II.2.5.

66. *See Tusculan Disputations,* 5.3. 8–9.

67. *Oratio* 27-*Theologica* I.2; PG 36:13B; LNPF, ser. 2, 7:285.

68. *The Life of Moses;* PG 44:377; SCh 1bis: 82; Malherbe and Ferguson, CWS and CS 31:96.

69. *Oratio* 28-*Theologica* 2.15; PG 36:45C; LNPF, ser. 2, 7:293ff.

70. See J. Lemaitre, DSp 2/2 (1953) 1802ff, and Jean Kirchmeyer, DSp 6 (1967) 847.

71. Evagrius, *Centuries,* 6.2; ed. Guillaumont, PO 28:216.

72. Clement of Alexandria, *Stromata* 3.5. 44; GCS 2:126; PG 8:1148B; ANF volume 2.

73. J. Lemaitre, DSp 2/2 (1953) 1811ff.

74. *De congressu,* 9.46. See the translation of F. H. Colson and G. H. Whitaker: *Philo* (Cambridge: Harvard University Press, 1949) 481: 'No knowledge is profitable to the possessors through the mere theory *(theoria psile)* if it is not combined with practice'

75. See p. 177.

76. *Homilia* 42.1; PG 34:769D; Maloney, CWS 218–219.

77. 'Vie de Syméon the Nouveau Théologien', *Orientalia Christiana* 12 (Rome, 1928), lxv. See Lemaitre, DSp 2/2 (1953) 1802ff.

78. See Justin, *Apologia I pro Christianis,* 39.3; PG 6:388B; translated Leslie W. Barnard, *St. Justin Martyr. The First and Second Apologies,* ACW 56 (New York, 1997).

79. *Centuries* 4.90.

80. *Epistola* 62; Frankenberg, 611.

81. Ed. M. Kmosko, *Patrologie syriaque,* vol. 3 (Paris, 1926) 777; translated Robert Kitchen and Martien Parmentier, *The Book of Steps: The* Syriac Liber Graduum, CS 196 (Kalamazoo: Cistercian Publications, 2004); partial translation by Sebastian Brock, *The Syriac Fathers on Prayer and the Spiritual Life* (Kalamazoo: Cistercian Publications, 1987) 41–61.

82. Špidlík, '"Fous pour le Christ"'. DSp 5 (1964) 752–761. Guy Oury, 'Idiota'. DSp 7/2 (1970) 1242–1248.

83. Maximus the Confessor, *Ad Thalassium, quaestio* 32; PG 90:372BC. Pseudo-Denys, *The Divine Names,* 2; PG 3:637C; Luibheid, *Pseudo-Dionysius: The Complete Works,* CWS, 58ff.

84. Ilias the Ekdidos, *Anthologion gnomikon* 157; PG 90:1437B and PG 127:1156A;, translated G. E. H. Palmer, Philip Sherrard, and Kallistos Ware 'A Gnomic Anthology' (selections) in *The Philokalia. The Complete Text,* 3 (London, 1984) 34ff.

85. Origen, *On the Song of Songs, prologue;* PG 3:73A; GCS 8:5; ACW 26:21ff.

86. Origen, *Homilia in Isaias,* 9; GCS 8:298, 20.

87. *Questiones ad Thalassium,* 65:PG 90:744ff.

88. *Ibid.,* 745D.

89. *Ibid.,* 372BC.

90. See Henri de Lubac, *Histoire et Esprit. L'intelligence de l'Écriture d'après Origène,* coll. Théologie 16 (Paris, 1950) 336ff.

91. *Contra Celsum,* 6.6; GCS 2:130, 20. *Ibid.,* 7.7;141, 22. ANF 4:575.

92. *Commentarium in Ioannem,* 19.22; GCS 4:324, 11; translated Ronald Heine, *Commentary on the Gospel According to John,* FCh 80 and 89.

93. *Ibid.,* 13.42; GCS 268,17.

94. Henri Crouzel, *Origène et la 'connaissance mystique'* (Paris-Bruges, 1960) 54ff.

95. *Commentary on John* 5.5; GCS 4:102, 29.

96. Origen, 'Fragmentum In Eph. VI', *The Journal of Theological Studies* 3 (1902) 241.

97. Henri de Lubac, *Histoire et Esprit* (above, n. 90), 336–373.

98. *On Leviticus, homily* 5.2; GCS 6:337.

99. *Commentary on John,* 5.5; GCS 4:102.

100. *Contra Celsum,* 5.42; GCS 2:461, 13; ANF 4:562.

101. Špidlík, *La sophiologie de S. Basile,* OCA 162 (Rome, 1961) 6ff.

102. *Homily 7 on the Hexamaeron,* 4; PG 29:157A; SCh 26:413; translated Agnes C. Way, *Saint Basil: Exegetic Homilies,* FCh 46 (1963).

103. *Homilia in psalmum* 28.3; PG 29:289B.

104. *Homily 9 on the Hexamaeron,* 2; PG 29:189C; SCh 26:483ff; FCh 46:136.

105. *Homily 2 on the Hexamaeron,* 7; 45BC; SCh 173ff; FCh 32ff.

106. *Ibid.,* 5, 1; 96A; 279. *Ibid.,* 5, 2; 97B; SCh, 285; FCh 67.

107. *Ibid.,* 7, 1; 148BC; SCh 393; LNPF 8:90.

108. *Ibid.,* 5, 4; 101C; SCh 293; FCh 71.

109. See Maximus the Confessor, *Questiones ad Thalassium,* 32; PG 90:372BC. See also Pseudo-Denys, *De divinis nominibus, cap.* 2; PG 3:637C [See above, note 83]. J. Lemaitre, DSp 2/2 (1953) 1818ff.

110. Basil, *Homily 7 on the Hexamaeron,* 4; PG 29:157A; SCh 26: 413; FCh 46:111ff.

111. Špidlík, *La sophiologie,* 27ff.

112. Basil, *Homily 7 on the Hexamaeron,* 4; PG 29:157A; SCh 26:409; FCh 46:111ff.

113. Symeon Metaphrastes, *Sermo 22—De Providentia* (a collection of texts by Basil); PG 32:1373A.

114. *Homilia in principium proverbiorum,* 3; PG 31:392A.

115. *Ibid.*

116. *Ibid.;* 392B.

117. See *A Systematic Handbook,* 129, 382.

118. Margherite Harl, *Origène et la fonction révélatrice du Verbe Incarné* (Paris, 1959) 129.

119. Špidlík, *La sophiologie,* 193ff.

120. *Systematic Handbook,* 65ff.
121. *Prosvetitel'* (Kazan, 1857) 370.
122. See *Trois Entretiens (L'Antéchrist)* (Paris, 1916).
123. *Smysl ljuibvi* [Works], 2nd ed., n.d. (rpt Brussels, 1966) 7:3–60; translated Jane Marshall, *The Meaning of Love* (London: Geoffrey Bles, 1946).
124. *Les fondements spirituels de la vie, Oeuvres,* vol. 3:299–430; translated Donald Attwater, *God, Man and the Church: The Spiritual Foundations of Life* (London, 1938). See Špidlík, 'Solov'ëv', *La mistica . . .* (Rome, 1984) 645–668.
125. Olivier Clément, *Transfigurer le temps* (Neuchâtel-Paris, 1959) 99.
126. Špidlík, *Théophane le Reclus,* 296.
127. Aimé Solignac, '"Nous" et "Mens"'. DSp 11 (1982) 459–469.
128. Plato, *The Republic,* VI, 490ab. *Ibid.,* VII, 519b, 522d. *Symposium,* 211de. *Phaedrus,* 247c.
129. *Phaedo,* 79a–81a; 84b. *Symposium* 212a.
130. *Metaphysics* 12.7.9; cf. translation of Hugh Tredennik, Loeb Classical Library (Cambridge, Mass.: Harvard University Press, 1962) 151, 165: Throughout eternity is the divine thought which has *itself* for its object.
131. *Enneads* IV.8.8; V. 1.10, VI.9.3. René Arnou, *Le désir de Dieu dans la philosophie de Plotin,* 2nd ed. (Rome, 1967) 233.
132. André-Jean Festugiere, *La révélation d'Hermès Trismégiste,* vol. 2 (Paris, 1936) 542ff.
133. *Ibid.,* 558–561.
134. *A Systematic Handbook,* 59ff.
135. Pseudo-Macarius (Macarius Aegyptius, Macarius the Egyptian), *Homily* 25.10; PG 34:673C; Maloney, CWS, 163f. See A. Schneider, 'Der Gedanke der Erkenntnis des Gleichen durch Gleiches in antiker und patristischer Zeit', *Beiträge zur Geschichte der Philosophie des Mittelalters,* Supplementsband 2 (1923) 65ff.
136. *Oratio* 28.17; PG 36:48C; LNPF, ser. 2, 7:288ff. See *Carminum liber* 2. I.17, v. 35; PG 37:1264.
137. *The Republic,* VII, 532C.
138. *Centuries,* Suppl. 4. Irénée Hausherr, *Les leçons d'un contemplatif* (Paris, 1960) 53.
139. Evagrius, *On Prayer*, 34a; Hausherr, 52; CS 4: 60.
140. *Ibid.;* 63; CS 4:65.
141. See p. 177.
142. See p. 250.
143. *Symposium,* 210e. *Letter* VII, 341cd.
144. *Symposium,* 211dff. *The Republic* VI, 4490. See Plotinus, *Enneads* V.3.17; V.5.7.
145. Michel Spanneut, *Le stoïcisme des Pères de l'Église* (Paris, 1957) 206ff.
146. *Ibid.*
147. Maximus the Confessor, *Centuries* 1.17; PG 90:1089AB. See Lemaitre, DSp 2/2 (1953) 1821ff.
148. Špidlík, *Théophane le Reclus,* 22ff.
149. Among the letters of Basil, *Epist.* 8.12; PG 32:265D; translated Agnes C. Way, *Saint Basil. Letters,* FCh 13.
150. Karl Rahner, 'Le début d'une doctrine des cinq sens spirituels chez Origène', RAM 13 (1932) 113–145. Michel Olphe-Gaillard, 'Le sens spirituel dans l'histoire de la spiritualité', *Nos sens et Dieu,* Études Carmélitaines (Desclée de Brouwer, 1954) 179–193.
151. *Centuries* 2.35; Frankenberg, 155. See DSp 2/2 (1953) 1843.
152. *A Systematic Handbook,* 20ff, 74ff.
153. See *Evagrius Ponticus: The Praktikos. Chapters on Prayer,* CS 4 (1970) Introduction, xc.

154. Symeon the New Theologian, *Ethical Discourses* 2, 243ff; SCh 122: 409; translated Alexander Golitzin, *St Symeon the New Theologian. On the Mystical Life: The Ethical Discourses,* 1:83ff.
155. *Life of Antony,* 63; PG 26:933A; translated Vivian and Athanassakis, CS 202:190–191.
156. See Ps 33:9. See Jozef G. Ziegler, *Dulcedo Dei. Ein Beitrag zur Theologie der griechischen und lateinischen Bibel* (Münster, 1937), and Pierre Adnès, 'Goût spirituel'. DSp 6 (1967) 626–644.
157. *A Systematic Handbook,* 72ff.
158. *On the Holy Spirit,* 8; PG 26:573–576. See Athanasius, *Epistola prima ad Serapionem;* PG 26:573–576; translated C. R. B. Shapland, *The Letters of Saint Athanasius Concerning the Holy Spirit* (London-New York, 1951). See also Gregory of Nazianzus, *Oratio* 31.3; PG 36:136BC; LNPF, ser. 2, 7:319.
159. Leon Veuthey, 'Illumination'. DSp 7 (1971) 1330–1346.
160. Michel Olphe-Galliard, 'Contemplation'. DSp 2/2 (1953) 1923–1925.
161. *Paedagogi.* I.6.31; PG 8:288; translated Simon P. Wood, *Clement of Alexandria: Christ the Educator,* FCh 23 (1954).
162. *Adversus haereses,* 4.5; PG 7:1035B; ANF 5, 9; translated F. R. Montgomery Hitchcock, *The Treatise of Irenaeus of Lugdunum Against the Heresies,* 2 vols. (London, 1916); translated D. J. Unger and J. J. Dillon, *Saint Irenaeus of Lyons Against the Heresies,* vol. 1, ACW 55 (New York: Paulist).
163. *On the Holy Spirit,* 26; PG 32:180C; SCh 17:226.
164. Paul Evdokimov, 'L'Esprit Saint et l'Église d'après la tradition liturgique', *L'Esprit Saint et l'Église,* Actes du symposium . . . (Paris: Fayard, 1969) 98.
165. *A Systematic Handbook,* 32ff.
166. *Antirrheticon, acedia* 16; Hausherr, *Les leçons d'un contemplatif* (Paris, 1960) 47.
167. Henri Crouzel, *Origène et la 'connaissance mystique'* (Bruges, 1960) 45ff. *Idem, Théologie de l'image de Dieu chez Origène* (Paris, 1956) 159ff.
168. Spanneut, *Le stoïcime,* 317.
169. Walther Völker, *Das Volkommenheitsideal des Origenes* (Tübingen, 1931) 90.
170. Karl Rahner, 'Le début d'une doctrine des sens spirituels chez Origène', *RAM* 13 (1932) 134.
171. Crouzel, *Origène,* 45.
172. Špidlík, *Grégoire de Nazianze,* 19.
173. *Comment. in Joannem,* 20.32 (26); GCS 4:362; translated Ronald E. Heine, *Origen. Commentary on the Gospel according to John,* Books 13–32, FCh 89. Crouzel, *Origène,* 449.
174. Crouzel, *Origène,* 474ff.
175. Špidlík, *Joseph de Volokolamsk,* 4ff.
176. For example, Rom 3:24–4:16.
177. See *Stromata* 5.13; GCS 2:334, 17; ANF 2:444ff.
178. Špidlík, *Grégoire de Nazianze,* 122ff.
179. *Capita practica et theologica,* 1.10; PG 120:604A; translated by Paul [John] McGuckin, *Symeon the New Theologian. The Practical and Theological Chapters,* CS 41 (Kalamazoo: Cistercian Publications, 1982) 35.
180. Col 1:9, 2:2-3. Eph 3:17-9. 2 Cor 4:6.
181. *To the Magnesians* 8.2–9.1; ANF 1:59ff.
182. Crouzel, *Origène,* 448.
183. *Ibid.,* 499.
184. Origen, *Fragmenta in Matt.,* 464; GCS 12:191.

185. *De perfectione* 91; SCh 5bis:153; translated G. E. H. Palmer, Philip Sherrard, and Kallistos Ware, 'On Spiritual Knowledge and Discrimination: One Hundred Texts', *The Philokalia. The Complete Text,* 1 (London: Faber and Faber, 1979) 289–290.
186. *The Ecclesiastical Hierarchy,* 1 and 2; PG 3:392C; Luibheid (above note 83), CWS, 195–208.
187. *La femme et le salut du monde* (Tournai-Paris, 1958) 14; translated by Anthony P. Gythiel, *Woman and the Salvation of the World* (Crestwood, New York: St. Vladimir's Seminary Press, 1994).
188. *Oratio* 29-*theologica* 3.21; PG 36:104A; LNPF, ser. 2, 7:301ff.
189. Jérome Gaïth, *La conception de la liberté chez Grégoire de Nysse* (Paris, 1953) 142ff.
190. *Dialectica* 1; PG 94:529A–532D; ed. Kotter, 53–55.
191. *Praktikos* 81; SCh 171: 671; CS 4:36. See Clement of Alexandria, *Stromata* 7.10.55; GCS 17:40, 25–27. Athanasius, *Life of Antony,* 77; PG 26:952A; CS 202:220–221.
192. Origen, *Fragmenta in Ioannem,* 93; GCS 4:556, 9.
193. *Century* 4.47; SCh 9:162; ACW 21:199.
194. Ladislas Szabó, 'Pur', VTB, 1068–1074; 'Pure', DBT, 477–479.
195. Plato, *Phaedo* 66d, 67bc, 70a. See René Arnou, *Le désir de Dieu dans la philosophie de Plotin* (2nd ed., Rome, 1967) 139ff.
196. *A Systematic Handbook,* 183.
197. Evagrius, *Praktikos,* 78; SCh 171:667; CS 4:36.
198. *A Systematic Handbook,* 183.
199. Maricio Gordillo, *Mariologia orientalis,* OCA 141 (Rome, 1954) 111ff.
200. Gregory Nazianzus, *Carminum liber,* 2. 45, v. 45; PG 37:1356.
201. Origen, *Commentary on Matthew,* 21; GCS 40:58; ANF 4:409–512. *A Systematic Handbook,* 248ff.
202. Evagrius, *Praktikos* 48; SCh 171:609; CS 4:29.
203. Evagrius, *Chapters on Prayer,* 4; Hausherr, 18; CS 4:56.
204. *A Systematic Handbook,* 252ff.
205. *Praktikos* 26; SCh 171: 561; CS 4:23. John Climacus, *Scala paradisi,* 9; PG 88:8400; CWS, 152.
206. *Chapters on Prayer,* 13; Hausherr, 28; CS 4:57.
207. *A Systematic Handbook,* 252ff.
208. *Ibid.,* 252.
209. *Ibid.,* 193ff.
210. *Chapters on Prayer,* 5; Hausherr, 19; CS 4:56.
211. *Ibid.,* 52; Hausherr 57; CS 4:63. *A Systematic Handbook,* 270ff.
212. *Cent.,* Suppl. 30; Hausherr, *Les leçons,* 77.
213. *Oratio* 20.1; PG 35:1065B.
214. See J. Lemaitre, in DSp 2/2 (1953) 1802.
215. *In Lucam fragmenta,* 39; ed. Rauer, GCS 9:252, 2. The same idea is contained in *Selecta in psalmos, Ps.,* 5.13; PG 12:1173.
216. *In Lucam homelia,* 1; Rauer, GCS 9:9–10. See Plotinus, *Enneads,* 3.8, and the note by Bréhier, 152. See René Arnou, *Le désir de Dieu dans la philosophie de Plotin* (2nd ed., Rome, 1967) 87.
217. Gregory Nazianzus, *Oratio* 20.12; PG 35:1080. Cassian, *Conferences,* 14.9; PL 49:696ff; SCh 54 (1958) 192ff; ACW 58:512; LNPF 11:438–439. *Scientia actualis* (practical knowledge) is a preparation for *scientia theoretica* (spiritual knowledge). See also Nicephorus, *De sobrietate et cordis custodia;* PG 147:948A; translated E. Kadloubovsky and G. E. H. Palmer, 'A Most Profitable Discourse on Sobriety and the Guarding of the

Heart', *Writings from the Philokalia on Prayer of the Heart* (London, 1979) 22ff, and Abba Philemon, in the *Philokalia, 2* (Athens, 1958) 250, 39; *The Philokalia, The Complete Text,* 2:349.

218. Origen, *Commentary on Matthew,* 12.14; GCS 10: 96, 30; ANF volume 4. Evagrius, *Praktikos* 90; SCh 171:691; CS 4:38–39.

219. John the Solitary (Pseudo-John of Lycopolis), *Dialogue sur l'âme et les passions des hommes,* edited and translated by Irénée Hausherr, OCA 120 (Rome, 1939) 32ff.

220. Isaac of Nineveh, *De perfectione religiosa,* Syriac edition by Paul Bedjan (Paris-Leipzig, 1909) 320; see 'Faith and Knowledge', in Hilarion Alfeyev, *The Spiritual World of Isaac the Syrian,* CS 175 (Kalamazoo: Cistercian Publications) 256ff.

221. Philoxenus of Mabbug, see Irénée Hausherr, 'Contemplation et sainteté', *RAM* 14 (1933) 186; *idem,* Hésychasme et prière, OCA 176 (Rome, 1966) 28ff. See 'Philoxenus of Mabbug', in *The Syriac Fathers on Prayer and the Spiritual Life,* CS 101 (Kalamazoo: Cistercian Publications, 1987) 101–122.

222. *Oratio* 2.15; PG 35:204A.

223. *Praktikos* 78; SCh 170:661 and 38 ff; CS 4:35.

224. Špidlík, *Grégoire de Nazianze,* 26.

225. See p. 283.

226. Gregory Nazianzus, *Oratio* 39—*In Sancta lumina,* 8; PG 36:344A; LNPF, ser. 2, 7:352ff.

227. See p. 243.

228. *A Systematic Handbook,* 283ff.

229. Gregory Nazianzus, *Oratio* 39-*In theophania,* 10; PG 36:345AB; LNPF, ser. 2, 7:347ff.

230. *Idem, Oratio* 38.12; PG 36:324BC. See LNPF, ser. 2, volume 7.

231. Evagrius, *Praktikos,* Prologue; SCh 171:492; CS 4:14.

232. Gregory Nazianzus, *Carminum liber* 1.2.25, v. 363; PG 37:838.

233. *Ibid.,* 1.2.10, v. 984; PG 751.

234. *Praktikos* 32; SCh 171:574; CS 4:25.

235. See Irénée Hausherr, 'Contemplation et sainteté. Une remarquable mise au point par Philoxène de Mabboug (décédé 523)', *RAM* 14 (1933) 18. *Idem, Hésychasme et prière,* OCA 176 (Rome, 1966) 31.

236. Evagrius, *Letter* 56; Frankenberg, 605.

237. See Špidlík, *Théophane le Reclus,* 58ff, 65, 68, 93.

238. *Serdce v christianskoj i indiiskoj mistike* [*The Heart in Christian and Indian Mysticism*] (Paris, 1929) 26.

239. Gregory Nazianzus, *Oratio* 6—*de pace,* 12; PG 35:737C. See *Oratio* 11.7; PG 35:841C.

240. *A Systematic Handbook,* 55ff.

241. *Fragmenta in Joannem,* 9; GCS 4:490, 24.

242. Henri Crouzel, *Théologie de l'image de Dieu chez Origène* (Paris, 1956) 239. See also, Crouzel, *Origen,* translated by A. S. Worrel (San Francisco: Harper & Row, 1989) 92ff.

243. *Oratio* 28—*Theologica* 2.3; PG 36:29A; LNPF, ser. 2, 7:289.

244. Špidlík, *Grégoire de Nazianze,* 96.

245. *Carminum liber* 2.2.4, v. 80ff.; PG 37:1511.

246. Gregory Nazianzus, *Oratio* 20.12; PG 1080B.

247. *Idem, Oratio* 30—*Theologica* 4.21; PG 36:132B; LNPF, ser. 2, 7:317.

248. René Arnou, *Praxis et Theoria. Étude de détail sur le vocabulaire et la pensée des Ennéades de Plotin* (Paris, 1921; 2nd ed. Rome, 1972) 25.

249. Arnou, *Praxis et Theoria,* 7. *Idem, Le désir de Dieu dans la philosophie de Plotin* (2nd ed., Rome, 1967) 231ff.
250. See p. 249.
251. Arnou (n. 248), *Praxis et Theoria,* 84.
252. Rudolf Bultmann, '*gignoskein,* to come to know, takes place in man's dealings with the world, in experience', in Kittel 1 (1964) 252.
253. Špidlík, 'L'eternità e il tempo, la zoè e il bios, problema dei Padri Cappadoci', *Augustinianum* 16 (1976) 107–116.
254. David Amand, *L'ascèse monastique de saint Basile* (Maredsous, 1949) 35.
255. *Systematic Handbook,* 243ff.
256. See Jean Lemaitre (Irénée Hausherr), in DSp 2/2 (1953) 1824.
257. *Centuries.* 3.19, 21; Frankenberg, 201, 203.
258. See Clement of Alexandria, *Stromata* 1.28.176, 1–2; PG 8:921–924; GCS 2:108; ANF 2: 299ff. Origen, *In Canticum canticorum, prologus;* PG 13:73A–77A; GCS 8:75–76; ACW 26.
259. *Centuries* 1.27; Frankenberg, 73. See *Letter* 7; 571 See also *Selecta in psalmos, ps.* 138; PG 12:1661C.
260. *Centuries* 1.99; SCh 9: 91;ACW 21:151.
261. *In Cantica canticorum, homilia* 11; PG 44:1000CD.; translated Casimir McCambley, *Saint Gregory of Nyssa, Commentary on the Song of Songs* (Brookline, MA: Hellenic College Press, 1987) 202.
262. Lemaitre, in DSp 2/2 (1953) 1807ff. Jean Kirchmeyer, in DSp 6. 852. Špidlík, *La sophiologie,* 11ff, 225ff.
263. *Homilies on the Hexaemeron,* 7.5; PG 29:157C; SCh 26:415; FCh 46:113–114.
264. Spanneut, *Le stoïcisme,* 275.
265. See the pseudo-aristotelian treatise *De mundo* VI, 399b: the deity lets himself be seen in his works like the invisible soul is manifested in her activities.
266. André-Jean Festugière, *La révélation d'Hermès Trismégiste,* vol. 2 (Paris, 1944–1954) xiiff. See *A Systematic Handbook,* 126ff.
267. *Homilies on the Hexaemeron,* 9.2; PG 29:189C; SCh 26:485; FCh 46:136–137.
268. *Ibid.,* 1.6; PG 16BC; FCh 10–11.
269. *Homilies on the Hexaemeron,* 6.1; PG 29:117B; SCh 26:325; FCh 46:83.
270. *My Life in Christ* (New York, 1994) 318.
271. J. Lemaitre, in DSp 2/2 (1953) 1820.
272. *A Systematic Handbook,* 21.
273. *Homilies on the Hexaemeron,* 5.7; PG 29:108D; SCh 26 (1950) 307; FCh 46:77.
274. *Homilies on the Hexaemeron,* 7.3; PG 153BC; SCh 402ff; FCh 109. See Yves Courtonne, *S. Basile et l'hellénisme* (Paris, 1934) 124ff.
275. Lemaitre, DSp 2/2 (1953).
276. *My Life in Christ* (New York, 1994) 285–286.
277. *Apologia,* I, 1–2; translated D. M. Kay, 'The Apology of Aristides the Philosopher', ANF 8: 263.
278. *Adversus haereses,* 1.9.1; Harvey I:272; ANF 1:369.
279. *Corpus Hermeticum,* 5.3–5; Nock-Festugière, 61–62, and 11.6–8; 149–150.
280. Placide Deseille, 'Gloire de Dieu. Dans l'Écriture et chez les Pères de l'Église jusqu'à saint Bernard', DSp 6 (1967) 422–462. *A Systematic Handbook,* 342.
281. *Commentarium in Joannem,* 13.42; GCS 4:268, 17; see ANF 9:297–408.
282. Lemaitre, in DSp 2/2 (1953) 1807.
283. *Apophthegmata,* Silvanus 2; PG 65:408CD; CS 59:222.

284. *Homilies on the Hexaemeron,* 3.10, PG 29:76C–77A; SCh 26:415; FCh 46:53.
285. *Homilia,* 2.7; PG 48AB; SCh 175; FCh 48.
286. *Homilia,* 3.10; PG 77A; SCh 241; FCh 53.
287. Yves Courtonne, *S. Basile et l'héllenisme* (Paris, 1934) 131ff.
288. *Commentarium in Isaiam prophetam,* 5.162; PG 30:385A.
289. *Ibid.,* 5.154; 372B.
290. See p. 363.
291. Špidlík, *La sophiologie de S. Basile,* 227ff.
292. Basil, *Homilia in psalmum* 44.5; PG 29:400.
293. Špidlík, *Théophane le Reclus,* 22, 51.
294. *Commentarium in Cantica,* Prol.; GCS 25, 21; ACW 26:40. See Henri Crouzel, *Origène et la 'connaissance mystique',* (Paris-Bruges, 1961) 62ff.
295. *Homilium in Jud.* 6.2; GCS 7:500, 9.
296. *Systematic Handbook,* 233ff.
297. *Praktikos* 48; SCh 171:609; CS 4:29.
298. *Systematic Handbook,* 244f.
299. *Cent chapitres gnostiques,* 28; SCh 5a:99; 'On Spiritual Knowledge and Discrimination: One Hundred Texts', *The Philokalia: The Complete Text,* vol. 1 (London: Faber and Faber, 1979) 260.
300. N. O. Losski, *Histoire de la philosophie russe des origines à 1950* (Paris, 1954) 92ff; *History of Russian Philosophy* (New York: International University Press, n.d.) 81ff.
301. J. Lemaitre, in DSp 2/2 (1953) 1825ff.
302. Albert Vanhoys, 'Accomplir'. VTB, 8; 'Fulfill'. DBT, 195–197.
303. Marc-François Lacan, 'Providence'. VTB, 1058–1060; 'Providence'. DBT, 474–475.
304. Ws 14:3, 17:2.
305. Michel Spanneut, *Le stoïcisme,* 401ff. *A Systematic Handbook,* 130ff.
306. *A Systematic Handbook,* 133.
307. E. Otto, *Der Vorwurf an Gott* (Wildesheim, 1951). Roger Rémondon, 'Égypte pharaonique', DSp 4/1 (1960) 504ff.
308. Irénée Hausherr, *Direction spirituelle en Orient autrefois,* OCA 144 (Rome, 1955) 42; translated by Anthony P. Gythiel, *Spiritual Direction in the Early Christian East,* CS 114 (Kalamazoo: Cistercian Publications, 1990) 32.
309. *Ibid.,* 90 (93).
310. *De virginitate,* 10; PG 46:360D; LNPF, ser. 2, 5:354–355.
311. Jean-Claude Guy, 'Examen de conscience chez les Pères de l'Église', DSp 4/2 (1961) 801–807.
312. J. Lemaitre, in DSp 2/2 (1953) 1825.
313. *A Systematic Handbook,* 193ff.
314. John Chrysostom, *Lettre d'exil,* 4.64; SCh 103: 81.
315. Hans Urs von Balthasar, 'Die gnostische Centurien des Maximus Confessor', *Freiburger theologischen Studien* 61 (Freiburg, 1941) 46ff. Antoine Guillaumont, *Les 'Kephalaia gnostica' d'Évagre le Pontique et l'histoire de l'origénisme chez les Grecs et chez les Syriens* (Paris, 1962).
316. André-Jean Festugière, *La révélation d'Hermès Trismégiste,* vol. 2 (Paris, 1944–1954) 598.
317. *The Republic* II, 379 a 5.
318. *Phaedrus,* 270a.
319. Festugière, *Hermès* (above, n. 316) 2:601.
320. *Quaestiones convivales* I,1, 4, 5.

321. Špidlík, *Grégoire de Nazianze,* 134ff.
322. *Oratio* 28-*Theologica,* 2.2ff, PG 36:29AB; LNPF, ser. 2, 7:288ff.
323. *Oratio* 20.12; PG 35:1080B.
324. *Oratio* 28-*Theologica,* 2.2; PG 36:28AC; LNPF, ser. 2, 7:289.
325. *Oratio* 27. 2; PG 36:13AB; LNPF, ser. 2, 7:284 ff.
326. *Oratio* 26-*In seipsum,* 5; PG 35:1233B.
327. *Oratio* 23-*De pace* 3.5; PG 35:1153C.
328. *Epistola* 185; PG 37:304C.
329. In a homily by Cyril of Alexandria (*Homily* 13; PG 77:1079AB), the children of Palm Sunday are called *theologoi paides,* children-theologians. Within the context, this can only be understood as the children who proclaim the divinity of the Messiah.
330. *Oratio* 21.12; PG 35:1080A. *Ibid.,* 5; 1069C; LNPF, ser. 2, 7:272.
331. Pierre Battifol, 'Théologia, Théologie', *Ephemerides Theologiae Lovanienses* 5 (1928) 275.
332. *Praktikos,* Prologue; SCh 171:501; CS 4:xc. *Ibid.,* 84; SCh 674;CS 4:37.
333. Origen, *In Mt* 17.19; GCS 10:640, 19–20; PG 13:1537A; ANF. 4:403–512.
334. For Moses, see Basil, *Homilia I in Hexaemeron,* 1; PG 29:5BC; FCh 46:3–4.
335. Jean Kirchmeyer, 'Grecque (Église), la "vision de Dieu"', DSp 6 (1966) 842.
336. *Ibid.*
337. Theodoret of Cyrrhus, *Ad Ephesios,* 2.7; PG 82:520D–521A.
338. Kirchmeyer, 'Grecque (Église)', DSp 6 (above, n. 335).

# 8

# MYSTICISM

## AT THE THRESHOLD OF UNKNOWING

### *Truth Is Mystical*

WHAT IS BEYOND THE PATTERN of common experience and eludes our powers of knowing is called 'mystical'. Yet according to a very common opinion, this is the foundation of truth.

On this subject, the analysis of the term 'truth' made by Pavel Florensky is significant.[1] The same sanskrit root *var* lies at the origin of the latin word for truth, *veritas,* the german verb *wehren* (to defend), the slavonic *vera* (faith), and the greek noun ἑορτή, a festival, as something venerable, hence forbidden to some; comparable to the Latin *reverendus* awe-inspiring, and *verenda* (to be feared). Knowledge bears witness to an immediate contact with the mystery, with religion, with worship. The hebrew noun for truth, *'emeth,* has the same root as the verb *aman,* to support, to believe (cf. *Amen*). Truth then would be defined as a revealed word, the object of faith. The slavonic term for truth, *istina* (cf. Sanskrit *asmi, asti* and the german verb *atmen,* to breathe, to live) expresses contact with a living reality known in a personal relationship.

The greek word for truth, ἀλήθεια, is entirely different. It is formed of the privative *a,* 'not', and of *lethos* or *lathos,* a forgetting (cf. λήθη [oblivion], λανθάνω [to be hidden]), λήθαργος [sleep]). Truth, then, is that which is no longer hidden, what is known, what has been 'un-covered'. The term expresses a gnoseological optimism. The philosopher rises above what is common, convinced of being able to discover the truth he tirelessly seeks: *Ens est intelligibile* (being is intelligible).[2] Man is able to know many things; he is therefore able also to know the Supreme Being.

This faith in the value of the human intellect was to waver in late antiquity, however. Greek rationalism devoured itself, so to speak. The same dialectical power which had built the structure also caused it to collapse. An entire class of 'sages' repudiated the great principles of classical philosophy and, in reaction, turned toward the irrational, toward mystery.[3] Can we say that the Fathers were influenced by the antirationalism of the era?

From a study of Origen's noetic vocabulary one may draw out the following teaching: mystery is an authentic reality; what is more, it is the first, independent, original reality. It is the only truth. Its hidden character is expressed by such words as μυστήριον, μυστικός, ἀπόρρητος, and words derived from the root κρύπτω (to conceal, keep secret). Mystery is ineffable. If it is an object of knowledge (νοητός), it is a knowledge so deep (βαθύς) that it is inexhaustible. Therein lies its fundamental paradox. Even the word *aletheia* (truth) is opposed to the logical conclusions of the philosophers. The ἀληθινὸς λόγος, the 'true reason', designates the *Logos* of God in his divinity; ἀγήλεια identified with μυστήρια, the mysteries.[4]

But in Origen, the sense of mystery is not the result of a philosophic defeatism that would lead to skepticism; by contrast, it serves as the foundation for arriving at a new, mystical knowledge which is typically christian.

## *The Christian Mystery*

The main unifier of the many meanings given the words *mysterion, mystikos,* and their equivalents in religious language is the concept that God communicates with the human person, and that the human person is initiated into God's plans.[5] According to Paul,[6] a 'mystery' is the fulfillment in Christ of a divine plan which was first hidden, then revealed to human persons. The contrast between the two aspects 'hidden-revealed' (or also 'shrouded in silence-announced and revealed') is essential to the concept of mystery. This contrast is indicated by the element of time (once hidden, now made manifest) but it also transcends time: even when known, the mystery always remains partly veiled.

The Fathers drew their fundamental inspiration from the pauline concept of mystery. Yet other influences were also at work. Since they had to translate the christian message into a language and a culture that were deeply imbued by 'mystery religions', they did not hesitate to use their vocabulary, in the process giving it new meaning: the *locus* where the mystery is accomplished is Jesus Christ; the mystery is known and lived in the Church, in the sacraments. As a consequence, the terms οἱ μυηθέντες and οἱ μεμυημένοι(the initiates) signify the baptized and, by extension, the communicants.[7] The great interpreter of the pauline teaching is John Chrysostom in his *Homily Seven on First Corinthians.*[8]

Ultimately, a mystery must be unfolded. Progress in understanding it ranges from the simple knowledge of faith to an experience of a higher order, *theognosia,* which is at one and the same time a knowledge of God and a lifestyle. Revelation is a progressive 'illumination' *(photismos).*[9] Subsequently, the darkened face of the mystery will be brought out more at the expense of its luminous face. Pseudo-Denys speaks of 'mystical theology', which he describes as 'the perfect knowledge of God gained through unknowing, by virtue of an incomprehensible union'.[10] From then on, the emphasis in 'mysticism' was to be more on what 'lies hidden' than on what is 'revealed'. What came to be emphasized is the dimension of unknowing, the need to go beyond images, figures, and even concepts to reach God in a 'mystic union'.

## *The Awakening of Mystical Awareness in the Fourth Century*

Although christian mystical literature abounds with concrete expressions, over the centuries it has retained a terminology which was linked to the structures put in place by the greek Fathers towards the end of the fourth century, especially by Gregory of Nyssa, who returned to the alexandrian tradition. Philo had emphasized strongly that the God of Scripture is infinitely beyond human thought and words (see Jb 42:3). His view that God is incomprehensible (ἀκατάληπτος) played an important role among the Fathers, especially Clement of Alexandria, Gregory of Nyssa, and John Chrysostom.[11]

'The greatest good', he writes, 'is to understand that God, according to his being (κατὰ τὸ εἶναι), is incomprehensible.'[12]

Among Christians, the question arose again in connection with the heresy of the Eunomians who, in the opinion of Gregory Nazianzus, had changed theology into disputatiousness (τεχνύδριον).[13] Confronted with interminable discussions on the Holy Trinity conducted in a dialectic spirit and using aristotelian terminology,[14] the Fathers of the late fourth century were led to reemphasize the incomprehensible character of the divine essence, while specifying that this essence remains mysterious, even to the mind enlightened by grace.[15] How could our limited understanding grasp the Limitless? 'To let oneself be apprehended in this manner would be a form of limitation', Gregory Nazianzus wrote.[16] Intelligibility is intimately linked to being: only like knows like.[17] The abyss separating the two categories of being, human and divine, determines the noetic inaccessibility of God with respect to creation.[18] More than one patristic text states that one should abandon altogether the idea of seeing God *as He is* and be satisfied with *knowing that He is*.[19]

But the anti-eunomian reaction did not only give rise to polemical writings and merely repeat formulations tinged with agnosticism; it led to a deeper awareness of the mystery of God which found expression above all in the mystical writings of Gregory of Nyssa. Taking up the tradition of Philo, Gregory shows that taking the spiritual path lets us discover that God eludes our grasp, and that the Incomprehensible must be understood as incomprehensible. His ideas would be taken over by Pseudo-Denys in his *Mystical Theology* and would have a profound influence on christian mysticism.

John Chrysostom tackled the problem of divine transcendence from the viewpoint of religious common sense. His influence in this area will be found in the eastern liturgy, where a feeling of sacred awe—a spirit of veneration and adoration—developed in an atmosphere of mystery.

### *Images of the Mystical Ascent*

Later tradition also owes the fourth-century Fathers the symbolic images that express the various stages of the soul's ascent to God.

The mystic ascent is symbolized by the 'ascent' of Israel from Egypt to Jerusalem,[20] and elsewhere, by the ascent of Mount Sinai.[21] It could just as well be 'the ascent of Mount Carmel'. While speaking of Mount Saint Auxentius, Stephen the Deacon wrote in *The Life of Saint Stephen the Younger:* 'If someone calls it the Mountain of God, or Mount Horeb, or Mount Carmel, or Mount Sinai, or Tabor, or Lebanon, or Holy City, as being located on the Mountain of the inhabitants of Jerusalem, he would not sin against propriety'.[22]

Another image just as easily developed is this: Imagine prayer rising up as 'Jacob's Ladder; its top reached heaven and on it the Lord leaned'.[23] In Egypt, the step-pyramid of Saqqara was conceived as an immense stairway built to facilitate the ascent of the king's soul to his father Ra, the sun-god. Pindar, too, imagined that one could ascend to heaven on a ladder. Christ recalled Jacob's ladder (Gn 28:12-13) when he said to the Apostles: 'You will see heaven open and the angels of God ascending and descending over the Son of man' (Jn 1:51). Philo saw in Jacob's ladder 'the ebb and flow of contemplation'.[24] Aphrahat wrote, 'The ladder which Jacob saw is a symbol of our Saviour, in that by means of him the just ascend from the lower to the upper realm'.[25] The syrian Jacobites were fond of composing *seblata* or 'ladder' hymns.[26]

The ladder became the classical image for spiritual progress in general, while for the mystic ascent, on the authority of Gregory of Nyssa's *The Life of Moses,* the image of the mountain prevailed.

## *The Ascent of Mount Sinai*

*The Life of Moses* is, without question, the classic mystical treatise that established a tradition. This book is often presented systematically by differentiating between the four stages of the ascent to the knowledge of God.

Let us imagine Mount Sinai. During the great divine epiphany, the people are standing on the plateau. They hear peals of thunder and see flashes of lightning. This is symbolic of the first knowledge of God, through fear. What the people become aware of is the power of Yahweh, of his 'hand'. 'The beginning of wisdom is fear of Yahweh' (Ps 110:11).

Moses, God's chosen one, begins the ascent of the mountain. He symbolizes positive theology. During this ascent, the soul moves from one concept to the other, from an imperfect to one that is perfect. The soul learns something new every day; her knowledge of the divinity increases. Up to what point?

This positive ascent is not endless. The moment arrives when Moses halts on top of the rock. One step forward and he would hurl himself into the abyss. He is overcome by dizziness. Having reached the intellectual heights, the prophet realizes that no concept can adequately express the knowledge of God. Only negation is appropriate, but it expresses a higher degree of knowledge, an experience of the divine incomprehensibility. This teaches that God is infinitely greater than anything our mind is able to grasp. Thus, our knowledge is in fact 'a not-knowing' *(agnoia),* but it is a 'learned' ignorance.[27]

The role of the human intellect ends with one last effort. If we think of the intellect as light, the light goes out. The darkness that invades the soul lights the fire of *eros,* desire, love. It is this love which gives the soul wings to fly and soar toward the heights. Through the intensity of her love, the soul begins to understand how great must be the One whom she so greatly desires. The darkness then becomes luminous, because love is knowledge. Having left the natural state of the mind, *stasis,* the human person goes to meet God in an *ex-stasis,* because love is, by nature, an ecstatic force which leads us to go beyond our human condition, to be united with the transcendent God.

This structure, explained in outline, looks easy, and could be illustrated with texts from Gregory of Nyssa or other mystical writers. However, its weakness consists of an over-simplification which eliminates some basic questions. Furthermore it is beyond dispute that an advance in knowledge moves from positive to negative theology, from the 'scholastic' to the 'mystic'. Could we not adopt another point of view and reverse the procedure?

We cannot deny that someone who opens his eyes to know reality initially acquires a number of 'positive' concepts. But these concepts remain intimately linked to creation. Religious knowledge, in the true sense of the word, possesses a mystical dimension from the beginning: the awareness that everything we grasp through our faculties is not God. This experience does not diminish over the course of the spiritual life; on the contrary, we move from minor negations to major ones.

But this knowledge of 'the abyss' goes hand in hand with the discovery of another movement, one that is revealed. The effort of the human mind is an *anabasis* (ascent), but, contrary to the platonic thesis, this leads, not to a knowledge of God in the light of our concepts, but to a 'not-knowing', an ecstasy which, in itself, would not be positive if it did not meet the *katabasis* (descent) of revealing, divine grace, the 'going-out *(exstasis)* of the Word', who 'emptied himself', who out of love for the human person did not jealously hold on to his divine condition (cf. Phil 2:6).

Thus, between ascent and descent there is a mysterious dialectic —an antinomy that finds its explanation in Christ, who humbled himself and was exalted to the glory of the Father. To repeat the beautiful formula of Gregory of Nyssa, is humility not 'a descent toward the heights?'[28] The numerous experiences of mystic souls can illustrate the various stages of this 'existential dialectic of the divine and the human'.[29]

## NEGATIVE THEOLOGY

### *The Apophatic Way*

If truth is found beyond human knowledge, the search for it will be made in the first place by *apophasis,* 'knowing by way of negation'. Vladimir Lossky describes apophatic theology like this:

> The negative way of the knowledge of God is an ascendant undertaking of the mind that progressively eliminates all positive attributes of the object it wishes to attain, in order to culminate finally in a kind of apprehension by supreme ignorance of him who cannot be an object of knowledge. We can say that it is an intellectual experience of the mind's failure when confronted with something beyond the conceivable.[30]

Is this already mystical knowledge in the strict sense? Not directly. Lossky specifies:

> In fact, consciousness of the failure of human understanding constitutes an element common to all that we can call *apophasis,* or negative theology, whether this which remains within the limits of intellection, simply declaring the radical lack of correspondence between our mind and the reality it wishes to attain.[31]

The apophatic element is present in all religious thinking, under different forms. Lossky continues:

> We can say as well that it is not foreign to sacred art, where failure of artistic means of expression, deliberately conspicuous in the very art of the iconographer, corresponds to the learned ignorance of the theologian.[32]

In the patristic tradition, negative theology first emerges from a simple material fact: the great number of negative expressions signify the incomprehensibility of the divine nature. In Gregory of Nyssa, for example, an entire vocabulary created by his predecessors converges. Certain terms are derived from the New Testament, especially from Saint Paul: 'invisible' (ἀόρατος, Rom 1:20), 'ineffable' (ἄρρητος, 2 Cor 12:4), 'inscrutable' (ἀνεξερεύνητος, Rom 11:33), 'unsearchable' (ἀνεξιχνίαστος, Rom 11:33), and 'unapproachable' (ἀπρόσιτος, 1 Tm 6:16). Others come from Philo; this is the case, for example, of certain favorite expressions: not only 'incomprehensible' (ἀκατάληπτος) but also 'inaccesible' (ἀνέφικτος),[33] and others.

One central idea emerges from the various biblical or philosophic expressions: the only knowledge we can have of the divine nature is to understand that it is incomprehensible. 'The true knowledge of God consists of this: understanding that knowledge of him transcends all knowledge, his incomprehensibility being inclosed on all sides as if by darkness.'[34]

Such a conclusion is not readily accepted by the rational being, aware of his or her vocation to understand whatever exists. What compels us to admit our weakness in this area are the innumerable wrecks that litter the road of the knowledge of God on the level of sensory knowledge as well as on that of reason.

*What Falls Under the Senses Is Alien to God*

The Fathers unhesitatingly took over this principle, generally accepted after Plato,[35] Proclus,[36] and Celsus.[37] 'Nothing seemed so desirable to me,' wrote Gregory Nazianzus, 'as to close the door of my senses. . . . I devote myself to conversing with myself and with God, with no admixture whatever of earthly, erring images . . . to capture light by light, the brighter light by the darker light, perceiving already, in hope the good of the age to come.'[38]

Spiritual writers of all times have tirelessly recommended freeing the mind from sensory images, using the senses only according to the needs of reason. Concretely, this principle will have numerous applications, as is true for the terms 'sense' and 'sensibly' in the vocabulary of the spiritual writers.[39]

*The Rejection of Images in Prayer*

The question was taken up within the context of contemplation. Here we need only quote one text which stands out on account of its radicalness and instills a sort of inner iconoclasm. It is a passage from Pseudo-Symeon the New Theologian, a well-known author in the history of hesychasm. Here is how he describes 'the first prayer', a manner of praying which, in his view, is entirely false:

> The distinctive features of the first method are as follows: . . . a man stands at prayer and, raising his hands, his eyes and his mind to heaven, keeps in mind divine thoughts, imagines celestial blessings, hierarchies of angels and dwellings of the just. . . . But this [thinking in this way of this method of prayer] is a sign of going astray *(prelest),* for the good is no longer good if it be not rightly done. If then such a man gives himself up to a solitary life without outward associations . . . he can scarcely avoid going mad. . . . It is a method which has led astray those who see light with bodily eyes, smell sweet scents, hear voices and experience many other similar phenomena. Some have become totally possessed by demons and in their madness wander from place to place. Others have been led astray, mistaking the devil for an angel of light . . . and have remained incorrigible to the end of their days. Some, at

> the devil's instigation, have committed suicide . . . . And who could enumerate all the various forms of diabolic deceit?[40]

*Imaginary Visions*

Contemplation is, by definition, a 'vision of God'. 'Someone who has not seen God cannot speak of him'.[41]

For the Messalians, this vision was a sensible reality which affected not only the soul, but also the body, sensibly and visibly (αἰσθητῶς καὶ ὁρατῶς), and led to the natural vision of the Trinity. Pseudo-Macarius classified such phenomena and in his *Homily* Seven, he differentiates between spiritual 'sense' (αἴσθησις), 'vision' (ὅρασις), 'enlightenment' (φωτισμός), and 'revelation' (αποκάλυψις).[42]

'Visionary' elements are found in the lives of the early monks.[43] An apophthegm states that 'the cell of a monk is [like] the furnace of the three young men, where they saw the Son of God' (see Dn 3:49), and 'like the dark cloud from which God spoke [to the Israelites]' (see Ex 2:21).[44] The ecstasies of Antony,[45] like those of Pachomius,[46] Silvanus,[47] John the Dwarf (Colobos),[48] and others, have the explicit character of a vision: ὅρασις (an act of sight), ὀπτασις (vision, apparition), φαντασία (image), θεωρία (a seeing, beholding).

The content of such visions varies greatly: prophetic anticipations, an awareness of spiritual realities, inner responses, apparitions of saints, the objectifying of the mystery being contemplated. Whatever their structure, the formulations instinctively used a visual terminology.

Without altogether banishing them, most spiritual authors—and not only the most intellectual—had deep reservations about visions for reasons of humility and especially out of fear of illusion. 'When the intellect attains prayer that is pure', Evagrius writes, 'the demons present to it an illusive vision in some image that is pleasing to the senses.'[49] It is vainglory which moves the mind to represent God in some form or image.[50] Hence this advice: 'Never desire nor seek to see any face or image during prayer. Do not wish for a sensory vision of angels.'[51]

The Syrians were equally severe. In Philoxenus of Mabbug we find a total rejection of physical visions and of the alleged revelations based upon them. His statement is categorical, and he puts it in the mouth of Saint Paul:

> Indeed, he says that all contemplations the tongue is capable of representing in the realm of corporeal beings are phantoms of the soul's thoughts, not the result of grace. Therefore, let your holiness be reminded of this also, and beware of the imaginations of deep thoughts [in modern idiom, the words might perhaps be rendered, 'of the subconscious']. For it is the solitaries with a more refined psychology, on a quest for vainglory and eager for novelties, who especially have to fight this type of warfare.[52]

Philoxenus mentions an anecdote that made the rounds in eastern monastic circles: the devil appeared in human form to a hermit and said to him, 'I am Christ'. To which the solitary responded, 'I do not want to see Christ in this world.'[53] Visions, Philoxenus concludes, can indeed lead only to the most lamentable illusions and pave the way either for heresy, as is shown by the example of Adelphus, the leader of the Messalians, or to suicide, as in the case of Assuana the Hymnographer.[54]

If, on the one hand, such precautions are justified, we understand, on the other, that the christian people were not equally severe and loved stories of saints' visions. Hagiography is full of them. But it was always trust in the person's holiness that assured the credibility of such visions.

### *Beyond Rational Concepts*

The value of 'aristotelian' concepts in theology was questioned by the Fathers right from the beginning.[55] During the byzantine era, this even became the subject of a dispute between Barlaam and Palamas.[56]

Since, according to Aristotle, all knowledge presupposes sense experience, and since the Godhead cannot be experienced in this manner, the two protagonists agreed: no 'aristotelian definition' expresses the essence of God, which is entirely other than that of creatures. But their views differed with respect to neo-platonism. Barlaam acknowledged a direct neo-platonic influence upon the

Fathers, particularly on Pseudo-Denys, and he concluded from this that the neo-platonist philosophers themselves had been 'enlightened' by God, since, on certain points, their thought was not different from that of the Fathers. Moreover, the illumination of the mind needed for a knowledge of God presupposes some 'knowledge of creation'. For Palamas, this attitude ran counter to the Gospel, which states that the truth is hidden 'from the learned and the clever', and revealed 'to little children' (Mt 11:25). For him, greek philosophy remained useless as long as it refused a 'new birth' through baptism. He illustrated his thought by using the image of venomous serpents: from them doctors can draw useful medicine, but only if they are first killed and dissected.[57]

As we can see, the protagonists moved on different levels. Barlaam's position was to be taken up again later, as a substantiation for symbolic theology. Here, we appeal to Palamas to describe the experience of the mystics on the *via negativa:* to seek God the Father, we must go beyond the concepts of human reason.

## *Learned Ignorance*

The phrase *docta ignorantia (Learned Ignorance),* the title of Nicolas of Cusa's best known treatise, is linked to an entire tradition.[58] In fact, the treatise was written after the author had made a voyage to Constantinople. While presenting the concept of 'learned ignorance' as a 'divine gift' received by grace on the ship that brought him back from Greece on the eve of the Council of Union (the Council of Ferrara-Florence), Nicolas of Cusa considered himself dependent above all on a meditation on dionysian works.[59]

Pseudo-Denys wrote: 'The most divine knowledge of God (ἡ θειοτάτη τοῦ θεου γνῶσις) is the one received by Unknowing (ἡ δἰ ἀγνωσίας γινωσκομένη)'.[60] How are we to interpret this concept of a knowledge generated through unknowing? The cessation of all cognitive activity clears the path for 'a communion which transcends the mind', Pseudo-Denys explains.[61] It generates a knowledge-communion that is 'beyond the mind' (ὑτὲρ νοῦν—mystical knowledge. But unknowing, the summit of negative theology, is itself already a knowing: it is the admission that God is 'beyond all essence and knowledge' (ὑπὲρ πᾶσαν οὐσίαν καί γνῶσιν)'.[62] In this sense, negation becomes an affirmation of the essential attribute of God.

## LUMINOUS DARKNESS

### *Entering the Darkness*

'Learned ignorance' is considered the apex of negative theology, and yet, it is not the last boundary of noetic renunciations. 'God is not only beyond knowledge, but also beyond unknowing', Gregory Palamas states in the *Triads (Defense of the Holy Hesychasts).*[63] While quoting the *Encomium of Saint Stephen* by Gregory of Nyssa,[64] Palamas writes that the first martyr did not see God 'either intelligibly or sensibly or by negation'.[65]

Paradoxically, unknowing is still knowing: only a rational being knows that he does not know. Because it is a form of knowledge, learned ignorance gives the mind a certain satisfaction. It is the cloud (νεφέλη) in which Moses ascended Mount Sinai, knowing that he was on his way to God.[66] But such a modest satisfaction cannot extinguish our soul's desire for Infinity. The highest degree of knowledge therefore presupposes a still more radical renunciation, a transcending of rationality itself, an entering into total darkness (γνόφος).

The famous fresco of Raphael entitled The School of Athens clearly illustrates this 'philosophers' discussion' about the appropriateness of this last step. Aristotle points to the earth, exhorting man to renounce deification and be satisfied with a limited human happiness; the hand of Plato, by contrast, points to heaven.

Making the most of the dialectic delineated by Plato in the *Phaedrus, Symposium,* and the *Timaeus,*[67] the Fathers sought to remove the fetters that weighed down the soul's wings and prevented her from ascending to God. Whether direct or not, the influence of Plotinus is evident. As an image of God, the soul tends by nature towards the Archetype, toward divine metamorphosis.[68] Hellenic antiquity, indeed all of antiquity, never knew anything more grandiose.

The human person, then, is a ζῶον θεούμενον, an animal called to intimacy with God, as Gregory of Nazianzus writes.[69] To the human person 'who knows', the divine metamorphosis is 'natural' (συγγενές), because the soul has a divine origin.[70] Gregory gave this advice to a young priest: 'Of the things that are beautiful, you are not ignorant of what comes first: to acquire God always and become God's possession through intimacy with him and by ascending *(dia tes anabaseos)* to him'.[71]

Texts such as these abound everywhere.[72] This desire for God is cherished as a very positive element in the spiritual life and, as such, it corresponds to the divine will. 'He [God] longs to be longed for (literally, 'God thirsts for us to thirst for him': διψῶν τὸ διψᾶσθαι).[73]

Unquestionably, and according to platonic teaching, this desire, this divine *eros,* is the first movement in the ascent of the mind and contemplation. Therein lies its initial merit, so to speak. We may wonder what fruit it will bear on the intellectual summit, at the moment when one realizes that the human *nous* (mind) is no longer able to follow the marked path. Plato was able to point bravely to heaven. His disciples believed that the human person, 'the third light', has his or her true home where 'the sun of the invisible world' shines—God.

Moses, by contrast, discovered that God dwells in darkness. The divine *eros* then manifests itself as an ecstatic force in the true sense of the term: it compels the human person to leave 'the domain of the intellect' and venture toward the unknown or rather the Unknowable.

This text by Philo of Alexandria had a direct influence on Gregory of Nyssa: 'Although he is aware that he loves a reality which is difficult to grasp and even inaccessible, Moses nevertheless seeks it. He enters into the darkness (γνόφος) where God dwells, that is, into the reflections on the Existent Being that are unapproachable and formless'.[74]

The key phrase here is, 'knowing that he loves'. It is therefore *eros,* desire, that compels the human person to transcend the limits of unknowing and put one's trust in the Beloved. As Gregory writes:

> By divine command, Abraham went out from his own country and kindred, on a journey worthy of a prophet eager for the knowledge of God. . . . But what does Scripture say about him? That

> he went out not knowing where he was going (Heb 11:8), not even able to learn the name of the One he loved, yet in no wise impatient or ashamed because of such ignorance (ἄγνοια). . . . Indeed, he took this as a sure indication of being on the right road—not to stop, during his ascent to God, at any of the things that are within reach of the mind, but to take as a token of his unfailing knowledge of God the belief that he is greater than any sign by which he may be known.[75]

## Eros *Becomes Knowledge*

Making a sharp distinction between the terms 'knowledge' and 'awareness' is not easy. However, language itself differentiates between them sufficiently to allow a description of the mystical experience of 'darkness'. The human person, goaded by divine *eros,* abandons the way of 'knowing' without losing the 'awareness' of the intensity of his or her desire. Paradoxically, we thereby acquire a new 'knowledge'. The ardor of the love we experience gives us an image of the One who is so greatly loved. The immensity of God is reflected in the expansion of the human heart.

To desire someone is in reality to give witness that one is aware of his or her value. As modern gnoseologies[76] confirm, then, true wisdom consists of 'value-knowledge'. Fervently desired, God then reveals to the spiritual 'sages' a value which transcends every other reality. *Amor ipse fit cognitio:* love itself becomes knowledge. The text of Gregory of Nyssa renders this mystical experience superbly: 'This truly is the vision of God: never to be satisfied in the desire to see him and never to find satiety to such a desire'.[77]

The 'darkness' is gradually brightened by an inner, mysterious light: God is known inwardly, in the heart, and this constitutes great progress in *theognosia* (knowledge of God).

## *The Critical Problem of Non-Christian Mysticism*

The flame of the heart's desire which illuminates the way to God has often been described masterfully by mystics throughout the world and all ages.[78] Even the terms that describe this experience differ little from those in the christian vocabulary. Yet this 'ecumenical' point of contact presents itself as a crossroads at which the ways begin to diverge in opposite directions.

Desire implies a duality between the desiring subject and the desired object. This presupposes an effort at interiorization which nonetheless does not suppress the inner split. The opposition can become painful, even tragic. Is Hell not viewed as an infinite desire which cannot ever be satisfied?

Theoretically, a twofold solution presents itself to resolve the tension between the two opposite poles. One is 'satanic', declaring oneself as the absolute, only desirable reality. In this sin of pride, this revolt against God, there is, as Dostoevsky demonstrates,[79] a certain 'mystique of the Infinite'. The other solution seems profoundly religious, and may be summarized in a few words: The opposition between the desiring subject and the desired Infinite is reconciled only by suppressing this duality. When a person is totally absorbed by the divine reality in a nirvana, a total self-negation, the flame of human desire dies out, and nothing is left but God, the sole value.[80]

## Eros *Satiated by Divine* Agape

If Christians do not have recourse to the spiritual 'suicide' of a nirvana, they must experience another solution to solve the problem. It is sensed from the beginning of the mystic way in the form of confidence that the desire for God can neither be fruitless nor end in frustration and the annihilation of the human person. The history of salvation is a mysticism of divine promises, the path on which human *eros* (desire) always encounters divine *agape* (love, charity).

In Plato's *Symposium,* God is presented as ardently desired, yet loving neither the world nor man.[81] Christians, by contrast, know that God first loved us.[82] It is God who implanted in human nature the desire for perfection. This is the call to *theosis,* deification. The One who is desired wishes to give himself, and from the beginning he already gives himself by communing with man through 'earnest-money' *(arrha)* and by means of symbols. The pre-eminent knowledge of God is the experience of God, who gives himself to us, for *agape* (love, charity) is the 'definition' of God (1 Jn 4:8-16). It is the knowledge of the great wonders of

God as revealed in Scripture and as the soul discovers within herself when she feels loved.

Can we speak then of a new knowledge of God by means of love, but this time on a plane essentially higher than that of *eros* (desire)? Indeed, the soul now not only desires the Godhead but feels herself being carried into the divine life, deified. While *eros* is a 'lift-off', *agape* is a descent, and the encounter between the two is the summit of mystical knowledge.[83]

At this moment, the 'darkness' becomes entirely light and this new splendor begins to illumine the world. Negative theology turns into 'symbolic theology', in which everything is seen in the 'light of Tabor'.[84] In the Novgorod icon of the Transfiguration, the darkened sun is brought to life by the figure of Christ enlightening the world and giving it new meaning. According to the Fathers, the Transfiguration prefigures the world to come.

As the soul begins to enter into the divine splendor, we have to ask whether this movement comes to an end or whether she sinks endlessly into the depths of God. The question was asked by Gregory of Nyssa in terms of the concept of *epektasis* (reaching out, stretching forth).

## Epektasis

The term ἐπέκτασις is borrowed from Gregory of Nyssa[85] and refers to a view of the christian life as progress, a tending without end. If God never ceases to be darkness, the soul advances eternally within this darkness, and the attraction exercised by God makes the soul go beyond herself. Furthermore, God gives the soul a vision that is forever new. The experience of God is that of an unending 'newness' which keeps the soul in a state of amazement and awe. From this perspective, the term *epektasis* allows us to see the unity of the mysticisms of darkness and of light by showing that they are two complementary aspects of a single, unique experience: the desire for God and its fulfillment.

On earth, the moments of such an experience are ephemeral and transient; the paradox of a 'stable movement' is achieved in heaven. The soul who has subdued the agitation of the passions acquires a stability founded on the rock which is Christ. The soul, however, 'uses her stability as if it were a wing'.[86] Such stability is viewed, not as immobility, but as the quiet flow of a river.[87]

> There is in you, Moses, an immense desire to tend toward what is ahead, and your race knows no weariness. . . . May you know that close to me there is a space so great that the one running in it is never able to see an end to his progress. But in another respect, this motion is a standing still. Indeed, it is said, 'you must stand on the rock'. This is the most paradoxical of all: that stability (στάσις) and movement (κίνησις) are one and the same.[88]

This thesis of Gregory of Nyssa was criticized by Maximus the Confessor.[89] Most authors would agree in seeing in the unending progress of faith the law of perfection here below, but only here below.[90] In the West, the teaching of Thomas Aquinas came to play a decisive role in this respect in subsequent ascetic theology: 'As long as we are in this world, there is no end to the movement of desire in us, because at every stage we can still draw nearer to God by grace. But when we come to perfect happiness, nothing will remain for us to desire.'[91]

As we can see, in Thomas Aquinas desire is essentially linked to the concept of insatiety. Gregory, by contrast, accepts a paradox: 'desire' and 'satisfaction' go hand in hand in the mysterious divine-human communion.

### *The Role of Christ in Mysticism*

In the economy of salvation, God gives himself through the Word made flesh. The role of Christ must therefore be manifest above all in moments when communion with God is intensely felt and lived. Even if tender devotion to the person of Christ is typical of all christian mystics, this is not always evident in the terminology or in the outlines of some authors. We may therefore ask what the role of the humanity of Christ is for them on the level where darkness reigns in the soul who is fully conscious of the incomprehensibility of God?[92]

This experience, we may reply, is linked to the immediate perception of the divine presence in the soul. If the soul communes with this presence as if in a mystical marriage,[93] this is because the soul knows she is attracted to the One who first came down to her: 'Indeed', Gregory of Nyssa expressly states, 'we cannot be raised to the Most High unless the Lord who uplifts the humble first bent down to what is below'.[94]

The contemplative becomes gradually identified with Christ.[95] And if Moses is his model, this is because, according to the Gospel, Moses was the first to discover the symbolism of the Burning Bush.[96] The texture of *The Life of Moses* and of the *Commentary on the Song of Songs* is, so to speak, interwoven with passages from the Gospel or from Saint Paul. It is therefore not unreasonable to indicate the degree to which, in Gregory, 'the content of the ecstasy is determined by the historic revelation'.[97]

### *Martyrdom and the Resurrection of the Mind*

The mystics' love for the person of Christ is often expressed by a veneration of his cross and passion. They establish a link between the humility of the Word who emptied himself of his glory (see Phil 2:7) and 'apophatic' (negative) theology, the path of intellectual renunciation. This is a true sacrifice: the human person who is by nature a rational being gives up the exercise of his or her essentially creative power and the concepts it engenders as its own offspring. To the one for whom knowledge is life, *apophasis* (renunciation) is a dying of the intellect. But this death is freely chosen and accepted for the love of God. It assumes the form of a spiritual martyrdom and will therefore be rewarded with a 'resurrection', like that which has known a physical death.

The christological dynamics of knowledge are entirely absent from the 'technical' speculations of Eunomius, who never managed to understand the insistence of the Cappadocians on the incomprehensibility of God. Quite the contrary. Would it not be a person's vocation to seek to understand God more and more clearly?

Gregory of Nyssa solved the problem by recalling a paradox of Scripture: at one and the same time, God is incomprehensible, and the human person has been created to know him.

> God is promised to the vision of those whose heart has been purified. But 'No man has ever seen God at any time', as says the great

> John (Jn 1:18). And the sublime mind of Paul confirms this verdict when he says, 'Whom no man has seen, nor can see' (1 Tm 6:16). God is the slippery, steep rock that affords no basis for our thoughts, which the teaching of Moses, too, declared to be so inaccessible that our mind can nowhere approach Him. For all possibility of apprehension is taken away by this explicit denial (ἀπόφασις).[98]

At the same time, Gregory admits that the antithesis between ignorance of and knowledge of God is similar to that between life and death. In the Old Testament, 'seeing God' meant death (see Is 6:5). This is why in the same text, Gregory continued: 'No man can see God and live. But to see God is life eternal.'[99] A terse statement—with content fraught with meaning. Negation *(apophasis),* intellectual renunciation pushed to the extreme, is like a spiritual death that leads to life, to the resurrection of our faculties. 'The Hand of the Word is stretched out also to us and confirms those who have lost their balance in the depths of their speculations. . . . for he says, "Blessed are the pure of heart, for they shall see God" (Mt 5:8).'[100]

The help of God is the hand which the Bridegroom of the Song extends through the open door of the house while he himself remains outside. God reveals himself through his activity in the world: all created reality becomes symbolic and is understood symbolically. 'The immensity of nature cannot be perfectly understood, and all the power of thought, all the signifying of words and names are not of a nature to even arrive at the true Word; but our mind, as if from foot-tracks and illustrations, guesses the Word. From the things that are understood, we infer through analogy that which cannot be understood.'[101]

Ecstasy is therefore the high point at which negative theology is converted into symbolic theology. But before we describe the latter, we have still to go more deeply into the concept of ecstasy as it is found in spiritual literature.

## ECSTASY

### *Ecstatic Phenomena*

It is very difficult to give a verdict on all the ecstatic phenomena that appeared among primitive peoples, in the hindu religious experience, in ancient Greece, or in muslim mysticism.[102] In this complex area, we need to distinguish between the phenomenal aspects (alienation of the senses, suspension of the empirical awareness, and so forth) and the metaphysical-religious dimension. There are, in addition, morbid states, not to mention the 'ecstasies' attained artificially through artificial techniques.

In the Septuagint the term *ekstasis* translates—more or less felicitously—twelve or thirteen hebrew terms. In none of the twenty-eight texts in which the word appears does it refer to ecstasy in the modern sense of the term. The same observation applies to the verb ἐξιστάναι (to be amazed). In the New Testament, the term *ekstasis* is used only seven times: four times meaning 'astonishment' or 'terror'; three times (in Acts) in the sense of ecstasy properly speaking. The verb itself takes on the following meaning: being out of one's senses; and being amazed. The documentation we have for a philological biblical study on the meaning of ecstasy is therefore meager. Furthermore, would it be illegitimate, we ask, to call 'ecstatic' all the persons who in the history of salvation generously followed the voice of God as he uprooted them from the conditions of normal life, especially the prophets and the 'charismatics' of the mother-community of Christians in Jerusalem?[103]

The language of the first monks presents the same use of the word *ekstasis* as does the New Testament. Ecstasy can refer to folly, terror, or rapture; the word occurs in contexts which make its religious meaning explicit. Moreover, the elements of 'enthusiasm' were less important in the life of the early monks than one is sometimes led to believe. Monasticism has known 'men of God', 'Spirit-bearers (Pneumatophores)', who subsequently became 'visionaries' and 'prophets': not that what they sought was ecstasy, but the means to save themselves.[104]

Gregory of Nyssa is unquestionably the first christian theoretician to pay serious attention to the phenomenon of ecstasy. He was able to isolate its characteristic elements and integrate them into a doctrine of the spiritual development of the soul. In this sense, and more than anyone else, he christianized ecstasy and established the ecstatic vocabulary which had had a long tradition among the greek philosophers.[105]

Pseudo-Denys borrowed his ecstatic vocabulary from, on the one hand, Philo and Gregory of Nyssa and, on the other, his neo-platonic predecessors. While his influence was apparently limited in the East, it appears, by contrast, to have been considerable in the West.[106]

Since this overview has no other aim than to serve as an introduction to a reading and study of the Fathers, we will isolate from the phenomenon of ecstasy only those aspects that will help us discover its essence and, at the same time, define the special character of christian ecstasy.

*Ecstasy: Objective Polarization*

The ecstatic phenomena that embellish the stories of holy monks belong most often to what is called the ecstasy of objective polarization.[107] This is a mental fixation polarized on an object of high value which brings about the blurring, even a more or less radical suspension, of various mental functions. Several texts closely link ecstasy and vision (ὅρασις, act of sight; ὀπτασία, vision; φαντασία image; θεωρία, a beholding). The ecstasies of Antony,[108] like those of Pachomius,[109] John Colobos,[110] and others, have the explicit character of a vision.[111] John Moschus uses the expression 'γίομαι ἐν ἐκστάσει καί θεωρῶ:, I fell into an ecstasy and I saw', like a refrain.[112] The ideal suggested by Bessarion or Pseudo-Macarius: 'The monk ought to be as the cherubim and the seraphim: all eye',[113] can then be explained in terms of ecstasy. John Climacus explains this attitude: 'A monk, properly speaking, is someone whose soul's eye does not look haughtily, and whose bodily feeling is unmoved. . . . A monk experiences unceasing rapture of mind'.[114] The attitude of the Greek Fathers toward visions of the imagination is well known.[115]

*Ecstasy: 'Possession'*

Reservations about visions were motivated by a fear of illusions. Unlike the science of modern psychology, the Fathers were not concerned with the sickly hallucinations of abnormal subjects. They were afraid, on the contrary, that a normal human being might be influenced of the Evil One. This type of 'ecstasy' is no longer caused by the attraction of an 'object', but by the suggestion of someone who imposes himself imperiously on the exercise of another's faculties.

Should Christians, however, not put themselves, analogically, under the influence of the Holy Spirit? Docility to the Spirit, far from being an invention of the Montanists or other enthusiasts, is one of the traits typical of the disciples of Christ.[116] One of the rare miracles of Montanus to have come down to us[117] compares divine inspiration to a plectrum that makes the lyre vibrate. The image is classical—it appeared in the *Odes of Solomon*[118]—and would be used by the commentators on the Psalter. But Montanus strongly emphasized the passivity of the inspiration.

Submitting oneself passively to the divinity is a source of new knowledge, but the means of arriving at it is a possession, a μανία (mania, frenzy). The explanation of ecstasy Socrates gives in Plato's *Phaedrus* was well known in antiquity: 'There is also a madness which is a divine gift, and the source of the greatest blessings granted to men'.[119] Such must have been the prophetic or 'mantic' inspiration attributed to Apollo and the ceremonies of initiation, the 'madness' produced by the ceremonies called τελεσταί, the 'mysteries'.[120]

It was along these lines that Tertullian proposed his explanation of montanist prophesying. What did he mean by 'ecstasy'? The latin equivalents of the greek term already let us understand: it is an *amentia* (insanity), an *excessus mentis* (being out of one's mind).[121] It certainly is a form of *amentia,* since responsibility and freedom no longer intervene and everything takes place in the margin of the intellect. But there is no total *amentia* because the memory subsists. Such an ecstasy is *operatrix prophetiae,* 'the operative virtue of prophecy'.[122] This, Tertullian believed, was the ecstasy of Peter on Mount Tabor: 'And therefore, because it was in the Spirit that he now spoke, and not in his natural sense, he could not know what he had said'.[123]

## *The Ecstasy of the Prophets*

Reaction against montanist prophesying was so strong that the term 'prophet' disappeared from the vocabulary of the christian communities.[124] At the same time, they began to reflect on the nature of biblical prophecy. It is typical of second century apologetics to contrast the prophet and the diviner or magician. Justin and Athenagoras, whose formulations recall Philo of Alexandria, were the only ones to associate the phenomenon of prophecy with ecstasy.[125] However, they did not fail to emphasize that such ecstasy did not show any of the traits of possession, the possessed person being, by contrast, a pseudo-prophet.[126]

A mental derangement, Origen would say, cannot be compared to true prophecy. The latter presupposes a presence (ἐπιδημία) of the divine Spirit, and far from beclouding the awareness, his presence, on the contrary, illumines it by making the mind more clear-sighted, more dioratic *(dioratikos).*[127] Origen's position is the opposite of Tertullian's: there is no 'possession of the mind' that is not diabolical. While the evil spirit alienates and depraves the conscience, the good Spirit liberates and enlightens.[128] After Origen, exegetes unanimously rejected any concept of inspiration which, by making of the prophet a mere tool or plaything of the divine, would destroy his personality.[129] It is true that the prophet is 'inhabited' (κατοικεῖν), 'compelled or moved' (κινεῖν, ἐνεργεῖν), by the Spirit, and that he is often called a 'Spirit-bearer', pneumatophore (πνευματοφόρος), but the authors avoided applying terms that would evoke the ancient *mania* too closely.

### *Ecstasy: The Psychological Suspension of the Faculties*

While the spiritual authors were not directly concerned with psychology when they described the various degrees of prayer, they nonetheless observed the repercussions of it on the human constitution. For them, prayer was psychologically integrated, and all the faculties were involved. But in the higher spheres of prayer, one faculty was not always able, because of human weakness, to follow the dizzying flight of another.

Here is the explanation of Theophan the Recluse. Perfection consists in harmonious cooperation between all the parts of the human composite: the body, the soul, and the Spirit.[130] For an inferior part, for example the body, to prevail to such a degree that the higher parts fall silent is unnatural; the opposite, by contrast, is praiseworthy. This is what happens in the highest contemplation, in ecstasy. The natural powers of the soul are suspended, but there is no suspension of the Spirit.[131]

In this Theophan already mentions the higher degree of ecstasy, which is achieved in various stages. The first, according to the definition of prayer given by Nilus of Sinai, is 'a rapture (ἁρπαγή) of the mind, a total separation from all sensory things'.[132] During such ecstasy, the mind may perfectly forget all that is not God; this is the attitude of a soul which is perfectly removed from distractions, which has become 'insensitive' to all things, except prayer.[133] The evagrian ecstasy is more radical still: it refers to apophatic (negative) theology. It is the 'infinite ignorance' or 'unknowing' of all partial concepts, of all concepts; a state of 'pure intellectuality'.[134] The 'mysticism of darkness' is a new stage: the last step of intellectual cognition has been mounted and the soul then takes another path, that of 'the wings of love'. This is a 'departure' from the intellectual state. But there still is, at least in theory, a still higher step: 'spiritual' ecstasy.

### *Spiritual Ecstasy*

The outline sketched by Theophan the Recluse starts from the assumption that the last step of ecstasy is the suspension of all the soul's powers and the action of the power of the Holy Spirit alone. It is from this perspective that Isaac the Syrian (Isaac of Nineveh) describes 'the entry into the spiritual sphere' *(ruhonuto):* the soul arrives at the threshold of the stage that is beyond the capability of human powers. Characteristic of this state is the loss of the use of the senses: the soul no longer guides but is guided by the Spirit.[135]

A problem then arises: how is this 'spiritual ecstasy' different from the 'ecstasy-possession' described by Tertullian? Answering this question would be difficult if one were to limit oneself, like Messalians, to a view of the Holy Spirit only as 'another', 'a divine host', whereas he becomes what is most sublime in us, our true self,[136] our 'formal cause' (εἶδος),[137] 'the soul of our soul'.[138] While he 'suspends' our human faculties, he does not destroy them, but in a mysterious way makes them more perfect. Isaac the Syrian correctly compares spiritual ecstasy to the resurrection.[139]

The personal indwelling of the Spirit in the soul is a participation in the life of the Holy Trinity. While considering this mystery of union, we are justified in insisting as well on the distinction between persons. The soul does not lose herself in some nirvana; on the contrary, she maintains her personality and develops it to the highest degree,[140] even if, for the moment and in full freedom, she has sacrificed the use of her human faculties.

Through this participation in the trinitarian life, according to Pavel Florensky, the human person has access to the highest degree of knowledge. Our mind knows reality by contrasting itself to it as an 'object', by distinguishing itself from it. And in this dissociation, we also wish, deep down, to remain united with reality at the same time. 'Natural mysticism' attempts to overcome this difficulty by blurring the boundary between the 'me' and 'the other', between subject and object. It advocates the individual's absorption into universal reality. Only a consideration of life in the Trinity enables us to move away from this dead end: the trinitarian mystery is indeed the mystery of the unity of nature and the distinction of Persons.[141] Did Evagrius not correctly identify the last degree of *gnosis* with 'the contemplation of the Holy Trinity'?[142] 'Ex-stasy' and 'en-stasy' (ἐνδημία, presence) become one.

In this typically christian concept of ecstasy, other problems also find a solution, especially that of the voluntary renunciation of one's own human powers, of 'passivity' with respect to God. Taken in isolation, these expressions could lead us astray, especially if we were to compare them mechanically to analogous terms in non-christian mystics. In fact, following the example of Maximus the Confessor, they should be placed in a christological context. Maximus borrowed his terminology from Pseudo-Denys, whose vocabulary is still strongly reminiscent of Plato's. He speaks of a needed 'leaving self behind' which, in the summits of prayer, is 'a death of the mind' but also, because it takes place in Christ, a 'deifying self-negation' (στέρησις θεοποιός),[143] a participation in the Lord's death and resurrection. The mystical themes are thereby inserted into a new synthesis, with the Incarnation at its center.[144]

## *Spiritual Prayer According to Isaac of Nineveh*

The great syrian mystic Isaac of Nineveh has given us a description of the various elements of ecstasy.

He differentiates between the three stages of the spiritual life: 1) The bodily stage *(duboro pagrono);* 2) The psychic stage *(napsono):* the struggle against alien thoughts; 3) The spiritual stage *(ruhonuto):* letting oneself be ruled entirely by the Holy Spirit.[145] At its highest degree, this ascendency of the Spirit is seen in 'spiritual prayer'. It is a state of total passivity with respect to the action of the Spirit: 'Once the Spirit's activity starts to reign over the intellect—the orderer of senses and thoughts—then the inborn, natural free choice is removed, and the intellect is then itself guided and no longer guides.'[146] The faculties are 'submerged (or baptized) in a profound inebriation'.[147]

The formulation 'free choice is removed' may seem suspect. Isaac explains it as follows: 'From then on, the mind is easily moved by what is called the one knowledge which, according to The Exegete [Theodore of Mopsuestia], is wonderment *(tehro)* in God, that is, the state of the high condition to come given in the freedom of the immortal life after the Resurrection.'[148] In other words, Isaac knows that the problem cannot be solved in our present state, by wanting to safeguard freedom of choice at any price. After the resurrection, the soul no longer has to choose one object or the other, but lives in uninterrupted 'wonderment'.[149] This state does not correspond to 'the ecstasy of polarization', during which the eye's gaze is fascinated by an external object; the wonderment is caused by the Spirit, who is inside the soul. Isaac compares this descent of the Spirit into the soul during prayer to the descent of the Spirit on the eucharistic Bread and Wine, when everyone is standing in prayer.[150] It is therefore a matter, not of an alienation of our being, but of its deification.

## SYMBOLIC THEOLOGY

### *The World: 'A Forest of Symbols'*

The mystic journey, as we have followed it, moves from apophaticism through the mystery of darkness to direct contact with the love of God who reveals himself. The human person is then able to return to the created world and discover the original meaning of it as revelation or as a 'school for souls',[151] and to understand its value as 'word' of God. Such knowledge is not a passive reception of impressions coming from outside. Spiritual understanding, which is a gift of God, is combined with personal creativity to build in everything that can be seen, a place of encounter, a temple. Only then does one truly know the created world.

In biblical language, knowing things is synonymous with 'naming' them. God put the finishing touches to creation by bestowing names (Gn 1:3-10). Pretending that man can do the same with respect to reality is impious. But with knowledge of God, God gives us the possibility of 'naming', that is, of giving a spiritual meaning to all that is visible (Gn 2:20). As a consequence, all concepts we elaborate about God on the basis of created things are not mere inventions, devoid of value: they are symbols of the Truth which reveals itself and of the divine mysteries.

The entire cosmos then becomes 'a forest of symbols' (to cite Baudelaire). Mystical events do indeed have a repercussion on the 'knowledge of beings'. In this forest then everyone picks a favorite flower. This is why 'symbolic theology' appears under extremely varied aspects: at one and the same time a symbolic explanation of texts from Scripture, of the visible cosmos, of the events of universal and personal history, of the structure of the human being, and so on. The alexandrian Fathers even insisted on the symbolic character of the humanity of Christ. Lastly, there is also a liturgical mysticism that develops a symbolism of church rites, the temple building, and icons.[152]

### *Scriptural Mysticism*

Mystics read the texts of Scripture according to their symbolic meaning. Thus, the key used by the first christian exegetes for reading the Old Testament could serve equally well for the New. The New Testament, the Fathers said, brought the truth and put an end to the images of the ancient Scriptures. The Incarnation has removed the veil that covered the Law. But, confronting such statements stands this antithesis: for as long as our knowledge is linked to our earthly condition and we see 'in a mirror dimly', the temporal gospel is still an image for us. Even the gospel itself has 'a letter', and as is true for the letter of the Law, one must move beyond it.[153]

Even if the ways of interpreting scriptural texts symbolically differ according to the various types of spiritual exegesis, the great rules drawn up by Origen remained valid norms for many centuries, and would inspire a never ending exploration of the meaning of Scripture hidden beneath the letter of the sacred text. Numerous examples from mystical literature prove that such ceaseless meditation raises the soul to the highest union with God.

### *The Symbolism of the Visible World*

While the mystery is spiritual and invisible, material creatures are sensory, corporeal, and visible. Unable to become the object of true knowledge, they are, above all, everything they symbolize, and serve as a foundation for spiritual knowledge.

According to Origen's terminology,[154] they are 'an image' (εἰκών), 'a shadow' (σκιά), 'a model' (ὑπόδειγμα, παραδείγμα), 'an imitation' (μίμημα), 'a type' (τύπος), 'a symbol' (σύμβολον), 'a riddle' (αἴνιγμα), and 'a sign' (σημεῖον) because they possess only imperfectly the reality to which they correspond.

Thus, the stars are 'signs' (unlike the fatalism which divines their movements), as are the earth, the animals and plants, and so forth—all the things that are the object of 'natural contemplation' *(theoria physike)*.[155]

In all those things which the soul earlier saw only as obstacles to her pure love for her Creator and Lord, God reveals many means to be found by which he shows his love, and which the soul, in turn, uses to love him. In this way, the soul is able to sing her 'Canticle of Creation'.[156]

The stories of famous russian pilgrims contain numerous examples of this type of praise. Here is one taken from the biographical memoirs of Archimandrite Spiridon:

> Every day, in the open field, we praised God. We spoke of him and of the kingdom of heaven. Our soul was happy. All of nature celebrated with us. I felt especially happy when we had to cross fields and woods. My soul rejoiced in the larks, the nightingales,

> the blackbirds, the goldfinches, the cranes and, generally, in all the birds, the animals, the trees and grasses, and at night in the stars of heaven.[157]

### *The Mysticism of Events*

While the Greeks sought God above all in the cosmos, the Hebrews found him while pondering their history. The 'contemplation of Providence' can feed this type of meditation on the events of one's personal life. Following the example of the authors of Scripture, the goal of the teaching of Isaac of Nineveh and other syrian mystics was to make the monk look at everything that happened around him with an eye that already anticipated vision in heaven in the world of the Resurrection.[158]

This outlook sets events in a new light; it changes our judgments and our assessment of reality: what appears great to men of the world will be of no consequence to the person of God, and conversely. When spiritual people write historic tales, the connection between facts is viewed from a distinctive angle: daily struggles became symbolic of the struggle of Christ against the Prince of Darkness. The cross and persecutions appear in transformation: they become a reason for joy, a sign of victory.

The famous expression of Dostoevsky, 'Suffering is good; through it everything is expiated', sums up a long tradition of the Russian *strasstoterpsy* (those who have suffered 'a passion'), that is, those who accepted any kind of unjust persecutions, seeing in them the signs of a special call for the purification of the world.

In the *Sacred Elegies* of Gregory of Nareg, we find a certain 'mysticism of sin' in a special, very positive sense: the sinner who repents finds even in the remembrance of his own aberrations an opportunity to experience mystically the immense mercy of God who loves humankind.[159]

### *The Vision of God Through the Vision of Self*

The Fathers spoke frequently, and in various circumstances, of the divine image and likeness in man.[160] As the most perfect image of God, the human person is the pre-eminent symbol of *theognosia,* knowledge of God. We arrive at the knowledge of God through self-knowledge. 'Knowing yourself', Basil writes, 'will lead to the knowledge of God.' 'Here is what the prophet says, "Such knowledge is beyond my understanding, so high that I cannot reach it" (Ps 138:6), that is, by knowing myself, I have learned the infinite wisdom that is in you'.[161] In the same sense, Gregory Nazianzus exhorts: 'Know yourself, O excellent one! Know who you are and where you come from. On this path, you will easily reach the beauty of the Archetype.'[162]

There is a great diversity of opinion about the nature of the divine image in man.[163] From the practical point of view of interest to the ascetic writers, the question was as follows: which human quality is most like God? That is the one which must be cultivated in the first place; it is there that God is found most easily.

For Evagrius the image of God consists in the cognitive faculty. In emphasizing this, he founded a tradition which, through Isaac of Nineveh and the other Syrians, reached down to the muslim mystics. 'Seeing God in oneself' is actualized 'when the rational nature contemplates itself',[164] when it sees 'the splendor that is proper to the *nous* and surrounds it at the time of prayer'.[165]

When we speak of such 'intellectual' mysticism, we should not forget that the greek *nous* does not entirely coincide with the concepts of 'mind' or 'reason' as they are used in the language of modern psychology, which gives them a narrower meaning which differentiates them from desire and will.[166] But this observation does not diminish the fact that the ability to know was what most astounded the Fathers, for they saw in this the unique privilege of humankind.[167] What obstacle prevents the human person who rejoices in knowing something, then, from seeing in his or her own knowledge, in the very fact that we are able to know, the image of God? According to the aristotelian definition, the actuality of thought *(nous)* is life, and God is that actuality.[168]

Amazement about the greatness of the rational human person is a frequent homiletic theme—for example, in Basil. 'You have been given a mind capable of understanding *(psychen noeran),* through which you gain knowledge of God. You investigate, with the aid of your reason, the nature of existing things. You pluck the exceedingly sweet fruit of wisdom.'[169]

In Descartes' *Cogito ergo sum,* 'I think' proves one's own existence ('therefore I am'). For the greek Fathers, 'I think' is the symbol of God's existence, for those who 'contemplate the reasons for creation can somehow understand the goodness of the Providence of God . . . ; the voice of the Lord dwells in them', Basil continues.[170]

### *The Symbols of Faith*

A rational human person exercises the cognitive faculty by forming notions and concepts. In the same way, too, a person strives to think of God. How valuable are such products of human intelligence? The problem of 'rational theology' was, and always will be, real.

In an Eunomius, a Gemisthus Plethon, a Barlaam of Calabria, and others, the greek tradition has known arid rationalism, an encyclopedism seldom attuned to spiritual problems. No wonder that simple people saw 'a diabolical invention' in theological learning![171] Furthermore, the East has never lacked great minds steeped in rational theology, even under the monastic habit. The days of theological controversy show, sometimes too vividly, that the resources of dialectic were at that time not to be ridiculed. It was Origen's vision to give the christian faith and its wisdom a dialectic, a ἀπόδειξις λογική—a proof by strict argument, similar to that of greek philosophy.[172]

What strife there was in formulating the conciliar 'definitions'! It would be wrong, certainly, to interpret such definitions in the manner of aristotelian 'definitions'. But it remains true that a high value was placed on 'precise concepts', on 'ideas' as expressions of the orthodox faith. If the Word, to reveal himself, did not disdain the flesh, why would he recoil from speaking to human persons endowed with reason by using rational concepts?

Yet spiritual authors always had to wonder: Why is it that some persons use rational reflections with great profit, even in their meditative prayers,[173] while for others the same exercise can be an obstacle to prayer?[174] The answer never varied: without charity and without humility the human person tends to view the products of the brain as precise, infallible notions that 'measure the Deity',[175] and thereby convert theology into 'logic-chopping' *(technologia).*[176]

The expression 'Symbol of the Faith' *(symbolum fidei)* is very appropriate. To understand a symbol presupposes having a vision of what is symbolized. So, 'the one who has not seen God cannot speak of God', as the highly speculative Evagrius declared. Such vision is given to those who are pure of heart. 'Only the one who has reached this degree (of perfection) does it befit to deal with questions concerning the Godhead . . .'[177], stated Philoxenes of Mabbug, bishop though he was.

The Russians of our day are fond of saying that christian truth is not *'illogical',* since one tries to understand it by means of concepts. It is *'meta-logical',* 'beyond logic', the object of mystical vision.[178] Mysticism is needed to save the value of knowledge. This is the main thesis in the thought of Vladimir Soloviev.[179]

*The Transcendent Value of the Desire for Happiness*

If the Greeks esteemed theoretical knowledge so greatly, it was because they realized that knowing satisfies a person's deepest desire. As a mysticism of the *nous,* platonic mysticism is at the same time a mysticism of the desire *(eros)* for God.[180] It is true, however, that the desire for one's own good is often characterized as egotism. Indeed, an egotist is someone who gives an absolute character to his or her smallest, solitary desire. But in this quest for a specific good, can one not see a nostalgia for infinite Blessedness? The essential quality of human desires lies in their insatiability; in this, they show the way to God, the absolute Good.

How important the desire for happiness was in Augustine's conversion is well known. His famous *Irrequietum cor* ('our heart is restless')[181] inspired Theophan the Recluse to a meditation on this point. The nostalgia for God, he says, is linked indivisibly to everything we desire, and it prompts 'a general discontent with every creature'.[182] The long road of the spiritual life is bracketed by this *irrequietum* and the *donec requiescat in te* ('until it rests in Thee'). The first temptation of the human person, Theophan continues, consists in lowering the eternal perspective to the level of ephemeral desires, in forgetting 'the universal tendency toward the most perfect good'.[183] For the spirit 'might possibly grow dull'.[184] The demon suggests to us thoughts 'that detain us in the world'.[185] The Holy Spirit, by contrast, kindles the flame of our desires and lets us understand that 'in this life, there is no life'.[186] The restlessness that accompanies all our desires becomes a sign that leads to the heights. The human person realizes that God is loved in this very love of the created.

### *The Symbolism of Carnal Love*

The Spirit, Theophan says, awakens the desire for the divine Infinite. Fleshly desires deaden it; but, conversely, the Spirit deifies the body and all its activity. Also, after successive purifications, even the desires described as 'carnal' can become an image of the spiritual ascent toward the divine reality.

The treatise by Vladimir Soloviev entitled *The Meaning of Love*[187] and several passages from his handbook on morality, *The Justification of the Good*[188] rank among the best examples of a mysticism of married love or of a 'spiritualization of sex love'. Soloviev himself summarizes his main ideas:

> In a true marriage the natural sexual tie is not abolished but transubstantiated. The necessary data for the moral problem of such transubstantiation are the natural elements of the sexual relation: 1) carnal desire; 2) being in love; 3) childbearing. Marriage remains the satisfaction of the sexual desire, but the object of that desire is no longer the satisfaction of the animal organism, but the restoration of the image of God in man.[189]

Soloviev's essential idea is this: we should follow the natural evolution of our own carnal life and seek to understand it as a material initiation into the spiritual evolution of souls, and of their desire to live in eternal union in a divinized life. 'The amorous state' of the young is especially rich in spiritual symbolism. It leads those to whom it is given to understand this, to choose virginity for the love of God and human persons.

### *The Symbolism of the Human Body*

Ascetic authors focused their attention chiefly on the temptations that are inherent in the inferior part of our being.[190] But all

Orthodox accept the participation of the body in the ascent of mind to God. They see in it a foretaste of the eschatological transformation that will bring with it a spiritualization of matter.

In practice, the spiritual symbolism of the body was incorporated into the liturgy from the beginning.[191] The role of the body during prayer was explicitly taken up as a theological problem by Gregory Palamas. In his *Defense of the Holy Hesychasts* against Barlaam, who had attacked the psycho-somatic methods of prayer, he apparently admitted the patristic concept of the primacy of the spirit in the human composite, but pointed out that this primacy does not destroy, but transfigures, the body: 'In the same manner, indeed, as the divinity of the Word is common to the body and soul [of Christ], so, with spiritual men, does the grace of the Spirit, transmitted to the body through the intermediary of the soul, also give it an experience of things divine.'[192] The body with its members, transformed into a glorious body (Phil 3:21), causes us to bear 'the likeness of the heavenly Adam' (1 Cor 15:49), and become an instrument of revelation, a sign, a visible word.[193]

## *The Mysticism of the Church*

Gregory of Nyssa noted that, in the context of the image of God, 'the human person' is to be understood especially as 'the human totality', the human *pleroma,* as it is sanctified in the Church.[194] He developed this symbolism of the Church on several occasions[195] and generally in this sense: 'The one who looks at the Church, looks at Christ'; the face of the Bride makes known the face of the Bridegroom.[196] The various stages of this vision are expressed by the following terms: ἐπιφάνεια (a manifestation, epiphany), διαλέγεται, (a discourse), and βλέπει (a seeing).[197]

The Church as the Bride of Christ is a concept that predominates in the syrian liturgy, western or eastern.[198] To the eastern imagination, nothing is more intimate than the union of bride and bridegroom. From this it follows that the syriac liturgy describes the relationships between Christ and the Church by analogy to the eastern customs of betrothal and marriage, and never tires of praising the beauty of the Bride of Christ by bringing into play all the poetic figures the eastern mind could invent. 'On your face, he has spread the splendor of his heavenly glory.'[199] As fullness *(pleroma),* the Church is a complex, universal reality. In mystical considerations, one aspect or the other predominates. There is a 'sacramental',[200] and a 'liturgical' mysticism,[201] a mysticism of icons[202] and of everything that conveys us from the visible to the invisible.

### *The Dangers of Symbolic Theology*

In dealing with the great problem of christian symbolism, Origen asked himself this fundamental question: Why does God speak to people in physical images, but gives them the truth only in obscure form? Here, in a few words, is his answer.[203]

The first reason is our corporeality: 'Human nature, dressed in skin and flesh, mingled with bones and nerves, can by its natural powers not tolerate naked Justice itself or pure Truth.'[204] The density of the flesh has resulted from the Fall; it stands before the human person's mind like an obstacle to a knowledge of the Truth.[205]

This is why Christ, Justice and Truth, took on the form of a slave, Origen continues. The Church-Bride desires to sit beneath the shadow of the apple tree, symbolizing her Bridegroom, the incarnate Christ. 'It seems that every soul, as long as she is in this present life, must by necessity sit in his shadow.'[206] According to 1 Cor 1:21, 'the foolishness of preaching' is the proclamation of Christ incarnate and crucified; it is 'the foolishness of God' which is wiser than all of human wisdom.[207]

Only by means of sensory forms could God speak to the human person, immured by the body, unable to understand except through the mediation of bodily organs. The entire divine economy demonstrated in Scripture is a pedagogy. God lets himself be represented in human form and speaks a human language. Christ achieves in his Incarnation what the Father carried out only *in figura*[208]; the Holy Spirit is compared to a master accepting an ignorant pupil *(suscipiens rudem discipulum).*[209]

Even so, Origen did not fail to warn of the dangers of symbolism in *theognosia.* The illusion consists in viewing the symbol, which is the point of departure, as the truth. The golden rule of symbolic theology is, therefore, to move beyond the symbol. Indeed, knowledge cannot rest in what is contingent and in the process of becoming: the symbol is not the ultimate object of knowledge. The vision of beings cannot linger at their sensory 'surface'. True 'knowledge' *(gnosis alethine)* consists in continually going beyond. Pretending to find the absolute where only the contingent exists is the deadly sin against knowledge, the sin of idolaters, of those who do not see that the Old Testament is 'shadow and figure'.[210]

Idolaters are the truly blind: 'They are unable to look up from the magnificence of the world . . . , and from the beauty of created things to see that they ought to worship and admire and reverence Him alone who created these things.'[211]

In the mystic ascent, certain types of idolatry are particularly insidious.

### *Carnal Idolatry*

'We cannot know God outside the economy in which he reveals himself,' writes Vladimir Lossky.[212] Since God reveals himself in what is sensory, the starting point of our knowledge will be the reality accessible to our physical senses. When dealing with this aspect of the problem, the Fathers are close to Aristotelianism. As an instrument of knowledge, the body brings a material element to the activity of the mind: the imagination. Consequently, incorporeal God is expressed through perceptions and words drawn from sensory experience: 'We transfer these to God', noted Gregory Nazianzus.[213]

'Transferring' images to God is difficult; it is hard work, Origen says.[214] And it is a dangerous enterprise, Gregory Nazianzus adds. We 'give chase' to transcendent realities with our senses, because we are their prisoners. But if we do not pay close attention, they carry us away at their whim and lead us astray because of the weakness of the flesh.

> They looked at visible things, and gave to one of them the name of God. . . . And this was the trick of the Evil One, who abused good to an evil purpose. . . . For he laid hold of their desire in its wandering in search of God, in order to distort to himself the power, and steal the desire.[215]

The idolatry of the sensory things and the seduction of 'appearances' are overcome by 'the power of the pure mind' (νοῦς καθαρός), capable of contemplating the Ideas—at least, this is what the ancient classical philosophers believed.[216] Christians know that the danger lies much deeper, for there is still another, more subtle 'idolatry' that resides in the realm of the intellect itself.

### *The Idolatry of Concepts*

The idolatry of rational concepts is indeed more subtle than the idolatry of sensory things. It is dangerous to recognize as God what is only the product of our intellectual activity.[217] 'Woe to the one who reduces theology to disputatiousness (τεχνύδριον)', exclaimed Gregory the Theologian against the Arians.[218] To explain what causes this aberration, he continued:

> Every rational being longs for God and for the First Cause, but without help is unable to grasp him.[219]
>
> Exhausted therefore by desire, and as it were restive and impatient of the disability, [the human person] tries a second course [and accepts the result of such reasoning as God]. The weakness of our argument is ascribed to the mystery itself; and thus, cleverness of language reduces the cross of Christ to nothing.[220]

Gregory's explanation is benevolent enough and of a psychological nature. Origen's judgment is much harsher: if the true knowledge of God is love and union, ignorance of God is caused by sin, obstinacy, and pride.[221] Hence the need for moral purification.[222]

But once such purification is accomplished, how can we overcome the feebleness of our human concepts? Gregory Nazianzus gives this advice: we should turn to 'the second navigation' *(deuteros plous),*[223] and move from a human understanding to that which only the Spirit can provide. And if we ask the spiritual writers the means by which we mount up to this kind of understanding, they have only one answer: through prayer. Reasoned reflection becomes theology when it becomes prayerful reflection: 'If you are a theologian you truly pray.'[224]

### *Anything Not God Can Become an Idol*

The varieties of idolatry are as numerous and diverse as created beings. The danger of 'idols' lurks everywhere, today as in former days. Nicolai Berdyaev vehemently warned moderns against 'objectifying' the world, institutions, even the forms of religion, and falling into enslavement to things. 'Man is in a state of servitude. He frequently does not notice that he is a slave, and sometimes he loves it.'[225] By contrast, 'A man who is free should feel himself to be not on the circumference of the objectified world, but at the center of the spiritual world.'[226]

To become free, the human person needs to plunge into 'ecstasy', which is in its depth nothing but the love of God which surpasses everything we encounter. Thus, 'in the spiritual liberation of man there is a movement in the direction of freedom, truth, and love'.[227] Only when the human person has made the transition from being enslaved by things to the freedom of the children of God, 'will the Second Coming of Christ take place, and then there will be a new heaven and a new earth—and the kingdom of freedom will come'.[228]

## THE MYSTICISM OF LIGHT

### *Two Types of Mysticism*

The path of the ascent to God we have followed till now is that of 'the mysticism of darkness'. Gregory of Nyssa originally expressed this experience, using the classic terms of an intellectual ecstasy. Another type of mysticism may, however, be contrasted to this, that of 'the light'. The most eloquent representative of this second type is Evagrius, for whom the gnostic life cannot be *'ek-static'* but *'kata-static'* ('settled'), because the *nous* is the image of God. Therefore, the mind does not 'move away from itself', but returns to its proper activity: at the intellectual summit, it 'reflects the light of the Holy Trinity'. Thus, this return to self is an ἀποδημία (inward journey), an ἐνδημία (presence), not an ἐκ-στασις ('a standing outside of one's self').[229]

Are these two positions really diametrically opposed? Actually, both have founded a tradition in the East, and, surprisingly, they often intertwine. To evaluate them properly, we should attentively observe the terms used to express them, while taking into account the context.

## *God Is Light*

'For as those who see the light are within the light and partake of its brilliancy; even so those who see God are in God and receive of his splendor. Those, therefore who see God, do receive life,' wrote Irenaeus.[230] In christian mysticism, the symbolism of light is very rich, from its beginnings to its continuation in Palamas. It starts in Scripture, especially in the Gospel of John.[231] God is Light as he is Life, as he is Holiness, Charity *(agape),* Infinite Goodness. Christians are children of the light. Light and darkness are terms that are often used to refer to the illumination of the mind.[232]

Clement of Alexandria applied to the divine light epithets which everyone took over: the light is without form, without image (φῶς ἀσχημάτιστον ἀνεικόνιστον).[233] Origen distinguished between the paternal light (φῶς πατρικόν), the radiance of Christ (ἀπαύγασμα), and the illumination of the Holy Spirit (ἔλλαμψις).[234] 'Any rational being partakes of this true light.'[235] For Symeon the New Theologian, 'the cloud' itself is not the mosaic cloud, the darkness, but 'a very luminous cloud', the glory of Tabor.[236]

## *Two Trends in the Mysticism of Light*

Ascetics who aspired to the luminous experience of God belonged to two groups: one of a more primitive mentality, the other closer to the intellectuals.[237] The former did not know the learned vocabulary and based themselves exclusively on the revelation of the Spirit promised in Scripture, as a continuation of the early charisms. This was the environment in which Messalianism developed. The transition from orthodoxy to heresy is often imperceptible. 'The soul that has become all light' is a concept that played a crucial role in the *Spiritual Homilies* of Pseudo-Macarius.[238] The mind is overwhelmed by light, great beams of light were perceived by some, and so on.

The other trend depends on Origen, at least in part. It is a matter no longer either of seeing external splendors or of feeling 'surrounded by light', but of becoming light oneself. It is in this sense that Gregory Nazianzus distinguishes between 'three lights': God, the angel, and the human person. 'The human being is called *phos* (light) because of the faculty of reason that is in us.'[239] Even when our intelligence has been illumined by the Spirit, this enlightenment remains inward, as 'art is potentially in the artist'.[240] The best interpreter of this tradition is Evagrius, for whom life is the life of the mind, and happiness the light that is proper to it.

### *Evagrius: The Nakedness of the Intellect The Condition for Seeing Pure Light*

To see the light, the intellect must purify itself of everything which the shadow produces in it. The evagrian purification is the most demanding of all: it requires a perfect nakedness of an intellect divested of all multiplicity, of its 'last vestment'.[241] We reach it by steps. The first step consists in leaving behind objects themselves.[242] The second, in banishing passionate thoughts and memories.[243] The third, in rising above simple thoughts. These last remain an obstacle, because they constitute a multiplicity (ποικίλλεσθαι) [from the word ποικίλια, embroidery], and because they are 'diversified thoughts'.[244] Perfect prayer is 'the rejection of concepts' (ἀπόθεσις νοημάτων).[245]

The reason for this last purification hangs on the vivid contrast between the absolute simplicity of God and contemplation of him through created beings. 'God is without quantity',[246] whereas 'the reasons' *(logoi)* of beings are a reflection of various divine attributes. This is why the inferior contemplations of the various *logoi* ('reasons') are an ascent from *gnosis* to *gnosis*[247] toward the 'uniform *gnosis* of the Holy Trinity'.[248] Evagrius had difficulty in harmonizing the doctrine of the Trinity with divine simplicity, but he found a solution: the Trinity is not a numerical Trinity[249] as it is beyond number.

'Pure prayer' (προσευχὴ καθαρά) therefore presupposes a 'nakedness of the intellect': 'The naked intellect is the one that is perfect in the sight of itself'.[250] It is the total absence of sensory impressions (ἀναισθησία) and of forms (ἀμορφία).[251] The contemplation of the Holy Trinity must be ἀνείδεος, without form of figure, like God himself.[252] Thus we must divest ourselves from thoughts that 'give to the mind an imprint (τυποῦσιν) and a form' (σχηματίζουσίν).[253] After acquiring a 'perfect formlessness',[254] the mind 'becomes free of all matter'.[255]

### *'Essential Knowledge': Seeing One's Own Light*

The reward for the ultimate denudation of faculties is great, Evagrius assures us: it is the 'essential knowledge of God' (γνῶσις οὐσιώδης),[256] 'a substantial knowledge of God'.[257] How is one to understand such knowledge? Manifestly, there can be no question here of a knowledge identical to that which God has of himself, which would presuppose that we are consubstantial with him.[258]

For the mind, such knowledge is typified as 'the vision of its own light'. Invoking Basil, Evagrius speaks of 'the splendor of the light which is proper to the mind and in which the most pure see themselves bathed at the time of prayer'.[259] The human *nous* which is in the image of God becomes pure light, and on this intellectual height it 'reflects the light of the Holy Trinity'.[260]

The mysticism of Evagrius is not a mysticism of ecstasy. Of the Pseudo-Dionysian formula ἑαυτοῦ καὶ πάντων ἔκστασις, 'a leaving behind of oneself and all things',[261] Evagrius would have accepted 'of all things', but not 'of oneself'. And he would not have said 'ecstasy': the word is not found in his writings except in a pejorative sense. For Evagrius, the gnostic life is the return to self,[262] but in this return 'the *nous* sees the Holy Trinity'.[263] What defines the *nous* as the image of God is in fact its relationship to the Trinity, more precisely, its ability to contemplate the Trinity. In one word, 'It pertains to the mind to be engaged in contemplation . . . because in this is its life'.[264] 'Prayer . . . prepares the spirit to put its powers into operation',[265] and 'of all the created things, only the mind can receive knowledge of the Holy Trinity'.[266]

In outline, Evagrius' thought is presented in a rather simple form, but it is precisely this apparent simplicity that gives rise to numerous objections. We can legitimately ask this question: does the elimination of concepts not destroy what Evagrius wanted to save—human intellectuality? Its resemblance to the mysticism of nirvana, which renounces all thought, is striking. This is why we should evaluate this teaching not simply in function of the terms used in it, but should also verify the value a Christian can attribute to them and the interpretation they were given by the subsequent tradition. Let us note above all that the term 'nakedness of the intellect' does not belong to Evagrius alone: it is a traditional one.

### *The Nakedness of the Intellect: A Traditional Term*[267]

In Scripture and rabbinic texts, the 'deprivation of a vestment' is a sign of a loss of identity, of a freedom that has been taken away: it is applied to captives, slaves, prostitutes, the demented, and the dead who were buried naked.[268]

In spiritual literature, we discern two traditions of nakedness in a positive sense. The first sees in it a form of evangelical poverty and finds its formulation in Jerome's aphorism 'naked, we follow the naked Christ' *(nudus nudum Jesum sequi)*[269]; the second trend, followed by contemplatives and mystics, viewed denudation as a complete purification of all the human faculties and activities as a means of attaining a mystical knowledge of God and union with him.

For Gregory of Nyssa, virginity is a return to the original nakedness of Adam and results in a restoration in the human person of the image of God in its original splendor: Adam was 'destitute of this covering of dead skins, but he could gaze with frankness *(parrhesia)* upon God's countenance'.[270]

Pseudo-Denys saw in 'the seraphs' discalced feet' (see Is 6:2) an indication that there is in these heavenly creatures 'a freedom, a being unattached, a not being held, a being pure of any outer appendage, an assimilation with the divine simplicity, as far as is permitted'. Among people, similarly, 'anyone who has a relationship with the One cannot live a divided life'.[271] What is more, the mysteries must be divested of their symbolic representations if we are to behold them 'naked and pure' *(gymna kai kathara)*.[272]

### *The Confrontation Between the Two Mystical Ways*

The nakedness of the intellect is a phrase which, in principle, agrees with the apophatic effort we described earlier. The objection we could make against Evagrius is that the renunciation he demands is at the same time insufficient and overly radical. While he does not wish to abandon intelligence, he reduces it to a state that seems to destroy it. Furthermore—and this is still more serious for the Christian—, we find hardly any place for Christ, and it is not clear how the function of charity *(agape)* could be inserted into his scheme. Can we find a satisfactory answer to these objections?

Let us begin with the last problem, the absence of charity. The concept of divesting oneself of everything not belonging to the state of pure intellectuality derives from the language of the Platonists. Its motive is the presence of *eros,* the intellectual desire to know divine reality. But from the point of view of knowledge, there is an essential difference between Plato and Evagrius. The God of the Christians is not the supreme Idea, but the Holy Trinity—which Evagrius emphasizes at every opportunity. But how could one 'know' the mysterious relationship between the Father, the Son, and the Holy Spirit, unless divine *agape* reveals it? Here the role of Christ is indispensable. Who else could lead human persons to a vision of the Holy Trinity? And how could we know the Father if not through the Son, in the Spirit? And only Christ can guarantee life to the intellect that has resolved to sacrifice its concepts, even if they are partial. All the authors who have written about obedience know that renouncing one's ideas is the most difficult sacrifice; there can be no other reason for it than the love of God.[273]

It could be said, certainly, that this interpretation of Evagrius is too generous, and that it moves away from the texts. Let us therefore turn to the successors of Evagrius, who clarify his thought. In Cassian the 'pure' prayer of Evagrius is called 'the fiery prayer' and it includes 'an ardent charity'.[274] Who assimilated the evagrian doctrine better than the great mystic Isaac the Syrian (Isaac of Nineveh)?[275] A quick reading of his *De perfectione religiosa* leaves no doubt that the doctrine of 'the wise among the saints', of 'the prince of gnostics', that is to say, Evagrius, had been assimilated in terms of a language that is typically christian. The state of 'pure intellectuality', when 'the intellect is moved from now on by what is called the only knowledge',[276] is called *ruhonuto,* a 'spiritual' state, when 'the Spirit's activity starts to reign over the intellect'.[277]

Better to understand the 'vision of the pure light' and the role attributed to Christ in it, nothing is more useful than reading about the conversion of 'the great mystic of light'—Symeon the New Theologian.

### *The Light in the Heart According to Symeon the New Theologian*

To understand how refreshing Symeon's spiritual experience was, we should read the texts he wrote himself. Here we must limit ourselves to highlighting the guiding concept. From the beginning of his conversion, Symeon sought neither 'rules' of life nor abstract ideas about divinity, but he learned how to 'listen to the voice of his own conscience', and he prolonged his nocturnal prayers with an adolescent zeal. The visions arrived, and he has given us an invaluable description of them.

'One night', he writes, 'he saw nothing but light all around him. . . . His mind ascended to heaven and beheld yet another light which was clearer than that which was close at hand.'[278] The vision passed quickly, and the young man returned to a life of worldly dissipation. But a second conversion proved more lasting. Symeon left the world and became a monk. He had new visions, but also gained an important experience: a mere vision of the light does not bring peace to the soul; it caused an intense weariness, a deceptive satisfaction.[279]

Finally, after apparitions and dry periods had repeatedly alternated, the decisive moment arrived: he discovered that in the light it was Christ who began to speak. 'And then for the first time, You deemed me worthy—me, the prodigal—of hearing your voice.'[280]

But his most important discovery was that Christ did not speak from outside. 'I knew that I possessed you consciously in me.'[281] What was the sign of this presence? 'The abiding Love which I possessed in me; yes, Love itself, which is indeed what you are, O God.'[282]

Here we discover one of the most important moments of Symeon's mystical development. He began to realize with certainty that it was not he himself, 'the brother-loving poor man' (πτωχός φιλάδελφος) who loved the brethren, but it was Christ, the true treasure, who in the heart of Symeon loves the human person. This is what is called knowing God by experiencing him inwardly. 'It is not of myself that I say this', Symeon continues,

> He who himself is the treasure has said, and still says, 'I am the resurrection and the life', 'I am the mustard seed that was hidden in the ground'; 'I am the pearl' that is bought by the faithful. . . . I am the luminous source of the immortal stream and river. In it those who love me with (all their) soul are washed by the water that flows from Me, not after death but hour by hour, and are cleansed from every stain in body and soul, so that they are completely radiant like a lamp and have the appearance of a sunbeam.[283]

While speaking of the mysticism of darkness, we made a distinction between 'knowledge' and 'awareness'.[284] The first we renounce, but the second remains in us; and this is proof, on the one hand, of the ardor of the heart's desire and, on the other, of its satisfaction by divine *agape*. The mysticism of light requires that we renounce the incomplete knowledge of objects; what remains is a vision of pure light. But, as we see from Symeon's story, does this pure light not resemble the 'awareness' of an encounter with Christ, in the sense of his presence in us, which is so strong that everything else is pushed into oblivion? The two mystic visions—of darkness and of light—merely express in antithetical terms a spiritual experience which is fundamentally the same.

## THE MYSTICISM OF THE HEART

### *The Importance of the Subject in Eastern Spirituality*

How many times have we come across the word 'heart' in the spiritual writings of the East! They speak of 'guarding the heart', 'attentiveness to the heart', 'purity of heart', 'the thoughts, desires, and resolutions of the heart', 'prayer of the heart', 'revelations of the heart', 'the divine presence in the heart, and on it goes.[285]

Russian authors are fond of making the heart a badge to dissociate themselves from the 'rationalist' West, which tends to forget that the heart is the foundation of the christian life. In his short work, *Peace in Christ,* P. Ivanov writes:

> To seek nourishment for the heart means turning to God, because God himself is a heart that enfolds everything. Only through the heart can we understand the secret of the universe, what Kant has called *Das Ding an Sich* [*The Thing in Itself*]. Therefore anyone who has a heart sees God, people, the animals, and nature. Only the heart is able to give peace to the mind.[286]

Another Russian, Boris Vyšeslavcev, states that if religion is a relationship with God, true contact with the deity is possible only 'in the depth of the heart, the "me", since God, according to Pascal,[287] is sensitive to the heart. Only there is an authentic religious experience possible, outside of which there is neither religion nor a true ethic.'[288] 'A human person without heart is one without love for religion; and ultimately, atheism is but a state without heart.'[289] Therefore, the same author believes, the concept of the heart occupies *the* central place in the mysticism, religion, and poetry of all peoples.[290]

The teaching in textbooks on dogma is no different. Let us quote, among others, Th. S. Ornatsky[291]—'Faith is an immediate disposition of the heart'; N. Malinovski[292]—'Faith can be understood only as the religion of feeling'; P. Sokolov[293]—'Faith is motivated by feeling'; J. Nikolin[294]—'Faith is born in the domain of feeling', and 'it must be kindled and nurtured by feeling'.[295]

### *The Ambiguity of the Term*

This insistence on the feelings of the heart is not without its dangers, in the opinion of western theologians. The most profound mystical experience or the most mundane truism, like a barely orthodox modernism, can be decked out with the same pompous ornament. Do all those people who so casually throw out impassioned phrases about the heart and the feelings always realize what they are referring to? True, the expressions some use can easily lead to the irrational and the sentimental. Faith would be totally opposed to scientific knowledge, and from that moment on one would not know what to do with 'the rational foundation' of the faith.[296]

The sin of the West, the Russians retort, is, by contrast, a rationalism which forgets that the heart is the foundation of the spiritual life. Theophan the Recluse saw the beginning of decadence in the humanism of the fifteenth century, first in Italy, then in England, France, and Germany. It is as if the devil, chained up for a thousand years (Rv 20:2) and suddenly unleashed, had begun by encouraging scholars to study ancient languages for the purpose of enticing their minds at the end into pagan pride.[297]

The Lord has commanded the faithful to shut themselves in their room to pray (Mt 6:6). This inner room, Theophan contends, is the heart. Consequently, it is the commandment of the Lord that requires us to pray in our heart.[298]

But is it easy to say which prayer is said in the heart? Vyšeslavcev, who has emphatically praised the function of the heart in religious life, refuses on principle to give details. 'The heart', he writes, 'is as mysterious as God himself, and is entirely accessible only to God. The prophet Jeremiah has said, "The heart is the most deceitful of all things, . . . who can fathom it? I, the Lord, search the mind and test the heart"' (17:9, 10).[299]

*The Heart in Scripture*

In Scripture, the word 'heart' *(lev* or *levav, kardia)* refers to the physical organ no more than perhaps ten times, whereas in the metaphorical sense it is used more than a thousand times, to indicate the seat of various psychological functions. It is the heart that thinks, reflects, conceives projects, makes resolutions and decisions, and assumes responsibilities. It is the heart, not the soul, that plays a central role in the inner life. The heart is the seat of the moral as well as the religious life. It is the heart that experiences fear of God; it is principally in the heart that loyalty to Yahweh resides (see 1 K 11:3-4).

In Scripture, the heart contains within itself the complete fullness of the spiritual life, which should involve the whole person, all faculties and all activities.[300]

But the heart escapes scrutiny. Normally, a person's conduct makes apparent what is in the heart. One knows the heart, indirectly, from the look on someone's face (Si 13:25), from someone's speech (Pr 16:23), from what someone's actions demonstrate (Lk 6:44ff). Yet instead of making the heart manifest, words and conduct can also conceal it (Pr 26:23-26; Si 12:16): the human being has the fearsome ability of double-mindedness.[301]

*The Heart in Christian Anthropology*

From the outset, christian anthropology differentiated between two levels in the human personality. At the same time, especially with the Alexandrians, it began to lean on the platonic doctrine of soul and body in order to define its position with respect to philosophical problems.[302]

To the Fathers, the biblical contrast between 'outer man' and 'inner man' seemed to correspond to the distinction between body and soul. Furthermore, the platonic dualistic view of the soul was interpreted during the patristic age as follows [303]: the *nous* is the higher, rational part of the mind; and the *psyche* is the lower, animal function, which Evagrius called 'the affective part of the soul'.[304]

We know that for Plato, the *nous* is 'what is best in the human being', 'the pilot of the soul', the faculty which is in contact with God.[305] This tradition, corrected and christianized, persists in the classical definition of prayer, 'an ascent of the mind *(nous)* to God'.[306] As the pupil of the eye is, so to speak, the point of intersection between two worlds, the outer and the inner, so—the Fathers thought—there must be in the human person a mysterious point through which God enters human life with all his riches.[307]

Faithful to the speculative tradition of their culture, the Greek Fathers certainly did not by chance substitute the *nous* (mind) for the biblical *lev, levav* (heart). According to Gregory Nazianzus, the 'clean heart' of Ps 50:2 is the διανοητικόν (intellect).[308]

From the latin Middle Ages we could cite a great number of texts in which the heart is identified with the intellect.[309] The twelfth century was in many respects the century of *affectus* (affective attachment). By endeavoring to define the relationship between the soul and God in the language of love, this century led christian spirituality in a new direction. And since the heart, which for the poets was already the place of love, remained that of devotional life and spiritual experience, it is not surprising that from then on the terms *cor* (heart) and *affectus* more frequently moved close to one another.[310] And since a contrast was made between *cordis affectus* and *intellectus,* Thomas Aquinas saw the evangelical counsel to love God wholeheartedly (see Lk 5:27) was merely 'an act of the will, which is indicated here by the heart' *(actus voluntatis quae hic significatur per cor).*[311]

Soon, however, a reaction against 'voluntarism' and in favor of 'feelings' was bound to occur, especially in popular piety. In russian spirituality, as we have seen, the 'part of the heart' and the 'part of feeling' are one and the same.[312]

At the source of this divergence lies the effort, praiseworthy but overhasty, to communicate spiritual experience in psychological terms. There have been attempts, principally, to locate the biblical 'heart' in the human person's metaphysical nature, and only then was the question asked: what function can such a 'heart' have in the spiritual life. The procedure should be reversed. In the religious realm, the heart has precedence.

## *The Ascent of the Mind to God*

Prayer is the pre-eminent religious problem. Prayer, Theophan the Recluse writes, 'is a totality. It summarizes everything.'[313] But the classical definition of prayer as 'an ascent of the mind *(nous)* to God' does not express this fullness of life without other explanations. When Christ taught us how to pray 'Our Father', he presented us with a mystery inaccessible to human thought—the trinitarian life of the Father, Son, and Holy Spirit. Consequently, if prayer is uttered 'in the Spirit',[314] it will be, more than an ascent of our spirit (lower case), an ascent of the Spirit (capital letter): it will be a 'breathing of the Spirit'.[315]

Prayer will be 'spiritual' in the true sense of the word. But is it still our own prayer? Does the Holy Spirit not remain outside our human soul? While it is true that there are symbols which express the arrival of this 'divine host' from outside, the Spirit is given to us so abundantly that he becomes what is most spiritual within us, our true self.[316] According to the trichotomy explained by Irenaeus, 'the perfect human person consists of three elements: flesh, soul, and Spirit'.[317] Prayer in the Spirit is therefore identified with our spiritual prayer.

*The Spirit in the Heart*

In which human faculty does the Spirit abide? What the mystics noted above all was the marked resemblance between a person's spiritual life and his or her experience of the visible world. As the pupil of the eye is, so to speak, the point of intersection between two worlds, outer and inner, so must there be in the human person a mysterious point through which God enters human life with all his riches, 'an organ of the Spirit'.[318]

The term 'organ', however, conceals a hidden danger. With good reason a reaction has set in against the ethical theory of the past century which made our relationship to God *one* of various social relationships. We cannot put obedience to our superiors, charity towards our neighbor, and religion on the same level, because the third of these is the foundation and the motive for the first two. This applies to our inward structure. For the Christian, all visual, intellectual and other activities should converge towards piety, because all human faculties, without exception, tend towards the Lord.

This is what the Fathers did not sufficiently realize when they debated the question about in which human faculty 'the image of God' is found. The later mystics did indeed shed more light on the problem, but without arriving at a definitive solution. They no longer spoke of an 'organ', a particular 'faculty', but of 'the ground of the soul', her 'center', her 'essence'. In Sermon Fifteen, *Homo quidam nobilis,* Meister Eckhart wrote: 'Truly you are the hidden God, in the ground of the soul *(seelengrunt),* where God's ground and the soul's ground are one ground'. True union with God is achieved only in the essence of the soul: 'As being true, *sub ratione veri,* God is understood by the intellect; as being good, *sub ratione boni,* by the will: the intellect and the will are the powers of the soul. As being, God penetrates into the intimacy of the soul's essence'. From this follows the conclusion: 'We ought not to think of building holiness upon action; we ought to build it upon a being, for our works do not sanctify us, we ought to sanctify our works'.[319]

Knowing how to interpret the terms 'essence' and 'being' is another, very delicate, question. Let us merely note that Eckhart sought to place the point of contact with grace in a region that is the very 'root' of life, the focus of all human powers, the center of life in its manifold activities. According to the ordinary language of people and of Scripture itself, this focus is in the heart, 'the throne of the Spirit'.[320]

### *The Heart As the Principle of Unity within a Person*

If the heart is the vital center of all human activity, it will be the principle of unity within the human person. Identified with the person, it will designate our integrity. 'The heart maintains the energy of the powers of the soul and of the body', Theophan the Recluse said.[321] To illustrate his statement, Theophan used a comparison borrowed from the theater. When an actor plays his role offstage, his acting loses a great deal. So it is with the exercise of an isolated faculty: it becomes unnatural, and its efficiency is decreased. In itself, however, this comparison is very weak, for the stage is an element entirely external to acting, while the heart participates actively in the role of the other faculties. 'Not only is it the scene on which the characters play their role: it takes part in the action itself. Through their movements, the other powers are reflected in it and, conversely, the heart is reflected in them.'[322]

Let us look at another aspect of this unity. If we were to call the first unity 'static', the second would be 'dynamic' or 'historical'. To define time, Gregory of Nyssa uses the term ἀκολουθία, an ordered sequence that governs development according to 'before' and 'after', and guides all beginnings to their end.[323] The present is but an unseizable instant in a fleeting swiftness. Our life is continually 'torn apart' by multiple activities. We cannot live one act which lasts forever. Bossuet detected here an error which wanted 'to put the perfection of this life in an act suited only to the life to come'.[324]

But the ideal of the christian East has always been 'the state (κατάστασις) of prayer', that is, an habitual disposition which somehow in itself deserves the name prayer, apart from the acts which it produces with more or less frequency.[325] This disposition is called the 'prayer of the heart', because the heart gives stability to the multiplicity of life's successive moments.

### *The 'State' of the Human Person*

Here we touch on one of the difficult problems of the spiritual life: the assurance of salvation. Each of the commonplace acts that make up our spiritual life possesses a certain independence. This is the very thing that saves the sinner. Unlike the angel, fallen man is not immutably held captive to his error: he can change his decision, do penance, and be reconciled with God. This independence, however, brings a fearful risk; and for the just, the successive moments of life always remain dangerous. Eighty years of virtuous living are no assurance of salvation! Who can be certain of dying in a state of grace? No one, the Saints reply. Listen to Teresa of Avila: 'How is it, my Lord, that we live a life so full of perils!'[326]

Christian writers frequently revert to the idea that salvation demands only one thing, 'good will', and nothing more. The will is free and master of its decisions. The will is not to satisfy its desires blindly. In the same manner in which they defended the freedom of God, the greek Fathers insisted on the human person's free responsibility: free will is the condition and the foundation of merit.

Even so, we should not identify a free act with an isolated act. Everything that goes on in us or happens to us creates an impression on the heart, leaves an imprint on it; and the heart draws into unity the great variety of feelings buried in it. A stable disposition is formed, which gives an orientation to future decisions: 'Notice how quickly we perform that which pleases us', Theophan writes, 'while the hands become heavy and the feet remain nailed to the ground when one has to perform a task that does not speak to the heart.'[327]

Always in motion, like a barometer during a storm, the heart nonetheless lies at the beginning of a stability of sorts. It leads our life in a set direction and fashions within the human person a well-determined inner structure. If good dispositions take root in the heart, this will be, in the present life, the only assurance of our future salvation. 'This is why the formation of the heart is of such great importance from the very beginning of the spiritual life.'[328]

### *Attentiveness to the Heart*

The tradition of the Eastern Church insists on the attentiveness to be given to the heart, 'the most important, fundamental work of the spiritual life'.[329] Performing good external actions is not enough; we should also conceive good thoughts and experience good feelings. We should acquire 'the art of governing the movements of the heart, what the saintly Fathers call "attentiveness", "sobriety", and "inner work"'.[330]

This attentiveness to the heart assumes, first of all, a negative aspect: keeping away any evil thought that comes from outside the heart. This is an 'oversight', an ἐπισκοπή.[331] It was represented as an angel standing before the gate of the Paradise of the heart.[332] The analogy works only in part: guarding the gate is not enough. We guard it in order to enjoy what is found inside, the paradisiacal life in dialogue with God. Attention to where the feelings of the heart are leading us prepares the way for contemplation. In his book *On Prayer,* Theophan cites among others, these words of Hesychius: it is 'in the heart' that believers see God.[333] Isaac the Syrian often spoke in the same vein.[334] For him, purification follows these stages: purification from the passions and unceasingly holding the remembrance of God. Then the heart becomes a source of revelation. If all the power of the Spirit is concentrated in it, the believer is dazzled by a great spiritual splendor and contemplates the Lord in his or her own heart.[335]

### *Knowledge of the Heart*

All the above is not yet conclusive, for an important question remains to be clarified. Let us present it in the form of an objection: 'We ought not to think of building holiness upon action', Eckhart taught. Now in the West, all handbooks of morality do no more than distinguish good *actions* from actions which are evil, or even indifferent *(adiaphora).* The degree of rebellion against God is measured by whether an *action* constitutes a venial or a mortal sin. Confessors prove to be great masters in making such distinctions. In the Christian East, by contrast, the 'spiritual fathers', the famous russian *startzy* (elders) took little interest in the detailed confession of their penitents. They had *kardiognosis* (knowledge of the heart), a clear-sightedness that reads the human heart. Psychologically speaking, we could say that they were more 'maternal' than 'paternal'. What is more, do we in the West in our own day not read critics who condemn a morality based on the perfection or imperfection of actions? This point of view is certainly considered responsible for the present-day crisis in spiritual direction.

Theophan's judgment is incomparably more balanced than that of a good number of our modern critics. He set great value on actions that result from free will and observing the commandments. For him, the question should not be the 'morality of actions *or* of the heart', but of 'actions *in* the heart'. 'Those who observe the commandments of God know that God is near them, for the commandments of God enter into their habits; they fashion in their soul various traits of likeness to God.'[336] In modern terms we could say that the morality of the commandments should become more and more a *morality of the heart*.

An easy exhortation, but difficult to describe! Actions are visible, tangible, and measurable—but the heart? 'I, the Lord, search the mind and test the heart' (Jer 17:9-10). For human beings, Vyšeslavcev writes, the heart is 'impenetrable to the gaze of another; but still more surprising, is that it is equally impenetrable to one's own gaze'.[337]

*Kardiognosis* presupposes, however, that we overcome such incommunicability. If we insist on knowing how we can know ourselves—and we are bound to do so—the answer is that the soul is present to herself: 'As these eyes of ours see the sun, so those who are enlightened see the image of the soul'.[338] Depending on the degree of her transparency, the soul has a direct intuition of herself. The concept of the heart, they say, includes a type of intuitive, integrated knowledge. These are the 'feelings' of the heart.

'The function of the heart', Theophan writes, 'consists in feeling everything that touches our being. Consequently, the heart always and unceasingly feels the condition of body and soul as well as the manifold impressions created by concrete activity, whether spiritual or physical, the things which surround us or cross our path and, in general, the course of life.'[339]

## *Spiritual Feelings*

All feelings of the heart obviously cannot have the same value. To find his bearings in a domain marked by countless gradations, Theophan the Recluse faithfully follows the tripartite division of the human person: there are feelings of the body, the soul, and the

Holy Spirit.[340] It goes without saying that the feelings of the body can coincide with natural desires, but it is also true that the corruption of nature through sin can be made more apparent here.[341]

The feelings of the soul are feelings of the heart which arise as a result of the changes produced in the soul through her own activity. We may distinguish between feelings that are 'theoretical', 'practical', and 'aesthetic', depending on whether they derive from the understanding or from the will, or whether they are the result of the heart reflecting on itself, returning to its own richness.[342]

In this context, Theophan explains the various 'intuitions' that guide us in our intellectual and moral activity, but particularly in an aesthetic appreciation of the values of life born in the heart through the appeal of beautiful objects.[343]

Above all, we should adorn ourselves with 'spiritual feelings', cultivate and develop them, increase our natural sympathy for 'God himself and the divine order of things or the spiritual world'.[344] From this 'intuitions' are born, perceived only by the person who has experienced them, while a knowledge of the divine mysteries becomes a specific good. 'By the full renewal of God's grace, there is in the person who has abandoned sin and turned to God a sympathy with the spiritual world.'[345] It is dependent upon the degree of kinship between man and God (*srodstvo,* Theophan says).[346] To be attentive to the voice of this 'connaturality' is to perceive the divine mysteries as they exist within us, as they enter our lives. The heart then becomes a wellspring of revelation. 'The air we feel around us will not be as close to our exterior senses as is the Spirit of God who is continuously in our hearts. Through him the memory of him is clear at every moment, and in this way he dwells all the more in us. . . .'[347]

In conformity then with the teaching of Theophan, who follows a long eastern tradition, especially that of the hesychasts, prayer will never be perfect if it does not descend 'from the mind into the heart'.[348] The Lord has commanded us to enter into our inner room to pray. This inner room is the heart.[349] 'Prayer is, in the true sense of the word, a sigh of the heart to God; if such fervor is lacking, there is no prayer.'[350] It should be like the natural breathing of the heart which longs for union with God spontaneously and through a natural intuition senses the presence of the

Holy Spirit in everything the human person does, thinks, and desires.[351] Such prayer is unceasing. It is, to the extent to which it is possible to feel and taste the presence of the Spirit in this life, an awareness of our state as children of God, of our deification.[352]

### *Spiritual Consolations*

'Feelings are the raiment of the mind.'[353] Progress in the spiritual life then is measured in terms of the constancy of good dispositions in the heart, like a tree that has grown deep roots in the soil.[354] Heavenly realities cannot be felt by the heart because of its impurity. The ultimate victory over sin is therefore gained only when we begin to experience feelings that are the opposite of temptations, when we become insensitive to the attractions of the world and savor only the divine.[355]

In this life, however, this sense of the divine is subject to numerous variations. Summarizing typical passages from Diadochus of Photice, Theophan explained the normal rule of the divine pedagogy: 1) divine grace is present from the beginning, forming, as it were, one substance with the soul;[356] 2) at the beginning of the spiritual life, grace often makes its presence felt as a consolation, a reward for labor; 3) later, this is often withdrawn and God lets his saints suffer and sense desolation in order to test and purify them; 4) finally, when the period of purification is over, God again grants his comfort and the fullness of the Holy Spirit.[357]

It is undeniably difficult to describe such feelings. Nonetheless, language has an entire range of analogical terms capable of giving some idea of what we 'feel' inwardly: warmth, peace, joy, and tears. In the East, tears are most frequently mentioned.

### *Tears*[358]

Certain emotions can trigger tears in greater or lesser profusion. In ancient ascetic language, 'having the gift of tears' meant to cry easily. Mystic sorrow, and still more, moral anguish, are the usual causes. We can also cry because of anger, frustration, pity, or at an aesthetic experience. That an intensely lived prayer can become a source of specific emotions and various feelings conveyed through tears is in itself not surprising.

John Cassian was the first to give us the classification of the phenomenon of tears. They are caused, he says, not only by a spiritual feeling, but also by a recollection and the desire for heaven or spring from fear of hell. 'There is another kind of tears stirred . . . by the hard-heartedness and sins of others . . . ; there are also tears on account of the worries . . . and the anxieties of life with which the just of this world are afflicted'.[359]

Among ancient easterners, tears and compunction go together so often that they became practically synonymous, through metonymy.[360] 'Is there a *penthos* (sadness) without tears?' Dorotheus of Gaza asks Barsanuphius, who limits himself to remarking that once self-will has been broken, thoughts will recollect themselves; once recollected, they bring about compunction in the heart, and compunction causes tears to flow.[361] The aim of compunction is not merely to obtain divine forgiveness, as mere repentance (μετάνοια) does: it endeavors to erase the consequences of sin, its traces and scars which always remain. This is why such tears never dry up.[362]

Eastern documents dealing with tears are numerous.[363] Ammonas sums up the doctrine of the Fathers on the healing power of *penthos* in one line: 'Without exception, *penthos* drives away all faults'.[364] Purified of their passions, those who always shed tears will enjoy true peace. Mourning will amount to consolation.[365]

While there are tears that are shed without effort on our part, there are others which arise from the will, declared John Climacus.[366] John Cassian held forced tears in low esteem.[367] On this point, he differed from his eastern masters, who taught that compunction, a gift of God, is occasionally given 'without effort, naturally' *(automatos).*[368] But to arouse and maintain it, we should use certain means and profit from external events, meditate on the last things, reject frivolity and laughter, create a suitable atmosphere, and practice poverty and bodily penance.[369]

Mystic tears are given to someone who 'has received the contemplation of the inaccessible light', wrote Nicetas Stethatos.[370] His master, Symeon the New Theologian, never ceased shedding a flood of tears during his most sublime visions.[371] Even so, most of the ancients warned against the temptation of vainglory. 'Do not glow conceitedly if you shed tears when you pray', says Mark the Ascetic.[372] We should use the fear of God to discern the cause of tears, John Climacus warns.[373] John the Solitary, a Syrian, had an original theory on the distinction of shedding tears using the three classes of people (somatic, psychic, and pneumatic); he admitted that tears stop flowing 'when the mind is in the region of the Spirit . . . ; [then] the angel does not weep'.[374] But it has always been very dangerous to view oneself as an angel! To weep over our sins is, by contrast, a commandment given to all, a general charism.[375]

## MYSTICAL EXPRESSIONS

### *The Language of the Spiritual Writers*

The language of spiritual writers is a form of the language of faith. It presupposes faith and helps make visible its content and possibilities. To the extent that mystical language is related to an experience, it should be viewed as a descriptive language: it attempts to describe a living reality through symbolic forms. It is therefore a specific form of the personal testimonial.

There are, to be precise, certain well-known language forms which allow us to speak of the various modalities of experience. Through language experience becomes communicable. Let us also note that certain expressions have become very frequent among eastern mystics. It goes without saying that such language cannot be isolated from the context in which it is found, especially the context of tradition and the life in which it originated.[376]

### *Spiritual Marriage*[377]

The concept of spiritual marriage and divine betrothal is not characteristic of Christianity. When God has relations with the soul, Philo of Alexandria, a Jew, taught, the soul receives the divine seed from which are born virtues and good deeds.[378] This text[379] is to be viewed as a milestone in the history of the theme of the marriage of God to the soul. It may have had a threefold origin: 'the sacred marriage' of the initiate to the deity, as practiced in certain pagan mystery religions; the biblical metaphor of the marriage of Yahweh to Israel; and Plato's *Symposium* in which the soul is united to the Beautiful to engender the virtues.

The valentinian gnostics had a mysterious initiation rite which they called spiritual marriage (πνευματικόν γαμόν).[380] It is probably to such heterodox circles that we should look for the first manifestation of this expression in a christian climate.

Among Christians, marriage is a sacrament, that is, an efficient symbol through which the grace of God is communicated. This very symbol therefore easily becomes an allegory of the most sublime realities. Origen,[381] it seems, is the father, the creator, of the mysticism which applies the concept of marriage to the summits of the spiritual life: ecclesiology and the sacraments, eschatology and virginity, and the mystic ascent during prayer are all areas to be considered.

From the beginning, the union of man and woman was transferred, in divine thinking, to the union of Christ and the Church which it represents and signifies. When things are viewed from on high, not from below, it is not the union of Christ and the Church which is derived from the creation of the human couple but quite the opposite: it is the relationship man-woman in marriage which has its concrete, living archetype in the union of Christ-the Church.

According to Gregory of Nyssa, the *Song of Songs* represents the loving union of God and the soul in the figure of a 'divine marriage' (θεῖος γάμος).[382] The nuptial union of the Christian with God is celebrated in baptism. Entirely typical in this respect is the first of John Chrysostom's eight *Baptismal Catecheses*.[383] Nuptial symbolism has been applied to eucharistic communion, although this idea is less frequent among the Fathers.[384]

Tertullian was the first to use the words *sponsa Christi* (bride of Christ) to designate the christian virgin.[385] This expression became current after the third and fourth centuries.

The last phase of the earthly development of the nuptial mystery of baptism is death, when the Bride arrives in person. It is possible to speak of a nuptial ecclesiology among the Fathers which is at the same time both individual and collective.[386]

The mariological theme of Mary, the Bride of Christ, has been developed in poetic lyricism.[387] The meditations on 'the eternal feminine' by Vladimir Soloviev or Vjaceslav Ivanov extend the symbol to all of creation in a cosmological mysticism.[388] These same authors exhort Christians to live the married life as a starting-point of eschatological mysticism.[389]

*Spiritual Inebriation*[390]

Several Fathers and numerous spiritual writers have used the phrase *spiritual inebriation* to designate one of the manifestations of the encounter between the human being and God. While inebriation of the body snatches the human person temporarily away from ordinary existence, that of the spirit makes us forget our limitations, our misery and trials (note the frequent connection between inebriation and forgetting), and gives us access to the experience of God. Strictly speaking, the concept is not biblical at all. Indeed, Scripture uses the word 'drinking' in a figurative sense to designate the acquisition of the salvation offered by God (Is 55:1; Pr 9:5; Jn 4:13-14; 7:37-39), but it does not describe the joy caused by such salvation in terms of spiritual inebriation. The source of the greek expression would be Philo[391] and gnostic circles rather than the cult of Dionysus. The oxymoron μέθη νηφάλιος (sober drunkenness)—rendered in Latin, with a slight shift of meaning, as *ebria sobrietas* (drunken sobriety)—is defined by Philo as an ecstasy of right reason caused by drinking divine wisdom.[392] Close to this philonian idea, the concept of Plotinus represents an interesting detail: ecstasy is an inebriation, not of the Intellect knowing, but of the Intellect loving (νοῦς ἐρῶν).[393]

Origen had a defining influence on the history of the theme of spiritual inebriation, especially through his commentary on *The Song of Songs* 2.4: 'Bring me into the house of wine'. That which inebriates is no longer the wisdom of God, an impersonal wisdom, as in Philo, but the Person of the *Logos,* 'the true vine' (Jn 15:1). As presented by John Chrysostom, spiritual inebriation is simply the joy of the believer who participates in the mysteries of God.[394] In Gregory of Nyssa the mystical character of 'the ascent from the lower to the higher world' reappears in the eucharistic celebration.[395]

The Greeks most frequently saw a specific effect of *sobra ebrietas* in the fact that it led to a knowledge of things unknown, in contrast to physical drunkenness which makes us forget things that are known.[396] They follow in the wake of Philo: the human person is intoxicated by *gnosis*. Something entirely different is found in the syriac Fathers: a description of perfect love by means of the metaphor of inebriation. A detailed description of the conduct and condition of a drunken person is found in the *Book of Perfection* by Martyrius Sahdona. The author clarifies:

> The same thing happens to someone who is drunk on divine love and aflame with love for the Lord: the movements of the soul are unceasingly occupied with God, and the heart is absorbed by him (Lk 10:39); the body walks on earth, but the mind dwells in heaven with Christ, for the body is dead to the world, but the soul is aflame with love of the things in heaven' (Col 3:1-3).[397]

Isaac of Nineveh follows the same line, with this one difference: he sometimes links spiritual inebriation not only specifically to love, but also to faith and hope.[398]

### *Watchful Sleep*

Sleep lends itself well to express ecstasy. It causes the mind to go out of itself. The soul is pulled away from herself, from the pathways of reason, and is subjected to dreams. This is 'ordinary' sleep. Mystical sleep submits the soul to the sovereign reality of the presence of the Holy Spirit.[399]

This can happen in a real dream. Origen attributes a prophetic value to certain dreams: 'It is a matter of belief that in a dream impressions are brought before the minds of many—some relating to divine things, and others to future events of this life, and this either with clearness or in an enigmatic manner—a fact which is manifest to all who accept the doctrine of providence'.[400] Examples of dream visions abound in hagiography.

But as a mystical expression, sleep is understood in a metaphoric sense. 'The voice of God', Basil writes, 'is this representation corresponding to that which frequently occurs in dreams.'[401] Of what does this analogy consist? What characterizes this state is first of all passivity. The action is directed by another who attracts the soul into a sphere where she is unprotected. But it is not a total passivity. The attention of the soul is entirely captivated by the intensity of the divine presence, but she is neither absorbed nor swallowed up. This is a wakeful sleep: 'My heart is awake' (see Sg 5:3). 'The reference here is to an unusual sleep, removed from ordinary reality', Gregory of Nyssa writes. It draws the soul away 'from the deceptive dreams which are the pleasures of the flesh and puts her in the presence of the one true reality'.[402]

Although sleep resembles death, Clement of Alexandria believed that this applies only to the body, and that the soul, as such, does not sleep. 'The soul whose senses are at rest abides with herself and participates more in the intellection'; while the body is absent, a 'concentration' of the soul occurs.[403]

This observation is certainly valid for mystical sleep, not for 'ordinary' sleep.

### *Seeing the Place of God*

From the stoic point of view, place *(topos, locus)* pertains to corporality.[404] Accordingly, Philo of Alexandria writes, 'the Deity, being contained by nothing, is of necessity itself its own place'.[405] The Fathers say the same thing.[406]

But this property does not isolate God from the world. In biblical thought, God is not only the 'Most High': he is also the one who is near (Ps 119:151). He is present in his creation (Ws 11:20) and in his people (Ex 19:4ff). God the Father is present in his Son (Rm 8:14, 28).[407] And so contemplatives who try to see God in everything gaze, like Moses, on the place of God.[408] Pseudo-Denys explains that by 'place', we are to understand the 'fundamental reasons' which are in beings.[409]

God wills to be present to the human person in a special way. If we, through sin, flee from his presence, the divine call continues to pursue us over the centuries: Adam and Eve, 'where are you?'(Gn 3:8ff). But if we 'hear' the voice of God in our heart, according to the 'visual' vocabulary of the Greek Fathers, we perceive the presence of God in ourselves as in an 'image'.[410] The Syrian Martyrius Sahdona combines the one aspect and the other. 'Like those who dwell in heaven, let us *speak* with God, stretching out towards him the *gaze* of the eyes of our heart (see Col 3:1-2); in a hidden way, let us *look* upon his majesty in awe, and behold "as though in a mirror" as it were the image of him who cannot be seen'.[411] The statement 'like those who dwell in heaven' illustrates the mutual indwelling of God in the human person and the human person in God.

That we now see 'as though in a mirror' (1 Cor 13:12) is common christian teaching.[412] But our contemplation is a vital, intimate union and as fruitful as that of branches on the vine (Jn 15:4-7). Indeed, the theology of 'the place of God' is given its full dimension in the Farewell Discourse at the Last Supper. The Fathers were fond of developing this theme of the mutual indwelling of the divine Persons. 'The Father is, so to speak, the natural place *(topos physikos)* of the Son', writes Cyril of Alexandria.[413] In his turn Jerome states: 'Certainly, the Son is the place of the Father *(Filius locus est Patris),* as the Father is the place of the Son *(sicut et Pater locus est Filius),* according to the words of the Lord, "I am in the Father and the Father is in me"' (Jn 14:10).[414]

To understand what Evagrius says about the vision of the place of God, let us recall the promise of Christ: 'I shall return to take you to myself, so that you may be with me where I am. You know the way to the place where I am going' (Jn 14:3-4). In this context, Evagrius, for all practical purposes, discovers a correspondence between the vision of the Trinity and that of his own state: 'Know that the Trinity is not signified either in the vision of bodies or in a contemplation of the bodiless powers; it is not counted in the knowledge of the soul'.[415] The image of God, Evagrius continues, exists only in beings able to know the Trinity and only in view of such knowledge.[416] Hence his insistence on the vision of one's 'own state' (νοῦ κατάστασις). If this is achieved, the intellect need only view itself in order to see God, not through an ontological identity, but through what Maximus the Confessor boldly called an 'identity through grace' (ἡ κατά χάριν αὐτότης).[417]

Among the conditions required for this vision, Evagrius emphasizes two in particular: moral purity; and the purity of partial and multiple concepts. 'The place of God is called peace . . . . The one who desires that God dwell in him must carefully purify his soul of all passions.'[418] Moreover, he must have 'a naked intellect', 'one that is reached in the vision of itself and deserves to commune in a contemplation of the Holy Trinity',[419] one that sees 'its own light', the 'pure light'.[420]

## *The Prayer of Fire*

This is a form of prayer which Cassian described succinctly as free and unforeseeable and beyond all human effort.[421] He defines it as 'a still more sublime and excellent condition which is shaped by the contemplation of God alone and by the fire of love'.[422] Like the 'pure prayer' of Evagrius,[423] Cassian's 'prayer of fire' excludes any imaginative representation, any human form and all discursive elements.[424] It is utterly silent, so that the demons do not know what the mind is thinking[425] because it is entirely non-attached: 'Prayer is not perfect when the monk is conscious of the fact that he is praying'.[426] The three heavenly figures of the Transfiguration are presented as models of this type of prayer: Moses, Elijah, and Christ himself praying on the mountain, alone.[427]

Cassian continues to be faithful to Evagrius, his master, when he describes ecstasy *(excessus mentis)* not as a 'going out' of the soul from herself, but, on the contrary, as an inward absorption: the Lord turns 'the eyes of the heart'[428] inward and the soul perceives that she is illumined by heavenly light. Here is how Cassian describes this grace:

> I feel that my spirit has once more found a sense of direction, that my thinking has grown purposeful, that because of a visit of the Holy Spirit my heart is unspeakably glad and my mind ecstatic. Here is a great overflow of spiritual thoughts, thanks to a sudden illumination and to the coming of the Savior. The holiest ideas, hitherto concealed from me, have been revealed to me.[429]

## *The Vision of God in His 'Energies'*

To be the object of our contemplation, God must somehow go out of himself, manifest his 'glory',[430] and transfigure our soul and the entire cosmos by his 'energies' (*energeia,* activity), his lights. The 'Taboric light' is the most characteristic effulgence of this divine energy. Such considerations lie at the heart of the palamite synthesis.[431] The distinction between the transcendent essence of God and his 'uncreated energies' was primarily a formulation of the contemplative experience by the 'holy hesychasts'.[432]

At the basis of this doctrine, there are two propositions which are strongly emphasized in the tradition of the Eastern Church: divine transcendence, on the one hand; and, on the other, the deification of the human person and of the cosmos.[433] 'No one, neither man nor angel, has seen God (Jn 1:18) nor will ever see him, for the creature sees only through the senses or through the intellect.'[434] The divine transcendence is beyond all possibilities of the created intellect. But the mystical experience adds a new dimension. 'In addition to this incomprehensibility [of God through the intellect], what is most divine and extraordinary in the very comprehension [the saints] may have, they possess incomprehensibly . . .for the Spirit by whom they see is incomprehensible.'[435]

The vision of God is therefore 'spiritual' in the true sense of the word, through a revelation of the 'energy' which is the mode in which the divine nature externalizes its existence. Gregory Palamas chose this generic term deliberately, because he was dealing with a complex and mysterious reality. On the one hand, it is a manifestation of God to the outside *(ad extra),* common to the three divine Persons, in the order of creation. On the other hand, God does not act in the world by virtue of a natural necessity. The deification of the human person, a free being, presupposes a *personal* encounter. 'When God was speaking with Moses, he did not say "I am the essence", but "I am that I am"' (Ex 3:14).[436] Creation is a motion of the will of God which is, beyond doubt, common to the three divine Persons. Nonetheless, 'the motion of the divine originates from the primary cause, the Father; it proceeds through the Son and is manifested in the Holy Spirit.'[437]

This encounter transforms the human person and the cosmos, just as the body of Christ permeated by divine energy becomes a source of deification and, consequently, of vision for those who share in it. Then 'this mysterious light, inaccessible, immaterial, uncreated, deifying, eternal, this radiance of the Divine Nature, this glory of the divinity, this beauty of the heavenly kingdom, is at once accessible to sense perception and yet transcends it.'[438]

We could say (perhaps by oversimplifying), therefore, that 'seeing God in his energies' represents the experiences of the encounters with him in the entire economy of salvation. This experience is manifestly diverse according to the various degrees of the spiritual life: it is produced when 'the entire Divinity comes to dwell in fullness in those deemed worthy'.[439]

### *'Anarchic' Mysticism, 'of Hope' and 'of Love' According to Vjaceslav Ivanov*

The mystical flight visible in art arises from *eros,* love of the beautiful, believed Vjaceslav Ivanov, the russian religious poet. But paradoxically, such love of beauty finds its first expression in an anarchistic 'No' to any reality that does not correspond to the ideal. This attitude is expressed by the figure of Christ in the fresco of the *Last Judgment* by Michelangelo: 'Depart from me, you doers of evil' (see Mt 25:41). Buddhist mysticism, which seeks to destroy in a nirvana all that is not absolute, is, according to Ivanov, an 'anarchistic' mysticism, one of negation.

After a period of 'anarchistic' youth, lovers of beauty arrive at the mysticism 'of hope' expressed by Raphael in *The Transfiguration:* it is a vision of the world to come—spiritual, but not yet realized. This is the mysticism of expectation.

Finally, the last degree of the mystical attitude can be seen in *The Last Supper* of Leonardo da Vinci. Jesus bows his head to say 'Yes' to everything that comes from the Providence of the Father, even the betrayal of Judas. He sees and knows that through his acceptance everything is transformed and that all the beauty longed for is already present. Ivanov concludes by saying: 'Here we see the suffering of the world, but also the gold of the cup; and through the narrow windows penetrates the bluish evening. The beauty of this azure peace descends in the supper-room of the sacrifice.'[440] The true mystics are those who know that they transform the universe by accepting the will of the Father.

## Notes

1. *Stolp i utverždenie istiny* [*The Pillar and Foundation of Truth*] (Moscow, 1914) 19ff. Špidlík, *Grégoire de Nazianze,* 1ff.

2. See Thomas Aquinas, *Contra Gentes,* II. 98.

3. André-Jean Festugière, *La révélation d'Hermès Trismégiste,* vol. 1 (Paris, 1944–1954) 63.

4. Henri Crouzel, *Origène et la 'connaissance mystique'* (Desclée de Brouwer, 1961) 25ff.

5. Aimé Solignac, 'Mystère', DSp 10 (1980) 1861–1974.

6. Especially 1 Cor 2:7-16, Rom 16:25-7, Eph 3:3-12, Col 1:25-7, 2:2-9.

7. Gregory Nazianzus, *Oratio 42-Supremum vale,* 16; PG 36:477A; LNPF, ser. 2, 7:385ff. John Chrysostom, *In Matthaeum,* homily 16. 9; PG 57:251A; LNPF 10.

8. *In epistolam I ad Cor.,* homily 7; PG 61:53D–57B; LNPF 12. See Aimé Solignac, 'Mystère', DSp 10 (1980) 1863ff.

9. Léon Veuthey, Íllumination', DSp 7/2 (1971) 1330–1346.

10. *De mystica theologia* 1; PG 3:997; translated by Colm Luibheid, *Pseudo-Dionysius: The Complete Works,* in CWS (New York: Paulist, 1987). See Eusebius, *Contra Marcellum* 1.4; GCS 4:29, 22 and 207, 5.

11. Jean Daniélou, *Philon d'Alexandrie* (Paris, 1958) 146.

12. *Poster.* 15.

13. *Oratio* 27-*Theologica,* I. 2; PG 36:13B; LNPF, ser. 2, 7:284ff.

14. Špidlík, *Grégoire de Nazianze,* 35ff.

15. Jean Daniélou, Introduction to John Chrysostom's *De incomprehensibili Dei natura, Sur l'incompréhensibilité de Dieu;* SCh 28bis:16; see the translation of Paul W. Harkins, *St. John Chrysostom: On the Incomprehensible Nature of God,* FCh 72 (1984).

16. *Oratio* 18-*Theologica* 2; PG 36:40A; LNPF, ser. 2, 7:288ff.

17. *A Systematic Handbook,* 332ff.

18. Špidlík, *Grégoire de Nazianze,* 39ff.

19. Basil, *Epistola* 189.2; PG 32:689C. For other texts, see DSp 4/1 (1960) 843ff. See also, Jean Daniélou's Introduction in SCh 28bis (above, n. 15):17.

20. Evagrius, *Centuries,* 6.49.

21. Symeon the New Theologian, *Éthique* XV. 64–67; SCh 129:448; translated Alexander Golitzin, *St Symeon the New Theologian. On the Mystical Life: The Ethical Discourses,* vol. 2 (New York, 1996) 173ff.

22. *Analecta graeca* of the Maurists (Paris, 1588) 417. See Irénée Hausherr, *Les leçons d'un contemplatif* (Paris, 1960) 54.

23. *Centuries* IV.43. See *Suppl.,* 43.

24. *De somniis,* 1.24, 153–155; translated by F. H. Colson and G. H. Whitaker in *Philo,* vol. 5, (Cambridge, Mass., 1958) 294ff.

25. *Demonstratio* 4.5; *Patrologie syriaque,* 1 (Paris, 1894) 145–148; translated Sebastian Brock, *The Syriac Fathers on Prayer and the Spiritual Life,* CS 101 (Kalamazoo: Cistercian Publications, 1987) 8–9.

26. Émile Bertaud and André Rayez, 'Échelle spirituelle', DSp 4/1 (1960) 62–86.

27. See p. 214.

28. *The Life of Moses;* PG 44:416D.

29. This refers to the title of a work by Nicolai Berdiaev, *Dialectique existentielle du divin et de l'human* (Paris, 1947); translated R. M. French, *The Divine and the Human* (London, 1949).

30. Translated John H. Erickson and Thomas E. Bird, *In the Image and Likeness of God,* (Crestwood, New York: St Vladimir's Seminary Press, 1985) 13.

31. *Ibid.*

32. *Ibid.,* 14.

33. *De posteritate Cain,* 15 and 4; translated F. H. Colson and G. H. Whitaker, in *Philo,* vol. 2 (Cambridge, Mass., 1950) 328ff.

34. *The Life of Moses;* PG 44:337A; Malherbe-Ferguson, CWS and CS 31:95.

35. *Politea* (The Republic), 273D.

36. *Alcibiades,* II, 90.

37. Origen, *Contra Celsum,* 7.36; PG 11:1472A; ANF. 4:395–669.

38. *Oratio 2-Apologetica,* 7; PG 35:413C–416A; LNPF, ser. 2, 7:204ff.

39. *A Systematic Handbook,* 331ff. Špidlík, *Grégoire de Nazianze,* 30ff.

40. Irénée Hausherr, 'La méthode d'oraison hésychaste', *Orientalia Christoama* 9/ 2, no. 36 (1927) 151–153. See 'On the First Method of Attention and Prayer', *Writings From the Philokalia on Prayer of the Heart,* translated E. Kadloubovksy and G. E. H. Palmer (London: Faber and Faber, 1979) 153–154.

41. Evagrius, *Centuries,* 5. 26.

42. *Homily* 7; PG 34:525D ; *Pseudo-Macarius, The Fifty Spiritual Homilies and The Great Letter,* translated George A. Maloney, in the series CWS (New York, 1992)].

43. Karl Heussi, *Der Ursprung des Mönchtums* (Tübingen, 1936) 1768.

44. Louis Leloir, *Paterica armeniaca* 7, 22b; CSCO 361, 156.

45. See especially PG 26:933C–936B.

46. François Halkin, *Sancti Pachomii Vitae graecae* (Brussels, 1932) 48; translated Armand Veilleux, *Pachomian Koinonia* I: *The Life of Saint Pachomius,* CS 45:297ff.

47. *Apophthegmata Patrum,* 2 and 3; PG 65:408D–409A; CS 59:222.

48. *Ibid.,* 14; PG 65:208C; PL 73:981A.

49. *Chapters on Prayer* 72; Hausherr, *Leçons,* 104; CS 4:63.

50. *Ibid.,* 116; Hausherr, 149.

51. *Ibid.,* 114–115; Hausherr, 144ff; *Early Fathers from the Philokalia,* 140.

52. See Irénée Hausherr, 'Contemplation et sainteté', *RAM* 14 (1933) 192. *Idem, Hésychasme et prière,* OCA 176 (1966) 34.

53. Published by François Nau in *Revue de l'Orient Chrétien* 17 (1912) 206. See *Verba Seniorum* 15.70–71; PL 68:965C.

54. Hausherr, 'Contemplation', 35.

55. Špidlík, *Grégoire de Nazianze,* 35ff.

56. Jean Meyendorff, 'Palamas (Grégoire), DSp 12 (1984) 90ff. For an overview of the dispute, see David N. Bell, *Many Mansions. An Introduction to the Development and Diversity of Medieval Theology,* CS 146 (Kalamazoo: Cistercian Publications, 1996) 175–184.

57. *Triades pour la Défense des saints hésychastes* 1.1.20; ed. Meyendorff, 2nd ed. (Louvain, 1974) 56ff; translated Nicholas Gendle, *Gregory Palamas: The Triads* (New York: Paulist Press, 1983).

58. Maurice de Gandillac, 'Docte ignorance', DSp 3 (1957) 1497–1501.

59. *Idem,* 'Denys l'Aréopagite', DSp 3:375–378.

60. *The Divine Names (De divinis nominibus),* 7.3; PG 3:872A; translated Colm Luibheid, *Pseudo-Dionysius: The Complete Works* (New York: Paulist Press, 1987) 108–109.

61. *Ibid.*

62. *Mystical Theology (De mystica theologia);* PG 3:997B; Luibheid (n. 60), 135.

63. *Triades* I.3.4; Meyendorff, 114ff; *The Triads,* CWS, 32.

64. *In Sanctum Stephanum protomartyrem;* PG 71:721.

65. *Défense des saints hésychastes, Triade* 1.3.30; Meyendorff, 177; *The Triads,* 52.

66. *In Cantica Canticorum, homily* 11; PG 44:1000C.

67. René Arnou, *Le désir de Dieu dans la philosophie de Plotin,* 2nd ed. (Rome, 1967).

68. See the end of book 7 of the *Enneads.*

69. *Oratio* 28—In theophania; PG 36:324A; LNPF, ser. 2, 7:345ff.

70. *Carminum, liber* 1.2.33, v. 222; PG 37:944. See Arnou, *Le désir,* 231ff.
71. *Epistola* 212, sacerdoti; PG 37:349C.
72. *Epist.* 66; PG 37:132A.
73. Gregory Nazianzus, *Carminum, liber* 1.2.33. v. 145; PG 37:938ff. Špidlík, *Grégoire de Nazianze,* 23ff.
74. *De posteritate Cain.* Translated M. A. Colson and G. H. Whitaker, 'On the Posterity of Cain and His Exile', Loeb Classical Library, *Philo,* 2:335 (Cambridge, MA: Harvard, 1950).
75. *Contra Eunomium, liber* 2; PG 45:940C–942B; LNPF, ser. 2, 5:33–248, 250–314.
76. See F. Bamberger, *Untersuchungen zur Entstehung des Wertproblems in der Philosophie des 19. Jahrhunderts* (Halle, 1924).
77. *The Life of Moses;* PG 44:404D; Malherbe and Fergusson, CWS and CS 31:116 (para. 239).
78. François Taymans d'Eypernon, 'Dieu (désir de)', DSp 3 (1957) 929ff.
79. Špidlík, 'Der anthropologische Aspekt der Freiheit bei Dostojevskij', *Festschrift für F. von Lilienfeld* (Erlangen, 1982) 294–316.
80. Jesús López-Gay, 'Le phénomène mystique', DSp 10 (1980) 1896.
81. *A Systematic Handbook,* 297.
82. *Ibid.,* 298.
83. *Ibid.,* 299.
84. See DSp 12/1 (1984) 96.
85. Jean Daniélou, 'Mystique de la ténèbre chez Grégoire de Nysse', DSp 2/2 (1953) 1882–1885. Daniélou, *Platonisme et théologie mystique* (Paris, 1953) 291–307. Placide Deseille, 'Épectase', DSp 4/1 (1960) 785–788.
86. *The Life of Moses;* PG 44:405CD; CWS and CS 31:118 (para. 244).
87. *Ibid.,* 977C.
88. *Ibid.,* 405BC; CWS-CS 31:117.
89. *Gnostic Centuries* 2.88; PG 90:1165D.
90. Symeon the New Theologian, *Chapitres théologiques, gnostiques et pratiques,* 1.7; SCh 51: 42; translated Paul [John] McGuckin, *The Practical and Theological Chapters,* CS 41 (Kalamazoo: Cistercian Publications, 1982) 34–35.
91. *Summa theologiae,* 2-II, 28, 3.
92. Charles Kannengieser, 'Contemplation de l'humanité du Christ', DSp 7/1 (1968) 1049.
93. See p. 261.
94. *In Cantica Canticorum, homily* 10; PG 44:988A; McCambley, 191.
95. *Homily* 3; *ibid.*
96. *The Life of Moses,* 37ff; SCh 1*bis*:37; CWS-CS 31:40ff.
97. Walther Voelker, *Gregor von Nyssa als Mystiker* (Wiesbaden, 1955) 214.
98. *De beatitudinibus, oratio,* 6; PG 44:1264; translated Hilda C. Graef, *Gregory of Nyssa: The Lord's Prayer. The Beatitudes,* ACW 18 (1954) 143.
99. *Ibid.*
100. *Ibid.,* 144.
101. *In Cantica canticorum homilia* I; PG 44:781D. Homily 13;1049D. Špidlík, 'La mistica del martirio secondo Gregorio di Nissa', in *I martiri della Val di Non e la reazione pagana alla fina del secolo* IV (Trent, 1985) 69–84.
102. See the articles in DSp 4/2 (1961) 2045–2189.
103. Michel de Goedt, 'L'Extase dans la Bible', DSp 4/2:2072–2087.
104. Jean Kirchmeyer, 'Extase chez les Pères de l'Église', DSp 4/2:2087–2113.
105. Jean Daniélou, 'Mystique de la ténèbre chez Grégoire de Nysse', DSp 2/2 (1953) 1872–1885. Walther Völker, *Gregor von Nyssa als Mystiker* (Wiesbaden, 1955).
106. René Roques, 'Contemplation, extase et ténèbre ches le pseudo-Denys', DSp 2/2 (1953) 1885–1911. Roques, *Structure hiérarchique du monde selon le Pseudo-Denis* (Paris, 1954). Walther

Völker, *Kontemplation und Extase bei Pseudo-Dionysius Areopagita* (Wiesbaden, 1958). Jean Vanneste, *Le mystère de Dieu. Essai sur la structure rationelle de la doctrine mystique de Pseudo-Denys l'Aréopagite* (Louvain, 1959).

107. Henri Gratton, 'Psychologie et extase', DSp 4/2 (1961) 2177.

108. *Life of Antony;* PG 26:933C–936A; CS 202:196–198.

109. François Halkin, *Sancti Pachomii Vitae graecae* (Brussels, 1932) 48; CS 45:110.

110. *Apophthegmata Patrum,* Colobos 14, PG 65:2864A; PL 73:981; translated Ward, *The Sayings of the Desert Fathers,* CS 59:88.

111. *Pratum Spirituale* 16; PG 87:2864A; Wortley, CS 139:12.

112. See other examples in DSp 4/2 (1961) 2104.

113. *Apophthegmata Patrum,* Bessarion 11; PG 65:141D; CS 59:42. Macarius, *Homily* 1; PG 34:452A; *Fifty Spiritual Homilies. St Macarius the Great.*

114. *Scala paradisi* 28; PG 88:969A; Moore translation,182.

115. See pp. 146, 211.

116. Joseph Lécuyer, 'Docilité au Saint-Esprit', DSp 3 (1957) 1471–1497.

117. Epiphanes, *Panarion* 48.4.1; ed. Karl Holl, GCS 2:224ff.

118. VI; translated J. Labourt and P. Battifol (Paris, 1911) 8.

119. 244a.

120. Edouard des Places, in DSp 4/2 (1961) 2061ff.

121. *De anima,* 45.3; CSEL 20:374; translated R. Arbesmann, *Tertullian: The Testimony of the Soul,* FCh 10 (1950) 131–143.

122. *De anima,* 11.4; CSEL 316.

123. *Adversus Marcionem,* 4.22; CSEL 47:493; ANF 3:383. See *Adversus Praxeam,* 15; CSEL 47, 255; ANF 3:610ff.

124. Irénée Hausherr, *Direction spirituelle en Orient autrefois,* OCA 144 (Rome, 1955) 43ff; *Spiritual Direction in the Early Christian East,* CS 116: 34ff.

125. Justin, *Dialogus cum Tryphone Judaeo,* 115.3; PG 6:741–744; *Dialogue with Trypho,* ANF 1:256. Athenagoras, *Legatio pro Christianis,* 9; PG 6:908A; *A Plea for the Christians,* ANF 2:133.

126. *Dialogus,* 68; PG 6:633BD; ANF 1:232.

127. *Contra Celsum,* 7.3–4; GCS 2, 154–156; ANF 4:611ff.

128. *De principiis,* 3.3.4; GCS 5:260–261; ANF 4:334ff.

129. Pseudo-Basil, *In Isaiam prophetam prooemium,* 5; PG 30:125BC. *Commentarium in Isaiam prophetam,* 13; PG 30:565–568.

130. *A Systematic Handbook,* 29ff.

131. *Pis̆ma o duchovnoj žizni* [*Letters on the Spiritual Life*] (Moscow, 1903) 251. S̆pidlík, *Théophane le Reclus,* 253.

132. *Ad Magnam* 27; PG 79:1004A.

133. Philoxenus of Mabbug, *'Exhortation à un juif converti';* translated M. Albert, *Orient Syrien* 6 (1961) 44, 5.

134. See p. 245.

135. Élie-Khalifé-Hachem, 'Isaac de Ninive', DSp 7/2 (1971) 2042ff. See also CS 101:259.

136. *A Systematic Handbook,* 29ff.

137. Basil, *Liber de Spiritu Sancto,* 26; PG 32:180C; SCh 17:225ff; LNPF 8:28ff.

138. *A Systematic Handbook,* 32.

139. Khalifé-Hachem, DSp 7/2 (1971) 2042ff.

140. *A Systematic Handbook,* 31ff.

141. *Stolp i Utverždenie Istiny* [The Pillar and Foundation of Truth] (Moscow, 1914) 51ff.

142. *Capitum theol. et oecon. Centuria,* 1.81; PG 90:1116B.

143. *Capitum de charitate Centuria,* 2.62; PG 90:1004–1005; ACW 21:165.

144. Jean Kirchmeyer, 'Extase chez les Pères de l'Église', DSp 4/2 (1961) 2103.

145. See Élie Khalifé-Hachem, in DSp 7/2 (1971) 2043ff.
146. Paul Bedjan, ed., *Mar Isaacus Ninivita. De perfectione religiosa* (Paris-Leipzig, 1909) 170; translated, in part, by Sebastian Brock, *The Syriac Fathers on Prayer and the Spiritual Life,* CS 101 (Kalamazoo: Cistercian Publications, 1987) 259.
147. *De perfectione religiosa;* Bedjan, 173ff; CS 101:262.
148. *De perfectione religiosa;* Bedjan, 304.
149. *A Systematic Handbook,* 99ff: Christian Freedom.
150. *De perfectione religiosa;* Bedjan, 172; CS 101:261.
151. *Homilia in Hexaemeron,* 6.1; PG 29:117; SCh 26:324; FCh 46:83.
152. See p. 301.
153. See p. 136.
154. Henri Crouzel, *Origène et la 'connaissance mystique'* (Desclée de Brouwer, 1961) 216ff.
155. See p. 183.
156. See DSp 10 (1980) 1979.
157. *Les grands mystiques russes* (Paris, 1979) 203.
158. See DSp 7/2 (1971) 2049.
159. SCh 78 (1961).
160. *A Systematic Handbook,* 87ff.
161. *Homilia in illud, Attende tibi ipsi,* 7; PG 31:213D; translated M. Monica Wagner, *Homily on the Words, 'Give Heed to Thyself',* FCh 9 (1950) 431ff.
162. *Carminum liber* 1.2.31, v. 7; PG 37:911.
163. *A Systematic Handbook,* 55ff.
164. *Centuries* 2.15; Frankenberg, 141.
165. *Gnosticon* 147; Frankenberg, 553.
166. *A Systematic Handbook,* 95ff.
167. *Ibid.,* 42ff.
168. *Metaphysics* XI, 7, 1072.
169. *Homilia in illud, Attende tibi ipsi,* 6; PG 31:212B [see above, note 161].
170. *Homilia in psalmum* 38.4; PG 29:293A.
171. E. Kourilas, *Historia tou asketismou* (Thessalonika, 1929) 54.
172. Margherite Harl, *Origène et la fonction du Verbe Incarné* (Paris, 1953) 355.
173. See p. 143.
174. See Irénée Hausherr, *Penthos,* OCA 132 (Rome, 19440 124ff; translated Anselm Hufstader, *Penthos. The Doctrine of Compunction in the Christian East,* CS 53 (Kalamazoo, Cistercian Publication, 1982) 114ff.
175. Gregory Nazianzus, *Oratio* 33.1; PG 36:216A; LNPF, ser. 2, 7:328ff.
176. See 240.
177. *Philoxeni Mabbugensis Tractatus de Trinitate et Incarnatione;* CSCO, series 2, vol. 27 (Rome, 1907) 4.
178. Sergius Boulgakoff (Bulgakov), *L'Orthodoxie* (Paris, 1932) 12 ; rev. translation by Lydia Kesich, *The Orthodox Church* (Crestwood, New York: St. Vladimir's Seminary Press, 1988) 10ff.
179. J. Palan, *The Theory of Religious Knowledge of Vladimir Soloviev* (thesis, Oxford, 1976). Tomaš Špidlík, 'Solov'ev', in *La mistica . . .* (Rome, 1984) I:645–668.
180. René Arnou, *Le désir de Dieu dans la philosophie de Plotin* (2nd ed., Rome, 1967).
181. *Confessions of Saint Augustine,* 1.1.1; PL 32:661; translated Vernon J. Bourke, FCh 21; translated Albert C. Outler, Library of Christian Classics 7:31. See François Bussini, 'Inquietude', DSp 7/2 (1971) 1776–1791.
182. *Čto ješť duchovnaia žizň* [*What the Spiritual Life Is*] (Moscow, 1897) 9:33.
183. *Ibid.,*
184. *Ibid.,* 2:5ff.

185. *Pisma* [*Letters*], 86, 26 (Moscow) 182, 443.
186. *Čto jesť duchovnaja žizň* [*What the Spiritual Life Is*] 3:7.
187. *Works*—in Russian (Brussels, 1966) 7:3–60; translated Jane Marshall, *The Meaning of Love* (London: Geoffrey Bles, 1946).
188. (Paris, 1933); translated Natalie A. Duddington, *The Justification of the Good: An Essay in Moral Philosophy* (New York: The Macmillan Company, 1918).
189. *Ibid.,* lxi.
190. *A Systematic Handbook,* 107ff.
191. See p. 97.
192. *Triades pour la Défense des saints hésychastes* II, 2, 12 (2nd ed., Louvain, 1974) 342; excerpts translated by Nicholas Gendle in *Gregory Palamas. The Triads,* (New York: Paulist Press, 1983).
193. See p. 75.
194. Roger Leys, *L'image de Dieu chez Saint Grégoire de Nysse* (Paris, 1951) 78ff.
195. G. I. Gargano, *La teoria di Gregorio di Nissa sul Cantico dei Cantici,* OCA 216 (Rome, 1981).
196. *Ibid.,* 218.
197. *Ibid.,* 210ff.
198. Gulielmus (Wilhelm) De Vries, 'Le sens ecclésial chez les Syriens (jacobites nestoriens)', DSp 41 (1960) 436–442.
199. Paul Bedjan, *Breviarium chaldaicum* (Rome, 1938) 3:394.
200. Nicolas Cabasilas, *The Life in Christ;* PG 150:493–725; translated C. J. deCatanzaro *The Life in Christ* (New York: St. Vladimir's Seminary Press, 1974).
201. *Idem, Explication de la divine liturgie;* SCh 4bis (1967); translated by J. M. Hussey and P. A. McNulty, *A Commentary on the Divine Liturgy,* (London: SPCK, 1960).
202. See p. 307.
203. Henri Crouzel, *Origène et la 'connaissance mystique* (Desclée de Brouwer, 1961) 262ff.
204. *Homilia in psalmum,* 38.2; PG 12:1402.
205. Crouzel, *Origène,* 409ff. See Špidlík, *Grégoire de Nazianze,* 37ff.
206. *Commentarium in Cantica,* 3; GCS 7:183, 5; ACW 26:184.
207. *Homilia in Jeremias,* 8.7–9; GCS 3:61, 15.
208. Crouzel, *Origène,* 257ff.
209. *Commentarium in epistolam ad Romanos,* 7.6; PG 14:1194D.
210. Crouzel, *Origène,* 273ff; see also, 'The Mystical Themes', in *Origen,* trans. by A. S. Worrall (San Francisco: Harper & Row, 1989) 121ff.
211. *Contra Celsum,* 3.77; GCS 1:268, 25; ANF 4:494ff.
212. *À l'image et à la ressemblance de Dieu* (Paris, 1967); *In the Image and Likeness of God.* Crestwood, New York, 1985) 15.
213. *Oratio* 28–*Theologica* 2.13; PG 36:41C; LNPF, ser. 2, 7:293.
214. Crouzel, *Origène,* 262ff.
215. *Oratio* 28—*Theologica* 2.13; PG 35:41Cff; LNPF, ser. 2, 7:294.
216. Plato, *Phaedo,* 66d, 67b, 70a.
217. Špidlík, *Grégoire de Nazianze,* 40ff. Gregory of Nyssa, *De vita Moysis,* PG 44:377; Malherbe-Ferguson, CWS, CF 31:93.
218. *Oratio* 27—*Theologica* 1.2; PG 36:13B; LNPF, ser. 2, 7:284ff.
219. *Oratio* 28—*Theologica* 2.15; PG 36:45C; LNPF, ser. 2, 7:288ff.
220. *Oratio* 29—*Theologica,* 3.21; PG 36:104A; LNPF, ser. 2, 7:302ff.
221. Crouzel, *Origène,* 514ff.
222. *Ibid.,* 438ff.
223. *Oratio* 28—*Theologica* 2.15; PG 35:15; LNPF, ser. 2, 7:288ff. See H. Stephanus, *Thesaurus Linguae Graecae* (Paris, 1842–1847) 6:1240. See also, Gregory Nazianzus, *De vita sua,*

5. 497; PG 37:1063; translated Denis M Meehan, *Saint Gregory of Nazianzus. Three Poems: Concerning His Own Affairs, . . . , Concerning His Own Life*, Fch 75 (1987) 77ff.

224. Evagrius, *Chapters on Prayer,* 60; PG 79:1180B; Hausherr, *Les leçons,* 85; CS 4:65.

225. N. Berdiaeff, *De l'esclavage et de la liberté de l'homme,* 276 (Paris, 1946); translated R. M. French, *Slavery and Freedom* (New York: Charles Scribner's Sons, 1944) 247.

226. *Ibid.,* 277 [247].

227. *Ibid.,* 284 [253].

228. *Ibid.,* 300 [268]; See Špidlík, *La spiritualità russa,* 146–155.

229. Jean Lemaitre (Irénée Hausherr), DSp 2/2 (1953) 1830ff.

230. *Contra haereses,* 4.20.5; PG 7:1035B; SCh 100:640;ANF 1:488.

231. Jules Lebreton, *Lumen Christi, La doctrine spirituelle du nouveau Testament* (Paris, 1947).

232. See Jean Lemaitre, DSp 2/2 (1953) 1847.

233. *Stromata,* 1.24,163; PG 8:909D; Stählin 2:102, 17–19; FCh 85:143.

234. *In Mattheum Commentarium, sermo* 134; GCS 12:278, 14–15.

235. *In Jeremiam homilia* 14.10; PG 13:416A; GCS 3:114.

236. *Vie de Syméon le Nouveau Théologien* (949–1022) *par Nicétas Stéthatos,* Greek text edition and French translation by Irénée Hausherr and Gabriel Horn, *Orientalia Christiana* 12, no. 45 (1928) 8–10.

237. Jean Lemaitre, DSp 2/2 (1953) 1849.

238. *Homily* 1.12; PG 34:461C. See *Intoxicated with God: The Fifty Spiritual Homilies of Macarius,* translated George A. Maloney (Denville, New Jersey: Dimension Books, 1978) 32.

239. *Oratio* 40.5—*In sanctum baptisma;* PG 36:364BC; LNPF, ser. 2, 7:360ff. Špidlík, *Grégoire de Nazianze,* 16ff.

240. *Liber de Spiritu Sancto,* 26; PG 32:185BC; SCh 17:226; LNPF, ser. 2, 8:38.

241. Evagrius, *Centuries,* 3.8.

242. *Centuries,* 1.78.

243. *Centuries,* 1.79.

244. *Centuries, Suppl.,* 52.

245. *Chapters on Prayer,* 70; Hausherr, *Leçons,* 120; CS 4:66. Cp. Maximus the Confessor, *Centuries,* 3.48; ACW 21:182.

246. *Chapters on Prayer,* 67; Hausherr, *Leçons,* 98; CS 4:66. See Gregory Nazianzus, *Oratio* 22—*De pace* 3; PG 35:1164. The godhead is *apoion* (formless), *aposon* (without quantity), *aperilepton* (incomprehensible).

247. *Centuries,* 2.1.21, 5.54, 57, 6. 22.

248. *Centuries,* 1.54.

249. *Centuries,* 6.10–13.

250. *Centuries* 3.6. See Lemaitre, in DSp 2/2 (1953) 1780.

251. *Chapters on Prayer,* 117 and 120; Hausherr, *Les leçons,* 152; CS 4:75.

252. *Ibid.,* 66, 99; CS 4:66. See *Vie de Plotin par Porphyre* (*The Life of Plotinus* by Porphyry), n. 23 (Bréhier, 1:26): 'By following the path prescribed by Plato, in the *Symposium* (210a), he saw the god who has neither form nor essence, because he resides above the intelligence and the intelligible'. See Maximus the Confessor, *Centuries* 2.61; ACW 21:165.

253. *De malignis cogitationibus,* 24; PG 79:1223ff; selections in 'On Various Evil Thoughts', *Early Fathers from the Philokalia,* translated and edited by E. Kadloubovsky and G. E. H. Palmer (London, 1963) 117ff.

254. *Chapters on Prayer,* 117; Hausherr, *Les leçons,* 150; CS 4:75.

255. *Ibid.,* 119; Hausherr, 154; CS 4:75. *Ibid.,* 66; Hausherr, 93; CS 4:66.

256. La 'science essentielle de Dieu', as Dom Joliet translates it in his version of *Chapters on Prayer,* chapter 73, *Saint Nil, Traité de la prière,* 485.

257. Marcel Viller, *Aux sources de la spiritualité de S. Maxime,* 248. See Jean Lemaitre, in DSp 2/2 (1953) 1838ff, and 1179.
258. *Adversus Eunomium,* 2,32; PG 29:648B. See Jean Kirchmeyer, DSp 4 (1961) 843.
259. *Liber gnosticus* 147. See Irénée Hausherr, *Les leçons d'un contemplatif,* 107.
260. See Maximus the Confessor, *Centuries,*1.97; ACW 21:151.
261. *De mystica theologia,* 1.1; PG 3:1017C; translated Colm Luibheid, *Pseudo-Dionysius: The Complete Works,* CWS (New York: Paulist Press, 1987) 135.
262. Hausherr, *Les leçons,* 153.
263. *Centuries* 3.30. See also 3.6, 12, 28, 32.
264. *Ibid.,* 4.62 and 2.5.
265. *Chapters on Prayer,* 83; Hausherr, *Leçons,* 115; CS 4:69.
266. *Ibid.,* 84; 117; CS 4:69.
267. Reginald Grégoire and Aimé Solignax, 'Nudité', DSp 11 (1981) 508–517.
268. E. Haulotte, *Le symbolisme du vêtement dans la Bible,* Théologie 65 (Paris, 1966) 79–89.
269. *Epist.* 52.5; ed. I. Hilberg, CSEL 54:422; LNPF, ser. 2, 6:89ff.
270. *De virginitate,* 12.4; SCh 119 (1966) 418–419; LNPF, ser, 2, 5:358. See E. Peterson, 'Pour une théologie du vêtement', coll. La Clarté-Dieu 8 (Lyon, 1943).
271. *De coelesti hierarchia,* 15.3; PG 3:332D; SCh 8:177–178; Luibheid, CWS, 186.
272. *Epist.* 9.1; PG 3:1104B; Luibheid, CWS, 280–281.
273. Špidlík, 'La mistica del martirio secondo Gregorio di Nissa', *I martiri della Val di Non* (Trent, 1985) 69–84.
274. See p. 267.
275. Élie Khalifé-Hachem, 'Isaac le Syrien', DSp 7/2 (1971) 2041–2054.
276. *De perfectione religiosa,* ed. Paul Bedjan (Paris-Leipzig, 1909) 170; Brock, CS 101:259.
277. *Ibid.,* Bedjan, 304; Brock, 259.
278. *Catecheses* 22,88; SCh 104 (1964) 372; translated C. J. deCatanzaro, *Symeon the New Theologian: The Discourses, CWS* (New York: Paulist Press, 1980) 426. See also,George A. Maloney, *The Mystic of Fire and Light: St. Symeon the New Theologian* (Denville, New Jersey: Dimension Books, 1975).
279. *Action de Grâce* 1.164–177; SCh 113 (1965) 319.
280. *Ibid.,* 2.226; 348.
281. *Ibid.,* 2.228; 352.
282. *Ibid.,* 2.272; 353.
283. *Discourse* 34, 305–342 (abridged); SCh 113:297ff; deCatanzaro, CWS, 356. See Basile Krivochéine, Introduction to *Catéchèses,* SCh 96 (1963) 16–54.
284. See p. 225.
285. See Index to the greek *Philokalia,* vol. 5 (Athens, 1963) 233–235.
286. *Smirenie vo Christe* (Paris, 1925) 97.
287. 'It is the heart which perceives God and not the reason'. *Pascal, Pensées,* translated by A. J. Krailsheimer (London: Penguin, 1995) 127.
288. *Serdce v christianskoj i indijskoj mistike* [*The Heart in Christian and Indian Mysticism*] (Paris, 1929) 5ff.
289. *Ibid.,* 11.
290. *Ibid.,* 5.
291. *Vozmožno li naučnoe zañatie religiej, Trudy* (Kiev, 1888) 3:228.
292. *Pravoslavnoe dogmatičeskoe bogoslavie,* vol. I (Sergev Posad, 1910) 215.
293. *Vera* (Sergev Posad, 1903) 13.
294. *Kurs osnovnogo bogoslovija ili Apologetiki* (Sergev Posad, 1914) 21.
295. *Ibid.,* 51.

296. Theophil Spáčil, *Doctrina theol. Orientis separati de revelatione, fide, dogmate* (Rome, 1935) 106ff.
297. *Slova* (Moscow, 1883) 157ff.
298. *Pis̀ma* (Moscow, 1892) 382.
299. Vyšeslavcev, *Serdce* [*The Heart*] 12.
300. Andre Lefèvre, 'Cor et cordis affectus, Usage biblique', DSp 2/2 (1953) 2278–2281.
301. Jean de Fraine and Albert Vanhoye, 'Coeur', VTB, 176–179; 'Heart', DBT, 228–229.
302. *A Systematic Handbook,* 90ff.
303. Michel Spanneut, *Le stoïcisme des Pères de l'Église de Clément de Rome à Clément d'Alexandrie* (Paris, 1957) 133ff.
304. *Praktikos* 84; SCh 17:674; CS 4:37.
305. *Phaedrus* 247c. *Timaeus* 51d.
306. See p. 33.
307. Špidlík, *Théophane le Reclus,* 292.
308. *Oratio* 40-*In sanctum baptisma* 39; PG 36:416AB; LNPF, ser. 2, 8:374.
309. See, for example, Cassiodorus, *Expositio in psalterium, psalmum* 72.26; PL 70:523CD; translated P. G. Walsh, *Cassiodorus. Explanation on the Psalms,* ACW 52 (1991) 207. See Peter Lombard, *Sententiarum libri quatuor, lib.* III, *dist.* XXVIII, *cap.* 5; PL 192:812.
310. Jean Chatillon, 'Cordis affectus au moyen âge', DSp 2/2 (1953) 2288–2300.
311. 2-II, 44, 5.
312. Špidlík, *Théophane,* 46ff.
313. *Načertanie christianskogo nravoučenija* [*Christian Moral Teaching*] (Moscow, 1895) 47.
314. See p. 39.
315. *Načertanie*, 406.
316. *A Systematic Handbook,* 31ff.
317. *Contra haereses,* 5.9.1–2; PG 7:1144; Harvey, 2:342; ANF 1:534.
318. Špidlík, *Théophane,* 40ff.
319. Héribert Fischer, 'Fond de l'âme, chez Eckhart', DSp (1964) 650–661.
320. Špidlík, *Théophane*, 40ff.
321. *Čto jest̀ duchovnaja žizǹ* [*What the Spiritual Life Is*] (Moscow, 1897) 25.
322. *Načertanie* [*Christian Moral Teaching*], 306.
323. *Contra Eunomium, lib.* I; PG 46:364C; 548D; LNPF, ser. 2, vol. 5.
324. *Instructions sur les estats d'oraison, livre* I, 20 (Paris, 1697) 26.
325. Fernand Jetté, 'État', DSp 4/2 (1961) 1372–1388.
326. *Obras completas* (Madrid, 1951) vol. 1: *Libro de la vida,* 624; translated E. Allison Peers, *The Complete Works of St Teresa of Jesus,* vol. 1: *Life*, chapter 6, London: Sheed and Ward, 1975) 36.
327. *Čto jest* [*Spiritual Life*] 26.
328. *Put ko spaseniju* [*The Way to Salvation*] (Moscow, 1908) 238.
329. *Načertanie,* 205.
330. *Slova,* 191ff.
331. *Constitutiones monasticae S. Basilii Magni,* cap. 2; PG 31:1337D–1340A.
332. John Moschus, Le pré spirituel; SCh 12 (1946) 162; translated John Wortley, *The Spiritual Meadow (Pratum Spirituale),* CS 139 (Kalamazoo: Cistercian Publications, 1992) 200.
333. *O molitve i trezvenni* (Moscow, 1889) 235.
334. *Ibid.,* 312.
335. *Ibid.*
336. *On Psalm* 118, v. 151 (Moscow, 1891) 443.
337. Vyšeslavcev, *Serdce* [*The Heart*], 43.

338. Pseudo-Macarius (Macarius of Egypt), *Homily* 7.5–6; PG 34:525–528; *Fifty Spiritual Homilies. St. Macarius the Great,* 63.
339. *Čto jest* [*Spiritual Life*]. 26.
340. Špidlík, *Théophane le Reclus,* 46ff.
341. *Ibid.,* 54.
342. *Načertanie,* 316.
343. *Ibid.,* 320.
344. *Načertanie,* 307.
345. *Ibid.,* 312.
346. *Ibid.,* 309. See the *cognitio per connaturalitatem* in Thomas Aquinas, *Summa theologiae,* 2-II. 45. 2. See also Jacques Maritain, *Art et scholastique,* 3rd ed. (Paris, 1935); translated Joseph W. Evans, *Art and Scholasticism* (New York: Charles Scribner's Sons, 1962).
347. Martyrius Sahdona, *Livre de la perfection;* CSCO 215 (Syri 91): 16, 11ff; 'The Book of Perfection', *The Syriac Fathers on Prayer and the Spiritual Life,* CS 101:225–226.
348. Špidlík, *Théophane le Reclus,* 58ff.
349. *Pisma* [*Letters*] (Moscow, 1892) 382.
350. *Recueil de lettres* (Moscow, 1898ff.) I:205.
351. Špidlík, *Théophane le Reclus,* 250ff.
352. *Ibid.,* 94ff.
353. *Ibid.,* 98ff.
354. *Načertanie,* 135.
355. *Put ko spaseniju* [*The Way to Salvation*] (Moscow, 1908) 146.
356. *A Systematic Handbook,* 32ff.
357. Špidlík, *Théophane le Reclus,* 102ff. *A Systematic Handbook,* 73ff.
358. Pierre Adnès, 'Larmes', DSp 9 (1976) 287–303.
359. *Conferences* 9.29; SCh 54:63–64; ACW 57:347–348; Luibheid, CWS 118–119.
360. Hausherr, *Penthos, La doctrine de la componction dans l'Orient chrétien,* OCA 132 (Rome, 1944); translated Anselm Hufstader, *Penthos: the Doctrine of Compunction in the Christian East,* CS 53 (Kalamazoo: Cistercian Publications, 1982).
361. *Letter* 284, *The Letters of Barsanuphius and John,* ed. (in Greek) by Schoinas (Volos, 1960) 168–169. See also *S. Dorothei Abbatis, doctrina* XXI; PG 88:1813AB; translated Eric P. Wheeler, *Dorotheos of Gaza: Discourses and Sayings,* CS 33 (Kalamazoo: Cistercian Publications, 1977) 249ff.
362. *A Systematic Handbook,* 194ff: Causes of Compunction.
363. *Ibid.*
364. *Instruction* 4.14; PO 11:476.
365. John Climacus, *Scala paradisi, gradus* 7; PG 88:801C; Luibheid and Russell, CWS, 136ff.
366. *Ibid.,* 805D, CWS 139–140.
367. *Conferences* 9.30; ACW 57:348; LNPF, ser. 2, 11:397ff.
368. Basil, *Regulae brevius tractatae* 16; PG 31:1092. See 'The Shorter Rules', in *The Ascetic Works of Saint Basil,* translated by W. K. L. Clarke (London: SPCK, 1925) 236.
369. *A Systematic Handbook,* 196.
370. *Practicorum capitum centuria* 1.71; PG 120:884BC.
371. *Life,* ed. Irénée Hausherr, OC 12, no. 45 (Rome, 1928) 8–11.
372. *De lege spirituali,* 12; PG 65:908A; 'On the Spiritual Law 15', *The Philokalia: The Complete Text,* 1:111.
373. *Scala paradisi-gradus* 7; PG 88:808BC; CWS 137.
374. French translation by Irénée Hausherr, *Dialogue sur l'âme et les passions des hommes,* OCA 120 (Rome, 1939) 40–42.

375. Gregory Nazianzus, *Oratio* 19.7 *(ad Julianum);* PG 35:1049–1052.
376. Jean Ladrière, 'Langage des spirituels', DSp 9 (1976) 204–217.
377. Pierre Adnès, 'Mariage spirituel', DSp 10 (1980) 388–408.
378. *De cherubim* 42–52; SCh, *Les Œuvres de Philon d'Alexandrie,* volume 3; translated F. H. Colson, G. H. Whitaker, *Philo,* Volume 2*: On the Cherubim. The Sacrifices of Abel and Cain. The Worse Attacks the Better. On the Posterity and Exile of Cain. On the Giants,* Loeb Classical Library (Cambridge: Harvard University Press).
379. André-Jean Festugière, *La révélation d'Hermès Trismégiste* (Paris, 1949) 2:459–550.
380. Irenaeus, *Adversus haereses.* 1.21.2; ed. W. Wigan Harvey, *Saint Irenaeus, Bishop of Lyons* (Cambridge, 1857, rpt. Gregg, 1965) 1:73; SCh 210; ANF 1:346]. See Antonio Orbe, 'Los valentinianos y el matrimonio espirituel', *Gregorianum* 58 (1977) 5–53.
381. Henri Crouzel, *Virginité et mariage selon Origène* (Paris, 1962).
382. *In Cantica canticorum, homily* 1; PG 44:765A; ed. H. Langerbech, *Gregorii Nysseni Opera.* Vol.6: *In Canticum canticorum* (Leiden: Brill, 1960) 15,5; translated Casimir McCambly, *St Gregory of Nyssa. Commentary on the Song of Songs* (Brookline, MA: Hellenic College Press, 1987) 43.
383. Ed. A. Wenger, *Huit catéchèses baptismales inédites,* SCh 50 (1957). See LNPF 9:159ff.
384. Theodoret of Cyrrhus, *In Canticum Canticorum,* 2.3; PG 81:128A.
385. Hal Koch, *Virgines Christi,* TU 31, 2 (Leipzig, 1907) 31.
386. Alfred C. Rush, 'Death as a Spiritual Marriage: Individual and Ecclesial Eschatology', *Vigiliae Christianae* 26 (1972) 81–101.
387. Henri Crouzel, 'La théologie mariale d'Origène', SCh 87 (1962) 11–64.
388. Tomaš Špidlík, 'To the Anthropological Background of the Truth-Theory of Wladimir Soloviev', *Kultur und Tradition, Festschrift für O. Nahodil,* Integrale Anthropologie 4 (Munich, 1983) 153–168.
389. See p. 236.
390. Hermann-Josef Sieben, 'Ivresse spirituelle chez les Pères de l'Église', DSp 7/2 (1971) 2312–2322. Hans Lewy, *Sobria ebrietas. Untersuchungen zur Geschichte der antiken Mystik* (Giessen, 1929).
391. *Vita Mosis* 1,187. *Legum allegoria* 1, 84 and 3, 82. *De fuga* 166. [Translations by F. H. Colson and G. H. Whitaker are available in the Loeb Classical Library series (Cambridge, MA: Harvard University Press, 1959). For a bibliography, see vol. 6: xix–xx.]
392. *De fuga,* 166. (Loeb, Philo, vol. 5).
393. *Enneads* 6.7, 35.
394. *De resurrectione D. N. Jesu Christi;* PG 50:436AB.
395. *In Cantica canticorum,* homily 10; PG 44:985C; Langerbeck (Leiden, 1960) 6: 308–309; McCambley, 194. [See above, n. 382].
396. Cyril of Jerusalem, *Catechesis* 17, *de Spiritu Sancto,* 18–19; PG 33:989B–992A; FCh 64: 107. See also PG 33:665AB.
397. 1.3, 149–153; ed. A. de Halleux, CSCO 201:71, 14–16.
398. See Hermann Josef Sieben, 'Ivresse spirituelle', DSp 7/2 (1971) 2321.
399. See Jean Daniélou, in DSp 2/2 (1953) 1879.
400. *Contra Celsum* 1.48; GCS 1:97, 24; ANF 4:416.
401. *Homilia in psalmum* 28.3; PG 29:289AB; FCh 46:199. See *Palladius: The Lausiac History,* 29; Butler, 85; ACW 34:88ff.
402. *In Cantica canticorum,* homily 10; PG 44:992C; McCambley, 194.
403. *Stromata,* 4.140, 1–2.
404. Emile Bréhier, *La théorie des incorporels dans l'Ancien Stoïcisme* (Paris, 1928) 38. Michel Spanneut, *Stoïcisme,* 356.
405. *De somniis,* 1.64; *Philo,* The Loeb Classical Library, vol. 5:329.

406. Spanneut, *Stoïcisme,* 356.
407. Marc-François Lacan, 'Présence de Dieu', VTB, 1019–1023; 'Presence of God', DBT, 455–457. Jules de Vaulx, 'Demeurer', VTB 254–257; 'Abide', DBT, 2–3.
408. Ex 24:9-11 (LXX) dominates the evagrian theory of the vision of God, as Ex 20:21 dominates the dionysian theory.
409. *Mystical Theology,* 1.3; PG 3:1000D; CWS, 137.
410. *A Systematic Handbook,* 55ff.
411. The *Book of Perfection* 2.8 (2); CSCO 253 (*Syri* 111):1; CS 101:202–203.
412. Clement of Alexandria, *Stromata,* 1.19.94; PG 8:809C; Stählin 2: 60, 20–25; ANF. 2:322.
413. *Thesaurus, assertio* VII; PG 75:85B.
414. *Commentariorum in Ezechielem,* 1.3; PL 25:38A.
415. *Letter* 29*;* Frankenberg, 587.
416. *Centuries,* 3.32; Frankenberg, 211.
417. *Quaestiones ad Thalassium,* 25; PG 90:33A.
418. *Centuries* 5.39; Frankenberg, 335.
419. *Ibid.,* 3.6. Irénée Hausherr, *Les leçons d'un contemplatif* (Paris, 1960) 145ff.
420. See p. 244.
421. Michel Olphe-Galliard, 'Cassien', DSp 2/1 (1953) 262ff.
422. *Conferences,* 9.18; PL 49:788; LNPF, ser. 2, 11:393; Luibheid, CWS, 111f; Ramsey, ACW 57: 340f.
423. See p. 243.
424. *Conferences,* 10.5; PL 49:826; ACW 57:373f.
425. *Ibid.,* 9.35; PL 816.; ACW 353.
426. *Ibid.,* 9.31; PL 807; ACW 349.
427. *Ibid.,* 9.25; PL 802; ACW 345–346.
428. *Ibid.,* 3.7; 566; ACW 124ff.
429. *Ibid.,* 10.10; PL 835; ACW 382; CWS, 135.
430. Donatien Mollat, 'Gloire', VTB, 504–511;'Glory', DBT, 202–205. Pierre Adnès, 'Gloire de Dieu', DSp (1967) 421–487.
431. Jean Meyendorff, 'Palamas (Grégoire)', DSp 12 (1986) 81–107. See also, John Meyendorff, *A Study of Gregory Palamas,* translated George Lawrence (London: Faith Press, 1964).
432. *Grégoire Palamas, Triades pour la Défense des saints hésychastes,* critical edition and French translation by Jean [John] Meyendorff, 2 vols., Spicilegium Sacrum Lovaniense, 29–30 (Louvain: 1959); 2nd rev. ed. (1973); excerpts in *Gregory Palamas: The Triads,* translated Nicholas Gendle, CWS (New York: Paulist Press, 1983).
433. *A Systematic Handbook,* 45ff.
434. Gregory Palamas, *Triad* 2. 3,31; Meyendorff, 499.
435. *Triad* 1.3.17; Meyendorff, 145; Gendle, CWS, 34.
436. *Traité apodictique,* 1.37; ed. Boris Bobrinskoy in the complete edition of P. Chrèstou (Thessalonika, 1962) 68.
437. *Physica, Theologica, Moralia et Practica Capita,* 112; PG 150:1197C; edition, translation and study by Robert E. Sinkewicz, *Saint Gregory Palamas: The One Hundred and Fifty Chapters* (Toronto, 1988).
438. *Triad* 3.1.22; Meyendorff, 599; Gendle, CWS, 80.
439. *Ibid.,* 26.109;83. See Maximus the Confessor, *Ambiguorum liber;* PG 91:1240A.
440. *Works,* vol. 3 (Brussels, 1979) 86.

# 9

## THE DISPOSITIONS FOR PRAYER

### *Preparing for Prayer*

TRUE PRAYER, all orthodox authors say, is a gift of God. Our guardian angel inspires it in us, writes Theophan the Recluse; it comes and goes. But in truth, the spirit of prayer is given to those who 'work' at prayer.[1] This has always been the thinking of the Fathers—Saint Macarius and Saint John Climacus, among others.[2] After saying that each virtue is the fruit of our effort, Macarius adds that this observation also holds for prayer.[3] To those who are overconfident, as if they already knew how to pray, prayer most frequently does not succeed.[4] By contrast, believers who pursue their 'work of prayer' with patience and perseverance will attain the highest degrees of prayer.[5]

In modern treatises on prayer a distinction is made between immediate and remote preparation. Remote preparation consists in a purification of the soul and the observance of an authentically christian life. The ancient ascetics dealt mostly with this. By contrast, the instructions for interior prayer disseminated in the West beginning with the sixteenth century focused chiefly on the 'immediate' preparation, and taught various methods of recollection and concentration. Such methods were, of course, not unknown in the East, where they were also indeed valued as profitable aids.

Our inner life, Theophan the Recluse writes, can be compared to an untuned musical instrument. Before playing on it, the strings must be tuned.[6] But can one adjust the heart as one tunes a harp? Is there such an art? What methods exist? Theophan the Recluse believed that such preparations are possible, because the Fathers prescribe 'rules' for pious exercises.[7]

While using such methods, however, one should be very careful not to become a 'spiritual Martha', overzealously driven to find the best system. There are several roads that lead to Moscow, but once a road has been taken and we are on the way, we should not turn back to take another one.[8] Moreover, an overly meticulous method could become a hindrance to piety. 'Someone who seeks spiritual nourishment needs no system; showing him how to act will be sufficient. An attitude of prayer will develop in his heart. A system might have the detriment of preventing the heart from being kindled by devotion.'[9]

In the East, the pre-eminent method was that of the hesychasts and we will speak about it at length.[10] Our concern in this chapter is to give an overview of the 'remote preparation', which is simply a description of the general principle that *praxis* leads to *theoria*.[11] Viewed negatively, *praxis* looks like purification, but seen positively it is the practice of the virtues. This outline will allow us better to coordinate the notes which follow, and to which we will add some comments about the place of prayer: the church building and the icons.

## THE PURIFIED HEART

### *Purification*

'The pure alone can grasp him Who is pure', Gregory Nazianzus says, along with many others.[12] Since God is reflected in the human spirit like the sun in a lake, the purer the spirit is, the clearer is the divine reflection.[13] Platonizers, Stoics, and Christians all insist on the need for purification to come near God. Differences arise only in determining concretely in what such purification consists. It is progressive and has stages. We will follow these according to the traditional terms through which such purification is expressed.

### *Ritual Purification*

Ancient religions knew purification through rites. According to the biblical faith which views all of creation as good, the concept of purity tends to become inward and moral.[14] Nonetheless, physical cleanness and the removal of what is unclean are included in the life of the holy community. Biblical prescriptions regulate the use of everything that is holy (Lv 4:22). The holy community itself commands respect. This dimension is reflected in the great number of monastic rules concerning dress, the manner of eating, and things like this. It goes without saying that Christianity, too, has rites of expiation and purification, even sacramentals. What is more, each prayer has a purifying power,[15] the source of which are the words and the sacrifice of Christ. Also, the spiritual authors, in the wake of the prophets (Is 1:51ff; Jer 7:21ff.), constantly declare that such rites have no value in themselves unless they are accompanied by an inner purification.

*Moral Purification, From Sin*

While interpreting Jn 9:31, 'God does not listen to sinners', the commentator explains how sin renders the intellect ignorant by taking understanding away from it and by hardening the heart, which cannot then ascend to the Lord. Origen views the presence of sin in our heart symbolically as the reign of Uzziah, who prevented Isaiah (the symbol of our spirit) from receiving divine inspirations.[16] At the opening of his first *Letter,* Ammonas explains the need for radical purification: 'You also know, my brothers, that since the transgression came to pass, the soul cannot know God if she does not withdraw from people and all distraction. Then she will see the adversary who struggles against her.'[17]

Apatheia

Pityrion, a disciple of Antony, warns that during prayer the demons seek to excite the passions in order to 'change our good proclivities into bad ones'.[18] These passions that blind the spirit are desires contrary to prayer. 'During prayer', Evagrius writes, the vices 'put to shame the humble mind and extinguish its blessed light.'[19] The passionate person resembles someone who has an eye disease and persists in staring at the sun in its noonday brilliance, without a screen.[20] *Apatheia,* the perfect purification from passions, is the equivalent of the 'kingdom of heaven' where prayer becomes a passionless state *(habitus)*.[21] In this state, Isaac of Nineveh maintains, the intellect acquires a special strength to defend itself. As soon as a passion begins to be dislodged, the understanding, in turn, becomes alert through a certain intellection that arises in the mind, and the passion vanishes with no ill effect.[22]

### Amnesikakia: *The Non-remembrance of Injury*

Of all the passions, anger is the one that most disturbs the normal activity of the mind.[23] This is why the remembrance of injuries (μνησικακία) is an obstacle to prayer. And thus, a man of the world who is meek is worth more than an angry monk.[24] 'He is worthy of all blame, who loves true prayer and yet is angry or resentful; for he is like a man who wants to see clearly, yet fills his eyes with dust.'[25] This conclusion of Evagrius agrees with several short sayings on this same point. But we should not forget the opposite: prayer, especially psalmody, calms the irascible part of the agitated soul.[26]

### *Sadness*

The flame of anger dies out sooner or later. The sadness that remains in the soul in its wake endures for a long time. In life in community, Mark the Hermit writes, 'those who sadden others make themselves sad by collecting sad thoughts. In this way, they exclude themselves from pure prayer'.[27] Among solitaries, sadness instills in the heart a hatred for the place where they live, and causes them to abandon contemplation.[28] The parish priest John of Kronstadt also views sadness as 'the death of the heart', 'a falling away from God', the obliteration of prayer.[29] 'Carnal' sadness[30] is healed by 'sadness according to God', *penthos* (compunction).[31]

### *The Purification of the Flesh*

'If you desire to pray in the spirit', advised Evagrius, 'then take nothing from the flesh so that you will not have some cloud darkening your vision at the time of prayer.'[32] In similar texts, and there are thousands of them, 'the flesh' is always contrasted to 'the spirit', which gives the soul wings to ascend to God.[33] Despite the fact that Platonism strongly influenced the terminology, christian thought is clearly different: 'the flesh' *(sarx)* is a generic, moral term that includes everything which is opposed to the Holy Spirit.[34] The 'subduing of the flesh' then becomes an indispensable requirement for prayer, but this in no way excludes the participation of the human body in prayer.[35]

### *Fasting*

In Scripture, prayer is often linked to fasting; it is a means of guaranteeing the efficacy of prayer.[36] The *Didache* addressed this invitation to young Christians: 'Pray for your enemies, and fast for those who persecute you'.[37] Hermas kept a fast regularly, on fixed days, to accompany and strengthen his prayer.[38]

Multiplying quotations to illustrate this link would be pointless. Let us give only one, by John of Kronstadt, who belongs to our age: 'Look how high was the flight of the ascetics and abstinents! They soared in the heavens like eagles; they, earth-born, lived by their intellect and heart in heaven, heard there unspeakable words, and learned there divine wisdom.'[39]

Several grounds recommend joining prayer to fasting. One of them is that fasting cannot be separated from the concrete exercise of charity, almsgiving. As the prophets of Israel already proclaimed, charity toward one's neighbor should always be linked to fasting: 'Faithful love is what pleases me, not sacrifice' (Hos 6:6). The Book of Tobit echoes this teaching:[40] 'Prayer with fasting and alms with uprightness are better than riches with iniquity' (Tb 12:8).[41] And so arose the trilogy—fasting, prayer, almsgiving—which the christian tradition would inherit. The Fathers constantly recall that fasting should allow Christians to satisfy their duty of almsgiving. With what is saved on food, we should be able to provide for the needs of the hungry.[42] The byzantine liturgy proclaims: 'To our bodily fasting, let us join spiritual fasting. Let us give bread to the hungry, and open our house to the homeless poor, to attract the great mercy of Christ.'[43]

Other links between prayer and fasting were very quickly established. In archaic cultures the fast was almost always connected to rites of initiation, bereavement, or renewal.[44] This is how we should understand the eucharistic fast which the ancient church prescribed before receiving communion: physical hunger here corresponds to a spiritual expectation of the fulfillment, to the openness of one's entire being to the joy that is to come.[45]

Hermas speaks from personal experience of exceptional fasts undertaken to prepare for a divine revelation or to assure the granting of a prayer. Hermas calls this fast 'keeping a station', an expression that was to enter christian literature.[46] In general, we should say that fasting, especially the lenten fast, takes on meaning in connection with Christ. The main goal of the fast in the early Church was to prepare the catechumens, newly converted Christians, for baptism. Indeed, the *Didache* prescribes: 'Before baptism let the baptizer and the one who is to be baptized and any others who can do so, fast'.[47]

This theme of conversion explains the wider use of the fast. The 'penitential' character of monastic prayers makes them inseparable from fasting practices which were often so severe that they had to be modified. Ignatii Brianchaninov wrote:

> Let us try to regulate our physical condition wisely by giving our body enough food and sleep so that it not be weakened and remains capable of ascetic efforts; however, give it rather little, so that it constantly carries death within and does not awaken the impulse of the flesh.[48]

Greek philosophy insisted strongly on fasting as a purification with a view to *theoria:* only the pure can reach the Pure.[49] These philosophic themes were taken over by the Fathers; their influence is visible especially in, among others, Clement of Alexandria, Basil of Ancyra, Basil of Caesarea, and Gregory of Nazianzus.[50]

However, the Fathers present purification in a wider context. Purity of heart represents a victory over the demons, a living experience of a person's communion with God, a restoration to the original state, a return to the beginning where one finds *parrhesia,* frankness with God. Athanasius writes: 'the fast is the life of the angels'.[51] For monks this life requires a preliminary struggle against the fallen angels. Fasting is a powerful weapon against them: 'Let the one who wants to master the demons and defeat Satan have in his heart and body these two twin workers, like a double armor, (namely) constant prayer in the heart and constant fast in the mouth' (see Eph 6:11).[52]

Let us conclude by quoting John of Kronstadt: 'To what end do fasting and penitence lead? For what purpose is this trouble taken? They lead . . . to peace of heart, to union with God; they fill us with devotion and sonship and give us boldness before God.'[53]

*The Purification of the Senses*

'Blessed is the mind which, during prayer, is insensible to all things.'[54] The term ἀναισθησία (insensibility) usually designates a vice, utter lukewarmness.[55] But here Evagrius understands the word in a positive sense, as a mortification of the bodily senses, the fruit of which is an awakening of the spiritual senses. In ascetic literature, the 'senses', like the 'heart', are a moral term used to designate deviation from attention to God.[56] In addition, renouncing the sensory impressions becomes part of the apophatic dynamic that leads to the heights of spiritual knowledge and conveys the 'resurrection of the senses'.[57] Thus, the numerous statements which proclaim the utter incompatibility of the senses with pure prayer are to be understood within their context and according to the intent of the one who uttered them.

*Flight from the World*

Flight from the world *(fuga mundi),* in the christian sense, presupposes a moral condition caused by sin. It does not imply a dualistic structure of reality.[58] According to the definition of Abba Isaiah, the world, in a moral sense, 'is the soul's attraction to sin',[59] the forgetting of God. Evagrius gives this advice: 'Do you wish to pray? Then banish the things of this world. Have heaven for your homeland and live there constantly (Ph 3:20).'[60]

Concretely, the world that hinders prayer is nothing other than the 'impact of worldly cares and all thoughts'.[61] 'The cares and desires of this world', Martyrius Sahdona writes, 'are a great obstacle to the soul's engaging in pure prayer addressed to God' (see Mt 13:22). Similarly, that holy teacher, beloved by God, John

Chrysostom said: 'Nothing so much perturbs and troubles the eye of the soul as the importunity of this world's cares and yearning'.[62] Flight from the world therefore coincides with *amerimnia* (freedom from anxiety, tranquillity).[63]

The spirit can 'enter the ecstasy of spiritual knowledge' only after rejecting the shadow of the world, Philoxenus of Mabbug observed.[64] For him, flight from the world was a generic term for what is designated under various names: abnegation, renunciation, chastity, and asceticism. Each of these expresses a special coloring[65] against a common backdrop: removing the obstacles to union with God. 'If you wish to pray worthily', Evagrius writes, 'deny yourself every hour.'[66] 'Do you long to pray? Renounce all things. You will then become heir to all.'[67]

### *The Purification of the* Νοῦς

We have seen that the purified *nous* is the organ of contemplation.[68] In that it is itself inaccessible to demons, they seek to make it deviate from its function 'by means of thoughts',[69] that is, 'passionate thoughts', *logismoi*. 'Thoughts', Saint Antony laments,[70] are the main weapons the demons use to prevent prayer. Discernment of thoughts, 'unseen warfare', 'inward *praxis*[71] are therefore the daily occupation of contemplatives. 'If Moses, when he attempted to draw near the burning bush, was prohibited until he should remove the shoes from his feet', wrote Evagrius, 'how should you not free yourself of every thought that is colored by passion, seeing that you wish to see One who is beyond every thought and perception?' [72] How many examples do we read in the lives of the saints of those who, while praying, were oblivious to everything, except God? The purification of the *nous,* as understood by Evagrius, had to be still more radical.[73] But for most spiritual authors, a purification of the distractions is enough to arrive at a humanly perfect prayer.

### *Distractions*

The spiritual life cannot escape any of the distractions that arise in various forms in daily life .[74] In John Cassian's *Conferences*[75] nothing is overlooked in an extremely accurate description of the unending flow of thoughts pouring into the mind 'like water on a mill wheel'—meanderings of which we are not even aware, but after which we are like those who awaken from sleep without knowing where they are, who seek to return to God, but run away again before they find him, and the moment passes. The picture he gives of the causes of our distractions and their objects is no less complete. These can be of a physical nature: worries about eating and drinking, indisposition, stomach aches, headaches and other pains, sleep or insomnia and their phantoms. Or there can be an effervescence of distractions caused by a simple scattering of the mind on vain images and memories, even aridity, anxiety-filled desolation—temptations of despair. The meandering of thoughts can be such that during psalmody the soul often hops from verse to verse, unable to remember, penetrate, or interiorize anything, and the mind seems to be the plaything of chance.

As a remedy, Conference Eleven advances as a principle the indispensable, mutual conditioning of the virtues and prayer. The perfection of the one cannot be separated from that of the other, so that to arrive at stability in purity, we should take care to remove from the mind the remembrance of earthly things, even on the pretext that they are honest and profitable. For the memory will make us in prayer like we were before: 'What we would be found at our prayer, that we ought to be before the time of prayer. . . . for the mind cannot help being affected by its previous condition.'[76]

Evagrius had developed an identical doctrine: 'Undistracted prayer is the highest act of the intellect'.[77] Other texts of the patristic tradition apparently add nothing essential to this teaching, except for an insistent emphasis on this or that detail, depending on the authors. All are in agreement on the need habitually to keep watch over one's thoughts. The pre-eminent remedy against distractions will therefore be attentiveness, vigilance, and sobriety. On this point, the hesychasts proved to be the undisputed masters.[78]

In practice, the exercise of guarding the heart implies an unending struggle against demons, and the examination of conscience.

### *The Struggle Against Demons*

Being aware of the value of prayer, the demon is the sworn enemy of it. 'The devil is greatly envious of one who prays, and uses many wiles to disturb that intention', wrote Evagrius.[79] In chapter ninety-one of his treatise *On Prayer,* he begins his description of a long series of diabolical tests of the contemplative. This is what has been called the 'demonism' of Evagrius.[80] Its influence is particularly evident in the demonology of Cassian.[81] Among monks, those who lead the solitary life have to undergo the most violent assaults. The demonology expressed in the *Life of Antony* became a classic of the desert, together with that of Evagrius and Cassian.

What strategy do the demons use in this warfare? Their usual weapons are evil thoughts, the *logismoi,*[82] temptations which the monk overcomes by guarding the heart *(phylake kardias, custodia cordis).*[83] Sometimes the demons use the flesh to arouse passions directly, 'that the spirit in this way should become dull and . . . rendered unfit to pray'.[84]

When the monk outmanœuvers the assault of thoughts then the demon tries to unsettle him 'by appearing to him'[85] in deceptive forms: these are the φαντασίαι, visions or hallucinations, the best known temptations of anchorites. Their aim is to frighten the ascetic and make him run away. 'Crashing sounds and roars and voices and beatings—all of these, coming from the devils, are heard by the man who pursues the practice of pure prayer. Yet he does not lose courage or his presence of mind'[86]; he ignores them 'through contempt.'[87]

The demons then take on the appearance of devout persons, even angels. Changing themselves into 'angels of light' (2 Cor 11:14), they impel the monk to excessive fasts or give him false counsels on moderation and the like. One of the highest means they use to establish their authority is making predictions. This is because they divine the future by reading the present, which they are able to conjecture.[88] They procure visions of light, but their light is merely borrowed from the eternal fire that is prepared for them.[89]

Exasperated by the ascetic's courage, the demons sometimes have recourse to physical violence. The observation of Evagrius, that they 'shall attack you like a wild beast and buffet your entire body' is to be taken literally.[90]

'When the depraved demon has done all he can and still finds that his efforts to prevent the prayer of the virtuous man are unavailing, he will let up for a time. But again after a while he avenges himself on this man of prayer.'[91] The characteristic of these phenomena is their suddenness.[92]

The strategy against the demons is the method of *antirrhesis* (counterstatement, refutation)[93]: doing exactly the opposite of what they suggest: against their evil thoughts, guarding the heart; against the passions, asceticism; against vain fears, the fear of God[94]; against hallucinations, humility; and against violence, patience. But the best means is prayer itself. If prayer is what the demons seek to prevent, it will, in turn, be prayer that chases them away. By its nature, the human spirit is a faculty that prays.[95] The action of the demons against it is only indirect, and the human person will gain the upper hand through purity, with the help of the angels, contemplative spirits.[96]

### *The Examination of Conscience*

Examination of conscience is not unique to Christianity. Found already in Confucius, it would be practised in Taoism,[97] the religions of India,[98] Egypt,[99] the greco-roman world, especially among the Pythagoreans and the Stoics,[100] and in rabbinic spirituality.[101] The muslim ascetic writers give it an important role. In the Old Testament examination of conscience was made at two critical moments: when the time came to begin the worship; and when misfortune came to signal divine anger.[102] In the New Testament, it is done before the Lord—more precisely before the Cross, a preaching that pierces the hearts and determines the saving repentance: 'What are we to do?' (Acts 2:37). The Cross is sin stripped bare and shows that divine forgiveness is always strongest.[103]

From more than one angle the preaching of the Fathers is an appeal to an examination of conscience in the presence of God and confronted by our own salvation. In this general but fundamental sense of the examination of conscience, the Fathers are in full agreement with Scripture. Stoic ethics, on the other hand, had a fairly well defined practice of the examination as a special exercise. Recommended first in the pastoral literature addressed to Christians living in the world, this means of fostering piety was soon to become one of the key elements of monastic asceticism. What is surprising, however, is that we have to wait until the fifth century before the need of this ascetic exercise was recognized universally.[104]

Of all the Fathers, it is John Chrysostom who discussed the subject most frequently. He compares the examination of conscience to the manner in which a conscientious financier manages his affairs: 'Following the example of merchants, let us examine our conscience and tally our accounts in order to know what profit we made this week, what last week, and what additional profit there will be next week.'[105]

The technique was gradually brought to perfection in syro-palestinian monastic circles. According to Barsanuphius, the traditional teaching was that there are two moments in the day when we recollect ourselves for an examination of conscience: in the morning, we examine the thoughts of the night; and in the evening before going to sleep we examine those of the day.[106] But the one who deals with the question most explicitly is unquestionably Dorotheos of Gaza.[107]

### *The Goal of Examination of Conscience*

Self-knowledge (γνῶθι σεαυτόν—'Know thyself'), 'paying attention to oneself' (πρόσεχε σεαυτῷ—*Attende tibi*), and watchfulness *(nepsis)* are frequent themes in patristic homiletics,[108] which focus most often on one or another aspect other of such practices.

In our own day it is often said that the main, if not exclusive, goal of self-examination is the discovery of our sins and faults so that we may do penance and make a resolution to better ourselves. An exercise which is always valid, but which has relative value. Some may well be surprised when reading texts by ancient spiritual directors who advise against an all-too detailed examination of faults, the remembrance of which might dishearten the sinner and diminish his faith in the mercy of God.[109]

The Desert Fathers, who knew the role of evil thoughts in the 'unseen warfare',[110] focused their examination of conscience on the following feature: keeping a daily account of the 'movements of the soul' (Saint Antony).[111] This is the means to learn about the discernment of thoughts and to verify the tactics of wickedness or, by contrast, divine inspirations.[112]

Being attentive to divine inspirations means to be aware of the presence of God in the heart. Viewed from this angle, the examination of conscience is an awareness of this reality, a reflection on this inward revelation.[113]

Finally, those who are attentive to God in their personal life discover his providential action in everything that happens at every moment of the day. The examination of conscience is then identified with 'a contemplation of Providence'[114]: it is the daily effort everyone makes to understand the 'sacred history' of the events that affect us.

If attention is focused above all on purification of the heart, the manner of self-examining will be according to what was later to be called the 'particular examination'.[115] The need to concentrate one's efforts against the dominant vice is clearly indicated by John Climacus: 'Someone who sees that some passion is getting the better of him, should first of all take up arms against this passion, and moreover against this passion alone . . . because until this passion is destroyed, we shall not derive any profit from the conquest of other passions'.[116] A more systematic explanation of this practice is found in Cassian, the pre-eminent witness of the tradition of the Desert Fathers.[117]

## THE VIRTUES

### *The Virtues in General*

Here we deal with the positive aspect of *praxis*.[118] 'The soul that is purified by the plenitude of virtues renders the spirit unshakable in its balance and makes it capable of possessing the state for which it longs', that is, contemplation, perfect prayer.[119] It is not surprising that the virtues render the mind steadfast since 'virtue is an excellent habit of the rational soul, through which the soul becomes hardly shaken by evil'.[120] According to this explanation of Evagrius, then, the virtuous life involves stability in prayer.

Here we will not deal with the virtues themselves. Our only intent is to illustrate by means of texts how the authors viewed the direct connection between prayer and the virtues. Moreover, they are hardly systematic on this point: what we find instead are short notes inserted into various discourses.

*Piety*

In modern spiritual literature, the word 'piety' has taken on a general meaning which encompasses various dispositions for prayer. Thus, we refer to 'pious feelings', 'pious manuals', and so on. The 'pious person' is 'devout'. Among ancient authors, the meaning of this term was more specific: it indicated one's professed religion. For Origen, piety (εὐσέβεια or θεοσέβεια) meant Christianity: piety then became orthodoxy. The work in which the term piety is found most frequently is *An Exhortation to Martyrdom*. Piety pertained to spiritual warfare.[121] Much later, especially in the West, the first meaning was to be the one indicated by Augustine in *The City of God*[122]: *cultus Dei,* the worship of God, prayer.

*Simple Faith, Hope*

The concatenation of virtues established by the ancient authors always began with faith,[123] the foundation of life in Christ. Prayer to the Father is the natural manifestation of this: 'If you have faith, everything you ask for in prayer, you will receive' (Mt 21:22). Since faith does not coincide with dialectical wisdom,[124] those who maintain the simplicity of a child while praying, 'receive knowledge and learn everything they hear'.[125]

In agreement with Scripture, the spiritual writers joined faith and hope in a single concept. To hope while praying is, as it were, to open the eyes of the mind: 'The one who looks at the hope of this world is blind, but if he surrenders and looks at the hope that is expected (Col 1:5; Heb 6:18), he sees'.[126]

*The Fear of God*

Of all the salutary effects of the fear of God *(phobos theou, timor Dei)* the most important is that it unseals the ears of those who had become deaf to the voice of God.[127] Fear of God predisposes the soul to dialogue in prayer: 'When you are silent, you should fear the encounter with God that precedes your breathing [or rather, goes together with breathing, and is unceasing]; . . . as long as you do not have fear in you, you are far from mercy'.[128]

### *Obedience*

As in several other languages, the greek term ὑπακοή, obedience, is inserted by its very nature into the context of prayer: it is derived from the verb *hypakouo,* meaning 'to give ear' [as similarly in Latin *obedire* is derived from *ob-audire*]. Inversely, the terms παρακοή, παρακούειν ('that which has been half heard', 'unwillingness to hear', disobedience) describe the conduct of someone who hears the word, but puts himself 'next to it', as it were, 'parallel to it'.[129] The One to whom the obedient person gives ear is in the first instance always God the Father, whose voice in prayer makes itself heard by inspirations, illuminations, and special calls coming from the Holy Spirit.[130] The Christian is, so to speak, under his influence. Athanasius expresses this evidence by asking: 'Where shall I go to escape from your Spirit?'[131]

Being fearful that prayer might turn into a *didaskalia* (an instruction, admonition),[132] a monologue, the authors often encouraged people to lend an attentive ear to these inner voices, not to harden their hearts (cf. Ps 94:8). They frequently spoke of 'docility to the Spirit'.[133]

On the other hand, the 'charismatic' element is only one of numerous aspects of a 'complete' obedience that hears the harmony among the various voices of God, who speaks 'at many moments in the past and by many means' (Heb 1:1).[134] In such inspirations it is not possible to grasp what is essential within the plan of salvation, if one fails to view them as they relate to the Church. Inspirations during prayer are therefore inconceivable outside Scripture, the patristic teachings, the concrete life in the monastery, the ecclesiastical environment. In short, the help of a wise spiritual father or mother is imperative in the higher stages of prayer, especially in the case of exceptional illuminations.[135]

### *Humility*

If, according to common teaching, humility is the condition of every virtue, of any action,[136] it is also the indispensable condition for prayer. Augustine writes that nothing is more apt to become an obstacle to God's mercy than lack of humility.[137] As we know,

Augustine, and several Latin Fathers with him, base the need for prayer on our sinful condition.[138]

But humility during prayer is also required by the greek Fathers for whom prayer pertains to a human nature elevated to dialogue with the Father, in the fullness of the Spirit. Indeed, as Basil says, humility is 'the means of restoration to [our] original human condition'.[139]

In prayer, humility therefore manifests itself in two ways: as a request for mercy; and as thanksgiving *(eucharistia)*, both the one and the other preventing the Christian from attributing the gifts of God to self. In the byzantine liturgy, the prayer before communion beautifully expresses these two aspects as a unity: gratitude for the grace of the sacrament to 'Christ who came into the world to save sinners, of whom I am chief'.[140]

Numerous sayings illustrate this conviction. The demons can be recognized because, on account of their lack of humility, they do not succeed in praying.[141] The words 'God opposes the proud but gives grace to the humble' (Jm 4:5) are often cited. And thus, Ignatius Brianchaninov writes, 'true prayer and true humility are the same thing'.[142]

## *Meekness, Patience*

These virtues are simply concrete applications of charity in contact with one's brothers and sisters: 'If you desire to pray as you ought, do not sadden anyone. Otherwise you run in vain.'[143] 'From meekness is born *gnosis* (knowledge), that is, contemplation; from rudeness, ignorance.'[144]

Meekness manifests itself above all in the readiness to forgive offenses. The Lord's Prayer strongly emphasizes forgiveness (Mt 6:12, cf. Mt 19:23-35). It is therefore standard for those who dealt with prayer to have commented often on its lines.[145] 'Learn a lesson from the man who owed ten thousand talents!' (Mt 18:23-25).[146]

Each act of patience at the weakness of others will have a blessed repercussion on prayer: 'Whatever difficulty you patiently endure through love of wisdom will reap ripe fruits at the time of prayer'.[147]

### *Bearing the Cross*

Bearing one's cross in following Christ is a universal rule of the christian life. It has its application in mysticism[148] and in prayer in general. According to Abba Isaiah, crucifying ourselves to outward things rouses the intellect against evil tendencies: 'What cross do we carry', he says, 'if it is not that the intellect should be vigilant at all times.'[149]

### Penthos

The eastern ascetics unanimously teach that holy mourning is a normal disposition for the those who seek consolation in prayer.[150] Among the things which cause us sadness, Abba Isaiah mentions mistakes made during prayer itself, the weakness of our 'mind that sees how the senses have carried it far from itself'. If the human person feels sad because of distractions in prayer, 'the goodness of God will lead us to a renewal; and henceforth there will be no adversary to impede it'.[151]

### *Joy*

If passionate thoughts cause sadness,[152] serenity is the normal state of the purified soul, and prayer can then be 'the fruit of joy'.[153] To console a cloistered nun, Seraphim of Sarov confided:

> When I was a novice and sang in the choir, I was always happy. Sometimes when I saw my brothers tired and sad, I tried to make them happy. Then they no longer felt their weariness. In the house of God, speaking words that are friendly and inspire joy causes all to have a happy, sadness-free soul. This is not a sin.[154]

### *Gratitude*

In everything that happens, God has no other aim than to let us arrive at prayer which, in this context, is 'the fruit of thanksgiving'.[155] This is why it is recommended that we thank God before asking him a favor.[156] John of Kronstadt writes, 'Many do not pray because it seems to them that they did not receive any gift from God when they prayed before'.[157] In order to gain more confidence in prayer, 'it is useful to remind ourselves of former innumerable experiences of mercy and grace bestowed upon men [in Holy Writ and in the lives of the saints] and upon ourselves'.[158]

### *Poverty*

The poor are exhorted to invoke the Lord in their tribulations (see Jb 34:28). According to Scripture, those who 'have been brought low' and are afflicted (the *anawim*) are the privileged heirs of the kingdom of God. They will therefore be more easily heard than will others.[159] But the connection between poverty and prayer can be seen as well from another angle. A monk living in a monastery is not indigent. Quite the contrary. All of life's necessities are provided to him. He can therefore be unattached to money and taste the sweetness of heaven.[160] The result of this attitude is *amerimnia,* freedom from care, the freedom needed for undistracted prayer.[161]

### *Almsgiving*

While the word ἐλεμοσύνη (mercy, compassion) is late, the concept of almsgiving is as old as biblical religion.[162] Almsgiving should be, not a mere gesture of philanthropy, but a religious gesture. It is often associated with liturgical celebrations (2 Sm 6:19; Neh 8:10ff). Since giving alms imitates God's acts, it is particularly appropriate to someone asking for mercy from on high (Mt 18:23-35).[163]

### *Virginity*

Beginning in the fourth century,[164] treatises on virginity proliferated in christian literature. The arguments in favor of this angelic virtue varied depending on the erudition of the authors, who were fond of taking their inspiration from platonic philosophy or even medical theories. But essentially their entire dialectic merely served to support the teaching of Saint Paul that sexual abstinence has as its aim perfection in prayer (see 1 Cor 7:15).

The treatise of Gregory of Nyssa, which became a classic, frequently reiterates the almost necessary connection between virginity and contemplation, as means to end. It is thanks to this 'life according to excellence', that one is 'able to ascend to the heights'. 'Virginity, and zeal of incorruptibility have no other goal than this: the power, because of them, of seeing God'.[165] The union of the virgin soul with her Lord constitutes a true spiritual marriage, an admirable union, 'the soul . . . cleaves to her Master so as to become with him one spirit'.[166]

## *Charity*

We have spoken of the need of charity for contemplation and of its role in mysticism.[167] It goes without saying that charity, which is 'the summit of the spiritual mountain of the virtues',[168] is the indispensable condition for all prayer in the Spirit. The concrete consequences of this truth are numerous and dependent on the condition of those to whom the discourse is addressed. On this subject the text of Mt 5:23-24 was often used: 'So then, if you are bringing your offering to the altar and there remember that your brother has something against you, leave your offering there before the altar, go and be reconciled with your brother first, and then come back and present your offering'.[169]

On this point, Maximus the Confessor has given us the most complete documentation: for him, as for Evagrius, the path to perfection runs from ignorance to *gnosis,* from forgetfulness of God to unceasing prayer. But he identifies, much more explicitly than Evagrius, the progression from self-love to perfect love *(philautia* to *agape).* In this way, 'A sincere lover of God prays wholly without distraction, just as the one who prays without distraction loves God sincerely'.[170] 'When, urged on by love, the mind soars to God, it has no sense either of itself or of anything existing. Illumined by the limitless divine light, it is insensible to everything created, just as the physical eye is to stars in the light of the sun.'[171]

## THE PLACE OF PRAYER

### *Every Place Is Appropriate for Prayer*

According to the Fathers, it is a privilege of christian prayer, as compared to jewish and pagan prayer, that it can be made anywhere. In the *Octavius* of Minucius Felix, the christian interlocutor explains this by saying: 'What temple shall I build to him, when this whole world which is his handiwork cannot contain him? . . . Were it not better that he should be dedicated in our mind, consecrated in our inmost heart?'[172]

Many Fathers say the same thing: 'Each place . . . in which we entertain the idea of God is sacred', wrote Clement of Alexandria[173] and Origen.[174] John Chrysostom describes prayer in the workplace, on the *agora,* in the shop, at the market, in the kitchen, for 'the place does not embarrass God'. But he already adds one condition, 'if one cannot go to church'.[175] In this same context, let us also recall the expression of the mystics who said that the human soul is 'the place of God'.[176]

### *Favorite Places*

Exhortations to pray anywhere do not in the least mean that certain places were not considered to be more appropriate for prayer than others. The gospel already gave preference to the solitary place and to 'secret' prayer (Mt 6:6). The countless crowd of solitaries followed the letter of the exhortation in choosing the desert as their preferred place for prayer.[177]

But paradoxically, along with this, the commendations of common prayer in church multiplied. The authors often seem to contradict themselves. The esteem John Chrysostom had for the solitaries was sincere, and yet in Constantinople he spoke quite differently:

> Yes, you can pray at home, but not as well there as you can in church. . . . Here, there is something more, namely harmony and unanimity, the bond of love, and the prayer of the priests. Indeed, the priests preside for this reason: that the prayers of the

> crowd which are weaker, may rise to heaven, joined to theirs, which are stronger.[178]

While the reasons for solitary prayer have a rather psychological nature, prayer in church became preferable because of the sacredness of the place. In the East, this awareness deepened over the centuries. The expression 'heaven on earth', familiar to the Russians as a definition of the church, is evidence of this.[179] Here is a recent eulogy:

> Truly, the temple is heaven upon earth; for where the throne of God is, where the awe-inspiring mysteries are celebrated, where the angels serve together with men, where the Almighty is unceasingly glorified, there is truly heaven, and the heaven of heavens.[180]
>
> O, holy temple, how good, how sweet it is to pray in thee! For where can there be ardent prayer if not within thy walls, before the throne of God, and before the face of him who sits upon that throne?[181]

But this attitude creates problems. The entire world can be deified: by isolating one of its fragments and declaring it sacred are we not backsliding into early paganism? Several people raised this question when, after the Peace of the Church, Constantine had great basilicas built. The syrian monks refused to visit them. The Fathers were often critical of their excessive sumptuousness. Listen to John Chrysostom, whose positive attitude toward prayer in church we have just mentioned: 'God has no need at all of golden vessels. . . . No one was ever blamed for not enriching our temples with such splendid ornaments; but those who will not give alms he threatens with the punishments of hell.'[182]

This sense of the sacredness of churches, of their beauty and also their richness, nowadays so visible in the East, is the result of an historic evolution. It is no doubt due to external circumstances, but the foundation of it is dogmatic and essentially christian.

### *The Christological Character of the Christian Temple*

The Bible presents two views of the temple. On the one hand, the Israelites were strictly forbidden to visit 'the hill shrines' considered sacred by the pagans.[183] By its very nature, no place could be considered 'sacred' because Yahweh who dwells in heaven cannot be linked to any local center. In the two great discourses in the Acts of the Apostles—that of Stephen in Chapter Seven and that of Paul in Chapter Seventeen—the speakers, the first addressing a jewish audience, the second a greek, declare that 'God does not live in shrines made by men' (Acts 7:48; 17:24). No one was thereby excluding God from the world, but, on the contrary, they were affirming that God is present everywhere. This is why the author of the Book of Revelation justifies the absence of a temple in the heavenly Jerusalem: 'The Lord God Almighty and the Lamb were themselves the temple' (21:22).

The entire world is a temple, not in a pantheistic sense, as in 'cosmic religions',[184] but because God himself has chosen to come among his people. While the descent of God is universal in the heavenly Jerusalem, in the history of salvation it is determined by a free choice, a call. The Jews were proud of their temple and of the liturgies performed in it, because the Most High selected Mount Zion to dwell among his people in a special way.[185]

What was new in christian prayer was essentially the result of the discovery, not so much of the divine omnipresence, as of the place held by Christ in the economy of salvation. Christ is the locus of the divine presence among human beings. The risen body of Christ is the temple from which streams of living water of the Spirit flow upon humanity (Jn 7:39). The adoration of God is therefore linked to the presence of Christ in this world, which has not yet received its eschatological perfection.

Christians experience the presence of Christ chiefly all in their own life, in their heart, and even more in their prayer and their oneness within the Church: a spiritual, ecclesial oneness constituting unity. At the beginning church buildings counted for little because they were viewed only as gathering places. But in time, places of worship became symbols, and represented in their structure the spiritual unity of the believers among themselves and with God. Christian symbols are sacred. The 'temple' came to be venerated therefore like a great icon, an icon of our encounters with God, symbolizing the various dimensions of God's descent among his people.

## *The Image of the One Church*

Every Christian is God's temple, and the body is a temple of the Spirit (1 Cor 6:19; cf Rom 8:11). We are members of the Body of Christ (1 Cor 6:5, 12:27). But the presence of Christ is felt especially where 'two or three have met together' in his name (Mt 18:20) in the assembly of the believers, the *ekklesia* which is God's creation, a building up of Christ, animated and inhabited by the Spirit (1 Cor 3:16; Eph 2:22).

To the building which is to be the gathering place of the assembly, people normally give the shape symbolic of its function. It is therefore natural that christian churches came to be viewed very early as a symbolic expression of the assembly of the believers: like an ark into which those who wanted to be saved took refuge, as in a ship *(navis)* on its way to the East.[186]

Byzantine churches are even more explicit in this regard. They are not merely places where Christians gather. From the iconographic point of view, the saints are the walls and the Apostles the columns. 'The image of a man on a column', Michail Alpatov writes, 'is like the identification of the human body with the column, the human person become stone.'[187] In gothic structures the stones, which by nature fall and crush, create the impression of carrying us to the heights. In byzantine sanctuaries, the same forward movement is symbolized by the position of the saints represented around the altar, inviting us to partake in their eternal *deësis* (supplication).

## *The Symbol of the Sanctified Universe Linked Together by Christ*

In the temple, the *ekklesia* gathers around the celebration of the Eucharist, with its two essential realities. According to Leonid Ouspensky,

> One is the redeeming sacrifice of Christ, the need to participate in this sacrifice, to commune with it in order to be saved, the need for every one to recapitulate, to renew, so to speak, this sacrifice in the soul. The other essential truth is the goal and the result, the very meaning of this sacrifice: the transfiguration of the human person, and thereby that of the entire visible world.[188]

It is said that in western churches the emphasis is put mainly on the first aspect, and thus the cross occupies the central place. In the construction of byzantine churches, it is instead the second truth that is the main object of the building's symbolism: it represents the transfigured world, the heavenly Jerusalem. Indeed, as John of Damascus writes, 'everything that has been instituted according to the law and according to our worship *(latreian)* has been created in view of the heavenly Jerusalem'.[189] Consequently that a church, even a small one, resembles the great cosmos is a marvelous thing, Maximus the Confessor says.[190] The great figure of the *Pantokrator* (the All-Ruler) dominates the heavenly dome which rests on the four pillars of the *mundus quadratus* (four-cornered world).[191]

Even so, the typically greek separation between two worlds, the visible and the invisible, the human and the divine, is not erased: by the grace of God it is transcended. The sanctuary, as the τόπος νοερός (place of perception, understanding),[192] and the place of the invisible God, is clearly separated from the nave. The iconostasis with its representations of saints at prayer, interceding that the gates of mercy be opened, replaces the veil of the old temple. The 'Royal Door' of the iconostasis is an eloquent symbol of this.[193]

The greek Fathers often characterized the fallen world as θόρυβος, noisy confusion, chaos.[194] Christ's activity is unifying, a harmony of opposites,[195] a concept which, according to Pavel Florensky,[196] is strongly emphasized in eastern churches by the separation of the sanctuary from the nave and, at the same time, by the liturgical communication between them. There one contemplates the cosmological union between heaven and earth, between the invisible and the visible world. From an anthropological perspective, the sanctuary symbolizes the soul and the nave the body. Christologically, the entire church is the Body of Christ; the sanctuary represents his invisible Divinity. As a barrier, the iconostasis accentuates the meaning of the transcendent mysteries, but through the images painted on it, it appears as their revelation: its 'Royal Door' gives access to *parrhesia* (frankness, confidence), intimacy with God.

Attempts have been made to deduce this twofold aspect of time from the twofold apostolic tradition. The latin Mass would be the direct continuation of the Last Supper of Christ with his apostles on the night before his Passion while the byzantine liturgy would extend Christ's meals with his disciples after the resurrection.[197] One thing is certain: the classical iconostasis represents the entire economy of salvation around the victorious cross.[198] In the light of this eschatological vision, all space in a church is considered sacred, sanctified.

### *Visible Preaching*

In the West, especially after the Reformation, the church came to be viewed more and more as a place where the word of God is preached. Attempts are being made in our day to find a balance between the liturgy of the word and the eucharistic liturgy. We would say that in the East,[199] the entire liturgy is viewed as teaching: the gospel is proclaimed not only through words but also through images. The entire church is a speaking, a teaching icon.

Patriarch Alexis of Moscow wrote in a letter:

> In a church, everything is different from that which we constantly see around us and in our houses. The images are not the same as those we have in our houses. The walls are painted with sacred images; everything shines brightly; everything raises the spirit and removes it from the usual thoughts and impressions of this world. . . . The holy Fathers, who not only established the rite and the worship, but also the external aspect and the internal arrangement, thought of everything. They foresaw and ordered everything so as to create in the faithful a special spiritual state, so that nothing impedes their flight toward the heavens, toward God, toward the celestial world whose reflection a church should be.[200]

### *The Place of Grace*

Like a great icon, a church, the place of colloquy with God, possesses a sanctifying power. On the one hand, everything in its structure is conducive to prayer; and on the other, prayer makes it sacred. Certain places, Origen noted, have been desecrated and are unsuitable for prayer because sins have been committed in them, and this implies that evil spirits are present.[201] In such cases, it is better to pray in church than at home, because prayer in church introduces the presence of angels, saints, and Christ himself.[202]

The rites for consecrating the building and, above all, the altar for the holy mysteries confirms this conviction of the christian people. 'From the moment that altar was consecrated', an angel reveals in the *Spiritual Meadow,* 'I was commanded to remain here.'[203] The view of the temple as God's dwelling place was reborn in the concept of the christian church, but in a new context: as a prefiguration, an anticipation of the future, the heavenly, Jerusalem.

Christians came to be proud of their churches, as is clear from this text by Eusebius:

> And now henceforth a day bright and radiant with rays of heavenly light, overshadowed by never a cloud, shone down upon the churches of Christ throughout the whole world. . . . Temples (were) rising once more from their foundations to a boundless height, and (were) receiving in far greater measure the magnificence of those that formerly had been destroyed. . . . After this there were festivals of dedication in the cities and consecrations of the newly built houses of prayer.[204]

### *The Veneration of Icons*

Because the sacred image occupies a special place in eastern spirituality, numerous icons adorn places of worship and cover the iconostasis. In private homes, there is always a little sanctuary, 'the corner of beauty' *(krasnyi ugol),* where the 'family icons' are kept. The children are blessed with them and people pray before them. 'It is absolutely impossible to imagine the smallest rite in the Orthodox Church without icons,' Leonid Ouspensky states.[205]

The artistry of icons obeys technical, aesthetic, and mystical laws that make the icon an art object, not merely an object of devotion, but truly a sacred object. The considerations that follow are limited to the fundamental question covered in this section: the function of the icon during prayer.

### *The Created: Symbol of the Uncreated*

The old and always present problem of art may be formulated as follows: how can something material become a sign and symbol of the immaterial? The body of the spirit? In sacred iconography, the problem is transposed to an essentially higher level: how can what belongs to created reality become a symbol of the divine? While fighting iconoclasm, those who venerated images extended to the icons what the Fathers had attributed to the humanity of Christ: 'the expression of the archetypal beauty, the immovable Seal, the unchanged Image, the Father's 'Definition' and 'Word' *(logos),* who comes to his own Image, and puts on flesh.'[206]

Even in our day, those who admire icons feel compelled to repeat this same truth. As Vladimir Lossky notes, 'An icon or a cross does not exist simply to direct our imagination during our prayers. It is a material center in which there reposes an energy, a divine force, which unites itself to human art.'[207]

No Christian can deny that it is lawful to extend the power of Christ's flesh to everything that must become 'Christ-like' at the end of the ages. Even so, the real problem always remains the degree of such 'Christoformity' at the present moment, when the church is still 'on the way' and ultimate perfection still appears far off. There are special cases: the seven sacraments, which are already sacred signs, the first-fruits of the heavenly Jerusalem. To express the distinction between image and sacrament, theologians speak of the power of the sacraments *(sacramenta)* as coming directly from Christ, while that of sacramentals *(sacramentalia)* is exercised only through the prayer of the Church, *per orationem Ecclesiae.*[208] But is the prayer of the Church not essentially the prayer of Christ himself? Should it not increase in power and intensity to transform the world and lead it gradually to its ultimate perfection?

According to the canons of the Eastern Church, prayer must indeed accompany all of the painter's work,[209] and, on the other hand, it is the prayer of the faithful that sanctifies the icons, even makes them 'miraculous', 'a living organ, the place of encounter between the Creator and the human persons'.[210]

### *The Priestly Function of the Icon Painter*

The legend of Saint Luke, evangelist and painter, illustrates how eastern Christians moved from oral teaching to teaching through images. It is possible to discuss the influence of the 'visual' mentality of the Greeks which supplanted the 'acoustic' comprehension of the Hebrews.[211] We can evaluate the psychological advantages of one or the other form of teaching.[212] From the dogmatic point of view, the ultimate reason for the use of sacred images is to be found in the fact that 'the Word became flesh' (Jn 1:14), that the disciples were 'eye witnesses' of the new revelation (Lk 1:2), and that the Word is an object of vision.[213]

It was from this that icon painters drew the fundamental justification for their artistic activity. Symeon of Thessalonica, the great defender of the tradition, addresses this exhortation to them: 'Teach with words, write with letters, paint with colors, as handed down by the tradition; the paintings are true, like that which is written in books. The grace of God is in them *(kai charis en autois esti theia),* since what is represented on them is holy.'[214]

According to the russian *Podlinnik*—an instruction manual for painters—the function of the iconographer resembles that of the priest: 'The sacred ministry of iconographic representation already began with the Apostles. . . . In the liturgical services, the priest, through the power of the words, presents to us the Body of Christ. . . . The painter does this through the image.'[215]

His analogy with words helps us to summarize the goal of iconographic art in two points: 1) the teaching of the truth, 2) the imparting of grace. They are one. The words of God do indeed exercise a function that is at the same time 'dianoetic' (containing a *nous,* a thought) and 'dynamic' (containing a *dynamis,* a force): they are filled with power.[216]

### *The Spiritual Vision*

The truth revealed by sacred painting is spiritual: it is a *theoria,* a vision of God in all created forms.[217] It is therefore not by chance that students at one of the painting schools on Mount Athos had to produce, accurately, as their first assignment, an icon of the Transfiguration: it had to look like the result of their real artistic experience of the 'taboric vision' of the world which comes from divine inspiration. Paul Evdokimov echoes Pavel Florensky[218]: 'If no one can say "Jesus is Lord except by the Holy Spirit" (1 Cor 12:3), no one is able to represent the image of the Lord, save through the Holy Spirit. He is the divine Iconographer.'[219]

When a painter expresses his spiritual vision in an image, he does this so that this 'incarnation' may be useful to others as a starting-point for their own spiritual ascent. This ascent requires in the one who prays an effort not unlike that of the painter, but the movement is reversed: it is in the form of an ascent by the mind from the wooden board to a spiritual vision.

This ascent may be visualized in several stages. According to the classical outline of contemplation three 'visions' succeed one another: the sensory; the intellectual; and the spiritual. The spirit of idolatry is displayed as a negation of the transition from one vision to the other. The idolatry of archaic people was material: the visible idol itself was the object of divine worship. The 'idolatry of concepts' is visible in those who stop at the 'intellectual' and do not move on to the 'spiritual'.[220] The veneration of icons, by contrast, requires a transition: from matter to forms and colors, from the sensory to the intelligible, through the iconographic symbolism and ultimately, from an intellectual to a spiritual vision.

The symbolic language of icons is admirable, but in itself it is not enough to move from the human to the divine. 'Mere' knowledge *(gnosis psile)*[221] becomes spiritual through love, which is an 'ecstatic' force. It is Love that united the human and the divine natures in Christ. The love that is shown in the veneration of God and his saints will join the human art of the icon to a spiritual vision and the imparting of grace. Thus, only veneration—prayer—crosses the last abyss because it stops neither at the forms nor at the concepts: it is turned toward the *living person*. If an icon is not venerated, it ceases to be an icon. Pavel Florensky has explained this by saying: 'Aside from its relationship to light, aside from its function, a window is, so to speak, nonexistent, dead. It is not a window; removed from the light, it is but wood and glass. . . . So it is with icons, the visible representations of mysterious, supernatural apparitions.'[222]

The one who truly prays before an icon must move from the *typos* to the *Prototypos,* and from there to the *Archetypos*. The Archetype is God the Father, to whom all prayer is ultimately addressed. The Prototype is Christ. He is discovered in the *typos,* that is, in his direct image, representing His Face or in the image of the saints, because it is only through Christ that we can enter into direct contact with the Father. The attitude of the person who prays before an icon is therefore the one that will be appropriate to the inhabitants of the heavenly Jerusalem, who are able to see God in everything.

### *Pilgrimages*

Visiting holy places is a form of devotion in all cultures and all eras. It is the story of a pilgrimage that brings us the first words of Christ (Lk 2:41ff.). Since the year 326, the date of the journey of the empress Helena to Jerusalem—which tradition links to the finding of the True Cross—pilgrimages have become for Christians a recognized form of devotion, almost a habit. In Russia, an entire class of people, called the *stranniki,* spent their life visiting sanctuaries, churches, and monasteries.

The pilgrimage is a special 'place' of prayer because it contains several elements which are like natural conditions which lift the soul to God. 'The open road', Dostoevsky writes, 'is something that stretches endlessly ahead, like a man's dream, a nostalgia for the infinite.'[223] A pilgrimage always demands an effort, a gift of one's time, a self-sacrifice. As a reward, the pilgrimage is a victory over time and also a liberation from the cares of daily life, a detachment, a desert. The aim of the march is to be with the created things, places, and icons through which God has achieved our salvation. A pilgrimage is therefore a profession of faith in the sanctification of matter, of the world.[224] Its constituent element is the 'remembrance' of events; it is a 'recollection' *(anamnesis)* that defeats time. But it is also an experience of the universality of the Church in space, an encounter with strangers. In former times, a pilgrimage was an effective form of ecumenism. Like prayer and alms, a pilgrimage is one of the natural forms of piety.[225]

## Notes

1. *Čto jest duchovnaja žizň* [*What the Spiritual Life Is*], 15 (Moscow, 1897) 176.

2. *Ibid.,* 48; 176. See Macarius of Egypt, *Epistola* 2; PG 34:433D. John Climacus, *Scala paradisi, gradus* 28; PG 88:1132Cff; Luidheid and Russell, CWS, 274–281.

3. *Homily* 5.4–5; PG 34:497. *Homily* 27; 753.*Homily* 19. 3–6; 644ff; Maloney, *Pseudo Macarius: The Fifty Spiritual Homilies*, CWS, 64–65, 174–184, 147–149.

4. *Čto jest duchovnaia žizň*, 71, p. 253.

5. *Písma o duchovnoj žizni* [*Letters on the Subject of the Spiritual Life*] (Moscow, 1903) 169. Špidlík, *Théophane 1e Reclus,* 256ff.

6. *Slova na Gospodskie, Bogorodičnye I toržestvennye dni* (Moscow, 1883) 149.

7. *Put ko spaseniju* [*The Way to Salvation*] (Moscow, 1908) 196ff.

8. *Sobranie pisem* [*Collection of Letters*], vol. I (Moscow, 1898) 124ff.

9. *O molitve i trezvenii* (Moscow, 1889) 6. Špidlík, *Théophane le Reclus,* 259.

10. See p. 319.

11. See p. 177.

12. *Oratio 2—apologetica,* 29; PG 35:447A; LNPF, ser. 2, 7:239.

13. Špidlík, *Grégoire de Nazianze,* 26ff. *A Systematic Handbook,* 182ff.

14. Ladislas Szabó, 'Pur', VTB, 1068–1074; 'Pure', DBT, 477–479.

15. See p. 80.

16. *Homilia in Isaiam* 1.1; GCS 8:242, 6ff.

17. Greek text, ed. by François Nau, PO 11 (1915) 432; Syriac text, ed. by M. Kmosko, PO 10 (1912) 603; English translation by Derwas J. Chitty, *The Letters of Ammonas* Oxford: Fairacres Press [available in the USA from Cistercian Publications], 1985) Letter XII, p. 16.

18. PO 11:425; Chitty,14.

19. *De diversis malignis cogitationibus;* ed. J. Muyldermans, *À travers la tradition d'Évagre le Pontique* (Louvain, 1932) 53; selections translated E. Kadloubovsky and G. E. H. Palmer 'On Various Evil Thoughts', *Early Fathers from the Philokalia* (London: Faber and Faber, 1963) 117ff.

20. *Chapters on Prayer,* 146; Hausherr, *Les leçons,* 178; CS 4:79; see also *Early Fathers from the Philokalia,* 142–143.

21. *Ibid.* 52; *Leçons,* 76; CS 4:63. A passionless *habitus,* that is, a stable, permanent condition (ἕξις), not merely a passing disposition (διάθεσις).

22. *Mar Isaacus Ninivita de Perfectione Religiosa,* ed.Paul Bedjan (Paris-Leipzig, 1909) 513; excerpts translated by Sebastian Brock in *The Syriac Fathers on Prayer and the Spiritual Life,* CS 101 (Kalamazoo: Cistercian Publications, 1987) 242–301.

23. *A Systematic Handbook,* 251ff.

24. See Evagrius, *Praktikos* 26; SCh 171:561; CS 4:23. John Climacus, *Scala paradisi,* gradus 9; PG 88:840Dff; CWS, 152–154.

25. See Evagrius, *Chapters on Prayer,* 64; *Leçons,* 35; CS 4:65; *Early Fathers From the Philokalia,* 135.

26. See Evagrius, *Praktikos* 15; SCh 171:537, and note; CS 4:20.

27. *Ad Nicolaum, praecepta salutaria;* PG 65:1032D.

28. *A Systematic Handbook,* 251.

29. *My Life in Christ,* translated E. E. Goulaeff (Jordanville, New York: Holy Trinity Monastery, 1994) 10. Used with permission.

30. *A Systematic Handbook,* 251.

31. *Ibid.,* 193ff.

32. Evagrius, *Chapters on Prayer,* 128; *Leçons,* 164; CS 4:76.
33. Gregory Nazianzus, *Oratio* 36—*De seipso,* 11; PG 36:269B.
34. *A Systematic Handbook,* 108ff.
35. See p. 74.
36. Jer 14:12, Neh 1:4, 9:1-3, Joel 1:14, 2:12.
37. *Didache* 1.3; translated Francis X. Glimm, *The Didache or Teaching of the Twelve Apostles* (New York, 1947) 171.
38. *Fifth Parable,* 3. See also Simitude 5; translated Graydon F. Snyder, The Apostolic Fathers, 6 (London:Thomas Nelson, 1968).
39. *My Life in Christ,* 318.
40. Is 58:6-7, Zec 8:19, Jl 2:12-13.
41. J. Behm, 'Νῆστις', Kittel 4 (1942) 925–935; (1967) 924–935.
42. *The Shepherd of Hermas,* Parable 5.3.1ff; Apostolic Fathers, 6:103–104.
43. Sticheron for Vespers for Wednesday of the first week of Lent.
44. Placide Deseille, 'Jeûne', DSp 8 (1974) 1165.
45. Alexander Schmemann, *Great Lent* (Crestwood, New York: St Vladimir's Seminary, 1969) 55.
46. VII.4.
47. Adalbert Haman, *La prière,* 2: *Les trois premiers siècles* (Tournai, 1963).
48. *Approches de la prière de Jesus* (Bellefontaine, 1983) 70; in russian (St Petersburg, 1865) 231; selections translated by Lazarus Moore, *On the Prayer of Jesus* (London: John M. Watkins, 1952).
49. See p. 283.
50. Deseille, 'Jeûne', DSp 8 (1974) 1172.
51. *De virginitate* 7; PG 28:260B.
52. Martyrius Sahdona, *Livre de la perfection,* 2.7 (38); CSCO 215 (*Syri* 91): 86; selections in CS 101:98–239.
53. *My Life in Christ,* 3.
54. Evagrius, *Chapters on Prayer,* 120; *Leçons,* 155; CS 4:75; *Early Fathers from the Philokalia,* 140.
55. Origen, *De principiis;* GCS 5:104; ANF 4:239ff. John Climacus, *Scala paradisi, gradus* 13; PG 88:932; CWS, 162ff. Philo, *De vita Mosis,* 1.44; *Philo,* 6, The Loeb Classical Library (Cambridge, MA: Harvard University Press, 1959).
56. *A Systematic Handbook,* 332ff.
57. See p. 231.
58. *A Systematic Handbook,* 206.
59. *Oratio* 21—*De poenitentia;* PG 40:1159; cp. 'Discourse 21', translated John Chryssavgis and Pachomios Penkett, *Abba Isaiah of Scetis: Ascetic Discourses,* CS 150 (Kalamazoo: Cistercian Publications, 2002) 151–152.
60. Evagrius, *Chapters on Prayer,* 142; *Leçons,* 174; CS 4:78.
61. *Ibid.,* 9; *Leçons,* 22; CS 4:57.
62. *Livre de la perfection* 2. 8 (44); CSCO 253 (*Syri* 111):12; CS 101:220. See John Chrysostom, *Expositio in psalmos,* 6.9; PG 55:77.
63. See p. 324.
64. 'Exhortation à un juif converti', translated M. Albert, in *L'Orient Syrien,* 6 (Paris, 1961) 44, no. 5.
65. *A Systematic Handbook,* 177ff.
66. *Chapters on Prayer,* 18; *Leçons,* 34; CS 4:58.
67. *Ibid.,* 36; *Leçons,* 54; CS 4:61. See also 17–28; *Leçons,* 13ff; CS 4:58ff.

68. See p. 175.
69. Evagrius, *Praktikos,* 48; SCh 171:609; CS 4:77.
70. *Apophthegmata Patrum,* Anthony 1; PG 65:76A; CS 59:1–2.
71. *A Systematic Handbook,* 233ff.
72. *Chapters on Prayer,* 4; *Leçons,* 18; CS 4:56. See also 133–135; *Leçons,* 166ff; CS 4:77.
73. See p. 243.
74. Robert Vernay, 'Distractions', DSp 3 (1957) 1347–1363.
75. *Conferences* 1.16–18; SCh 42 (1955) 98ff; ACW 57:56–59; CWS, 51–52; LNPF, ser.2, 11:303–304. *Conferences,* 7.3–8; SCh 246ff; ACW 248–255; LNPF 362–263. *Conference* 10.10–12; SCh 54:93ff; ACW 378–385; CWS, 132–138; LNPF 405–408.
76. *Ibid.,* 10.14; SCh 95ff; ACW 386; CWS, 139–140; LNPF 409.
77. Vernay, 'Distractions', DSp 3:1350. Hausherr, *Les leçons d'un contemplatif* (Paris, 1960).
78. See p. 326.
79. *Chapters on Prayer,* 46; *Leçons,* 68; CS 4:62; *Early Fathers From the Philokalia,* translated by E. Kadloubovsky and G. E. H. Palmer (London, 1963)133.
80. *Ibid., Leçons,* 125ff.
81. Antoine and Claire Guillaumont, 'Démon dans la plus ancienne littérature monastique', DSp 3 (1957) 189–212.
82. *A Systematic Handbook,* 237ff.
83. *Ibid.,* 242ff.
84. Evagrius, *Chapters on Prayer,* 50; *Leçons,* 72; CS 4:63.
85. *Sancti Pachomii Vitae graecae, Vita Prima* 18, critical edition by François Halkin, Subsidia hagiographica 19 (Brussels, 1932) 12; translated Armand Veilleux, *Pachomian Koinonia* I, *The Life of Saint Pachomius,* CS 45 (Kalamazoo: Cistercian Publications, 1980) 308–309.
86. Evagrius, *Chapters on Prayer,* 97; *Leçons,* 133; CS 4:71.
87. *Chapters on Prayer,* 99; *Leçons,* 135; CS 4:72.
88. Guillaumont, 'Démon' (above, n. 81), 194.
89. *Apophthegmata patrum, Antonius* 12; PG 65:77C.
90. *Chapters on Prayer,* 91; *Leçons,* 125; CS 4:70.
91. *Chapters on Prayer,* 47; *Leçons,* 69; CS 4:62.
92. Evagrius, *Antirrheticus,* 'Sadness', 56, 58.
93. *A Systematic Handbook,* 243ff.
94. Evagrius, *Chapters on Prayer,* 100; *Leçons,* 136; CS 4:72.
95. See p. 168.
96. Evagrius, *Chapters on Prayer,* 96; *Leçons,* 131–133; CS 4:71.
97. Hasso Jaeger, 'Examen de conscience dans l'antiquité et les religions non-chrétiennes', DSp 4/2 (1961) 1790–1791.
98. *Ibid.,* 1791–1792.
99. É. Drioton, 'Sur la sagesse d'Aménéopé', *Mélanges bibliques André Robert* (Paris, 1957) 254–280.
100. Jaeger, 'Examen de conscience', DSp 4/2:1792–1744.
101. *Ibid.,* 1794–1797. J. Goldziher, 'Die Zurechtweisung der Seele', *Studies in Jewish Literature, Mélanges Kaufman Kohler* (Berlin, 1913) 133ff.
102. Jacques Guillet, 'Examen de conscience dans la Bible', DSp 4/2 (1961) 1799–1801.
103. *Ibid.*
104. Jean-Claude Guy, 'Examen de conscience chez les Pères de l'Église', Dsp 4/2:1801–1807.

105. *In Genesim,* homily 11.2; PG 53:93. See also 4.6–7 and 23.6; PG 53 and 206; translated Robert C. Hill, *Saint John Chrysostom: Homilies on Genesis,* Fch 74 and 82.
106. *Letter* 288, ed. Nicodemus the Hagiorite (Venice, 1816) 155.
107. *Doctrina,* 11.5 (PG 88:1740B); 4.5 (1664D); 10.7 (1733BC); 1793D. Translated Eric P. Wheeler, *Dorotheos of Gaza: Discourses and Sayings,* CS 53 (Kalamazoo: Cistercian Publications, 1977) 173, 119, 167.
108. See p. 326.
109. Irénée Hausherr, *Direction spirituelle en Orient autrefois,* OCA 144 (Rome 1955) 153; translated by Anthony P. Gythiel, *Spiritual Direction in the Early Christian East,* CS 116 (Kalamazoo: Cistercian Publications, 1990) 155–156.
110. *A Systematic Handbook,* 233ff.
111. *Life of Antony,* 55; PG 26:924AB; CS 202:176–177; ACW 10.
112. *A Systematic Handbook,* 244ff.
113. See p. 232.
114. See p. 188.
115. Antanas Liuma and André Derville, 'Examen particulier', DSp 4/2 (1961) 1838–1849.
116. *Scala paradisi, gradus* 15; PG 88:887D; CWS, 171ff; Moore translation, 152.
117. *Conferences* 5.4, and 14.5–6; PL 49:959–960; SCh 42:204ff; ACW 57:183–185, 507–508; LNPF, ser. 2, 11:345, 436.
118. *A Systematic Handbook,* 228ff.
119. Evagrius, *Chapters on Prayer,* 2; *Leçons,* 15ff; CS 4:56.
120. Evagrius, *Centuries,* 6.21.
121. André Méhat, 'La piété antique', DSp 12/2 (1986) 1694–1714.
122. *De civitate Dei,* 10.1.3; PL 41:279; translated Gerald Walsh and Grace Monahan, *Saint Augustine: The City of God,* Books VII–XVI, FCh 14.
123. *A Systematic Handbook,* 335.
124. See p. 188.
125. Abba Isaiah, *Asceticon* 19, 1b; CSCO 293 (*Syri* 122): 344.
126. See Evagrius, *Chapters on Prayer*, 80; *Leçons,* 112; CS 4:68.
127. Špidlík, *La sophiologie de S. Basile,* 67ff.
128. Abba Isaiah, *Asceticon,* 25.6; CSCO 293 (*Syri* 122): 427.
129. Jean-Marie Tillard, 'Obéissance', DSp 11 (1982) 536.
130. Andre de Bovies, 'Inspirations divines', DSp 7/2 (1970) 1791–1803.
131. *Epistola* I *ad Serapionem,* 26; PG 26:592C; SCh 15:131; translated C. R. B. Shapland, *The Letters of Saint Athanasius Concerning the Holy Spirit* (London, 1951).
132. Origen, *Commentarium in Mattheum,* 12.6; GCS 10:77, 30; ANF 9:453–454.
133. Joseph Lécuyer, 'Docilité au Saint-Esprit', DSp 3 (1957) 1471–1497.
134. *A Systematic Handbook,* 283ff.
135. See p. 346.
136. *A Systematic Handbook,* 88ff.
137. *De libero arbitrio,* 3.10.29; PL 32:1286A; *Saint Augustine: The Teacher. The Free Choice of the Will,* FCh 59:192ff.
138. See p. 31.
139. *Homilia* 20, *De humilitate,* 1; PG 31:528B.
140. See John Chrysostom, *De incomprehensibili Dei natura,* 5. 6; PG 48:745A; SCh 28: 295; translated Paul W. Harkins, *St. John Chrysostom. On the Incomprehensible Nature of God,* FCh 72.
141. Louis Leloir, *Paterica armeniaca* 18, 25; CSCO 377:60–61.

142. *Approches de la prière de Jésus* (Bellefontaine, 1983) 97 (in Russian [St Petersburg, 1865] 264).
143. Evagrius, *Chapters on Prayer,* 20; *Leçons,* 35; CS 4:58.
144. Evagrius, *Rerum monachalium rationes* no. 99; Hausherr, *Leçons,* 29.
145. Origen, *De oratione* 8.1; GCS 3:317; FCh 19:37. *Ibid.,* 28.7; 379; 110.
146. Evagrius, *Chapters on Prayer,* 104; Hausherr, *Leçons,* 140; CS 4:102.
147. *Ibid.,* 19; 39; 58.
148. See p. 221.
149. *Asceticon* 14, 25; CSCO 293 (*Syri* 122): 258.
150. *A Systematic Handbook,* 193.
151. *Asceticon* 16, 33–34; CSCO (*Syri* 122):343.
152. *A Systematic Handbook,* 251.
153. Evagrius, *Chapters on Prayer,* 15; Hausherr, *Leçons,* 29ff; CS 4:58.
154. Ivan Kologrivof, *Essai sur la sainteté en Russie* (Bruges, 1953) 424.
155. Evagrius, *Chapters on Prayer,* 15; Hausherr, *Leçons,* 29ff; CS 4:58.
156. See p. 53.
157. *My Life in Christ* (New York, 1994) 12.
158. *Ibid.,* 12.
159. Léon Roy, 'Pauvre', VTB, 927–932; 'Poor', DBT, 436–438. *A Systematic Handbook,* 208.
160. John Climacus, *Scala paradisi,* gradus 17; PG 88:927D; Luibheid-Russell, CWS, 189–190.
161. *Ibid.,* 27; 1096ff.
162. Claude Wiéner, 'Aumône', VTB, 95–98; 'Almsgiving', DBT, 10–12.
163. John Chrysostom, *De paenitentia seu de eleemosyna,* homily 3; PG 49:291–300.
164. *A Systematic Handbook,* 220ff.
165. SCh 119:190ff; LNPF ser. 2, 5:357ff.
166. *Ibid.,* 193ff; 361.
167. See pp. 178, 217.
168. John Chrysostom, *De perfecta caritate,* PG 56:279–290.
169. See p. 284.
170. *Second Century on Love,* 1; SCh 9:92; *Early Fathers from the Philokalia,* 299.
171. *Ibid.,* I, 10; SCh, 71.
172. *Octavius,* 32,1–3; ANF 4:193.
173. *Stromata,* 7.7; PG 9:460B; ANF 2:532ff.
174. *De oratione,* 3.1; GCS 2:395, 24–55; ACW 19:130. *Ibid.,* 31.4; GCS 397, 21–22; ACW 132.
175. *De Anna,* Sermon 4; PG 54:668.
176. See p. 265.
177. See p. 322.
178. *De incomprehensibili Dei natura,* 3; PG 48:726; translated Paul W. Harkins, *St. John Chrysostom. On the Incomprehensible Nature of God,* FCh (1984) 95ff.
179. Serge Boulgakov, *Le ciel sur la terre* (Munich, 1928).
180. John of Kronstadt, *My Life in Christ* (New York, 1994) 314.
181. *Ibid.,* 291.
182. *In Matthaeum,* homily 50; PG 58:509; LNPF 10.
183. 1 Kgs 3:2-3.
184. *A Systematic Handbook,* 126.
185. Francois Amiot, 'Temple', VBT, 1266–1273;'Temple', DBT, 594–597.

186. G. Badmann, 'Kirche, Kirchenbau', *Lexikon der christlichen Ikonographie* 2 (1970) 514–529.
187. Michail Alpatov, *Le icone russe, Problemi di storia e di interpretazione artistica* (Turin, 1976) 76.
188. Leonid Ouspensky, *Essai sur la théologie de l'icône dans l'Église Orthodoxe* (Paris, 1960) 24; translated Elizabeth Meyendorff and Anthony Gythiel, *Theology of the Icon,* vol. 1 (Crestwood, NY: St. Vladimir's Seminary Press, 1992) 21.
189. *De imaginibus oratio,* 2.23; PG 94:1309D; translated D. Anderson, *On the Divine Images* (Crestwood, NY: St. Vladimir's Seminary Press, 1980).
190. *Mystagogia* 3; PG 91:672A; translated Julian Stead, *The Church, The Liturgy and The Soul of Man: The Mystagogy of St. Maximus the Confessor* (Still River, MA: St Bede's Publications, 1982) 71.
191. Paul Evdokimov, *L'art de l'icône, Theologie de la beauté* (Desclée de Brouwer, 1972) 124; translated Steven Bigham, *The Art of the Icon: A Theology of Beauty* (Redondo Beach, California: Oakwood Publications, 1990).
192. Pavel Florensky, *Le porte regali, Saggio sull'icona* (Milan, 1977) 56; translated from the russian *Ikonostas* by Donald Sheehan and Olga Andrejev, *Iconostasis* (New York: St Vladimir's Seminary Press, 1996).
193. N. Labrecque-Pervouchine, *L'iconostase, Une évolution historique en Russie* (Montréal, 1982) 237ff.
194. *A Systematic Handbook,* 188.
195. *Ibid.,* 36.
196. *Le porte regali* (above, n. 193), 56.
197. J. Klinger, 'Chrystus Zmartwych wstal', *Jednota* 15:4 (1971) 3ff.
198. See Leonid Ouspensky, *Theology of the Icon,* vol. 2 (Crestwood, NY: St Vladimir's Seminary Press, 1978, 1992) 275–276.
199. See p. 98.
200. Calendar of the Patriarch of Moscow, quoted in Leonid Ouspensky, *Theology of the Icon,* vol. 1 (Crestwood, NY: St Vladimir's Seminary Press, 1978, 1992) 31–32.
201. *De oratione* 31.5–7; GCS 2:338ff; translated J. J. O'Meara, ACW 19 (1953).
202. *Ibid.,* 31.4, 31.6; GCS 399ff.
203. *Pratum spirituale,* 4; SCh 12:50; CS 130:6.
204. *Historiae ecclesiasticae,* 10.1; PG 20:845; translated J. E. Oulton, *Eusebius. The Ecclesiastical History* (Cambridge MA: Harvard University Press, 1964) 393–395.
205. *Essai,* 10 [*Theology,* vol. 1:8].
206. Gregory Nazianzus, *Oratio* 38, *In theophania,* 13; PG 36:325B; LNPF, ser. 2, 7:349.
207. Vladimir Lossky, *Essai sur la théologie mystique de l'Église d'Orient* (Paris, 1944) 185; *The Mystical Theology of the Eastern Church* (Crestwood, NY: St. Vladimir's Seminary Press, 1976) 189.
208. See Magnus Löhrer, 'Sakramentalien', *Sacramentum mundi,* vol. 6 (1969) 341–347; in English, 'Sacramentals', *Sacramentum mundi,* vol. 5 (1970) 375–378.
209. Pierre Miquel, Théologie de l'icône', DSp 7/2 (1971) 1229ff.
210. I. Kireïevsky, quoted by Nikolai Arseniev in *Das heilige Moskau* (Paderborn, 1940) 98ff.
211. Tomaš Špidlík, *Grégoire de Nazianze, Introduction à l'étude de sa doctrine spirituelle,* OCA 189 (Rome, 1971) 1ff.
212. Pierre Miquel, 'Image (culte des)', DSp (1971) 1503–1519.
213. See Symeon the New Theologian, *Ethical Discourse 3.231ff:* 'The holy Scripture thus habitually uses the vision of God to mean hearing and hearing to mean vision.' SCh

122:406ff; Golitzin, The Third Ethical Discourse, *St Symeon the New Theologian,* vol. 1:125.

214. *Dialogus contra haereses,* 23; PG 155:113CD.

215. Ed. T. Bolšakov (Moscow, 1903) 3.

216. O. Procksch, '"Wort Gottes" im AT', Kittel 4 (1942) 89ff; '"The Word of God" in the Old Testament', Kittel 4 (1967) 91–100.

217. See p. 152.

218. *Le porte regali* (above, n. 193), 74ff.

219. *L'art de l'icône* (Bruges-Paris, 1970) 13; translated Steven Bigham, *The Art of the Icon: A Theology of Beauty* (Redondo Beach, Calif.: Oakwood Publications, 1990).

220. Gregory of Nyssa, *De vita Moysis;* PG 44:377; translated Malherbe-Ferguson, *Gregory of Nyssa: The Life of Moses,* CWS–CS 31 (1978).

221. See p. 161.

222. *Le porte regali* (above, n. 193), 58ff.

223. *The Devils,* Part 3, chapter 7.

224. See *Le pèlerinage de l'hégoumène Daniel en terre sainte de l'a. 1106–1108,* ed. Vebevitinov (1883–1885; rpt Munich, 1970).

225. Léon Zander, 'Le Pèlerinage', *L'Église et les Églises . . . études et travaux offerts à Dom Lambert Beauduin,* vol. 2 (Editions de Chevetogne, 1955) 469–486.

# 10
# HESYCHASM

## MAIN CHARACTERISTICS

### *The History of Hesychasm*

WHEN WE SPEAK OF HESYCHASM today, we usually think of a specific method of prayer whose form was codified during the thirteenth and fourteenth centuries in the monastic world of Mount Athos. But we often forget that hesychasm, in the proper and traditional sense, is actually a spiritual trend which is so old that it coincides with the very beginnings of monasticism. In outline we may single out five main periods:

1) the era of the Desert Fathers;
2) the 'sinai school';
3) the legacy of Symeon the New Theologian (b. 949);
4) athonite hesychasm;
5) in more recent times, the 'philokalic' movement.[1]

While Antony is the real father of all monks, for hesychasts it is Arsenius.[2] After leaving the imperial palace, he became an anchorite and heard a voice from heaven saying, 'Flee, be silent, remain quiet'(ἡσυχαζε).[3] The ideal he embodied was recommended by numerous monks of the patristic period.

The spirituality of the sinaite authors of the sixth and seventh centuries (Nilus of Sinai, John Climacus, Hesychius, and Philotheus) centered around προσοχή (attention) and προσευχή (prayer), the guarding of the heart or the intellect with a view to mental prayer. Better than their predecessors had done, they analyzed the importance of thought for the state of the heart.[4]

The Sinaites had advocated the advantages of *hesychia* (stillness) as a preparation for *theoria,* the 'vision' of God. Now if the kingdom of God is indeed in the heart, as Symeon the New Theologian (†1022) thought, we need to be aware of this. Those who have not seen God, he argued, can have neither love nor hope, nor even faith. Knowing the divine inspirations in the purified heart is no longer a charism reserved to sacred authors, but the model of grace to be sought by all Christians.[5]

In the fourteenth century, a Sinaite named Gregory[6] came down from his mountain for the spiritual conquest of Athos and its greek, balkan, and russian monasteries. When he arrived at Mount Athos he found only three monks who had some understanding of mental prayer. He subsequently gathered numerous disciples who became so influential that their doctrine—a resurgence of the hesychast ideal of pure contemplation—soon triumphed. They recommended the 'Prayer of Jesus' (or better said, the prayer to Jesus) with special emphasis; and soon its practice was accompanied by a veritable psychosomatic technique. A detailed description of this technique is recorded by Nicephorus the Hesychast[7] as well as by Gregory the Sinaite and pseudo-Symeon, who are its oldest known theoreticians.[8] The diffusion of the method led to an acrimonious controversy. The method offended the sensibilities of a humanist, the italian-greek Barlaam of Seminaria, called the Calabrian (†1348). But Gregory Palamas, the future archbishop of Thessalonica (†1359), then a monk of Athos, took up the defense of the hesychasts and inserted this prayer into his theological synthesis.[9]

At the end of the eighteenth century, after three centuries of lethargy, the Greek Church experienced a spiritual renaissance, the main architects of which were the authors of the *Philokalia.*[10] This 'philokalic' movement bore fruit especially in the monasteries of Romania and Russia.[11] Their piety had been deeply affected by Paisij (Paisius) Velichkovsky (†1794). We may even speak in recent times of a neo-hesychasm, thanks to the numerous editions and translations into western languages of the *Philokalia* and of *The Candid Narrations of a Russian Pilgrim to His Spiritual Father.*[12]

From this quick overview we see that hesychasm is a great spiritual movement running through the entire history of eastern spirituality. The hesychasts devoted their life to prayer. We owe them numerous texts on prayer, every aspect of which they pondered. Here we will seek to bring out what is characteristic of them.

### *The Meaning of the Word* Hesychia[13]

The etymology of *hesychia* is uncertain. It is linked, perhaps, to ἧσθαι, to be seated. In philosophic Greek, the term refers to the state of calmness, to the cessation of external causes of trouble or to the absence of inner agitation.[14] *Hesychia* also refers to solitude, solitary retreat.[15]

The word *hesychia* and its derivatives are found frequently in the Greek of the Septuagint, where they kept the same meaning as in philosophic Greek. But *hesychia* also consists of abstaining from useless words and movements (Prv 11:12, 7:11).

In the New Testament, the verb ἡσυχάζειν means 'to be silent' (Lk 14:4), 'to observe the Sabbath rest' (Lk 23:56), 'to stop inconveniencing others' (Acts 21:14; 11:18).

Paul exhorts his readers 'to live quietly' (*hesychazein:* 1 Th 4:11), 'to do their work in quietness' (2 Th 3:12). It was his wish that, in church, 'a woman keep silence' (1 Tim 2:11-12). Peter, in turn, urges women to adorn themselves in their inmost heart 'with the ornament of a meek and quiet spirit' (1 Pt 3:4). This constellation of different yet coherent meanings allows us to predict what hesycham was to become and what ideal it would pursue.

We may define hesychasm, then, as a form of spirituality based on *hesychia,* and state that its orientation is essentially contemplative. Hesychasm, however, did not view peace or quietness as an end in itself, as Stoicism viewed *apatheia* (dispassion).[16] Like any other current in Christianity, *hesychia* was a means, perhaps a preeminent and at any rate an excellent means of arriving at the goal: union with God, unceasing prayer.

A distinction should of course be made between two forms of stillness: one external; the other internal; one in things, the other in the human person. The two do not necessarily go together. But from many of the representative spiritual authors of this tradition, we gain the impression that holy quiet and solitude merge, and that, in general, the former presupposes the latter. The pure and simple synonymy of—or at least the connection and the parallelism between—the words *hesychia* and *anachoresis* (withdrawal) or between desert *(eremos)* and *hesychia*—is frequent, while the distinction between the two realities was nonetheless sufficiently known and sensed.

Leading the life of a hesychast—ἡσυχάζειν in the language of the Byzantines—is characteristic of the monk who had settled in the desert and cultivated silence. 'The great and angelic solitary '(ὁ μέγας καὶ ἰσάγγελος ἡσυχαστής) Arsenius'[17] exemplifies this type of life.

## *The Tranquillity of Solitude*

From the sages of antiquity we could collect volumes of maxims in favor of solitude.[18] The aim was clear: 'Instruction and philosophy require great solitude, a place of retreat', noted Dion Chrysostom.[19] Yet in antiquity people were afraid of being ostracized, of being deprived of communication with those to whom they were close. The death penalty was often replaced by condemnation to exile. In vain did the great philosophers assure their contemporaries that the beatitude provided by philosophy greatly surpassed that produced by human conversation. Rational eudemonism (from *eudaimonia,* the aristotelian 'happiness') was a noble form of hedonism, and thus of egotism which gives happiness to no one.[20]

This problem did not exist for christian solitaries. The goal of their withdrawal was 'christian philosophy'—prayer, which is, by definition, a conversation with God. Thus, the one who converses with God is, even when he or she is separated from all, at the same time united to all.[21] This is why the praises of the solitary life were much more sincere among monks than they were among philosophers; and *anachoresis* was not merely recommended, but fervently desired.[22]

The christian anchorites did not feel alone in their solitude, and had no wish to live in isolation from the community of the Church. By virtue of their special calling, which was never intended for everyone, they believed they were able to actualize a person's social nature on a level more profound than the one provided by physical contact. While they viewed solitude as the condition for prayer, they transcended solitude through this very prayer.

*Silence*

There are various degrees of solitude. We are alone when we do not risk running into someone in the space in which we move. This is the 'flight from people' in the material sense. We are also alone as long as we do not converse with another. This is the solitude of silence.

Like material solitude, silence is itself a denial of the natural prerogative of rational beings *(logikoi).* To reduce someone to silence is to deprive that person of human dignity, for we are beings endowed with the gift of speech.[23] On the other hand, certain forms of silence are important as the condition for quiet communication. When someone speaks to us and we are ready to listen, we ask that others be silent.

The person who prays is attentive to the One whose words are more precious than any and all other audible voices. Nothing then is more natural than to require silence during readings, psalmody, and the liturgy. We also understand why the general rule for all conversation in the monastery must be that of Basil:

> *Question:* Which words are to be considered useless?
>
> *Answer:* In general, every word which adds nothing to the proposed goal in the service of God is idle; even if what is said would be good in itself; the danger of that kind of word is so great that if it is not directed toward the edification of faith, the one who has uttered it cannot escape this danger, not even through the goodness of the word; it will sadden the Holy Spirit in so far as it would have contributed nothing to edifying faith.[24]

But do heroic forms of silence—an almost complete break with human conversation—examples of which the *Lives* of the 'silent saints'[25] give us—not sin through inverse excess? Do they not contradict the Spirit who speaks to human persons through other inspired persons? The objection becomes even more serious if we remember that the hesychasts, as it were, reduced to silence God himself—the One who speaks in psalms and in spiritual readings. They gradually simplified their prayer to 'the prayer of silence'.[26]

It goes without saying that similar forms of silence are not for everyone. To appreciate their value, we should remember that of all the inspired words the most precious is the voice of God, heard in the silence of the heart.

## Amerimnia: *Inner Silence*

Solitude and silence do not make a hesychast. As Nicodemus the Hagiorite, that great advocate of hesychast spirituality, said one day: 'Within us there is an inner discourse by which we reason and compose works, make judgments, and read entire books in silence, as the mouth does not speak'.[27] Most people reason or talk nonsense, silently, depending on how they feel.

In his quest for God, the hesychast has an enemy more formidable than human society or outer distractions: it is the dissipation of a heart that remains agitated, perturbed, tugged at by attachments, preoccupations, and thoughts—an entire arsenal the hesychast carries with him when he withdraws. *Hesychia* (stillness) therefore requires *apatheia* (dispassion).[28] In general, however, hesychasm does not express itself in terms of *apatheia,* except in evagrian circles. Among the truly authentic hesychast writers, the term *apatheia* never predominates over *amerimnia,* freedom from care.[29]

The detachment to which *amerimnia* refers is neither uncaringness in the guilty sense—a negligence about the things of God, listlessness *(akedia)*[30]—nor unconcern in the messalian sense, taking pleasure in a life of idleness and false security (ἀσφάλεια). It is a good disengagement which Pseudo-Ephrem characterizes by calling 'an unconcern with earthly things'.[31] It is to this that Dorotheos of Gaza alludes frequently, explaining that it consists in 'neglecting worldly affairs and being occupied with God alone and, as is said of the unmarried girl, being "both diligent and without distraction"' (1 Cor 7:34-35).[32]

It is to this that John Climacus devotes Step Twenty-seven of *The Ladder of Divine Ascent,* where he says, 'The main work of *hesychia* is freedom from care *(amerimnia)* in all things, whether reasonable or not'.[33] John Climacus realizes that his statement is too radical, and therefore justifies his sentence with two psychological reasons. First, one concern summons up another.[34] Secondly, inner quiet is a state of the undivided soul: 'A small hair disturbs the eye, and a small care ruins *hesychia*'.[35] But Climacus goes even further. For him, *hesychia* is not only 'the elimination of reasonable cares': it is also 'the banishment of thoughts' (ἀπόθεσις νοημάτων).[36] This is the evagrian expression that qualifies the height of contemplative prayer.[37] At stake here is therefore a mystical detachment that is justified by God's special calling and not a quietist urge.

### Nepsis—Antirrhesis *(Watchfulness—Counter-statement)*

To acquire and preserve *hesychia* in the heart, prudence demands that 'we immediately slaughter the children of Babylon',[38] that is to say, evil thoughts *(logismoi).*[39] The treatises therefore speak of 'guarding the heart', 'guarding the mind', and 'attentiveness' (προσοχή).[40] To be watchful we must be sober and vigilant, 'neptic' (see 1 Pt 5:8),[41] 'attentive'. As early as Pseudo-Macarius (†390), *hesychia, nepsis, prosoche,* and *proseuche* (stillness, watchfulness, attentiveness, and prayer) are often intimately linked.[42]

But it was principally the school at Sinai that insisted on this vigilance. For the author of the *Centuries,* known by the name Hesychius the Sinaite, or 'of Vatos', all asceticism could apparently be reduced to watchfulness (νῆψις) which he defined as 'the spiritual method which, if sedulously practiced over a long period, completely frees us, with God's help, from impassioned thoughts, impassioned words, and evil actions'.[43]

'Guarding the entrance to the heart'[44] is above all a defensive method of repelling intrusive thoughts immediately by means of *antirrhesis* (counter-statement).[45] Tempted by the demon, Christ replied to his suggestions with texts from Scripture (Mt 4:3-11). The ascetics knew how to react to every diabolical suggestion with an appropriate counter-quotation from Scripture. The classical manual of this art is the *Antirrheticus* of Evagrius, divided into eight parts corresponding to the same number of vices.[46] To each thought, there is a countering biblical text to drive it away.

What mental labor for an uneducated monk to learn all this! But practice simplifies. Invoking the name of Jesus is enough 'to drive away all the demons'. In hesychasm, the 'Jesus Prayer' replaces the complex classifications. 'Among the mysterious, powerful properties of the name of Jesus', Ignatii Brianchaninov writes, 'is the power and property of expelling demons. This property was disclosed by the Lord himself. He said that those who believe in him, "in His name they will cast out demons" (Mk 16:17).'[47]

### *Attentiveness:* prosoche

By its simplest definition, attentiveness is an application of the mind, a statement that makes the role of attentiveness in spirituality clearly evident.[48] Here Christians may refer to the greatest philosophic authorities: Epictetus has an entire chapter 'On Attention'.[49] One day Saint Antony received a warning from heaven: 'Keep your attention on yourself' (πρόσεχε σεαυτῷ).[50] This simple injunction, written on the opening page of the *Apophthegmata Patrum* and one which the monks had to know by heart, has had a greater impact than the long discourses of Basil and other preachers. Even so, another statement, this time by Evagrius, would be quoted just as frequently: 'When attention seeks prayer it finds it. For if there is anything that marches in the train of attention it is prayer, and so it must be cultivated.'[51] This engraves itself on the memory, both through the promise it contains and the suggestive alliteration of the two words προσοχή (attentiveness) and προσευχή (prayer). The hesychasts would therefore write treatises entitled *Peri prosoches kai proseuches, 'On Attentiveness and Prayer'*.[52]

As an application of the mind, attentiveness has a screening function: it can even exclude everything that is not desirable. In prayer, this occurs at various levels.

The first degree of attentiveness is called verbal: it bears upon the very pronunciation of the words of the prayer and upon the immediate meaning of the text. Since the early centuries, the scourge of distraction has prompted repeated moral exhortations, like the one given by John Chrysostom: 'Many enter church. They recite countless lines of prayer and leave; but they do not know what they said. Their lips move, but they do not hear. You do not listen to your own prayer yourself, and you expect God to hear it?'[53]

Everyone felt compelled to repeat such admonitions, which all considered unrealistic, if applied with the utmost rigor. The hesychasts had the courage to say so openly. Nicephorus called this method of attentiveness the 'second prayer', and defined it in this way:

> The second method is this: a man tears his mind away from all sensed objects and leads it within himself, guarding his senses and collecting his thoughts, so that they cease to wander amid the vanities of this world; now he examines his thoughts, now ponders over the words of the prayer his lips utter, now pulls back his thoughts . . . ; now with great labor and self-exertion (he) strives to come back into himself, after being caught and vanquished by some passion. The distinctive feature of this method is that it takes place in the head. . . . In this struggle against himself, a man can never be at peace in himself, nor find time to practise virtues in order to gain the crown of truth.[54]

Everyone knows that multiplicity causes weariness. Methods were then suggested to simplify such 'verbal attentiveness'.

The second type of attentiveness may be called 'meditative' or 'contemplative'. Such attentiveness is aptly defined in the words of Richard of Saint Victor: 'Contemplation is the free, more penetrating gaze of a mind, suspended with wonder concerning manifestations of wisdom'.[55] The mind no longer feels compelled to follow everything the lips utter; it freely chooses to concentrate on what will profit piety.

The third attentiveness has been defined in the West as 'mystical' or 'affective'.[56] In the East, the classical term is 'guarding the heart'. It operates at various levels.

'Where does such uninterrupted dissipation of the mind come from?' Basil asked. And he replied: 'The mind wanders about when it is indolent, and not occupied with things that are necessary'. Where does such inertia come from? 'The mind becomes careless and lazy because of a lack of faith in the presence of God who searches the heart and the reins.'[57] Like so many others, Basil was deeply convinced that all such distractions can be cured by a vivid awareness of the presence of God.

Here is another testimony left to us by the solitaries of Egypt:

> The disciple of Abba Amoun related: One day while saying the office, my mind was troubled and I omitted a word from the psalm. When we had finished, the Old Man spoke again and said to me: 'When I say the office, I imagine that I am standing on fire and burning, and my mind cannot deviate either to the right or the left, and you—where was your mind when we were saying the office and you omitted a word (a line) from the psalm? Did you not know that you were standing before God and were speaking to God?'[58]

In this case, would it not be better to center one's entire attention on the presence of God and view everything else as being secondary? All the experts of the spiritual life would answer this question in the affirmative. To succeed in this effort, several recommendations were made.

The awareness of the presence of God may assume an imaginative form: 'I beheld the Lord ever before me, for he is at my right hand, that I might not be shaken' (Ps 15:8). Imagining a judge before whom one must give an account of one's work was always recommended to monks who cultivated compunction *(penthos),*[59] while a vision of the One who is always at our right hand gives courage to the weak. While this form of attention was considered useful, several spiritual writers pointed out its relative value, and the hesychasts sometimes sought to eliminate it as an aberration.[60]

Basil, however, was already aware of the imperfection of all images that locate God outside ourselves, whereas he is present in us, in our heart. The practice of attentiveness to God thus became an exhortation to 'pay heed to oneself'. We have an entire homily of Basil on this phrase,[61] and from Ephrem an instruction with a prologue and twelve chapters.[62] This theme was to be a favorite, especially with the pre-eminent champions of attentiveness, the hesychasts. However, we should keep in mind that their vocabulary clearly identifies 'oneself' with the heart: the center of the human person, and the seat where God dwells.[63]

### *The Vision of the Taboric Light*

While the 'prayer of the heart' was well known in eastern spirituality, the hesychasts made it the key to their mysticism. It forms 'the third method of prayer' suggested by the famous treatise *Three Methods of Attentiveness and Prayer.*[64] Its principle was not 'collecting the thoughts and invoking the help of heaven' (the first method of attentiveness),[65] nor 'imagining celestial blessings' (the second method).[66] 'True attention' consisted of the following:

> The mind should be in the heart. . . . It should guard the heart while it prays, revolve, remaining always within. . . . When the mind, there, within the heart, at last tastes and sees that the Lord is good, . . . then it will no longer wish to leave this place in the heart (then it will say the words of the Apostle Peter: 'It is good for us to be here' (Mt 17:4).[67]

From this brief description we discover some distinctive features of the 'prayer of the heart'. It is not imaginative: the author advocates an authentic inner iconoclasm. It is not 'conceptual' either, knowing that a multiplicity of thoughts does not go together with stillness *(hesychia).* Moreover, the one who prays 'sees himself entirely illumined'.[68] All this allows us to discern that an evagrian inspiration lies behind it and that hesychast mysticism belongs to the 'mysticism of light' type.[69]

Indeed, in hesychast literature there are numerous texts that speak of visions of light. The most famous is that of Maximus Kapsokalyivitis.[70] Inexperienced readers could easily interpret such visions as sensory. Consequently, Nicephorus protests vehemently against this error. On the other hand, however, we do not have the impression that what is referred to there is a vision of the 'pure light' as described by Evagrius, without object and form, for Nicephorus saw in this state the 'illumined self'. In the other texts, 'everything' is illumined: the whole world, in a manner similar to what the Apostles saw during the Lord's Transfiguration.

Symeon the New Theologian exhorted hesychasts to be 'like those who ascended Mount Tabor with Jesus and who saw his radiance flash with light like lightning, and his raiment changed, and the light of his face',[71] or, among other models from which the hesychast might take inspiration, like Moses, going to the peak of the mountain by himself and entering into the cloud.

> If he becomes such a one, he will not see just 'the back parts', but will be consciously present before the face of God and, looking on God himself alone and being seen by him in turn, and hearing his voice, he will be instructed in the mystery of the heavenly kingdom, and then will set down the law for others. He will be enlightened, and will lighten others.[72]

We have noted two crucial things in these visions of Symeon[73]: he identifies the light with Christ, and Christ lives in the human heart above all through charity. This concept explains why the hesychasts attached such great importance to the invocation of Jesus.

### *The Remembrance of Jesus*

To practice the 'prayer of the heart', the early monks uttered ejaculatory invocations so that their prayer would be *monologistos,* a pure remembrance of God.[74] Among the hesychasts, remembrance 'of God' received its concrete form as a remembrance 'of Jesus'. They strongly insisted on this. For Hesychius of Vatos, the constant invocation of the Lord Jesus should be as habitual as breathing (note the expression 'as breathing'), for without Christ one can do nothing.[75]

This aspect brings the christological character of prayer into strong relief. God does not reveal himself to the human person except through Christ; and if he illumines the heart, it is because his image most clearly appears there. The goal of prayer will therefore be unceasingly to join our heart to Jesus, and with Jesus in our heart, to be united with the Father and with everything that exists.

The ejaculatory prayer of the hesychasts was to be the 'Prayer to Jesus' (or the 'Jesus Prayer'). In its traditional form, that invocation would become one of the most distinctive features of hesychast piety.

THE JESUS PRAYER

*History of the Jesus Prayer*[76]

This form of prayer, used widely among byzantine Christians, particularly the Slavs, has for centuries been expressed in the following manner: 'Lord Jesus Christ, Son of God, have mercy on me'. To this the Russians add, 'a sinner'. We usually speak of the Jesus Prayer, which is a literal translation of the Russian *molitva Jisusova,* the equivalent of the Greek εὐχὴ Ἰησοῦ, where the name *Jesou* is an objective genitive: prayer *to* Jesus.

The roots of this prayer are to be sought in eastern monasticism, in the trend that practised guarding the heart *(phylake kardias),* unceasing prayer, and the sense of mourning *(penthos).*

'Guarding the heart'[77] presupposes a struggle against evil thoughts *(logismoi).* The pre-eminent method consisted of *antirrhesis*',[78] that is, being able to answer each diabolical suggestion with sacred texts. The classical handbook on this art is the *Antirrheticus* of Evagrius,[79] who cites four hundred and eighty-seven biblical texts. But practice was to simplify the principle. The appropriate invocation of Jesus was to be enough to 'drive away all the demons'[80]; and the Jesus Prayer came to replace catalogues of texts. The prayer is therefore an antirrhetic formula.

Monastics also practised unceasing prayer by 'meditating'[81] upon a repeated formula. Such formulas were extremely varied, but from the fifth century on, the ascetics (Nilus of Ancyra and Diadochus of Photice) assigned a special place to the invocation of Jesus without a specific formula. In the century that followed, two formulas were found among the monks in the desert of Gaza: one was of the 'catanyctic' (remorseful) type ('Have mercy on me!'), the other of the 'auxiliary' type ('Help me!').[82]

An important influence in the history of the Jesus Prayer is generally attributed to the Sinaites, but in fact neither Climacus nor Hesychius nor Philotheus prescribed a fixed formula, even though they insisted on the *monologistos* Jesus Prayer.[83] In the *Meterikon* by the twelfth or thirteenth century Abba Isaiah,[84] the formula was still both catanyctic and auxiliary. It had been reduced to its purely catanyctic aspect by an Abba Philemon, unknown in the chronicles of the desert, whose *Most Profitable Narrative* is found in the *Philokalia*[85] and presented as a remedy against the mind's inconstancy by eliminating all things except the remembrance of God. This short work antedates the twelfth century.[86]

Among the athonite hesychasts, this prayer was accompanied by a psychosomatic technique.[87] Nicodemus the Hagiorite inserted these texts in the *Philokalia* and attributed remarkable results to this 'mental prayer': detachment from the things of sense, humility, compunction, tears, a clear vision of self as in a mirror, perfect purity, and ineffable joy.[88]

Among the Russians the practice of the Jesus Prayer took on an original tonality. It is especially the *Candid Narrations of a Russian Pilgrim*[89] that celebrate its extraordinary prayer to lead souls to union with God. The catanyctic formula is preserved, but more intensely sought was a sense of the divine presence, more specifically Christ's presence, everywhere in the world. More attention was paid therefore to the importance of invoking the name of Jesus. 'Not only is God invoked by this Name, but he is already present in the invocation',[90] as 'in an icon'.[91]

At the end of the nineteenth century, an excessive veneration of Jesus' name *(onoma)* led to an 'onomolatric' doctrine. The controversy surrounding the 'Adorers of the Name' troubled the Russian Church during the years 1912 and 1913. But in our day, the Jesus Prayer has regained the place it once had in hesychast prayer.[92] Even so, a theoretical doubt remains. The Jesus Prayer is composed of two elements: the invocation of the name; and the request for mercy. Which element is considered more important?

Let us first indicate the reasoning of those who opt for the power of the divine name.

### *The Power of the Name of Jesus According to Certain Russian Authors*

In a little work *On the Prayer of Jesus,* Bishop Ignatii Brianchaninov maintained that 'the spiritual power of the prayer of Jesus is contained in the divine name itself of the God-man, our Lord Jesus Christ'.[93] 'The name by its external form is limited, but it represents an unlimited object, God, from whom it borrows infinite, divine value of worth, the power and properties of God.'[94] This is why 'we see the unbounded faith of the holy Apostles in the name of the Lord Jesus'.[95]

Without identifying the name with the Person, as did the 'Adorers of the Name', Sergius Bulgakov, who had intervened in the controversy, developed, in turn, a theory according to which the divine name invoked in the Prayer contains the presence of God dynamically and in a quasi-sacramental manner. The 'names-voices of the universe' resound in human language.[96] When the name of Jesus, 'a name belonging to both God and man', resounds in the human heart, it 'gives it the power of deification which our Redeemer accorded us'.[97] Bulgakov contrasted this mystical theory of the name to what he calls 'the more rationalistic and nominalistic view' of school theology.[98]

Ivan Kologrivof was inspired by this when he said that the name of Jesus 'reveals and represents the Lord; that is, makes him present as he is present in the holy icon or in any other sacramental'.[99]

Whatever the case may be, several authors warn us that the conclusions of such theories ought not to be exaggerated. They are not traditional. André Scrima writes that 'We would be hard pressed to find a basis in the tradition of the hesychast prayer for the modern russian trend of devotion to the name of Jesus'.[100]

Theophan the Recluse himself was opposed to those who wanted to attribute an almost sacramental value to the name: 'the power of this prayer [is to be attributed] not to the repetition of certain words, but to the turning of the mind and heart towards the Lord'.[101]

> It is said of the fruit of this prayer, that there is nothing higher in the world: This is wrong. As if it were some talisman! Nothing in the words of the prayer and their uttering can alone bring forth its fruit. All fruit can be received without this prayer, and even without any oral prayer, but merely by directing the mind and heart towards God.[102]

### *The Invocation of the Divine Name in Scripture and Among the Early Christians*

Advocates of the power of the name had frequent recourse to texts of Scripture. To the semitic mind, a name indeed appears as an emanation of the one who bears it. But we should make an appropriate distinction between the noetic value of a name (the name as a source of knowledge and understanding, *noesis*) and the dynamic value (the name as a source of power, *dynamis*).[103] To pronounce the name, or names, of God is therefore to gather within our faith the full religious experiences of a people.

Among Christians, the name of Jesus acquired the same value. The text of Joel: 'Everyone who invokes the Lord by name will be saved' (3:5) played an important role in early christian theology. Peter invited his audience to call upon the name of the Lord in order to be saved. Christians were designated by an expression taken from this very same prophetic text: 'those who invoke the name' (Acts 9:14, 21; Rom 10:12-14; 1 Cor 1:2).[104]

Archeology attests to the honor simple Christians gave Jesus by inscribing his name on documents or objects.[105] Later, the treatise by Pseudo-Denys entitled *The Divine Names (De divinis nominibus)*[106] would exercise a considerable influence in this area.[107]

In addition, as has been correctly noted,[108] to call on the name of Jesus does not mean just saying 'O Jesus'. The early Christians loved to confess their faith by saying: 'Jesus Christ', 'Jesus Messiah', 'Son of God', and especially 'Lord'. The first Christians who simply said 'Jesus' in their devotions were the Syrians. While the gnostics were fond of making all sorts of mystic speculations about the name of Jesus, the orthodox were suspicious of such a verbal faith. Without works, any name or title is worth nothing. A text of Origen states this clearly: 'When the works themselves *(ta erga)* cry out and say, "Lord, Lord", one says, "Lord" perfectly. It is therefore clear that someone who invokes the Lord must have uprightness *(dikaiosynen echei),* and true uprightness.'[109]

## *'Have Mercy on Me'*

Spiritual authors admitted unanimously that the principal merit of short prayers lay in helping create a state of the heart, a steadfast disposition of the spirit.[110] The great variety of ejaculatory prayers derives from this.[111] But Cassian had already made his choice when he saw the line *Deus in adiutorium meum intende* ('O Lord, make haste to help me', Ps 69:1) as a 'formula of piety' capable of creating in us all necessary devout feelings.[112]

The monastic tradition in general also made a choice. The monks arrived at the conclusion that out of love for prayer one should become a beggar before God, like the tax collector who beat his breast and went home justified (Lk 18:10ff). Indeed, the formula 'Have mercy on me, a sinner' was repeated with innumerable variants. From this it follows that 'the Jesus Prayer did not begin with the name of Jesus. It had its beginning in *penthos,* in mourning, in sorrow for sin'.[113]

This does not, of course, exclude a tender devotion to Christ. We have seen how Symeon the New Theologian lived this, and yet no one had a higher opinion of tears than did he. He saw in them the true baptism of the Spirit, the great illumination *(photismos)* through which the human person becomes fully light.[114] He had witnessed its sanctifying and illuminating effect on his spiritual father, Symeon the Pious (the Studite). After the latter's death, he addressed this prayer to him: 'Holy Symeon, having been conformed to the image of Jesus Christ through the participation of the Holy Spirit, arrayed in the shining garment of *apatheia* thanks to a long ascesis, bathing in your own tears which were so abundant that they equaled the fountain of baptism. . . .'[115]

In our day, we easily speak of devotional practices to renew baptism. Gregory Nazianzus was convinced that the last baptism to be required is that of tears, which consist of 'washing our couch and our coverlet every night with our tears'. And he also wondered 'how many tears we must contribute before they can add up to the baptismal font?'[116]

Seen in the light of this eastern tradition, the *Kyrie eleison* ('Lord, have mercy') is a summary of the Jesus Prayer. According to the *Philokalia,* an explanation of this invocation is 'highly profitable for every Christian', because the formula 'Lord Jesus Christ, have mercy on me', or more succinctly, 'Lord, have mercy' has been given to Christians 'since the time of the Apostles'.[117]

In the same vein, Brianchaninov writes:

> The choice of the Jesus Prayer as a meditation formula is fully justified, because the name of the Lord Jesus Christ contains a special

> divine power, and also because during the practice of the Jesus Prayer, the remembrance of death, of the tortures inflicted by the spirits that are in the air, of the last judgment pronounced by God, and of eternal torments, begins at a given moment to arrive by itself. The remembrance arises so vividly that it plunges the ascetic into abundant, inexhaustible tears . . .[118]

### *God and the Human Sinner*

The discussion on the historical priority of the first or the second element of the Jesus Prayer is undoubtedly very useful in understanding the dissemination of the formula in the East. On the other hand, a too specific description of the content is not profitable. The meaning of a prayer, especially one that is repeated frequently, is seen more in the inward disposition of the one who prays than in the words alone.

In reading *The Way of a Pilgrim,* as well as several other texts of our own day, we have the impression that the sense of *penthos* is somehow fading. By reciting the formula of the Jesus Prayer, the pilgrim seeks to become aware of God's presence everywhere and in everything, in the beating of the heart as in the breathing of the universe.[119]

This is a feeling proper to ancient and modern 'cosmic religions'.[120] Among Christians it is marked by a special trait: an awareness of the dialogue between us, human beings, and God, who is near us. But at the same time and paradoxically, God appears extremely remote, not only because of his transcendence but also because of our sins. These two words 'God—sin' epitomize the experience of the english author of a famous medieval mystical text when confronted by the fullness of reality.[121] Nonetheless, a Christian also experiences another feeling that is inseparable from the first: an awareness that the abyss is overcome—on the one hand, by the grace of our Lord, the incarnate Son of God and, on the other, by our confession and our prayer asking for mercy.

In this context, it is not surprising that after the fourteenth century certain authors, whether included in the *Philokalia* or not, tried to outdo each other in celebrating the excellence of the formula whose destiny it was to reconcile all of life's contradictions: 'Lord Jesus Christ, Son of God, have mercy on me, a sinner!'

*The Stages of the Jesus Prayer*

According to traditional teaching, all prayer progresses in three stages: oral recitation; mental attention to or understanding of the content; and feelings of the heart. As far as the Jesus Prayer is concerned, the second stage is greatly reduced because we are dealing with a simple invocation, even though, as early as the fourteenth century, certain authors artificially have celebrated its doctrinal depth.[122] The advantage of short invocations is, by contrast, that they help in moving directly from oral recitation to the prayer of the heart.

The byzantine and russian monks have associated the Jesus Prayer with the use of a rosary *(kombologion, komboskoinon, lestovka, vervitsa, tchotki)* which helps in counting the invocations and the bows that accompany them.[123] Thus, the first stage of the Jesus Prayer is oral recitation, which unquestionably has value. However, serious authors have protested with good reason against those who have wanted to make of it an almost magical formula. Theophan the Recluse noted that 'It is said of this prayer that there is nothing higher in the world. This is wrong. As if it were some talisman! Nothing in the words of the prayer and their uttering can alone bring forth its fruit. All fruit can be received without this prayer, and even without any oral prayer, but merely by directing the mind and heart towards God.'[124] *The Way of A Pilgrim* is more enthusiastic on this point, as are those who advocate the value of the name of Jesus.

From the lips we move directly to the heart, the authors often say. The passage through the mind is, as we noted, not important. Nonetheless, Ignatii Brianchaninov speaks of it, but from a negative point of view. The short prayer does not awaken reasoning; on the contrary, it causes us to be silent inwardly:

> At first the practice of the prayer of Jesus appears to be extraordinarily dry . . . There are degrees of action in the Jesus prayer. At first it acts only on the mind, leading it into a state of silence and attention. Afterwards it begins to penetrate into the heart, awakening it from the sleep of death. . . . As it goes deeper still, it gradually begins to act upon all parts of the soul and body.[125]

*Does It Replace Other Prayers?*

The question arises as to whether this formula should dominate prayer life to the extent of being substituted for all other prayers, particularly the Divine Office. According to Theophan the Recluse, the Jesus Prayer should be viewed as a complement: it does not replace other prayers, even private, fixed by the Rule.[126] 'Certainly, it is possible to replace meditation by the Jesus Prayer, but what need is there to do so?' he replied to a nun under his direction who practised mental prayer.[127] On the other hand, however, illness, lassitude, or weariness encourage this substitution.[128] Theophan holds that it is worthwhile to replace a recitation of something which is not understood and which leaves the heart unmoved with 'bows and the Jesus Prayer or some other short prayer'.[129]

There is another reason that argues in favor of this invocation, the same which in the West lies behind praying the rosary. Joseph of Volokolamsk prescribed the Jesus Prayer for uneducated monks unable to recite psalms when they moved from the church to the refectory.[130]

All such recommendations are but particular applications of general principles of prayer. The question to be resolved hinges on canon law: can a monk or priest who is obligated by the Rule to recite the Office substitute the Jesus Prayer for it? Theophan approved of the possibility: 'It has been admitted from ancient times that all other prayers may be replaced by this one'.[131] One fact is clear: even the *Služebnik,* edited in 1942 in Rome,[132] foresees that Vespers may be replaced by one hundred Jesus prayers and twenty-five *metanias* (profound bows); Nocturns (Vigils) by one hundred Jesus prayers and twenty-five *metanias;* Compline by twenty-five prayers and twelve *metanias;* Matins (Lauds) by three hundred prayers and fifty *metanias;* the Hours by fifty prayers and seven *metanias,* and the Typika by one hundred prayers and ten *metanias.*

For Ignatii Brianchaninov, replacement of the canonical Office by the Jesus Prayer is 'incomprehensible for beginners, and cannot be explained to them in a satisfactory manner'.[133] We must first acquire an experience of the prayer of the heart: 'A beginner can learn the prayer of Jesus with special ease during the long monastic services. When present at them, what is the use of fruitlessly and harmfully allowing one's thoughts to wander everywhere? . . . Busy yourself with the prayer of Jesus. It will prevent the mind from wandering.'[134] In other words, we should grow used to reciting this ejaculatory prayer during the Offices, not in place of them.

## THE PSYCHOSOMATIC METHOD

### *Pseudo-Symeon*

The psychosomatic technique is described in Nicephorus the Hesychast (the Solitary), Gregory of Sinai, and Pseudo-Symeon, the oldest known theoreticians. Pseudo-Symeon may have been a contemporary of the fourteenth-century Nicephorus, if not Nicephorus himself. Here is a translation of the famous passage:

> Then, sitting in a quiet cell, apart in a corner, do what I tell you: close the door, and raise your mind above every vain and transitory object. Then, pressing your beard against your chest, and turning your bodily eye and with it your entire mind upon the center of your belly—also called the navel—compress the inhalation of air passing through the nostrils so that you do not breathe easily; and mentally explore the insides of your bowels in search of the heart, where all the powers of the soul like to gather. In the beginning, you will find darkness, a stubborn opaqueness, but if you persevere, and perform this exercise day and night, you will experience—O wonder!—a boundless bliss. Indeed, as soon as the mind finds the place where the heart is, it perceives the air at the heart's center, and it perceives itself as being entirely flooded with light and filled with discernment. And from then on, as soon as a thought arises, even before such a thought takes on a form, the mind chases it away and destroys it by invoking the name of Jesus Christ. From that moment on, the mind, in its hatred of demons awakens the anger that is in its nature,[135] and hunts down these spiritual enemies. With God's help, you will learn the rest, by keeping your mind attentive and in your heart holding Jesus. Indeed, as has been said, 'sit down in your cell, and your cell will teach you everything'.[136]

### *'External Aids'*

There are variants to the method, and if we look at certain descriptions,[137] the practice of it seems to become increasingly complex. But sometimes, with one stroke, the procedure is simplified. Several elements come into play. What is needed, first, is a quiet, closed cell and a specific bodily position: sitting on a low seat, a footstool. One's beard is to be pressed against the chest, 'turning the bodily eye and with it the entire mind upon the center of the belly'. A regulated slowing down of breathing is required, as well as a mental exploration of the visceral 'self' in search of 'the place of the heart'; the unification of the human faculties and the repeated, persevering invocation of the name of Jesus. The early theoreticians do not say, at least not explicitly, that the repetition of the formula should be synchronized with the slower breathing rhythm or with the beating of the heart, as is described in *The Way of A Pilgrim.*[138] Several hesychasts had a vision of the light.[139]

Ignatii Brianchaninov, who tried to collect the elements of this exercise, speaks of seven material aids 'for the assistance of beginners in the practice of the prayer of Jesus': 1) a chaplet or *lestovka;* 2) great or little prostrations and bows *(metanias);* 3) keeping the eyes closed; 4) holding the left hand on the chest; 5) a dark cell; 6) sitting on a low stool; 7) cooling oneself with water or applying 'towels soaked in water to the places where there is blood-congestion'.[140]

### *A Darkened Cell*

Monastic literature praises the cell.[141] It is a happy 'desert', even in the midst of town. In order to avoid 'images', the Fathers recommended to the hesychasts a somewhat dark cell, 'with curtained windows, to keep the mind from distraction and to help it descend from the head to the heart'.[142]

### *A Low Chair*

For the ancient Fathers, sitting down during prayer was a concession in cases of illness or for another serious reason.[143] In hesychasm, by contrast, it was the favored position, and was part of the 'physical method'.

> Hesychasts are advised to sit on a low stool, firstly because attentive prayer requires a restful position, and secondly after the example of the blind beggar mentioned in the Gospel who sat on the roadside and cried to the Lord, 'Jesus, Son of David, have mercy on me' (Mk 10:47), and was heard and healed. Also this stool represents the dunghill on which Job sat (Jb 2:8). . . . A monk should see himself crippled, deformed, torn by sinfulness, . . .[144]

### *Breathing*

'One must breathe very slowly. In general all stirrings of flesh and blood must be restrained, and both body and soul must be held in a restful position, in a state of calm. . . . Experience will soon teach that checking the breathing (that is, an infrequent and gentle inhalation of breath) greatly assists the recollection of the mind from wandering.'[145]

The breathing technique of the athonite hesychasts has been compared to the respiration rhythm of a hindu yoga, the *pranayama,* who seeks to 'unify' the awareness and prepares for meditation. If there has been an influence of indian yoga on the hesychasts' method, it can only be indirect; by contrast, it is said that there are striking parallels between the Muslim *dhikr* and the method of Nicephorus.[146]

But such resemblances can also be explained through common experience. In this sense, Vladimir Solovyov writes:

> Breathing is the fundamental condition of life and the constant means of communication between our body and its environment. For the power of the spirit over the body it is desirable that this fundamental function should be under the control of the human will. Consequently there arose long ago and everywhere different ascetic practices with regard to breathing.[147]

### *Localizing Attentiveness in the Upper Part of the Heart*

Let us leave it to physicians and psychologists to evaluate what is produced in our feelings by an attentiveness that is focused on certain 'centers' of the body.[148] Let us merely convey the experience (sometimes associated with questionable theories) that has traditionally been repeated by spiritual authors.

> We should try to ensure that the prayer acts in the very summit of the heart where the power of speech resides according to the teaching of the Fathers, and where divine worship should therefore be performed.[149]
>
> The human heart has the shape of an oblong bag which widens upwards and narrows towards the base. It is fastened by its upper extremity which is opposite the left nipple of the breast, but its lower part which descends towards the end of the ribs is free; when shaken, this shaking is called the beating of the heart. Many, having no idea of the arrangement of the heart, think that their heart is where they feel its beating. In undertaking on their own the practice of the prayer of the heart and in trying to lead their breathing into their heart, they direct it to just that part of the heart and cause carnal excitement there. Then when this greatly increases the beating of the heart they invite it to themselves and thrust on themselves a wrong state and delusion.[150]
>
> The power of speech (reason), or the spirit of the human person is present in the breast and in the upper part of the heart; the power of fervor in the middle part; and the power of desire or natural cupidity in the lower part.[151]
>
> It is also helpful to hold the left hand on the chest, over the left nipple of the breast, a little above it. This technique helps one to feel the power of speech which is in the breast.[152]

The hesychasts have sometimes been blamed for introducing confusion in their use of words in the texts that speak of the 'attention to the heart'. Among listeners, the 'heart' has a complex, but exclusively metaphorical, significance. Why then is there that insistence on concentrating on the physical organ?

Those who study the hesychast method from psychological and medical points of view justify a 'localization' of the attention scientifically.[153] But this 'learned' tendency had already appeared in Gregory Palamas. Some of his considerations are philosophical, others psychological. A distinction should be made, he says, between the mind itself (νοῦς) and its operation (or energies). The mind has its seat in the heart, but through its operation it tends to be 'scattered' outwardly on the objects of sense. This state of dispersion should be brought to a halt by 'gathering' the mind, by bringing it from 'the outside' *(exothen)* to 'the inside' *(endothen),* to the heart. After this 'return to itself', the mind acts in itself, and sees itself in a kind of circular motion.

That breath control favors contemplation is easily confirmed. To increase the efficacy of the procedure, why, Palamas asked, would there not be great profit in fixing the eye on the breast? He replies that the inner person tends to model himself or herself on the outer person. By adopting a position of physically leaning forward, which conforms to a circular motion, we recall to the heart a power which is ever flowing outwards through the eyes.[154]

Theophan the Recluse who relied on simple personal observations states only that the physical organs naturally follow the inner attention: the tension of the muscles is somehow concentrated on the heart—the eyes no longer carry their gaze outwards. He adds that it is not easy either to prescribe or to describe this effort.[155]

We can, however, easily surmise the spiritual reason why the hesychasts were attached to this practice. 'Pure prayer', as conceived by Evagrius, renounces all forms and all thoughts in order to savor in the human person the presence of God alone.[156] But human awareness is of necessity linked to some symbol. Could beating the heart not become an eloquent symbol of this presence of the Saviour in the human person?

## *The Russian Pilgrim*

In the *Narrations* it is possible to follow the russian pilgrim's method step by step. The story opens by posing the crucial question that had preoccupied the monks for centuries: unceasing prayer.[157] 'I came into church . . . The reading was from Paul's First Letter to the Thessalonians, which says in part, "Pray constantly" (5:16).'[158] 'What shall I do? I thought. Where can I find a person who will explain this mystery to me?'[159] Having found the usual teaching on prayer insufficient, the pilgrim finally meets a *staretz* (elder) experienced in the 'Jesus Prayer' as taught in the *Philokalia*. He speaks with him. The *staretz* said to him:

> The ceaseless Jesus Prayer is a continuous, uninterrupted call on the holy name of Jesus Christ with the lips, mind, and heart; and in the awareness of his abiding presence it is a plea for his blessing in all undertakings, in all places, at all times, even in sleep. The words of the prayer are: 'Lord Jesus Christ, have mercy on me!' Anyone who becomes accustomed to this prayer will experience great comfort as well as the need to say it continuously. He will become accustomed to it to such a degree that he will not be able to do without it and eventually the Prayer will of itself flow in him.[160]

The ideal had been outlined, but it had to be realized gradually. The first step is to acquire the habit of reciting the formula orally. The pilgrim accepts the order to say the Prayer three thousand times a day. 'For two days it was somewhat difficult. Then it became so easy and pleasant that when I was not saying the Prayer a need arose within me to say it.' The *staretz* then suggests that he recite the Prayer six thousand times a day and finally twelve thousand times. He gets so accustomed to it that the habit moves from the state of being awake to that of sleep. 'Once, early in the morning the Prayer seemed to awaken me . . . .'[161]

The pilgrim felt happy and began to think that he had already arrived at unceasing prayer. But he had to take another step: moving from the lips to the tongue ('I stopped moving my lips and said the Prayer only with my tongue'). Of course, this was somewhat contrived. Then came the last stage which, according to the *Philokalia*, consists of making the Prayer move from the lips to the heart:

> Imagine your heart; direct your eyes as though you were looking at it through your breast, see the heart as vividly as you can, and listen attentively to its rhythmic beat. And when you have become accustomed to this, then begin to say the words of the Prayer, while looking into your heart, to the rhythm of your heartbeat. With the first beat say 'Lord', with the second 'Jesus', with the third 'Christ', with the fourth 'have mercy', and with the fifth 'on me'. And repeat this very frequently.[162]

This describes the pilgrim's method clearly. To express itself, vocal prayer uses a word like a symbol. The word can, of course, be replaced by a gesture linked to a thought through the laws of association. But when the words are linked to breathing and to the beating of the heart, prayer becomes inseparable from life itself.[163] At least, this is how the pilgrim understands the Prayer. In it he finds happiness and a solution to his problems.

*The Natural Phenomena Accompanying the Practice of This Method*

At the end of the first story, the russian pilgrim relates what 'happened to him'.

> So now I walk and say the Jesus prayer without ceasing and it is more precious and sweet to me than anything else in the world. Sometimes I walk seventy or more verses a day and I do not get tired; I am only conscious of praying. When the cold air chills me, I begin saying the Prayer with greater intensity and I warm up. When hunger begins to overcome me, I begin saying the name of Jesus Christ more frequently and I forget that I wanted to eat. When I become sick and feel rheumatic pain in my back and legs, I pay greater attention to the Prayer and I do not feel the pain. When someone offends me, I remember how sweet the Jesus Prayer is and the offense and anger disappear and I forget everything. I walk in a semiconscious state without worries, interests, and temptations. My only desire is for solitude and ceaseless recitation of the Jesus Prayer. This makes me happy. God knows what this is all about.[164]

Similar experiences are attested to by others devoted to hesychast prayer.[165] It is not easy to differentiate between what is presented as a result of prayer in itself—that is, of the soul's union with God—and what is to be attributed to a strong mental concentration, and finally, what is derived from the method. Among the phenomena most directly linked to psycho-physical exercises are found above all visions of the light and a feeling of warmth.[166]

*Controversies Surrounding the Method*

The value of the method continues to be the subject of discussions up to our own day. From the point of view of religious psychology, the importance of the discussion should not be made light of. The technique of the athonite hesychasts has been compared to hindu yoga.[167] Theories have been developed on the links between psychic activity and various centers of the body.[168] Hesychast prayer is sometimes compared to the ignatian *Spiritual Exercises,* which attach great importance to surroundings and bodily postures.[169] While some scholars strongly emphasize bodily concentration and the powers of attention, others seek to decant the method of its materiality by reducing the heart-mind relationship to some kind of symbol.[170] What was the judgment of the spiritual masters of the East? The psycho-physical method was certainly put into practice by the eastern ascetics. But to what extent? Concrete facts elude us. On the other hand, the summary evidence by classical authors and recognized spiritual masters reflects an extremely valuable living experience. Their observations—practical admonitions, for the most part—may be summarized in a few points.

1) The physical method is only an adaptation of the body to prepare for true, inner prayer of the heart that is, according to Theophan the Recluse, a gift of God to the pure of heart.[171] 'Physical phenomena' must be viewed as the effects of 'nature', not as a manifestation of the presence of the Spirit. 'Certainly, all this is on the sensual level, or, as the late elder said, it is a natural and artificial result of habit. I am not yet ready to make the inward prayer of the heart my own, because I am ignorant and unworthy.'[172]

2) Someone who has learned discernment can profitably use a propitious atmosphere to pray without distraction. It remains true that the spiritual masters warn that, in the realm of 'spiritual feelings', the dangers of delusion are great.[173] While practising the physical method, we may be tempted to take as the action of grace 'not only the gross carnal feelings of the old person, but also the more subtle, sometimes extremely refined, feelings that arise from the motions of the blood'.[174] Great russian spiritual masters such as Paisius Velichkovsky 'say that many of their contemporaries harmed themselves by misusing material aids'.[175]

But is this practice so terribly complicated? Ignatii Brianchaninov states the opposite: 'Sublime spiritual activity is extraordinarily simple. To accept it, one needs only a childlike simplicity and faith.

But we have become so complicated that this very simplicity is the reason we need a guide to lead us out of our complexity. . . .'[176]

Finding a good spiritual director has always been difficult.[177] Brianchaninov also complained about this: 'It often happens that inexperienced directors mistake a pernicious attachment for great progress'.[178] He adds, however, that the masters are not always to be blamed for the problem. We can succumb to delusion while reading patristic books that are insufficiently understood, or by having contact with the greatest servants of God and by listening to their holy doctrine, if presumption makes the soul impervious to repentance.[179]

3) A distinction between 'physical' and 'spiritual' reality helps forestall confusion. Palamas was right, nevertheless, in insisting on their interpenetration, which is the result of deification *(theosis)*.[180] The sensory then appears as a symbol, a participation in the spiritual. To evaluate concrete cases from this point of view requires, of course, extraordinary prudence. But we should not reject *a-priori* as delusions or aberrations the experiences of 'the holy hesychasts' whose defense he undertook.[181]

What had to be explained above all was the dual effects which are frequently mentioned: luminous sensations and warmth.

## *The Dual Light*

In the teaching of the hesychasts, the Christophany at the Transfiguration was the manifestation of a humanity deified and permeated by divine light. Does the physical method lead to a vision of the light? Can we trust such a 'vision'? It was on this point that the anti-palamites attacked the hesychasts and accused them of serious aberrations. The hesychasts replied with what was, in principle, a rather simple distinction: the divine light is spiritual and internal, not sensory and external.[182] But Palamas added that such a spiritual vision did not exclude some reflections in the physical senses: 'From this is clear that, contrary to the view of the Calabrian [Barlaam] and the Latins, this light is not material but spiritual, and that it opens the eyes of the soul and is seen by them, although it also acts on the bodily eyes, as it did in the case of the holy Apostle Paul (see Acts 9:3)'.[183]

### *The Dual Warmth*

After some time, the physical method produces an inner warmth. Like others, Theophan the Recluse warned against those who wanted to identify such natural manifestations with the grace of God.[184] He did not, however, believe that a feeling of warmth was itself evil if it created a sensation of well-being in a cold monastic cell. Ignatii Brianchaninov was more severe. Better to be rid of all this, he believed, so as not to confuse things with the true warmth of the spirit.

'In the case of special physical exertions to acquire the prayer of the heart, a warmth begins to act in the heart. . . . Precaution is necessary because this warmth, being of the blood, not only passes to various places in the breast, but can also very easily drop to the lower parts of the stomach and can cause there the most violent excitement and burning.'[185]

'Ascetics who practice mental activity sometimes have to pour cold water on themselves or apply towels soaked in water to the places where there is blood-congestion. The water should be at summer temperature, and on no account very cold as that only increases the heat.'[186]

In certain individuals, 'mental' activities tend to produce fever: 'spiritual' grace is different:

> When divine grace overshadows the labor of prayer to unite the mind with the heart, then material blood warmth completely vanishes. Then the sacred action of prayer undergoes a great change. It becomes as it were natural, perfectly light and free. Then there appears in the heart another warmth, subtle, immaterial, spiritual, . . . it induces unutterable love for God and men.[187]

An ancient symbol for the seat of the life of the soul,[188] blood and its circulation are of special importance for the balance of health. What the hesychasts sought to avoid was 'effervescence of the blood'—an indication of carnal motions.

> Thanks to spiritual influences, those of the blood upon the soul are definitely overcome; the blood begins to fulfill its natural func-

> tion inside the human composite, having ceased to serve—contrary to its original destination—as an instrument of sin and the devil. The Holy Spirit warms the human person spiritually, while covering with dew and freshness the soul that up to then had been familiar only with the effervescence of the blood.'[189]

## *Concluding Comments*

All professions and human undertakings organize their structure, sooner or later, according to the requirement or the usefulness of the goal they pursue. That the religious life were exempt from this law would be amazing! Eremitism, monasticism, and classical hesychasm arose out of the need to respond to the demands of prayer or to remove distractions and their causes. Prayer being a dialogue with God, its 'environment' is defined by two elements as well as by its 'physical performance': respect for God to whom one prays; and the psychology of the human person who is praying. In reality, the two are frequently joined, but sometimes they are separate or one prevails over the other.[190]

Eastern monasticism, with its ideal of 'pure',[191] unceasing prayer[192] has generally followed the second path. In this choice, respect for God and his will was, in the final analysis, uppermost, but in practice, and clear conscience, what was emphasized most was an aspiration towards a state of prayer characterized by a cluster of psychological and experimental factors. With differing gradations and to different degrees, universal monasticism has as its goal experiences of this type. We say 'universal monasticism'—a term which is applicable to a large number of practices, from hindu yoga to the *Exercises* of Ignatius of Loyola.

Among the dangers that threaten the spiritual person when using any method, the most insidious is this: that in the grip of being scrupulously faithful to method, we put this concern so squarely in the center of our attention that we forget the respect we owe God to whom we pray and whose will we seek. The dialogue with God then degenerates into a monologue, and to go on calling such a meditation 'transcendental' is a contradiction in terms.

Moreover, it is hard to disentangle a technique-ridden and quibbling mentality from a tendency to think in terms of the 'efficient cause': consequently, we ask what could *cause* the breath control, the repetition of a formula, and so forth. This is to reduce methods to purely psychological means, and to neglect their spiritual character. In the East, by contrast, people prefer to view things from the angle of 'exemplary causality', and when faced with phenomena, ask what is their meaning.'[193]

This attitude is fundamental to the use of methods of prayer: the elements they bring into play fulfill only the role of 'holy images' which—in the dialogue with God to whom all prayer is addressed—we must continually transcend if we are to move from the 'type' to the Archetype. While idolatry may lurk in sense impressions or intellectual concepts, the idolatry of one's body will be the most deadly. To this, it is so easy to fall prey.[194]

Through sensory consolations, we imagine the state of intimate union with God symbolically. But if our moral life does not go hand in hand with the stage of prayer, this incoherence may cause some type of spiritual schizophrenia, even madness, as Pseudo-Symeon warned.[195] 'As long as we are not purified and renewed by the Spirit', Ignatii Brianchaninov wrote, 'prudence consists in not recognizing as correct any sensation, any feeling of the heart, except the feeling of repentance, a salutary sorrow for sin, mixed with hope in the mercy of God.'[196]

Such deviations and dangers should not discourage those here below who seek to rediscover the original harmony between the spiritual and the material, a deification of the whole person. Cassian has outlined this ideal: 'This should be the aim and purpose of the solitary: to seek to possess, even in the body, an image of the blessedness to come, and to have a foretaste, in this mortal body, of that heavenly life and glory'.[197]

## *Notes*

1. On hesychasm, see *A Systematic Handbook,* 211f and bibliography, 395ff, 430.

2. See Nicetas Stethatos, *Vie de Syméon le Nouveau Théologien* (949–1022), 25, 15 and 55, 5; critical edition by Irénée Hausherr, *Orientalia Christiana* 12:45 (Rome, 1928).

3. *Apophthegmata Patrum,* Arsenius 2; PG 65:88C; CS 59:9. See *Synaxaire arabe jacobite* 13, *mois de Bachons,* ed. René Basset, PO 16 (Paris, 1922) 1022.

4. Irénée Hausherr, 'La méthode d'oraison hésychaste', *Orientalia Christiana* 9:2 (Rome, 1927) 119ff.

5. *Ibid.,* 120ff.

6. Jean Darrouzès, in DSp 6 (1967) 1011–1014.
7. Daniel Stiernon, in DSp 11 (1982) 198–203.
8. Hausherr, 'La méthode', 120. See Pierre Adnès, in DSp 8 (1974) 1135ff.
9. Adnès, Dsp 12:1138. Jean Meyendorff, 'Palamas (Grégoire)', DSp 12 (1984) 81–107. See also John Meyendorff, *A Study of Gregory Palamas,* translated George Lawrence (London: the Faith Press, 1964; Crestwood, NY: St Vladimir's Seminary Press, 1974).
10. See p. 482.
11. A monk of the Romanian Orthodox Church (Scrima), 'L'avènement philocalique dans l'Orthodoxie roumaine', *Istina* (1958) 295–328, 443–474.
12. See p. 490.
13. Pierre Adnès, 'Hésychasme', DSp 7/1 (1969) 382ff. Hausherr, 'La méthode', 5ff. and OCA 176 (1966) 163ff.
14. Herodotus, *History* I, 66, VI, 150. Plato, *The Apology* 37a, and *The Republic* X, 604e.
15. Xenophon, *Memorabilia* II, 1, 21.
16. *A Systematic Handbook,* 270ff.
17. John Climacus, *Scala paradisi, gradus* 27; PG 88:112D; CWS, 270; Moore, 246.
18. Irénée Hausherr, 'L'Hésychasme, Étude de spiritualité', OCP 22 (1958) 19ff. *Idem.,* 'Hésychasme et priere', OCA 176 (1966) 177ff.
19. *Dionis Prusaensis quae extant omnia,* ed. J. de Arnim (Berlin: Weidemann, 1893-1896; rpt 1962) vol. 2:261.
20. René-Antoine Gauthier, 'Eudémonisme', DSp 4/2 (1961) 1660–1674.
21. Evagrius, *On Prayer* 124; *Leçons,* 158; CS 4:76.
22. Hausherr, 'Hésychasme et prière', OCA 176 (1966) 176ff. *A Systematic Handbook* 211ff and 395.
23. Špidlík, *Grégoire de Nazianze,* 144ff.
24. *Regulae brevius tractatae,* interrogatio 23; PG 31:1098D–1099A; translated W. K. L. Clarke, *The Ascetic Works of Saint Basil* (London, 1925).
25. Hausherr, 'L'hésychasme', 247ff, 199ff. *A Systematic Handbook,* 215ff, 397.
26. See p. 213.
27. *Encheiridion symbouleutikon* (A Handbook of Counsel on Guarding the Five Senses) 10 (Vienna, 1801) 157; extracts in C. Cavarnos, *St. Nicodemos the Hagiorite* (Belmont, 1974) 142ff. See Pierre Adnès, DSp 7/1 (1969) 389ff, and Hausherr, 'L'hésychasme', 262, and OCA 176:214ff.
28. *A Systematic Handbook,* 270.
29. The words *hesychia* and *amerimnia* are linked frequently. See, for example, Diadochus of Photice, *Cent chapitres* 16 (Sch 5*ter:* 92, 20. See also 'On Spiritual Knowledge: One Hundred Texts', *The Philokalia: The Complete Text,* 1:257.
30. *A Systematic Handbook,* 252.
31. Pseudo-Ephrem, *Ad renunciantes,* ed. Joseph Assemani (Venice, 1732) vol. 3:323ff.
32. *Instructions* 1.15; SCh 92:172, 35; CS 33: 86-87.
33. *Scala paradisi,* gradus 27; PG 88:1109B; Luidheid-Russell translation, CWS, 268: The first task of stillness is disengagement from every affair good and bad. . . .
34. *Ibid.*
35. *Ibid.,* 1109; CWS 269 (Moore translation, 245).
36. *Ibid.,* 1112A; Moore, 245.
37. See p. 244.
38. Origen, *In Librum Jesu Nave,* homily 13.1; GCS 7:373. *Ibid.,* homily 15.3; 387. Dorotheos, *Instructions* 11.117; SCh 92:363; CS 39:174.
39. *A Systematic Handbook,* 237ff.

40. *Ibid.,* 242.
41. Hence the title, the *Philokalia ton hieron neptikon* (of the Neptic [watchful] Fathers.
42. *Homily* 6.1 (PG 34:517C) and 6.3 (520B); see *Intoxicated with God: The Fifty Spiritual Homilies of Macarius,* translated George A. Maloney (Denville, New Jersey: Dimension Books, 1987.
43. *De temperantia et virtute,* century 1.1; PG 93:1480D; 'On Watchfulness and Holiness', *The Philokalia: The Complete Text,* vol. 1 (1979) 162.
44. *A Systematic Handbook,* 242.
45. *Ibid.,* 243.
46. Syriac edition by Wilhelm Frankenberg, *Evagrius Ponticus* (Berlin, 1912) 47–544.
47. *On the Prayer of Jesus,* translated Lazarus Moore (London: John M. Watkins, 1965) 29.
48. Robert Vernay, 'Attention', DSp 1 (1937) 1058–1077.
49. Arrian, *Diatribes* 4, 12 [translated W. A. Oldfather, *Epictetus.* The Discourses as reported by Arrian, the Manual, and Fragments, Loeb Classical Library, 2 vols. (Cambridge MA: Harvard University Press, 1959–1961].
50. *Apophthegmata Patrum,* Antonius 2, PG 65:76B; *The Sayings of The Desert Fathers,* CS 59 (Kalamazoo: Cistercian Publication, 1975) 2.
51. *Praktikos,*149; PG 40:1233B; SCh 171:614; CS 4:79.
52. See Pseudo-Symeon, *Méthode de la sainte oraison et attention,* ed. Irénée Hausherr, *Orientalia Christiana* 36 (Rome, 1927) 150ff.
53. *De Chananaea* 10; PG 52:458.
54. 'La méthode d'oraison hésychaste', ed. Irénée Hausherr, *Orientalia Christiana* 9:2 (Rome, 1927) 154 (58). See *Writings from the Philokalia on Prayer of the Heart,* 154.
55. *Benjamin Major,* 1.4; PL 196:67D; translated Grover A. Zinn, *Richard of St Victor, The Mystical Ark,* CWS (New York: Paulist Press, 1979) 157.
56. See François de Sales, 'Amour de Dieu' 6, 2, *Oeuvres* (Annecy, 1844) 4:306; translated John K. Ryan, *Treatise on the Love of God,* 2 vols., (Rockford, Illinois: 1974).
57. *Regulae brevius tractatae,* interrogatio 21; PG 31:1097B (See above, n. 24). Cf. Ps 26:2.
58. *Apophtegmes syriaques* 23; PO 11:422-423.
59. Irénée Hausherr, Penthos. La doctrine de la componction dans l'Orient chrétien,. OCA 132 (Rome, 1944) 75ff; *Penthos. The Doctrine of Compunction in the Christian East,* CS 53:65ff.
60. Hausherr, *La méthode d'oraison hésychaste,* 151 (55)ff.
61. *Homilia in illud, Attende tibi ipsi;* PG 31:197-217; translated Monica Wagner, 'Homily on the Words, "Give Heed to Thyself"', FCh 9: 431ff.
62. (Rome, 1732), vol. 3:230–254.
63. See p. 254.
64. Critical edition by Irénée Hausherr, 'La méthode d'oraison hésychaste', *Orientalia Christiana* 9:2, (Rome, 1927) 150–172; translated (from the Russian) by E. Kadloubovsky and G. E. H. Palmer, *Writings from the Philokalia on Prayer of the Heart* (London: Faber and Faber, 1979) 152–161.
65. *Ibid.,* 157; 154.
66. *Ibid.,* 152; 153.
67. *Ibid.,* 159ff; 157.
68. *Ibid.,* 165.
69. See p. 242.
70. *Philokalia,* vol. 5 (Athens, 1963) 104ff.

71. *Ethica,* 15.41-43; SCh 129:446; translated Alexander Golitzin, 'Fifteenth Ethical Discourse', *St Symeon the New Theologian. On the Mystical Life: The Ethical Discourses,* 1:165 (Crestwood, NY: St. Vladimir's Seminary Press, 1996).

72. *Ibid.,* 15.64-67; 448;176. See also *Chapitres théologiques, gnostiques et pratiques,* 1.79; SCh 51:64; CS 41:56.

73. See p. 247.

74. See p. 364.

75. *De temperantia et virtute,* century 1.99; PG 93:1512A, and 1.32;1492B. [See 'On Watchfulness and Holiness', in *The Philokalia. The Complete Text,* vol. 1.163-198.]

76. Pierre Adnès, 'Jésus (prière à)', DSp 8 (1974) 1126-1150. Irénée Hausherr, *Noms du Christ et voies d'oraison,* OCA 157 (Rome, 1960); translated Charles Cummings, *The Name of Jesus,* CS 44 (Kalamazoo: Cistercian Publications, 1978). See *A Systematic Handbook,* 316, 410, 441.

77. *A Systematic Handbook,* 242ff.

78. *Ibid.,* 243ff.

79. Syriac edition by Wilhelm Frankenberg, *Evagrius Ponticus* (Berlin, 1912) 47-544.

80. See Tomaš Špidlík, 'Gesù nella pietà dei Cristiani orientali', in Ermanno Ancilli, *Gesù Cristo—mistero e presenza* (Rome: Teresianum, 1971) 398.

81. See p. 364.

82. *Vie de saint Dosithée,* 10; SCh 92 (1963) 138ff.

83. *Scala paradisi, gradus* 15; PG 88:889CD; CWS 171–186 [178].

84. See Daniel Stiernon, in DSp 7/2 (1971) 2080–2082.

85. Vol. 2 (Athens, 1958) 244; see *Writings from the Philokalia on Prayer of the Heart* (London: Faber and Faber, 1979) 402–416.

86. J. Gouillard, in *Échos d'Orient* 38 (1939) 268–269.

87. See p. 339.

88. 2nd ed. (Athens, 1885) 121ff; 'A Manual of Counsel on the Guarding of the Five Senses, of the Imagination, of the Intellect and of the Heart', extracts in C. Cavarnos, *St. Nicodemus the Hagiorite* (Belmont, 1974) 142–45.

89. See p. 343.

90. Bernhard Schultze, 'Der Streit um die Göttlichkeit des Namens Jesu in der russischen Theologie', OCP 17 (1951) 321–394. *Idem,* 'Untersuchungen über das Jesus-Gebet', OCP 18 (1952) 319–343. *Idem,* 'Auf den Bergen Kaukasus', *Geist und Leben* 32 (1959) 116–127.

91. Serge Bulgakov, *L'Orthodoxie* (Paris, 1932) 206; revised translation by Lydia Kesich, *The Orthodox Church* (Crestwood, New York: St. Vladimir's Seminary Press) 147.

92. André Scrima, 'Réflexions sur les rythmes et la fonction de la tradition athonite', *Le millénaire du Mont Athos* (1964) 2:301-324.

93. *On the Prayer of Jesus,* translated Lazarus Moore (London: John M. Watkins, 1965) 22; *Approches de la prière de Jésus,* 114 (in Russian, 278).

94. *On the Prayer of Jesus,* 19; *Approches,* 104 (in Russian, 274).

95. *Ibid.,* 19; *Approches,* 110 (in Russian, 274).

96. *Filosofija imeni* [*The Philosophy of the Name*] (Paris, 1953) 25ff. A. Wenger analyzes this work in *Revue des études byzantines* 13 (1955) 176–177. Bulgakov's teaching is found again in Paul Evdokimov in *L'Orthodoxie* (Paris, 1959) 114–115, and in *La connaissance de Dieu selon la tradition orientale* (Lyon, 1967) 67–69.

97. *L'Orthodoxie* (Paris, 1932) 206; *The Orthodox Church,* 147.

98. *Ibid.,* 208; 148.

99. *Essai sur la sainteté en Russie* (Bruges, 1953) 393.

100. 'Réflexions' (above, n. 92), 310, note 14.
101. *Pïšma o duchovnoj žizni* [*Letters on the Spiritual Life*] (Moscow, 1903) 211.
102. *Sobranie pisem* [*Collection of Letters*] (Moscow, 1898ff.) vol. 12:17. See *The Art of Prayer: An Orthodox Anthology,* compiled by Chariton of Valamo, and translated by E. Kadloubovsky and E. M. Palmer (London: Faber and Faber, 1966) 98.
103. Édouard Cothenet, 'Nom', DSp 11 (1982) 397.
104. Iréné Noye, 'Jésus (nom de)', DSp 8 (1974) 1109ff. Aimé Solignac, 'Les noms de Dieu dans la spiritualité', DSp 11 (1982) 407–410.
105. M. Schulzberger, 'Le symbole de la croix et les monogrammes de Jésus chez les premiers chrétiens', *Byzantion* 2 (1925) 337–448.
106. PG 3:585-984; translated Colm Luibheid, *Pseudo-Dionysius: The Complete Works,* CWS (New York: Paulist Press, 1987) 47–131; translated C. E. Rolt, *Dionysius the Areopagite: The Divine Names and The Mystical Theology* (London: SPCK, 1920, 1940) 50–190.
107. P. Scazzoso, *Richerche sulla struttura del linguaggio dello Pseudo-Dionigi* (Milan, 1967). V. Muñoz Rodriguez, *Significado de los nombres de Dios en el Corpus Dionysiacum* (Salamanca, 1975) presents new insights on the basis of the methods of structural linguistic analysis.
108. Hausherr, *Noms du Christ,* OCA 157:118;, CS 44:104-105.
109. *Selecta in Psalmos,* Psalm 4.2; PG 12:1136C.
110. See p. 366.
111. See p. 364.
112. *Conferences,* 10.10; SCh 54:88ff; ACW 57:378-383; CWS, 132ff. See the commentary by A. Gazet in PL 49:832D.
113. Hausherr, *Noms du Christ,* 118; CS 44:104.
114. *Chapitres pratiques et théologiques,* nos. 68, 69, 74, 75; translated Paul McGuckin, *Symeon the New Theologian: The Practical and Theological Chapters,* CS 41 (1982) pp. 51, 53. See also, George A. Maloney, trans., *The Mystic of Fire and Light. St Symeon the New Theologian* (Denville, New Jersey: Dimension Books, 1975).
115. Vie de Syméon le Nouveau Théologien, no. 90, critical edition and french translation by Irénée Hausherr and Gabriel Horn, *Orientalia Christiana* 12, no. 45 (1928) 124.
116. *Oratio* 39, *In sancta lumina,* 17; PG 36:356; LNPF, ser. 2, 7:352ff. *Oratio* 40, *In sanctum baptisma* 9; PG 36:369; LNPF, ser. 2, 7:360ff.
117. *Philokalia* (ed. Venice, 1782) 1186ff; see *Writings from the Philokalia on Prayer of the Heart,* 402ff.
118. *Approches de la prière de Jesus,* 57 (Russian, 216).
119. See p. 344.
120. *A Systematic Handbook,* 126.
121. *The Cloud of Unknowing,* translated Clifton Wolters (Penguin Classics, 1982). See P. Dubourg in RAM 7 (1926) 188-199.
122. Hausherr, *Noms du Christ,* 276; *The Name of Jesus,* CS 44:318.
123. A monk of the Eastern Church [Lev Gillet], *The Jesus Prayer* (Crestwood, New York: St. Vladimir's Seminary Press, 1987) 72ff.
124. *Letters,* vol. I, 2 (Moscow, 1898) 19; *The Art of Prayer,* 98.
125. *On the Prayer of Jesus,* 35; *Approches,* 129 (Russian, 291).
126. *Letters* (Moscow, 1898) 372. Špidlík, *Théophane le Reclus,* 284ff.
127. *Sobranie pisem* [*Collection of Letters*] (Moscow, 1898-ff.), vol. I:114.
128. *Letters,* 342.
129. *Ibid.,* 33ff.
130. *Monastic Rule,* in Makarij, *Velikija Minei Četii,* September volume (St Petersburg, 1869) 593; translated David M. Goldfrank, *The Monastic Rule of Iosif Volotsky,* edited

and translated by David M. Goldfrank, CS 36 (Revised, second edition, Kalamazoo: Cistercian Publications, 2000) 276.
131. *On Psalm 118* (Moscow, 1891) 167.
132. Page 689.
133. *Approches de la Prière de Jésus,* 50 (Russian, 207).
134. *On the Prayer of Jesus,* 58; *Approches,*155 (316).
135. In the *Scholia* to *Scala paradisi, gradus* 24; PG 88:985B, John Climacus states that 'it is the nature of the irascible power to fight against the demons'; *Handbook,* 251.
136. *La méthode d'oraison hésychaste,* ed. by Irénée Hausherr, *Orientalia Christ*iana 9:2 (Rome, 1927) 164ff. See 'Three Methods of Attention and Prayer', *Writings From the Philokalia on Prayer of the Heart* (London: Faber and Faber, 1979) 158–159.
137. Pierre Adnès, 'Jésus (prière à)', DSp (1974) 1135ff.
138. See p. 343.
139. See DSp 12/1 (1984) 96.
140. *On the Prayer of Jesus* 88-90; *Approches,* 187ff; (Russian, 346ff.).
141. Louis Gougaud, 'Cellule', DSp 2/1 (1953) 396–400.
142. Brianchaninov [Briančaninov], *On the Prayer of Jesus; Approches,* 188 (Russian, 374).
143. Origen, *Libellus de oratione,* 31.1; PG 11:552A; translated Rowan A. Greer, *Origen: An Exhortation to Martyrdom, Prayer,* CWS (New York: Paulist Press, 1974) 165.
144. Brianchaninov, *On the Prayer of Jesus,* 89.
145. *Ibid.,* 71; *Approches,* 169ff (Russian, 3).
146. Pierre Adnès, 'Jésus (prière à)', DSp 8 (1974) 1147ff.
147. *La justification du bien,* 1.2.6 (Paris, 1933) translated Natalie A. Duddington, *The Justification of the Good: An Essay in Moral Philosophy* (New York: Macmillan, 1918) 49.
148. Anthony Bloom, 'Contemplation et ascèse: contribution orthodoxe', *Technique et contemplation,* Études Carmélitaines (1949) 55.
149. Brianchaninov, *On the Prayer of Jesus,* 92; *Approches,* 191 (Russian, 350).
150. *Ibid.,* 95; *Approches,* 193 (353).
151. *Ibid.*
152. *Ibid.,* 89; *Approches,* 188 (347).
153. *Défense des saints hésychastes,* critical edition by Jean Meyendorff (Louvain, 1959; 2nd ed., 1974). Major extracts may be found, translated Nicholas Gendle, in *Gregory Palamas. The Triads,* CWS series, (New York: Paulist Press, 1983).
154. *Défense* I.2.8; 89–91. See *Triads,* CWS 46. Jean Meyendorff, 'Le thème du "retour en soi" dans la doctrine palamite du XIVe siècle', *Revue d'Histoire des religions* 145 (1954) 188–206. Meyendorff, *Introduction à l'étude de Grégoire Palamas* (Paris, 1959) 195–200; translated George Lawrence, *A Study of Gregory Palamas* (London: Faith Press, 1964) 134-156. Meyendorff, 'Palamas (Grégoire)', DSp 12 (1984) 81–107.
155. *Put ko spaseniju* [*The Way to Salvation*] (Moscow, 1908) 206.
156. See p. 243.
157. See p. 361.
158. Among available translations are *The Way of a Pilgrim* and *The Pilgrim Continues His Way,* translated by Helen Bacovcin (New York: Doubleday, Image Books, 1992), and *The Pilgrim's Tale,* translated T. Allan Smith, CWS (New York: Paulist Press, 1999).
159. *Ibid.,* 13.
160. *Ibid.,* 18.
161. *Ibid.,* 22.
162. *Ibid.,* 83.
163. *Ibid.,* 26–27.

164. *Ibid.,* 24.
165. *Umnoe delanie o molitve Isusovoj* (Valaam, 1936); *The Art of Prayer,* compiled by Hegumen Chariton and translated by E. Kadloubovsky and G. E. Palmer (London: Faber and Faber, 1966).
166. *Ibid.,* Index.
167. See Mircea Eliade, *Yoga. Essai sur les origines de la mystique indienne* (Paris 1936) 86–88. *Idem, Le yoga. Immortalité et liberté* (Paris, 1954) 75–78; translated Willard R. Trask, [*Yoga: Immortality and Freedom,* Bollingen Series 56:63-65(Princeton, New Jersey: Princeton University Press, 1969). Endre von Ivanka, 'Byzantinische Yogis'? *Zeitschrift der deutschen Morgenländischen Gesellschaft* 102 (1952) 234–239 (summary in *Revue des études byzantines* 13 (1955) 175). W. Nölle, 'Hesychasmus und Yoga', *Byzantinische Zeitschrift* 47 (1954) 95–103. Jules Monchanin, 'Yoga et hésychasme', *Axes* 4 (April 1969) 13–21. Pierre Adnès, 'Jésus (prière à)', DSp 8 (1974) 1147ff.
168. Anthony Bloom, 'Contemplation et ascèse: contribution orthodoxe', *Technique et contemplation,* Études carmélitaines (1949) 54-56. *Idem,* 'L'hésychasme: Yoga chrétien'? *Yoga. Science de l'homme intégral, Les Cahiers du Sud* (Paris, 1953) 177–195.
169. Irénée Hausherr, 'Les Exercises Spirituels de saint Ignace et la méthode d'oraison hésychaste', OCP 20 (1954) 7–26; OCA 176 (Rome, 1966) 134–153.
170. Piere Adnès, 'Jésus (prière à)', DSp 8 (1974) 1147.
171. Špidlík, *Théophane le Reclus,* 285ff.
172. See p. 2.
173. Andre Derville, 'Illusions', DSp 7/2 (1971) 1392–1401.
174. Brianchaninov, *Approches de la prière de Jésus,* 80 (in Russian, 243).
175. *On the Prayer of Jesus,* 95; *Approches,* 194 (Russian, 354).
176. *Ibid.,* 43; *Approches,* 138 (301). Translated from the French.
177. Irénée Hausherr, *Direction spirituelle en Orient autrefois,* OCA 144 (Rome, 1955) 178ff; translated Anthony P. Gythiel, *Spiritual Direction in the Early Christian East,* CS 116 (Kalamazoo: Cistercian Publications, 1990) 185ff.
178. Brianchaninov, *On the Prayer,* 86.; *Approches,* 185.
179. *Ibid.*
180. See Jean Meyendorff, 'Palamas (Grégoire)', DSp 12/1 (1984) 95.
181. *Ibid.*
182. *Ibid.,* 102.
183. Brianchaninov, *On the Prayer,* 102; *Approches,* 202 (Russian, 363).
184. *On Ps.* 118 (Moscow, 1891) 167ff. *Letters* (Moscow, 1898-ff.) I:18.
185. Brianchaninov, *On the Prayer,* 90–91; *Approches,* 189ff (Russian, 384ff.).
186. *Ibid.*
187. *Ibid.*, 92; 91 (350).
188. E. Jacob, 'Psyché', Kittel 9 (1969) 615ff; (1974) 619ff.
189. Brianchaninov, *Approches,* 85 (Russian, 49). See the conversation of Maximus of Kapsokalyvia with Gregory the Sinaite, in *The Philokalia,* vol. 5 (Athens, 1963) 104ff.
190. Irénée Hausherr, 'Les Exercises Spirituels de Saint Ignace et la méthode d'oraison hésychaste', OCP 20 (1954) 7–26; OCA 176 (Rome, 1966) 134–153.
191. See p. 175.
192. See p. 361.
193. See Yves Congar, *Chrétiens désunis, Principes d'un oecuménisme catholique,* Unam Sanctam 1 (Paris 1937) 252; translated M. S. Bousfield, *Divided Christendom: A Catholic Study of the Problem of Reunion* (London: Geoffrey Bles, 1939) 200.

194. Špidlík, 'Il metodo esicastico', *Rivista di vita spirituale* 32 (1978) 506–24; rpt in Ermanno Ancilli, ed., *Alla recerca di Dio, Le techniche della preghiera* (Rome, 1979) 197–215.
195. See p. 339.
196. *Approches,* 80ff (Russian, 244).
197. *Conferences,* 10.7; SCh 54:81ff; ACW 57:376; CWS, 130; LNPF, ser. 2, 11:404.

# CONCLUSION

PRAYER', wrote Martyrius Sahdona, 'may do what it likes—just as God can. It gives orders on earth, it holds back in heaven. Prayer is a god amongst human beings.'[1] All the spiritual authors of the Christian East would be ready to sign such a statement, for they were in no doubt about the power of prayer. With one voice, they confessed that prayer is the occupation most necessary to the human person.[2] Thus, Theophan the Recluse writes: 'Prayer forms a whole. It summarizes all things: faith, living according to faith, salvation.'[3] There is indeed a close link between prayer and perfection. Can they be identified? The answer will vary, depending on how one views prayer, and depending on the content one gives to this term which is universally human yet nonetheless is given very different meanings and gradations. To conclude, then, let us summarize the aspects which we have seen brought out into high relief in the East. Only then will we be able to give a satisfactory answer to the question about the identity of prayer and perfection.

### *Petition Addressed to the Father in the Trinitarian Life*

Addressing petitions to God is not distinctive to Christians. It is the natural consequence of belief in a personal God. The revelation of the gospel solemnly confirms that God is truly Father. But at the same time, Christ brings in something new, because it is through him and his Spirit that we are introduced to this dialogue, which of its very nature seems impossible. In christian worship the awareness that prayer is essentially christological and 'charismatic' has been strong from the beginning.

The great merit of the Greek Fathers is that they were not afraid to deal with the metaphysical and scientific difficulties which determined the attitude of human persons coming out of the cultural tradition of antiquity. They have shown that the Christian who speaks freely to the Father in the intimate life of the Trinity can continue to proclaim the necessity of the world's natural laws. The dialogue they engaged in with the Creator does not result in damaging the order of the world. *Theologia,* 'contemplation of the Trinity' leaves the *logikon* (reasoning) of human thought intact.[4] Paradoxically, the treatises on prayer by the alexandrian Fathers were needed to save the hellenistic tradition of human sciences in the acceptance of the simple faith of children of God.

### *Vocal Prayer*

Dialogue is conducted primarily with words. The first form of prayer is therefore oral, vocal prayer. Even here, Christians were not original. Certain invocations and rites go back to the most archaic ages.[5] Through the channel of Scripture, semitic expressions left the strongest impression on the formation of the christian language used in the conversation with God. Yet these expressions were translated into various languages, and each time they took on new shades of meaning.

Soon activity was not limited to translations. While Gregory Nazianzus promised to make Christ speak Greek, he put the gift of his mother tongue at the service of the *Logos* (Word),[6] and he became the pre-eminent witness to the many-sided wisdom of God (Eph 3:10), which is attested to in the ancient tradition by which the Eastern Churches 'praise God in their own language'.[7] Each language expresses an experience of its own, and each experience enriches human language. The religious and human treasures enshrined in the prayers of the Eastern Churches cannot be numbered.

### *Liturgical Prayer*

Words have a social function. Not only do they condition communion among persons, but they also reflect the manner and the degree of such union. In the Church, they are liturgical and share in the power of divine words. The eastern liturgies, in the richness of their variety—the fruit of the creativity and peoples' tradition—witness to the belief that the Spirit is incarnate in the most diverse historical forms. A plurality of languages does not prevent spiritual communion; a multitude of symbols is able to form one 'commemoration', the sacred *anamnesis,* the remembrance of the whole work of salvation. If the visual element of ceremonies is brought into full relief, this means that the 'word' is by nature not limited to the acoustic signs alone, but that it embraces all external human experiences.

### *Contemplation*

Corporeal beings communicate by means of sensory signs. The ancient Greeks believed that 'man' (*anthropos,* 'the human person'), enters into the divine world by thoughts, by raising the human spirit to God. On the one hand, the Greek Fathers took over this definition of inward prayer, and thereby remained rooted in the native soil of what was best in their culture, which taught man to ascend from the material to spiritual reality. On the other hand, they understood from the beginning that the 'spiritual', in the christian sense, did not coincide with the immaterial activity of the human soul.

Christian contemplation must therefore be the ascent, not merely of the spirit (with a small s, the human spirit, *nous,* the mind), but above all of the Spirit (with a capital S). The Spirit has his abode in the human heart; this expresses the integrity of the human person and at the same time a spiritual intuition, a gift of those who pray assiduously. This is why the teaching on contemplation, despite its intellectualistic greek terminology, could easily advance to other peoples of the Christian East and be assimilated by the simplest ascetics. The entire monastic life was therefore structured with a view to contemplation.

### *The Mystical Ladder*

Ascent to heaven is an image known in the history of religions.[8] Through their interpretation of Jacob's dream (Gn 18:12-13) or the vision of Moses on top of Mount Sinai (Es 2:4), christian authors were able to make a familiar mystical experience their own.

At the same time, they were aware that Jacob's ladder differs essentially from the Babylonian *ziggurat* (Gn 11): in the biblical dream, the angels ascend but also descend.

The mysticism inspired by Plato offered the Fathers magnificent descriptions of the 'ascent' of the mind, of the 'ecstatic power' of *eros,* human love and desire. The christian mystics emphasized more the benevolence of divine love *(agape),* which descends to let us ascend. In the teaching common among the Syrians,[9] Jacob's ladder symbolizes the Cross of Christ, a sublime expression of the love of God, of the economy of salvation. God gives himself through the Word made flesh. A tender devotion to the person of Christ is therefore typical of christian mysticism. The participation in his death and resurrection justifies the various ecstatic experiences all along the journey towards God.

### *Methods of Prayer*

In palamite terminology, *energeia* (activity, operation) is a general term for the divine gifts. It brings about human *synergeia* (cooperation). Prayer is therefore also an *ergon, opus,* work. The intelligent person works with prudence and according to certain methods. Experience has proven from the beginning that one way of reading is more profitable than another, and that one way of praying corresponds better to the psychological structures of people than do other spiritual exercises. The pre-eminent method of prayer was developed in hesychasm. It does not represent the entire spirituality of the Christian East but it nonetheless exhibits a common trait: the tendency that, as one progresses, prayer becomes simpler, becoming inseparable from life itself, from its root, from breathing. The human person is by nature a 'dialogical' creature. The first principle of perfection is to develop one's nature; to actualize one's nature means to pray unceasingly.

### *The Apostle's Instruction: 'Pray Without Ceasing' (1 Thes 5:17)*

Successive generations of monks have meditated on this text, which they considered the norm of their life. This is echoed by the russian Pilgrim:

> On the twenty-fourth Sunday after Pentecost I came to church to attend the Liturgy and entered just as the epistle was being read. The reading was from Paul's First Letter to the Thessalonians, which says in part, 'Pray constantly'. These words made a deep impression on me and I started thinking of how it could be possible for a man to pray without ceasing when the practical necessities of life demand so much attention. I checked my Bible and saw with my own eyes exactly what I had heard, that it is necessary to pray continuously (1 Thes 5:17); to pray in the Spirit on every possible occasion (Eph 6:18); in every place to lift your hands reverently in prayer (1 Tm 2:8). I thought and thought about these words, but no understanding came to me.
>
> What shall I do? I thought. Where can I find a person who will explain this mystery to me?[10]

This was the problem that had confronted the monks from ancient times.

### *Solutions to the Problem*

Eastern monks have always striven to follow the precept to pray without ceasing. They were never in doubt that unceasing prayer was an obligation and that it was possible.[11] Jesus prayed constantly, Origen notes[12], and the Christian has to do the same if he expects his prayers to be heard. The problem is how to achieve this. Spiritual writers have given divergent interpretations to these two words 'pray' and 'always'.

The Messalians[13] took these words literally. For them, praying meant always reciting prayers; it meant never doing anything but pray. Hence their name *mesaliane, precatores, euchitai* ('prayers'). They refused to mix any secular work with prayer.

The solution of the *Acoemeti* was doubtless naive and yet it was successful in Constantinople.[14] These monks sought to arrive at unceasing prayer through collaboration: a part of the community was always in church reciting the Offices, and so the impression was created that these pious men 'never slept'—hence their name ἀ-κοίμιται, 'non-sleepers'. But this solution did not satisfy everyone: *each person*—not just moral persons in monasteries and confraternities—has been ordered by Christ to always pray.

Origen gives the orthodox solution to the problem: 'Someone prays unceasingly who combines prayer with necessary deeds and the deeds with prayer. It is only in this way that the injunction to "pray without ceasing" can be made real.' [15] The entire life of the Christian is to be viewed as a totality, as 'one great continuous prayer'; what we usually call 'prayer' is but a part of this great prayer.

This was to become common doctrine: it is shared by Augustine,[16] Aphraates (Aphrahat),[17] and the famous motto *Ora et Labora* (Work and Pray) of benedictine monasticism. Of course, the terms can be reversed, as Basil had already done. Since we will be judged before the tribunal of God according to our deeds, good or bad, the Christian's first obligation is 'to abound in the work of God'.[18] In this context, prayer was one of the most important works, an *opus divinum* (divine work).[19]

### *The Pre-eminence of Contemplation?*

This classic solution does not yet solve all the problems, the first of which may be presented as follows: works are also prayer, and prayer is work, but would contemplation not be essentially superior? Does a human person not have to be more contemplative than 'practical', according to his potential? Does contemplation as such coincide with holiness?

This identification can be accepted easily if one remains within the circle of terms suggested by Evagrius. If 'God knows what he is',[20] the created intellect is what it knows.[21] This is one of the great principles that dominates the thought of Evagrius: knowledge is a real assimilation of the knower with the known. 'As in things sensory, sensation changes according to the diversity of the colors, so the intellect transforms itself according to the differences in what it contemplates.'[22] Pushing this principle to its ultimate conclusion, Evagrius writes; 'When the mind has been admitted to a knowledge of the Holy Trinity, then it is called God by grace, as having arrived at the full image of its Creator'.[23]

Would this transformation not already be a sign of perfection? Most of the ascetics were afraid of this delusion, and with good reason. A text by Philoxenus of Mabbug (*fl.* 500) is not without interest, because it deals explicitly with this subject and concludes that holiness differs from contemplation, and for two reasons: 1) because contemplation can exist without holiness; 2) because holiness can exist without contemplation. The ultimate reason for such distinctions is the freedom of God, who grants contemplation as a free gift. But this gratuitous *theoria* is inferior to that obtained by the normal channel of ascetic purification, for charity alone gives value to everything, whether contemplation itself or works.[24]

## Diathesis Agathe: *A Good Disposition*

In theory, the problem may be viewed as having been solved: it is charity that determines the correct relationship between action and contemplation, between works and prayer. In practice, however, the problem always remains a difficult one. Experience teaches that it is precisely the fervor of charity that dwindles when we devote ourselves to the work of God without prudence.

In order for a 'work' to keep its spiritual value, Basil suggests that it be performed with a good inner disposition (διάθεσις ἀγαθή).[25] This disposition is nourished by explicit prayers. This is why monks always sought to enrich their practice of prayer.

What was required was fidelity to the canonical hours, to the 'rule of prayer' agreed upon with one's spiritual director. Psalms were recited during work; the practice of ejaculatory prayers had a very long history.[26] Cassian did not misrepresent the Fathers' teaching on frequent short prayers, their use and efficacy. He merely made a choice among them and recommended his formula, as others would later praise the Jesus Prayer.[27] For him, the invocation 'O God, make speed to save me; O Lord, make haste to help me' (Ps 69:2) was a 'sacred formula' (a *formula pietatis*).[28] But for Basil, the pre-eminent means to transform works into contemplation is 'mindfulness of God'.

## *The Remembrance of God in the Thought of Basil*

The word *theoria* (seeing, beholding) is virtually banished from Basil's vocabulary; he based the monastic life exclusively on Scripture. By contrast, an appeal to the 'continual remembrance of God' is one of the unchanging factors in basilian spirituality.[29] But are there substantial differences between 'seeing God' (the definition of *theoria*) and 'remembering God'? *Theoria* conveys the impatient desire of the Greeks to acquire a direct experience of what is seen. Scripture confesses on every page that we do not have a direct vision of God. But Israel remembered Yahweh by mentioning, recalling, preserving, and invoking God's mighty deeds.[30]

In everyday language we call certain objects 'souvenirs'—trivial things sometimes, but things to which we attach memories of a person or a trip. It is through this remembrance that the object has value. In Basil's cosmic thought, the entire world in its multiplicity, its rhythm, and its marvelous order has no other objective than to be a 'remembrance' of our contacts with God. While the human mind was created to remember God, material things, in turn, were destined to evoke this remembrance. This is their nature.[31] Evagrian 'intellectual' mysticism presupposes that the human intellect returns to its proper nature when it 'divests itself' of all sensory impressions and all partial concepts.[32] Basil, by contrast, was convinced that we arrive at the 'contemplation of beauty' by fixing our gaze on creation. This was the situation in Paradise.[33] Contemplation is the return to the original state of human innocence, which presupposes 'a soul looking around everywhere in order to catch a thought of God' *(ennoian tou theou)*.[34]

Mindfulness of God, being a simplified contemplation in the midst of the world, is acquired through the frequent practice of 'natural contemplation' *(theoria physike)*.[35] If you meditate frequently on creation, wrote Theophan the Recluse,

> everything will become a sacred book for you or a chapter from this book. The smallest object, the slightest occupation, and the most unimportant work will always suggest to you the thought of God. From then on, you will walk in the visible world as in a spiritual domain; all things will speak to you of God, and everything will support the attention given to God.[36]

Theophan admits that certain images help in this effort, but also that they can easily become an obstacle. Some represent God as a Father whose gaze, full of solicitude, rests on everything we do.[37] Others see themselves surrounded by an entirely spiritual light. All this matters little, Theophan added, since it is only a means; God has no visible face.[38]

If we need to conceive some vision, it is better to represent God in the heart, to let ourself 'be encircled by the memory of God who dwells in us',[39] to retire to the cell of the *hegemonikon* (reason, the leading principle of action).[40] This is what the hesychasts practised,[41] in accordance with the teaching of the orthodox Fathers who viewed evil as coming 'from outside', while seeing grace as part of our being.[42]

The human make-up possesses a 'consciousness' (*con-scientia,* 'a joint knowledge') of his or her state. And if the Holy Spirit firmly establishes his throne in the heart of the Christian, the latter becomes more and more 'conscious' of his 'dialogical' state and feels included in the eternal dialogue of the divine Persons. This 'feeling' is compatible with an attention to created things, but it does not reduplicate the act of knowing but deepens it, becoming an enduring disposition, a state of the heart.

### *The State of Prayer*

In the West, authors in recent years have reserved the expression 'state of prayer' to mystical states, to 'infused prayer of some duration'.[43] In the East, the word κατάστασις (state) has been used in the broad sense to designate the attitude of prayer, the manner of praying[44] or again the state of the spiritual life, the soul's moral disposition or simply a peaceful state of soul.[45] Yet in Evagrius Ponticus, the term has a specific technical meaning, indicating the pre-eminent state; it designates 'the state of prayer', defined as 'a passionless state in which supreme love transports on high a wisdom-loving, spiritual mind'.[46] This evagrian notion was taken over by Maximus the Confessor.[47] Cassian uses the expression in a less intellectual sense: for him it is simply steadfastness of soul, centered on God by a constant remembrance of him.[48]

Depending on the various points of view, this perfect state of prayer will be defined as a 'passionless state' *(katastasis apathes),* a 'peaceful state' *(eirenike katastasis),* an 'angelic or primeval state' *(archike katastasis),* because it is a return to man's first condition, that is the 'natural state' of the soul created in the image of God. A 'state' *(stasis)* is therefore essentially long-lasting. But its second characteristic is that of connaturality. The term *katastasis* was therefore translated into Latin as *collocatio rei in sua sede*,[49] that is, 'something established in its proper place', where it should be.[50] Thus, the 'state of prayer' *(orationis status)*[51] is a habitual, natural disposition which somehow deserves the name 'prayer' in itself, aside from the acts it produces more or less frequently. It is an implicit prayer, always ready to become explicit; it is a 'state of the heart',[52] 'the state of perfection'.[53]

If we give the word 'prayer' the profound meaning of a 'filial' and 'dialogical' relationship with the heavenly Father, without being preoccupied with how it is manifested on the outside, then prayer and holiness coincide. Theophan the Recluse can therefore write that 'prayer is the quickening of the spirit, in some way its deification'.[54]

> As the lungs expand to attract the life-giving elements of air by breathing, so do the depths of our soul open and expand during prayer, and so does our spirit ascend to God to receive the gift that allows us to be united with him. And as the oxygen received by the blood is then conveyed to the entire body to vivify it, so does the gift received from God permeate everything that is in us and vitalize our entire inner being.[55]

Prayer is therefore the life of the Spirit.

Or, as John of Kronstadt writes, each fervent prayer 'will bring Christ into your heart, with the Father and the Holy Spirit'.[56] The Spirit, on his part, is crying in the depth of our heart, '*Abba,* Father!' (Rom 8:15; Gal 4:6).

## Notes

1. The *Book of Perfection,* 2.(40); CSCO 253 (*Syri* 111) 11:32–34; translated Sebastian Brock, *The Syriac Fathers on Prayer and the Spiritual Life,* CS 101 (Kalamazoo: Cistercian Publications, 1987) 218–219.

2. See p. 31.

3. *Načertanie christianskogo nravoučenija* [*Christian Moral Teaching*] (Moscow, 1895) 41. Špidlík, *Théophane le Reclus,* 239.

4. See p. 213.
5. Friedrich Heiler, *Das Gebet* (Munich, 1923); translated Samuel McComb, *Prayer: A Study in the History and Psychology of Religion* (London: Oxford University Press, 1932).
6. *Oratio* VI, *de pace,* 1.5; PG 35:728B. See Špidlík, *Grégoire de Nazianze,* 138ff.
7. *Vita Constantini,* 16.1–59; ed. F. Grivec and Fr. Tomšiè, *Radovi staroslovenskog instituta,* kniga 4 (Zagreb, 1960) 134ff.
8. Émile Bertaud and André Rayez, 'Échelle spirituelle', DSp 4/1 (1960) 62–86.
9. *Ibid.,* 67.
10. *The Way of a Pilgrim,* translated Helen Bacovcin (New York: Doubleday, Image Books, 1992) 13.
11. *A Systematic Handbook,* 307ff.
12. *Libellus de oratione,* 12; PG 11:452; CWS 104ff (see also *Origen: Prayer. Exhortation to Martyrdom,* translated John J. O'Meara. ACW 19 [1954]).
13. Antoine Guillaumont, 'Messaliens', DSp 10 (1980) 1074–1083.
14. Venance Grumel, 'Acémètes', DSp 1 (1937) 169–175.
15. *Libellus de oratione,* 12; PG 11:452 (see note 12).
16. *De haeresibus* 57; PL 42:40; translated G. Müller, *The 'De haeresibus' of St. Augustine.* Patristic Studies 90 (Washington, 1956).
17. *Demonstratio* 4.14–17; Patrologia syriaca 1 (1894) 169ff; translated Sebastian Brock, Aphrahat, *Demonstration* IV, On Prayer, *The Syriac Fathers on Prayer and the Spiritual Life,* trans. by Sebastian Brock. CS 101 (Kalamazoo: Cistercian Publications, 1987) 5ff.
18. *Regulae brevius tractatae, interrogatio* 290; PG 31:1286; see *The Ascetic Works of Saint Basil,* translated W. K. L. Clarke (London: SPCK, 1925).
19. Irénée Hausherr, *Opus Dei,* OCP 13 (1947) 195–218. Hausherr, *Études de spiritualité orientale,* OCA 183 (Rome, 1969) 121–144.
20. Evagrius, *Letter* 8; Irénée Hausherr, *Les leçons d'un contemplatif* (Paris, 1960) 74.
21. André-Jean Festugière, *Contemplation et vie contemplative selon Platon* (Paris, 1936) 108ff.
22. Evagrius, *Centuries,* 2.83; Hausherr, *Leçons,* 74.
23. *Centuries,* 5.31; Hausherr, 74.
24. Irénée Hausherr, '*Contemplation et sainteté. Une remarquable mise au point par Philoxène de Mabboug* (*décédé,* 523), *RAM* 14 (1933) 171–195. Hausherr, *Hésychasme et prière,* OCA 176 (Rome, 1966) 13–57.
25. See Špidlík, *La sophiologie de S. Basile,* 49.
26. Irénée Hausherr, *Noms du Christ et voies d'oraison,* OCA 157 (Rome, 1960) 177ff; translated Charles Cummings, *The Name of Jesus,* CS 44 (Kalamazoo: Cistercian Publications, 1978) 191ff.
27. See p. 331.
28. Hausherr, *Noms du Christ,* 187ff; *The Name,* CS 44:203ff.
29. Tomaš Špidlík, 'L'idéal du monachisme basilien', in P. J. Fedwick, *Basil of Caesarea, Christian, Humanist, Ascetic* (Toronto, 1981) I:361–374.
30. See Dt 4:9, 8:11, 9:7.
31. See Špidlík, *La sophiologie de S. Basile,* 45.
32. See p. 243.
33. *Quod Deus non est auctor malorum* 7; PG 31:344C.
34 *Homilia in Hexaemeron* 1; PG 29:3A; translated Agnes Clare, *Saint Basil: Exegetic Homilies,* FCh 46:3ff.
35. See p. 183.
36. *Čto jest duchovnaja žizň* [*What the Spiritual Life Is*], no. 51 (Moscow, 1884) 186. *Ibid.,* 50, 184.

37. Origen, *On Prayer,* 9.2; GCS 3:319, 4–8; CWS 99 and 8.2; 317, 25ff; CWS 98; also translated John J. O'Meara, *Origen: Prayer. Exhortation to Martyrdom,* ACW 19 (1954). *Constitutiones monasticae* (attributed to Basil) 1; PG 31:1333AB. John Chrysostom, *De Anna, sermo* 2; PG 54:645. John Climacus, *Scala paradisi, gradus* 28; PG 88:1129D; CWS [See *John Climacus. The Ladder of Divine Ascent,* trans. by Colm Luibheid and Norman Russell (New York: Paulist Press, 1982) in the series CWS].

38. Theophan, *Načertanie christianskogo nravoučenija* [*Christian Moral Teaching*] (Moscow, 1895) 389.

39. Basil, *Epistolarum classis* I. *ep.* 2; PG 32:230B; translated Agnes Way, FCh 13 (1951) and FCh 28 (1955)].

40. Origen, *De oratione,* 20.2; GCS 2:344–345 (see above, note 37).

41. See p. 325.

42. *A Systematic Manual,* 135ff.

43. R. Garrigou-Lagrange, *Les trois âges de la vie intérieure,* vol. 2 (Paris, 1938) 863; translated M. Timothea Doyle, *The Three Ages of the Interior Life: Prelude to Eternal Life,* vol. 2 (St Louis: Herder, 1948; rpt., Rockford, Illinois, Tan Bks and Publishers, 1991) 595.

44. Origen, *Libellus de oratione* 1 and 8; PG 11:417B and 441B.

45. Dorotheus, *Doctrina,* 17.2; PG 88:1801C; CS 33: 239 (under 18).

46. *On Prayer,* 52; Hausherr, *Leçons,* 76; PG 79:1177; CS 4:52; *Early Fathers From the Philokalia,* 133.

47. *Capitum de charitate, centuria* 2.61; PG 90:1003C; translated Polycarp Sherwood, *St. Maximus the Confessor: The Ascetic Life. The Four Centuries on Charity,* ACW 21:165.

48. *Conferences,* 10.14; PL 49:842A; SCh 54 (1958) 95ff; ACW 57:386–387; LNPF, ser. 2, 1:409]; see Salvatore Marsili, *Giovanni Cassiano ed Evagrio Pontico. Dottrina sulla carità e contemplazione,* Studia anselmiana 5 (Rome, 1936).

49. E. F. Leopold, *Lexicon Graeco-Latinum manuale* (Leipzig, 1911).

50. See Thomas Aquinas, *Summa theologiae,* 2–II. q. 183, a. 1.

51. Cassian, *Conferences,* 10.14; PL 49:842A; ACW 57:386; NPNF 11:409.

52. Hausherr, *Noms du Christ,* 137; *The Name,* CS 44:139.

53. See *S. Basilii magni sermo asceticus;* PG 31:877A.

54. *Načertanie christianskago nravoučenija* [*Christian Moral Teaching*] (Moscow, 1895) 407.

55. *Ibid.,* 406.

56. *My Life in Christ* (New York, 1994) 18.

# TABLE OF ABBREVIATIONS

| | |
|---|---|
| ACW | Ancient Christian Writers. Westminster, Maryland-New York, 1946ff. |
| ANF | Ante-Nicene Fathers. Edinburgh-New York, 1885ff. Rpt. Grand Rapids, Michigan. Rpt. Peabody, Massachusetts. |
| CS | Cistercian Studies. Spencer, Washington, Kalamazoo, 1969ff. |
| CSCO | *Corpus Scriptorum Christianorum Orientalium.* Louvain-Paris, 1903ff. |
| CSEL | *Corpus Scriptorum Ecclesiasticorum Latinorum.* Vienna, 1866ff. |
| CWS | Classics of Western Spirituality. New York, 1978ff. |
| DACL | *Dictionnaire d'Archéologie Chrétienne et de Liturgie,* ed. F. Cabrol and H. Leclercq. Paris, 1907–1953. |
| DBT | Xavier Léon-Dufour, ed. *Dictionary of Biblical Theology,* a translation of VTB, revised and enlarged. New York, 1973. |
| DESp | *Dizionario Enciclopedico di Spiritualità,* 1–2. Ed. Ermanno Ancilli, Rome, 1975. |
| DHGE | *Dictionnaire d'Histoire et de Géographie Ecclésiastiques,* ed. by A. Baudrillart. Paris, 1912ff. |
| DIP | *Dizionario degli Istituti di Perfezione.* Rome, 1973. |
| DP | *Dizionario Patristico e di Antichità Cristiane,* ed. Angelo Di Berardino, 1–2. Rome, 1983. [See also EEC] |
| DSp | *Dictionnaire de Spiritualité,* ed. M. Viller. Paris, 1932ff. |

| | |
|---|---|
| DThC | *Dictionnaire de Théologie Catholique.* Paris, 1903–1950. |
| EEC | *Encyclopedia of the Early Church,* 2 volumes. A translation of DP 1–2 by Adrian Walford. Cambridge (UK)-New York, 1992. |
| EF | *Encyclopédie de la Foi,* ed. by Heinrich Fries, 1–4. Paris, 1956–1957. |
| FCh | Fathers of the Church. New York-Washington, D.C., 1947ff. |
| GCS | Die griechischen christlichen Schriftsteller der ersten Jahrhunderte. Berlin-Leipzig, 1897ff. |
| *Grégoire de Nazianze* | Tomaš Špidlík, *Grégoire de Nazianze. Introduction à l'étude de sa doctrine spirituelle,* OCA, 189. Rome, 1971. |
| *Handbuch der Ostkirchenkunde* | Edd. Endre Von Ivanka, Julius Tyciak, and Paul Wiertz. Düsseldorf, 1971. |
| HTG | *Handbuch theologischer Grundbegriffe,* 1–2. Ed. Heinrich Fries. Munich, 1963. |
| *Joseph de Volokolamsk* | Tomaš Špidlík, *Joseph de Volokolamsk. Un chapitre de la spiritualité russe,* OCA 146. Rome, 1956. |
| JTS | The Journal of Theological Studies. London, 1899ff. |
| Kittel | Gerhard Kittel, *Theologischer Wörterbuch zum Neuen Testament,* 1–9. Stuttgart, 1933. English translation by Geoffrey W. Bromiliy, *Theological Dictionary of the New Testament,* 1–10. Grand Rapids, 1964–1974. |
| *La sophiologie de S. Basile* | Tomaš Špidlík, *La sophiologie de S. Basile.* OCA 162. Rome, 1961. |
| LNPF | A Select Library of Nicene and Post-Nicene Fathers, New York, 1886–1900. Rpt. Grand Rapids, Michigan; Peabody, Massaschusetts. |
| $LThK^2$ | *Lexikon für Theologie und Kirche,* 2nd ed. Freiburg im Breisgau, 1957–1966. |
| OC | *Orientalia Christiana.* Rome, 1923–1934. |
| OCA | *Orientalia Christiana Analecta.* Rome, 1935ff. |
| OCP | *Orientalia Christiana Periodica.* Rome, 1935ff. |

| | |
|---|---|
| PG | *Patrologia Graeca,* ed. J.-P. Migne. Paris, 1844–1855. |
| PL | *Patrologia Latina,* ed. J.-P. Migne. Paris, 1857–1866. |
| PO | *Patrologia orientalis,* edd. R. Griffin and F. Nau. Paris, 1903. |
| RAM | *Revue d'Ascétique et de Mystique*. Toulouse, 1920ff. |
| RHE | *Revue d'histoire ecclésiastique*. Louvain, 1900ff. |
| RHR | *Revue de l'histoire des Religions*. Paris, 1880ff. |
| RSR | *Recherches de Science Religieuse*. Paris, 1910ff. |
| SCh | *Sources chrétiennes*. Paris, 1941ff. |
| M. Spanneut *Le stoïcisme des Pères* | Michel Spanneut, *Le stoïcisme des Père de l'Église de Clément de Rome à Clément d'Alexandrie*. Patristica Sorbonensia. Paris, 1957. |
| SVF | Hans von Arnim, *Stoicorum Veterum Fragmenta,* 1–4. Leipzig, 1921–1924. |
| *Manuel* | Tomaš Špidlík, *La spiritualité de l'Orient chrétien. Manuel systématique,* OCA 206. Rome, 1978. |
| *A Systematic* | Tomaš Špidlík, *The Spirituality of the Christian East. A Systematic Handbook,* translated Anthony P. Gythiel. CS 79. Kalamazoo, 1986. |
| *Théophane le Reclus* | Tomaš Špidlík, *La doctrine spirituelle de Théophane le Reclus, Le coeur et l'esprit*. OCA 172. Rome, 1965. |
| TU | Texte und Untersuchungen zur Geschichte der altchristlichen Literatur. Leipzig-Berlin, 1882ff. |
| VTB | Xavier Léon-Dufour, *Vocabulaire de Théologie biblique*. Paris, 1970. |
| ZAM | *Zeitschrift für Aszese und Mystik.* (Innsbruck) Wurzburg, 1926ff. |
| ZKTh | Zeitschrift für katholische Theologie. Vienna, 1877ff. |

# SOURCE CITATIONS FOR FREQUENTLY CITED WORKS

*The Art of Prayer.*

*The Art of Prayer. An Orthodox Anthology*, compiled by Chariton of Valamo, translated by E. Kadloubovsky and G. E. H. Palmer. London: Faber and Faber, 1966.

*L'art de la prière. Anthologie de textes spirituels sur la prière du coeur*, Spiritualité orientale, 18. Begrolles-en-Mauge: Bellefontaine, 1976.

Russian original, *Umnoe delanie, O molitve Iisusivoj, Sbornik poučenii svjatych Otcov I opytnych dejatelej*. Valamo, 1936.

Athanasius. *Life of Antony.*

*Athanse d'Alexandrie. Vie d'Antoine*. Ed. G. J. M. Bartelink. SCh 400 (1994).

*Athanasius of Alexandria: The Life of Antony. The Coptic Life and The Greek Life*. Translated Tim Vivian and Apostolos N. Athanassakas, CS 202. Kalamazoo, 2002.

*The Life of Anthony*. Translated Robert T. Meyer. ACW 10 (1950).

'The Life of St Anthony', translated Mary E. Keenan. *Early Christian Biographies*. FCh 15 (1952).

LNPF, 2nd series. Volume 4.

Basil of Caesarea. *Commentary on the Hexaemeron.*

PG 29.

*Basil de Césarée. Homélies sur l'Hexaéméron*. Ed. S. Giet. SCh 26:415 (2nd edition, 1994).

*St. Basil. Exegetic Homilies.* Translated Agnes Clare Way. FCh 46 (1963).

———. *On the Holy Spirit.*

*Basile de Césarée. Traité du Saint-Esprit.* Ed. B. Pruche. SCh 17*bis* (2nd edition, 1968).
*St Basil of Caesarea. On the Holy Spirit.* Crestwood, New York, 1980.
LNPF, 2nd series. Volume 8.

*Brianchaninov, Ignace. Approches de la prière de Jesus.*

Russian edition in *Sočinenija,* 2:209–375. Saint Petersburg, 1965.
*Approches de la prière de Jesus.* French translation by Hieromonk Simeon. Spiritualité orientale, 35. Bégrolles-en-Mauges: Abbaye de Bellefontaine, 1983.
*Ignatius Brianchaninov. On the Prayer of Jesus.* Selections translated by Lazarus [Moore]. London: John M. Watkins, 1952.

Cassian. See John Cassian.

Clement of Alexandria. *Stromata,*

*Clément d'Alexandrie. Stromates,* Edd. C. Mondésert, M. Caster, P.-T. Camelot, A. Le Boulluec. Five volumes. SCh 30 , 38, 278 (1981), 279 (1981), 428 (1997)
*Stromata or Miscellanies.* ANF, volume 2.

Cyril of Jerusalem. *Catecheses.*

Cyrille de Jerusalem. *Catéchèses mystigogiques.* Edd. A. Piédagnel and P. Paris. SCh 126 (1988).
*St Cyril of Jerusalem, Works,* 1. Translated by Leo P. McCauley and Anthony P. Stephenson. FCh 61 (1969).
LNPF, 2nd series. Volume 7.

Dorotheus of Gaza. *Instructions.*

*Dorothée de Gaza. Œuvres spirituelles.* Ed. L. Regnault, J. de Préville. SCh 92 (1963).
*Dorotheos of Gaza. Discourses and Sayings.* Translated Eric P. Wheeler. CS 33. (1977).

Evagrius Ponticus. *Chapters on Prayer.*

Hausherr, Irénée. *Les leçons d'un contemplatif. Le Traité de l'oraison d'Évagre le Pontique*. Paris, 1960.
*Evagrius Ponticus: The Praktikos. Chapters on Prayer,* translated by John Eudes Bamberger. CS 4 (1970).

Gregory of Nyssa. *The Life of Moses.*

*Grégoire de Nysse. Vie de Moïse*. Ed. J. Daniélou. SCh 1*bis*. (4th edition, 1987).
*Gregory of Nyssa. The Life of Moses*. Translated Abraham Malherbe and Everett Ferguson, CWS and CS 31 (1978).

Gregory Palamas, *Défense des saints hésychastes*

Edited and translated by Jean [John] Meyendorff. Spicilegium sacrum Lovaniense, Etudes et documents, fasc. 30–31. Louvain, 1959.
*Gregory Palamas. The Triads.* An anthology of texts from Meyendorff's edition translated by Nicholas Gendle. CWS (1983).

Hazzâyâ, Rabban Jausep. *Briefe.*

*Briefe über das geistliche Leben und verwandte Schriften.* Introduced and translated into German by Gabriel Bunge in the series Sophia, Quellen östlicher Theologie, vol. 21. Trier, 1982.
See also *Lettre sur les trois étapes de la vie monastique,* édition critique du texte syriaque, traduction et introduction par Paul Harb et François Graffin. Turnhout, 1992. *Patrologia Orientalis,* vol. 45, fasc. 2=no. 202.
Critical edition and English translation of the short version of the 'Letter of the Three Stages of the Monastic Life', by G. Olinder, *A Letter of Philoxenus of Mabbug Sent to a Friend.* Acta Universitatis Gotoburgensis, Göteborgs Högskolas Årsskrift, 46 (1950:1). Göteborg, 1950.
See also E. J. Sherry, 'The Life and Works of Joseph Hazzâyâ', in *The Seed of Wisdom. Essays in Honor of T. J. Meek*. London, 1964. 78–91.

Irenaeus. *Adversus haereses*

Irenée de Lyons. *Contra les hérésies,* edd. A. Rousseau and L. Doutreleau. Seven volumes. SCh 263 and 264 (1979), SCh 293, 294 (1982), SCh 210, 211, SCh 100 (1985).
*Irenaeus Against Heresies.* ANF, volume 1.

Isaac the Syrian. *Discourses.*

*Isaac le syrien. Œuvres spirituelles. Les 86 discours ascétiques: les lettres.* Préface d'Olivier Clément; introduction du Père Basile; avant-propos, traduction et notes de Jacques Touraille. Paris: Desclée de Brouwer, 1981.
*The Ascetical Homilies of Saint Isaac the Syrian.* Translated by D. Miller. Boston: Holy Transfiguration Monastery, 1984.
Translated (from the Syriac) by A. J. Wensinck, *Mystic Treatises of Isaac of Nineveh.* Amsterdam, 1923.

John Cassian. *Conferences.*

Jean Cassien. Conférences. Ed. E. Pichery. Three volumes. SCh 42 (1966), 54 (1967), 64 (1971).
*John Cassian. The Conferences.* Translated Boniface Ramsey. ACW, 57. New York, 1997.
*John Cassian. Conferences* [1–3, 9–11, 14–15, 18]. Translated Colm Luibheid. CWS (1985).
LNPF, volume 11.

———. *Institutes.*

*Jean Cassien. Institutes cénobitiques.* Ed. J.-C. Guy. SCh 109 (1965).
*John Cassian. The Institutes.* Translated Boniface Ramsey. ACW, 58 (2000).
LNPF, volume 11.

John Climacus, *Scala paradisi.*

PG 88.
*John Climacus: The Ladder of Divine Ascent.* Translated Colm Luibheid and Norman Russell. CWS (1982).
*St. John Climacus: The Ladder of Divine Ascent.* Translated by Lazarus Moore. London, 1959. Rpt. Willits, California, 1973. Revised edition, Boston, 1978.

John Moschus, *Pratum spirituale.*

Jean Moschus. Le Pré Spirituel. Edited M.-J. Rouët de Journal. SCh 12.
*John Moschus. The Spiritual Meadow.* Translated John Wortley. CS 139 (1992).

*Life of Melania.*

*Vie de saint Melanie. Ed. D. Gorce. SCh* 90 (1960)
'The Life of Holy Melania by Gerontius.' Translated Joan M. Petersen, *Handmaids of the Lord*, CS 143:311–361 (1996).

*Macarius. See Pseudo-Macarius.*

Nicholas Cabasilas. *Commentary on the Divine Liturgy.*

*Explication de la divine liturgie,* edd. S. Salaville, R. Bornert, J. Gouillard, P. Perichon, 2nd edition. SCh 4*bis* (1967)
*A Commentary on the Divine Liturgy*. Translated J. M. Hussey and P. A. McNulty. London, 1960. Crestwood, New York, 1977.

Nicholas Cabasilas. *The Life in Christ.*

*La vie en Jésus Christ.* Ed. M.-H. Congourdeau. Two volumes. SCh 355 (1989), 361 (1990).
*The Life in Christ.* Translated Carmino J. deCatanzaro. Crestwood, New York, 1974, 1997.

Origen. *Commentary on the Gospel according to Matthew.*

*Origène. Commentaire sur l'Évangile selon Matthieu, X–XI.* Ed. R. Girod. SCh 162 (1970).
ANF, volume 10. [Second Book, 2, 10–14]

———. *Homilies on Luke.*

*Origène. Homélies sur S. Luc.* Edd. H. Crouzel, F. Fournier, P. Périchon. SCh 87 (1962).

———. *Commentary on John*

*Origène. Commentaire sur saint Jean.* Ed. C. Blanc. SCh 120*bis* (2nd ed., 1996)
*Origen. Commentary on the Gospel According to John. Books 1–10.* Translated Ronald E. Heine. FCh 80 (1989).
ANF, volume 10.

———. *Contra Celsum.*

*Origène. Contre Celse.* Ed. M. Borret. 5 volumes. SCh 132 (1967), 136 (1968), 147 (1969), 150 (1969), 227 (1976).
*Contra Celsum.* Translated Henry Chadwick. Cambridge (UK), 1953.
*Selections from the Commentaries and Homilies of Origen*, translated. R. B. Tollinton. London, 1929.
ANF, volume 4.

———. Origen. *Homilies on Leviticus.*

*Origène.Homélies sur le Lévitique.* Ed. M. Borret. SCh 286, 287 (1981).
*Origen. Homilies on Leviticus 1–16.* Translated Gary W. Barkley. FCh 83 (1990).

———. *Homilies on Numbers.*

*Origène. Homélies sur les Nombres,* Ed. A. Méhat. SCh 29 (1951).
Homily XXVII on Numbers, translated Rowan A. Greer. *Origen. An Exhortation to Martyrdom, Prayer,* Prologue to the *Commentary on the Song of Songs,* Homily XXVII on Numbers. CWS (1979).

———. *Homilies on the Song of Songs.*

*Origène. Homélies sur le Cantique des Cantiques.* Ed. O. Rousseau. SCh 37*bis* (2nd ed., 1966).
*Origen. The Song of Songs: Commentary and Homilies.* Translated R. P. Lawson. ACW 26 (1957).

———. *De oratione (On Prayer).*

PG 11.
*Origen. An Exhortation to Martyrdom, Prayer . . . .* Translated Rowan A. Greer. CWS (1979).

*Philokalia.*

*The Philokalia. The Complete Text.* 4 volumes. Translated and edited G. E. H. Palmer, Philip Sherrard, Kallistos Ware. London-Boston, 1979–1998.

*Early Fathers from the Philokalia,* together with some writings of St. Abba Dorotheus, St. Isaac of Syria, and St. Gregory Palamas. Selected and translated from the Russian text *Dobrotolubiye* by E. Kadloubovsky and G. E. H. Palmer. London, 1954.
*Writings from the Philokalia on Prayer of the Heart.* Edited and translated E. Kadloubovsky and G. E. H. Palmer. London, 1979.

Pseudo-Athanasius. *Life of Syncletica. On Virginity.*

*Vie de sainte Synclétique.* Translated J. Bouvet. Bégrolles-en-Mauge: Abbaye de Bellefontaine, 1972.
'The Life and Activity of the Holy and Blessed Teacher Syncletica', translated Elizabeth Castelli, in Vincent L. Wimbush, ed., *Ascetic Behavior in Greco-Roman Antiquity. A Sourcebook,* Studies in Antiquity and Christianity. Minneapolis, Minnesota, 1990.

Pseudo-Denys. *The Celestial Hierarchy.*

*Denys l'Aréopagite. La Hiérachie céleste.* Ed. J. Szymusiack, 2nd ed. SCh 58*bis* (1970).
*Pseudo-Dionysius: The Complete Works.* Translated Colm Luibheid. CWS (1992).

Pseudo-Macarius. *Homilies.*

*Die 50 Geistlichen Homilien des Makarios,* edd. Hermann Dörries, Erich Klostermann, Matthias Kroeger. Patristische Texte und Studien, 6. Berlin, 1964.
*Pseudo-Macaire. Œuvres spirituelles.* Ed. V. Duprez. SCh 275 (1980).
*Pseudo-Macarius. The Fifty Spiritual Homilies and the Great Letter.* Translated George A. Maloney, CWS (1992).
*Intoxicated with God.* Translated George A. Maloney. Denville, New Jersey, 1978.
*Fifty Spiritual Homilies. St Macarius the Great.* Translated A. J. Mason, London, 1921. Rpt. Willets, California, 1973.

Romanos Melodios. *Hymns.*

*Romanos le Mélode. Hymnes.* Edd. J. Grosdidier de Matons. Five volumes. SCh 99 (1964), 110 (1965), 114 (1965), 128 (1967), 283 (1981).

*Kontakia of Romanos, Byzantine melodist.* Two volumes. Translated and annotated by Marjorie Carpenter. Columbia, Missouri, 1970–1973.

Symeon the New Theologian. *Discourses.*

*Syméon le Nouveau Théologien. Catéchèses.* Edd. Basil Krivochéine and J. Paramelle. Three volumes. SCh 96 (1963), SCh 104 (1964), SCh 113 (1965)
*Symeon the New Theologian: The Discourses.* Translated Carmino J. de-Catanzaro, CWS (1980).

Symeon the New Theologian. *Discourses. [Ethiques, Livre de théologie]*

*Syméon le Nouveau Théologien. Traités théologiques et éthiques.* Ed. J. Darrouzès. Two volumes. SCh 122 (1966), 129 (1969).
*Symeon the New Theologian: The Practical and Theological Chapters and The Three Theological Discourses.* Translated Paul McGuckin. CS 4 (1982).
*St Symeon the New Theologian. The Ethical Discourses.* Two volumes. Translated Alexander Golitzin. Crestwood, New York, 1996.

Symeon the New Theologian. *Hymns.*

*Syméon le Nouveau Théologien. Hymnes,* ed. J. Koder, J. Paramelle, L. Neyrand. Three volumes. SCh 156 (1969),174 (1971), 196 (1973).
*Hymns of Divine Love,* edited and translated George A. Maloney. Denville, New Jersey. 1976.

Theodoret of Cyrrhus, *Historia religiosa.*

PG 82:1283–1496.
*A History of the Monks of Syria: The Religious History of Theodoret of Cyrrhus.* Translated by R. M. Price. CS 88 (1985).

# A SELECTED BIBLIOGRAPHY

For full bibliographic details, see Abbreviations and Source Citations

## CLASSIFIED BY TOPICS

### General bibliographical entries in encyclopedias


Greeven, Heinrich and Johannes Herrmann. 'εὔχομαι . . .', Kittel 2 (1964) 775–808.

Fonck Anton. 'Prière', DThC 13/2 (1936) 169–244.

Leclercq, Henri. 'Orant, Orante', DACL 12/2 (1936) 2291–2322

———. 'Papyrus', DACL 13/1:1382–1400.

Heiler, F., C. Westermann, J. Elbogen, O. Bauernfeind, H.L. Kulp, and H. Beintker. 'Gebet', in *Religion in Geschichte und Gegenwart,* 3rd ed., vol. 2:1209–1234. Tübingen, 1957–1965.

Thum Beda, Willibrord Hillmann, Karl Rahner, Friedrich Wulf, and Gebhard Frei. 'Gebet', LThK 4 (1960) 537–551.

*A Patristic Greek Lexicon,* ed. by Geoffrey William H. Lampe, s.v. Εὐχή [*Euche*], 380–385. Oxford, 1961.

Bernard, Ch. *Indications bibliographiques de théologie spirituelle.* Rome, 1965.

Dimitropoulos, Ch. and V. Moustakis. 'Προσευχή' in *Threstike kai ethike enkyklopaideia* 10 (1966) 640–646.

Boccassino, Renato, ed. *La preghiera,* 3 vols. Milan, 1966.

Wulf, F. 'Prière', in Heinrich Fries, EF 3 (Paris, 1966) 475–88. HTG 1, 424–435.

Sudbrack, Josef. 'Gebet', *Sacramentum mundi,* 2 (Freiburg-Basel-Vienna, 1968) 158–174.

———. 'Prayer', *Sacramentum mundi,* 5 (New York: Herder and Herder, 1970) 74–81.

Seib, G. 'Gebet', in *Lexikon der christlichen Ikonographie* 3 (1971) 332–334.

Severus, E. von. 'Gebet', in *Reallexikon für Antike und Christentum* 8 (1972) 1134–1158.

Michel, O. and Th. Klauser. 'Gebet II (Fürbitte)', *ibid.*, 9/1 (1973) 18–34.

Ancilli, Ermanno. 'Preghiera', in DESp 2, 1481–1497.

*Ecclesia orans. Mélanges Adalbert G. Hamman, Augustinianum* 20, 1–2 (1980), especially the contributions by Vittorino Grossi, H. Savon, and Victor Saxer.

Michel Dupuy. 'Oraison (Oratio, Oración)', DSp 11 (1982) 831–846.

Gribomont, Jean, Antoine Guillaumont, Tomaš Špidlík, and Adalbert de Vogüé. 'Preghiera', DIP 7 (1983) 582–606.

Martimort, Aimé-Georges. *L'Église en prière, 4. La liturgie et le temps,* bibliog., 176. Paris, 1983. Translated Matthew J. O'Connell, *The Church at Prayer,* 4:The Liturgy and Time, 153–155. Collegeville, Minnesota, 1986.

Hamman, Adalbert and Tomaš Špidlík. 'Preghiera', DP II, 2890–2899. EEC II, 706–708.

Lebrun, René and Marie-Joseph Seux. 'Prière: Les religions antiques', DSp 12/2 (1986) 2196–2202.

Méhat, André. 'La prière dans le monde gréco-romain', DSp 12/2: 2202–2217.

Grélot, Pierre. 'La prière dans la Bible', DSp 12/2: 2217–2247.

Méhat, André. 'La prière dans la tradition chrétienne: Du 2e siècle au concile de Nicée (325)', DSp 12/2: 2247–1256.

Solignac, Aimé. 'La prière: le Pères de l'Église du 4e au 6e siècle', DSp 12/2:2256–71.

## Prayer among the Church Fathers

*A Systematic Handbook,* 307–325, 407ff. (bibliog.), 439ff. (useful texts).

von der Goltz, E. *Das Gebet in der ältesten Christenheit.* Leipzig, 1901.

Genet, D. *L'enseignement d'Origène sur la prière.* Cahors, 1903.

Dibelius, Otto. *Das Vaterunser: Umrisse zu einer Geschichte des Gebetes in der alten und mittleren Kirche.* Giessen, 1903.

Sandreau, A. 'La prière chez les moines de l'antiquité', *La vie spirituelle* 8 (1923) 288–293.

Dölger, Franz Josef. *Sol salutis. Gebet und Gesang im christlichen Altertum mit besonderer Rücksicht auf die Ostung in Gebet und Liturgie.* 2nd ed. Münster, 1925.

Leclercq, Henri. 'Orant, Orante', DACL 12/2 (1936) 2291–2322; 'Papyrus', DACL 13/1:1382–1400.

Camelot, Pierre Thomas. 'L'oraison des Pères du désert', *L'Oraison*. Cahiers de la Vie spirituelle. Paris, 1947.

Olphe-Galliard, Michel. 'Cassien: Contemplation et prière', DSp 2/1 (1953) 261ff.

Jay, Eric G. *Origen's Treatise on Prayer. Translation and Notes with an Account of the Practice and Doctrine of Prayer from New Testament Times to Origen*. London, 1954.

Hausherr, Irénée. 'Comment priaient les Pères', RAM 32 (1956) 33–58, 284–296.

Perler, Othmar. 'Das Gebet der Frühkirche', *Anima* (Olten 1946–1965, for the year 1966: *Diakonia*) 14 (1956) 13–22.

Hamman, A[dalbert]. 'Genèse et signification de la prière aux origines chrétiennes', TU 64 (1957) 468–484.

Vischer, Lukas. 'Das Gebet in der alten Kirche', in *Evangelische Theologie* (Munich, 1934ff.) 17; (1957) 531–546.

Calati, B. 'Il metodo monastico della preghiera', *Vita monastica* 13 (1959) 147–157.

Hamman, Adalbert. *La prière,* vol. 2: *Les trois premiers siècles*. Tournai, 1963 (vol. 1 [1959], *Le* NT). [See also, *Early Christian Prayers,* ed. by Adalbert Hamman, and translated by Walter Mitchell. London, 1961].

Hausherr, Irénée. *Les leçons d'un contemplatif. Le Traité de l'oraison d'Évagre le Pontique*. Paris, 1960. See *Evagrius Ponticus: The Praktikos. Chapters on Prayer,* translated by John Eudes Bamberger. CS 4. Spencer-Kalamazoo, 1970.

Guy, Jean-Claude. *Jean Cassien. Vie et doctrine*. Paris, 1961.

Papadopoulos, N.G. 'Prayer According to Origen' (in Greek), *Gregorios Palamas* 45 (1962) 46–51, 124–129.

Weiss, B., ed. *Gebete und Betrachtungen der Kirchenväter*. Munich, 1963. [See also, Tomaš Špidlík, *Breviario Patristico* (1971), translated by Paul Drake as *Drinking from the Hidden Fountain: A Patristic Breviary. Ancient Wisdom for Today's World,* CS 148. Kalamazoo, 1994.]

Vedernikov, A. 'Der heilige Johannes Klimakos als Lehrer des Gebetes', *Stimme der Orthodoxie* (Berlin) 4 (1964) 43–49; 5 (1964) 46–52.

Vagagini, Cipriano, Gregorio Penco, *et al. La preghiera nella Bibbia a nella tradizione patristica e monastica*. Rome, 1964.

Gribomont, Jean. 'La preghiera secondo S. Basilio', *ibid.,* 371–97.

Hausherr, Irénée. *Prière de vie—vie de prière*. Paris, 1965.

———. *Hésychasme et Prière,* OCA 176. Rome, 1966 (rpt of articles).

Simpson, Robert L. *The Interpretation of Prayer in the Early Church.* Philadelphia, 1965.

Cerfaux, Lucien. 'La prière dans le christianisme primitif', in A. Plé, ed., *La prière,* 2nd ed. London-Cambridge, 1968.

Khalifé-Hachem, E. 'La prière pure et la prière spirituelle chez Isaac de Ninive', *Memorial G. Khouri-Sarkis,* 157–173. Louvain, 1969.

Jungmann, Joseph Andreas. *Christliches Beten in Wandel und Bestand.* Munich, 1969. Translation by John Coyne, *Christian Prayer Through the Centuries.* New York, 1978.

Fischer, B. 'La prière ecclésiale et familiale dans le christianisme ancien', *La Maison-Dieu* 116 (1973) 41–58.

Regnault, Lucien. 'La prière continuelle "monologistos" dans la littérature apophtegmatique', *Irénikon* 47 (1974) 467–493.

Gessel, Wilhelm. *Die Theologie des Gebetes nach 'De oratione' von Origenes.* Munich-Paderborn-Vienna, 1975.

Benito y Duran, A. 'La oración en pensamiento y en la Regla de S. Basilio Magno', *Teologia espiritual* 20 (1976) 33–159.

Cristiano, C. *La preghiera nei Padri,* coll. La spiritualità cristiana, Studi e Testi 4. Rome, 1981.

THE NECESSITY OF PRAYER, P. 31.

Aphraates. *Demonstration 4, On Prayer; Patrologia Syriaca* 1 (1984) 137; translated Sebastian Brock, *The Syriac Fathers on Prayer and the Spiritual Life.* CS 101:5–25.

Evagrius, *Chapters on Prayer,* 150; Hausherr, *Leçons,* 181ff; CS 4:79.

Mark the Monk. 'Controverse avec un avocat', 7, *Spiritualité orientale,* 4:161ff. Bellefontaine, 1985.

Hazzâyâ, Rabban Jausep. *Briefe,* 248ff.

See PG 46:361 *(precatio),* 329 *(oratio)—Index in opera S. Joannis Chrysostomi.*

Fonck, Anton. 'Prière', DThC 13/2 (1936) 199ff.

THE DEFINITIONS OF PRAYER, P. 33.

Evagrius, *Chapters on Prayer,* 35 and 3; Hausherr, 53, 16ff; CS 4:60, 56.

Hazzâyâ, R. J. *Briefe,* 247.

Bolshakoff, Sergei. 'Theophan the Recluse', *I mistici russi,* 211ff. Turin, 1962. Sergius Bolshakoff, *Russian Mystics,* CS 26:196ff. Kalamazoo 1976.

*The Art of Prayer,* 16–17, 50, 53, 93; *L'art de la prière,* 15ff, 62, 66, 123.

THE VARIOUS TYPES OF PRAYER, P. 35.

Irenaeus. *Adversus haereses* 4.1.1ff; SCh 100 (1985) 292ff; ANF 1:463ff.
Cyril of Jerusalem. *Catecheses,* 7; translated Leo P. McCauley and Anthony P. Stephenson. FCh 61:170–179.
Philoxenus of Mabbug. *Homily* 2.28; SCh 44 (1956) 59ff.
Nicholas Cabasilas. *A Commentary on the Divine Liturgy,* 31; *Explication de la divine liturgie,* SCh 4*bis:* 198ff; translated J. M. Hussey and P. A. McNulty, 79ff. London, 1960. Crestwood, New York, 1977.
See Solignac, Aimé. 'Pater noster: Inventaire des commentaires', DSp 12/1 (1984) 389ff.
*A Systematic Handbook,* 42, 369 (bibliog.), 417 (texts).
Berrouard, Marie-François. 'Enfance spirituelle: dans l'Écriture et chez les Pères', DSp 4/1 (1960) 682–705.
Lefèbvre, Georges. 'Familiarité avec Dieu', DSp 5 (1964) 47–61.
Jeremias, Joachim. *Das tägliche Gebet im Leben Jesu und in der ältesten Kirche. Abba. Studien zur neutestamentlichen Theologie und Zeitgeschichte.* Göttingen, 1965.
Traets, Charles. 'Voir Jesus et le Père en lui selon l'évangile de S. Jean', *Analecta Gregoriana* 159. Rome, 1967.
Marchel, Witold. *Abba, Père. La prière du Christ et des chrétiens.* Rome, 1971.
Galot, Jean. 'Il "padre" nella preghiera liturgica', *La Civiltà cattolica* I (1972) 8–17.
Schenker, A. 'Gott als Vater—Söhne Gottes', *Freiburger Zeitschrift für Philosophie und Theologie* 25 (1978) 1–55.
Marchel, Witold and Jean Ansaldi. 'Paternité de Dieu', DSp 12/1 (1984) 413–437.
Galot, Jean. *Découvrir le Père. Esquisse d'une théologie du Père.* Louvain, 1985. Translated M. Angeline Bouchard, *Abba, Father, We Long to See Your Face: Theological Insights into the First Person of the Trinity.* New York, 1992.

'PATER NOSTER' ('OUR FATHER'), P. 36.

Dibelius, Otto. *Das Vaterunser: Umrisse zu einer Geschichte des Gebetes in der alten und mittleren Kirche.* Giessen, 1903.
Walter, G. *Untersuchungen zur Geschichte der griechischen Vaterunser-Exegese.* Leipzig, 1914.
Chase, Frederic Henry. *The Lord's Prayer in the Early Church,* coll. Texts and Studies 3. Cambridge, 1891; rpt Nendeln, 1967.

Hamman, Adalbert, ed. *Le Pater expliqué per les Pères*. Paris, 1952; enlarged ed., 1962 (a selection of texts in translation).

———. 'Le Notre Père dans la catéchèse des Pères de l'Église', *La Maison-Dieu,* 85 (1966), 41–68.

Carmignac, J. *Recherches sur le 'Notre Père'*. Paris, 1969.

Sorsoli, C. 'Padre nostro', DESp II, 1361–1365.

Sabugal, S. 'El "Padre nuestro", tradiciòn litteraria y commentarios patristicos', *Revista augustiniana de espiritualidad* 21 (1980) 47–72.

Solignac, Aimé. 'Pater noster', DSp 12/1 (1984) 388–413.

Pollastri Alessandra. 'Padre nostro', DP, 2565–7; 'Lord's Prayer', EEC 1:506.

Légasse, S. 'Oraison dominicale', Catholicisme 10:112–124.

PRAYER THROUGH THE SON, P. 37.

Evagrius. *Chapters on Prayer,* 38; Hausherr, *Leçons,* 82ff; CS 4:64.

Gregory Palamas. *Défense des saints hésychastes,* II, 3, 46. Louvain, 480ff.

Gregory of Nareg. *Le livre de prières* 57; SCh 78 (1961) 307ff.

Nicholas Cabasilas. *A Commentary on the Divine Liturgy,* 44; *Explication de la divine liturgie,* SCh 4*bis:*252ff; translated Hussey and McNulty, 100ff. London 1960. Crestwood, New York 1077.

———. *La vie en Jésus Christ.* Chevetogne, 1960; translated Carmino J. deCatanzaro, *The Life in Christ.* Crestwood, New York, 1974, 1997.

Irina Goraïnov, 'Seraphim of Sarov', *Saint Séraphim de Sarov: Sa vie; Entretien avec Motovilov et Instructions spirituelles* (Bellefontaine, 1973) 182ff. See also the Index, s.v. Prayer, in Constantine Cavarnos and Mary-Barbara Zeldin, *St. Seraphim of Sarov.* Modern Orthodox Saints, no. 5. Belmont, Massachusetts, 1980.

The Art of Prayer, 193ff; *L'art de la prière,* 242ff.

DEVOTION TO THE HUMANITY OF CHRIST, P. 41.

*A Systematic Handbook,* 38, 44 (contemplating the mysteries of the life of Christ), 366 (bibliog.).

Noye, Irénée. 'Enfance de Jésus (dévotion à l')', DSp 4/1 (1960) 652–682.

Robilliard, Jean-Augustin. 'Face (Dévotion à la sainte Face)', DSp 5 (1964) 26–33.

Noye, Irénée and Paul Agaësse. 'Humanité du Christ (Dévotion et contemplation)', DSp 7/1 (1969) 1033–1053.

Loeser, Werner. 'Mystères de la vie du Christ', DSp 10 (1980) 1874–1886.

CONTEMPLATING THE MYSTERIES OF THE LIFE OF CHRIST, P. 43.

Symeon the New Theologian. *Catéchèses* 22.268ff; SCh 113:118ff; *The Discourses,* CWS, 284ff. New York, 1980.

———. Eighth Discourse, 21ff; *Éthiques,* SCh 129 (1967) 204ff; translated Alexander Golitzin, *St Symeon the New Theologian. The Ethical Discourses,* vol. 2:103ff. Crestwood, New York, 1996.

Nicholas Cabasilas. *The Life in Christ,* 6. New York, 1974, 49ff; *La vie en Jésus-Christ* (Chevetogne, 1960) 152ff.

Symeon of Thessalonika. *Treatise on Prayer,* 16ff. Brookline, Massachusetts, 1984.

PRAYER IN THE SPIRIT, P. 39.

Basil. *On the Holy Spirit,* 25–26; *Traité du Saint-Esprit,* SCh 17*bis:* 456ff; LNPF, 2nd ser., 8:37ff; *On the Holy Spirit.* Crestwood, New York, n.d.

Evagrius. *Chapters on Prayer,* 62; Hausherr, 88ff; CS 4:65.

Hazzâyâ, Rabban Jausep. *Briefe,* Sophia, vol. 21:333ff.

Irina Goraïnov. 'Seraphim of Sarov', *Saint Séraphim de Sarov* (Bellefontaine, 1973) 188ff. [For a description of prayer in the Spirit, see also 'A Conversation with the Saint by Nicholas A. Motovilov', in Constantine Cavarnos and Mary-Barbara Zeldin, *St. Seraphim of Sarov* (Belmont, Mass., 1980) 93ff.]

The Art of Prayer, 181ff; *L'art de la prière,* 238ff.

*A Systematic Handbook,* 29, 94, 365 (bibliog.) 416 (texts).

Fonck, Anton. 'Prière', DThC 13/2 (1936) 220ff.

Galtier, Paul. 'Le Saint-Esprit en nous d'après les Pères grecs', *Analecta Gregoriana,* theol. ser. 35 (Rome, 1946).

Bieder, W. 'Gebetwirklichkeit und Gebetmöglichkeit bei Paulus. Das Beten des Geistes und das Beten im Geiste', *Theologische Zeitschrift* (Basel, 1945ff.) 4 (1948) 22–40.

Lécuyer, Joseph. 'Docilité au Saint-Esprit', DSp 3 (1957) 1471–1494.

Bertaud, Émile and André Rayez. 'Dévotion au Saint-Esprit', DSp 3 (1957) 274ff.

Vandenbroucke, François. 'Esprit Saint: dans la liturgie', DSp 4/2 (1961) 1283–1296.

Niederwinner, K. 'Das Gebet des Geistes (Röm 8,26f.)', *Theologische Zeitschrift* 20 (1964) 252– 265.

*Théophane le Reclus,* 239ff.

Siman, E. P. *L'Expérience de l'Esprit par l'Église d'après la tradition syrienne d'Antioche,* coll. Théologie historique 15 (Paris, 1971).

Behler, Gebhard-Maria. 'Prier dans l'Esprit et prier sans cesse selon le nouveau Testament', *La Maison-Dieu,* 109 (1972) 31–50.

Bobrinskoy, Boris, 'Quelques réflexions sur la pneumatologie du culte', *Mélanges liturgiques . . . B. Botte* (Louvain, 1972) 19–29.

De Goedt, M. 'Die Interzession des Geistes im christlichen Gebet (Röm 8, 27)', *Concilium* 8 (1972) 654–660.

*Ökumenische Prospektiven. Wiederentdeckung des heiligen Geistes. Der heilige Geist in der chrismatischen Erfahrung und theologischen Reflexion. Ökumenische Prospektiven* 6, Frankfurt am Main, 1974.

Afasanieff, N. *L'Église du Saint-Esprit.* Paris, 1975.

*Conférences Saint-Serge. Le Saint-Esprit dans la liturgie. Conférences Saint-Serge,* XVIe *Semaine d'études liturgiques* (Paris, July, 1969) Rome, 1977.

*Convegno di studio. Spiritu Santo e catechesi patristica. Convegno di studio* (Rome, March 6–7, 1982) Rome, 1983.

Sullivan, Francis A. 'Pentecôtisme', DSp 12/1 (1984) 1036–1052.

Epiclesis, p. 40.

Cyril of Jerusalem. *Catéchèses,* 3.3; SCh 126 (1966) 124; FCh 61:109ff.

Brightman, Frank Edward. *Liturgies Eastern and Western; Being the Texts, Original or Translated, of the Principal Liturgies of the Church,* 386ff. and 404ff. Oxford, 1896. (The Liturgy of Saint John Chrysostom and of Saint Basil.)

Nicholas Cabasilas. *A Commentary on the Divine Liturgy,* 19.1; Explication de la divine liturgie, SCh 4*bis:*178ff; Hussey-McNulty translation, 57ff. Crestwood, New York, 1960.

*A Systematic Handbook,* 33.

Salaville S[évérin]. 'Épiclèse'. DThC 5 (1913) 194–300.

Cabrol, Fernand. 'Épiclèse'. DACL 5/1 (1922) 142–184.

Lukman, F. K. 'La doctrine de N. Cabasilas et de Symeon de Thessalonique sur l'Épiclèse' (in Slovenian), *Bogoslovni Vestnik* 7 (Ljubljana, 1927) 1–14.

Atchley, Edward G. *On the Epiclesis of the Eucharistic Liturgy and in the Consecration of the Font.* Alcuin Club 31. London, 1935.

Goldhammer, Kurt. *Die eucharistische Epiklese in der mittelalterlichen abendländischen Frömmigkeit.* Marburg, 1941 (Dissertation).

Chavasse, A. 'L'épiclèse eucharistique dans les anciennes liturgies orientales', *Mélanges de sciences religieuses* 3 (1946) 197–206.

Salaville, Sévérin. 'Épiclèse eucharistique', *Catholicisme* 4 (1956) 302–307.

De Jong, Johannes Petrus. 'Epiklese', LThK 3 (1959) 935–937 (bibliog.).

L'Huillier, Pierre. 'Théologie de l'épiclèse', *Verbum Caro* 56 (1960) 307–328.

Lager, J. 'Epiklesis', *Reallexikon für Antike und Christentum* 5 (1962) 577–599 (bibliog.).

Gouillard, J. Introduction to *L'Explication de la divine liturgie* by N. Cabasilas, SCh 4*bis* (1967), 31–36, and 312ff.

Heiler, Friedrich. *Die Religionen der Menschheit. Le religioni dell'umanità,* 324–326. Milan, 1958.

THE INTERCESSION OF THE SAINTS, P. 46.

Theodoret of Cyrrhus. *Thérapeutique des maladies helléniques,* VIII; SCh 57 (1958) 310–335 (the cult of the martyrs). See also, *Sermo* VIII; PG 83:1008ff.

Symeon the New Theologian. *Catéchèses,* 6; SCh 104:12ff; CWS (1980) 119ff.

———. 'The First Discourse', 6.1ff and 10. 81; *Livre d'éthique,* SCh 122:224ff, 252ff; *St Symeon the New Theologian . . . : The Ethical Discourses,* 1 43ff. Crestwood, New York, 1996.

Nicholas Cabasilas. *A Commentary on the Divine Liturgy*, 49; *Explication de la divine liturgie,* SCh 4*bis:*274ff, 347ff; Hussey-McNulty translation, 268ff; 108ff.

Nerses-Šnorhali. *Jésus Fils unique du Pere;* SCh 203 (1973) 196ff.

*A Systematic Handbook,* 41, 158, 388.

Lucius, E. *Les origines du culte des saints dans l'Église chrétienne.* Paris, 1908.

Peeters, D. 'La canonisation des saints dans l'Église russe', *Analecta Bollandiana* 33 (1914) 380–420; 38 (1920) 172–176.

Delehaye, Hippolyte. *Sanctus. Essai sur le culte des saints dans l'antiquité.* Subsidia Hagiographica 17. Brussels, 1927, rpt 1954.

Hild, J. 'Le mystère des saints dans le mystère chrétien', *La Maison-Dieu* 52 (1957) 5–18.

Denis-Boulet, N. M. *Le calendrier chrétien,* coll. Je sais, je crois 112. Paris, 1959.

Ware, Timothy [Kallistos]. 'The Communion of Saints', in A. J. Philippou, *The Orthodox Ethos,* 140–149. Oxford, 1964.

Trembelas, P. N. *Dogmatique de l'Église orthodoxe catholique,* vol. 2:439–53. Desclée de Brouwer and Editions de Chevetogne, 1967.

Noret, Jacques. 'Ménologes, Synaxaires, Ménées. Essai de clarification d'une terminologie', *Analecta Bollandiana* 86 (1968) 21–24.

Wiertz, P. 'Zur religiösen Volkskultur der orientalischen und orthodoxen Kirchen. Volksglauben und Volksgebrauch', *Handbuch der*

*Ostkirchenkunde,* 569–632. Düsseldorf, 1971; and 'Die Volkstümliche Heiligenverehrung', *ibid.,* 584–589.

Nicolas, Marie-Joseph. 'Intercession', DSp 7/2 (1971) 1858–1870.

Saxer, Victor. *Morts. Martyrs, Reliques en Afrique chrétienne aux premiers siècles: les témoignages de Tertullien, Cyprien et Augustin à la lumière de l'archéologie africaine.* Théologie historique 55. Paris, 1980.

Jounel, Pierre. 'L'année', Aimé-George Martimort, *L'Église en prière,* vol. 4:124–145. Paris, 1983; 'The Year', A. G. Martimort, *The Church at Prayer:* An Introduction to the Liturgy, vol. 4:31–76. Collegeville, Minnesota, 1986.

Saxer, Victor. 'Santi (intercessione)', DP 2, 3079–3081; 'Saints (intercession of)', EEC 2:752– 753.

Chapungco, Anscar. 'Intercessione', DP 2:1786–1787; 'Intercession', EEC 1:410.

VENERATION OF THE MOTHER OF GOD, P. 47.

*A Systematic Handbook,* 158, 388 (bibliog.), 425 (texts).

Špidlík, Tomaš. 'La devozione alla Madre di Dio nelle Chiese orientali', *Scripta de Maria* 4 (1981) 123–157.

———. 'Maria e lo Spirito santo nella Chiesa orientale', *Maria e lo Spirito Santo* (Acts of the Fourth International Mariological Congress, Rome, October, 1982) 104–132. Bologna, 1984.

Jounel Pierre. 'Le culte de Marie', Aimé-George Martimort, *L'Église en Prière,* vol. 4:146–166. Desclée, 1983; 'The Veneration of Mary', A. G. Martimort, *The Church at Prayer,* vol. 4:130–150. Collegeville, Minnesota, 1986.

*Handbuch der Marienkunde,* ed. Wolfgang Beinert and Heinrich Petri. Regensburg, 1984.

THE ANGELS, P. 48.

Origen. *Homélies sur S. Luc,* 12.3; SCh 87 (1962) 200ff.

———. *Homélies sur les Nombres,* 11; SCh 29 (1951) 211ff. See also, *Selections from the Commentaries and Homilies of Origen,* translated. R. B. Tollinton. London, 1929.

———. *Contra Celsum,* 5.52; SCh 147 (1969) 146ff; ANF 4:566ff.

Evagrius. *Chapters on Prayer,* 80ff; Hausherr, *Leçons,* 112ff; CS 4:68ff.

Pseudo-Denys. *The Celestial Hierarchy,* SCh 58*bis* (1970); translated Colm Luibheid, *Pseudo-Dionysius: The Complete Works,* CWS. New York, 1987.

Theodoret of Cyrrhus, *Thérapeutique des maladies helléniques,* 3.87ff; SCh 57 (1958) 196ff.

Hazzâyâ, Rabban Jausep. *Briefe,* 155ff.

Gregory of Nareg, *Le livre de prières,* 81; SCh 78 (1961) 432ff.

Gregory Palamas, *Défense des saints hésychastes,* II, 3, 28ff; Louvain, 442ff.

Symeon of Thessalonike, *Treatise on Prayer,* 9ff. Brookline, Massachusetts, 1984.

Grundman, Walter, 'ἄγγελος in the Greek and Hellenistic World', Kittel 1 (1964) 74–87.

*Varii.* 'Angels', *Catholicisme* 1 (1948) 538–548.

Daniélou, Jean. *Origène,* s.v. 'Angélogie', 219ff. Paris, 1948; translated Walter Mitchell, *Origen,* 'Angelology', 220–245. New York, 1955.

Recheis, A. *Engel, Tod und Seelenreise. Das Wirken der Geister beim Heimgang des Menschen in der Lehre der Alexandrinischen und Kappadokischen Väter.* Rome, 1958.

Detlef, C. and G. Müller. *Die Engellehre der koptischen Kirche. Untersuchungen zur Geschichte der christlichen Frömmigkeit in Aegypten.* Wiesbaden, 1959.

Struggnel, J. 'The Angelic Liturgy at Qumran', *Vetus Testamentum Supplementa* 7 (1960).

Trembelas, Panagiotis N. *Dogmatique de l'Église orthodoxe catholique,* vol. 1:462–498. Chevetogne: Desclée de Brouwer, 1966.

Heiser, Lothar. *Die Engel im Glauben der Orthodoxie,* coll. Sophia 13. Trier, 1976.

THE PRAYER OF SUPPLICATION, P. 53.

Evagrius. *Chapters on Prayer,* 31ff; Hausherr, *Leçons,* 49ff; 89, 123; CS 4:60, 70.

Isaac the Syrian. 44th Discourse; *Oeuvres spirituelles,* 252ff. See also, *Mystic Treatises by Isaac of Nineveh,* translated A. J. Wensinck. Amsterdam, 1923, rpt Wiesbaden, 1969; and *The Ascetical Homilies of Saint Isaac the Syrian,* translated Sebastian Brock. Boston, 1984.

Symeon the New Theologian. *Hymn* 38; *Hymnes,* SCh 174:458ff; *Hymns of Divine Love,* translated George A. Maloney, 197–198.

Nicholas Cabasilas. *A Commentary on the Divine Liturgy,* 12 and 17; *Explication de la divine liturgie,* SCh 4*bis:*106ff, 132ff; Hussey-McNulty translation, 43ff and 54ff.

Symeon of Thessalonika, *Treatise on Prayer* 46, 62ff. Brookline, Mass., 1984.

*A Systematic Handbook,* 309.
Fonck A[nton]. 'Prière', DThC 13/2 (1936) 278ff.
Baumstark, Anton. 'Litanies de demande', *Liturgie comparée,* 3rd ed. (Chevetogne, 1953) 80–90: translated F. L. Cross, *Comparative Liturgy.* Westminster, Md., 1958.
Ruppolt, L. *Die theologische Grundlage des Bit-Gebetes im NT.* Leipzig, 1953 (dissertation).
Derville, André. 'Ennemies: prier pour ses ennemies', DSp 4/1 (1960) 757ff.
Fischer, Balthasar, 'Litanies', DSp 9 (1976) 865–72 (bibliog.).
Guillet, Jacques. 'Parole de Dieu', DSp 12/1 (1984) 237–52.
Heiler, Friedrich. *Die Religionen der Menschheit. Le religioni dell'umanita* (Milan, 1985) 313–340.

THANKSGIVING P. 53.

Basil. *Homilia de gratiarum actione,* PG 31:217–237.
Evagrius. *Chapters on Prayer,* 15; Hausherr, *Leçons,* 29; CS 4:58.
Cassian. *Conferences,* 9.14; SCh 54:51ff; translated Ramsey, 338; translated Luibheid, CWS, 109.
Pseudo-Macarius. *Homily* 17.3; SCh 275 (1980) 212ff; translated George A. Maloney, *Intoxicated with God: The Fifty Spiritual Homilies of Macarius,* 118ff, rpt as *Pseudo Macarius: The Fifty Spiritual Homilies and The Great Letter,* CWS, 136. New York, 1992.
John Chrysostom. *In Epistola ad Romanos, Homily* 2.1; PG 60:401.
Mark the Monk. *À Nicolas,* 2 and 6, Spiritualité orientale 41:134ff, 139ff. See *Letter to Nicolas* in *The Philokalia. The Complete Text,* 2:147ff.
Nicholas Cabasilas. *Explication de la divine liturgie,* 41 and 56; SCh 4*bis:* 236ff, 296; *A Commentary on the Divine Liturgy,* 94.
Boobyer, G. B. '*Thanksgiving' and the 'Glory of God' in Paul.* Leipzig, 1929.
Monier-Vinard, H. 'Action de Grâce', DSp 1 (1936) 178–185.
Westermann, Claus. *Das Lob Gottes in den Psalmen,* 2nd ed. Göttingen, 1916; 4th ed., 1968; translated Keith R. Crim and Richard N. Soulen, *Praise and Lament in the Psalms.* Atlanta, 1981.
Hausherr, Irénée. 'La prière perpetuelle du chrétien', in *Laïcat et Sainteté,* vol. 2 (Rome, 1965) 111–160; Hausherr, OCA 176 (1966) 255–306.
Deseille, Placide. 'Gloire de Dieu', DSp 6 (1967) 421–463.
Saint-Jean, Raymond. 'Gratitude', DSp 6 (1966) 776–781.

Trémeau, T. 'La louange de Dieu. Sa valeur théologique et spirituelle', *Esprit et Vie* (1971) 266–269.

Ridouard André and Jacques Guillet. 'Action de grâces', VTB, 12–15; 'Thanksgiving', DBT 598–600.

Gaillard, Jean. 'Louange', DSp 9 (1976) 1020–1034.

Hamman, Adalbert. 'Dossologia', DP I:1042–1043; 'Doxology', EEC 1:252.

PRAYER FOR THE FORGIVENESS OF SINS, P. 63.

Cassian. *Conferences,* 9.22 and 20; SCh 54:59ff; Ch 64: 56–72; Ramsey, ACW 57: 343, 693–704; Luibheid, CWS 114–115; LNPF, 2nd ser., 11: 496ff.

Romanos Melodios. *Hymn* 55; SCh 283 (1981) 512ff; translated M. Carpenter, *Kontakia of Romanos,* 2 vols. Columbia, Missouri, 1970–1973.

Nicholas Cabasilas. *A Commentary on the Divine Liturgy,* 34; *Explication de la divine liturgie,* SCh 4*bis:* 212ff; Hussey-McNulty translation, 85ff.

Symeon of Thessalonika, *Treatise on Prayer* 29. Brookline, Mass., 1984, 42ff.

See Compunction, *penthos* in *A Systematic Handbook,* 193ff. 394 (bibliog.)

PRAYING FOR OTHERS, P. 64.

Evagrius. *Chapters on Prayer,* 103 ('against others'); Hausherr, *Leçons,* 139ff; CS 4:72.

John Chrysostom. *In Epistolam ad Philipp. cap.* I, *homily* 3.4; PG 62:203ff. (for the dead). See *Homily* III *on Philippians,* LNPF 13:193ff.

Gregory of Nareg. *Le livre de prières,* 83; SCh 78 (1961) 442ff. (for enemies and friends).

Nicholas Cabasilas. *A Commentary on the Divine Liturgy,* 23.1ff; SCh 4*bis:*158ff; Hussey-McNulty, 62ff.

PRAYERS FOR THE DEAD, P. 66.

Gregory of Nareg. *Le livre de prières,* 86; SCh 78 (1961) 454.

Nicholas Cabasilas. *A Commentary on the Divine Liturgy,* 42; SCh 4*bis:*240ff, see also 345ff; Hussey-McNulty, 96ff.

Symeon of Thessalonike, *De ordine sepulturae.* PG 155:669–96.

Harden, J. M., trans. *The Ethiopic Didascalia.* chapter 34. New York, 1920. 166ff.

Rush, A. C. *Death and Burial in Christian Antiquity*, Studies in Christian Antiquity 1. Washington D.C., 1941.

*Le mystère de la mort et sa célébration*, coll. Lex orandi 12. Paris, 1951.

Wiertz, P. 'Tod und Begrabnis', *Zur religiösen Volkskultur der orientalischen und orthodoxen Kirchen. Volksglauben und Volkbrauch*. Düsseldorf, 1971. 569–632; 624ff.

*La maladie et la mort du chrétien dans la liturgie. Conférences Saint-Serge* XXI, 1974. Coll. *Bibliotheca Ephemerides liturgicae, Subsidia* 1. Rome, 1975; translated M. J. O'Connell, *Temple of the Holy Spirit. Sickness and Death of the Christian in the Liturgy*. New York, 1983.

Adnes, Pierre. 'Liturgie de la mort', DSp 10 (1980) 1769–1777 (bibliog.).

Sicard, Damien, 'La mort du chrétien', Aimé-Georges Martimort, *L'Église en prière,* vol. 3:238–258. Descleé de Brouwer, 1984; 'Christian Death', A. G. Martimort, *The Church at Prayer,* vol. 3:221ff. Collegeville, Minn., 1987.

Saxer, Victor. 'Morti (culto dei)', DP 2:2303–2306; 'Dead, Cult of the,' EEC 1:221–222.

PERSEVERING IN THE REQUEST, P. 67.

Origen. *On Prayer,* 12; *Libellus de oratione,* PG 11:452ff; translated Rowan A. Greer, *Origen: An Exhortation to Martyrdom, Prayer . . .* , CWS, 104ff. New York, 1979.

Evagrius. *Chapters on Prayer,* 34 and 88; Hausherr, *Leçons,* 51,122; CS 4: 60, 69–70.

John Chrysostom. *In Matthaeum homilia,* 22.5; PG 57:306; LNPF 10:150ff.

Saint-Jean, Raymond. 'Persévérance', DSp 12/1 (1984) 1178–1184.

See Pray Unceasingly, p. 361.

MIRACLES, P. 68.

Origen. *Contra Celsum,* 1.66 and 2.48; SCh 132 (1967) 258ff, 390; ANF 4:426; 449.

Origen. *Commentary on the Gospel according to Matthew,* 10.19; SCh 162 (1970) 228ff; ANF 9:426ff.

Athanasius. *On the Incarnation of the Word,* 38; SCh 199 (1973) 398ff; translated A Religious of CSMV, *The Incarnation of the Word of God.* Crestwood, New York, 1946.

Cassian. *Conferences,* 20.7ff; SCh 54 (1954) 230; translated Ramsey, ACW 57: 697–698; LNPN, 2nd ser. 11:448.

*Life of Saint Melania,* 62ff; SCh 90 (1962) 246ff; translated Joan M. Petersen, *Handmaids of the Lord,* CS 143:283ff. Kalamazoo, 1996.

Romanos Melodios. *Hymn* 18 *on the wedding at Cana;* SCh 110 (1965) 300ff; translated M. Carpenter, *Kontakia of Romanos, Byzantine Melodist,* I: *On the Person of Christ;.* II: *On Christian Life,* Columbia, Missouri, 1970, 1973.

Isaac the Syrian. 36th Discourse; *Oeuvres,* 221ff (Desclée de Brouwer, 1981); translated A. J. Wensinck, *Mystic Treatises by Isaac of Nineveh.* Amsterdam, 1923, repr. Wiesbaden, 1967.

*A Systematic Handbook,* 74.

Hausherr, Irénée. *Direction spirituelle en Orient autrefois,* OCA 144 (Rome, 1955) 51ff; translated Anthony P. Gythiel, *Spiritual Direction in the Early Christian East,* CS 116 (Kalamazoo, 1990) 58ff.

Rodé, F. *Le miracle dans la controverse moderniste,* coll. Théologie historique 3, Paris, 1965.

Metz, Johann Baptist and Louis Monden. 'Miracle', *Sacramentum Mundi* 4 (1969) 44–49.

Sabourin, L. *The Divine Miracles Discussed and Defended.* Rome, 1977.

Latourelle, René. 'Miracolo', *Nuovo Dizionario di Teologia* (Rome, 1977) 931–945.

Léon-Dufour, Xavier, *et al. Les miracles de Jésus selon le Nouveau Testament.* Paris, 1977.

Latourelle, René. 'Miracle', DSp 10 (1980) 1274–1286 (bibliog.).

Saxer, V[ictor]. 'Fulminata (legio XII)'; DP I, 1410–1411; EEC 1:332.

Heiler, Friedrich. *Die Religionen der Menschheit. Le religioni dell'umanità* (Milan, 1985) 3301ff.

THE BODY DURING PRAYER, P. 74.

Hippolytus of Rome. *The Apostolic Tradition,* 36 (on the sign of the Cross); SCh 11: 37ff; translated Gregory Dix, *The Treatise on the Apostolic Tradition of St. Hippolytus of Rome.* London, 1934; translated B. S. Easton, *The Apostolic Tradition of Hippolytus.* Cambridge, 1924; translated Alistair Stewart-Sykes, *On the Apostolic Tradition, Hippolytus.* Crestwood, New York, 2001.

Evagrius. *Chapters on Prayer,* 105, 152; Hausherr, *Leçons,* 140, 84; CS 4:73, 80.

Cassian. *Institutes* 2.12; SCh 109 (1965) 78ff; LNPF, 2nd ser., 11:210.

Gregory Palamas. *Défense des saints hésychastes,* I, 2, 1ff and II, 2,14; Louvain, 75ff, 348ff; translated Nicholas Gendle, *Gregory Palamas: The Triads,* CWS, pp. 41, 53.

Symeon the New Theologian, *Catéchèses,* 4.207ff; SCh 96 (1963) 332ff. *Catéchèses,* 25.168ff; SCh 113 (1965) 62ff; translated C. J. DeCatanzaro, *Symeon the New Theologian,* CWS, 41, 53. New York, 1980.

Brianchaninov, Ignace. *Approches de la prière de Jésus,* 99; selections translated by Lazarus [Moore] in *Ignatius Brianchaninov: On the Prayer of Jesus.* London, 1952, 1965.

The Art of Prayer, 60ff; *L'art de la prière,* 80ff;

*A Systematic Handbook:* the body, 107ff, 380ff (bibliog.), 422ff (texts).

P. K. 'The Raising of Hands During Prayer as a Habit of the Early Christians' (in Russian). *Dušepoleznoe čtenie* 17/3 (1876) 461–468.

Leroy, O. *La splendeur corporelle des saints.* Paris, 1936.

Ohm, Thomas. *Die Gebetsgebärden der Völker und das Christentum.* Leiden, 1948.

Gorce, Denys. 'Corps . . . ; Le corps qui prie', DSp 2/2 (1953) 2375–2378.

Martimort, Aimé-Georges. 'L'intelligence des rubriques, attitudes et gestes liturgiques', *Bulletin du comité des études de Saint-Sulpice,* April-June 1955, 52–59.

Noirot, M. 'Gestes de la prière', *Catholicisme* 4 (1956) 1902–1904.

Bertaud, Émile. 'Danse religieuse', DSp 3 (1975) 21–37 (bibliog.).

Hänggi, Anton. 'Liturgische Körperhaltung', LThK 6 (1961) 1102–1103.

Metz, J. P. 'Corporalité', EF 1 (1967) 273–280.

Jousse, Marcel. *L'anthropologie du geste. La manducation de la parole.* Paris, 1969.

Crouzel, Henri. 'Le thème platonicien du "véhicule de l'âme" chez Origène', *Didaskalia* 7 (1977) 225–237.

Bellini, E. 'Il corpo a la salvezza dell'uomo nelle riflessione dei Padri,' *Communio* 54 (1980) 18–26.

Ladocci, G[aspar]. 'Oriente-orientamento', DP 2:2515–2517; 'East-Orientation', EEC 1:257.

GENUFLECTIONS, P. 78.

Lesêtre, H. 'Génuflexion', *Dictionnaire de la Bible* 3 (1903) 192–193.

Leclercq, Henri. 'Génuflexion', DACL 6 (1924) 1017–1021.

Rücker, A. 'Die feierliche Kniebeugungszeremonie an Pfingsten in den orientalischen Riten', *Heilige Ueberlieferung. . . offerts à Odo Casel,* coll. Beiträge zur Geschichte des alten Mönchtums (Munster, 1938) 139–211.

Schlier, H[einrich]. 'Γόνυ, γονυπρετέω', Kittel 1 (1964) 738–40.

Crawley, Alfred Ernst. 'Kneeling', *Encyclopedia of Religion and Ethics,* 7 (Edinburgh, 1959) 745–747.

Greeven, Heinrich. 'Προσκυνέν, προσκυνητής', Kittel 6 (1968) 758–766.

Lampe, Geoffrey William H. 'Γονυκλισία', *A Patristic Greek Lexicon,* fasc. 2 (Oxford, 1962), 321–322; 'Μετάνοια', fasc. 3 (1964) 855–858.

Bertaud, Émile. 'Génuflexions et métanies', DSp (1967) 214–226.

ORAL PRAYER, P. 80.

Isaac the Syrian. 68th Discourse; *Oeuvres* (Desclee de Brouwer, 1981) 350; translated A. J. Wensinck, *Mystic Treatises by Isaac of Nineveh.* Amsterdam, 1923, rpt Wiesbaden, 1967.

Brianchaninov, Ignace. *Approches de la prière de Jésus,* 45–51 (in Russian, 201–208). Excerpts translated by Lazarus [Moore], *Ignatius Brianchaninov: On the Prayer of Jesus,* London, 1965.

The Art of Prayer, 21ff, 45, 55–59, 66–67, 275; *L'art de la prière,* 21ff., 53ff., 69–75, 79ff, 377ff.

*A Systematic Handbook,* 311, 440 (texts).

Heinisch, P. *Das 'Wort' im AT und im alten Orient.* Münster, 1922.

Gaskell, G. A. *Dictionary of Sacred Language of all Scriptures and Myths.* London, 1923.

Jousse, M. 'Le style oral rythmique et mnémotechnique chez les verbomoteurs', *Archives de philosophie* 2 (1925) fasc. 4.

Dürr, L. *Die Deutung des göttlichen Wortes im AT und in dem alten Orient.* Leipzig, 1928.

Fonck, Anton. 'Prière', DThC 13/2 (1936) 185ff.

Mensching, Gustav. *Das heilige Wort, eine religionsphänomenologische Untersuchung.* Bonn, 1937.

Cappua, F. 'Osservazioni sulla lettura e sulla preghiera ad alta voce presso gli antichi', *Rendiconti della academia di archeologia* 28 (Naples, 1953) 59–99.

*Théophane le Reclus,* 245ff.

Aron, Robert. *Ainsi priait Jésus enfant* (Paris, 1968) 115–131; translated Agnes H. Forsyth and Anne-Marie de Commaille, *The Jewish Jesus* (New York, 1971).

Heiler, Friedrich. *Die Religionen der Menschheit. Le religioni dell'umanità.* Milan, 1985. 275–345.

THE POWER OF WORDS, P. 80.

Procksch, Otto. 'The Word of God in the Old Testament,' Kittel 4 (1967) 91–100.

Kittel, Gerhard. 'Word and Speech in the New Testament', Kittel, 4:100–143.

Bulgakov, Sergius. *Filosofia imeni*. Paris, 1953.

*Grégoire de Nazianze,* 138ff.

The 'magic' power of words, see the bibliography in Friedrich Heiler, *Le religioni dell'umanità* (Milan, 1985) 315. Originally published as *Die Religionen der Menschheit in Vergangenheit und Gegenwart* (Stuttgart, 1959).

GLOSSOLALIA, P. 84.

Irenaeus. *Adversus haereses* 5.6.1; SCh 153 (1969) 72ff; ANF1:531ff; translated and annotated by Dominic J. Unger, with further revisions by John J. Dillon, *Saint Irenaeus against the Heresies,* ACW 55. New York, 1992–.

Cyril of Jerusalem. *Catéchèses baptismales et mystagogiques* 17.16; FCh 64:106.

John Chrysostom. *In epistolam I ad Corinthios,* homily 29; PG 61:239B; LNPF 12:168–169.

Consult the exegetical commentaries on Acts and 1 Corinthians and standard biblical dictionaries: Kittel 1 (1964) 719–727: 'γλῶσσα', by Johannes Behm.

Lombard, E. *De la glossolalie chez les premiers chrétiens et des phénomènes similaires.* Études d'exégèse et de psychologie. Lausanne, 1910.

Kelsey, Morton T. *Tongue Speaking. An Experiment in Spiritual Experience*. Garden City, New York, 1964; 2nd ed., *Speaking With Tongues*. London, 1965.

Bittlinger, A. *Glossolalia. Wert und Problematik des Sprachredens*. Schloss Graheim, 1969.

Kildahl, J. P. *The Psychology of Speaking in Tongues*. New York, 1972.

Samarin, W. J. *Tongues of Men and Angels: The Religious Language of Pentecostalism*. New York, 1972.

Sullivan, Francis A. 'Langues (Don de)', DSp 9 (1976) 223–227 (bibliog.).

LONG OR SHORT PRAYERS? P. 85.

Evagrius. *Chapters on Prayer*, 98, 151; Hausherr, *Leçons,* 134,183ff; CS 4:71, 80.

Cassian. *Institutes* 2.10; SCh 109:74ff; translated Boniface Ramsey, *John Cassian. The Institutes,* New York, 2000; LNPF, 2nd ser., 11:208.

John Climacus. *Scala paradisi, gradus* 27; PG 88:111; CWS translation, 261ff. See Irénée Hausherr, *'monologistos euche' Noms du Christ et voies d'oraison,* OCA 157 (Rome, 1960) 247–283; *The Name of Jesus,* CS 44 (Kalamazoo, 1978) 220–233.

Ilias the Ekdidos, in *Petite Philocalie,* 164 *(monologistos).* Paris, 1953.

Gregory Palamas. *Défense des saints hésychastes,* I, 3, 2 *(monologistos);* Louvain, 108.

RECITATION IN COMMON, P. 87.

Fonck, Anton. 'Prière: Prière publique et prière privée', DThC 13/2 (1936) 192ff.

Cuming, Geoffrey. 'La base néotestamentaire de la prière commune', *La Maison-Dieu,* 116 (1973) 19–40.

Clément, Olivier. Boris Bobrinskoy, Elisabeth Behr-Siegel, and Myrrha Lor-Borodine. *Douloureuse joie, Aperçus sur la prière personelle de l'Orient chrétien.* Bellefontaine 1974.

See Liturgical Prayer—Communal Nature.

CHANT, P. 87.

Eusebius of Caesarea. *La préparation évangélique* 12.20ff; SCh 307 (1983) 96ff. English translation by E. H. Gifford. *Eusebiou tou Pamphilou Euangelikes proparaskeues logoi 15 / Eusebii Pamphili Evangelicae praeparationis libri XV.* 4 vols. Oxford, 1903.

Hazzâyâ, Rabban Jausep. *Briefe,* 146ff: Der Dämon, genannt der 'Liederdichter' [The Demon called 'the poet of songs']. [Critical edition and english translation of the short version of the 'Letter of the Three Stages of the Monastic Life', by G. Olinder, *A Letter of Philoxenus of Mabbug Sent to a Friend.* Acta Universitatis Gotoburgensis, Göteborgs Högskolas Årsskrift LVI (1950:1) Göteborg, 1950. See also E. J. Sherry 'The Life and Works of Joseph Hazzâyâ', in The Seed of Wisdom. Essays in Honor of T. J. Meek, 78–91. London, 1964].

*L'art de la prière,* 71–75. *The Art of Prayer,* 91ff.

Gevaert, F. A. *Origines du chant liturgique.* Ghent, 1890.

Quasten, Johannes. *Musik und Gesang in den Kulten der heidnischen Antike und christlichen Frühzeit.* Munich, 1930.

Orlov, S. P. 'La musique religieuse en Russie', *Irénikon* 8 (1931) 439–456.

Raes, Alphonse. 'Le chant liturgique dans le rite byzantin', *Introductio in liturgiam orientalem,* 249–273. Rome, 1947.

Fellerer, Karl-Gustav. *Einführung in die Musik-Wissenschaft.* 2nd ed. Hamburg, 1953.

———. 'Musik', LThK 7 (1962) 699–701.

Otto, W. F. *Die Musen und der göttliche Ursprung des Singens und Sagens.* Düsseldorf-Cologne, 1955.

*Musik des Ostens, Sammelbände der K.G. Herder-Forschungsstelle für Musikgeschichte.* Kassel, 1962ff.

Seaman, G. R. *History of Russian Music.* New York-Washington, 1967.

Powne, Michael. *Ethiopian Music, An Introduction. A Survey of Ecclesiastical and Secular Ethiopian Music and Instruments.* London, 1968.

von Gardner, J. 'Stile und Formen liturgischer Musik in der Orthodoxen Kirche', *Handbuch der Ostkirchenkunde,* 457–482; bibliog. 799–803. Düsseldorf, 1971.

Totzke, I. 'Die Musik der nichtchalkedonischen Kirchen', *ibid.,* 444–456.

Gardner, J. *System und Wesen des russisches Gesanges,* Schriften zur Geistesgeschichte des östlichen Europa. Wiesbaden, 1976.

*Kamar,* a collection of armenian music, directed by H. Vahramian. London, 1980ff.

Mathon, G. 'Musique', *Catholicisme* 9 (1982) 865ff.

Chupungco, A[nscar]. 'Canto (e antifona)', DP 2:384–386; 'Chant and Antiphon', EEC 1:160.

Pizzani, U[baldo]. 'Musica', DP 2:2327–2328; 'Music', EEC 1:576.

Heiler, Friedrich. *Die Religionen der Menschheit. Le religioni dell'umanità,* 275–279 (bibliog.) Milan, 1985.

PSALMS, P. 88.

Evagrius. *Chapters on Prayer,* 82ff, 85; Hausherr, *Leçons,* 119, 144; CS 4:69.

Cassian. *Institutes* 2.1ff; SCh 109 (1965) 58ff; translated ACW 55:37; LNPF, 2nd ser., 11:205ff.

Hazzâyâ, Rabban Jausep. *Briefe,* 172ff.

Gregory of Sinai, in Gouillard, *Petite Philocalie,* 250ff, 261ff. Paris, 1953. Translated by E. Kadloubovsky and G. E. H. Palmer, 'Instructions to Hesychasts', n. 5, *Writings from the Philokalia on Prayer of the Heart,* 76ff. London, 1979.

Brianchaninov, Ignace. *Approches de la prière de Jésus,* 116–122 (in Russian, 279–285). Selections translated Lazarus [Moore], *On the Prayer of Jesus,* London, 1965.

Commentaries on the Psalter among the Fathers, see W. Werbeck, in *Religion in Geschichte und Gegenwart* 5:684ff. Tübingen, 1961.

*A Systematic Handbook,* 408 (bibliog.).

Bouyer, Louis. 'Les Psaumes, prière du peuple de Dieu', *La vie spirituelle* 80 (1949) 579–597.

Drijvers, Pius. *Les Psaumes*. Paris, 1958. English translation, *The Psalms: Their Structure and Meaning*. Freiburg, New York, 1965.
De Vregille, Bernard. 'Écriture . . . , Psautier', DSp 4/1 (1960) 179–182.
Colombás, Garcia M. *Paradis et vie angélique,* 203ff. Paris, 1961.
de Langhe, Robert, ed. *Le Psautier, Ses origines, Ses problèmes littéraires, son influence: Études presentées*. Louvain, 1962.
Mateos, J. 'La psalmodie dans le rite byzantin', *Proche Orient Chrétien* 15 (1965) 107–126.
George, A. *Prier les Psaumes*. Paris, 1965.
*Psaumes,* DThC, Tables générales 3 (1972) 3820–3825.
Gelineau, Joseph. 'Les psaumes à l'époque patristique', *La Maison-Dieu* 135 (1978) 99–116.
Girard, M. 'Les Psaumes, Analyse structurelle et interprétation', vol. I:1–50, coll. Recherches, Nouvelle série 2. Montreal, 1984.
Gribomont, J[ean]. 'Salmi (libro dei)', DP 2:3063–3066; 'Psalms', EEC 2:722–723.
Gribomont. 'Salmodia', DP 2:3066–3067; 'Psalmody', EEC 2:722.

LITURGICAL PRAYER, P. 94.

Cyril of Jerusalem. *Mystagogical Lectures; Catéchèses mystagogiques,* SCh 126 (1966); translated Leo P. McCauley, *The Works of Saint Cyril of Jerusalem,* vol. 2, FCh 64 (1970).
Maximus the Confessor. *Mystagogia,* PG 91:657–718; translated George C. Berthold, 'The Church's Mystagogy', in *Maximus the Confessor: Selected Writings,* CWS. New York, 1985; also translated Julian Stead, *The Church, The Liturgy, and The Soul of Man: The* Mystagogia *of St Maximus the Confessor*. Still River, Massachusetts, 1982.
Sophronius of Jerusalem. *Commentarius liturgicus;* PG 87, III, 3981–4012
Theodorus Andinensis. *Commentatio liturgica;* PG 140:417–468.
Nicholas Cabasilas. *A Commentary on the Divine Liturgy; Explication de la divine liturgie,* SCh 4*bis* (1967); translated J. M. Hussey and P. A. McNulty, London, 1960, Crestwood, NY, 1984.
Symeon of Thessalonike. *De sacra liturgia;* PG 155:253–304; translated H. L. N. Simmons. *Treatise on Prayer. An Explanation of the Services Conducted in the Orthodox Church,* Brookline, Massachusetts, 1984.
*A Systematic Handbook,* 7, 312, 408 (bibliog.), 440 (texts).
Numerous articles on the various liturgies may be found in the journals *L'Orient chrétien* (Paris, 1956–1968), *Parole d'Orient* (University of Kaslik, Lebanon, 1970–); and *Proche-Orient chrétien* (1951–).

Sauget, Jean-Marie. *Bibliographie des Liturgies Orientales* (1900–1960). Rome, 1962.

Janeras, S. *Bibliografia sulle Liturgie Orientali* (1961–1967). Rome, 1969.

Gogol, Nikolai V. *Razmyšlenija o Božestvennoj liturgii*. Petersburg, 1902. *Meditations on the Divine Liturgy of the Holy Eastern Orthodox and Apostolic Church*. Rpt. New York, 1964.

Janin, Raymond. *Les Églises orientales et les rites orientaux*. Paris, 1929.

Hanssens, J. M. *Institutiones liturgicae de ritibus orientalibus,* vols. 2–3 (eucharistic liturgies). Rome, 1930–1932.

Bulgakov, Sergius. *The Orthodox Church,* 149–160. London, 1935; revised, Crestwood, New York, 1988.

Mercenier, P. E. *La prière des Églises de rite byzantin,* 2nd ed. revised by monks of Chevetogne. Chevetogne, 1972ff.

Casper, J. *Welterklärung im liturgischen Geiste der Ostkirche*. Freiburg im Breisgau, 1939.

Raes, Alphonse. *Introductio in liturgiam orientalem*. Rome, 1940.

King, Archdale A. *The Rites of Eastern Christendom,* 2 vols. London, 1950. [The chapters on the liturgies and the Syrian and Chaldean Churches have been adapted in *Liturgie d'Antioche*. Paris, 1967.]

Bouyer, Louis. 'Les catholiques occidentaux et la liturgie byzantine', *Dieu vivant* 21 (Paris, 1952) 15–31.

Bobrinskoy, Boris. 'Molitva i bogosluženie v žizni pravaslovnoj Cerkvi', in S. Verchovskoj, ed., *Provoslavie v žizni*, 241–273. New York, 1953.

Baumstark, Anton. *Liturgie comparée. Principes et Méthodes pour l'étude historique des liturgies chrétiennes,* 3rd ed. rev. by Bernard Botte. Chevetogne, 1953. Translated by F. L. Cross, *Comparative Liturgy*. Westminster, Md., 1958.

Dekkers, E. 'Les anciens moines cultivaient-ils la liturgie?, *La Maison-Dieu* 51 (1957) 31–54.

Dalmais, Irénée Henri. *Initiation à la liturgie*. Bruges-Paris, 1958 (bibliog.). Translated Roger Capel, *Introduction to the Liturgy*. London, 1961.

Evdokimov, Paul. *L'Orthodoxie,* 230–62. Neuchâtel-Paris, 1959.

Beck, Hans-Georg. *Kirche und theologische Literatur im byzantinischen Reich,* 240ff. Munich, 1959.

Trembelas, Panagiotis. 'Der orthodoxe christliche Gottesdienst', in P. Bratsiotis, *Die orthodoxe Kirche in griechischer Sicht,* vol. 1:157–168. Stuttgart, 1959.

Vagaggini, Cipriano (adapted by P. Rouillard and R. Gantoy). *Initiation théololique à la liturgie,* 2 vols. Loppem-lez-Bruges, 1959–1963. See also, Vagaggini, *Il senso teologico della liturgia. Saggio di liturgia pastorale generale*. Rome, 1965[4]. Translated L. J. Doyle and W. A.

Jurgens, *Theological Dimensions of the Liturgy: A General Treatise on the Theology of the Liturgy*. Collegeville, Minnesota, 1976.

Liesel, Nikolaus. *Die Liturgien der Ostkirche*. Freiburg im Breisgau, 1960. Translated David Heimann, *The Eucharistic Liturgies of the Eastern Churches*. Collegeville, Minnesota, 1963. French translations have appeared in *Les liturgies catholiques orientales* (Rome, 1958) and *Liturgies eucharistiques par l'image*. Paris, 1959.

Dalmais, Irénée-Henri. *Eastern Liturgies,* translated by Donald Attwater. New York, 1960.

Hamman, Adalbert. 'Mystère eucharistique', DSp 4/2 (1961) 1553–1586.

Martimort, Aimé-Georges. *Handbuch der Liturgiewissenschaft,* rev. E. J. Lengeling. 2 vols. Freiburg, 1963–1965.

Zernov, N. 'The Worship of the Orthodox Church', A. J. Philippou, *The Orthodox Ethos,* 115–121. Oxford, 1964.

Hamman, Adalbert. *La Messe, Liturgies anciennes et textes patristiques*. Paris, 1964.

Hayek, M. *Liturgie maronite, histoire et textes eucharistiques*. Paris, 1964.

Martimort, Aimé-Georges. *L'Église en prière, Introduction à la liturgie,* 3rd ed., Paris, 1965 (bibliog.). Translated Austin Flannery and Vincent Ryan, *The Church at Prayer: Introduction to the Liturgy*. New York, 1968.

Bornet, A. *Les commentaires byzantins de la divine liturgie du VII^e au XV^e siècle*. Paris, 1966.

Schmemann, Alexander. *Introduction to Liturgical Theology*. London, 1966. Crestwood, New York, 3rd ed., 1997.

Evdokimov, Paul. *La prière des Églises d'Orient. La liturgie de saint Jean Chrysostome*. Mulhouse, 1966.

Veilleux, Armand. *La liturgie dans le cénobitisme pachômien au quatrième siècle,* Studia Anselmiana 57. Rome, 1968.

Lécuyer, Joseph. 'Les assemblées liturgiques et le culte religieux des premiers siècles', *Concilium* 42 (1969) 23–36.

Patrinacos, N. D. *The Individual and His Orthodox Church,* 32–42. Oxford, 1970.

*Handbuch der Ostkirchenkunde,* 793–803 (bibliog.). Düsseldorf, 1971.

Tarby, A. *La prière eucharistique de l'Église de Jérusalem,* Théologie historique 17. Paris, 1972.

Vandenbroucke, François. 'Théologie de la liturgie', *Catholicisme* 7 (1975) 882–889.

Castellano, J. 'Liturgia', DESp 2:1086–1104.

Grélot, Pierre. 'La liturgie dans l'Écriture', DSp 9 (1976) 873–884.

Lanne, Emmanuel. 'Liturgie eucharistique en Orient et en Occident (1^er^–4^e^ siècles), DSp 9:884–999.

Bobrinskoy, Boris. 'Liturgies orientales', DSp 9:914–923.

Viaud, Gerard, *La liturgie des Coptes d'Égypte*. Paris, 1978.

Andronikoff, Constantine. 'Liturgie et spiritualité', in S. Ch. Agouridès, *Deuxième congrès de théologie orthodoxe,* 79–91. Athens, 1978.

Jevtic', A. 'Liturgy and Spirituality', *ibid.,* 112–128.

Muzj, M. G. *La preghiera eucaristica nella spiritualità d'Oriente e d'Occidente*. Rome, 1979.

Bria, I. 'La vie', in M. A. Vosta de Beauregard and I. Bria, *L'orthodoxie, hier-demain,* 189–260. Paris, 1979.

Dalmais, Irénée-Henri. *Les liturgies d'Orient, 'Rites et Symboles'.* Paris, 1980. Translation of the 1959 edition by Donald Attwater, *Eastern Liturgies.* New York, 1960.

Miquel, Pierre. *La liturgie une oeuvre d'art. L'œuvre de Dieu célébrée par son peuple,* Vie monastique 13. Bellefontaine, 1981.

Meyendorff, John. 'The Liturgy: A Clue to the Mind of Worldwide Orthodoxy', in Demetrios J. Constantelos, *Orthodox Theology and Diakonia*. Brookline, Mass., 1981. 79–90.

Felmy, K. Ch. *Die Deutung der göttlichen Liturgie in der russischen Theologie, Wege und Wandlungen russischer Liturgie-Auslegung,* Arbeiten zur Kirchengeschichte 30. Berlin-New York, 1984.

Taft, Robert. *Beyond East and West. Problems in Liturgical Understanding*. Washington, D.C., 1984.

Various authors. 'Liturgie', DP 2:1973–2019; EEC 1:494–505.

Grisbrook, W. Jardine. 'Liturgia: Libri liturgici orietali', DP 2:2003–2008; 'Liturgy, Eastern liturgical books', EEC 1:501–502.

Triacca, Achille M. 'Improvvisazione eucologica', DP 2:1994–1997; 'Euchological improvisation', EEC 1:498–499.

Fahey, Patrick. 'Messa', DP 2:2232–2238; 'Mass', EEC 1:540–542.

Studer, Basilio. 'Mistagogia', DP 2:2264–2265; 'Mystagogy', EEC 1:576–577.

Peretto, Elio. 'Acoluthia', DP 1:37–38; 'Acoluthia', EEC 1:8.

Gelsi, Danielle. 'Anafora', DP 1:539–546; 'Anaphora', EEC 1:33–35.

Dalmais, Irénée Henri. 'Egitto: Liturgia', DP 1:112–114; 'Egypt, Liturgy', EEC 1:264–265.

Kilmartin, Edward J. *Theology of Worship*. Sheed & Ward, 1987.

THE CHRISTIAN ASSEMBLY AT PRAYER, PP. 94FF.

Aphrahat, *Demonstrationes,* 4.11; *Patrolologia syriaca* 1 (1894) 159ff. Translated Sebastian Brock, 'Aphrahat, Demonstration IV, On Prayer', *The*

*Syriac Fathers on Prayer and the Spiritual Life,* CS 101:15ff. Kalamazoo, 1987.

John Chrysostom. *In Epistolam II ad Corinthios,* Homily 18.3 and 2.14; PG 61:527, 398; LNPF 12 (1899) 365.

Nicholas Cabasilas, *A Commentary on the Divine Liturgy,* 20,3 and 38,1; *Explication de la divine liturgie,* SCh *4bis:*146ff, 230ff; (Explication des rites, 12) 378ff; Hussey-McNulty translation, 58, 91f, 43ff.

Mersch, Émile. 'Communion des saints', DSp 2 (1853) 1292–1294.

Elert, W. *Abendmahl und Kirchengemeinschaft in der alten Kirche hauptsächlich des Ostens.* Berlin, 1954.

Tena, Pedro, *et al.,* 'Église', DSp 4/1 (1960) 370–479.

Neuenzeit, Paul. *'Koinonia',* LThK 6 (1961) 368ff.

Daniélou, Jean and H. Vorgrimmler. *Sentire Ecclesiam. Das Bewusstsein von der Kirche als gestaltende Kraft der Frömmigkeit.* Freiburg im Breisgau, 1961.

Congar, Yves. 'L'Ecclesia' ou communauté chrétienne, sujet intégral de l'action liturgique', *La liturgie après Vatican II,* Unam Sanctam 66:241–282. Paris, 1967.

Veilleux, Armand. *La liturgie dans le cénobitisme pachômien au 4^e^ siècle,* Studia Anselmiana 57. Rome, 1968.

Zizioulas, John D. *La communauté dans la divine eucharistie et en l'évêque aux trois premiers siècles* (in Greek). Athens, 1965; a summary by P. C. Bori in RHE 65 (1970) 56–58.

Sieben, Hermann Josef, *et al. 'Koinônia',* DSp (1972) 1743–1769.

Erni, R. and D. Papandreou. *Eucharistiegemeinschaft. Der Standpunkt der Orthodoxie.* Freiburg, Switzerland, 1974.

Basil of Stavronikita. *Chant d'entrée. Vie liturgique et mystère de l'unité dans l'Église Orthodoxe,* Perspective Orthodoxe 2. Geneva, 1980.

Guillaume, Paul Marie. 'Peuple de Dieu', DSp 12/1 (1984) 1230–1246.

THE DOXOLOGICAL CHARACTER OF THE LITURGY, P. 96.

Steinheimer, M. *Die* doxa tou theou *in der römischen Liturgien.* Munich, 1951.

Deseille, Placide. 'Gloire de Dieu . . .', DSp 6 (1967) 421–463.

THE LITURGY AS AN INSTRUCTION OF THE TRUTH, P. 97.

Tyciak, Julius. *Die Liturgie als Quelle östlicher Frömmigkeit,* Ecclesia orans, 20. Freiburg, 1937.

Tarchnišvili, Michele. *Die byzantinische Liturgie als Verwirklichung der Einheit und Gemeinschaft im Dogma.* Würzburg, 1939.

Federer, Karl. *Liturgie und Glaube. Eine theologiegeschichtliche Untersuchung*. Freiburg, Switzerland, 1950.

Vawter, Bruce and E. Vilacroza. 'Le développement de la foi dans la communauté de prière', *Concilium,* 82 (1973) 25–42.

THE CONTEMPLATIVE DIMENSION OF THE LITURGY, P. 98.

Casper, J. *Weltverklärung im liturgischen Geiste der Ostkirche,* Ecclesia orans 22. Freiburg, 1939.

von Balthasar, Hans Urs. *La prière contemplative,* 113–114. Bruges, 1959. Translated (from the German original, *Des Betrachtende Gebet*) A. V. Littledale, *Prayer,* 88–103. New York, 1961.

Bouyer, Louis. *Le rite et l'homme, Sacralité naturelle et liturgie*. Paris, 1962. Translated M. Joseph Coastelloe, *Rite and Man. Natural Sacredness and Christian Liturgy*. Notre Dame, Indiana, 1963.

Arseniev, Nicholas. 'Traits majeurs de la vie liturgique, contemplative et sacramentelle', *Contacts* 14 (1962) 38–39, 135–158.

Bouyer, Louis. *Le Fils éternel, Théologie de la parole de Dieu et christologie*. Paris, 1974. Translation Simone Inkel and John F. Laughlin, *The Eternal Son: A Theology of the Word of God and Christology*. Huntington, Indiana, 1978.

Grammont, Paul. 'Liturgie et contemplation', DSp 9 (1976) 927–932.

THE MYSTICAL NATURE OF THE LITURGY, P. 98.

Hendrix, P. 'Der Mysteriencharacter der byzantinischen Liturgie', *Byzantinisiche Zeitschrift* 30 (1921) 333ff.

Barsotti, Divo. *Vie mystique et vie liturgique*. Paris, 1954.

Bouyer, Louis. *La vie de la liturgie, Une critique constructive du mouvement liturgique*. Paris, 1956. Translated as *Liturgical Piety* (Notre Dame, 1955) and as *Life and Liturgy* (London, 1956).

Dalmais, Irénée Henri. *Initiation theologique à la liturgie*. Translated Roger Capel, *Introduction to the Liturgy*. Baltimore, 1961.

Vagaggini, Cipriano. *Initiation théologique à la liturgie,* 2 vols., Bruges, 1959–1963.

Bouyer, Louis. *Le rite et l'homme*. Paris, 1962. Translated Joseph Coastelloe, *Rite and Man,* Notre Dame, 1963.

Bornert, R. *Les commentaires byzantins de la divine liturgie du VIIe au XVe siècle*. Paris, 1966.

Gelineau, Joseph. 'Liturgie et vie chrétienne', DSp 9 (1976) 923–927.

Bobrinskoy, Boris. 'Liturgies orientales', DSp 9: 914–923.

Grammont, Paul. 'Liturgie et contemplation', DSp 9:927–932.

THE ALLEGORICAL EXPLANATION OF THE LITURGY, P. 99.

Symeon the New Theologian. Ethical Discourses,14, 89ff; *Éthique,* SCh 129 (1967) 428ff; translated Alexander Golitzin, 'Fourteenth Discourse', *St Symeon the New Theologian: The Ethical Discourses,* 1:175ff. Crestwood, New York, 1996.

Symeon of Thessalonika, *Expositio de divino templo,* PG 155:697–750.

Nicholas Cabasilas, *A Commentary on the Divine Liturgy, passim; Explication de la divine liturgie,* SCh *4bis* (1967). Translated J. M. Hussey and P. A. McNulty. London, 1960, Crestwood, New York, 1977.

Pseudo-Germanus of Paris, *Expositio liturgiae gallicanae,* ed. E. C. Ratcliff. London, 1971 (the first witness in the West of the allegorical exegesis of the liturgy).

Schultz, H. J. 'Kultussymbolik der byzantinischen Kirche', in F. Hermann, ed. *Symbolik des orthodoxen und orientalischen Christentums.* Symbolik der Religionen, 10:3–51. Stuttgart, 1963.

———. *Die byzantinische Liturgie. Glaubenszeugnis und Symbolsgestalt,* Sophia 5, 2nd ed. Trier, 1989. Translated M. J. O'Connell, *The Byzantine Liturgy. The Development of Its Symbolic Form.* New York, 1986.

Bornert, René. 'Les commentaires byzantins de la divine liturgie du VIIe au XVe siècle', *Archives de l'Orient chrétien* 9. Paris, 1966.

Felmy, K. Ch. *Die Deutung der göttlichen Liturgie in der russischen Theologie. Wege und Wandlungen russischer Liturgie-Auslegung,* Arbeiten zur Kirchengeschichte 54. Berlin-New York, 1984.

THE BEAUTY OF THE LITURGY, P. 100.

Bulgakov, Sergius. 'Le ciel sur la terre', *Una Sancta.* Munich, 1928.

von Balthasar, Hans Urs. *Herrlichkeit. Eine theologische Ästhetik.* Einsiedeln, 1961–1969. Translated Joseph Fessio and John Riches, *The Glory of the Lord; A Theological Aesthetics.* San Francisco, 1982–1989.

Evdokimov, Paul. *L'art de l'icône. Théologie de la beauté.* Desclée de Brouwer, 1972. Translated Steven Bigham, *The Art of the Icon: A Theology of Beauty.* Redondo Beach, California, 1990.

THE TRADITIONAL TEACHING, P. 101.

*A Systematic Handbook,* 1, 6, 359 (bibliog.).

Bulgakov, Sergius. *L'Orthodoxie,* 12–50. Paris, 1932. Translated Elisabeth Cram, *The Orthodox Church.* London, 1935. Translation revised by Lydia Kesich. Crestwood, New York, 1988.

Ouspensky, Leonid and Vladimir Lossky. *Der Sinn der Ikonen,* 11–23. Bern-Olten, 1952. Translated G. E. H. Palmer and E. Kadloubovsky, *The Meaning of Icons.* Boston, 1956.

Evdokimov, Paul. *L'Orthodoxie,* 195–197. Neuchâtel-Paris, 1959.

Lossky, Vladimir. *À l'image et à la resemblance de Dieu,* 139–166. Paris, 1967. Translated John H. Erickson and Thomas E. Bird, *The Image and Likeness of God.* Crestwood New York, 1985.

Špidlík, Tomaš. *Les grands mystiques russes,* 111ff, 205ff. Paris, 1979.

———. *La spiritualità russa,* 13ff. Rome, 1981.

———. 'Orthodoxe (spiritualité), DSp 11 (1982) 974 (spiritualité traditionelle).

*ANAMNESIS*, P. 103.

Hippolytus. *La tradition apostolique* 4; SCh 11 (1946) 32–33. Translated Gregory Dix, *The Treatise on the Apostolic Tradition of St. Hippolytus of Rome.* London, 1934. Translated B. S. Easton, *The Apostolic Tradition of Hippolytus.* Cambridge, 1924; translated Alistair Stewart-Sykes, *On the Apostolic Tradition, Hippolytus.* Crestwood, New York, 2001.

Nicholas Cabasilas. *A Commentary on the Divine Liturgy,* 7 and 33; *Explication de la divine liturgie,* SCh 4*bis:* 84ff, 206ff; Hussey-McNulty translation, 35, 83f. London, 1960–Crestwood, New York, 1977.

Arseniev, Nikolaj. *Das Leiden und die Auferstehung des Herrn in Kirchengesangen der Orthodoxen Kirche des Ostens.* Wernigerode, 1938.

Dahl, N.A. '*Anamnesis:* Mémoire et commémoration dans le christianisme primitif', *Studia theologica,* 69–95. Copenhagen, 1947.

Salaville, J. 'Anamnèse', *Catholicisme,* 1 (198) 505–506.

Thurian, Max. *L'Eucharistie, mémorial du Seigneur, Sacrifice d'action de grâces et d'intercession.* Neuchâtel-Paris, 1959. Translated J. G. Davies, *The Eucharistic Memorial.* Richmond, Virginia, 1962.

Ligier, Louis. 'Autour du sacrifice eucharistique. Anaphores orientales et anamnèse juive de Kippur', *Nouvelle revue théologique* 82 (1960) 405.

Tillard, Jean Marie. *L'Eucharistie, pâque de l'Église,* Unam Sanctam, 44. Paris, 1964.

Lanne, Emmanuel. 'L'histoire du salut dans la liturgie byzantine', in F. Christ, ed., *Oikonomia, Heilsgeschichte als Thema der Theologie,* Mélanges O. Cullmann. Hamburg, 1967.

Ligier, Louis. *Célébration divine et anamnèse dans Eucharisties d'Orient et d'Occident,* Lex orandi 46:139–178. Paris, 1970.

THE FEASTS, PP. 104–105.

*The Epistle of Barnabas,* 15; *Epître de Barnabé,* SCh 172:182ff; ANF 1:146–147.

Origen. *Homélies sur les Nombres* 23; SCh 29 (1951) 435ff.

Harden, J. M. *The Ethiopic Didascalia Translated,* 178ff. London-New York, 1920.

Isaac the Syrian, 74e Discourse; *Oeuvres spirituelles,* 377ff. Paris, 1981. Translated D. Miller, *The Ascetical Homilies of Saint Isaac the Syrian.* Boston, 1984; also translated (from the syriac text) A. J. Wensinck, *Mystic Treatises by Isaac of Nineveh.* Amsterdam, 1923; rpt Wiesbaden, 1969.

Symeon the New Theologian. *Ethical Discourses,* 14.1ff; *Éthiques,* SCh 129 (1967) 422ff; translated Alexander Golitzin, 'Fourteenth Discourse', *St Symeon the New Theologian . . . : The Ethical Discourses,* 1:172ff. Crestwood, New York, 1996.

Cabrol, Fernand. 'Fêtes chrétiennes', DACL 5 (1922) 1403–1412.

Nielen, J. M. *Das Zeichen des Herrn. Sabbat und Sonntag in biblischer Bezeugung.* Freiburg im Breisgau, 1940.

Martimort, Aimé-Georges, Bernard Botte, *et al.* 'Fêtes humaines et liturgie', *La Maison-Dieu,* 30 (1952) 79–100.

Daniélou, Jean. *Bible et liturgie,* Lex orandi, 11. Paris, 1951. Translation, *The Bible and the Liturgy.* Notre Dame, Indiana, 1956.

Chavasse, A. 'Sanctoral et année liturgique', La Maison-Dieu, 52 (1957) 89–97.

Gaillard, Jean. 'Dimanche', DSp 3 (1957) 948–982.

Clément, Olivier. *Transfigurer le temps. Notes sur le temps à la lumiere de la tradition orthodoxe.* Neuchâtel-Paris, 1959.

Various authors, *La sanctification du temps,* in Aimé-Georges Martimort, *L'Église en prière,* Paris, 1961, 4:671–785. English translation, *The Liturgy and Time,* vol. 4 of Martimort, *The Church at Prayer.* Collegeville, Minnesota, 1986.

Hild, Jean. 'Fêtes', DSp 5 (1964) 221–247 (bibliog.).

Van Goudoever, J. *Biblical Calendars.* Leiden, 1961.

Mosna, C. *Storia della domenica dalle origini fino agli inizi del V secolo.* Rome, 1969.

Schulz, Hans Joachim. 'Liturgie, Tageszeiten und Kirchenjahr des byzantinischen Ritus', *Handbuch der Ostkirchenkunde,* 332–385.

Wiertz, Paul. 'Zur religiösen Volkskultur der orientalischen und orthodoxen Kirchen. Volksglauben und Volksbrauch', *ibid.,* 6061–6019.

Rohrdorf, Willy. *Der Sonntag. Geschichte der Ruhe-und Gottesdiensttages im ältesten Christentum.* Zurich, 1962. Translated A. A. K. Graham,

*Sunday. The History of the Day of Rest and Worship in the Earliest Centuries of the Christian Church.* Philadelphia, 1968.
Miquel, Pierre. *La liturgie une oeuvre d'art. L'oeuvre de Dieu célébrée par son peuple,* Vie monastique, 13:169–194. Bellefontaine, 1981.
Rohrdorf, Willy. 'Sabato', DP 2:3042–3045; 'Sabbath', EEC 2:748.

LITURGICAL ESCHATOLOGISM, P. 107FF.

de Montcheuil, Yves. 'Signification eschatologique du repas eucharistique', RSR 33 (1946) 10–43.
Tyciak, Julius. *Maranatha. Die Geheime Offenbarung und die kirchliche Liturgie.* Warendorf, 1947.
Cuttaz, François. 'Ciel (désir du)', DSp 2/1 (1953) 890–897.
Gaillard, Jean. 'Dimanche et eschatologie', DSp 3 (1957) 977ff.
Colombás, Garcia M. *Paraíso y vida angélica. Sentido escatológico de la vocación cristiana.* Montserrat, 1958.
Galot, Jean. 'Eschatologie', DSp 4/1 (1960) 1020–1059.
Evdokimov, Paul. 'Eschatological Transcendence', in A.J. Philippou, *Orthodoxy: Life and Freedom. Essays in Honour of Archbishop Iakovos,* 31–47. Oxford, 1973.

THE DIVINE OFFICE, P. 109.

Pseudo-Athanasius. *De la virginité,* 14ff., in *Vie de sainte Synclétique,* 131ff. Bellefontaine, 1972. Translated Elizabeth A. Castelli, 'Pseudo-Athanasius: The Life and Activity of the Holy and Blessed Teacher Syncletica', in Vincent L. Wimbush, ed., *Ascetic Behavior in Greco-Roman Antiquity. A Sourcebook,* Studies in Antiquity and Christianity. 265ff. Minneapolis, 1990.
Cassian. *Institutes,* 3; SCh 109 (1965) 90ff; ACW 58:59ff; LNPF, 2nd ser., 11:212.
Egeria. *Diary,* 24ff (the liturgy at Jerusalem); *Journal de voyage,* SCh 296 (1982), 234ff; translated George E. Gringas, *Egeria: Diary of a Pilgrimage,* ACW 38:89ff, New York, 1970. Also translated John Wilkinson, *Egeria's Travels.* London, 1971.
Symeon the New Theologian. 26th Discourse.*2ff; Catéchèses,* SCh 113:70ff; translated C. J. deCatanzaro, *Symeon the New Theologian,* CWS, 274ff. New York, 1980.
Symeon of Thessalonika. *De sacra precatione;* PG 155:535ff; translated as *Treatise on Prayer* 17, 26ff. Brookline, Massachusetts, 1984.
Marcus Ephesinus. *Expositio officii ecclesiastici;* PG 160:1163–1194.

Baumstark, Anton. *Liturgie comparée . . .*, rev. ed. Chevetogne, 1939; 3rd ed. rev. by Bernard Botte. Chevetogne, 1953. Translated F. L. Cross, *Comparative Liturgy*. Westminster, Maryland, 1958.

Salmon, Pierre. *L'Office divin, Histoire de la formation du Bréviaire,* Lex orandi 27. Paris, 1959. Translated David Mary, *The Breviary Through the Centuries*. Collegeville, Minnesota, 1962.

Mateos, J. 'L'office monastique à la fin du IV^e siècle, Antioche, Palestine, Cappadoce', *Oriens Christianus* 47 (1963) 53–88.

Mgr. Cassien, Bernard Botte, *et al. La prière des heures,* Lex orandi, 35. Paris, 1963.

Besret, B., M. M. Croisset, L. Deiss, *et al. Célébrer l'Office divin*. Paris, 1967.

Labarre, Albert. 'Heure (Livre d'Heures)', DSp 7/2 (1969) 410–431.

Bertaud, Émile. 'Horloges spirituelles', DSp 7/1 (1969) 745–763.

Join-Lambert, Michel and Pierre Grélot. 'Temps', VTB, 1273–1284; 'Time', DBT 600–606.

Oury, Guy-Marie. 'Office divin: en Occident', DSp 11 (1982) 685–707 (bibliog.).

Arranz, Miguel. 'Office divin: en Orient', DSp 11:707–720 (bibliog.).

Martimort, Aimé-Georges, *La prière des Heures,* in Martimort, *L'Église en prière,* 4; *La liturgie et le temps,* 167–293. Paris, 1983. Translated Matthew J. O'Connell, *The Church at Prayer,* vol. 4, *The Liturgy and Time,* 'The Liturgy of the Hours', 151–275. Collegeville, Minnesota, 1986.

Rohrdorf, Willy. 'Settimana', DP 2:3174–3175; 'Week', EEC 2:876–877.

Taft, Robert. *The Liturgy of the Hours in East and West. The Origins of the Divine Office and Its Meaning for Today*. Collegeville, Minnesota, 1986.

THE TIME FOR PRAYER, P. 110.

Hippolytus of Rome. *The Apostolic Tradition,* 35 (suitable hours for prayer); *La tradition apostolique,* SCh 11 (1946) 68ff; translated Gregory Dix, *The Treatise on the Apostolic Tradition of St. Hippolytus of Rome*. London, 1937. Also translated: B. S. Easton, *The Apostolic Tradition of Hippolytus*. Cambridge, 1924. Alistair Stewart-Sykes, *On the Apostolic Tradition, Hippolytus*. Crestwood, New York, 2001.

Origen. *On Prayer,* 12; PG 11:452ff; translated Rowan E. Greer, *Origen: An Exhortation to Martyrdom, Prayer, . . .*, CWS, 104–105. New York, 1979.

Cassian. *Institutes,* 2.17; SCh 109:88; ACW 58:48; LNPF, 2nd ser., 11:212.

Isaac the Syrian. 28^e Discourse, *Oeuvres,* 181ff. Desclée de Brouwer, 1981. Translated D. Miller, *The Ascetical Homilies of Saint Isaac the*

*Syrian*. Boston, 1984; also translated (from the Syriac) A. J. Wensinck, *Mystic Treatises of Isaac of Nineveh,* 136ff. Amsterdam, 1923.

Symeon the New Theologian. 3rd Discourse, 1ff (vigils); *Catéchèses,* SCh 96:280; translated C. J. deCatanzaro, *Symeon the New Theologian. The Discourses,* CWS 60ff. (rising at night time).

SACRAMENTS, P. 111.

Denzinger, Heinrich. *Ritus orientalium Coptorum, Syrorum et Armenorum in administrandis sacramentis*. 2 vols. Würzburg, 1963.

Nicholas Cabasilas. *The Life in Christ,* 1 and 6; La *vie en Jésus-Christ,*. 27ff, 149ff. Chevetogne, 1960. Translated C. J. deCatanzaro, *The Life in Christ*. New York, 1974. Crestwood, New York, 1974.

Symeon of Thessalonika. *De sacramentis;* PG 155:175–237.

Arcudius, P. *De concordia Ecclesiae occidentalis et orientalis in septem sacramentorum administratione libri VII.* Paris, 1626, 1672.

Lot-Borodine, Myrrha. 'La grâce déifiante des Sacrments d'après Nicolas Cabasilas', *Revue des Sciences Philosophiques et Théologiques,* 2:26 (1937) 693–713.

De Vries, W. *Sakramententheologie bei den Nestorianern,* OCA 133. Rome, 1947.

Roques, René. 'Denys l'Aréopagite (pseudo-)', DSp 3 (1957) 276ff.

Evdokimov, Paul. *L'Orthodoxie,* 262–299. Neuchâtel-Paris, 1959.

Beck, Hans-Georg. *Kirche und theologische Literatur im byzantinischen Reich,* (bibliog.): 'Sakramentenlehre', 282ff. Munich, 1959.

Crouzel, Henri. 'Origène et la structure du sacrement', *Bulletin de littérature ecclésiastique,* 81–104. Toulouse, 1962.

Sherrard, Philip. 'The Sacrament', in A. J. Philippou, *The Orthodox Ethos,* 133–139. Oxford, 1964.

Trembelas, Panagiotis N. *Dogmatique de l'Église orthodoxe catholique,* 3:8–78. Chevetogne-Desclée de Brouwer, 1968.

Patrinacos, N. D. *The Individual and His Orthodox Church,* 1–31. Oxford, 1970.

Dalmais, Irénée Henri. 'Die Sakramente: Theologie und Liturgie', *Handbuch der Ostkirchenkunde,* 415–443. Düsseldorf, 1971.

Meyendorff, John. *Byzantine Theology: Historical Trends and Doctrinal Themes,* 191–211. New York, 1974.

Villalón, J. R. *Sacraments dans l'Esprit. Existence humaine et théologie existentielle,* Théologie historique, 43. Paris, 1977.

Kleinheyer, B., E. V. Severus, and R. Kaczynski, *Sakramentliche Feiern,* 2. Regensburg, 1984.

Martimort, Aimé-Georges. *L'Église en prière,* 3: *Les sacrements.* Desclée de Brouwer, 1984. Translated Matthew J. O'Connell, *The Church at Prayer,* 3: *The Sacraments.* Collegeville, Minnesota, 1988.

Nocent, A[drien]. 'Sacramenti', DP 2:3051–3059; 'Sacraments', EEC 2:749–751.

BAPTISM, P. 114.

Hippolytus of Rome. *The Apostolic Tradition,* 20; *La tradition apostolique,* SCh 11: 47ff. Translated Gregory Dix, *The Apostolic Tradition of Hippolytus of Rome.* London, 1937. Translated B. S. Easton, *The Apostolic Tradition of Hippolytus.* Cambridge, 1924. Translated Alistair Stewart-Sykes, *On the Apostolic Tradition, Hippolytus.* Crestwood, New York, 2001.

*Trois antiques rituels du baptême;* SCh 59 (1958).

Basil. *Traité du Saint-Esprit,* 15; SCh 17*bis* (1968) 364ff; *On the Holy Spirit.* Crestwood, New York, n.d.; LNPF, 2nd ser., volume 8.

Cyril of Jerusalem. *Catéchèses mystagogiques,* SCh 126 (1966). Translated Leo P. McCauley and Anthony A. Stephenson, *Mystagogical Lectures, The Works of Saint Cyril of Jerusalem,* 1, FCh 61:153ff. New York, 1969.

John Chrysostom. *Baptismal Instructions; Huit Catéchèses baptismales inédites;* SCh 50*bis* (1970); translated Paul W. Karkins, *John Chrysostom: Baptismal Instructions,* ACW 31 (1963).

Romanos Melodios. *Hymn* 52; SCh 283 (1981) 342ff. Translated M. Carpenter, *Kontakia of Romanos, Byzantine Melodist,* 2 volumes. Columbia, Missouri, 1970, 1973.

Mark the Monk. *On Baptism.* Translated into French by C. A. Zirnheld, *Le baptême,* Spiritualité orientale, 41: 91–132. Bellefontaine, 1985.

*Nicholas Cabasilas. The Life in Christ, 2; La vie en Jésus Christ,* 45ff. Chevetogne, 1960. Translated C. J. deCatanzaro, *The Life in Christ.* Crestwood, New York, 1974.

*L'art de la prière,* 155. *The Art of Prayer,* 150, 170.

Dietrich, G. *Die nestorianische Taufliturgie.* Giessen, 1903.

Staerk, Antonius. *Der Taufritus in den orientalischen Kirchen: sein apostolischer Ursprung und seine Enwicklung.* Freiburg, 1903.

Rahner, Karl. 'Taufe und geistliches Leben bei Origenes', ZAM 7 (1932) 205–223.

Delay, E. 'Baptême', DSp 1 (1936) 1218–1230.

Lundberg, Per Ivar. *La typologie baptismale de l'ancienne Église.* Upsala-Leipzig, 1942.

Daniélou, Jean. 'Le symbolisme des rites baptismaux', *Dieu vivant* 1:15–43. Paris, 1945.

Lampe, Geoffrey William H. *The Seal of the Spirit. A Study in the Doctrine of Baptism and Confirmation in the New Testament and the Fathers.* New York, 1951.

Benoît, André. *Le baptême chriétien au second siècle. La théologie des Pères.* Paris, 1953.

Hambye, E. 'Le baptême dans les Églises syriennes de l'Inde', *L'Orient Syrien* 1 (1956) 255–266.

Khouri-Sarkis, Gabriel. 'Prières et cérémonies du baptême selon le rite de l'Église syrienne', *L'Orient Syrien* 1:158–184.

Botte, Bernard. 'Le baptême dans l'Église syrienne', *L'Orient Syrien* 1:137–157.

Daniélou, Jean. *Théologie du judéo-christianisme,* 359–393. Tournai, 1958. Translated, with additions and expansions, John A. Baker, *The Theology of Jewish Christianity*. London, 1964.

Segovia, A. *La illuminación baptismal en el antiguo cristianismo.* Grenada, 1958.

Beck, Hans-Georg. *Kirche und theologische Literatur im byzantinischen Reich,* 282 (bibliog.). Munich, 1959.

Evdokimov, Paul. *L'Orthodoxie,* 273–277. Neuchâtel-Paris, 1959.

Camelot, Pierre-Thomas. *Spiritualité du bapteme,* Lex orandi, 40. Paris, 1960.

Gaillard, Jean. 'Eau', DSp 4/1 (1960) 8–29.

Hamman, Adalbert. *L'initiation chrétienne,* Lettres chrétiennes, 7. Paris, 1963.

Daniélou, Jean. *L'entrée dans l'histoire du salut, Baptême et Confirmation,* Foi vivante, 36. Paris, 1967.

Trembelas, Panagiotis N. *Dogmatique de l'Église orthodoxe catholique,* 3:79–129. Chevetogne–Desclée de Brouwer, 1968.

Bobrinskoy, Boris. 'Le mystère pascal du Baptème', in A. Benoît, *et al., Baptême, sacrement d'unité,* 85–144. Paris, 1971.

Duffels, Y. C. and C. Geay, *Le baptême dans l'Église copte,* Liturgie et catéchèse, 1–2. Cairo, 1973.

Trumpp, E. *Das Taufbad der aethiopischen Kirche*. Munich, 1978.

Mouhanna, Augustin. *Les rites de l'initiation dans l'Église maronite,* OCA 212. Rome, 1980.

Winkler, Gabriele. *Das Armenische Initiationsrituale: entwicklungsgeschichtliche und liturgievergleichende Untersuchung der Quellen des 3. bis 10. Jahrhunderts,* OCA 217. Rome, 1982.

Bobrinskoy, Boris. 'Onction baptismale et Trinité dans la tradition syrienne ancienne', *Mens concordet voci pour Mgr. A.G. Martimort,* 559–568. Desclée, 1983.

Lanne, Emmanuel. 'L'acqua e l'unzione nelle Chiese orientali', *I simboli dell'iniziazione cristiana,* Studia Anselmiana, 87:37–156. Rome, 1983.

Mouhanna, Augustin. 'Le symbolisme dans les rites de l'initiation de l'Église maronite', Studia Anselmiana, 87:105–121.

Cabié, R. 'L'initiation chrétienne', in A.G. Martimort, *L'Église en prière,* 3:21–114. Desclée, 1984. Translated Matthew J. O'Connell, 'Christian Initiation', *The Church at Prayer,* 3:11–100. Collegeville, Minnesota, 1988.

Hamman, Adalbert, Ernst Dassmann, Russell J. de Simone. 'Battessimo', DP 1:500–508; 'Baptism', EEC 1:107–109.

Hamman, Adalbert. 'Iniziatione cristiana', DP 2:1779–1781; 'Initiation, Christian', EEC 1:409.

CONFIRMATION, P. 115.

Cyril of Jerusalem. *Mystagogical Lectures,* 3; *Catéchèses mystagogiques,* SCh 126 (1966)120ff; translated Leo P. McCauley and Anthony A. Stephenson, *Mystagogical Lectures, The Works of Saint Cyril of Jerusalem,* vol. 2, FC 64 (1979).

Nicholas Cabasilas. *The Life in Christ,* 3; *La vie en Christ,* 87ff. Chevetogne, 1960. Translated C. J. deCatanzaro. *The Life in Christ,* The Third Book,103ff. Crestwood, New York, 1974.

Chaine, M. 'Le rite éthiopien de la confirmation et du mariage', *Bessarione,* 24 (1913) 249–283.

Grébaut, S. 'Ordre du baptême et de confirmation dans l'Église éthiopienne', *Revue de l'Orient chrétien,* 20 (1927–1928) 105–189.

Cuttaz, François. 'Confirmation (effets)', DSp 2/2 (1953) 1412–1422.

Evdokimov, Paul. *L'Orthodoxie,* 277ff. Neuchâtel-Paris, 1959.

Verghese, Paul. 'Relation between Baptism, 'confirmation' and Eucharist in the Syrian Orthodox Church', *Studia liturgica,* 4 (1965) 81–93.

Ligier, Louis. *La confirmation. Sens et conjoncture oecuménique hier et aujourd'hui,* Théologie historique, 23 (bibliog.) Paris, 1973.

Neunheuser, Burkhard. 'Confermazione', DP 1:753–756; 'Confirmation', EEC 1:189–190.

THE EUCHARIST, PP. 115FF.

Hippolytus of Rome. *The Apostolic Tradition,* 7, 32; *La tradition apostolique,* SCh 11:35ff, 66ff. Translated Gregory Dix, *The Treatise on the Apostolic Tradition of St. Hippolytus of Rome*. London, 1937. Translated B. S. Easton, *The Apostolic Tradition of Hippolytus*. Cambridge, 1924. Translated Alistair Stewart-Sykes, *On the Apostolic Tradition, Hippolytus*. Crestwood, New York, 2001.

Cyril of Jerusalem. *Mystagogical Lectures,* 4; *Catéchèses mystagogiques,* SCh 126 (1966) 134ff. Translated Leo P. McCauley and Anthony A. Stephenson, *Mystagogical Lectures, The Works of Saint Cyril of Jerusalem,* vol. 2, FC 64 (1979).

Pseudo-Chrysostomus. *On Easter* 3; *Sur le Pâque* 3, SCh 36 (1953) 102ff.

Symeon the New Theologian, 4th Discourse, 5; *Catéchèses,* SCh 96 (1963) 312ff; deCatanzaro, CWS, 74–75. New York, 1980.

———. *Livre d'éthique* 3.41ff; SCh 122 (1966) 420ff (Contemplation et Eucharistie). Translated Alexander Golitzin, 'Third Discourse', *St Symeon the New Theologian*: *The Ethical Discourses,* 1:118ff. Crestwood, New York, 1996.

———. *Hymn* 26; *Hymnes,* SCh 174:68ff; translated George A. Maloney, *Hymns of Divine Love*. Denville, New Jersey, n.d.

Nicholas Cabasilas. *The Life in Christ,* 4; *La vie en Jésus-Christ,* 97ff. Chevetogne, 1960. Translated C. J. deCatanzaro, *The Life in Christ*. Crestwood, New York, 1974.

Arseniev, Nikolai S. *La piété russe,* 41. Neuchâtel, 1931. Translation A. Moorhouse, *Russian Piety*. 2nd ed. Crestwood, New York, 1975.

Daniélou, Jean. 'La catéchèse eucharistique chez les Pères de l'Église', *La messe et sa catéchèse,* Lex orandi, 7:73–85. Paris, 1946.

Kern, Kiprian. *Evcharistia*. Paris, 1947.

Duhr, Joseph. 'Communion fréquente', DSp 2 (1953) 1234–1292.

Betz, Johannes. *Die Eucharistie in der Zeit der griechischen Väter,* 1–2. Freiburg im Breisgau, 1995, 1961.

Evdokimov, Paul. *L'Orthodoxie,* 244ff, 265ff. Neuchâtel-Paris, 1959.

Bertaud, Émile. 'Dévotion eucharistique', DSp 4/2 (1961) 1621–1637.

Longpré, Éphrem. 'Eucharistie et expérience mystique', DSp 4/2:1593–1621.

Penco, G. 'La partecipazione alla via eucaristica presso il monchesimo antico', *Revista liturgica* 48 (1961) 184–192.

Kilmartin, Edward. *The Eucharist in the Primitive Church*. Englewood Cliffs, 1965.

———. *Church, Eucharist and Priesthood: A Theological Commentary on 'The Mystery and Worship of the Most Holy Eucharist'*. New York, 1981.

Bouyer, Louis. *Eucharistie. Théologie et spiritualité de la prière eucharistique*. Paris, 1966. Translation Charles Underhill Quinn, *Eucharist. Theology and Spirituality of the Eucharistic Prayer*. Notre Dame, Indiana, 1968.

Rohrdorf, Willy, *et al. L'Eucharistie des premiers chrétiens,* Le point théologique, 17. Paris, 1976.

Sánchez Caro, J. M. *Eucaristia y Historia de la Salvation, Estudio sobre la plegaría eucarística oriental,* Biblioteca de Autores Cristianos, 439. Madrid, 1983.

Felmy, K. Ch. *Die Deutung der göttlichen Liturgie in den russischen Theologie. Wege und Wandlungen russischer Liturgie-Auslegungen,* Arbeiten zur Kirchengeschichte, 54. Berlin-New York, 1984.

Hamman, Adalbert. 'Eucaristia', DP 1:1261–1266; 'Eucharist', EEC 1:292–293.

CONFESSION, P. 119.

Aphrahat. *Demonstrations,* 7: *De paenitentibus; Patrologica Syriaca* 1 (1894) 313–360.

Basil. *Canonical Letters* 188, 199, 217; PG 32:664ff, 716ff, 793ff; translated Agnes C. Way, *Saint Basil: The Letters,* 2 (186–368), FCh 28. New York, 1955.

Gregory of Nyssa. *Canonical Letters;* PG 45:221ff.

Symeon of Thessalonika. *De paenitentia;* PG 155:469–504.

Denzinger, Heinrich J. *Ritus orientalium . . . in administrandis sacramentis . . . .* Würzburg, 1863. 100ff.

*A Systematic Handbook,* 191, 428 (bibliog.).

Raes, Alphonse. 'Les formulaires grecs du rite de la pénitence', *Mélanges en l'honneur de Mgr. Adrien,* 365–732. Strasbourg, 1956.

Evdokimov, Paul. *L'Orthodoxie,* 288–292. Neuchâtel-Paris, 1959.

*Théophane le Reclus,* 273ff.

Trembelas, Panagiotis N. *Dogmatique de l'Église orthodoxe catholique,* 3:255–303. Chevetogne–Desclée de Brouwer, 1968.

Karpp, H. La Pénitence. *Textes et commentaires des origines de l'ordre pénitentiel de l'Église ancienne.* Neuchâtel, 1970.

*Liturgie et rémission des péchés. Conférences Saint-Serge,* XXe *Semaine d'études liturgiques* (Paris, July 2–5, 1973). Rome, 1975.

Papathanassiou-Ghinis, D. *Théologie et pastorale des pénitences selon l'Église orthodoxe* (bibliog.) Strasbourg, 1981.

Amato, A. *Il sacramento della Penitenze nelle Teologia Greco-Ortodossa* (16°–20° s.), Analecta Vlatadon, 38. Thessalonike, 1982.

Adnès, Piere. 'Pénitence', DSp 12/1 (1984) 943–1010 (bibliog.).

Vogel, C[yril]. 'Penitenza e riconciliazione', DP2:2742–2746; 'Penitence and Reconciliation', EEC 2:667–668.

THE ANOINTING OF THE SICK, P. 120.

Denzinger, Heinrich J. *Ritus orientalism . . . in administrandis sacramentis . . .*, Würzburg, 1863. 184–190.

Spáčil, Theophil. *Doctrina Orientis separati de infirmorum unctione.* Rome, 1931.

De Clercq, Charles. *Ordre, mariage, extrême onction. Bibliotheque catholique de sciences religieuses.* 1939.

De Vries, Wilhelm. *Sacramenten theologie bei den Nestorianen,* OCA 133:281–283. Rome, 1947.

Poschmann, Bernard. 'La pénitence et l'onction des malades', *Histoire des dogmes,* 4/3. Paris, 1966. Original title, *Busze und Letzte Ölung.* Freiburg im Breisgau, 1951. Translated (from the 2nd revised edition) Francis Courtney, *Penance and the Anointing of the Sick.* New York, 1964.

Dauvillier, J. 'Extrême-onction dans les Églises orientales', *Dictionnaire de droit canonique,* 5 (1953) 725–789.

Didier, J. C. 'Extrême-onction', *Catholicisme* 4 (1956) 987–1005.

Philippeau, H. R. *Catholicisme* 4:1005–1014: histoire du rite.

Lanne, Emmanuel. 'Liturgie alexandrine et liturgie romaine. L'onction des martyrs et la benediction de l'huile', *Irénikon* 31 (1958) 138–155.

Rondet, Henri. 'Extrême-onction', DSp 4/2 (1961) 2189–2200 (bibliog.).

*La maladie et la mort du chrétien dans la liturgie* (*Conférences Saint-Serge, 21e semaine d'études liturgiques, Paris, 1974).* Rome, 1975. Translated M. J. O'Connell, *Temple of the Holy Spirit. Sickness and Death of the Christian in the Liturgy.* New York, 1983.

Arranz, M. 'Christologie et ecclésiologie des prières pour les malades de l'Eucologe slave du Sinaï', *L'Église dans la liturgie,* Conférences Saint-Serge, 179:19–66. Rome, 1980.

Martimort, Aimé-Georges. 'Prière pour les malades et onction sacramentelle', in A.G. Martimort, *L'église en prière,* 3:132–153. Desclée, 1984. Translated by Matthew J. O'Connell, 'Prayer for the Sick and Sacramental Anointing', in *The Church at Prayer,* 3:117–137. Collegeville, Minnesota, 1988.

Neunheuser, Burkhard. 'Olio', DP 2:2464–2466; 'Oil', EEC 2:611.

———. 'Unzione, DP 2:3529–3532; 'Anointing', EEC 2:41–42.

MARRIAGE, P. 121.

John Chrysostom. *On Marriage; Traité sur le mariage unique,* SCh 138 (1968) 160–201. Translated Catherine P. Roth and David Anderson, *On Marriage and Family Life.* Crestwood, New York, 1997.

Symeon Thessalonicensis, *De matrimonio;* PG 155:503–516.

Denzinger, Heinrich J. *Ritus orientalium . . . in administrandis sacramentis. . . .*, 2: 364–482. Würzburg, 1963 (anastatic rpt. Graz, 1961).

Raes, Alphonse. *Le mariage, Sa célébration et sa spiritualité dans les Églises d'Orient,* Irénikon. Chevetogne, 1959.

*A Systematic Handbook,* 112, 219, 398 (bibliog.), 431 (texts).

Dalmais, Irénée Henri. 'La liturgie du mariage dans les Églises orientales', *La Maison-Dieu,* 50 (1957) 58–69.

Evdokimov, Paul. *L'Orthodoxie,* 292–298. Neuchâtel-Paris, 1959.

Trembelas, Panagiotis N. *Dogmatique de l'Église orthodoxe catholique,* 3:339–367. Chevetogne-Desclée De Brouwer, 1968.

Ritzer, K. *Formen, Riten und religiöses Brauchtum der Eheschliessung in der christlichen Kirchen des ersten Jahrtausends.* Münster, 1962. 2nd ed., 1982.

Dalmais, Henri Irénée. 'Die Eheliturgie', *Handbuch der Ostkirchenkunde,* 438–443. Düsseldorf, 1971.

Wiertz, Paul. 'Zur religiösen Volkskultur der orientalischen und orthodoxen Kirchen. Volksglauben und Volksbrauch', *Handbuch der Ostkirchenkunde,* 569–632, 621–624: Hochzeit.

Špidlík, Tomaš. 'La concezione cristologica del matrimonio nelle liturgie orientali', *Bessarione,* 1:139–152. Rome, 1979.

Passarelli, Gaetano. 'Le cerimonie dello stefanoma (incoronazione) nei riti matrimoniali bizantini secondo il codice Cryptense G.B. VII (X° secolo), *Ephemerides Liturgicae,* 93 (1979) 381–391.

Évenou, Jean. *Le mariage,* in A. G. Martimort, *L'Église en priere,* 3:201–224. Desclée de Brouwer, 1984. Translated Matthew J. O'Connell, 'Marriage', in Martimort, *The Church at Prayer,* 3:185–207. Collegeville, Minnesota, 1988.

Crouzel, H[enri], *et al.* 'Matrimonio', DP 2:2181–2190; 'Marriage', EEC 1:528–530.

ORDINATIONS, P. 121.

Hanssens, Jean Michel. 'Les oraisons sacramentelles des ordinations orientales', OCP 18 (1952) 297–318.

Botte, Bernard. 'La formule d'ordination "La grâce divine . . ." dans les rites orientaux', *Orient syrien* 2 (1957) 285–296.

Dalmais, Irénée Henri. *Les liturgies d'Orient,* Je sais, Je crois, 88–97. Fayard, 1959. Translated Donald Attwater, *Eastern Liturgies.* New York, 1960.

Lanne, Emmanuel. 'Les ordinations dans le rite copte, leurs relations avec les Constitutions apostoliques et la Tradition de saint Hippolyte', *Orient syrien* 5 (1960) 81–106.

Botte, Bernard. 'Les ordinations dans les rites orientaux', *Bulletin du Comité des études* 3 (1962) 13–18.

Dalmais, Irénée Henri. 'Ordinations et ministères dans les Églises orientales', *La Maison-Dieu,* 102 (1970) 73–81.

Kilmartin, Edward J. 'Ministère d'ordination dans l'Église chrétienne primitive', *La Maison-Dieu,* 138 (1979) 49–92.

Lécuyer, Joseph. *Le sacrement the l'ordination: recherche historique et théologique,* Théologie historique, 65. Paris, 1983.

Jounel, Pierre. 'Les ordinations', in A. G. Martimort, *L'Église en prière,* 3:154–200. Desclée, 1984; 'Ordinations', *The Church at Prayer,* 3:139–179. Collegeville, Minnesota, 1988.

Vogel, Cyril. 'Imposizione delle mani', DP 2:1768–1770; 'Laying on of Hands', EEC 1:477.

Nocent, Adrien. 'Ordine-Ordinatione', DP 2:2496–2501; 'Orders, Ordination', EEC 1:615–616.

Lécuyer, Joseph. 'Ministeri (ministri ordinati)', DP 2:2251–2259; 'Ministries, Ordained Ministers', EEC 2:560–562.

Heiler, Friedrich. *Die Religionen der Menschheit. Le religioni dell'umanità,* 257ff. Milan, 1985.

THE PRIESTHOOD, P. 121.

Hippolytus of Rome. *Apostolic Tradition,* 8; *La tradition apostolique,* SCh 11:37ff. Translated Gregory Dix, *The Treatise on the Apostolic Tradition of St. Hippolytus of Rome*. London, 1937. Translated B. S. Easton, *The Apostolic Tradition of Hippolytus*. Cambridge, 1924. Translated Alistair Stewart-Sykes, *On the Apostolic Tradition, Hippolytus*. Crestwood, New York, 2001.

John Chrysostom. *On the Priesthood; Sur le sacerdoce,* SCh 272 (1980); LNPF 9 (1903) 33ff.

Symeon the New Theologian. *Hymn* 19; SCh 174: 94ff. Translated George A. Maloney, *Hymns of Divine Love by St. Symeon the New Theologian,* 85ff. Denville, New Jersey, n.d.

Symeon Thessalonicensis, *De sacris ordinationibus;* PG 155:361–469.

Denziger, Heinrich J. *Ritus orientalium . . . in administrandis sacramentis . . . .* Würzburg, 1863 (rpt. Graz, 1961) 2:1–363.

Blondeel, M. *Les ordinations chez les Melkites*. Harissa, 1946.

Dalmais, Irénée Henri. 'Formules les plus caractéristiques des ordinations orientales', *Bulletin du Comité des études,* 38 (1962) 384–393.

Khouri-Sarkis, Gabriel. 'Le rituel du sacre des évêques et des patriarches dans l'Église syrienne', *Orient syrien* 8 (1963) 137–212.

'Prières d'ordination de l'Église ancienne', *La Maison-Dieu,* 138 (1979) 143–149.

Bardy, Gustave. *Le sacerdoce chrétien du 1er au 5e siècle,* Unam Sanctam, 28. Paris, 1954.

Daniélou, Jean. 'Le ministère sacerdotal chez les Pères grecs', *Études sur le sacrement de l'Ordre,* 147–165. Paris, 1957.

Lécuyer, Joseph. *Le sacrement dans le mystère du Christ,* part 5. Paris, 1957.

Evdokimov, Paul. *L'Orthodoxie.* Neuchâtel, 1959. 164ff.

Breydy, M. *Le concept du sacerdoce, Essai de théologie syro-maronite.* Beirut, 1964.

Colson, Jean. *Ministre de Jésus-Christ ou le sacerdoce de l'évangile,* Théologie historique, 4. Paris, 1966.

Dalmais, Irénée Henri. 'Die Sakramente: Theologie und Liturgie', *Handbuch der Ostkirchenkunde,* 415–456, 431ff (Die Weiheriten). Düsseldorf, 1971.

Ruiz Jurado, M. 'La espiritualidad sacerdotal en los primeros siglos cristianos', *Teología del sacerdotio,* 9:277–305. Burgos, 1977.

Lamarche, Paul. 'Presbytérat: Nouveau Testament et période subapostolique', DSp 12/2 (1986) 2069–2077.

Solignac, Aimé. 'Presbytérat: le 3e diècle', DSp 12/2:2077–2081.

Esquerda Bifet, Juan. 'Presbytérat: Du 4e au 6e siècle', DSp 12/2: 2081208–7.


LECTIO DIVINA, P. 130.


*Life of Melania the Younger,* 22ff; *Vie de sainte Mélanie,* SCh 90:172ff; translated Joan M. Petersen 'The Life of the Holy Melania by Gerontius', *Handmaids of the Lord,* CS 143:327ff. Kalamazoo, 1996.

Isaac the Syrian. 34e Discourse, *Oeuvres,* 210ff. Desclée de Brouwer, 1981. Translated A. J. Wensinck, *Mystic Treatises by Isaac of Nineveh.* Amsterdam, 1923.

Nicholas Cabasilas. *A Commentary on the Divine* Liturgy, 22; *Exposition de la divine liturgie,* SCh 4*bis:*154ff; translated Hussey-McNulty, 61–62. London, 1960.

*The Art of Prayer,* 106–107, 130, 246–247; *L'art de la prière,* 144ff; for additional texts, see DSp 9 (1976) 474.

*A Systematic Handbook,* 7, 41, 74.

Gorce, D. 'La "lectio divina"' . . . *S. Jérôme et la lecture sacrée* . . . . Paris-Wépion, 1925.

Leclercq, Jean. 'La lecture divine', in *La Maison-Dieu* 5 (1946) 21–33.

Jousse, M. *La manducation de la leçon dans le milieu ethnique palestinien.* Paris, 1950.

Bouyer, Louis. *Le sens de la vie monastique,* 257–272. Paris, 1950. Translated Kathleen Pond, *The Meaning of the Monastic Life.* New York, 1955.

Bacht, Heinrich. '"Meditatio" in den ältesten Mönchsquellen', *Geist und Leben* 28 (1955) 360–373.

Špidlík, Tomaš. 'L'autorità del libro per il monachesimo russo', *Monachesimo orientale,* OCA 153:159–179. Rome, 1958. Rpt. *Les grands mystiques russes,* 205–238. Paris, 1979. See DSp 11 (1982) 975ff.

Aron, Robert. *Les années obscures de Jesus,* 72–86. Paris, 1960. Translated as *Jesus of Nazareth: The Hidden Years.* New York, 1962.

Leclercq, Jean. 'Les caractères traditionnels de la "lectio divina"', *La liturgie et les paradoxes chrétiens,* 243–257. Paris, 1963.

———. 'Les caractéristiques de la spiritualité monastique', *Aux sources de la spiritualité occidentale,* 276–277, 309ff. Paris, 1964.

Špidlík, Tomaš. 'Der Enfluss cyrillo-methodianischer Uebersetzungen auf die Mentalität der russischen Mönche', *Annales Instituti Slavici,* I/4:95–105. Wiesbaden, 1968.

Rouillard, P. 'Lectio divina', *Catholicisme* 7 (1969) 170–171.

Meyer, Robert T. '"Lectio divina" in Palladius', *Kyriakon (Festschrift J. Quasten)* 2:580–584. Münster, 1970.

Perrot, Charles. *La lecture de la Bible dans la synagogue: les anciennes lectures palestiniennes du Shabbat et des fêtes.* Hildesheim, 1973.

Rousse, Jacques. 'La lectio divina', DSp 9 (1976) 470–87 (bibliog.).

Sieben, Hermann Josef. 'De la lectio divina à la lecture spirituelle', DSp 9:487–496.

Gribomont, Jean. 'Lectio divina', DP 2:1918–1920; 'Lectio divina', EEC 1:478.

Canart, Paul. 'Libro', DP 2:1956–1959; 'Book', EEC 1:125–126.

Řezáč, Joannes. 'Lectio divina', DIP 5 (1978) 561–562.

Giurisato, G. *Lectio divina oggi,* (bibliog., 29–38). Parma, 1966. 2nd ed., Praglia, 1987.

THE READING OF SCRIPTURE, P. 132.

Origen. *Homilies on Joshua,* 20.1ff; *Homélies sur Josué;* SCh 71:406ff.

———. *Homilies on Genesis,* 12.5; *Homélies sur la Genèse,* SCh 7:211ff; translated Ronald E. Heine, *Origen. Homilies on Genesis and Exodus,* FC 71 (1982) 180ff.

———. *Letter to Gregory; Lettre à Gregoire le Thaumaturge,* SCh 148:192ff; ANF 4:393ff.

Theophilus of Antioch. *Three books to Autolycus,* 2; *Trois livres à Autolycus,* SC 20 (1948) 94ff; ANF 2:89ff.

Pseudo-Macarius. *Homilies,* 28.5; SCh 275 (1980) 338ff; translated Maloney, *Pseudo-Macarius: Fifty Spiritual Homilies . . . ,* CWS 185. New York, 1992.

Hazzâyâ, Rabban Jausep. *Briefe,* 126ff, 155.

Symeon the New Theologian. Tenth Discourse, 370ff; *Éthique,* SCh 129 (1967) 286ff; translated Alexander Golitzin, *St Symeon the New Theologian . . . : The Ethical Discourses,* 1:142ff. Crestwood, New York, 1996.

*A Systematic Handbook,* 5, 237, (against the demons), 377 (bibliog.), 415 (texts).

Florovsky, Georges. 'La bible et l'Église', *Dieu vivant* 21 (1952) 95–102.

Daniélou, Jean. *Origène comme exégète de la Bible,* Studia Patristica, 1, TU 63 (1957).

Evdokimov, Paul. *L'Orthodoxie,* 187ff. Neuchâtel, 1959.

Lefèvre, André. 'La Bible—livre spirituel', DSp 4/1 (1960) 128–132.

Kirchmeyer, Jean. 'Écriture Sainte et vie spirituelle: dans l'Église orientale', DSp 4/1:242–247.

Crouzel, Henri. 'Origène, précurseur du monachisme', *Théologie de la vie monastique,* 15–18. Paris, 1961.

Colombás, Garcia. 'La Bibbia en la espiritualidad del monacato primitivo', *Yermo* 1 (1963) 3–20, 149–170, 271–286.

*Théophane le Reclus,* 264ff.

Stramare, T. 'Mensae duae. Studio biblico-patristico su S. Scrittura ed Eucaristia', *Seminarium* 18 (1966) 1020–1034.

Tamburrino, P. 'Bibbia a vita spirituale negli scritti di Orsiesi', *Bibbia e spiritualità.* Rome, 1967. 83–120.

Recchia, V. *L'iniziazione biblica negli autori cristiani antichi.* Bari, 1969.

Leloir, Louis. 'La lecture de l'Écriture selon les anciens Pères', RAM 47 (1971) 183–199.

———. 'La Bible et les Pères du désert d'après les deux collections arméniennes des Apophthegmes', *La Bible et les Pères,* 113–134. Paris, 1971.

*La Bible et les Pères* (Colloque de Strasbourg, 1–3 October, 1969). Paris, 1971.

Burton-Christie, Douglas. *The Word in the Desert. Scripture and the Quest for Holiness in Early Christian Monasticism.* New York, 1993.

Kaczynski, K. *Die Predigten des Johannes Chrysostomus als Zeugnis für die Rolle der Schrift in Gottesdienst und Alltag seiner Gemeinden.* Trier, 1971.

Todde, M. 'Lettura a meditazione della Scrittura secondo la tradizione patristica', *Servitium* 7 (1973) 515–526.
Špidlík, Tomaš. 'L'obbedienza tra carisma e istituzione', *Vita monastica* 24 (1974) 36–49.
Rousse, Jacques. 'La lectio divina', DSp 9 (1976) 470–487.
Angelini, M. I. *Il monaco e la parabola. Saggio sulla spiritualità monastica della lectio divina.* Brescia, 1981.
Guillet, Jacques. 'Parole de Dieu', DSp 12/1 (1984) 237–252.
Secondin, B., T. Zecca, and B. Calati, edd. *Parola di Dio e Spiritualità,* Bibl. di Scienze Religiose 62. Rome, 1984.
Gribomont, Jean. 'Scrittura (sacra)', DP 2:3118–3124; 'Scripture, Holy', EEC 2:762–764.

READING THE FATHERS, P. 134.

*A Systematic Handbook,* 6ff, 360 (bibliog.).
Kern, Kiprian. *Les traductions russes des textes patristiques. Guide bibliographique.* Chevetogne, 1957.
Richard, Marcel. 'Florilèges spirituels grecs', DSp 5 (1964) 475–512.
Barré, Henri, and Réginald Grégoire. 'Homéliaires', DSp 7/1 (1969) 597–617.

BIOGRAPHIES OF SAINTS, P. 135.

Bardy, Gustave. 'Biographies spirituelles: Antiquité chretienne', DSp 1 (1936) 1624–1634.
Hausherr, Irénée. 'Biographies spirituelles: Époque byzantine', DSp 1:1634–1646.
Kologrivof, Ivan. *Essai sur la sainteté en Russie,* 19ff. Bruges, 1953.
Beck, Hans-Georg. *Kirche und theologische Literatur im byzantinischen Reich,* 267ff. (Hagiographie). Münster, 1959.
Velat, Bernard. 'Éthiopie: Hagiographie', DSp 4/2 (1961) 1465.
Pétré, Hélène. 'Exemplum: Époque patristique', DSp 4/2 (1961) 1885–1892.
Garitte, Gérard. 'Géorgienne' (littérature spirituelle), DSp 6 (1967) 244–256.

THE SEARCH FOR THE SPIRITUAL SENSE, P. 136.

Origen. *Contra Celsum* 1.48; SCh 132 (1967) 200ff; ANF 4:416ff.
———. *Homilies on Genesis,* 9.1; *Homélies sur la Genèse,* SCh 7*bis:* 236ff; translated Ronald E. Heine, *Origen. Homilies on Genesis and Exodus,* FCh 71 (1982).

———. *Homilies on Leviticus,* 1.1, 4.1, 5.1; *Homélies sur le Lévitique,* SCh 286 (1981) 66ff, 162ff; 204ff; translated Gary W. Barkley, *Origen. Homilies on Leviticus* 1–16, FCh 83 (1990).

———. *Homilies on Joshua,* 8.1; *Homélies sur Josué,* SC 71 (1960) 218ff.

———. *Commentary on John,* 10.10ff; *Commentaire sur saint Jean,* SCh 157:386ff; translated Ronald E. Heine, *Origen. Commentary on the Gospel According to John*. Books 1–10, FCh 80 (1989).

Didymus the Blind. *On Zachary* 4.1; *Sur Zacharie,* SCh 85:804ff.

Hazzâyâ, Rabban Jausep. *Briefe,* 180ff.

Symeon the New Theologian, *Catecheses,* 24; SCh 113 (1965) 34ff; de-Catanzaro, CWS, 261ff.

Gregory Palamas. *Défense des saints hésychastes,* 2.1.11 (Louvain, 1959) 246ff.

Mondésert, Claude. *Clément d'Alexandrie. Introduction à l'étude de sa pensée religieuse à partir de l'Écriture,* Théologie, 4. Paris, 1944.

de Lubac, Henri. 'Sens spirituel', RSR 36 (1946) 542–576.

Daniélou, Jean. 'L'Unité des deux Testaments dans l'oeuvre d'Origène', RSR 22 (1948) 27–56.

———. Histoire et Esprit. *L'intelligence de l'Écriture d'après Origène,* Théologie, 6. Paris, 1950.

Olphe-Galliard, Michel. 'Cassien', DSp 2/1 (1953) 259ff.

Gruber, Winfried. *Die pneumatische Exegese bei den Alexandrinern. Ein Beitrag zur Noematik der Heiligen Schrift*. Graz, 1957.

Kamenicky, E. 'Vom Wort Gottes, Grundlagen spiritueller Schriftauflegung', *Mystische Theologie,* 5/1 (1959) 9–118.

Gögler, Rolf. *Zur Theologie des Biblischen Wortes bei Origenes*. Düsseldorf, 1963.

Kerrigan, A. 'The Objects of the Literal and Spiritual Senses of the New Testament According to St. Cyril of Alexandria', *Studia Patristica* 1, TU 63 (1957) 354–374.

Crouzel, Henri. *Origène et la 'connaissance mystique'*. Paris-Bruges, 1961. [In English, see A. S. Worrall's translation of the author's 1985 work, *Origène: Origen,* Part Two: Exegesis, 61ff. San Francisco, 1989.]

von Balthasar, Hans Urs. *La gloire et la croix,* Théologie, 61. Paris, 1965. (A translation of *Herrlichkeit: Eine theologische Ästhetik*. Einsiedeln, 1961.) Translated Erasmo Leiva-Merikakis, *The Glory of the Lord: A Theological Aesthetics*. San Francisco, 1982–1989.

Calati, B. 'La conversione dell'intelligenza spirituale alla Scrittura', *Vita monastica* 23 (1969) 139–154.

Simonetti, M[anlio]. 'Esegesi patristica', DP 1:1211–1123; 'Exegesis, patristic', EEC 2:309–311.

Allegorical and typological exegesis, p. 138.

Irenaeus. *Adversus haereses* 4.26.1; SCh 100 (1965) 712ff; ANF 1:496ff.

Origen. *Homilies on Genesis,* 5.5 and 9.2; *Homélies sur la Genèse,* SCh 7:141ff, 178ff; translated Ronald E. Heine, *Origen: Homilies on Genesis and Exodus,* FCh 71:117ff.

———. *Homilies on Joshua,* 8.6, 12.1, 17.1; *Homélies sur Josué,* SCh 71:232ff, 294ff, 370ff.

Didymus the Blind. *Sur Zacharie,* 1, 375ff; SCh 83 (1962) 392ff.

Basil. *Homilies on the Hexameron,* 3.9 (a critique of allegorical interpretation); *Homélies sur l'Hexaméron,* SCh 28*bis:* 234ff; translated Agnes C. Way, *Saint Basil. Exegetic Homilies,* FCh 46 (1963) 51ff.

Cassian. *Conferences,* 14.11 (on the many meanings of Scripture); SCh 54 (1954) 197ff; translated Ramsey, ACW 57:515–517; translated Luibheid, CWS, 165ff.

Heinisch, P. *Der Einfluss Philos auf die älteste christliche Exegese,* Alttestestamentliche. Abhandlungen 1, 2. Munster, 1908.

Hoornaert, R. 'Allégorie', DSp 1 (1936) 310–314.

de Lubac, Henri. 'Typologie et allégorisme', RSR 34 (1947) 180–226.

Daniélou, Jean. *Sacramentum futuri. Études sur les origines de la typologie biblique.* Paris, 1950; translated Wulstan Hibberd, *From Shadows to Reality. Studies in the Biblical Typology of the Fathers.* London, 1960.

Kerrigan, A. *St. Cyril of Alexandria Interpreter of the Old Testament. Anal. biblica* 2. Rome, 1952.

Cavallera, Ferdinand. 'Cantique des Cantiques: Histoire de l'interprétation spirituelle', DSp 2/1 (1953) 93–101.

Daniélou, Jean. *Origène comme exégète de la Bible,* Studia patristica 1, TU 63 (1957) 280–290.

Hanson, Richard Patrick C. *Allegory and Event. A Study of the Sources and Significance of Origen's Interpretation of Scripture.* London-Richmond, Virginia, 1959.

Daniélou, Jean, *et al.* 'Écriture et vie spirituelle dans la tradition: époque patristique (2e–6e siècles)', DSp 4/1 (1960) 132–169.

Daniélou, Jean. 'Exégèse et typologie patristique', DSp 4/1 (1960) 132–138.

———. *Typologie et allégorie chez Clement d'Alexandrie,* Studia patristica 4, TU 79:50–57.

Daniélou, Jean. *Etudes d'exégèse judeo-chrétienne (les Testimonia).* Paris, 1966.

Pépin, J. *Mythe et allegorie. Les origines grecques et les contestations judeo-chrétiennes.* 2nd ed. Paris, 1976.

de Margerie, Bernard. *Introduction à l'histoire de l'exégèse* I. *Les Pères grecs et orientaux*. Paris, 1980; translated Leonard Maluf, *An Introduction to the History of Exegesis,* vol. 1: *The Greek Fathers*. Petersham, Mass., 1991.

Gargano, G. I. *La teoria di Gregorio di Nissa sul Cantico dei cantici. Indagine su alcune indicazione di metodo esegetico,* OCA 216. Rome, 1981.

Canévet, M. *Grégoire de Nysse et l'herméneutique biblique. Études des rapports entre le langage et la connaissance de Dieu,* Part IV: 289–361: Symbolisme et exégèse. Paris, 1983.

MORAL EXEGESIS, P. 138.

Gribomont, Jean. *Les Règles Morales de saint Basile et le Nouveau Testament,* Studia Patristica 2, TU 64 (1957) 416–426.

Guy, Jean-Claude. 'Écriture Sainte: dans le monachisme', DSp 4/1 (1960) 159–164.

Boularand, Ephrem. 'Écriture Sainte: Saint Jean Chrysostome', DSp 4/1:150–153.

MYSTICAL EXEGESIS, P. 139.

Kirchmeyer, Jean. 'Écriture Sainte: Isaac de Ninive', DSp 4/1 (1960) 243–244.

See Scriptural Mysticism, p. 230.

MEDITATION, P. 140.

Isaac the Syrian. 31st and 35th Discourses, *Oeuvres,* 195ff, 218ff. Desclée de Brouwer, 1981. Translated Wensinck, *Mystic Treatises by Isaac of Nineveh*. Amsterdam, 1923.

Nicholas Cabasilas. *The Life in Christ,* 6–7; *La vie en Jesus-Christ,* 152ff. Chevetogne, 1960. Translated deCatanzaro, Crestwood, New York, 1974.

*The Art of Prayer,* 75–79 ('secret meditation'); *L'art de la prière,* 98ff.

Muyser, Jacob. *Quelques indices sur l'existence de la méditation spontanée 'non méthodique' dans la première école de spiritualité chrétienne, celles des Pères du Désert*. Cairo, 1951 (excerpts in *Les Cahiers Carmélitains,* vol. II).

von Severus, Emmanuel. 'Das Wort "meditari" im Sprachgebrauch der Heiligen Schrift', *Geist und Leben* 26 (1953) 365–375.

Rabbow, Paul. *Seelenführung. Methodik der Exerzitien in der Antike.* Munich, 1954.
Bacht, Heinrich. '*Meditatio* in den ältesten Mönchsquellen', *Geist und Leben* 28 (1955) 360–373.
Hausherr, Irénée. *Noms du Christ et voies d'oraison,* OCA 157 (Rome, 1960) 171; translated Charles Cummings, *The Name of Jesus,* CS 44. Kalamazoo, 1978.
Kirchmeyer, Jean. 'Ecriture Sainte: Syméon le Nouveau Théologien', DSp 4/1 (1960) 244–245.
*Théophane le Reclus,* 267ff.
von Severus, Emmanuel and Aimé Solignac. 'Méditation: De l'Écriture aux auteurs médievaux', DSp 10 (1980) 907–914.

LEARNING BY HEART, P. 140.

Michel, O. μιμνήσικομαι. . . ', Kittel 4 (1967) 675–683.
Bacht, Heinrich. '"Meditari" in den ältesten Mönchsquellen', *Geist und Leben* 28 (1955) 360–373.
Kirchmeyer, Jean. 'Sainte Écriture: Évagre et l'antirrhétique', DSp 4/1 (1961) 164–167.
Rousse, Jacques. 'La lectio divina', DSp 9 (1976) 470–487.
Solignac, Aimé. 'Mémoire: dans l'Écriture, dans la tradition augustinienne', DSp 10 (1980) 991–1002.

THE 'TESTIMONIES' OF SCRIPTURE, P. 142.

de Vregille, Bernard. 'Écriture Sainte: L'âge des florilèges', DSp 4/1 (1960) 176–187.
Daniélou, Jean. *Études d'exégèse judeo-chrétienne (Les Testimonia),* Théologie, 5. Paris, 1966.
Gribomont, Jean. 'Testimonia', DP 2:3435–3436; 'Testimonia', EEC 2:821.

THE USE OF THE IMAGINATION IN PRAYER, P. 146.

Isaac the Syrian. 36e Discourse; *Oeuvres,* 221ff. Desclée de Brouwer, 1981. Translated A. J. Wensinck, *Mystic Treatises by Isaac of Nineveh.* Amsterdam, 1923.
*The Art of Prayer,* 25, 33, 68, 96, 100–101, 115, 182–183, 223; *L'art de la prière,* 26ff, 38ff, 87–90, 129, 134ff, 155, 251ff, 304.
Maréchal, J. 'Application des sens', DSp 1 (1936) 810–828.

Lemaitre, J (Hausherr), 'Contemplation imaginative', DSp 2/2 (1953) 1959ff.

Selig, Karl Ludwig. 'Emblèmes religieux', DSp 7/2 (1971) 1529–1535.

Rayez, André. 'Imaginerie et dévotion', DSp 7/2 (1971) 1529–1535.

Blasucci, Antonio. 'Images et contemplation', DSp 7/2 (1971) 1472–1490.

Musurillo, Herbert A. 'Méthode d'Olympe: méthodes de méditation', DSp 10 (1980) 1113ff.

CONTEMPLATION, PP. 152FF.

See the terms 'contemplation' *(theoria)* and 'knowledge, spiritual' *(gnosis, epignosis)* in the Index of the *Philokalia. The Complete Text,* vol. I (London, 1979).

Cassian. *Conferences,* 14 (spiritual knowledge); SCh 54:182ff; translated Ramsey, ACW 57:503–534; translated Luibheid, *John Cassian. Conferences,* CWS, 114ff.

Diadochus of Photice. *One hundred Gnostic Chapters,* 67ff; *Cent chapitres gnostiques,* SCh 5ter:127ff; translated G. E. H. Palmer, Philip Sherrard, Kallistos Ware, 'On Spiritual Knowledge and Discrimination: One Hundred Texts', *The Philokalia. The Complete Text,* I: 275ff. London, 1979.

Mark the Monk. 'On Those who Think that They are Made Righteous by Works: Two Hundred and Twenty-Six Texts', *The Philokalia,* 1 (1979) 125ff; 'De ceux qui pensent être justifiés 135ff, *Spiritualité orientale* 41, 55. Bellefontaine, 1985.

Isaac the Syrian. 65th Discourse, *Oeuvres,* 340ff. Desclée de Brouwer, 1981. Translated A. J. Wensinck, *Mystic Treatises of Isaac of Nineveh.* Amsterdam, 1923.

Symeon the New Theologian. Third Discourse, 1ff; *Livre d'éthique,* SCh 122:390ff; translated Alexander Golitzin, *St Symeon the New Theologian . . . : The Ethical Discourses,* 1:21ff. Crestwood, New York, 1996.

Gregory Palamas. *Défense des saints hésychastes,* I.1.1ff ; Louvain, 4ff; translated Gendle, *The Triads,* CWS, p. 25. New York, 1983.

*The Art of Prayer,* 64, 66, 72–73, 175; *L'art de la prière,* 95ff.

*A Systematic Handbook,* 327ff, 441 (bibliog.).

Honoré de Sainte Marie. *Tradition des Pères et des auteurs ecclésiastiques sur la contemplation.* Paris, 1708.

Lebreton, Jules. 'Les degrés de la connaissance religieuse d'après Origène', RSR 12 (1922) 254–296.

Bremond, Jean. *Les Pères du Désert,* 445–570. Paris, 1927.

Festugière, Jean. *Contemplation et vie contemplative selon Platon.* Paris, 1936.

Hausherr, Irénée. *Gregorii monache Cyprii De theoria sancta,* OCA 110. Rome, 1937.

Rudberg, G. 'Hellenisches Schauen', *Classica et Medievalia* 5 (1942) 159–186.

Daniélou, Jean. *Platonisme et théologie mystique. La doctrine spirituelle de saint Grégoire de Nysse,* Théologie, 2 (1944, 1953) 152–182.

Grilli, Albert. *Il problema della vita contemplativa nel mondo greco-romano.* Milan, 1953.

Lebreton, Jules. 'Clément d'Alexandrie: la perfection chrétienne et la contemplation', DSp 2/1 (1953) 954ff.

'Contemplation . . .', articles in DSp 2/2 (1953) 1643–2193, particularly J. Lemaitre (Hausherr) 1762–1787 ('contemplation chez les Grecs at autres orientaux').

von Balthasar, Hans Urs. *La prière contemplative.* Paris, 1958. English translation, based on the german original, *Das Betrachtende Gebet* (1957), by A. V. Littledale: *Prayer.* New York, 1961.

Rendina, S. *La contemplazione negli scritti di S. Basilio Magno.* Rome, 1959.

Hausherr, Irénée. *Les leçons d'un contemplatif. Le traité de l'Oraison d'Évagre le Pontique.* Paris, 1960. See also, *Evagrius Ponticus. The Praktikos. Chapters on Prayer,* translated by John E. Bamberger. CS 4. Kalamazoo, 1970.

Crouzel, Henri. *Origène et la 'connaissance mystique', Museum Lessianum, Section théologique* 56. Paris-Bruges, 1961.

Colombás, G. M. *Paradis et vie angélique,* 180ff. Paris, 1961.

von Balthasar, Hans Urs. *Kosmische Liturgie, Das Weltbild des Maximus Confessor.* Freiburg im Breisgau, 1941; 2nd rev. ed., Einsiedeln, 1962.

Van der Aalst, Patricius. 'Contemplation et Hellénisme', *Proche-Orient Chrétien* 14 (1964) 151–168.

von Ivánka, Endre. *Plato christianus. Uebernahme und Umgestaltung des Platonismus durch die Väter.* Einsiedeln, 1964.

Völker, Walther. *Maximus Confessor als Meister des geistlichen Lebens.* Wiesbaden, 1965.

*Théophane le Reclus,* 251ff.

Kirchmeyer, Jean. 'Grecque (Église)', DSp 6 (1967) 848–856.

Camelot, Pierre Thomas. 'Hellénisme: la contemplation', DSp 7/1 (1969) 156–162.

Špidlík, Tomaš. 'La contemplazione nella spiritualità cristiana orientale', *Enciclopedia delle religioni,* 2:385–390. Firenze, 1970.

Altissimo, C. *La contemplazione nell'Oriente cristiano.* Vicenze, 1979.

Solignac, Aimé and L. Donnat. 'Marthe et Marie', DSp 10 (1980) 664–673.

Couilleau, Guerrie. 'Perfection: Pères et premiers moines', DSp 12/1 (1984) 1081–1118.

CONTEMPLATION: TERMS, P. 155.

*A Systematic Handbook: gnosis,* 70, 76, 114, 178, 208, 275, 296, 327, 336, 343, 375 (bibliog.).

Stephanus, Henricus. *Thesaurus Graecae Linguae* 4 (1841) 349–353: θεωρέω, θεωρία, etc.

Arnou, René. Πρᾶξις et θεωρία, *Étude de détail sur le vocabulaire et la pensée des Ennéades de Plotin.* Paris, 1921. Rpt. Rome, 1972.

Ziehen, L. *'Theoria',* Pauly-Wissowa, *Real-encyclopädie der classischen Altertumswissenschaft* 10 (1934) 2228–2233.

Arnou, René. 'La contemplation chez les anciens philosophes du monde gréco-romain', DSp 2/2 (1953) 1717–1742.

Lemaitre, J. (Hausherr), 'Contemplation . . . Étude de vocabulaire', DSp 2/2:1762–1768.

Bouyer, Louis. 'Gnosis. Le sens orthodoxe de l'expression jusqu'aux Pères alexandrins', *The Journal of Theological Studies,* New Series (1953) 188–203.

Michaelis, [Wilhelm]. ὁράω, . . . , Kittel 5 (1967) 315–382.

Colpe, C., E. Haenchen, G. Kretchmar. *'Gnôsis', Die Religion in Geschichte der Gegenwart,* 3rd ed., Tubingen, 1958. Vol. 2:1648–1661.

Rahner, Karl. 'Gnosis', LThK 4 (1960) 1019–1021.

Bouyer, Louis. *La spiritualité du Nouveau Testament et des Pères,* 262–337. Paris, 1960; translated Mary P. Ryan, *The Spirituality of the New Testament and the Fathers.* 211–255. New York, 1963.

Lampe, Geoffrey W. H. *A Patristic Greek Lexikon:* s.v. θεωρέω, θεωρία, 647–649; γνῶσις, 318–320. Oxford, 1961.

Emmet, Dorothy. 'Theoria and the Way of Life', *The Journal of Theological Studies* 17 (1966) 38–52.

Crouzel, Henri. *Origène et la 'connaissance mystique',* 395ff (les divers termes grecs). Paris-Bruges, 1961.

Hausherr, Irénée. 'Τὴν θεωρίαν ταύτην, Un hapax eirémenon et ses conséquences', OCS 176 (1966) 247–253 (rpt. from *Bolletino Regina Mundi,* no. 11).

Camelot, Pierre Thomas. 'Gnose chrétienne', DSp 6 (1967) 509–523.

Daniélou, Jean. *L'être et le temps chez Grégoire de Nysse,* 1–17 *(theôria).* Leiden, 1970.

*Grégoire de Nazianze,* 113ff.

Špidlík, Tomaš. 'La theoria et la praxis chez Grégoire de Nazianze', *Studia Patristica* 14, Tu 117 (Berlin, 1976) 358–364.

Filoramo, Giovanni. 'Gnosi-gnosticismo', DP 2:1642–1650; 'Gnosis-Gnosticism', EEC 1:353–354.

THE OBJECT OF CONTEMPLATION: LOGOS, SOPHIA, PP. 158FF.

Lieske, Aloysius. *Die Theologie der Logosmystik bei Origenes.* Münster, 1938.

Loosen, J. *Logos und Pneuma in begnadeten Menschen bei Maximus Confessor.* Münster, 1941.

de Lubac, Henri. *Histoire et Esprit, l'Intelligence de l'Ecriture d'après Origene.* Paris, 1950.

Dalmais, Irénée Henri. 'La théorie des "Logoi" des creatures chez s. Maxime le Confesseur', *Revue des Sciences Philosophiques et Théologiques* 36:244–249. Paris, 1952.

Lemaitre, J. 'Contemplation . . .', DSp 2/2 (1953) 1801ff, 1818ff.

von Balthasar, Hans Urs. *Parole et mystère chez Origène.* Paris, 1957.

Harl, Marguerite. *Origène et la fonction révélatrice du Verbe incarné,* Patristica Sorbonensia 2. Paris, 1958.

*La sophiologie de S. Basile,* OCA 162. Rome, 1961.

Gögler, Rolf. *Zur Theologie des biblischen Wortes bei Origenes.* Düsseldorf, 1963.

Thunberg, Lars. *Microcosm and Mediator. The Theological Anthropology of Maximus the Confessor.* Copenhagen-Lund, 1965.

*Grégoire de Nazianze,* 3ff.

Solignac, Aimé. 'Logos', DSp 9 (1976) 958–960.

Florenskij, Pavel. *Stolp i Utverzhenie Istiny—Opyt Pravoslavnoi v Dvenadtsati Pismakh* [*The Pillar and Foundation of Truth. An Essay in Orthodox Theodicy in Twelve Letters*]. Moscow, 1914. French translation by C. Andronikof, *La colonne et le fondement de la vérité: essai d'une théodicée orthodoxe en douze lettres.* Lausanne, 1975. Pp. 209–254. [See also Robert Slesinski, *Pavel Florensky. A Metaphysics of Love,* Index, s.v. *Logos, Sophia.* Crestwood, New York, 1984].

*Handbuch der Ostkirchenkunde,* 784 (bibliog.: sophiology). Düsseldorf, 1971.

THE ORGAN OF CONTEMPLATION: *NOUS,* PP. 168FF.

Evagrius. *Chapters on Prayer,* 63, 84; Hausherr, *Leçons,* 90; 84ff; CS 4, 65, 69.

Isaac the Syrian. First Discourse, *Oeuvres,* 59ff. Desclée de Brouwer, 1981. *Mystic Treatises of Isaac of Nineveh,* 1ff. Amsterdam, 1923.

Gregory Palamas. *Défense des saints hésychastes,* II, 3,63 and II, 3,48; Louvain, 516ff, 484ff.

*The Art of Prayer,* 17–8, 22, 26, 68–9, 181–198; *L'art de la prière,* 21ff, 87–90, 258ff, 378.

*A Systematic Handbook,* 310, 322, 332, 377 (bibliog.).

Festugière, André Jean. *Contemplation et vie contemplative selon Platon,* 28ff. Paris, 1936.

Arnou, René. 'La contemplation chez les anciens philosophes gréco-romains', DSp 2/2 (1953) 1716–1742.

Armstrong, Arthur Hilary. 'The Plotinian Doctrine of ΝΟΥΣ in Patristic Theology', *Vigiliae christianae,* 8 (1954) 234–238.

Rendina, Sergio. *La contemplazione negli scritti di S. Basilio Magno.* Rome, 1959.

von Ivánka, Endre. *Plato christianus. Übernahme und Umgestalltung des Platonismus durch die Väter.* Einsiedeln, 1964.

Arnou, René. *Le désir de Dieu dans la philogophie de Plotin.* 2nd ed. Rome, 1967.

Camelot, Pierre Thomas. 'Hellénisme', DSp 7/1 (1969) 145–164; especially, 158ff.

Špidlík, Tomaš. *Grégoire de Nazianze. . .*, OCA 189:25ff. Rome, 1971.

Bacht, Heinrich. 'Logismos', DSp 9 (1975) 955–958.

Solignac, Aimé. '"*NOUS*" et "*Mens*"', DSp 11 (1982) 459–469.

Lilla, S[alvatore]. 'Nous', DP 2:2423–2433; 'Nous', EEC 1:601–603.

THE INTUITIVE *NOUS*, P. 170.

Leisegang, H. *Der heilige Geist. Das Wesen und Werden der mystisch-intuitiven Erkenntnis in der Philosophie und Religion der Griechen,* vol. I. Leipzig, 1919.

Pourrat, Pierre. 'Clairvoyance spirituelle', DSp 2/1 (1953) 922–929.

Lemaitre, J. (Hausherr). 'Contemplation . . . , DSp 2/2 (1953) 1805ff.

de Bovis, André. 'Inspirations divines', DSp 7/2 (1971) 1791–1803.

Derville, André. 'Paroles intérieures', DSp 12/1 (1984) 252–257.

See Heart, The Spiritual Senses.

THE SPIRITUAL SENSES, P. 171.

Origène. *Homilies on Leviticus,* 3.7; *Homélies sur le Lévitique,* SCh 286:150; translated Gary W. Barkley, *Origen. Homilies on Leviticus 1–16,* FCh 83 (1990).

Gregory of Nyssa. *The Life of Moses;* SCh 1*bis:*75ff; PG 44:372ff; translated Malherbe and Ferguson, *Gregory of Nyssa. The Life of Moses,* CWS, CS 31:31ff. New York, Kalamazoo, 1978.

Pseudo-Macarius. Homilies, 15.1; *Homélies,* SCh 275:172; translated Maloney, *Pseudo-Macarius: The Fifty Spiritual Homilies . . . ,* CWS, 1008. New York, 1992. Also translated A. J. Mason, *Fifty Spiritual Homilies. St. Macarius the Great.* Willits, California, 1974.

Didymus the Blind. *Sur Zacharie,* 1.146; SCh 83 (1962) 270ff.

Diadochus of Photice. *One hundred Gnostic Chapters,* 29ff; *Cent chapitres gnostiques,* SCh 5*ter:* 99ff; 90ff, 150ff; 'On Spiritual Knowledge and Discrimination: One Hundred Texts', *The Philokalia. The Complete Text,* vol. 1 (1979) 260ff, 90ff, 289ff.

Ephrem the Syrian, *Commentaire de l'évangile concordant ou diatesseron,* 5.3; French translation by Louis Leloir, SCh 121 (1966) 140ff.

Isaac the Syrian. 72nd Discourse, *Oeuvres,* 365ff. Desclée de Brouwer, 1981. Translated Wensinck. *Mystic Treatises by Isaac of Nineveh.* Amsterdam, 1923.

*A Systematic Handbook,* 94, 377 (bibliog.), 420 (texts); the consciousness of grace, 419; heart, 354.

Dörr, Friedrich. *Diadochus von Photike und die Messalianer.* Freiburg im Breisgau, 1937.

Daniélou, Jean. *Platonisme et théologie mystique,* 235–266. Paris, 1944.

Mouroux, Jean. *L'Expérience chrétienne,* Théologie, 24. Paris, 1952. Translated George Lamb, *The Christian Experience. An Introduction to Theology.* New York, 1954.

Olphe-Galliard, Michel. 'Les sens spirituels dans l'histoire', *Nos sens et Dieu, Les Études carmélitaines* 1 (1954) 179–193.

Fraigneau-Julien, B. *Les sens spirituels et la vision de Dieu selon Syméon le Nouveau Théologien,* Théologie historique, 67. Paris 1985.

THE ILLUMINATED *NOUS,* P. 172.

Evagrius. *Chapters on Prayer,* 74ff, 80; Hausherr, *Leçons,* 108ff, 112ff; CS 4:67ff, 68ff.

Cyril of Jerusalem. *Baptismal Cathecheses,* 16.16; *Catéchèse baptismales et mystagogiques,* 373ff. Namur, 1962. Translated Leo P. McCauley, *The Works of Saint Cyril of Jerusalem,* FCh 64. 1970. Vol. 2: 85ff.

Didymus the Blind. *Sur Zacharie,* 5.71, 5.128; SCh 85:1008ff, 1042.

Pseudo-Macarius. *Homilies* 12 and 16.2; SCh 275: 254ff, 178ff; translated Maloney, CWS 97–104, 129–130; translated A. J. Mason, 89ff, 135.

Symeon the New Theologian, 24th Discourse, 101ff, 22nd Discourse, 157ff; *Catéchèses,* SCh 113:42ff, SCh 104:376ff; deCatanzaro, CWS, 263ff, 247ff.
———. *Livre de théologie,* 1.155ff; SCh 122:108ff. See The First Theological Discourse, translated Paul McGuckin, *Symeon the New Theologian: The Practical and Theological Chapters and The Three Theological Discourses,* CS 4:107ff. Kalamazoo, 1982.
Gregory Palamas. *Défense des saints hésychastes,* I, 3,16 and II, 3, 52. Louvain, 1959. 142ff, 490ff.
*A Systematic Handbook,* 32 (The Spirit-Enlightener), 35 (Jesus-Light).
*Illuminations et sécheresses. Études carmélitaines,* 1937.
*Lemaitre J.* (Hausherr). 'Contemplation: La saisie du logos des choses est le don de Dieu', DSp 2/2 (1953) 1821–1824.
———. 'Mystique dioratique', DSp 2/2:1856–1858.
Ratzinger, Joseph. 'Licht und Erleuchtung', *Studium generale,* 13 (1960).
Beierwalters, W. 'Die Metaphysik des Lichtes in der Philosophie Plotins', *Zeitschrift für philosophische Forschung* 15 (1961) 334–362.
Gribomont, Jean. 'Esprit Saint chez les Pères . . . : lumière de la gnose', DSp 4/2 (1961) 1269–1272.
Camelot, Pierre Thomas. 'Gnose chrétienne', DSp 6 (1967) 509–523.
Veuthey, Léon. 'Illumination: origines de la doctrine de l'illumination', DSp 7/2 (1971) 1330–1346.
See The Mysticism of Light.

FROM FAITH TO *GNOSIS*, P. 173.

Clement of Alexandria. *Stromata,* 2.4.12 and 5.1.1ff; *Stromates,* SCh 38: 42ff, SCh 278:24ff; ANF 2:349ff, 444ff.
Origene. *Homilies on Luke,* 1.3; *Homélies sur S. Luc,* SCh 87 (1962) 104ff.
Theodoret of Cyrrhus. *Thérapeutique des maladies helléniques,* I.107ff; SCh 57:131ff.
Symeon the New Theologian. *Discourses,* 22.87ff; *Catéchèses,* SCh 104:372ff; translated deCatanzaro, CWS, 245ff.
*A Systematic Handbook,* 76, 335, 442.
Lebreton, Jules. 'La théorie de la connaissance religieuse chez Clément d'Alexandrie', RSR 18 (1928) 457–488.
Camelot, Pierre Thomas. *Foi et Gnose. Introduction à l'étude de la connaissance mystique chez Clément d'Alexandrie,* Études de théologie et de l'histoire de la spiritualité. Paris, 1945.

Völker, Walther. *Der wahre Gnostiker nach Klemens von Alexandrien,* TU 27. Berlin, 1952.

Camelot, Pierre Thomas. 'Gnose chrétienne', DSp 6 (1967) 509–523 (bibliog.).

Derville, André. 'Le gnosticisme', DSp 6:523–542.

THE PURIFIED *NOUS*, P. 175.

Clement of Alexandria. *Stromata,* 5.11.71.7; *Stromates,* SCh 278:142ff; ANF 2 (1885).

Gregory of Nyssa. *The Life of Moses,* 2.19; SCh 1*bis* (1955) 37ff; translated Malherbe and Ferguson, CWS / CS 31:59ff.

Cassian. *Conferences,* 14.14ff; SCh 54:201ff; translated Ramsey, ACW 57: 519; translated Luibheid, CWS, 168–169.

Pseudo-Macarius. *Homilies,* 4. 2; SCh 275:96ff; translated Maloney, CWS, 50ff.

Isaac the Syrian. 83rd Discourse; *Oeuvres,* 405ff. Desclée de Brouwer, 1981.

Gregory Palamas. *Défense des saints hésychastes* I, 3, 9 and I, 3, 52. Louvain, 1959. Pp. 126ff, 220ff.

*A Systematic Handbook:* purification from sin, 182, 428; of the passions, 267, 402 (bibliog.); 436 (texts).

Olphe-Galliard, Michel. 'La pureté de coeur d'après Cassien', RAM 17 (1936) 28–60.

George, Augustin. '"Heureux les coeurs purs, ils verront Dieu"', *Bible et vie chrétienne* 13 (1956) 74–77.

Agulles, J. *Bienventurados los puros de corazón.* Valencia, 1965.

Raasch, Juana. 'The Monastic Concept of Purity of Heart and its Sources', *Studia Monastica* 8 (1966) 7–33, 183–213; 10 (1968) 7–55; 11 (1969) 269–314; 12 (1970) 7–41.

Camelot, Pierre Thomas. 'Hellénisme (et spiritualité patristique)', DSp 7/1 (1969) 145–164.

Dupont, Jacques. *Les béatitudes,* Bruges, 195. Rev. ed., Études bibliques, 3 (Paris, 1973):557–603.

Rodriguez, I. 'Purificazione', DESp 2:1539–1547.

PURE PRAYER, P. 175.

Evagrius. *Chapters on Prayer,* 66ff; Hausherr, *Leçons,* 93ff, 69ff, 100ff, 117ff, 150ff, CS 4:66ff, 75.

Isaac the Syrian. 32nd Discourse; *Oeuvres,* 197. Desclée de Brouwer, 1981. See Wensinck, *Mystic Treatises of Isaac of Nineveh,* 146ff.

Hazzâyâ, Rabban Jausep. *Briefe,* 276ff, 283ff.

Ilias the Ekdidos, in J. Gouillard, *Petite Philocalie,* 162ff. Paris, 1953. See also, Ilias the Presbyter, *Gnomic Anthology,* Part II (Prayer), translated and ed. by G. E. H. Palmer, Philip Sherrard, and Kallistos Ware, in *The Philokalia. The Complete Text,* vol. 3 (1984) 43–46.

*The Art of Prayer,* 25, 117–118; *L'art de la prière,* 25, 159.

Hausherr, Irénée. 'Par delà l'oraison pure grâce à une coquille à propos d'un texte d'Évagre', RAM 13 (1932) 184–188; OCA 176 (1966) 8–12.

Békés, Gerardus. 'Pura oratio apud Clementem Alexandrinum', *Studia Benedictina in memoriam gloriosi ante saecula XIV transitus S. P. Benedicti,* Studia Anselm. 18–19 (1947) 157–172.

Olphe-Galliard, Michel. 'Cassien: la "prière pure"', DSp 2/1 (1953) 262ff.

Hausherr, Irénée. *Noms du Christ et voies d'oraison.* 150 (Deux sortes d'oraison pure), OCA 157. Rome, 1960. Translated Charles Cummings, *The Name of Jesus.* CS 44:151–158. Kalamazoo, 1978.

Khalifé-Hachem, Élie. 'La prière pure et la prière spirituelle selon Isaac de Ninive', *Memorial Gabriel Khouri-Sarkis,* 157–173. Louvain, 1969.

———. 'Isaac de Ninive', DSp 7/2 (1971) 2041–2054.

See The Mysticism of Evagrius.

*PRAXIS* LEADS TO *THEORIA,* PP. 177FF.

Origen. *Homilies on Luke,* 1.5; *Homélies sur S. Luc,* SCh 87 (1962) 106ff.

Gregory of Nyssa. *The Life of Moses,* 2.189ff; SCh 1*bis:* 91ff; translated Malherbe and Ferguson, CWS/ CS 31:103ff.

Cassian. *Conferences,* 14.9; SCh 54 (1954) 192ff; translated Ramsey, ACW 57: 511f; translated Luibheid, CWS, 162ff.

*The Life of Syncletica,* 79; *Vie de sainte Synclétique,* 69. Bellefontaine (1972) 69. See also, *Vita Sanctae Syncleticae,* PG 28:1533B. Translated Elizabeth A. Castelli, 'The Life and Activity of the Holy and Blessed Teacher Syncletica', in Vincent L. Wimbush, ed., *Ascetic Behavior in Greco-Roman Antiquity. A Sourcebook,* Studies in Antiquity and Christianity. Minneapolis, 1990. 297ff.

Symeon the New Theologian. *Catecheses,* 24.54ff and 8.147ff; *Catéchèses,* SCh 113: 38ff, SCh 104:98ff. Translated Alexander Golitzin, *St Symeon the New Theologian. The Ethical Discourses,* 2 volumes. Crestwood, New York, 1996.

———. *Livre de théologie* I.303ff; SCh 122:119ff; translated Paul McGuckin, CS 41: 107ff.

———. *Livre d'éthique* I.12.1ff; SCh 122:272ff; 'First Discourse', translated Alexander Golitzin, *St Symeon the New Theologian . . . : The Ethical Discourses,* vol. 1:55ff. Crestwood, New York, 1996.

*A Systematic Handbook,* 333.

Arnou, René. Πραχις et Θεωρία, *Étude de detail sur le vocabulaire et la pensée des Ennéades de Plotin*. Paris, 1921. Rpt. Rome, 1972.

Olphe-Galliard, Michel. 'Vie contemplative et vie active d'après Cassien', RAM 16 (1935) 252–98.

Lemaitre, L. (Hausherr). 'Contemplation . . .', DSp 2/2 (1953) 1810ff.

von Balthasar, Hans Urs. 'Aktion und Kontemplation', *Verbum Caro,* 245–249. Einsiedeln, 1960.

*Grégoire de Nazianze,* 49ff.

Völker, Walther. *Praxis und Theoria bei Symeon dem Neuen Theologen. Ein Beitrag zur byzantinischen Mystik*. Wiesbaden, 1974.

Špidlík, Tomaš. 'La theoria et la praxis chez Grégoire de Nazianze', *Studia patristica* 14, TU 117: 358–364. Berlin, 1976.

CHARITY, THE 'DOOR TO GNOSIS', P. 178.

*A Systematic Handbook,* 295, 406 (bibliog.), 438 (texts).

Hausherr, Irénée. *Philautie. De la tendresses pour soi à la charité, selon Maxime le Confesseur,* OCA 137. Rome, 1952.

Armstrong, Arthur Hilary and R. A. Markus. *Christian Faith and Greek Philosophy,* 79–96. London, 1960.

Camelot, Pierre Thomas. 'Gnose chrétienne', DSp 6 (1967) 509–523.

Kirchmeyer, Jean. 'Grecque (Église); la charité', DSp 6:857–872 (bibliog.).

Le Guillou, M. J. 'Lumière et charité dans la doctrine palamite de la divinisation', *Istina,* 3 (1974) 329–338.

Garrigues, J. M. *Maxime le Confesseur. La charité, avenir divin de l'homme,* Théologie historique, 38. Paris, 1976.

NATURAL CONTEMPLATION, P. 183.

Basil. *Homilies on the Hexameron* 6.1; *Homélies sur l'Hexahéméron,* SCh 26bis:326ff; translated Agnes Clare, *Saint Basil: Exegetic Homilies,* FCh 46:83ff. Washington, 1963.

Athanasius. *Contra Gentes,* 2.2; *Contre les païens,* SCh 18*bis:*166ff; LNPF, 2nd series, 4:20ff.

Hazzâyâ, Rabban Jausep. *Briefe,* 215ff.

Gregory Palamas. *Défense des saints hésychastes,* I, 1, 20, and II, 3, 44. Louvain, 1959. 56ff, 476ff. 1.1.20 translated Gendle, *The Triads,* CWS, p. 28.

Tikhon of Zadonsk. *Sokroviščе duchovnoe ot mira sobiraemoe,* in *Tvorenija* [Works] vol. 4. Moscow, 1889. (Excerpted in Tomaš Špidlík, *Les grands mystiques russes,* 65–72. Paris, 1959.)

*A Systematic Handbook,* 336, 442 (texts).
von Balthasar, Hans Urs. *Kosmische Liturgie, Das Weltbild des Maximus Confessor.* Freiburg im Breisgau, 1941; 2nd rev. ed., Einsiedeln, 1962. Translated as *Cosmic Liturgy: The Universe According to Maximus the Confessor.* Fort Collins, Colorado, 2003.
de Lubac, Henri. *Histoire et Esprit. L'intelligence de l'Écriture d'après Origène,* Théologie, 16. Paris, 1950.
Lemaitre, Jean. *'Contemplation: la theôria physike',* DSp 2/2 (1953) 1806–1927.
Crouzel, Henri. *Origène et la 'connaissance mystique'.* Bruges, 1961.
Thunberg, Lars. *Microcosm and Meditator. The Theological Anthropology of Maximus the Confessor,* 363ff. Lund, 1875.
Kirchmeyer, Jean. 'Grecque (Église)', DSp 6 (1967) 852ff.
Solignac, Aimé. 'Nature et vie spirituelle', DSp 11 (1962) 44–55.

THE CONTEMPLATION OF INVISIBLE BEINGS, P. 187.

Origen. *Homilies on Luke,* 3.1; *Homélies sur S. Luc,* SCh 87 (1962) 120ff.
Isaac the Syrian. 84e Discourse; *Oeuvres,* 411ff. Desclée de Brouwer, 1981.
Hazzâyâ, Rabban Jausep. *Briefe,* 181ff, 188ff.

THE CONTEMPLATION OF PROVIDENCE AND OF THE JUDGMENT, PP. 188–189.

Origen. *Homilies on Luke,* 35.1; *Homélies sur S. Luc,* SCh 87:412ff. (judgment).
Theodoret of Cyrrhus. *Thérapeutique des maladies helléniques,* 6 (Providence); SCh 57 (1958) 254–287.
John Chrysostom. *On God's Providence; Sur la Providence de Dieu,* SCh 79 (1961).
Isaac the Syrian. 40e Discourse; *Oeuvres,* 234ff (Providence). Desclée de Brouwer, 1981. See the translation by A. J. Wensinck, *Mystic Treatises by Isaac of Nineveh.* Amsterdam, 1923.
*Ebed-Jesu Sobensis Carmina Selecta ex libro Paradisus Eden,* a latin translation by H. Gismondi: *Carmen* 6 (De decretis divinis). Beirout, 1888. Pp.18ff.
Hazzâyâ, R. J. *Briefe,* 189, 227 (on judgment and Providence).
*A Systematic Handbook,* 130, 330 (bibliog.), 423 (texts).
Koch, Harl. *Pronoia und Paideusis. Studien über Origenes und sein Verhältnis zum Platonismus.* Berlin-Leipzig, 1932.

Lemaitre, Jean. 'Contemplation de la providence et du jugement', DSp 2/2 (1953) 1825ff.

Spanneut, Michel. *Le stoïcisme des Pères de l'Église de Clément de Rome à Clément d'Alexandrie,* 326ff. Paris, 1957.

Loi, Vincenzo. 'Provvidenza', DP 2:1942–1945. 'Providence', EEC 2:720–721.

*THEOLOGIA,* P. 190.

Diadochus of Photice. *Cent chapitres gnostiques,* 57ff; SCh 5*ter:*127ff; 'On Spiritual Knowledge and Discrimination: One Hundred Texts', *The Philokalia. The Complete Text,* 1:270ff. London, 1979.

Hazzâyâ, R. J. *Briefe,* 214ff., 339ff.

Symeon the New Theologian. *Theological Discourses* 1.1ff, 2.1ff; *Livre de théologie,* SCh 122: 96ff, 130ff; translated Paul McGuckin, The First Theological Discourse, *Symeon the New Theologian. The Practical and Theological Chapters and The Three Theological Discourses,* CS 41:107ff, 123ff. Kalamazoo, 1982.

———. *Hymns* 31, 38; Hymnes, SCh 174:384ff, 466ff; translated George A. Maloney, *Hymns of Divine Love by St. Symeon the New Theologian,* 173ff., 189ff. Denville, New Jersey, n.d.

*A Systematic Handbook,* 338, 411 (bibliog.).

Battifol, Pierre. '*Theologia,* Théologie', *Ephemerides Theologicae Lovanienses,* 5 (1928) 205–220.

Jaeger, Werner. *À la naissance de la théologie. Essai sur les Présocratiques.* Paris, 1966. See also Werner Jaeger, *The Theology of the Early Greek Philosophers,* translated by Edward S. Robinson. Oxford, 1947, Westport, Connecticut, 1980.

*Grégoire de Nazianze,* 134ff.

Constantinidis, Ch. 'La théologie au renouveau de la vie de l'Église. La réflexion critique des applications de la théologie', in S. Ch. Agourides, *Deuxième congrès de théologie orthodoxe . . . ,* 385–412. Athens, 1978.

Romanides, John. 'Critical Examination of the Applications of Theology', *ibid.,* 413–453.

Koev, Totju. 'Die Theologie als Ausdruck des Lebens und des Bewusstseins der Kirche', *ibid.,* 215–235.

Studer, Basilio. 'Teologia', DP 2:3408–3409. 'Theology', EEC 2:831.

THE VISION OF GOD, P. 191.

Irenaeus. *Adversus haereses,* 4.20.9ff; SCh 100:654ff; ANF 1:487ff.

Origen. *Homilies on Genesis,* 11.3; *Homélies sur la Genèse,* SCh 8*bis:*286ff; translated Ronald E. Heine, *Origen. Homilies on Genesis and Exodus,* FCh 71:168ff. Washington, D.C., 1982.

Gregory of Nyssa. *The Life of Moses,* 2.170ff; SCh 1*bis:*84ff; Malherbe–Ferguson translation, CWS/ CS 31:97ff.

*Vision de saint Diadoque,* SCh 5*ter:*168ff.

Symeon the New Theologian, Discourse 14.169ff; *Catéchèses,* SCh 104:216ff; translated C. J. deCatanzaro, *Symeon the New Theologian. The Discourses,* CWS, 191ff.

———. *Hymns* 25, 45; SCh 174:254ff, SCh 196: 102ff; translated George E. Maloney, *Hymns of Divine Love by St. Symeon the New Theologian.* Denville, New Jersey. n.d.

Gregory Palamas. *Défense des saints heyschastes,* I, 3,21ff (Louvain, 152ff), I, 3, 43 (202ff), II, 3,16ff (418ff), II, 3,31ff (448ff); excerpts translated in *Gregory Palamas. The Triads,* CWS, pp. 37, 60.

Seraphim of Sarov, in I. Goraïnoff, *Saint Séraphim de Sarov,* 194ff. Bellefontaine, 1973; see 'A Conversation with the Saint by Nicholas A. Motovilov', in Constantine Cavarnos and Mary-Barbara Zeldin, *St. Seraphim of Sarov,* Modern Orthodox Saints no. 51, 93ff. Belmont, Massachusetts, 1980.

*A Systematic Handbook,* 3338, 412 (bibliog.), 442 (texts).

Ammann, A. M. *Die Gotteschau im palamitischen Hesychasmus. Ein Handbuch der spätbyzantinsichen Mytik,* Das östliche Christentum, Heft 6–7. Wurzburg, 1938.

Alonso, J. M. 'Estudios de la teologia positiva entormo la visión beata', *Estudioss* 6 (1950) 35–56, 237–303; 7 (1951) 29–71.

Lossky, Vladimir. 'Le probleme de la "vision face à face" et la tradition patristique de Byzance', *Studia Patristica* 2, TU 64:512–537. Berlin, 1957.

Lanne, Emmanuel. 'La vision de Dieu dans les oeuvres de saint Irénée', *Irenikon* 33 (1960) 311–320.

Baert, E. 'Het thema van de zalige godsaanschouwing in de griekse patristiek tot Origenes', *Tijdschrift voor theologie* 1 (1961) 289–308.

———. 'Le thème de la vision de Dieu chez S. Justin, Clément d'Alexandrie et S. Grégoire de Nysse', *Freiburger Zeitschrift für Philosophie und Theologie* 12 (1965) 439–497.

Lossky, Vladimir. *The Vision of God,* translated by Asheleigh Moorhouse. London, 1963.

Kirchmeyer, Jean. 'Grecque (Église)', DSp 6 (1967) 842–846 (bibliog.).

Orbe, Antonio. 'Visión del Padre e incorruptela segun san Ireneo', *Gregorianum* 64/2 (1983) 199–241.

Ciccarese, Maria Pia. 'Visione', DP 2:3601–3603 (bibliog.), 'Vision', EEC 2:872–873.

MYSTICISM, P. 203.

*A Systematic Handbook,* 22, 337, 412 (bibliog.), 442 (texts).

Arseniev, Nikolai S. *Ostkirche und Mystik.* Munich, 1925, 1943[2]; translated Arthur Chambers, *Mysticism and the Eastern Church.* London, 1926. Rpt New York, 1979.

von Ivánka, Endre. 'Vom Platonismus zur Theorie der Mystik. Zur Erkenntnislehre Gregors von Nyssa', *Scholastik* 11 (1936) 163–195.

Viller, Marcel and Pierre Pourrat. 'Abandon', DSp 1 (1936) 2–49.

Daeschler, R. 'L'anéantissement mystique', DSp 1:562ff.

Evdokimov, Paul. *L'amour fou de Dieu,* 41–61. Paris, 1937.

Viller, Marcel and Karl Rahner. *Aszeze und Mystik in der Väterzeit.* Freiburg im Breisgau. 1939.

Wunderle, Georg. *Wesenszüge der byzantinischen Mystik aufgezeichnet an Symeon dem Jüngeren.* Regensburg, 1939.

Lossky, Vladimir. *Essai sur la théologie mystique de l'Église d'Orient.* Paris, 1944. *The Mystical Theology of the Eastern Church.* London, 1957.

Daniélou, Jean. *Platonisme et théologie mystique. Essai sur la doctrine spirituelle de saint Grégoire de Nysse,* Théologie, 2. Paris, 1944.

Camelot, Pierre Thomas. *Foi et gnose. Introduction à l'étude de la connaissance mystique chez Clément d'Alexandrie.* Paris, 1945.

Stolz, Anselm. *Théologie de la Mystique.* Chevetogne, 1947. Originally published in German as *Theologie der Mystik.* Regensburg, 1938. English translation by Aidan Williams, *The Doctrine of Spiritual Perfection.* London, 1946.

Otto, Rudolf. *Mystique d'Orient et mystique d'Occident.* Paris, 1951. German original: *West-östliche Mystik.* Gotha, 1926. English translation by Bertha L. Bracey and Richenda C. Payne, *Mysticism East and West: A Comparative Analysis of the Nature of Mysticism.* New York, 1962.

Leys, R. *L'image de Dieu chez saint Grégoire de Nysse.* Bruges, 1951.

Völker, Walther. *Gregor von Nyssa als Mystiker.* Wiesbaden, 1955.

Crouzel, Henri. *Théologie de l'image de Dieu.* Paris, 1956.

Lemaitre, J. 'Contemplation: Syméon le Nouveaux Théologien', DSp 2/2 (1953) 1851ff.

Roques, René and André Rayez. 'Denys l'Aréopagite (le pseudo-)', DSp 3 (1957) 244–318.

Crouzel, Henri. 'Grégoire de Nysse est-il fondateur de la théologie mystique?, in RAM 83 (1957) 189–202.

Reypens, Leonce. 'Dieu (connaissance mystique)', DSp 3 (1957) 883–929.

Gardet, L. *Thèmes et textes mystiques, recherche de critères en mystique comparée.* Paris, 1958.

Evdokimov, Paul. *L'Orthodoxie,* 107–119. Neuchâtel, 1959.

Theodorou, A. *Die Mystik in der orthodoxen Ostkirche,* in Panagiotis Bratsiotis, *Die orthodoxe Kirche in griechischer Sicht,* vol. I. Stuttgart, 1959.

Widengreen, George. 'Researches in Syrian Mysticism. Mystical Experiences and Spiritual Exercises', *Numen,* 8 (1961) 161–198.

Crouzel, Henri. 'Origène et la 'connaissance mystique'. *Museum Lessianum, Section théologique* 56. Paris-Bruges, 1961.

Mühlenberg, E. *Die Unendlichkeit Gottes bei Gregor von Nyssa.* Göttingen, 1965.

Joly, R. 'Sur deux thèmes mystiques de Grégoire de Nysse', *Byzantion,* 46 (1966) 127–143.

Canevet, Mariette. 'Grégoire de Nysse', DSp 6 (1967) 971–1011.

Levasti, A. 'Clemente Alessandrino iniziatore della mistica cristiana', *Revista di ascetica e mistica,* 12 (1967) 127–147.

Agaësse, Paul. 'Liberté: expérience des mystiques', DSp 9 (1976) 824–838.

Solignac, Aimé. 'Mystère (μυστήριον, μυστικός)' DSp 10 (1980) 1861–1874.

Agaësse, Paul, *et al.* 'Mystique', DSp 10 (1980) 1889–1984.

Gagey, Jacques. 'Phénomènes mystiques', DSp 12/1 (1984) 1259–1274.

Ruhbach, Gerhard and Josef Sudback. *Grosse Mystiker, Leben und Wirken.* Munich, 1984.

Špidlík, Tomaš. 'Solovëv', in E. Ancilli and M. Paparozzi, *La mistica,* vol. I:645–668. Rome, 1984.

Špidlík, Tomaš. 'Mistica', DP 2:2266–2268; 'Mysticism', EEC 1:577–578.

Bernard, Charles André. 'La doctrine mystique de Denys l'Aréopagite', *Gregorianum* 68/3–4 (1987) 523–566.

THE CHRISTIAN TRUTH IS MYSTICAL, P. 203.

Origen. *Homilies on Joshua,* 25.4; *Homélies sur Josué,* SCh 71: 486ff.

Gregory of Nyssa. *The Life of Moses;* SCh 1*bis:*112ff; *De vita Moysis,* PG 44:408ff; Malherbe and Ferguson translation, CWS/CS 31. New York-Kalamazoo, 1978.

Pseudo-Denys. *The Celestial Hierarchy,* 2.2; *La hiérarchie céleste,* SCh 58*bis:*76ff; translated Colm Luibheid and Paul Rorem in *Pseudo-*

*Dionysius. The Complete Works,* in the series CWS, 145–191. New York, 1987.

Symeon the New Theologian. Discourse 14.108ff; *Catéchèses,* SCh 104:212ff; translated C. J. deCatanzaro, *Symeon the New Theologian. The Discourses,* CWS, 186ff. New York, 1980.

THE ASCENT OF THE MYSTICAL MOUNTAIN, P. 207.

Origen. *Homilies on Genesis,* 15.1 (mystical ascents and descents); *Homélies sur la Genèse,* SCh 7:237ff; translated Ronald E. Heine, *Origen. Homilies on Genesis and Exodus,* FCh 71:203ff.

Gregory of Nyssa. *The Life of Moses;* SCh 1*bis:*77ff; PG 44:372ff (the mountain of *theognosis*). Malherbe and Ferguson, 'The Mountain of Divine Knowledge', *Gregory of Nyssa. The Life of Moses,* CWS/CS31: 91–94. New York-Kalamazoo, 1978.

Didymus the Blind. *Sur Zacharie,* 2.237; SCh 84:538ff (the holy mountain).

Hazzâyâ, Rabban Jausep. *Briefe,* 187ff.

Gregory Palamas. *Défense des saints hésychastes,* II, 3, 54; Louvain, 496ff.

Leclercq, Henri. 'Échelle du ciel', DACL 4/2 (1921) 1717–1719.

Roques, R. *L'univers dionysien,* Théologie 29:94–100, 174–196. Paris, 1954.

Bertaud, Émile and André Rayez. 'Échelle spirituelle', DSp 4/1 (1960) 62–86.

THE APOPHATIC WAY, P. 209.

Clement of Alexandria. *Stromata,* 5.12.78.1; *Les Stromates,* SCh 278:152ff; ANF 2: 462ff.

Basil. *Adversus Eunomium,* 1.12ff; *Contre Eunome,* SCh 299:212ff; PG 29:497–669.

John Chrysostom. *On the Incomprehensible Nature of God, Sur l'incompréhensibilité de Dieu,* Hom. 1–5, SCh 28*bis* (1970). English translation by Paul W. Harkins, *St. John Chrysostom. On the Incomprehensible Nature of God,* FCh 72:51ff. Washington D.C., 1984.

Pseudo-Macarius. *Homily* 18.1–2; SCh 275:218ff and *Homily* 12.1; SCh 275:254ff. Translated George A. Maloney, *Pseudo-Macarius. The Fifty Spiritual Homilies,* CWS 141–142 ,97; translated A. J. Mason, *Fifty Spiritual Homilies. St. Macarius the Great,* 151ff, 89ff.

Symeon the New Theologian. *Hymn* 23; SCh 174:189ff; translated George A. Maloney, *Hymns of Divine Love by St. Symeon the New Theologian,* 113ff. Denville, New Jersey, n.d.

Gregory Palamas. *Défense des saints hésychastes,* I, 3, 4 (Louvain, 112ff), I, 3,19 (150ff), II, 3, 5 (394ff), II, 3, 25 (436ff), II, 3, 31 (456ff), II, 3, 53 (492ff), II, 3, 65 (520ff).

Norden, E. *Agnostos Theos.* Leipzig-Berlin, 1923.

de Lubac, Henri. *De la connaissance de Dieu.* 2nd ed. Paris, 1948. Translated Alexander Dru, *The Discovery of God.* New York, 1960. [*The Discovery* is a translation of *Sur les chemins de Dieu,* itself the third expanded edition of *De la connaissance.*]

Plagnieux, Jean. *Saint Gregoire de Nazianze Théologien,* 276ff. Paris, 1952.

Dodds, Eric Robertson. *The Greeks and the Irrational,* Sather Classical Lectures, 25. Los Angeles, California, 1951.

Lossky, Vladimir. *L'apophase de la théologie trinitaire* (mimeographed) Paris, 1952.

Lemaitre, J., René Roques, Marcel Viller. 'Contemplation chez les Orientaux chrétiens', DSp 2/2 (1953) 1786ff, 1832ff.

Festugière, Andre Jean. *La révélation d'Hermès Trismégiste,* vol. IV: *Dieu inconnu et la Gnose.* Paris, 1954. [See also, George R. S. Stow, translator, *Thrice-greatest Hermes . . . .* 3 vols. London, 1906.]

Cuttat, Jacques Albert. *La rencontre des religions,* 133ff. Paris, 1957. Translated Pierre de Fontnouvelle and Evis McGrew, *The Encounter of Religions,* 112ff. New York, 1960.

de Gandillac, Maurice. 'Docte ignorance', DSp 3 (1957) 1497–1501.

Bardy, Gustave. 'Dépouillement', DSp 3 (1957) 455–468.

Evdokimov, Paul. *L'orthodoxie,* 174ff. Neuchâtel-Paris, 1959.

Lossky, Vladimir. *Théologie négative et connaissance de Dieu chez Maître Eckhart,* Études de philosophie mediévale. Paris, 1960.

———. *Vision de Dieu.* Neuchâtel, 1962. (This was a course given at the Sorbonne, 1945–1946.) English translation by Asheleigh Moorhouse, *The Vision of God.* London, 1963.

———. *Théologie dogmatique* (a course given in 1945), in *Messager de l'exarchat du Patriarche russe en Europe occidentale,* nos. 46–50, 1964–1965.

Segundo, Juan Luis. *Berdiaeff. Une réflexion chrétienne sur la personne,* Théologie, 53 (Paris, 1963)129ff, 365ff.

Thunberg, Lars. *Microcosm and Mediator. The Theological Anthropology of Maximus the Confessor,* 432ff. Lund, 1965.

Nicolas, Jean Hervé. *Dieu connu comme inconnu, Essai d'une critique de la connaissance théologique.* Paris, 1966.

Lossky, Vladimir. *À l'image et à la resemblance de Dieu,* 7–23. Paris, 1967; translated John H. Erickson and Thomas E. Bird, *In the Image and Likeness of God.* Crestwood, New York, 1974.

Giannaras, Chrestos. [*The Theology of the Absence and Unknowability of God*] (in Greek). Athens, 1967.

———. *De l'absence et de l'inconnaissance de Dieu d'après les écrits aréopagites et Martin Heidegger*. Paris, 1971.

———. 'Teologia apofatica e architettura bizantina', in T. Moschopoulos and P. Scazzoso, *Simposio cristiano,* 104–112. Milan, 1971.

Evdokimov, Paul. *La connaissance de Dieu selon la tradition orientale*. Lyon, 1968.

*Grégoire de Nazianze,* 35ff.

Evdokimov, Paul. *L'art de l'icône. Théologie de la beauté,* 195–204. Desclée de Brouwer, 1972. Translated Steven Bigham, *The Art of the Icon: A Theology of Beauty*. Redondo Beach, California, 1990.

Gouhier, Alain. 'Néant', DSp 11 (1982) 64–80.

Meyendorff, Jean. 'Palamas (Grégoire)', DSp 12/1 (1984) 92ff.

THE REJECTION OF IMAGES, P. 211.

Evagrius. *Chapter on Prayer,* 68, 72, 92, 94, 115ff; Hausherr, *Leçons,* 99ff, 104ff, 126ff, 125ff, 147ff; CS 4: 66, 67, 70, 71, 74.

Didymus the Blind. *Sur Zacharie,* 1.317; SCh 83:360ff.

Diadochus of Photice. *Cent chapitres gnostiques* 36ff; SCh 5*ter:*104ff; 'On Spiritual Knowledge and Discrimination: One Hundred Texts', in *The Philokalia. The Complete Text,* 1:263ff. London, 1979.

Isaac the Syrian. 85th Discourse; *Oeuvres,* 429ff. Desclée de Brouwer, 1981.

Hazzâyâ, Rabban Jausep. *Briefe,* 108ff.

Gregory of Sinai, in J. Gouilliard, *Petite Philocalie,* 255. Paris, 1953. Texts by Gregory of Sinai are translated and edited by E. Kadloubovsky and G. E. H. Palmer in *Writings from the Philokalia on Prayer of the Heart,* 37ff. London, 1979.

Gregory Palamas. *Défense des saints hésychastes,* I, 3, 48 (Louvain, 212ff), II, 3, 58f (508ff).

*A Systematic Handbook,* 77.

Jaffe, A. *Apparitions. Fantômes, rêves et mythes*. Paris, 1983.

Voigt, M. *Beitrage zur Geschichte der Vision-Literatur im Mittelalter*. Leipzig, 1924.

de Tonquédec, J. 'Apparitions', DSp 1 (1936) 801–809.

Monden, Louis. 'Erscheinungen', LThK$^2$ 3 (1959) 1047–1050.

Rahner, Karl. *Visionen und Prophezeiungen*. Freiburg, 1960.

Pax, A[lpidius]. 'Vision. In der Bibel', LThK$^2$ 10 (1965) 811–812.

Benz, Ernst. *Die Vision, Erfahrungsformen und Bilderwelt*. Stuttgart, 1969.

Ancilli, Ermanno. 'Vizioni e rivelazioni', DESp 2:208–212.

Postel, J. 'Le psychiatre devant les visions des mystiques', *Nouvelles,* 1:73–93 (bibliog.). Institut catholique de Paris, 1976–1977.

LEARNED IGNORANCE, P. 214.

Hausherr, Irénée. *Ignorance infinie.* OCP 2 (1936) 351–362; *Hésychasme et prière,* OCS 176 (1966) 38–49.

Losskii, Nikolai O. *Histoire de la philosophie russe des origines à 1950,* 313–29. (L. P. Karsavin) Paris, 1954; *History of Russian Philosophy.* New York: International Universities Press, 1951.

de Gandillac, Maurice. 'Docte ignorance', DSp (1957) 1497–1501.

Walsh, James. 'Nuage de l'inconnaissance (en anglais, *The Cloud of Unknowing*)', DSp 11 (1982) 497–508.

———. ed., trans. *The Cloud of Unknowing,* CWS. New York, 1981

Meyendorff, Jean. 'Palamas (Gregoire)', DSp 12/1 (1984) 92ff.

LUMINOUS DARKNESS, P. 215.

Origen. *Commentary on John, Commentaire sur saint Jean,* SCh 120*bis:*296ff, 312ff; translated Ronald E. Heine, *Origen. Commentary on the Gospel According to John. Books 1–10,* FCh 80: 130ff., 136ff. Washington, D.C., 1989.

Gregory of Nyssa. *The Life of Moses,* 18ff; SCh 1*bis:*18ff, 80ff; PG 44:316, 376ff; Malherbe-Ferguson translation, CWS/CS 31: 94ff.

Didymus the Blind. *Sur Zacharie,* 1.172ff; SCh 83 (1962) 284ff.

Pseudo-Macarius. *Homily* 3.3 and 26.5; SCh 275:90ff, 304ff; Maloney translation, CWS, 48, 165.

Symeon the New Theologian. Discourse, 15.1 and 23.150ff; *Catéchèses,* SCh 104:122ff and SCh 113:140ff; translated C. J. deCatanzaro, *Symeon the New Theologian. The Discourses,* CWS 198–199, 254ff. New York, 1980.

Gregory Palamas. *Défense des saints hésychastes,* I, 12, 36ff and II, 3, 54; Louvain, pp. 36ff, 496.

*The Art of Prayer,* 261; *L'art de la prière,* 358ff.

*A Systematic Handbook,* 340; see Ecstasy, 339ff.

Koch, K. 'Das mystische beim H1. Gregor von Nyssa', *Theologische Quartalschrift,* 80 (1898) 397–420.

Horn, G. 'Le mirroir et la nuée. Deux modes de connaissance chez S. Grégoire de Nysse', RAM 8 (1927) 113–131.

*Nuit mystique. Études carmélitaines,* 1938.

Puech, Henri Charles. 'La ténèbre mystique chez le Pseudo-Denys l'Aréopagite et dans la tradition patristique', *Nuit mystique. Études carmélitaines* (1938) 33–53.

Daniélou, Jean. *Platonisme et théologie mystique; Essai sur la doctrine spirituelle de saint Grégoire de Nysse,* 201–211. Paris, 1944, rev., 1954.

Hausherr, Irénée. 'Les Orientaux connaissent-ils les "nuits" de saint Jean de la Croix?', OCP 12 (1946) 5–46; OCS 176 (1966) 87–128.

Lemaitre, J. (Hausherr). 'Contemplation . . . : Mystique extatique', DSp 2/2 (1953) 1862–1872.

Daniélou, Jean. 'Mystique de la ténèbre chez Grégoire de Nysse', DSp 2/2:1972–1985.

Roques, René. 'Contemplation, extase et ténèbre chez le Pseudo-Denys', DSp 2/2: 1885–1911.

Daniélou, Jean. *La colombe et les ténèbre*. Paris, 1954. [See also, Herbert Musurillo, *From Glory to Glory: Texts from Gregory of Nyssa's Mystical Writings,* selected with an Introduction by Jean Daniélou. New York, 1961.]

Völker, Walther. *Gregor von Nyssa als Mystiker*. Wiesbaden, 1955.

———. *Kontemplation und Ekstase bei Pseudo-Dionysius Areopagita*. Wiesbaden, 1958.

Stanescu, N.V. 'Le progrès dans la connaissance de Dieu plus spécialement d'après S. Grégoire de Nysse', *Studii theologice* (Bucharest,1958) 14ff.

Vanneste, Jan. *Le mystère de Dieu. Essai sur la structure mystique du Pseudo-Denys l'Aréopagite*. Brussels, 1959.

Lossky, Vladimir. *Théologie négative et connaissance de Dieu chez Maître Eckhart*. Paris, 1960.

———. *Vision de Dieu*. Neuchâtel, 1962; translated Asheleigh Moorhouse, *The Vision of God*. London, 1963.

———. *À l'image et à la ressemblance de Dieu,* 25–37. Paris, 1967; translated John H. Erickson and Thomas E. Bird, *In the Image and Likeness of God*. Crestwood, New York, 1974.

Joly, R. 'Sur deux thèmes mystiques de Grégoire de Nysse', *Byzantion* (1966) 127ff.

Brontesi, A. *L'incontro misterioso con Dio, Saggi sulla Teologia affermativa e negativa nello Pseudo-Dionigi. Note di una lettura*. Brescia, 1970.

Dupuy, Michel. 'Nuit (Ténèbres)', DSp 11 (1982) 519–525.

HUMAN EROS SATIATED BY DIVINE AGAPE, P. 218.

Origen. Homilies on the Song of Songs, 2,.8 ('wound of love'); *Homélies sur le Cantique des Cantiques,* SCh 37*bis:* 132ff; translated R. P. Lawson,

*Origen. The Song of Songs: Commentary and Homilies,* ACW 26:148ff. Washington, D.C.-London, 1957.

Pseudo-Macarius. *Homily* 7 ('true love for God cannot be satisfied'); SCh 275:128ff; translated George A. Maloney, *Pseudo-Macarius. The Fifty Spiritual Homilies. . . ,* CWS 78–80; translated A. J. Mason, *Fifty Spiritual Homilies. St Macarius the Great,* 61ff.

Diadochus of Photice. *Oeuvres spirituelles,* SCh 5*ter* (1966) 90ff.

Abba Isaiah. *Asceticon,* Logos 9; CSCO 293, Syri 122, 118ff.

Isaac the Syrian. 24e Discourse; *Oeuvres spirituelles* (Desclée de Brouwer, 1981) 164. Wensinck, *Mystic Treatises.*

Symeon the New Theologian, Discourse 18; *Catéchèses,* SCh 104:254ff; translated C. J. deCatanzaro, *Symeon the New Theologian. The Discourses,* CWS 209ff. New York 1980.

———. *Hymn* 39; SCh 174: 476ff; translated George A. Maloney, *Hymns of Divine Love by St. Symeon the New Theologian,* 202ff. Denville, New Jersey, n.d.

Nicholas Cabasilas. *The Life in Christ,* 7; *La vie en Jésus-Christ* 217ff; deCatanzaro.

*The Art of Prayer,* 156, 169, 274; *L'art de la prière,* 56ff., 990ff., 202ff.

Arnou, René. *Le désir de Dieu dans la philosophie de Plotin. Contribution à l'histoire des idées religieuses aux premiers siècles de l'ère chrétienne.* Paris, 1921. 2nd ed., Rome, 1967.

Horn, G. 'L'amour divin. Note sur le mot "eros" chez S. Grégoire de Nysse', RAM 6 (1925) 378–389.

Daniélou, Jean. *Platonisme et théologie mystique,* 274–326 (ecstatic love). Paris, 1944.

Nygren, Anders. *Eros und Agape. Gestaltwandlungen der christlichen Liebe.* Gütersloh, 1937. Translated Philip S. Watson, *Agape and Eros.* London, 1953.

D'Arcy, Martin C. *The Mind and Heart of Love: A Study in Eros and Agape.* London, 1945.

Arnou, René. 'Contemplation ches les anciens philosophes gréco-remains', DSp 2/2 (1933) 1716–1742, particularly 1722 and 1729.

Daniélou, Jean. 'Mystique de la ténèbre chez Grégoire de Nysse', DSp 2/2 (1953) 1872–1885; 1880ff (impassible eros).

Martin, Henri. 'Désirs', DSp 3 (1957) 606–623.

Taymans d'Eypernon, François. 'Dieu (désir de)', DSp 3:929–947.

Rist, John M. *Eros and Psyche: Studies in Plato, Plotinus and Origen.* Toronto, 1964.

———. 'A Note on Eros and Agape in Pseudo-Dionysius', *Vigiliae christianae* 20 (1966) 235–243.

EPEKTASIS, P. 218.

Gregory of Nyssa. *The Life of Moses* 2.219; SCh 1*bis:*102ff; Malherbe and Ferguson, CWS/CS 31:111.
Daniélou, Jean. *Platonisme et théologie mystique* . . . , 291–307, Théologie, 2, 2nd ed., Paris, 1954.
———. 'Mystique de la ténèbre chez Grégoire de Nysse', DSp 2/2 (1953) 1882ff.
von Balthasar, Hans Urs. *Parole et mystere chez Origène,* 23ff. Paris, 1957.
Deseille, Placide. 'Épectase', DSp 4/1 (1960) 785–788.
Hausherr, Irénée. 'La prière perpétuelle du chrétien', *Laïcat et Sainteté,* vol. 2:111–166. Rome, 1965; *Hésychasme et prière,* 255–306 (304ff: basilian *epektasis*), OCS 176. Rome, 1966.
Meyendorff, Jean. 'Palamas (Grégoire)', DSp 12/1 (1984) 93.

THE ROLE OF CHRIST IN MYSTICISM, P. 220.

Origen. *Homilies on Luke,* 3.3–4; SCh: 124ff.
Pseudo-Macarius. *Homily* 16. 6 (SCh 275:200ff), *Homily* 3.1 (84ff), *Homily* 26.7ff (208ff). Maloney, CWS, 131f, 47, 166; Mason, 137, 16, 188. .
Nersès Šnorhali. *Jésus Fils unique du Père,* SCh 203 (1973) 125ff.
Symeon the New Theologian, *Discourses* 28.300ff (*Catéchèses,* SCh 113: 152ff) , 2.68ff (SCh 96:424ff), 20.1 (SCh 104:330ff).
———. *Éthiques* 8.99ff; SCh 129:208ff; Eighth Discourse, translated Alexander Golitzin, *St Symeon the New Theologian . . . : The Ethical Discourses,* vol. 2:104ff. Crestwood, New York, 1996.
Gregory Palamas. *Défense des saints hésychastes,* III, 1, 16ff; Louvain, 588ff; translated Gendle, *The Triads,* CWS, p. 76.
Völker, Walther. *Das Vollkommenheitsideal des Origenes,* 98–116. Tübingen, 1931.
Salaville, Sévérien. 'Le Christocentrisme de Nicolas Cabasilas', *Échos d'Orient* 35, June 1936.
Lieske, Aloysius. *Die Theologie der Logosmystik bei Origenes.* Münster, 1938.
———. *Die Theologie der Christusmystik Gregors von Nyssa.* Innsbruck, 1949 (first published in *Zeitschrift für katholische Theologie,* 70 [1948]).
Rahner, Hugo. 'Die Gottesgeburt. Die Lehre der Kirchenväter von der Geburt Christi im Herzen des Gläubigen', *Zeitschrift für katholische Theologie* 59 (1935) 333–418; rpt. *Symbole der Kirche, Die Ekklesiologie der Väter,* 11–87. Salzburg, 1964.

Roques, René. 'Denys l'Aréopgagite', DSp 3 (1957) 280ff.
Bertrand, Frédéric. *Mystique de Jésus chez Origène,* Théologie, 23. Paris, 1951.
Gögler, Rolf. 'Die christologische und heiltheologische Grundlage der Bibelexegese des Origenes', *Theologlische Quartalschrift* 136 (1956) 1–13.
Kirchmeyer, Jean. 'Écriture Sainte: Nicolas Cabasilas', DSp 4/1 (1961) 245ff.
Solignac, Aimé. 'Logos', DSp 9 (1976) 958–960.
Meyendorff, Jean. 'Palamas (Grégoire)', DSp 12/1 (1984) 95ff.
See The Jesus Prayer.

ECSTASY, P. 222.

Origen. *Homilies on Numbers,* 27.12; *Homélies sur les Nombres,* SCh 29:554ff; translated Greer, CWS, 261ff.
Cassian. *Conferences,* 9.31; SCh 54:66; translated Ramsey, SCW 57: 349; LNPF, 2nd ser., 11:398.
Hazzâyâ, R. J. *Briefe,* 189ff, 252ff, 263ff.
Symeon the New Theologian, Discourse 16; *Catéchèses,* SCh 104:236ff.
*The Art of Prayer,* 23, 52, 64, 131; *L'art de la prière*, 83ff, 179.
Holl, Karl. *Enthusiasmus und Bußgewalt beim griechischen Mönchtum.* Leipzig, 1898.
de Labriolle, Pierre. *La crise montaniste.* Paris, 1913.
Delatte, Armand. 'Les conceptions de l'enthousiasme chez les philosophes présocratiques', *L'antiquité classique* 3 (1934) 5–79; offprint, Paris, 1935.
Lemaitre, J. (Hausherr). 'Contemplation chez les orientaux chrétiens: Mystique extatique', DSp 2/2 (1953) 1862–1872.
Roques, René. *L'univers dionysien.* Paris, 1954.
Sherwood, P. *The Earlier Ambigua of St. Maximus the Confessor,* Studia Anselmiana, 36. Rome, 1955.
Thurston, Herbert. *Die körperlichen Begleiterscheinungen der Mystik.* Lucerne, 1956. English edition by J. H. Crehan, *The Physical Phenomena of Mysticism.* Chicago, 1952.
Völker, Walther. *Kontemplation und Ekatase bei Pseudo-Dionysius Areopagita.* Wiesbaden, 1958.
Pfister, F. 'Ekstase', *Reallexikon für Antike und Christentum* 4 (1959) 944–987.
des Places, Edouard. 'L'estasi nella Grecia antica', *La civiltà cattolica,* 1 (1960) 603–614.

Goetz, Joseph, *et al.* 'Extase', DSp 4/2 (1961) 2045–2189.
Gratton, Henri. 'Psychologie et extase', DSp 4/2 (1961) 2171–2182.
Leroy, Olivier. 'Faits extraordinaires occasionellement associés à l'extase', DSp 4/2:2182–86.
Kirchmeyer, Jean. 'Extase chez les Pères de l'Église', DSp 4/2:2087–2113.
Scazzoso, P. 'Rivelazioni del linguaggio pseudo-dionysiano intorno ai temi della contemplazione e dell'estasi', *Rivista di filosofia neoscolastica* 56 (1964) 37–66.
Greely, Andrew M. *Ecstasy: A Way of Knowing*. Englewood Cliffs (NY) 1974.
Rodriguez, Isaias. 'Ligature des puissances', DSp 9 (1976) 845–850
Gagey, Jacques. 'Phénomènes mystiques', DSp 12/1 (1984) 1259–1274.
Solignac, Aimé. 'Passivité (dans l'expérience mystique)', DSp 12/1:357–60.
Messalians, see *A Systematic Handbook,* 374.

SPIRITUAL PRAYER, P. 227.

Pseudo-Macarius. *Homily* 27.5 (the Spirit unifies human thoughts); SCh 275:324ff; Maloney translation, CWS, 176; Mason translation, 202ff.
Isaac the Syrian. 39e Discourse; *Oeuvres* (Desclée de Brouwer, 1981) 232ff. English translation by A. J. Wensinck, *Mystic Treatises of Isaac of Nineveh,* 197ff. Amsterdam, 1923.
Hazzâyâ, Rabban Jausep. *Briefe,* 295ff.
*The Art of Prayer*, 52, 53, 94; *L'art de la prière,* 65ff., 93ff., 125.

SYMBOLIC THEOLOGY, PP. 229FF.

On jewish-christian symbols, see Jean Daniélou, *Theologie du judéo-christianisme*. Tournai, 1958.; translated John A. Baker, *The Theology of Jewish Christianity*. London, 1964.
The *Physiologus,* ed. by Francesco Sbordone (Milan, 1936) is a great repertoire of patristic symbols; Meisenheim: O. Offermans, 1966.
Gregory Palamas. *Défense des saints hesychastes,* II, 3, 55 (Louvain, 500ff), II, 3, 72 (536ff), III, I,13ff (582ff).
Lossky, Vladimir. 'La notion des "analogies" chez Denys le Pseudo-Aréopagite', *Archives d'histoire doctrinale et littéraire du moyen age* 5 (1930) 279–309.
Pourrat, Pierre. 'Arributs divins (méditation des)', DSp 1 (1936) 1078–98.
Mondésert, Claude. 'Le symbolisme chez Clément d'Alexandrie', RSR 26 (1936) 158–180.

Daniélou, Jean. *Platonisme et théologie mystique,* 142–151. Paris, 1944.
Semmelroth, Otto. 'Die θεολογία συμβολική des Ps. Dionysius Areopagita', *Scholastik* 27 (1952) 1–11.
Rahner, Karl. 'Zur Theologie des Symbols', *Schriften zur Theologie,* 4:275–313. Einsiedeln, 1960. Translated Kevin Smith, 'The Theology of the Symbol', *Theological Investigations,* 4:221ff. London, 1966.
Ampe, Albert. 'Exemplarisme', DSp 4/2 (1961) 1870–1878.
Various authors in F. Herrmann, ed. *Symbolik der orthodoxen und orientalischen Christentums,* Symbolik der Religionen. Stuttgart, 1962.
Lossky, Vladimir. *À l'image et à la ressemblance de Dieu.* Paris, 1967 (a collection of essays); *In the Image and Likeness of God.* Crestwood, New York, 1974.
Schmemann, Alexander. 'Symbols and Symbolism in the Orthodox Church', in D. J. Constantelos, *Orthodox Theology and Diakonia,* 91–102. Brookline, Massachusetts, 1981.
Voicu, Sever J. and Carlo Carletti. 'Simboli – simbolismo', DP 2: 3196–3203. 'Symbol– symbolism', EEC 2: 802–803.

SCRIPTURAL MYSTICISM, P. 230.

Daniélou, Jean. 'Les sources bibliques de la mystique d'Origène', RAM 23 (1947) 126–141; reprinted in *Origène,* 287–301. Paris, 1948.
de Lubac, Henri. *Histoire et Esprit, L'intelligence de l'Écriture d'après Origène,* Théologie, 16. Paris, 1950.
Vilnet, Jean. 'L'Écriture et les mystiques', DSp 4/1 (1960) 247–260.
Crouzel, Henri. *Origène et la 'connaissance mystique',* Museum Lessianum. Brussels-Paris, 1961.

THE MYSTICISM OF EVENTS AND OF SUFFERING, P. 232.

Origen. *Commentary on the Gospel according to Matthew,* 10.18 (the suffering of the prophets); *Commentaire sur l'évangile selon Matthieu,* SCh 162:224ff; ANF 9:424ff.
John Chrysostom. *Letter from Exile*; *Lettre d'exil* (*Quod nemo laeditur nisi a seipso),* SCh 103 (1964) 56ff.
Pseudo-Macarius. *Homily* 3.4; SCh 275:86ff; translated Maloney, CWS, 48; translated Mason, 17–b.
Mark the Ascetic. *Controversy with a Lawyer (Controverse avec un avocat),* 16; french translation by C. A. Zirnheld, in the series Spiritualité orientale, 41:170ff. Bellefontaine, 1985.

Isaac the Syrian. 46th Discourse; *Oeuvres,* 259ff.; translated Wensinck, 221ff.

Symeon the New Theologian. *Hymn* 36 (thanksgiving for tribulations); SCh 174: 450ff; translated George A. Maloney, *Hymns of Divine Love by St. Symeon the New Theologian,* 194ff. Denville, New Jersey, n.d.

———. *Discourses* 2.207f (Sch 96:254f), 28.36f (Sch 113:130ff). See the translation of C. J. deCatanzaro, *Symeon the New Theologian. The Discourses,* CWS. New York, 1980.

Arseniev, Nikolai S. *La piété russe,* 28ff. Neuchâtel, 1963; translated A. Moorhouse, *Russian Piety.* 2nd ed. Crestwood, New York, 1975.

Ray, L. 'Blessure d'amour', DSp 1 (1936) 1724–1729.

Lot-Borodine, Myrrha. 'Warum kennt das christliche Altertum die mystischen Wundmale nicht?', *Benediktinische Monatschrift* 21 (1939) 23–32.

Hausherr, Irénée. 'Les Orientaux connaissent-ils les 'nuits' de S. Jean de la Crox?', OCP 12 (1946) 5–46; *Hésychasme et prière,* OCA 176:87–128. Rome, 1966.

Olphe-Galliard, Michel. 'Croix (dévotion à la' DSp 2/2 (1953) 2606–2623.

de la Trinité, Philippe. 'Épreuves spirituelles', DSp 4/1 (1960) 911–925.

Leroy, Julien. 'ΕΓΚΑΤΑΛΕΙΨΙΣ (la dérélection chez les Orientaux)', DSp 4/1 (1960) 344–357.

Stockmeier, P. *Theologie und Kult des Kreuzes bei Johannes Chrysostomus. Ein Beitrag zum Verständnis des Kreuzes im IV. Jahrhundert,* Theologische Studien, 18. Trier, 1966.

Nowak, Edward. *Le chrétien devant la souffrance. Étude sur la pensée de Jean Chrysostome.* Paris, 1972.

Gielen, H. and F. Nackaerts. *Bibliographie Stauros. Souffrance humaine et Passion du Christ.* Louvain, 1975ff. (semi-annual fascicules).

Alszeghy, A. and M. Flick. *Sussidio bibliografico per una teologia della croce.* Rome, 1975.

*La sapienza della croce oggi. Atti del Congresso Internazionale* (Rome, October 1975), 3 vols. Turin, 1976.

Špidlík, Tomaš. *Les grands mystiques russes,* 13–27. Paris, 1979.

di Bernardo, Flavio. 'Passion (mystique de la)', DSp 12 (1984) 312–338.

THE VISION OF GOD THROUGH A VISION OF SELF, P. 232.

Athanasius. *Contra gentes,* 2.1; *Contre les paiens,* SCh 18*bis* (1983) 150ff; LNPF, 2nd ser., 4:20.

Pseudo-Macarius. *Homily* 19.1; SCh 275:228ff; translated Maloney, CWS, 146.

Isaac the Syrian. 43rd Discourse; *Oeuvres* (Desclée de Brouwer, 1981), 243ff; Wensinck, *Mystic Treatises,* 210ff. Amsterdam, 1923.

Hazzâyâ, Rabban Jausep. *Briefe*, 217ff, 224.

Nicetas Stethatos. *Opuscules et lettres, Traité de l'âme;* SCh 81 (1961) 64ff.

Gregory Palamas. *Défense des saints hésychastes,* I, 2, 4 and I, 3, 45; Louvain, 80ff, 208; partial translation in *Gregory Palamas. The Triads,* CWS, 43.

*The Art of Prayer*, 256; *L'art de la prière,* 303ff.

*A Systematic Handbook,* 87, 376 (bibliog.), 420 (texts).

Florenskij, Pavel. *Voprosi religionznogo samopoznaija* [*Questions of Religious Self-knowledge*]. Sergiev Posad, 1907.

Arnou, René. *Le désir de Dieu dans la philosophie de Plotin.* Rome, 1921, 1967.

Reypens, Léonce. 'Âme (son fond, ses puissances et sa structure d'apres les mystiques)', DSp 1 (1936) 433–469.

Schoemann, J. B. 'Gregors von Nyssa theologische Anthropologie als Bildtheologie', *Scholastik* (1943) 31–53, 175–200.

Daniélou, Jean. *Platonisme et theologie mystique, La doctrine spirituelle de saint Grégoire de Nysse,* Théologie, 2:223–225. Paris, 1944.

Festugière, André-Jean. *La révélation d'Hermès Trismégiste,* 2:575ff. Paris, 1944–1945.

Mouroux, Jean. *Le sens chrétien de l'homme*. Paris, 1945; translated A. H. G. Downes, *The Meaning of Man.* New York, 1948.

Leys, R. *L'image de Dieu chez saint Grégoire de Nysse.* Paris-Brussels, 1951.

de Bazelaire, Louis. 'Connaissance de soi', DSp 2/2 (1953) 1511–1544.

Lemaitre, J. (Hausherr). 'Contemplation . . .', DSp 2/2 (1953) 1836ff.

Meyendorff, Jean. 'Le thème du "retour en soi" dans la doctrine palamite du XVe siècle', RHR 145 (1954) 188–206.

Reypens, Léonce. 'Dieu (connaissance mystique): vision speculaire et vue par assimilation d'amour', DSp (1957) 886ff.

Puech, Henri Charles. 'Les themes gnostiques "se rassembler en soi, se concentrer sur soi"', *Annuaire de l'École pratique des Hautes Etudes,* Section des Sciences religieuses, 84–86, 1962–1963.

Dupuy, Michel. 'Introversion', DSp 7/2 (1971) 1904–1918.

Blasucci, Antonio. 'Images et contemplation', DSp 7/2:1904–90.

Courcelle, Pierre. *Connais-toi toi-même de Socrate à saint Bernard,* Études augustiniennes. 3 vols. Paris, 1974–1975.

THE MYSTICISM OF THE CHURCH, P. 237.

Hermas. *The Shepherd; Pasteur,* Introduction, SCh 53*bis* (1997) 34ff; translated Joseph M.-F. Marrique, in *The Apostolic Fathers,* FCh 1:225ff. New York, 1947.

Basil. *On the Holy Spirit,* 29; *Sur le Saint-Esprit* 9, SCh 17*bis* (1968) 510ff; LNPF, 2nd ser., 8:44ff. Also translated as *St Basil the Great: On the Holy Spirit*. Crestwood, New York, n.d.

Gregory of Nyssa. *The Life of Moses,* 2.184ff; SCh 1*bis*:89ff; Malherbe and Ferguson, CWS/CS31:101ff.

Nicholas Cabasilas. *A Commentary on the Divine Liturgy,* 37. 6; SCh 4*bis:* 228ff; Hussey and McNulty, 91ff.

*A Systematic Handbook,* 158, 387 (bibliog.), 424 (texts).

de Lubac, Henri. *Méditation sur l'Église,* Théologie, 27. Paris, 1953. English translation, based on the 2nd edition, by Michael Mason, *The Splendour of the Church*. New York, 1956.

Jourjon, Maurice. 'Le sens ecclésial de l'Église chez les Pères de l'Église', DSp 4/1 (1960) 402–11.

de Vries, Guillaume. 'Le sens ecclésial chez les Syriens (jacobites et nestoriens)', DSp 4/1: 436–42.

Broutin, Paul. '"Mysterium Ecclesiae"', DSp 4/1:468–479.

Brunet, Robert. 'Figures et images de l'Église', DSp 4/1: 384–401.

Nissiotis, N. A. 'The Importance of the Doctrine of the Trinity for Church Life and Theology . . . , in A. J. Philippou, *The Orthodox Ethos,* 60–65. Oxford, 1964.

Rahner, Hugo. *Symbole der Kirche. Die Ekklesiologie der Väter*. Salzburg, 1964. [See also, *Kirche und Staat im frühen Christentum,* translated Leo D. Davis, *Church and State in Early Christianity*. San Francisco, 1992.]

Afanassieff, N. *Cerkov Ducha Svjatogo*. Paris, 1970.

Chênevert, Jacques. *L'Église dans le Commentaire d'Origène sur le Cantique des Cantiques*, Studia, 24. Desclée de Brouwer, 1969.

Rancillac, Ph. *L'Église, manifestation de l'Esprit chez saint Jean Chrysostome*. Dar El-Kalima (Lebanon), 1970.

Robitaille, L. *L'Église, épouse du Christ, dans l'interpretation patristique du Psaume* 44 [45]. Quebec, 1971.

Murray, R. *Symbols of Church and Kingdom. A Study in Early Syriac Tradition*. Cambridge, 1975.

THE MYSTICISM OF LIGHT, P. 241.

Pseudo-Macarius. *Homily* 3.4; SCh 275:91; Maloney translation, CWS, 48–49; Mason translation, 18.

Hazzâyâ, Rabban Jausep. *Briefe,* 228ff.

Symeon the New Theologian, *Discourses,* 2.353ff (SCh 96:270ff), 11. 67ff (SCh 104:228ff); deCatanzaro translation, CWS, 56, 168–169.

———. *Livre de théologie,* 3.133ff; SCh 122:164ff; The Third Theological Discourse, translated Paul McGuckin, CS 41:135ff.

———. *Hymn* 8; SCh 174:74ff; translated George A. Maloney, *Hymns of Divine Love by St. Symeon the New Theologian,* 30ff.

Gregory Palamas. *Défense des saints hésychastes,* I, 3, 7 (Louvain, 120ff), I, 3, 27 (166ff).

Seraphim of Sarov, in Irina Gorainoff, *Saint Séraphim de Sarov,* 205ff. Bellefontaine, 1973. [See 'A Conversation with the Saint by Nicholas A. Motovilov', in Constantine Cavarnos and Mary-Barbara Zeldin, *St. Seraphim of Sarov,* 93ff. Belmont, Massachusetts, 1980. Modern Orthodox Saints no. 5. See also, Frandlin Jones, ed., *The Spiritual Instructions of Saint Seraphim of Sarov*. Los Angeles, 1973].

*The Art of Prayer,* 66, 73, 157; *L'art de la prière,* 214ff.

Wetter, G. P. Φῶς. *Eine Untersuchung über hellenistische Frömmigkeit.* Uppsala, 1915.

Dölger, Franz Josef, 'Lumen Christi . . .' , *Antike und Christentum,* 5:1–44.

Pulver, M. 'Die Lichterfahrung im Johannesevangelium, in Corpus Hermeticum, in der Gnosis und in der Ostkirche', *Eranos-Jahrbuch* 10 (1943) 253–296.

Lossky, Vladimir. *Essai sur la théologie mystique de l'Orient,* 215–234. Paris, 1944. *The Mystical Theology of the Eastern Church,* 217–235. London, 1957.

Bultmann, Rudolf. 'Zur Geschichte der Lichtsymbolik im Altertum', *Philologus* 97 (1948) 136ff.

Olphe-Galliard, Michel, 'Cassien: une mystique intellectualiste', DSp 2/1 (1953) 225–229.

Lemaitre J. (Hausherr). 'Mystique catastatique ou mystique de la lumiere', DSp 2/2 (1953) 1830–1855.

Beierwalters, W. 'Die Metaphysik des Lichtes in der Philosophie Plotins', *Zeitschrift für philosophische Forschung* 15 (1961) 334–367.

Martinez, M. *Teología de la luz en Origenes*. Comillas, 1962.

Pelikan, Jaroslav. *The Light of the World, A Basic Image in Early Christian Thought*. New York, 1962.

Melia, Élie. 'Le thème de la lumière dans l'hymnographie byzantine de Noël'; Dalmais, Irénée Henri. 'Le thème de la lumière dans l'office du matin des Églises syriennes-orientales', in *Noël-Épiphanie, retour du Christ,* Lex orandi, 40:237–256, 257–76. Paris, 1967.

Deseille, Placide. 'Gloire de Dieu', DSp 6 (1967) 421–463.

Lossky, Vladimir. À l'image et à la ressemblance de Dieu, 25–38. Paris, 1967. *In the Image and Likeness of God,* 31ff. New York, 1974.

Rius-Camps, Josef. *El dinamismo trinitario en la divinización de los seres racionales según Origenes,* OCA, 158. Rome, 1970.

———. 'Consideración catafática de la naturaleza de Dios . . . , φῶς, πῦρ, πνεῦμα, OCP 38 (1972) 430–453.

*Grégoire de Nazianze,* 15: Les trois lumières [the three lights].

Moreschini, C. 'Luce e purificazione nella dottrina di Grigorio Nazianzeno', *Augustinianum* 13 (1973) 535–549.

Mathieu, Dominique. 'Lumière: Étude biblique', DSp 9 (1976) 1142–1149.

Camelot, Pierre-Thomas. 'Lumière: Étude patristique', DSp 9:1149–1158.

Studer, Basilio. 'Illuminazione', DP 2:1755–1756; 'Illumination', EEC 1:405.

Sfafeni Gasparro, Giulia. 'Luce (symbolismo)', DP 2:2041–2042; 'Light, Symbolism of', EEC 1:489.

THE MYSTICISM OF EVAGRIUS, P. 243.

Bousset, Wilhelm. *Apophthegmata, Studien zur Geschichte des ältesten Mönchtums.* 281–341. Tübingen, 1923.

Rahner, Karl. 'Die geistliche Lehre des Evagrius Pontikus', ZAM 8 (1933) 21–38.

Hausherr, Irénée. 'Une énigme d'Évagre le Pontique', RSR 12 (1932), 321–325; OCA 183 (1969) 1–10.

———. 'Par delà l'oraison pure grâce à une coquille. À propos d'un texte d'Évagre', RAM 13 (1932) 184–188; OCA 176 (1966) 8–12.

———. 'Le "De oratione" de Nil et d'Évagre', RAM 14 (1933) 196–198.

———. 'Le Traité de l'Oraison d'Évagre le Pontique (Pseudo-Nil)', RAM 15 (1934) 34–93, 113–170; rpt., RAM 25 (1959) 3–26, 121–146, 241–265, 361–385; and as, *Les leçons d'un contemplatif.* Paris, 1960.

———. '"Ignorance infinie"', OCP 2 (1936) 351–362; OCA 176 (1966) 38–49.

———. 'Ignorance infinie ou science infinie?' OCP 25 (1959) 44–52; OCA 176 (1966) 238–246.

———. 'Le "De oratione" d'Évagre le Pontique en syriaque et en arabe', OCP 5 (1939) 7–71.

———. 'Nouveaux fragments grecs d'Évagre le Pontique', OCP 5:229–233.

Marsili, Salvatore. *Giovanni Cassiano ed Evagrio Pontico. Dottrina sulla carità e contemplazione*. Rome, 1936.

von Balthasar, Hans Urs. 'Metaphysik und Mystik des Evagrius Ponticus', ZAM 14 (1939) 31–47.

———. 'Die Hiera des Evagrius', in *Zeitschrift für katholische Theologie* 63 (1939) 86–106, 181–205.

Draguet, René. 'L'histoire lausiaque, une oeuvre ecrite dans l'esprit d'Évagre', RHE 41 (1946) 321–364; 42 (1947) 5–49.

Chadwick, Owen. *John Cassian. A Study in Primitive Monasticism,* 82–87. Cambridge, 1950. 2nd ed., Cambridge, 1969. [See also, Philip Rousseau, *Ascetics, Authority and the Church* (bibliog.). Cambridge, 1978.]

Lemaitre, J. (Hausherr). 'Contemplation . . .', DSp 2/2 (1953) 1775ff.

Guillaumont Antoine and Claire Guillaumont. 'Évagre le Pontique', DSp 4/2 (1961) 1731–1744.

Guillaumont, Antoine. *Les 'Kephalaia Gnostica' d'Évagre le Pontique et l'histoire de l'Origénisme chez les Grecs et les Syriens,* Patristica Sorbonensia, 5. Paris, 1962.

———. 'Evagrius Ponticus', *Reallexikon für Antike und Christentum* 6 (1966) 1088–1107.

———. 'Evagrius Ponticus', *Theologische Realenzyclopädie,* 10:565–570. Berlin-New York, 1982.

———. 'La "preghiera pura" di Evagrio e l'influsso del neoplatonismo', DIP 7 (1983) 591–595.

Dempf, A. 'Evagrius Ponticos als Metaphysiker und Mystiker', *Philosophisches Jahrbuch der Görres-Gesellschaft* 77 (1970) 297–319.

Grillmeier, Aloys. 'Evagrius Ponticus (als Origenist)', *Jesus der Christus im Glauben der Kirche,* I:561–8. Freiburg im Br., 1979.

Bunge, Gabriel. 'Évagre le Pontique et les deux Macaires', *Irénikon* 56 (1983) 215–226, 323–360.

Gribomont, Jean. 'Evagrio Pontico', DP 1:1313–1314; 'Evagrius of Pontus (Ponticus)', EEC 1:306.

SYMEON THE NEW THEOLOGIAN, P. 247.

Biedermann, Hermegild M. *Das Menschenbild bei Symeon dem Jüngeren Theologen (949–1022)*. Wurzburg, 1949.

———. 'Symeon der Neue Theologe (949–1022)', in G. Ruhbach and J. Sudbrack, *Grosse Mystiker,* 93–106. Munich, 1984.

Stathopoulos, D. *Die Gottesliebe bei Symeon dem neuen Theologen*. (Dissertation, Bonn, n.d.).

———. *Das göttliche Licht (Aus der Theologie des Ostens).* Athens, 1971.

Völker, Walther. *Praxis und Theoria bei Symeon dem Neuen Theologen, Ein Beitrag zur byzantinischen Mystik.* Wiesbaden, 1974.

Krivošein, Vasilii, archbishop. *Prepodobnyi Simeon Novyj Bogoslov (949–1022).* Paris, 1980.

———. *Dans la lumière du Christ, Saint Syméon le Nouveau Théologien (949–1022).* Chevetogne, 1980. Translation Anthony P. Gythiel, *In the Light of Christ. Saint Symeon the New Theologian (949–1022): Life-Spirituality-Doctrine.* Crestwood, New York, 1986.

Fraigneau-Julien, B. *Les sens spirituels et la vision de Dieu selon Syméon le Nouveau Théologien,* Théologie historique, 67. Paris, 1985.

THE HEART, PP. 248FF.

Origen, *Homilies on Joshua,* 19.2; SCh 71 (1960) 384ff.

Mark the Monk (Mark the Ascetic). *À Nicolas,* 5, in Spiritualité orientale, 41, 138ff. Bellefontaine, 1985. *Letter to Nicolas the Solitary,* in *The Philokalia. The Complete Text,* I:1, 147ff. London, 1979.

Maximus the Confessor, in J. Gouillard, ed., *Petite Philocalie,* 158ff. Paris, 1953. [See also Polycarp Sherwood, trans., *St. Maximus the Confessor. The Ascetic Life. The Four Centuries on Charity,* ACW 21. New York, 1956.]

Isaac the Syrian. *83rd Discourse; Œuvres* (Desclée de Brouwer, 1981) 409.

Symeon the New Theologian. Discourse 16.152ff; *Catéchèses,* SCh 104:250ff.; translated deCatanzaro, *Symeon the New Theologian. The Discourses,* CWS, 202–203. New York, 1980.

Gregory Palamas. *Défense des saints hésychastes,* I, 2, 3; Louvain, 78; translated Gendle, *The Triads,* CWS, pp. 42–43.

Brianchaninov, Ignace. *Approches de la prière de Jésus,* 177ff; *On the Prayer of Jesus.* London, 1952.

*L'art de la prière,* 75ff, 146ff; *The Art of Prayer:* see Index, s.v. Heart.

*A Systematic Handbook,* 105, 237 (maintaining guard over the heart, custody of the heart), 397 and 400 (bibliog.), 422 and 433 (texts).

Špidlík, Tomaš. 'El corazón en la spiritualidad del oriente cristiano', in Roger Vekemans, ed., *Cor Christi . . . ,* 145–157. Bogota, 1980.

———. "Il cuore nella spiritualità russa', in R. Faricy and E. Malatesta, *Cuore del Cristo: cuore dell'uomo,* 49–73. Naples, 1982.

THE PRAYER OF THE HEART, PP. 248FF.

*A Systematic Handbook,* 311, 440 (Texts).

dc B., H. *La prière du Coeur.* Paris, 1952.

*Théophane le Reclus,* 249ff.
Serr, Jacques. *La prière du coeur,* Spiritualité orientale, 6. Bellefontaine, 1970.
Lefebvre, G. *Prière pure et Pureté du coeur d'après S. Grégoire . . . et J. de la Croix,* 2nd ed. Paris, 1959.
Antoniadou, A. 'Le thème du coeur dans la Philocalie', *Contacts* 34 (1982) 235–247, 323–327.

SPIRITUAL FEELINGS, P. 256.

Pseudo-Macarius. *Œuvres spirituels,* SCh 275:361 (Index) s.v. αἴσθησις, αἰσθάνομαι.
Diadochus of Photice. *Cent chapitres gnostiques,* 87ff; SCh 5*ter:*146ff; 'On Spiritual Knowledge and Discrimination: One Hundred Texts', *The Philokalia. The Complete Text,* 1:286ff. London, 1979.
Isaac the Syrian. 69th Discourse; *Oeuvres,* 352ff. Desclée de Brouwer, 1981; translated A. J. Wensinck, *Mystic Treatises of Isaac of Nineveh,* 321ff. Amsterdam, 1923.
*The Art of Prayer,* 25–7, 52, 60, 67, 86; *L'art de la prière,* 77ff.

THE CONSCIOUSNESS OF GRACE, P. 257.

Pseudo-Macarius. *Homily* 16.2; SCh 275:188ff. *Homily* 25. 6; 284ff. Translated Maloney, CWS, 129–130, 162; translated Maloney, *Intoxicated with God,* 112, 145.
Diadochus of Photice. *Cent chapitres gnostiques,* 75ff; SCh 5*ter:*133ff; 'On Spiritual Knowledge and Discrimination: One Hundred Texts', *The Philokalia. The Complete Text,* 1:278ff. London, 1979.
Symeon the New Theologian. *Éthique,* 5.1ff; SCh 129:78ff; Golitzin, The Fifth Discourse, *St Symeon the New Theologian . . . : The Ethical Discourses,* 2:44ff. Crestwood, New York, 1996.
———. *Hymn* 34; SCh 174:426; translated George A. Maloney, *Hymns of Divine Love by Symeon the New Theologian,* 187ff. Denville, New Jersey. n.d.

SPIRITUAL CONSOLATIONS, P. 259.

Evagrius. *Chapters on Prayer,* 93; Hausherr, *Leçons,* 128; CS 4:71.
Pseudo-Macarius. *Homily* 3.1.4; SCh 275:87ff; Maloney, CWS 47, Mason, 16ff. *Homily* 25.6.1; 285ff; CWS 162; Mason, 108ff.

Diadochus of Photice. *Cent chapitres gnostiques,* 31ff; SCh 5*ter:*100ff; 'On Spiritual Knowledge and Discrimination: One Hundred Texts', *The Philokalia. The Complete Text,* I:261ff. London, 1979.

Symeon the New Theologian. Discourse 9; *Catéchèses,* 9,367ff; SCh 104:134ff; deCatanzaro, CWS, 160ff.

*The Art of Prayer,* 25–27, 52, 60, 67, 86; *L'art de la prière,* 325ff.

Daeschler, René. 'Aridité', DSp 1 (1936) 845–855.

Pourrat, Pierre. 'Affective (spiritualité)', DSp 1:2406.

Ziegler, Josef. *Dulcedo Dei, Ein Beitrag zur Theologie der griechischen und lateinischen Bibel.* Münster, 1937.

Lot-Borodine, Myrrha. 'L'aridité, "Siccitas" dans l'antiquité chrétienne', *Études carmélitaines* (1937) 191–201.

Truhlar, C. *De experientia mystica.* Rome, 1952.

Mouroux, Jean. *L'expérience chrétienne,* Théologie, 26. Paris, 1953. Translated George Lamb, *The Christian Experience. An Introduction to a Theology,* New York, 1954.

Poullier, Louis. 'Consolation spirituelle', DSp 2/2 (1953) 1617–1634.

Vernay, Robert. 'Découragement', DSp3 (1957) 58–65.

Martin, Henri. 'Dégoût spirituel', DSp 3:99–104.

———. 'Déréliction', DSp 3:504–517.

———. 'Désolation', DSp 3:631–645.

Chatillon, Jean. 'Dulcedo, dulcedo Dei', DSp 3:1777–1795.

Léonard, Augustin. 'Expérience spirituelle', DSp 4/2 (1961) 2004–2026.

Bussini, François. 'Joie', DSp 8 (1974) 1236–1256.

Michael, Pierre and Vincent Desprez. 'Plèrophoria', DSp 12/2 (1986) 1813–1821.

Bernard, Ch. *Teologia affetiva.* Ed. Paoline, 1985.

TEARS, P. 259.

Evagrius. *Chapters on Prayer,* 5ff.; Hausherr, *Leçons,* 19ff.; CS 4:56ff.

Pseudo-Athanasius. *De la virginité* 17, in *Vie de sainte Synclétique,* 135ff. Bellefontaine, 1972; translated Elizabeth Castelli, in Vincent L. Wimbush, ed., *Ascetic Behavior in Greco-Roman Antiquity. A Sourcebook,* Studies in Antiquity and Christianity, 276ff. Minneapolis, 1990.

Cassian. *Conferences,* 9.28; SCh 54:63ff; Ramsey, ACW 57:347; Luibheid, CWS, 118ff.

Isaac the Syrian. 33rd Discourse; *Oeuvres,* 208ff. Desclée de Brouwer, 1981; Wensinck, 111ff. Amsterdam, 1923.

Hazzâyâ, Rabban Jausep. *Briefe,* 101ff, 181ff.

Symeon the New Theologian. Discourses 2.216ff (*Catéchèses,* SCh 96:262ff), Discourse 4, 402ff (436ff), Discourse 29, 181ff (SCh 113:180ff); deCatanzaro, CWS, 54, 80ff, 230. New York, 1980

Gregory Palamas. *Défense des saints hésychastes,* II, 2, 17; Louvain, 354ff.

'Larmes (Don des)', *Dictionnaire de mystique chrétienne de Migne,* 739–740. Paris, 1858.

Hello, Ernest. *Paroles de Dieu, Réflexions sur quelques textes sacrés,* s.v. Les larmes dans l'Écriture. Paris, 1919 (rpt).

Leclercq, Henri. 'Larmes (dans la prière)', DACL 8 (1928) 1393–1402.

Gardeil, Ambroise. 'La béatitude des larmes', *La vie spirituelle* 39 (1934) 129–136.

Lot-Borodine, Myrrha. 'Le mystère du "don des larmes" dans l'Orient chrétien', *La vie spirituelle* 48 (1936) 65–110, and in *La douloureuse joie,* Spiritualité orientale, 14:131–195. Bellefontaine, 1974.

Gillet, Lev. 'The Gift of Tears', *Sobornost* (December, 1937).

Steidle, Basilius. 'Die Tränen, ein mystisches Problem im alten Mönchtum', *Benediktinische Monatschrift* 20 (1938) 181–187.

Hausherr, Irénée. *Penthos. La doctrine de la componction dans l'Orient chrétien.* Rome, 1944. Translated Anselm Hufstader, *Penthos. The Doctrine of Compunction in the Christian East,* CS 53. Kalamazoo, 1982.

Schulte, R[aphael]. 'Tränengabe', LTHK 10 (1965) 305.

Théron, M. 'Larmes', *Catholicisme* 6 (1966) 1849–1851.

Mary, Sylvia. 'St Symeon the New Theologian and the Way of Tears', *Studia Patristica* 10, TU 107 (1970) 431–436.

Kahle, W. 'Die Tränen der Frommen in der Gottesbegegnung (Ein Beitrag zur oekumenischen Spiritualität)', *The Ecumenical World of Orthodox Civilisation,* 3:91–119. The Hague-Paris, 1974.

Adnès, Pierre. 'Larmes', DSp 9 (1976) 287–303.

The language of the spiritual writers, pp. 261ff.

Güntert, Herman. *Von der Sprache der Götter und Geister. Bedeutungsgeschichtliche Untersuchungen zur homerischen und eddischen Göttersprache.* Halle, 1921.

Beth, H. 'Göttersprache', in H. Bächtold-Stäubli, ed., *Handwörterbuch des deutschen Aberglaubens* (1927–1942) 3:962ff.

*Grégoire de Nazianze,* 138ff.

Canévet, Mariette. *Grégoire de Nysse et l'herméneutique biblique. Études des rapports entre le langage et la connaissance de Dieu,* 31–64. Paris, 1983.

Heiler, Friedrich. *Die Religionen der Menschheit. Le religioni dell'umanità,* 269–283. Milan, 1985.

Špidlík, Tomaš. 'Y a-t-il un pluralisme théologique en Grégoire de Nazianze? Le théologie est-elle une poésie ou une science?', *Studia Patristica* 16 (1985) 428–432.

SPIRITUAL MARRIAGE, P. 261.

Origen. *Homilies on Genesis,* 10.5; SCh 7*bis:*270ff; FCh 71: 165ff.

———. *Commentary on Matthew,* 17.21; GCS 10.643; ANF 9 (1908).

———. *Homilies on the Song of Songs,* 1; SCh 37:60ff (see the Introduction by O. Rousseau, 35ff); *Origen. The Song of Songs: Commentary and Homilies,* ACW 26:266ff.

Gregory of Nyssa. *La columbe et la ténèbre. Textes extraits des 'Homélies sur le Cantique des Cantiques',* translated [into French] by M. Canévet, 21, 112. Paris, 1967. [See Jean Daniélou, 'Mystical Marriage', in Herbert Musurillo, *From Glory to Glory. Texts of Gregory of Nyssa's Mystical Writings,* 153ff. New York, 1961.]

———. *On Virginity,* 20.1; *Traite de la virginité,* SCh 119 (1966) 492ff; LNPF, 2nd ser., 5:365ff.

Pseudo-Athanasius. *De la virginité* 2, in *Vie de sainte Synclétique,* 112ff. Bellefontaine, 1972; translated Castelli, in Wimbush, *Ascetic Behavior,* 276ff.

Theodoret of Cyrrhus. *Explanatio in Canticum Canticorum,* preface; PG 81:27ff.

Wilpert, Josef. *Die gottgeweihten Jungfrauen in den ersten Jahrhunderten der Kirche*. Freiburg im Breisgau, 1892.

Koch, Hugo. *Virgines Christi: die Gelübde der gottgeweihten Jungfrauen in der ersten drei Jahrhunderten,* TU 31, fasc. 2:31ff. Leipzig, 1907.

Engberding, J. 'Die Kirche als Braut in der ostsyrischen Liturgie', OCP 3 (1937) 5–48.

Vonier, Anscar. *The Spirit and the Bride*. London, 1935.

Daniélou, Jean. *Bible et Liturgie,* Lex orandi, 11, chapter 12, pp. 259–280. Paris, 1951. Translated Michael A. Mathis, *The Bible and the Liturgy*. Notre Dame, Indiana, 1956.

Cavallera, Ferdinand. 'Cantique des cantiques: Histoire de l'interprétation spirituelle', DSp 2/1 (1953) 93–101.

Gummersbach, Joseph, and Marcel Viller. 'Confirmation en grâce et le mariage mystique', DSp 2/2 (1953) 1436–1441.

Münster, Ludwig. *Die Hochzeit des Lammes. Die Christusmystik der Jungfrauenweihe*. Düsseldorf, 1955. Translated Basil Stegman and

M. Margretta, *Christ in His Consecrated Virgins: The Marriage of the Lamb*. Collegeville, Minnesota, 1957.

Brunet, Robert. 'Figures et images de l'Église: l'Épouse', DSp 4/1 (1960) 392–396.

de Vries, Guillaume. 'Le sens ecclésial . . . chez les Syriens (jacobites et nestoriens)', DSp 4/1 (1960) 436–442.

Grant, Robert M. 'The Mystery of Marriage in the Gospel of Philip', *Vigiliae christianae* 15 (1961) 129–140.

Crouzel, Henri. *Virginité et mariage selon Origène*. Desclée de Brouwer, 1963.

Heiler, Friedrich. *Die Religionen der Menschheit. Le religioni dell'umanità,* 252–256. Milan, 1985.

Rush, A. C. 'Death as a Spiritual Marriage: Individual and Ecclesial Eschatology', *Vigiliae christianae,* 26 (1972) 81–101.

Harl, Marguerite. 'Cadeaux de fiançailles et contrat de mariage pour l'Épouse du "Cantique des Cantiques" selon quelques commentateurs grecs', *Mélanges . . . offerts à H. Ch. Puech,* 243–261. Paris, 1974.

Alvarez, A. 'Matrimonio spirituale', DESp 2:1163–1166. Rome, 1975.

Crouzel, Henri. 'Le thème du mariage mystique chez Origène', *Studia missionalia* 26 (1977) 37–57.

Adnès, Pierre. 'Mariage spirituel', DSp 10 (1980) 388–408.

SPIRITUAL INEBRIATION, P. 263.

Origen. *Homilies on Leviticus,* 7.1; *Homélies sur le Lévitique,* SCh 286:302ff; translated Gary W. Barkley, *Origen. Homilies on Leviticus* 1–16, FCh 83:129ff.

Cyril of Jerusalem. *Catechesis* 17.18; *Catéchèses baptismales et mystagogiques,* translated [into French] J. Bouvet (Namur, 1962) 403ff. English translation by Leo P. McCauley and Anthony A. Stephenson, *The Works of Saint Cyril of Jerusalem,* 1, FCh 61:107ff.

Pseudo-Denys. *Letter* 9.5; PG 3:1111; translated by Colm Luibheid and Paul Rorem, *Pseudo-Dionysius. The Complete Works,* CWS, 287ff. New York, 1987.

Isaac the Syrian. *24th Discourse; Oeuvres* (Desclée de Brouwer, 1981), 164; Wensinck, Chapter 27, *Mystic Treatises of Isaac of Nineveh,* 136. Amsterdam, 1923.

Symeon the New Theologian. *Discourse* 23, 157ff; *Catéchèses,* SCh 113:24ff; deCatanzaro, CWS, 258ff.New York, 1980.

Lewy, Hans. Sobra ebrietas. *Untersuchungen zur Geschichte der antiken Mystik*. Giessen, 1929.

Daniélou, Jean. *Platonisme et théologie mystique,* 290–308. Paris, 1944.
———. 'La mystique de la ténèbre chez Grégoire de Nysse', DSp 2/2 (1953) 1872–1875.
Leclercq, J. 'Jours d'ivresse', *La vie spirituelle* 76 (1947) 574–591.
Raymond, Johanny. *L'eucharistie centre de l'histoire du salut chez Ambroise de Milan,* Théologie historique, 9, 211ff. Paris, 1968.
Lebeau, P. 'La signification ecclésiologique de la coupe eucharistique d'après les Peres', *Studia Patristica,* 10, TU 107:366–373. Berlin, 1970.
Sieben, Hermann Josef. 'Ivresse spirituelle', DSp 7/2 (1971) 2312–2322 (bibliog.).
Meloni, P[ietro]. 'Ebrietà', DP 1:1048–1049; 'Drunkenness', EEC 1:255.
Špidlík, Tomaš. 'La mistica del sangue inebriante', *Il sangue che rivela l'amore,* 201–208. Rome, 1987.

WATCHFUL SLEEP, P. 264.

Daniélou, Jean. *Platonisme et théologie mystique,* 290–308.
———. 'Mystique de la ténèbre chez Grégoire de Nysse', DSp 2/2 (1953) 1879–1880.

THE 'PLACE' OF GOD, P. 265.

Dupuy, Michel. 'Introversion', DSp 7/2 (1971) 1904–1918.
———. 'Présence de Dieu', DSp 12/2 (1984) 2107–2136.

THE PRAYER OF FIRE, P. 267.

Origen. *Homilies on Genesis,* 15.2; SCh 7*bis:*354; translated Ronald E. Heine, *Origen. Homilies on Genesis and Exodus,* FCh 71 (1982).
Pseudo-Macarius. *Homily* 26.4; SCh 175:302; Maloney, CWS, 108–109; Mason, 186.
Hazzâyâ, Rabban Jausep. *Briefe,* 159ff.
Symeon the New Theologian. *Hymns,* 30; SCh 174:340ff; Maloney, *Hymns of Divine Love,* 160ff.
Gregory Palamas. *Défense des saints hésychastes,* I, 3, 8; Louvain, 124ff; translated Gendle, *The Triads,* CWS, p. 57.
*The Art of Prayer,* 52–53, 94; *L'art de la prière,* 28, 203–16.
Olphe-Galliard, Michel. 'Cassien', DSp 2/1 (1953) 262–264.
Gaillard, Jean. 'Feu', DSp 5 (1964) 247–273.

THE VISION OF GOD IN HIS 'ENERGIES', P. 267.

Gregory Palamas. *Défense des saint hésychastes,* II, 3, 9ff (Louvain, 404ff), II, 3, 66 (524ff), III,1, 9 (572ff), III, 2, 7) (654ff); selections translated by Gendle, *The Triads,* CWS.

Krivošein, Vasilii, monk. 'Asketičeskoe i bogoslovskoe učenie sv. Grigorija Palamy', *Seminarium Kondakovianum,* 8. Prague, 1936.

———. *Die asketische und theologische Lehre des hl. Gregorius Palamas (1296–1359),* Das östliche Christentum, 8. Würzburg, 1939.

———. (Archbishop). 'The Ascetic and Theological Teaching of Gregory Palamas', offprint from *The Eastern Churches Quarterly,* 4 (1938). London, 1954.

Meyendorff, Jean. *St. Grégoire Palamas et la mystique orthodoxe.* Paris, 1959. Translated M. Adele Fiske, *St. Gregory Palamas and Orthodox Spirituality.* Crestwood, New York, 1974.

Malevez, Léopold. 'Essence de Dieu (vision de l')', DSp 4/2 (1961) 1333–1345.

Lossky, Vladimir. *Vision de Dieu.* Neuchâtel, 1962. Translated Asheleigh Moorhouse, *The Vision of God.* London, 1963.

———. *À l'image et à la ressemblance de Dieu,* 39–66. Paris, 1967. *In the Image and Likeness of God.* Crestwood, New York, 1974.

Deseille, Placide. 'Gloire de Dieu', DSp 5 (1967) 421–463.

Nadal, J. S. 'La critique par Akindynos de l'herméneutique patristique de Palamas', *Istina,* no. 3 (1974) 297–328.

Hussey, M. Edmund. 'The Person-energy Structure in the Theology of St. Gregory Palamas', *St. Vladimir's Theological Quarterly* 18 (1974) 22–43.

Yannaras, Christos. 'The Distinction between Essence and Energies and its Importance for Theology', *St Vladimir's Theological Quarterly,* 19 (1975) 232–245.

Podalsky, G. *Theologie und Philosophie in Byzanz.* Munich, 1977.

Wendebourg, D. *Geist oder Energie. Zur Frage der innergöttlichen Verankerung des christlichen Lebens in der byzantinischen Theologie.* Munich, 1980.

Meyendorff, Jean. 'Palamas (Grégoire)'. DSp 12/1 (1984) 81–107.

———. [*Introduction à l'etude de Grégoire Palamas.* Paris, 1959. Translated George Lawrence, *A Study of Gregory Palamas.* London, 1964. Crestwood, New York.

PREPARING FOR PRAYER, P. 282.

Origen. *On Prayer,* 31; PG 11:549ff; translated Rowan A. Greer, *Origen. An Exhortation to Martyrdom, Prayer . . . ,* CWS, 164ff. New York, 1979.

Aphrahat. *Demonstrations,* 4. On Prayer; translated Sebastian Brock, in *The Syriac Fathers on Prayer and the Spiritual Life,* CS 101:17ff. Kalamazoo, 1987.

Evagrius. *Chapters on Prayer,* 65; Hausherr, *Leçons,* 92ff; CS 4:65ff.

Abba Isaiah. *Asceticon, Logos* 1; CSCO 293, Syri 122, 15.

PURIFICATION, PP. 283FF.

Clement of Alexandria. *Stromata,* 5.11.67, 1ff; SCh 278:136ff; ANF 2:460ff.

Origen. *Homilies on Leviticus,* 5.9; SCh 286:248ff; Barkley, *Origen. Homilies on Leviticus* 1–16, FCh 83:115.

Evagrius. *Chapters on Prayer,* 37, 39; Hausherr, *Leçons,* 55ff, 58; CS 4:61.

Philotheus of Sinai, in J. Gouillard, *Petite Philocalie,* 145. Paris, 1953. ['Forty Texts on Sobriety', *Writings from the Philokalia on Prayer of the Heart,* 339.]

Symeon the New Theologian. Discourse 4, 670ff; SCh 96:368ff; DeCatanzaro, CWS, 87ff.

———. *Livre de théologie,* I, 338ff; SCh 122:122ff; McGuckin, The First Theological Discourse, CS 41:107ff.

*A Systematic Handbook,* 182, 267 (purif. of the passions). 393 (bibliog.), 428 (texts).

Špidlík, T[omaš]. 'Purificazione', DP 2:2955–2956; 'Purification', EEC 2:725.

Solignac, Aimé. 'Passions et vie spirituelle', DSp 12/1 (1984) 339–357.

Heiler, Friedrich. *Die Religionen der Menschheit. Le religioni dell'umanità,* 195–213. Milan, 1985.

APATHEIA, P. 284.

Gregory of Nyssa. *The Life of Moses,* 2.256ff, 291ff; SCh 1*bis*:114ff, 124ff; CWS/CS 31:120, 129.

Evagrius. *Chapters on Prayer,* 4, 17, 141; Hausherr, *Leçons,* 18, 103ff, 172ff; CS 4: 56, 58, 78.

Dorotheus of Gaza. *Instruction* 11; SCh 92:356ff; translated Eric P. Wheeler, *Dorotheos of Gaza. Discourses and Sayings,* CS 33:172ff. Kalamazoo, 1977.

Symeon the New Theologian. *Éthique,* 4; SCh 129:8ff; Golitzin, Fourth Discourse, *St Symeon the New Theologian . . . : The Ethical Discourses,* 2:12ff. Crestwood, New York, 1996.

Gregory Palamas. *Défense des saints hésychastes,* II, 21, 19; Louvain, 360ff.
*The Art of Prayer,* 199–220; *L'art de la prière,* 272ff.
*A Systematic Handbook,* 100, 270ff., 403 (bibliog.), 437 (texts).
Solignac, Aimé. 'Passions et vie spirituelle', DSp 12/1 (1984) 339–357.

*AMNESIKAKIA*, THE NON-REMEMBRANCE OF INJURY, P. 284.

Evagrius. *Chapters on* Prayer, 13ff, 21, 40, 147; Hausherr, *Leçons,* 28ff, 36ff, 40ff, 179ff;. CS 4:57, 58, 61, 79.
Cassian. *Institutes,* 8; SCh 109: 334ff; Ramsey, ACW 58:191–204; LNPF, 2nd ser. 11: 257ff.
*Vie de sainte Synclétique* 63ff; Bellefontaine, 56ff; Castelli, *Ascetic Behavior,* 291ff.
Dorotheus of Gaza. *Instructions,* 8; SCh 92:306ff; CS 33:149ff.
*The Art of Prayer,* 218ff; *L'art de la prière,* 288ff.
*A Systematic Handbook,* 251 (anger), 435 (texts).
de Bovis, André. 'Haine', DSp 7/1 (1969) 29–50.
Marty, François. 'Pardon', DSp 12/1 (1984) 208–222.

SADNESS, P. 285.

Evagrius. *Chapters on Prayer,* 16, 42, 78ff, 144; Hausherr, *Leçons,* 30ff, 63, 110ff, 176; CS 4:58, 61, 68, 78.
Cassian. *Conferences,* 9.26ff; SCh 54:62ff; Ramsey, ACW 57: 346; Luibheid, CWS, 117; LNPF, 2nd ser., 11:396ff.
———. *Institutes,* 9; SCh 109:368ff; Ramsey, ACW 58:209-214; LNPF, 2nd ser., 11:264ff.
*Vie de sainte Synclétique* 40ff, Bellefontaine (1972) 36ff; Castelli, *Ascetic Behavior,* 283ff.
Isaac the Syrian. *50th Discourse; Oeuvres,* Desclée de Brouwer, 1981, 276ff; Wensinck, 230ff.
Hazzâyâ, R. J. *Briefe,* 143ff.
Symeon the New Theologian. *Discourse 5; Catéchèses,* SCh 96:374ff; DeCatanzaro, CWS, 90ff.
*The Art of Prayer,* 266; *L'art de la prière,* 311ff.
*A Systematic Handbook,* 251 (sadness), 193 *(penthos),* 402 (bibliog.: sadness), 394 (bibliog.: *penthos*), 429 (texts: sadness) 400 (texts: *penthos*).

THE PURIFICATION OF THE FLESH, P. 285.

*A Systematic Handbook,* 111ff, 217 (renunciation of the flesh), 380 (bibliog.), 398 (bibliog.), 422 (texts), 431 (texts).

FASTING, P. 286.

*Letter of Barnabas,* 3; *Épître de Barnabé,* SCh 172 (1971) 88ff; translated Francis X. Glimm, FCh 1, (1947) 193ff.
Cassian. *Institutes,* 5; SCh 109:186ff; Ramsey, ACW 58:113–141; LNPF, 2nd ser., 11:235ff.
Gerontius, *The Life of Melania the Younger,* 24ff; Vie *de sainte Mélanie,* SCh 90:176ff; Petersen, CS 143: 327ff.
*The Ethiopic Didascalia,* translated by J. M. Harden, 122ff. New York, 1920.
Romanos the Melode. *Hymne* I, *d'Adam et Eve;* SCh 99 (1964) 74ff. English translation by M. Carpenter, *Kontakia of Romanos,* 2 vols. Columbia, Mo., 1970–1973.
Brianchaninov, Ignace. *Approches de la prière de Jesus,* 70ff. (in Russian, 231ff.); selections translated Lazarus [Moore], *Ignatius Brianchaninov. On the Prayer of Jesus.* London, 1952.
Solovyov, Vladimir. *Duchovnyja osnovy žizni, Oeuvres* 3:315ff. Brussels, 1966.
*Dossier patristique sur le jeûne,* see DSp 8 (1974) 1175–1179.
*A Systematic Handbook,* 224, 399 (bibliog.), 432 (texts).
Deseille, Placide and Hermann-Josef Sieben. 'Jeûne', DSp 8 (1974) 1164–1179.

THE PURIFICATION OF THE SENSES, P. 288.

Basil of Ancyra (Pseudo-Basil of Caesarea), *Liber de vera virginitatis integritate,* 4–22; PG 30:669–716 (a treatise on guarding the senses, for use by a virgin).
Gregory Palamas. *Défense des saints hésychastes,* II,2, 5 (not all the sensory is to be rejected); Louvain, 326ff.
Nicodemus the Hagiorite. Συμβουλευτικὸν ἐγχειρίδιον περὶ φυλακῆς τῶν πέντε αἰσθησειων, τῆς τε φαντασίας τοῦ νοὸς καὶ τῆς καρδίας 2nd ed. Athens, 1885.
*A Systematic Handbook,* 331, 411 (bibliog.) 442 (texts).
Adnès, Pierre. 'Garde des sens', DSp 6 (1967) 117–122.

FLIGHT FROM THE WORLD, P. 288.

Evagrius. *Chapters on Prayer,* 18ff, 36, 124; Hausherr, *Leçons,* 34, 54ff, 158ff; CS 4: 58, 61, 76.
Cassian. *Conferences,* 3; SCh 42:138ff; Ramsey, ACW 57:119ff; Luibheid, CWS, 81ff; LNPF, 2nd ser., 11:319ff.

*Life of Melania,* 30ff; SCh 90:184ff; Petersen, CS 143:323ff.
Theoleptus of Philadelphia, in J. Gouillard, *Petite Philocalie,* 122. Paris, 1953. See 'A Word', in E. Kadloubovsky and G. E. H. Palmer, trans., *Writings from the Philokalia on Prayer of the Heart,* 385ff. London, 1979.
*A Systematic Handbook,* 205ff, 395 (bibliog.), 429 (texts).

THE PURIFICATION OF THE *NOUS*, P. 289.

*A Systematic Handbook,* 332ff, 411 (bibliog.), 442 (texts).

DISTRACTIONS, P. 289.

Evagrius. *Chapters on Prayer,* 34a, 46; Hausherr, *Leçons,* 53ff, 64ff, 68ff; CS 4:60, 62.
Cassian. *Conferences,* 10.13ff; SCh 54:90; Ramsey, ACW 57:385–386; Luibheid, CWS, 138–139; LNPF, 2nd ser., 11:408.
Isaac the Syrian. *33rd Discourse; Oeuvres,* 206; Wensinck, *Mystic Treatises,* 118ff.
Brianchaninov, Ignace. *Approches de la prière de Jesus;* translated Lazarus [Moore], *On the Prayer of Jesus.* London, 1952.
*The Art of Prayer,* 127ff; *L'art de la prière,* 172ff.
*A Systematic Handbook,* 233 (spiritual warfare), 400 (bibliog.), 432 (texts).
Vernay, Robert. 'Dissipation', DSp 3 (1957) 1346–1347.
———. 'Distractions', DSp 3:1347–1363.

THE STRUGGLE AGAINST DEMONS, P. 290.

Evagrius. *Chapters on Prayer,* 91ff; Hausherr, *Leçons,* 125; CS 4:70ff.
Cassian. *Conferences,* 7; SCh 42:242ff; Ramsey, ACW 57:247–272; LNPF, 2nd ser., 11:375ff.
Pseudo-Macarius. *Homilies,* 25.4.2; SCh 275:158ff; Maloney, CWS, 159ff; *Intoxicated with God,* 144.
Diadochus of Photice. *Cent chapitres gnostiques* 96ff; SCh 5*ter:*158ff; 'On Spiritual Knowledge and Discrimination: One Hundred Texts', *The Philokalia. The Complete Text,* 1:293ff.
Brianchaninov, Ignace. *Approches de la prière de Jésus,* 123–132; translated Moore, *On the Prayer of Jesus.*
*The Art of Prayer,* 211, 216; *L'art de la prière,* 272ff, 288., 295.
*A Systematic Handbook,* 233ff, 400 (bibliog.), 432 (texts).

THE EXAMINATION OF CONSCIENCE, P. 292.

Athanasius. *Life of Antony,* 55; PG 26:924AB; Vivian-Athanassakas, CS 202:175–179; translated Meyer. ACW 10:66ff; NPNF, 2nd ser., 4:210–211.

*Catéchèse copte de Pacôme,* edited by L.Th. Lefort, CSCO 160:23.

John Chrysostom. *Baptismal Catecheses,* 4.32, 5.27; *Catéchèses baptismales,* SCh 50 (1985) 98ff, 213; partial translation in LNPF 9:159–171.

Pseudo-Macarius. *Homily* 25.3; SCh 275:274ff; Maloney, CWS, 160–161; Mason, 179ff.

Symeon the New Theologian, *Discourses,* 31.5ff; SCh 113:224ff; deCatanzaro, CWS, 329ff.

Brianchaninov, Ignace. *Approches de la prière de Jésus,* 84ff; *On the Prayer of Jesus,* 93ff

Other texts in DSp 4/2, 1804–6.

*A Systematic Handbook,* 247, 401 (bibliog.), 434 (texts).

Nepper, Marius. 'Comptabilité spirituelle', DSp 2/2 (1953) 1326–1333.

Cabassut, André. 'Défauts', DSp 3 (1957) 68–88.

Jaeger, Hasso. 'L'examen de conscience dans les religions non-chrétiennes et avant le christianisme', *Numen,* 6 (1959) 175–233; summarized in DSp 4/2 (1961) 1790–1799.

Guillet, Jacques. 'Examen de conscience dans la Bible', DSp 4/2:1799–1801.

Guy, Jean-Claude. 'L'examen de conscience chez les Pères de l'Église', DSp 4/2:1801–1807.

Liuma, Antanas and André Derville. 'Examen particulier', DSp 4/2:1838–1849.

*Théophane le Reclus,* 273ff.

Schmidt, Margot. 'Mirroir', DSp 10 (1980) 1290–1303.

THE VIRTUES, PP. 294FF.

Evagrius. *Chapters on Prayer,* 1ff, 101; Hausherr, *Leçons,* 13ff, 137ff; CS 4:55ff, 72.

Mark the Monk (the Ascetic). *Controversy with a Lawyer,* 8; *Controverse avec un avocat,* Spiritualité orientale, 41:162ff. Bellefontaine, 1985.

Dorotheus of Gaza. *Instructions,* 14; SC 92:420ff; CS 33:201ff.

Isaac the Syrian. *37th Discourse; Oeuvres,* 224ff; Wensinck, *Mystic Treatises,* 188ff.

Gregory of Sinai, in J. Gouillard, *Petite Philocalie,* 239. Paris, 1953. 'Texts on Commandments and Dogmas', *Writings from the Philokalia on Prayer of the Heart,* 37ff.
*A Systematic Handbook,* 288, 405 (bibliog.), 438 (texts), 334 (the virtues lead to spiritual knowledge).

PIETY, P. 295.

Curran, J. 'Dévotion (fondement théologique)', DSp 3 (1957) 716–727.
Chatillon, Jean. 'Devotio', DSp 3:702–716.
Bertaud, Émile and André Rayez. 'Dévotions', DSp 3:747–777.
de Bovis, André. 'Loyauté', DSp 9 (1976) 1091–1099.
Méhat, André. 'Piété', DSp 12/1 (1986) 1694–1714.
Peretto, E[lio]. 'Pietà', DP 2:2778–2780; 'Piety', EEC 2:687.

SIMPLE FAITH, HOPE, P. 295.

Philoxenus of Mabbug. *Deux Homélies sur la foi;* SCh 44 (1956) 45ff.
Isaac the Syrian. *19th Discourse;* (*Oeuvres,* 128ff), *18th Discourse* (124ff); Wensinck, *Mystic Treatises,* 105ff., 95ff.
Gregory of Nareg. *Le livre de prière,* 10–11; SCh 78 (1961) 94ff.
Barhebraeus. *Le candélabre du sanctuaire, Onzième base,* chapters 3–4: *De la comparaison de la foi avec les oeuvres, Patrologia Orientalis* 41 (1983) 313–318.
Seraphim of Sarov, in Irina Goraïnoff, *Saint Séraphim de Sarov,* 216ff. Bellefontaine, 1973. [See A. F. Dobbie-Bateman, *St. Seraphim of Sarov. Concerning the Aim of the Christian Life*. London, 1936. See also, Index, s.v. Hope, in Constantine Cavarnos and Mary-Barbara Zeldin, *St. Seraphim of Sarov,* Modern Orthodox Saints, 5. Belmont, Massachusetts, 1980.]
Viller, Marcel. 'Confiance', DSp 2/2 (1953).
de Bovis, André. 'Foi', DSp 5 (1964) 529–603.
Duplacy, Jean. 'Foi', VTB, 476–486; 'Faith', DBT, 135–140.
Miquel, Pierre. 'Parrhesia', DSp 12/1 (1984) 260–267.
See *From Faith to Gnosis,* 173–175.

THE FEAR OF GOD, P. 295.

Evagrius. *Chapters on Prayer,* 28; Hausherr, *Leçons,* 44ff.; CS 4:59.
Dorotheus of Gaza. *Instructions,* 4; SCh 92 (1963) 220ff.; CS 33:109ff.
Symeon the New Theologian. *Hymn* 17; SCh 179:14ff; Maloney, *Hymns of Divine Love,* 60ff.

*The Art of Prayer,* 130–131, 163; *L'art de la prière,* 168ff, 177ff.
*A Systematic Handbook,* 143.
Boularand, Éphrem. 'Crainte', DSp 2/2 (1953) 2463–2511.
*La sophiologie de S. Basile,* 67ff.

OBEDIENCE, P. 296.

Diadochus of Photice. *Cent chapitres gnostiques,* 41ff; SCh 5*ter:*108ff; 'On Spiritual Knowledge and Discrimination: One Hundred Texts', *The Philokalia. The Complete Text,* 1:265ff.
Dorotheus of Gaza. *Instructions* 1.21ff; SCh 92:178ff; CS 33:77ff.
Hazzâyâ, Rabban Jausep. *Briefe,* 91ff.
*The Art of Prayer,* 437; *L'art de la prière,* 329ff (texts).
*A Systematic Handbook,* 284, 403 (bibliog.), 437 (texts).
Tillard, Jean-Marie. 'Obéissance', DSp 11 (1982) 535–563.

HUMILITY, P. 296.

Mark the Monk (the Ascetic). *À Nicolas,* Spiritualité orientale 41:142ff; 'Letter to Nicolas the Solitary', *The Philokalia. The Complete Text,* 1:147ff.
Dorotheus of Gaza. *Instructions,* 2; SCh 92:186ff; CS 33:94ff.
Isaac the Syrian. *20th Discourse; Oeuvres,* 137ff; Wensinck, *Mystic Treatises,* 109ff.
Symeon the New Theologian. *Hymn* 24; SCh 174:226ff; Maloney, *Hymns of Divine Love,* 126ff.
Gregory of Nareg. *Le livre de prières,* 72; SCh 78 (1961) 378.
*The Art of Prayer,* 237–238, 271–274; *L'art de la prière,* 155ff, 371ff.
*A Systematic Handbook,* 88, 255, 420 (texts).
Adnès, Pierre. 'Humilité', DSp 7/1 (1969) 1136–1187 (bibliog.).

MEEKNESS, PATIENCE, P. 297.

John Chrysostom. Texts on patience, DSp 12/1 (1984) 447.
Isaac the Syrian. *25th Discourse; Oeuvres,* 166ff; Wensinck, *Mystic Treatises,* 124ff.
Nicholas Cabasilas. *The Life in Christ,* 6; Chevetogne (1960) 180ff; deCatanzaro, 159ff.
Brianchaninov, Ignace. *Approches de la prière de Jesus,* 173ff; *On the Prayer of Jesus.* London, 1952.
Spanneut, Michel. 'Patience', DSp 12/1 (1984) 438–476 (bibliog.).

Bearing the cross, p. 298.

*Letter of Barnabas,* 11; SCh 172 (1971) 158ff; translated Francis X. Glimm, *The Apostolic Fathers,* FCh 1: 208ff.

Origen. *Commentary on the Gospel according to Matthew,* 11.5; SCh 162:290ff; ANF 9:434ff.

John Chrysostom. *Letters to Olympias; Lettres à Olympias,* SCh 13*bis* (1968); translated W. R. W. Stephens, LNPF 9:302ff.

*The Art of Prayer,* s.v. Suffering, 117, 231, 249; *L'art de la prière,* 158ff., 173ff.

Joy, p. 298.

Evagrius. *Chapters on Prayer,* 153; Hausherr, *Leçons,* 184; CS 4:80.

Nicholas Cabasilas. *The Life in Christ,* 7; Chevetogne,. 206ff; deCatanzaro, 195ff.

Auer, Alfons. 'Freude', LTHK 4 (1960) 361–363.

Hausherr, Irénée. *Prière de vie, vie de prière.* Paris, 1965.

Jacquemet, G. and G. Marsot. 'Joie', *Catholicisme* 6 (1967) 922–929.

Bussini, Francois. 'Joie', DSp 8 (1974) 1236–1256.

Gratitude, p. 298.

Aphrahat. *Demonstrations,* 4.17; *Patrologia syriaca* 1 (1984) 175; Brock, *The Syriac Fathers on Prayer,* CS 101:21ff.

Isaac the Syrian. *30th Discourse; Oeuvres,* 188ff;. Wensinck, *Mystic Treatises,* 141ff.

Poverty, p. 299.

Evagrius. *Chapters on Prayer,* 171; Hausherr, *Leçons,* 31ff; CS 4:58.

Pseudo-Macarius. *Homilies,* 6.4; SCh 275:112ff; Maloney, CWS, 77; Mason, *Fifty Spiritual Homilies,* 58ff.

Symeon the New Theologian, *Catéchèses* 9. 214ff; SCh 104:122ff; deCatanzaro, *The Discourses,* CWS,156ff.

Légasse, Simon Aimé. 'Pauvrete chrétienne: Écriture Sainte', DSp 12/1 (1984) 613–634.

Solignac, Aimé. 'Pauvreté: Pères de l'Église et moines des origines', DSp 12/1:634–647.

Alms, p. 299.

For texts by the Church Fathers, see DTHC 1/2 (1923) 2564.

Solovyov, Vladimir. *Les fondements spirituels de la vie* (prayer-fasting-alms). Tournai-Paris, 1948. English translation by Donald Attwater, *God, Man and the Church: The Spiritual Foundations of Life*. London, 1938.
*A Systematic Handbook,* 167, 193, 224, 390 (bibliog.), 426 (texts).

VIRGINITY, P. 299

Methodius of Olympus. *The Symposium;* Le *Banquet,* SCh 95 (1963); translated Herbert Musurillo, *St. Methodius. The Symposium: A Treatise on Chastity,* ACW 27. New York-London, 1958.
Gregory of Nyssa. *On Virginity,* 11.6 (virginity leads to the vision of God); *Traité de la virginité,* SCh 119 (1966); LNPF, 2nd ser., 5:355ff.
Cassian. *Institutes,* 6.6–18; SCh 109 (1965) 282; Ramsey, ACW 58:155-161; (not translated in NPNF series).
John Chrysostom. *La virginité,* SCh 125 (1966); translated Sally Rieger Shore and Elizabeth A. Clark, *John Chrysostom. On Virginity. Against Remarriage.* Lewiston, New York, 1083.
*Life of Syncletica,* 23; Bellefontaine, 20ff; Castelli, *Ascetic Behavior,* 276–277.
*A Systematic Handbook,* 220, 398 (bibliog.), 432 (texts).

CHARITY, P. 300.

Evagrius. *Chapters on Prayer,* 20ff; Hausherr, *Leçons,* 35ff; CS 4:58.
Diadochus of Photice. *Cent chapitres gnostiques* 12ff; SCh 5*ter* (1966) 90ff; 'On Spiritual Knowledge and Discrimination: One Hundred Texts', *The Philokalia. The Complete Text,* 1:255ff. London, 1979.
Maximus the Confessor. *Four Centuries on Charity; Centuries sur la charité,* SCh 9 (1943). Translated Polycarp Sherwood, *St. Maximus the Confessor. The Ascetic Life. The Four Centuries on Charity,* ACW 21. Westminster, Maryland-London, 1955.
Symeon the New Theologian. *Catéchèses,* 1, 8; SCh 96:222ff, SCh 104:36ff. Translation deCatanzaro, *Symeon the New Theologian. The Discourses,* CWS. New York, 1980.
*A Systematic Handbook,* 77, 167, 297, 334, 390 (bibliog.), 426 (texts).
Kirchmeyer, Jean. 'Grecque (Église): la charité', DSp 6 (1967) 857–871 (bibliog.).

THE PLACE OF PRAYER, PP. 301FF.

Aphrahat. *Demonstrations,* 4.1; *Patrologia syriaca,* 1 (1984) 158ff; Brock, *The Syriac Fathers on Prayer,* CS 101:5–6.

Origen. *On Prayer,* 31; PG 11:552ff; Greer, *Origen. An Exhortation to Martyrdom, Prayer . . .* , CWS, 164ff.
Evagrius. *Chapters on Prayer,* 67 (the place of God); Hausherr, *Leçons,* 96ff; CS 4:66.
Cassian. *Conferences,* 9.35 (in a room); SCh 54:71ff; Ramsey, ACW 57:353; Luibheid, CWS, 123ff.
John Chrysostom. *Expositio in Psalmum* 4.2; PG 55:42. *In Psalmum 123;* PG 55:387.

THE TEMPLE, P. 302.

*Letter of Aristeas to Philocratus,* 6.84ff (description du temple de Jerusalem); *Lettre d'Aristée à Philocrate,* SCh 89 (1962) 142ff; 'The Letter of Aristeas', § 83–91, in R. H. Charles, ed., *The Apocrypha and Pseudepigrapha of the Old Testament in English,* 103ff. Oxford, 1913.
*Letter of Barnabas,* 16; SCh 172:188ff; *The Apostolic Fathers,* FCh 1:216ff.
Irenaeus. *Adversus haereses,* 4.9.2; SCh 100 (1965) 480ff; ANF 1: 472ff.
Origen. *Homilies on Leviticus,* 5.3 ('a holy place'); SCh 286 (1981) 218; FC 83:93ff.
Sozomen. *Ecclesiastical History,* 2.3 (the temples built by Constantine the Great); *Histoire ecclésiastique,* SCh 306 (1983) 236; LNPF, 2nd ser., 2.
Egeria. *Diary,* 48ff (Feast of the Dedications); *Journal de voyage,* SCh 296 (1982) 316ff; *Egeria: Diary of a Pilgrimage,* ACW 38:126ff. New York, 1970.
Photius. *Homilia* III-*In dedicatione novae basilicae,* PG 102:563–573.
Symeon of Thessalonika. *De sacro templo,* PG 155:305–361.
———. *Expositio de divino templo et . . . de divina missa, ibid.,* 697–749.
Nicholas Cabasilas. *The Life in Christ,* 5; *La vie en Jésus-Christ,* Chevetogne, 139ff; deCatanzaro, 149ff.
de Puniet, P. 'Dédicace des Églises', DACL 4 (1920) 374–405.
Leclercq, Henri. 'Église', DACL 4:2220–2238; 'Églises', 2279–2299; 'Dominicum', 1385–1386; 'Domus (Dei, Ecclesiae, orationis . . .) 1442–1443.
Rust, H. *Heilige Stätten.* Leipzig, 1933.
Daniélou, Jean. *Le signe du Temple.* Paris, 1942. Translated Walter Roberts, *The Presence of God.* Baltimore, Maryland, 1959.
Schmidt, M. *Prophet und Tempel.* Basel, 1948.
Ratzinger, Joseph. *Volk und Haus Gottes in Augustinuslehre von der Kirche.* Munich, 1954.
Michel, Otto. 'Οἶκος', Kittel 5 (1967) 119ff.

Gaillard, Jean. *'Domus Dei'*, DSp 3 (1957) 1551–1567.

Congar, Yves Marie Joseph. *Le mystère du temple,* Lectio divina, 22. Paris, 1958. Translated Reginald F. Trevett, *The Mystery of the Temple.* London, 1962.

Evdokimov, Paul. *L'orthodoxie,* 210ff. Neuchâtel, 1959.

Brunet, Robert. 'Figures et images de l'Église: Temple', DSp 4/1 (1960) 386–389.

Ouspensky, Léonide. *Essai sur la théologie de l'icône dans l'Église orthodoxe.* Translated Elizabeth Meyendorff, *Theology of the Icon.* Crestwood, New York, 1978. Revised translation by Anthony Gythiel, *Theology of the Icon,* volume I. Crestwood, New York, 1992.

———. *La théologie de l'icône.* Paris, 1980. Translated Anthony Gythiel, *Theology of the Icon,* volume II. Crestwood, New York, 1992.

Lohmeyer, Ernst. *Lord of the Temple. A Study of the Relation Between Cult and Gospel.* London, 1961.

Ouspensky, Léonide. 'The Symbolism of the Church', in A. J. Philippou, *The Orthodox Ethos,* I:153–168. Oxford, 1964.

Cavarnos, Constantine. 'Iconographic Decoration in the Orthodox Church', in Philippou, 169–185.

Bandmann, G. 'Kirche, Kirchenbau', *Lexikon der christlichen Ikonographie* 2 (1970) 415–529.

Evdokimov, Paul. *L'art de l'icône. La théologie de la beauté,* 119–140. Desclée de Brouwer, 1972. Translated Steven Bigham, *The Art of the Icon: A Theology of Beauty.* Redondo Beach, California, 1990.

Pigna, A. 'Tempio', DESp II (1975) 1841–1844.

Saxer, V[ictor]. 'Dedicazione delle chiese', DP 1:902–904; 'Dedication of Churches', EEC 1:224.

Duval, Noël. Edificio di culto', DP 1:1067–1095; 'Church Buildings', EEC 1:168–175.

Heiler, Friedrich. *Die Religionen der Menschheit. Le religione dell'umanità,* 135–137. Milan, 1985.

ICONS, PP. 307FF.

For patristic texts on the veneration of images, see Ch. Schoenborn, *L'icône du Christ, Fondements théologiques élaborés entre le Ier et IIe Concile de Nicée,* 325–787, Paradosis, 24. Freiburg, 1976.

Theodore the Studite. *On the Holy Icons,* translated C. P. Roth. Crestwood, New York, 1981.

Symeon of Thessalonika. *Treatise on Prayer,* 61. Brookline, Massachusetts (1984) 91ff.

*A Systematic Handbook,* 313, 408 (bibliog.), 440 (texts).

Léonard, P. M. 'Art et spiritualité', DSp 1 (1936) 899–934.

Myslivec, J. *Ikona.* Prague, 1947.

Ouspensky, Léonide. *L'icône, vision du monde spirituel. Quelques notes sur son sens dogmatique.* Paris, 1948.

——— and Vladimir Lossky. *Der Sinn der Ikonen.* Bern–Olten, 1952. Translated G. E. H. Palmer and E. Kadloubovsky, *The Meaning of Icons.* Crestwood, New York, 1982.

Evdokimov, Paul. *L'orthodoxie,* 216–238. Neuchâtel, 1959.

Beck, Hans Georg. *Kirche und theologische Literatur im byzantinischen Reich,* 296–306 (Der Bilderstreit [Iconoclasm]). Munich, 1959.

Aurenhammer, Hans. *Lexikon der christlichen Ikonographie.* Vienna, 1959ff.

Šumilin, I. N. *Zur Psychologie der Ikonenverehrung.* Munich, 1960.

Dwirnyk, J. *Rôle de l'Iconostase dans le culte divin.* Montreal, 1960.

Ouspensky, Léonide. *Essai sur la théologie de l'icone dans l'Église orthodoxe.* Translated Elizabeth Meyendorff, *Theology of the Icon.* Crestwood, New York, 1978. Revised translation by Anthony Gythiel, *Theology of the Icon,* I. Crestwood, New York, 1992.

———. *La théologie de l'icône.* Paris, 1980. Translation Anthony Gythiel, *Theology of the Icon,* 2. Crestwood, New York, 1992.

Nyssen, W. *Das Zeugnis des Bildes im frühen Byzanz.* Freiburg im Breisgau, 1982.

———. 'Zur Theologie des Bildes', *Handbuch der Ostkirchenkunde,* 473–482; bibliog.: 803–806. Düsseldorf, 1971.

Kalokyris, Konstantinos D. *He ousia tes Orthodoxou eikonographias.* Translated Peter Chamberas, *The Essence of Orthodox Iconography.* Brookline, Massachusetts, 1971.

Trubetskoi, Eugene N. *Icons: Theology in Color.* Crestwood, New York, 1973.

Alpatov, M. *Drevnerusskaja ikonopis.* Moscow, 1974. Italian translation, *Le iconi russe. . .* Turin, 1976.

Sollazzo, F. *La teologia dell'icone dal I all'VIII secolo.* Bari, 1975.

Beck, Hans Georg. *Proplematice delle icone.* Centro Tedesco di Studi Veneziani, Quaderni 3. Venice, 1977.

*Iconoclasm,* Papers given at the Ninth Spring Symposium of Byzantine Studies, University of Birmingham, March 1975, edited by A. Bryer and J. Herrin. Birmingham, 1977.

Thon, N. *Ikone und Liturgie,* Sophia, 19. Trier, 1979.

Donadeo, M. *Le icone, immagini dell'Invisibile.* Brescia, 1980.

Melchiore, V. *Icona dell'invisibile. Studi per una interpretazione simbolica di Gesù Cristo.* Milan, 1981.

Sendler, Egon. *L'icône, image de l'invisible. Éléments de théologie, esthétique et technique*. Paris, 1981.
Galignani, P. *Il mistero e l'immagine, l'icona nella tradizioni bizantina*. Milan, 1981.
Galavaris, George. *The Icon in the Life of the Church, Liturgy, Devotion*. Leiden, 1981.
Onasch, Konrad. *Kunst und Liturgie der Ostkirche in Stichworten, unter Berücksichtigung der Alten Kirche*. Vienna, 1981.
Labrecque-Pervouchine, N. *L'iconostase—une évolution historique en Russie*. Montreal, 1982.
Meier, J. *Mit anderen Augen, vor Ikonen beten*. Würzburg, 1983.
Crouzel, H[enri]. 'Immagine', DP 2:1758–1766; 'Images', EEC 1:405–407.
Fiocchi Nicolai, V[incenzo]. 'Pittura', DP 2:2806–2818; 'Painting', EEC 1:629–632.

PILGRIMAGE, P. 311.

*Life of Melania the Younger*, 34ff; *Vie de sainte Mélanie* 34ff; SC 90 (1962) 190ff; Petersen, CS 143:325ff.
Egeria. *Diary;* SCh 296 (1982); *Egeria: Diary of a Pilgrimage*. ACW 38. New York, 1970.
Ephrem. *Die Homilie über das Pilgerleben,* edited by A. Haffner, Sitzungsberichte der Kaiserlichen Akademie der Wissenschaften in Wien, 135 (IX). [See also, *On Our Lord,* LNPF, 2nd ser., 13:305–330.]
*Récits de pèlerins,* see DSp 12/1 (1984) 908.
*The Art of Prayer,* 256ff. ('Retreat within yourself); *L'art de la prière,* 96ff.
Folliet, J. *La spiritualité de la route*. Paris, 1936.
Leclercq, Henri. 'Pèlerinages aux lieux saints', DACL 14/1 (1939) 65–176.
Köttig, B. *Peregrinatio religiosa. Wallfahrten in der Antike und das Pilgerleben in der alten Kirche*. Regensburg-Münster, 1960. 2nd ed., 1980.
Dax, W. 'Bittprocession', *Reallexikon für Antike und Christentum* 2 (1954) 422–429.
Zander, L. 'Le pèlerinage', *L'Église et les Églises (Travaux offerts à L. Beauduin),* 2:469–486. Chevetogne, 1955.
Louvel, François. 'Les processions dans la Bible', *La Maison-Dieu* 43 (1955) 5–28.

Hofinger, Jean. 'The Pilgrimage, Symbol of the Christian Life', *Lumen Vitae* 13 (1958) 256–269.

Venece, M. *Storia e spiritualità dei pelegrinaggi cristiani nell'alto Medioevo*. Dissertation, Gregorian University, Rome, 1970.

Harms, W. *'Homo viator in bivio'. Studien zur Bildlichkeit des Weges*. Munich, 1970.

Catret, J.V. 'Para una espiritualidad del camino: "la busqueda de una persona", nota común en la peregrinación de los monjes cristianos y budistas en la Edad Media', *Manresa* (1972) 349–360.

George, A[ugustin]. 'Pèlerinage', VTB, 947–949; 'Pilgrimage', DBT, 430–432.

Sumption, Jonathan. *Pilgrimage. An Image of Medieval Religion*. London, 1975.

Seemann, K. D. *Die altrussische Wallfahrtsliteratur. Theorie und Geschichte eines literarischen Genres*. Munich, 1976.

Dupont, A. 'Pèlerinages et lieux sacrés', *Encyclopedia Universalis* 12 (1976) 729–734.

Bourdeau, François. *La Route du pardon. Pèlerinage et réconciliation*. Paris, 1982.

Chellini, J. and H. Branthomme. *Les chemins de Dieu. Histoire des pèlerinages chrétiens des origines à nos jours*. Paris, 1982.

Évenou, Jean. 'Procession, pèlerinages, religion populaire', in Aimé-George Martimort, *L'Église en prière,* 3:259–281. Desclée, 1984. Translated Matthew J. O'Connell, 'Processions, Pilgrimages, Popular Religion', in Martimort, *The Church at Prayer,* 3:241–262. Collegeville, Minnesota, 1988.

Solignac, Aimé, *et al.* 'Pèlerinages', DSp 12/1 (1984) 888–940.

Vogt, H[ermann] J. 'Pelegrinaggi (Peregrinatio)', DP 2:2638–2641; 'Pilgrim-Pilgrimage (Peregrinatio)', EEC 2:688.

Saxer, V[ictor]. 'Itinerari', DP 2:1881–1884; 'Itineraries', EEC 1:426–427.

HESYCHASM, PP. 319FF.

*A Systematic Handbook,* 25, 161, 211, 311, 395–6 (bibliog.).

Špidlík, Tomaš. 'Il metodo esicastico', in Ermanno Ancilli, *Alla ricerca di Dio, Le technice della preghiera,* 197–215. Rome, 1978.

Paparozzi, M. *La spiritualità dell'Oriente cristiano*. Rome, 1981.

Stiernon, Daniel. 'Nicéphore l'hésychaste', DSp 11 (1982) 198–203.

Meyendorff, Jean. 'Palamas (Grégoire)', DSp 12/1 (1984) 81–107.

THE PHILOKALIA, P. 320.

*A Systematic Handbook,* 13.

A monk of the Romanian Orthodox Church [A. Scrima]. 'L'avènement philocalique dans l'Orthodoxie roumaine', *Istina* (1958) 295–328, 443–474.

Le Guillou, Marie Joseph. 'Aux sources des mouvements spirituels de l'Église orthodoxe de Grèce: la renaissance hésychaste', *Istina* 7 (1960) 114–120.

Un moine de l'Église d'Orient. *La prière de Jesus. Sa genèse et son développement dans la tradition spirituelle byzantino-slave,* 62ff. 3rd ed., Chevetogne, 1963. A monk of the Eastern Church [Lev Gillet, archimandrite]. *The Jesus Prayer,* revised edition with a foreword by Kallistos Ware, Bishop of Diokleia. Crestwood, New York, 1987.

Pascal, P. *'Sulla 'filocalia' e le sue fortune nella Russia del XIX secolo', Anonimo russo: La vita di un pellegrino.* Milan, 1972. Rpt *Russia cristiana,* 125 (1972) 19–32.

Ware, Kallistos. 'Philocalie', DSp 12/1 (1984) 1336–1352 (Greek editions, editions in other languages, content, notes on the authors).

See also, DSp 2:1799–1801; DSp 8:1140–1141; DSp 10:10; DSp 11:235.

Among translations are:

*Philocalie des Pères neptiques,* Abbaye de Bellefontaine, 1979ff.

*Writings from the Philokalia on Prayer of the Heart.* Translated from the Russian text, *Dobrotolubiye,* by E. Kadloubovsky and G. E. H. Palmer. London, 1969.

*The Philokalia, The Complete Text,* 4 volumes, translated and edited by G. E. H. Palmer, Philip Sherrard, and Kallistos Ware. London, 1979ff.

HESYCHIA, P. 321.

Cassian. *Conferences,* 1.7; SCh 42:84ff; Ramsey, ACW 57:45–46; Luibheid, CWS, 41ff.

Didymus the Blind. *Sur Zacharie,* 1.43; SCh 83 (1962) 213ff.

Isaac the Syrian. *12th Discourse* and *79th Discourse; Oeuvres,* 107ff, 388ff; Wensinck, *Mystic Treatises,* 82ff., 361ff.

Seraphim of Sarov, in Irina Goraïnoff, *Saint Séraphim de Sarov,* 232ff. Bellefontaine, 1973. [See Index, s.v. Solitude, in Constantine Cavarnos and Mary-Barbara Zeldin, *St. Seraphim of Sarov,* Modern Orthodox Saints, 5. Belmont, Massachusetts, 1980. See also, Chapter V: 'The

Distant Hermitage', in Lazarus Moore, *St. Seraphim of Sarov: A Spiritual Autobiography,* 83ff. Blanco, Texas: New Sarov Press, 1994.]

See Index of *The Philokalia. The Complete Text,* vol. I, s.v. Hesychasm, Stillness *(hesychia).*

Förster, Werner. 'εἰρήνη', Kittel 2 (1964) 400–420.

Hausherr, Irénée. 'L'hésychasme . . . , OCP 22 (1956) 5–40, 427–485; OCA 176 (1966) 163–237.

Adnès, Pierre. 'Hésychasme', DSp 7/1 (1969) 382ff.

Leclercq, Jean. *'Otia monastica. Étude sur le vocabulaire de la contemplation au moyen âge',* Studia Anselmiana, 51. Rome, 1963.

Coste, René. 'Paix', DSp 12/1 (1984) 40–56.

Sieben, Hermann Josef. 'La paix intérieure', DSp 12/1:56–73.

SOLITUDE, P. 322.

Cassian. *Institutes,* 6.3–4; SCh 109:264ff; Ramsey, ACW 58:154–155.

Isaac the Syrian. *3rd Discourse: Oeuvres,* 69ff; Wensinck, *Mystic Treatises,* 14ff.

Symeon the New Theologian. *Éthiques* 15, 94ff; SCh 129:450ff; Golitzin, Fifteenth Discourse, *St Symeon the New Theologian . . . The Ethical Discourses,* 2:173ff.

Verkhofskoi, Zosima, in Sergei Bolshakoff, *I mistici russi,* 247ff. Turin, 1962. Sergius Bolshakoff. *Russian Mystics,* CS 26:168ff. Kalamazoo, 1977.

*The Art of Prayer,* 250–256; *L'art de la prière,* 342ff.

*A Systematic Handbook,* 21, 161, 429 (texts); flight from the world, 206ff, 395 (bibliog.), 429 (texts).

Bremond, Jean. *Les Pères du désert,* 106–154. Paris, 1927.

Lialine, Clement. 'Erémitisme en Orient', DSp 4/1 (1960) 936–953.

SILENCE, P. 323.

Origen. *Homilies on Luke,* 5.1; SCh 87 (1962) 136ff.

Cassian. *Institutes,* 2.12; SCh 109:85ff; Ramsey, ACW 58:67–68; LNPF, 2nd ser., 11:210.

———. *Conferences,* 9.36 (silent prayer); SCh 54:72; Ramsey, ACW 57:353–354; Luibheid, CWS, 124.

Isaac the Syrian. *3rd Discourse,* 34th Discourse; *Oeuvres,* 71ff, 213ff; Wensinck, *Mystic Treatises,* 14ff, 149ff.

Symeon the New Theologian. *Discourse 12,* 168ff; *Catéchèses,* SCh 104:182ff; deCatanzaro, CWS, 173ff.

*The Art of Prayer,* 153, 163, 185, 186, 250–256; *L'art de la prière,* 78ff, 160.
*A Systematic Handbook,* 215, 397 (bibliog.), 431 (texts).
Hephner, C. *The Fellowship of Silence Being Experienced in the Common Use of Prayer Without Words.* London, 1915. 12th ed., 1925.
———. *The Fruit of Silence Being Further Studied in the Common Use of Prayer Without Words.* London, 1924.
Casel, O. *De philosophorum graecorum silentio mystico.* Giessen, 1919.
Heiler, Friedrich. *Das Gebet,* 289ff. Munich, 1921 (4th ed.). English translation by Samuel McComb, *Prayer. A Study in the History and Psychology of Religion,* 277ff. London, 1932.
Mensching, Gustav. *Das heilige Schweigen, eine religionsgeschichtliche Untersuchung.* Giessen, 1926.
Gebhard-L'Estrange, A. H. *Tradition of Silence in Myth and Legend.* London, 1940.
Bouyer, Louis. *Le sens de la vie monastique,* 215–220. Paris, 1950. Translated Kathleen Pond, *The Meaning of the Monastic Life.* New York, 1956.
van Rijnberg, G. *Le langage par signes chez les moines.* Amsterdam, 1953.
Hausherr, Irénée. 'L'hésychasme, Étude de spiritualité', OCP 11 (1956) 247–262; OCA 176 (1966) 199–214.
Mensching, Gustav and E. Hertzsch. 'Schweigen', *Die Religion in Geschichte und Gegenwart* 5 (1961) 1605–1606.
Kemmer, Alfons. 'Schweigen', LThK 9 (1964) 540–541.
Heiler, Friedrich. *Die Religionen der Menschheit. Le religioni dell'umanità,* 340–345. Milan, 1985.
Dupuy, Michel. 'Présence de Dieu', DSp 12/2 (1986) 2107–2136.

*AMERIMNIA*, INNER SILENCE, P. 323.

Evagrius. *Chapters on Prayer,* 9ff; Hausherr, *Leçons,* 22ff; CS 4:97.
Isaac the Syrian. *13th Discourse; Oeuvres,* 111ff; Wensinck, *Mystic Treatises,* 84ff.
Branchaninov, Ignace. *Approches de la prière de Jésus,* 101ff; *On the Prayer of Jesus.* London, 1952.
Hausherr, Irénée. 'L'hésychasme, Étude de spiritualité', OCP 22 (1956) 262–273; OCA 176 (1966) 214–225.
Adnès, Pierre. 'Hésychasme: Hésychia et amerimnia', DSp 7/1 (1969) 389–391.

*NEPSIS, ANTIRRHESIS,* P. 324.

*Life of Syncletica,* 46ff; *Vie de sainte Synclétique,* Bellefontaine, 41ff; Castelli, *Ascetic Behavior,* 286.

Dorotheus of Gaza. *Instruction 10;* SCh 92:336ff; CS 33:163ff.

Hesychius of Batos, in J. Gouillard, *Petite Philocalie,* 124ff. Paris, 153; 'On Watchfulness and Holiness', *The Philokalia. The Complete Text,* I:163–198.

Cabasilas, N. *The Life in Christ,* 7; Chevetogne, 198ff; deCatanzaro, 195ff.

*The Art of Prayer,* 124ff; *L'art de la prière,* 175ff.

*A Systematic Handbook,* 243, 400–1 (bibliog.), 433 (texts).

Hausherr, Irénée. 'L'hésychasme, Étude de spiritualité', OCP 22 (1956) 273–278; OCS 176 (1966) 225–230.

Adnès, Pierre. 'Garde du Coeur', DSp (1967) 100–107.

———. 'Hésychasme: Hésychia et nepsis', DSp 7/1 (1969) 391–392.

———. 'Nepsis', DSp 11 (1982) 110–118.

ATTENTIVENESS, P. 326.

John Chrysostom. *On Virginity,* 32.1ff; SCh 125 (1966) 194ff.

Pseudo-Macarius. *De custodia cordis;* PG 34:821–841.

Abba Isaiah. *Asceticon, Logos* 24, CSCO 294 (*Syri* 122) 417–424.

Symeon the New Theologian. *Discourse Four,* 155ff; SCh 96:326ff; de-Catanzaro, *Symeon the New Theologian: The Discourses.* New York, 1980.

Brianchaninov, Ignace. *Approches de la prière de Jésus,* 156–164; excerpts translated Lazarus [Moore], *On the Prayer of Jesus.* London, 1952.

*The Art of Prayer,* 124ff; *L'art de la prière,* 168ff.

See Watchfulness-Attentiveness *(prosoche)* in the Index of *The Philokalia. The Complete Text,* vol. I. London, 1979.

*A Systematic Handbook,* 107, 222, 379 (bibliog.), 422 (texts).

Fonck, A[nton]. 'Prière', DThC 13 (1936) 213ff.

Vernay, Robert. 'Attention', DSp 1 (1936) 1058–1077.

Hausherr, Irénée. L'Hésychasme, Étude de spiritualité', OCP 22 (1956) 269–285; OCA 176 (1966) 231–237.

THE TABORIC LIGHT, P. 329.

Zielinski, Bronislaus. 'De Doxa Christi transfigurati', *Verbum Domini* 26 (1948) 291–303.

Dupont, Jacques. 'Le chrétien, miroir de la gloire divine d'après 2 Cor 3, 18', *Revue biblique* 56 (1949) 392–411.

Deseille, Placide. 'Gloire de Dieu', DSp 5 (1967) 421–463 (bibliog.).

Meyendorff, Jean. 'Palamas (Grégoire)', DSp 12/1 (1984) 95ff.

THE JESUS PRAYER, PP. 331FF.

Symeon of Thessalonika. *Treatise on Prayer* 4. Brookline, Mass., 1984, 14ff.

Kallistos II [Xanthopoulos]. *Das Herzesgebet, Mystik und Yoga der Ostkirche, Die Centurie der Mönche Kallistus und Ignatius.* Munich, 1955; Kadloubovsky and Palmer, 'The Monks Callistus and Ignatius of Xanthopoulos, "Directions to Hesychasts, in a Hundred Chapters"', *Writings from the Philokalia on Prayer of the Heart,* 164–270.

'Bishop Theophane the Recluse', in Sergius Bolshakoff, *Russian Mystics,* CS 26:196ff. Kalamazoo, 1977; 'Théophane le Reclus', in Serge Bolshakoff, *I mistici russi,* 213ff. Turin, 1962.

Brianchaninov, Ignace. *Approches de la Prière de Jésus.* Selections translated by Lazarus [Moore], *On the Prayer of Jesus,*. London, 1952.

*The Art of Prayer,* 75ff; *L'art de la prière,* 98ff.

*A Systematic Handbook,* 316, 410 (bibliog.).

Orlov, A. S. 'The Jesus Prayer in Russia in the Sixteenth Century' [in Russian], *Pamjatniki drevnej pĭsmennosti i iskusstva,* 185. 1914.

Jugie, Martin. 'Les origines de la méthode d'oraison hésychaste', *Echos d'Orient* (Paris, April-June 1931)179–239.

Gorodetzky, Nadejda. 'The Prayer of Jesus', *Blackfriars,* 23, nos. 262 to 273 (February 1942) 74–78.

Behr-Sigel, Elisabeth. 'La Prière à Jésus ou le Mystère de la spiritualité monastique orthodoxe', *Dieu vivant* 8 (1947) 68–94.

Gardet, Louis. 'Un problème de mystique comparée . . . ', *Revue Thomiste,* 52 (1952) 642–679; 53 (1953) 197–216.

de B., H. 'La prière du Coeur', *Messager de l'Exarchat Russe en Europe Occidentale* 4 (13–40). Paris, 1953.

Recheis, A. 'Das Jesusgebet', *Una Sancta* 9 (1954) 1–25.

Saint-Servais, Ch. 'Sur la Prière de Jésus', *Contacts* 15 (1963) 249–253.

Deseille, Placide. 'La prière de Jésus dans la spiritualité hésychaste', *Assemblée du Seigneur* 12 (Bruges, 1964) 60–71.

Leclercq, Jean, François Vandenbroucke, and Louis Bouyer, *A History of Christian Spirituality,* vol. 2: *The Spirituality of the Middle Ages,* 576ff.London, 1968. Translated by the Benedictines of Holme Eden Abbey, Carlisle, from *Histoire de la spiritualité chrétienne,* 2 (Paris, 1961) 680–695; vol. 3 (1965) 63–64, 76–77.

*Théophane le Reclus,* 285–291.

Serr, Jacques. *La Prière du coeur,* Spiritualité orientale, 6. Bellefontaine, 1970. [See also, Serr, Jacques and Olivier Clément, *La Prière du coeur.* Bellefontaine, 1977 (bibliog.).]

Sjögren, Per-Olof. *Jesusbonen*. Translated by Sydney Linton, *The Jesus Prayer*. London-Philadelphia, 1975; London, 1986, 1996 (bibliog.).
Staniloaë, Dumitru. *Prière de Jésus et expérience du Saint-Esprit*. Desclée de Brouwer, 1981.
Maloney, George. *The Prayer of the Heart*. Notre Dame, Ind., 1981.
Goetmann, Alphonse and Rachel. *Prière de Jesus: Prière de Coeur*. Paris, 1995. Translated by Theodore J. and Rebecca Nottingham, *Prayer of Jesus: Prayer of the Heart*. Greenwood, Indiana, 1996.
Guillaumont, André. 'The Jesus Prayer Among the Monks of Egypt', *Eastern Churches Review* 6 (1974) 66–71.

THE POWER OF THE NAME OF JESUS, P. 332.

Origen. *Homilies on Joshua,* 1.1; SCh 71 (1960) 95ff.
———. *Homilies on the Song of Songs,* 1.4; SCh 37*bis:*80ff; translated R. P. Lawson, *Origen. The Song of Songs: Commentary and Homilies,* ACW 26:272ff.
Diadochus of Photice. *Cent chapitres gnostiques* 59ff; SCh 5*ter:*119ff; 'On Spiritual Knowledge and Discrimination: One Hundred Texts', *The Philokalia. The Complete Text,* I:253ff.
*The Art of Prayer,* 88ff., 275; *L'art de la prière,* 117ff, 338ff.
*Collection of Documents Concerning the Disturbances of the 'Adorers of the Name' on Athos* (in Russian). Petrograd, 1916.
A Monk of the Eastern Church. *On the Invocation of the Name of Jesus.* London: Fellowship of St Alban and St Sergius.1950.
———. 'L'invocation du nom de Jésus dans la tradition byzantine', *La vie spirituelle* (1952) 38–45. [See also, by the same author, Archimandrite Lev Gillet, *The Jesus Prayer,* revised edition with a foreword by Kallistos Ware, Bishop of Diokleia. Crestwood, New York, 1987.]
Bulgakov, Sergei N. *Filosofia imeni*. Paris, 1953.
Evdokimov, Paul. *L'Orthodoxie*, 114ff. Neuchâtel–Paris, 1959.
Vanucci, G. *Invocazioni del Nome di Gesù*. Florence, 1961.
Ware, Kallistos. *The Power of the Name. The Jesus Prayer in Orthodox Spirituality*. Oxford, 1981.
Lanne, Emmanuel. 'Le nom de Jésus-Christ et son invocation chez saint Irénée de Lyon', *Irénikon* 48 (1975) 447–467, 49 (1976) 34–53.
de Leon, L. *De los nombres de Cristo en tres libros por el maestro Fray Luys de León*. Salamanca, 1595. Translated Edward J. Schuster, *The Names of Christ by Louis of León*. St Louis, Missouri, 1955.
Cothenet, Édouard and Aimé Solignac. 'Nom', DSp 11 (1982) 397–410.
Vanyó, L[azló]. 'Nome', DP 2:2413–5; 'Name, *onoma*', EEC 2:579–580.

Scholem, Gershom. *Le Nom et les symboles de Dieu dans la mystique juive*. Paris, 1983.

THE PSYCHO-SOMATIC METHOD, P. 339.

Evagrius. *Chapters on Prayer,* 69, 73; Hausherr, *Leçons,* 99ff; 106ff; CS 4:66, 67.

Hazzâyâ, Rabban Jausep. *Briefe,* 114ff (life in the cell—a symbol of the promised land).

Gregory the Sinaite, in J. Gouillard, *Petite Philocalie,* 249 (on breathing). Paris, 1953.

Gregory Palamas. *Défense des saints hésychastes,* I, 3, 3 (two lights), II, 2, 7 (physical sensations), III, 1, 20 (warmth); Louvain, 110ff, 330ff, 594ff; *The Triads,* CWS, pp. 31, 49f, 78f. See also, Appendix I, 'On the Blessed Hesychasts', in Kadloubovsky and Palmer, *Early Fathers from the Philokalia,* 401ff.

Callistus and Ignatius of Xanthopoulos, in *Petite Philocalie,* 288ff. 'Directions to Hesychasts, in a Hundred Chapters', in Kadloubovsky and Palmer, *Writing from the Philokalia on Prayer of the Heart,* 193ff.

For late witnesses, see *Petite Philocalie,* Part Three, 401ff.

Brianchaninov, Ignace. *Approches de la prière de Jésus,* 185–195 (material aids), 146ff. 'Material Aids', *On the Prayer of Jesus,* translated by Lazarus [Moore], 86ff.

*The Art of Prayer,* 51ff (cell), 93–95 (warmth), 97ff (the importance of technique), 104–105 (breathing techniques), 159ff (two types of warmth), 22, 190ff. (finding the place of the heart), 99ff, 197–198 (the place of mechanical methods). *L'art de la prière,* 51ff (cellule), 123–127 (la chaleur), 131ff (l'importance d'une technique), 138–141 (les techniques respiratoires), 217ff (deux sortes de chaleur), 261 (trouver la place du coeur); 270ff (le rôle des méthodes méchaniques).

Paparozzi, M. *La spiritualità dell'Oriente cristiano*. Rome, 1981.

*A Systematic Handbook,* 318.

Hausherr, Irénée. 'Note sur l'inventeur de la méthode hésychaste', OCP 20 (1930)179–182; OCA 176 (1966) 4–7.

Bloom, Anthony. 'L'Hésychasme . . . yoga chrétien?, *Cahiers du Sud,* 1933 (a special edition devoted to yoga).

[See also, 'Christian Yoga?', in John Meyendorff, *A Study of Gregory Palamas,* translated by George Lawrence, 139ff. London, 1964].

Leroy, O. 'La splendeur corporelle des saints', *La vie spirituelle* (November–December 1935), 65–85, 139–160, *Ibid.,* (January 1936) 29–43. Offprint, Paris, 1936.

Hausherr, Irénée. 'À propos de spiritualité hésychaste: controverse sans contradicteur', OCP 3 (1937) 260–272; OCA 176 (1966) 50–62.

Bloom, Anthony. 'Contemplation et ascèse, Contribution orthodoxe', *Technique et Contemplation, Études carmélitaines* 28 (1949) 49–67.

______. *Asceticism (Somatopsychic Techniques),* Guild Lecture 95. London: The Guild of Pastoral Psychology, 1957.

Wunderle, Georg. 'La technique psychologique de l'hésychasme byzantin', *La nuit mystique, Études carmélitaines* 23/2 (1938) 61–67.

———. *Zur psychologie des hesychastischen Gebetes.* Das östliche Christentum, Neue Folge, 2. Würzburg, 1949.

Hausherr, Irénée. 'Les Exercices Spirituels de Saint Ignace et la méthode d'oraison hésichastique', OCP 20 (1954) 7–26; OCA 176 (1966) 134–153.

———. 'Variations récentes dans les jugements sur la Méthode d'oraison des Hésychastes', OCP 19 (1953) 424–428; OCA 176 (1966) 129–133.

Nölle, W. 'Hesychasmus und Yoga', *Byzantinische Zeitschrift* 47 (1954) 95–103.

Déchanet, Jean Marie. *Yogin du Christ, 'la voie du Silence'.* Bruges, 1956; *Christian Yoga.* London-New York, 1960; *Yoga and God: An Invitation to Christian Yoga.* Saint Meinrad, Indiana 1974.

_____. *Journal d'un Yogi,* 1967. Translated by Sarah Fawcett, *Yoga and God. An Invitation to Christian Yoga.* Saint Meinrad, Indiana, 1974.

Courel, F. 'Y a-t-il des techniques de prière?', *Christus* 19 (1958) 188–194.

Thurston, Herbert. *The Physical Phenomena of Mysticism.* Chicago, 1952.

Leclercq, Jean. 'Sedere', A propos de l'hésychasme en Occident', *Le millénaire du Mont Athos,* 1:253–264. Chevetogne, 1963.

Zigmud-Cerbu, A. 'Lumières nouvelles sur le yoga et l'hésychasme', *Acta Phil. Theol.* 2:505–527. Rome, 1964; *Contacts* 26 (1974) 272–289.

*Théophane le Reclus,* 285ff.

Adnès, Pierre. 'Jésus (prière à)', Dsp 8 (1974) 1126–1150.

Blasucci, Antonio. 'Lumineux (phénomènes)' DSp 9 (1976) 1184–1188.

Špidlík, Tomaš. 'Il metodo esicastico', *Rivista di vita spirituale* 32 (1978) 506–524; rpt in *Alla ricerca di Dio,* edited by Ermanno Ancilli, 197–215. Rome, 1978.

Dupuy, Michel. 'Méthodes et vie spirituelle', DSp 10 (1980) 1117–1125.

Sudbrack, Josef. 'Méditation aujourd'hui', DSp 10 (1980) 927–934.

Paparozzi, M. *La spiritualità dell'Oriente cristiano,* La spiritualità cristiana, 11. Rome, 1981.

Stiernon, Daniel. 'Nicéphore l'hésychaste', DSp 11 (1982) 198–203.

THE RUSSIAN PILGRIM, P. 343.

*A Systematic Handbook,* 318, 410 (bibliog.).
Hausherr, Irénée. 'Un pèlerin russe de la prière intérieure', *Orientalia Christiana* 6 (1926) 174–176; OCA 176 (1966) 1–3.
Adnès, Pierre. 'Jésus (prière à)', DSp 8 (1974) 1306–1310.
Rocheau, V. 'Étude analytique des "Récits du pèlerin russe"', *Plamia* (Meudon, France) no. 45, September 1976.
Špidlík, Tomaš. *Les grands mystiques russes,* 282–290. Paris, 1979.
Solignac, Aimé. 'Pèlerin russe (Récit d'un)', DSp 11/1 (1984) 885–871.
Translations, see DSp 11/1:890. English translations include, *The Way of a Pilgrim and The Pilgrim Continues His Way,* translated by Helen Bacovcin. New York, 1992; and *The Pilgrim's Tale,* edited Aleksei Pentkovsky, translated T. Allan Smith, Preface Jaroslav Pelikan, CWS. New York, 1999.

PRAY UNCEASINGLY, P. 361.

Cassian. *Conferences,* 1.2ff (SCh 42:90ff; Ramsey, ACW 57:41–42; Luibheid, 46ff). 10.10 (SCh 54:85ff; Ramsey, ACW 57: 378–383; Luibheid, 132ff).
Maximus the Confessor, in J. Gouillard, *Petite Philocalie,* 157ff. Paris, 1953. 'Four Centuries on Love', in *Early Fathers from the Philokalia,* 286–346.
Symeon the New Theologian, in Gouillard, 173ff. 'St. Simeon the New Theologian, Practical and Theological Precepts', in *Writings from the Philokalia on Prayer of the Heart,* 97–161. London, 1979.
Gregory Palamas. *Défense des saints hésychastes,* II, 1, 30ff; Louvain, 282ff.
Brianchaninov, Ignace. *Approches de la Prière de Jésus,* 54ff; *On the Prayer of Jesus,* 59ff.
*The Art of Prayer,* 23, 49–50, 54, 63–64, 77, 80–87, 95, 102, 154; *L'art de la prière,* 23, 60–62, 67, 82ff, 101, 105–116, 128ff, 137, 210ff.
*A Systematic Handbook,* 315, 409 (bibliog.), 439 (texts).
Marx, Michael J. *Incessant Prayer in Ancient Monastic Literature*. Rome, 1946.
Hausherr, Irénée. 'Opus Dei', OCP 13 (1947) 195–218; OCA 183 (1969) 121–144.
Olphe-Galliard, Michel. 'Cassien', DSp 2/1 (1953) 264–266.
Kerkhoff, Radbert. *Beiträge zur Lehre des unablässigen Betens im Neuen Testament*. Rome, 1951.
———. *Das unablässige Gebet des Herrn*. Freiburg, 1954.

*Théophane le Reclus,* 276ff.
Behler, Gebhard-Maria. 'Prier dans l'Esprit et prier sans cesse selon le nouveau Testament', *La Maison-Dieu,* 109 (1972) 31–50.
*'Priez Sans Cesse', La Maison-Dieu,* 64 (1960); articles on the teaching of the Fathers and the practice of ancient monasticism by Adalbert Hamman, Philippe Rouillard, Irénée H. Dalmais, and Jean Mateos.
Ancilli, Ermanno. 'Presenza di Dio', DESp 2:1498–1504.
Dupuy, Michel. 'Présence de Dieu', DSp 12/2 (1986) 2107–2136.
Gribomont, Jean. 'Acemeti (insonni)', DP 1:33–34; 'Acoemetae (Sleepless Ones)', EEC 1:8.

EJACULATORY PRAYERS, P. 362.

Cassien. *Conferences,* 9.36; SCh 54:72; Ramsey, ACW 57: 353–354; Luibheid, 124ff.
Augustine. *Epistola* 130.20; PL 33:501; translated Wilfrid Parsons, *Saint Augustine. Letters,* vol. 2 (83–130), FCh 18:376ff. New York, 1953.
*The Art of Prayer,* 48–50; *L'art de la prière,* 59–62.
Plus, Raoul. *Comment toujours prier.* Toulouse, 1926.
Fonck, Anton. 'Prière', DThC 13/2 (1936) 197ff.
Vansteenberghe, E. 'Aspirations', DSp 1 (1936) 1017–1025.
Hausherr, Irénée. *Noms du Christ et voies d'oraison,* OCA 15:177ff. Rome, 1960; translated Charles Cummings, *The Name of Jesus,* CS 44:191ff. Kalamazoo, 1978.
*Théophane le Reclus,* 276ff.
Rayez, André. 'Jaculatoires (oraisons)', DSp 8 (1974) 66–67.

THE REMEMBRANCE OF GOD, P. 364.

Mark the Monk. 'De ceux qui pensent être justifiés', *Spiritualité orientale,* 41:54; '226 Texts: To Those who Think to be Justified by Deeds', in Kadloubovsky and Palmer, *Early Fathers from the Philokalia,* 86ff.
Diadochus of Photice, *Cent chapitres gnostiques,* 59; SCh 5*ter:*119; 'On Spiritual Knowledge and Discrimination: One Hundred Texts', *The Philokalia. The Complete Text,* I:270ff.
Isaac the Syrian, *33rd Discourse; Oeuvres,* 204ff; Wensinck, *Mystic Treatises,* 148ff.
Gregory Palamas. *Défense des saints hésychastes,* II, 1, 31; Louvain, 285ff.
Theoleptus of Philadelphia, in J. Gouillard, *Petite Philocalie,* 226ff. Paris, 1953; 'A Word', in Kadloubovsky and Palmer, *Writings from the Philokalia on Prayer of the Heart,* 383ff.

Brianchaninov, Ignace. *Approches de la prière de Jésus,* 52ff. Selections in *On the Prayer of Jesus,* translated by Lazarus [Moore]. London, 1965.
*The Art of Prayer,* 30, 98, 118–121, 163, 166, 185, 202; *L'art de la prière,* 34, 132, 160–67, 223, 254, 276ff.
*A Systematic Handbook,* 340.
Otto, Rudolf. 'Mystische und gläubige Frömmigkeit', *Das ganz Andere, Aufsätze das Numinose betreffend,* 82–107. Gotha, 1923.
Hausherr, Irénée. *Noms du Christ et voies d'oraison,* OCA 157:156ff; Cummings, *The Name of Jesus,* CS 44:158ff.
A Monk of the Eastern Church. *Gegenwart des Herrn.* Lucerne, 1963; translated from the 2nd French edition, *Présence du Christ,* by A Monk of the Western Church, *A Day with Jesus.* New York, 1964.
*Théophane le Reclus,* 278ff.
Hausherr, Irénée. 'La prière perpétuelle du chrétien', *Laicat et Sainteté,* 111–166. Rome, 1965; OCA 176 (1966) 255–306, particularly 275–288.
Adnès, Pierre. 'Hésychasme: Hésychia et souvenir de Dieu', DSp 7/1 (1969) 392–394.
Sieben, Hermann Josef. *'Mneme Theou',* DSp 10 (1980) 1407–1414.
Solignac, Aimé. 'Mémoire', DSp 10:991–1002.
Dupuy, Michel. 'Présence de Dieu', DSp 12/2 (1986) 1207–1236.
Quacquarelli, A[ntonio] and V[ittorino] Grossi. 'Memoria', DP 2:2213–2216; 'Memory', EEC 1:552–553.

THE STATE OF PRAYER, P. 366.

Hausherr, Irénée. *Noms du Christ et voies d'oraison,* OCA 157:137ff; translated Cummings, *The Name of Jesus,* CS 44:136ff.
Jetté, Fernand. 'État', DSp 4/2 (1961) 1372–1388.
Fisher, Heribert. 'Fond de l'âme: chez Eckhart', DSp 5 (1964) 650–661.
*Théophane le Reclus,* 281ff.
Pinkaers, Servais. 'Habitude et habitus', DSp 7/1 (1969) 2–11.
See HEART.

# TOPICAL INDEX

# NAMES INDEX

Cistercian Publications publishes books in four series—Cistercian Fathers, Cistercian Studies, Cistercian Liturgy, and Monastic Wisdom—and in the following areas:

## Monastic Texts in English Translation

- Sermons and treatises by twelfth & thirteenth-century cistercian spiritual writers
- Classic texts from the monastic wisdom of both the eastern and western Churches

## Monastic Life, History, Spirituality, Architecture, and Liturgy

- For those with a personal interest in contemplative prayer and monastic lifestyle
- For students exploring monastic tradition
- For scholars specializing in aspects of monastic history, art, liturgy, or theology

- Reflections by contemporary monks and nuns
- Specialized studies by scholars
- Overviews of patristic & medieval doctrine
- Cistercian music and retreat addresses on CD and audio-cassette
- Video / DVD visits to contemporary abbeys

## Editorial Offices & Customer Service

- Cistercian Publications: Editorial Offices
  WMU Station, 1903 West Michigan Avenue
  Kalamazoo, Michigan 49008-5415 USA

  Telephone 269 387 8920
  Fax 269 387 8390
  e-mail cistpub@wmich.edu

- Cistercian Publications: Customer Service
  Liturgical Press
  Saint John's Abbey
  Collegeville, MN 56321-7500

  Telephone 800 436 8431
  Fax 320 363 3299
  e-mail sales@litpress.org

## Canada

- Bayard-Novalis
  49 Front Street East, Second Floor
  Toronto, Ontario M5E 1B3 CANADA

  Telephone 800 387 7164
  Fax 416 363 9409

## UK and Europe

- The Columba Press
  55A Spruce Avenue
  Stillorgan Industrial Park
  Blackrock, Co. Dublin IRELAND

  Telephone 353 1 2942556
  Fax 353 1 2942564
  e-mail info@columba.ie

## Website

- www.cistercianpublications.org

To explore the range of titles in our series of texts and studies in the monastic tradition, please request our free complete catalogue from customer service or visit our website.

Original CIP data, subject to revision:

**Library of Congress Cataloging in Publication Data**

Spidlik, Tomas.
The spirituality of the Christian East.
(Cistercian studies series: no. 79)
Translation of: La spiritualité de l'Orient chrétien
Includes bibliographies and index.
1. Spirituality—Eastern churches. 2. Eastern churches—Doctrines. I. Title. II. Series.
BX106.2.S5513 1986 231'.15 84-29348
ISBN 0-87907-879-0